SEX AND DESTINY

SEX AND DESTINY

*The Politics of
Human Fertility*

Germaine Greer

Secker & Warburg
London

First published in England 1984 by
Martin Secker & Warburg Limited
54 Poland Street, London W1V 3DF

Copyright © 1984 by Germaine Greer

British Library Cataloguing in Publication Data

Greer, Germaine
  Sex and destiny.
  1. Fertility, Human—Social aspects
  I. Title
  304.6'32   HB903.F4

ISBN 0–436–18801–5

Printed and bound in Great Britain by
Richard Clay (The Chaucer Press) Ltd,
Bungay, Suffolk

For my god-children
Baal Krishna and Purushottam

Contents

Author's Acknowledgments

My thanks are due to hundreds of people whose names I have never known, and to a few whose names are very well known to me but ought not to be mentioned here, because I have made my own judgments and drawn my own conclusions about an intimate part of their lives. The people who helped me despite the strong probability that they would jeopardise their careers or job security by so doing are all remembered. I show my appreciation of their courage and honesty if I do not name them in this connection.

The book could never have been written without the help of Penny Kane, and later Graham Peck, of IPPF International Office in London, both of whom are committed to the belief that the corrective to error is not censorship. They are, of course, not responsible for the use I have made of the masses of information they sent my way.

The staffs of Bombay University Library, the London Library, the Cambridge University Libraries, the Family Planning Information Service (London) and the British Library have all given patient, prolonged and indefatigable help.

The Family Planning Association of India, under the distinguished leadership of Mrs Avabai Wadia, put personnel, vehicles and their library at my disposal; I can only hope that I have done justice to the reality that they showed me. Dr Seshagiri Rao, projects director at Bombay headquarters, and Mr Sreenath in Bangalore, both showed great faith in my ability to tell a hawk from a handsaw, and I hope I shall not embarrass them. I must also salute Dr Indumati Parikh of the Streehitikarini Clinic in Bombay, Dr Rajnikant Arole of the Rural Health Project in Jamkhed, Dr M. N. Shete of the Primary Health Centre in Dehu, and Drs Sangle, Gune and Godbole at the Waghole PHC. Special thanks are due to Gita Mehta and Ajit Singh who found ways round logistical problems for me, to Mira Savara of the Feminist Resource Centre and to Mr Shankar Menon.

In Sudan, Mrs Rashida Mutalib and her colleagues, and in Colombia, Clorinda Zea de Morales both helped me to come a little closer to the heart of the matter. Ron Hall and William Shawcross both gave me windfalls of unique material. Drs R. D. Catterall, R. C. Ravenholt and Herbert Reiss all tolerated the fumbling enquiries of an amateur. Tarzie Vittachi, Elizabeth Reid and Susan Kedgeley gave understanding and encouragement when it was most needed. My agent, Gillon Aitken, shepherded this book and me through a travailed publishing history. If there are any blunders in the editing of the copy they will not be the fault of John Byrne, who gave up a sorely needed summer holiday to check each comma.

Warning

It is sometimes thought, mostly perhaps by people who do not read many books, that books should be incitements to action. They write letters to authors, demanding to know, "What is it you want me to do?" and, further, "How exactly do you suggest that I go about it?" The author is obliged either to throw the letter away, as simply evidence that her reader has begun to think, or to answer carefully, "Dear reader, why should you do what I would have you do? Do as you would when you have considered the case I make." Astonishingly, people still write to some hapless authors, accusing them of superhuman achievements: "Your book changed my life." "No, no," replies the author in despair, "You changed your life. Nobody else should or can."

Some books are incitements to action, none of them good books, for the principal function of writing, even polemical writing, is to stimulate thought, to stimulate creative thought in particular. That means producing confusion in place of certainty, melting concepts so that they may reform and coagulate in new relationships. The way of doing this may be quite violent, for settled certainties resist corrosion and demand vitriol. They are shrunken and crusty and need roasting or scalding to make them germinate new forms.

You may think, dear reader, that I have overstated my case. The attack upon my own culture is, indeed, extreme, but the weight of custom is heavy as life and its hide is thick. The hearts of my readers may be of more penetrable stuff than I think, and so my challenge overshoots its target and falls harmlessly beyond, or leaves an exit wound that hardens into scar tissue.

Some judicious people will say that I should have made a better case if I had been less emotionally involved, but I am not now writing for fun or for profit. I have written this book because I had to. If I had felt less strongly about the subject I should not have written at all, much less crept into the storehouses of arcane technical literature, waded through the bales of family planning propaganda, wandered around hospitals with no glass in the windows and stained sheets on the beds or tramped round graveyards full of fresh graves three feet long.

What is this subject so grandiosely labelled *Sex and Destiny*? It might just as well have been labelled *The Fate of the Earth* or *Civilisation and Its Discontents* or *Sons and Lovers*. In fact, this book is a plea for a new intellectual order, written in the full consciousness that there is less likelihood of the development of such a thing than there is of the coming to pass of a new economic order. The cultural values of consumer society have developed as a consequence of changes in economic and political structure: they are not absolutes. At the same time that traditional societies are buffeted in the slip-stream of economic development to the point of capsizing, they are also assailed by Western culture, carried by emissaries with unequalled powers of penetration and persuasion. The economic development is a fraud, but the cultural onslaught is real and irresistible.

The very paradigm of first, second and third worlds, of developed and undeveloped or developing countries, is based upon unquestioning arrogance. It is conceptually identical with the assumption of a degree of inequality undreamt of by the most arrant feudalism. Nowhere is this bland condescension more apparent than in the designs and executions of our foreign aid programmes, even though the flower of our intellect and benevolence may give its life to them. The dilemma of this book is the dilemma of the people who care, who have long suspected that the system which they represent is fundamentally inhuman and can neither change nor cease its depredations. The dilemma is real. One book like this will not resolve it. This book does not seek to provide a formula for the resolution of the dilemma, but rather to gore the reader slightly with its horns.

What is our civilisation that we should so blithely propagate its discontents? How can we teach due care for children when we cannot care for our own? Why should we erect the model of recreational sex in the public places of all the world? Who are we to invade the marriage bed of veiled women? Do we dare drive off the matriarch and exterminate the peasantry? Why should we labour to increase life expectancy when we have no time or use for the old? Why should we care more about curbing the increase of the numbers of the poor than they do themselves? Who are we to decide the fate of the earth?

These are some of the questions. I have no hope of having answered them, but only of having asked them so poignantly that they cannot be ignored or forgotten.

Chapter One

A Child is Born

> After the first, I didn't ever want to have another child, it was too
> much to go through for nothing, they shut you in a hospital, they shave
> the hair off you and tie your hands down, and they don't let you see,
> they don't want you to understand, they want you to believe it's their
> power, not yours. They stick needles in you so you won't hear anything,
> you might as well be a dead pig, your legs are up in a metal frame, they
> bend over you, technicians, mechanics, butchers, students clumsy or
> sniggering practising on your body, they take the baby out with a fork
> like a pickle out of a pickle jar. After that they fill your veins up with
> red plastic, I saw it running down the tube. I won't let them do that
> to me ever again.
>
> *Margaret Atwood*, Surfacing

In World Population Year, the location chosen for the international
conference was Bucharest. The choice was perhaps unfortunate, for the
raison d'être behind the whole jamboree was fear of the population explosion and the promotion of birth-control programmes. Just the year
before the Rumanian government had outlawed abortion and banned the
sale of contraceptives, because the decline in population growth and the
increasing senility of the population had been construed as a threat to
the country's economic future. When the Foreign Minister met the Press,
among the questions he was asked was whether such Draconian measures
were not tantamount to forced childbirth. The minister had trouble understanding the question, which was re-phrased for him. "Does that mean
that unwanted children are being born in Rumania?" "Of course not!"
snapped the minister. The question was based upon the common Western
assumption that the only people who want children are those who conceive them. The minister's answer might have been based upon a different
premise, that a child wanted by someone, in this case the Rumanian
government, could not have been called unwanted. On the other hand,
he might have been referring to the fact that, after an initial baby boom,
during which the country literally ran out of napkins and baby foods,
the birth rate had settled back at its earlier, unsatisfactory level.[1]

The Rumanian example is just one of many which could be cited to
show that even the governments of totalitarian countries cannot counteract
the profound lack of desire for children which prevails in Western society,
especially among upwardly mobile social groups. Governments may

present themselves as pro-children; governments however are not interested in children themselves but in recruiting the workforce of the future.
The methods they may adopt are extremely limited, for no suggestion
of forced childbirth will be tolerated, even in conspicuously unfree
societies like Rumania. "Every child a wanted child" is the slogan, but
the modern Western infant is wanted by fewer people than any infants
in our long history – not only by fewer parents, but by smaller groups
of people. Historically, babies have been welcome additions to society;
their parents derived prestige and joy and satisfaction from their proximity
and suffered little or no deterioration in the quality of their lives, which
could even have been positively enhanced by the arrival of children.
Parents, themselves still relatively junior in the social hierarchy, had no
need to cudgel their brains to decide if they were ready for the experience, for they were surrounded by people who watched their reproductive career with passionate interest, who would guide them through
the fears and anguish of childbirth and take on a measure of responsibility
for child-rearing. Historically, human societies have been pro-child;
modern society is unique in that it is profoundly hostile to children. We
in the West do not refrain from childbirth because we are concerned about
the population explosion or because we feel we cannot afford children,
but because we do not like children.

Conventional piety is still such that to say such a thing is shocking.
Parents will point angrily to the fact that they do not beat or starve or
terrorise their children but struggle to feed, house, clothe and educate
them to the best of their ability. Our wish that people who cannot feed,
house, clothe and educate their children adequately should not have them
is born of our concern for the children themselves, or so most of us would
claim. At the heart of our insistence upon the child's parasitic role in
the family lurks the conviction that children must be banished from adult
society. Babies ought not to be born before they have rooms of their own:
when they are born they must adhere to an anti-social time-table. Access
to the adult world is severely rationed in terms of time, and in any case
what the child enters is not the adult's reality but a sort of no-man's-
land of phatic communication. Mothers who are deeply involved in ex-
ploring and developing infant intelligence and personality are entitled to
feel that such a generalisation is unjust, but even they must reflect that
they share the infant's ostracised status. No one wants to hear the
fascinating thing that baby said or did today, especially at a party. Mother
realises she is becoming as big a bore as her child, and can be shaken
by the realisation. The heinousness of taking an infant or a toddler to
an adult social gathering is practically unimaginable; as usual the discomfort and uneasiness are manifested as concern. A baby may be produced and brandished momentarily but then it must disappear, otherwise
well-meaners begin cooing about it being time for bed: the more baby

chirps and chatters and reaches for necklaces and earrings, the more likely it is to be told that it is a poor little thing. Restaurants, cinemas, offices, supermarkets, even Harrods auction rooms, are all no places for children. In England restaurants mentioned in the *Good Food Guide* boldly advise parents to leave "under-fourteens and dogs at home": the object in doing so is to increase their patronage by vaunting their child-free condition.[2] The placing of children in the same category as dogs is risqué, but no one will object.

Adults cannot have fun while kids are around; kids must be "put down" first. Drinking and flirting, the principal expressions of adult festivity, are both inhibited by the presence of children. Eventually our raucousness wakes them and they watch our activities through the stair-rails and learn to despise us. In lieu of our real world we offer them a fake one, the toy world. Parents shocked by some family crisis try to mend the cracks in the nuclear family by dating their children, abjectly courting them. The scale and speed of our world is all anti-child; children cannot be allowed to roam the streets, but must run a terrifying gauntlet to get to the prime locus of their segregation, school. They cannot open doors or windows, cannot see on top of counters, are stifled and trampled in crowds, hushed when they speak or cry before strangers, apologised for by harassed mothers condemned to share their ostracised condition.

As we shall see, the state's desire for children is powerless against the anti-child thrust of the Western lifestyle. Western industrialised society is gerontomorphic. Life has become so complex that induction into adult society takes many years and effectively isolates the socialised adult from the unsocialised child. There is so little interpenetration between the worlds of the child and the adult that we can easily call to mind whole parts of our commercial districts where no child should ever be seen. The adult who elects to spend time with a child must take time off from his immediate interests and make a special effort. Communication is strained, artificial and often illusory, and the children less often fooled about the real nature of the case than their egregious parents. The general tendency to separate children from parents, which has always characterised north-western Europe, has intensified with the development of consumer society. The most privileged people in protestant Europe have tradition-ally seen least of their children, and upwardly mobile groups have assumed the upper-class pattern. The new baby has its own room, is put to bed awake and not picked up until the time is right and routine says it will not thereby be "spoiled". The child goes away to school and learns "self-reliance". Children learn to treat adults, all of whom stand in paternal authoritarian relationship to them, with a sort of hypocritical deference. All their spontaneous contacts are with their peer group, with whom they are quite likely to share anti-social ritual behaviour. The child world is further alienated from the adult world by the creation of the buffer state, "teenage", while old age is absurd, isolated, disgusting, so alien that it serves as a bait for juvenile thugs to bash, rape and rob.

If the truth is, we of the industrialised West do not like children, the corollary is equally true, our children do not like us. It is blasphemy to deny that parents love their children (whatever that may mean) but it is nevertheless true that adults do not like children. People of different generations do not consort together as a matter of preference: where a child and an old person develop any closeness, we are apt to suspect the motives of the older person. Most social groupings tend to be formed of individuals in the same age set and social circumstances, and even within the family, parents and children spend very little time in each other's company. The family which sits down at the table together most nights in the week is now an exception in many of the well-to-do suburbs in the United States. Food advertising often shows mothers preparing single-portion frozen dinners for individual family members. Families used to meet only to eat; nowadays a commoner pattern has the kids' being fed earlier and on different foods from those which will be eaten later by the adults.

We generally try to explain our separation from our children as a system adopted for their own good; they must not work but learn, and so they are passive subordinates in the family structure. Serious matters are not discussed with them because it might confuse and worry them; they are offered a kind of conversational pabulum out of consideration. So much adult amusement stems from matters ribald or malicious that even light-hearted conversation is censored for the younger generation. The children capitulate by concealing their own diversions; where once parents sent them to bed before a party, now they wait until their parents are in the Bahamas before planning their jubilee.

The inability to enjoy the company of children is for many adults a source of guilt. Because children spend most of their time with their peers, they are quite unable to participate intelligently in an adult conversation. They have not learned to listen and learn from unselfconscious discussions which are not primarily directed at them. Children paraded in front of adults are too often silent and coy, or else dominate the conversation with tedious twaddle unenlivened by complexity or spontaneity. It is anathema to admit being bored by one's own children, but it is understood that one's children will bore anyone else who has to spend time with them and that the company of the children of others is all the things one would never admit about the company of one's own.

The gulf that yawns between adult society and the world of children in the "Anglo-Saxon" West is by no means universal. There are societies where adults and children laugh at the same jokes, where adults would not dream of eating their evening meal without their children about them and would not inhibit discussion of serious matters because children were present. In fact such societies are still more populous than our own. There are huge cities which are practically run by children, children who support their parents and their brethren by their skills and initiative, where children and adults inhabit the same cruel world and survive by clinging to each other. But these are the societies whose children, we think, should not be born.

The state's institutionalised desire for children is, obviously, a desire for productive adults rather than for children themselves. This pressure is expressed through other institutions which deal directly with the production of these A-grade humans, and which are constantly struggling to improve the product by further sophistication of the technology. The most fantastic elaboration of this process would bypass the role of mother altogether. When asked on an ABC television programme whether he thought that artificial wombs were a possibility, Professor Joseph Fletcher replied:

> Yes, yes. I foresee it with urgent approval ... if I were an embryologist I should be eager for the day when I could actually see, let's say through a glass container, a conceptus develop from fertilisation through to term ... it seems to me that what is known as artificial gestation ... in such a non-uterine container is the most desirable thing in the world for me to imagine ... Great thing ... I hope it comes soon. I think it will.

His co-guest on the programme, Dr Helleger, ventured to suggest a different point of view:

> I have a misgiving about what I would call the increasing objectivisation of children ... children as a product of artifice. I think it's already terribly difficult for an American child today to come home with a C-minus instead of an A and I think this intolerance towards imperfection, I have some considerable misgivings about.[3]

The "objectivisation" or reification of which Dr Helleger was speaking is already far advanced. He would draw the line at trying to screen out children of C-minus academic ability *in utero*, but he would be out of line with the consensus if he did not accept "therapeutic" abortion in some cases, perhaps even including the relatively minor cases of Down's syndrome, and he would almost certainly endorse the drive towards perfectibility in correcting minor disfigurements and straightening teeth. People who cannot afford to pay orthodontists' huge bills had better not have children. Reproduction in the highly developed world has become a kind of manufacture; doctors do not want children for themselves, they want better children just as industry demands a better mousetrap, or a bigger, brighter, more regularly formed, utterly flawless (and tasteless) tomato. Such a desire is not tantamount to an encouragement to any woman to bear a child; it functions instead as a challenge and a multifarious source of anxiety.

If we continue along the path of trying to see who, if anyone, wants children around, we come next to the child's kin-group. It used to be a truism of feminist theory that women were railroaded into motherhood by the expectations of their parents and their in-laws. In the view of this writer such forms of persuasion and pressure as the kin-group can bring to bear pale into utter insignificance next to the powerful disincentives which are offered by the actual social context in which the would-be child-bearer lives. A distant mother or a mother-in-law who is plainly waiting around for the good news can be disregarded. Only in the rarest instance does she have any economic power to coerce the birth of a grandchild, and she is hardly any more likely to be actively involved in the rearing of a grandchild, especially in the socially mobile groups which characterise the American (and the EEC) dream. None of us thinks that one generation has a right to the children of the next, not only because it gives no help in raising children but because in our view the exercise of such a right would represent an intolerable intrusion into the rights of the individual. Only two people have the right to want a child – its parents – and even then, the father has no *a priori* right to want a child from an unwilling woman.

One of the reasons why we so firmly believe that the only people with the right to want a child are its parents, is that we see quite clearly that bearing and raising a child is an ordeal. The individuals whom we have painstakingly inducted into child-free society and established there, with a life-style centred entirely upon achievement and self-gratification, have now to disrupt that pattern. The sacrifice is enormous, and they are to expect no reward or recompense. If the management of childbearing in our society had actually been intended to maximise stress, it could hardly have succeeded better. The child-bearers embark on their struggle alone; the rest of us wash our hands of them.

From conception, pregnancy is regarded as an abnormal state, which women are entitled to find extremely distressing. Such an attitude is itself the product of the fact that Western women are pregnant so seldom, but even so, pregnancy is not simply viewed as a natural, if rather peculiar condition, but as an illness, requiring submission to the wisdom of health professionals and constant monitoring, as if the foetus were a saboteur hidden in its mother's soma. Though some women will freely admit that they feel more comfortable pregnant than they ever felt when enduring the monthly cycle of depression, tension, Mittelschmerz and menstruation, their number is not likely to be increased by the fact that most women expect to feel rotten and look worse. The well-documented disabilities – morning sickness, caries, cravings, incontinence, toxaemia, thrombosis, fluid retention, skin eruptions, piles, sleeplessness, varicose veins – range from the undignified to the unbearable and, bitterest irony of all, of the palliatives offered by the medical profession for the disorders of pregnancy, so many of them the result of cultural practices and not of the condition itself, there is hardly one effective drug which is not also damaging to the development of the foetus.[4] The pregnant woman also finds that she is to forgo the drugs upon which our society depends, alcohol, caffeine and nicotine.

Perhaps more difficult to bear than the physical discomforts of pregnancy is the psychic discomfort of feeling unattractive. The feeling has less to do with the behaviour of the woman's mate, than it has to do with the accepted aesthetic of female appearance. Societies which place a high premium on child-bearing feature styles of female dress which accept breasts and bellies, whether softly accentuated by the sari, rounding out the salwar or pushing out the high-waisted front-opening full-skirted frocks of the vanishing European peasantry. The preferred shape of Western women, narrow-hipped and small-breasted is desirable partly because of its denial of fecundity. Even those few women who feel at ease with their own soft and ample bodies are sorely tried whenever they are obliged to choose clothes. Women who want to breast-feed will find that very few clothes which will open to free the breast can be found, so we have the multiple irony that they are forced to make a display of what most people would rather not see. Because the pregnant woman is unlikely to have seen pregnancy in her immediate family, she is ill-prepared for the changes her body goes through, from the swelling, darkened nipples and engorged veins of early pregnancy to the wallowing bulk of the last weeks, and she may well find them alarming and disgusting.

It is to be hoped that there are very few men who react as violently as Maurice Utrillo to the physical signs of pregnancy; when he saw pregnant women in the street, "he would chase them and pull their hair and try to kick them in the stomach".[5] Unfortunately this extreme behaviour may not be altogether rare. Dr Anson Shupe of the Centre for Social Research and Dr William Stacey of the Centre on Domestic Violence at the University of Texas at Arlington, found that of 2,638 women who entered shelters for battered wives in Dallas and Denton or used the shelter hot lines, fully 42% had been attacked when they were pregnant.[6] The roles of sex object, as stereotyped in our culture, and mother, as it is biologically determined, are antagonistic. Men may be baffled and enraged when their playmate becomes a parturient monster, but women are even more bamboozled by the demands of the dual role. Should they or should they not engage in sexual intercourse during pregnancy? Not to is to "let the child come between them"; there is no helpful rule which says that a father must nourish the foetus with his seed, or that he must protect it by practising self-control. If husbands grow fractious pregnant wives are to try to placate them; if wives are desirous they may court rejection.

While the pregnant woman does not have to be protected from exertion, for like most people in our society she is more likely to take too little exercise than too much, she ought to be protected from anxiety. There are too many genuinely unknowable aspects of childbirth for a mother to be unaware of risk, yet genuine psychoprophylaxis is the last thing that modern obstetrics can offer. Most Western women face a pregnancy fundamentally alone. They sally forth alone on their endless round of visits to the obstetrician, the clinic, the hospital, abandoning their own environment and entering a series of unfamiliar settings in a submissive posture. The women who have given up paid employment to have a baby move from gossipy collectivity to isolation and introspection in an empty house, at a time when neither isolation nor introspection is good for them. Women who fear the consequences of loneliness and brooding fight to remain at jobs they are perfectly capable of doing, even to the extent of concealing their pregnancies almost to the end. As soon as a pregnancy is admitted, the mother-to-be is bombarded with contradictory advice, and not only from well-meaning amateurs, but from the health professionals themselves. Some doctors routinely prescribe diuretics, others detest the idea. Some are so keen on small babies that they keep the mothers half-starved and increase the risk of toxaemia. Some urge women to undergo amniocentesis when others would oppose it.

Childbirth in our society is not conducted in an orderly predictable way but half experimentally. It is a hand-to-mouth business, changing weekly according to fads and fashions which sweep the medical world, bringing riches and fame to their proponents. Every fad is presented as the newest medical breakthrough, the meticulously researched result of increased technological know-how, and each gains a measure of acceptance because of woman's anxiety. Within the span of one woman's child-bearing years we have seen diethylstilboestrol administered for bigger and better babies, decompression chambers for easier labour and smarter children, Thalidomide and its sister-catastrophes, the Lamaze or gymnastic approach, every kind of anaesthesia and induction and the see-sawing battle between high forceps and caesarians, to name but a few. Women who have "been through it" naturally seek to find converts to the methods used on them, in order to allay their own anxiety. Women whose experiences caused rage and bitterness are expected to hold their tongues. Fortunately perhaps, once the immediate interest in the management of childbirth has waned, very few women trouble to read the rueful follow-up information about the methods they chose. There is after all nothing they can do to right the consequences of an induction, or to restore to their children those first days passed in a drugged daze or the brain cells that died while technicians disagreed.[7] The women who have still to become pregnant will not have the benefit of their collective experience; they must pick a haphazard course across terrain which has been charted in various and contradictory ways and which guide they choose is simply, shockingly, a matter left to chance.

The fortuitousness of the method of management of childbirth stands in sharp contrast to the deliberateness with which the prospective parents must approach the child-bearing project, timing it carefully, making sure that they can afford it. From the beginning child-bearing involves invest-ment, as the mother-to-be acquires her special wardrobe and the infant's layette is assembled and the doctor is paid and the hospital is booked and so forth and so on endlessly. In the case of a student of mine in the United States the doctor demanded to be paid in advance before he would agree to preside at the delivery. Everything about the wanted child's arrival is calculated; everything, that is, except how he and his mother shall be treated. If ours was a society which welcomed and enjoyed children, and if each parturient woman was surrounded by people who wanted her child even more than she did, she could ease her feelings of responsibility and inadequacy. If ours was a society with collective notions of normative behaviour for parents, parents could escape the crushing responsibility for the ills that befall the children, they would be aware that they had fulfilled all expectations. Where there are no shared expectations there can be no feeling of having done the right thing. Western mothers enter on childbirth punctiliously – the ones who are not feckless that is – and consciously, self-consciously, strive to go about it intelligently and carefully, but even that is not forgiven them. The very people who exploit their conscientiousness to increase their own influence – and income – will be the first to tell them that their lack of spontaneity is in itself a cause of uncomfortable pregnancy or tension during the birth or difficulties with feeding or failure to caress the baby adequately.

The gestation period of humans is only nine months, too short a time for any individual to get a grasp of the whole spectrum of ideas about pregnancy management and her own place in it. The decisions which any mother makes are partly rational and informed and partly irrational and emotional. Eventually the mother may wish to say that she behaved in certain ways instinctively, but in fact intelligence and emotion play a more significant part in mothering than does instinct. Mothering be-haviour is learned, but not in our society by custom and example. Each mother has, as it were, to re-invent childbirth: she has joined the competi-tion for the bigger, better, brighter baby. On the widely accepted principle that parenthood is too important a function to be left to amateurs, the Swedish government has instituted a nationwide scheme to teach Swedes how to do it, although there is no more agreement about the right way to do it in Sweden than there is anywhere else in the Protestant world.

It follows from the muddle of conflicting demands made upon her that the mental strain of pregnancy for an intelligent, self-regulating female must be much more upsetting than the physical concomitants of her con-dition. The stress can only be increased by the fact that, although every-one agrees that the woman who has wished this extraordinary dilemma upon herself must bear the total responsibility for the outcome, she will not be allowed complete freedom of choice in the matter. Her family doctor will have ideas of his own about the best management of her pregnancy; after all he is much more used to pregnancies than she is. Her first problem is to find out what her doctor's fixed ideas are and whether they are acceptable to her or not. Her doctor may agree to discuss them frankly with her but he is much more likely to try to extort confidence in himself at the expense of minimising the disagreements among the members of his profession. The more experience he has the more likely he is to want a biddable patient, especially if she is too intelligent to be fobbed off with oversimplified accounts of why he is choosing a certain course of action. He also comes in with the considerable advantage of knowing what he wants, while his "patient" is still trying to find out what she wants. As an expert, and a detached professional he will make decisions which she, not he, has to live with. The doctor who counsels a woman to accept a method of birth which has adverse consequences for her or her child may do so with impunity. The woman who trusts him has only herself to blame, for no one can be found who will share the blame with her. The more malpractice suits proliferate, the more conservative the procedures doctors will choose; the much higher proportion of caesarians carried out in the USA can probably be explained by some such irrelevant factor. Babies plucked out of opened abdomens escape many of the perils of the struggle down the birth-canal, but they are born anaesthetised and their mothers have missed out on the experience too. The first days of life are poisoned.

The woman who demands the right to make her own decisions will find herself conducting a running battle with health professionals. There are good grounds, for example, for giving birth at home, but a woman who chooses to do so may find herself abandoned by the people who should help her. In some parts of North America she may be breaking the law; if she can find a midwife to attend her the midwife may go to gaol.[8] On the other hand she may find herself in worse danger because the only help she can find is inexpert. Obstetricians may refuse to attend her at home for fear of eventual malpractice suits. Home is less bacterially pathogenic than the hospital, is a less stressed and stressing environment, yet for more and more women birth at home is not a realistic possibility.[9] A primipara might be told that if she gives birth at home she is solely responsible for the consequences, so that the advantages of home confinement are effectively negated by the imposition of anxiety. The British home confinement system is being wound down; the flying squads which would attend home births if any difficulty arose no longer exist. The official policy is to have all births carried out in hospitals, as they are in Sweden, which has an extremely low rate of perinatal complication and death, and in the United States, where the consequences are much less impressive.[10]

Much has been written on the inappropriateness of the hospital as the setting for the birth of children, but the logistics of delivery of health services force the continuation and intensification of the trend to manage births in the atmosphere of crisis and disease. Even when induction and caesarian sections are not performed on slight justification with appalling results for mother and child, hospital birth takes place among strangers and is subordinated to their routine. There is no room for the family to celebrate one of the climactic points in its life-cycle. The only other family member allowed to be present is the mother's lover or husband, or someone purporting to be one or the other; the presence of a sex partner as the only lay helper in the birthplace is an unusual circumstance, in historical terms, and it dramatises the fact that the basic unit of consumer society is not the family, but the couple.

Ironically, because hospitals are geared to deal with crises, a birth which presents no complications may be worse attended in hospital than it would have been at home. The commonest complaint of women undergoing hospital childbirth in Britain as long ago as 1947, and ever since, was that they had been left alone during labour.[11] Labour, as its name implies, is very hard work; a labouring woman needs support and sustenance and reassurance. Writhing like a beached whale on a trolley in a corridor is no way to get any of these. Even when hospitals have taught women what to expect in pre-natal classes, the staff is still capable of telling a woman who knows that she is in second-stage labour and that dilation is well advanced, that she has hours to go and mustn't be naughty and clamour for assistance when the need of others is so much greater. Nevertheless the woman who can get on with the business without interference is in better shape than the one who has been taken over by the doctors, fighting to stay aware in theatres which exist to deliver drugs and surgical procedures, helpless in the stupid lithotomy position, befuddled, bamboozled and humiliated.

Yet women continue to want to bear children. They may say that they want to experience childbirth. What they can mean by that when there is no telling whether they will be allowed to experience it, given the aggressiveness of childbirth management, or whether the experience will not simply consist of torture and terror, is not at all clear. Far too many women have no experience of birth at all, but simply of anaesthesia. Others have a confused, hallucinatory recollection which has more to do with narcotics than any natural event; others felt fear and loneliness and resentment, humiliation and defeat, and pain natural and induced. Some speak of an experience dramatic, rewarding, deeply pleasurable, a vast whole-body orgasm. Having had one child does not mean that one will know about it next time; it is probably true to say that no two births are the same, yet the degree of contrast between one birth and the next in the child-bearing career of a single Western woman can be utterly disorienting and unpredictable. Women who want the experience of childbirth are in the curious position of desiring the unknown.

If the only persons to suffer in the chaos of childbirth management were the mothers, female stoicism might override self-preservation, as always, in the interest of better babies. Instead, an increasing number of voices can be heard sternly insisting on the importance of the birth experience for the future development of the child, its capacity for bonding, affection, orgasm, sociability and so forth. Again we have the typical mix of impotence and responsibility which characterises the twentieth-century Western parent. The threat of damage to the child's future is much more disturbing to women than the prospect of pain or torment or disfigurement to themselves. The very women who would take their responsibility most seriously in this regard are the ones who would experience the most stress in fulfilling it. Proponents of birth control often point to the phenomenon that the birthrate falls as the educational level rises, and see in that a sign that literacy and investigative intelligence lead to informed choices and a greater measure of control. They could interpret the phenomenon in a less positive way: the more women know about childbirth the more likely they are to refuse to undergo it. Further, educated women are more likely to encounter institutionalised, sophisticated health care, so the reality of the experience is actually different for them and has very little to recommend it. When we encounter eugenists lamenting the unwillingness of the brightest women to reproduce we might suggest to them that they give some thought to making childbirth less of an ordeal.

The closer women draw in social and economic status to the male level, the more disruptive childbirth becomes. In order to compete with men Western woman has joined the masculine hierarchy and cultivated a masculine sense of self. The acknowledgment of her pregnancy means that she must step down from all that and enter the psychological equivalent of the birth hut; what happens to her there can have convulsive effects upon what she has come to think of as unalterable, her personality. In exchange for her settled self-image she has a body which inexorably goes about its own business, including biochemical changes in the brain. The period following the birth of a child has been called a fourth trimester; mother and child remain attached as it were by an invisible umbilical cord.[12] A mother is no longer self-sufficient but at the mercy of the child's indomitable love and egotism. The drastic nature of the psychological process has never been explained, but there is a growing body of evidence that carrying a child to term results in a bond which cannot be broken without causing enduring anguish to the mother. Adoption at birth is much less manageable in terms of emotional sequelae than abortion.[13] Miscarriage and stillbirth are also experienced as disasters, although society callously ignores them.[14] The woman who becomes a mother vastly increases her capacity for pain and her vulnerability. From henceforth her attention will be divided. If she returns to work and brings baby to the office, the divided nature of her attention is obvious. She may encounter support as she breastfeeds in the boardroom but she will also encounter ridicule. If she stays at home for her two years paid leave (supposing she has such an unusual privilege) and returns to work without loss of seniority, she is not the same worker who left to bear a child. Asking her to continue as if nothing had happened is absurd. Contemplated through the eyes of the ostracised dyad mother-and-child, the world of business may well seem cruel and silly, and a key to the executive washroom a poor reward. Meanwhile the child's development is taken over by professionals: the mother begins her long struggle with guilt.

The woman who becomes a mother suffers a crushing loss of status; as a "patient" she was at the bottom end of the health professionals' social hierarchy. At home she is a solitary menial. Fewer and fewer women can expect the support of another family member during their maternal isolation, and fewer still could expect or would welcome the help and support of neighbours. Modern dwellings are arranged in such a way that housewives carry out identical tasks in isolation from one another, in suburbs which are deserted by day except for their lonely selves and their babies. The mother who has a car may break out of her isolation without too much difficulty; she will also have a place to feed baby which is not a public lavatory. If she has to rely on public transport the ordeal of escaping from her suburb may well prove too intimidating. Watching mothers trying to juggle their parcels and the baby while stowing their strollers on London transport buses is an unedifying pastime. Watching airline stewardesses ignoring women with children and fawning on businessmen is equally unedifying, especially as time was when mothers with infants were given special attention. Outside English supermarkets rows of parked baby-carriages can be seen, because the merchants who take billions of pounds from mothers' purses cannot be bothered to design a facility to accommodate them. Instead they have the gall to announce that perambulators and strollers are not permitted inside the store. Feminists are often accused of downgrading motherhood. The accusation is ridiculous: motherhood hit rock-bottom long before the new feminist wave broke. The wave itself was caused by the groundswell.

As a mother, the young woman who once moved freely through her varied and stimulating environment as a working girl, now finds herself segregated and immobilised. The collapse in the quality of her life will have to be expiated by her infant who has to deal with the barrage of her full attention. The best mother in the world cannot continue for long on a diet of dreary routine chores and insatiable infant demand: if she is not to suffer from serious psychic deprivation she must have stimulation and communication from supportive peers, as well as rest. The unfamiliarity of the mothering situation itself makes for anxiety; isolation and exhaustion complicate the picture. Women who planned their babies, and therefore believe sincerely that they wanted them, find themselves driven to desperation. They did not know that motherhood was like this: how could they have known? They write angry books about the lie of mother-love. Human societies before our own have known that mother-love does not well up unbidden to lull women into bearing the unbearable. The mother who will love her child must be allowed to take pleasure in it. Caressing and cuddling are behaviours which must be reinforced, not forced. The baby who brings its mother new prestige, new leisure, prettier clothes and better food is vastly more lovable than the baby attended by loneliness, drudgery and anxiety. If mothering is not positively reinforced, women will cease to do it, whether contraception and abortion are legal or illegal, easy or dangerous. In our immediate past mothering was negatively reinforced by the severe limitations on women's options; in our arrogant ethnocentricity we have interpreted the popularity of motherhood in other cultures as reflecting nothing but the paucity of options. It is logical and sensible for a Western woman to wish to avoid childbirth, but it is wrongheaded of her to judge women in contrasting circumstances and assume that childbearing is as profitless and unreasonable for them as it would be for her.

Sophisticated Caucasians are a shrinking proportion of all human beings, for reasons which should be becoming obvious. People for whom pregnancy is not a strange and disorienting condition already outnumber us and threaten to do so by an ever-increasing margin. In their societies a woman's body is not the more admired the less of it there is. Even in comparatively sophisticated Tuscany, a woman with a gap between her thighs is called *secca*, dry; the word is the same as is used for dead plants.[15] Only in consumer society is the famished female type admired, partly because it is so rare. North African women pity slim Western women because they fear that their husbands will tire of them. The days are past when brides were fattened for marriages, yet Indian film stars and Egyptian belly-dancers are fat by Western standards. Obviously in countries where most people live at subsistence level or below, fatness is a sign of success and wealth, but the different aesthetic has deeper roots still. The most prevalent notions of beauty are those of fecundity.

Among naked nations pregnancy is a familiar state. Women who wear *cortes* or *huipiles* or saris or jellabas or *salwar kameez* or any other ample garments can swell and diminish inside them without embarrassment or discomfort. Women with shawls and veils can breastfeed anywhere without calling attention to themselves, while baby is protected from dust and flies. In most non-Western societies, the dress and ornaments of women celebrate the mothering function. Ours deny it. (The Western aesthetic of the virgin breast is catching on, alas, for the brassiere and artificial baby foods have virtually conquered the world.) In societies where women give birth as soon as they have attained maturity, the changes of pregnancy cannot be as disorienting as they are for Western women whose body-image is fixed (although probably erroneously). Because mothers are younger the changes of pregnancy are less likely to leave permanent unsightly signs like stretchmarks. Such mothers are more likely to see pregnancy as the culmination of their development than as the ruination of a mature body. There are those who will compliment the young mother-to-be on having reached the pinnacle of female beauty.

The ways of managing childbirth in traditional societies are many and varied; their usefulness stems directly from the fact that they are accepted culturally and collectively so that the mother does not have the psychic burden of re-inventing the procedures.[16] Even though the potential catastrophes are alive in the memory of her community and the index of anxiety high, a ritual approach to pregnancy which hems the pregnant woman about with taboos and prohibitions helps to make the anxiety manageable. A woman who observes all the prohibitions and carries out all the rites will be actively involved in holding the unknown at bay. She will have other reinforcements, for many of the ritual observances of pregnancy involve the participation of others who should support her, primarily her husband, then her kinsfolk and then the other members of her community. Some of these behaviours will be sensible and useful, others magical, but they will all increase her sense of security and her conviction that she is conducting the pregnancy, not that it is conducting her. The remnants of this kind of prophylaxis can be found in the persistence of old wives' tales about pregnancy even in our own superrational and confused lifestyle. One university graduate of my acquaintance who approached her pregnancy as if it were her term assignment, meticulously footnoting every development, clung to her pre-natal exercises as a form of ritual observance as well as a helpful preparation for the physical exploit of childbirth, performing them in deep silence and total recollection at the same time every day come hell or high water. As well, she observed the old diehard superstition that acquiring equipment and apparel for baby before the birth was bad luck, and so one of my godchildren shot into the world without crib or napkins. Considerable effort had gone into seeing that the mother had every opportunity to enjoy her baby, but, after her training for unmedicated childbirth for months, in the event the hospital refused to believe she was in second-stage labour until her daughter's head had appeared and she had a long spiral tear in her vagina, which took a lot of the fun out of the next few days. The hospital staff was so uncooperative about breast-feeding that mother and daughter discharged themselves after two days.

This birth was virtually unattended. In non-technocratic societies, except for remarkable accidents, birth is always attended. The commonest arrangement is that the mother sits or crouches, her back rounded, supported by another person, with another to "catch the baby", an expression common in folk dialects around the world. It is a sobering fact that in all the masses of anthropological literature there are very few accounts of the management of childbirth. Anthropologists are usually men, and even when they are women they are often treated as men. Women all over the world will cover their babies' faces if foreigners appear, because the presence of strangers may pervert the course of potentially dangerous situations.[17] No environment is more difficult of access to an alien than the birth chamber, except of course in a Western hospital. Whereas birth in traditional societies is always attended by a strictly specified group of people – midwife, female relatives, other women who have borne children and the like – birth in a hospital is semi-public, carried out among strangers and passers-by who may or may not be health professionals with a duty to attend. In the Egyptian village in which Hamed Ammar grew up, birth was a social event, but not a public one:

> Immediately the birth pangs are felt close female relatives are called upon, and soon the house teems with other women coming to offer their help ... For delivery the pregnant woman is seated on three stones ... The mother usually supports the back, while two other women each hold a leg, and another two the outstretched arms...[18]

Western women might well say that they would rather that only strangers saw them through the ordeal, for then their demeanour during it would not be remembered. The Egyptian women know that there is pain (as the male obstetrician cannot know) and they also know that it will end. Brigitte Jordan's account of the help given by other women in a difficult birth in Yucatan is expressed in an appropriately unsentimental manner, but it is clear that what she participated in was a profoundly moving experience:

> When a woman needs encouragement to renew her flagging strength, helpers respond to her with what we came to call "birth talk". At the onset of a contraction casual conversation stops. A rising chorus of helpers' voices pours out an insistent rhythmic stream of words whose intensity matches the strength and length of the contraction. "*Ence, ence, mama*", "*jala, jala, jala*", "*tuuchila*", "*ko'osh, ko'osh*" come from all sides of the hammock. With the "head helper" behind her, not only holding her but physically matching every contraction, the laboring woman is surrounded by intense urging in the touch, sight and sound of those close to her ...
> When the mother is on the chair, the physical involvement of the "head helper" is at its most intense. Most of the weight of the woman giving birth rests on her. When a contraction comes and the woman begins to push, there is a matching exertion visible in the helper's body. She covers the laboring woman's

nose and mouth with her hand, holds her own breath, and pushes herself until they both run out of air ...

The intense physical and emotional involvement of the helpers in a long and demanding birth is mirrored in the strain on their faces and in the signs of fatigue that become evident in them as well as the mother ...[19]

From the beginning of her labour the mother has been the centre of attention; no one has hurried her, instead they have sat around with her talking and enjoying being together. As time off manual work, the attendance at a childbed is a festival and the woman giving birth is at the centre of it. Her head helper may be her husband or her mother, or both at different stages in her labour. Their presence and participation in her exertions is an enactment of the fact that her baby is the result of a collective effort and desired by a collective will.

Brigitte Jordan's field work in the Yucatan was based upon the guidelines set out by Margaret Mead and Niles Newton in a 1967 article on "Cultural Patterning of Perinatal Behaviour" which pointed out that information on childbirth as a social event was scarce and misleading in that it was either medically oriented or narrowly anthropological.[20] None of the people now working in the field would permit herself to draw the kinds of conclusions about Western practices that a polemicist might do, but there seems to be evidence available to anyone who suspected that Western practices were bound to discourage women from undergoing birth and to reinforce the technological production paradigm. The insistence on removing the woman from her own territory to the unfamiliar environment of the hospital has a frightening and disorienting effect which is intensified by the further insistence on moving her from place to place once labour is well under way. Instead of being aided by familiar figures whom she trusts and who have nothing else to do for the time being but assist her, she is competing for the attention of professionals, who will not give her their undivided attention unless she earns it by turning into a medical emergency. Hospitals do not encourage competence in giving birth because they do not recognise it, let alone reward it. Much of what they routinely do is calculated to diminish the woman's efficiency, such as forcing her into the passive lithotomy position.[21] The justification for such procedures is that they reduce infant mortality but there is no hard evidence that they do. Contractions are more efficient, pain less, labour shorter and blood supply to the placenta better if the mother is squatting or crouching rather than wallowing on her back. To lengthen labour and diminish the blood supply to the placenta is to increase the risk to the infant. To further drug the mother (and therefore the infant) is to place further obstacles in the way of the birth of a healthy, alert baby. The evidence for all kinds of obstetric procedures is contradictory, but the contradictions are not registered as significant. The motivation behind the procedures is not after all rational or "scientific" but superstitious. Through our proxies, the medical professionals, who are now the only priests or shamans that *homo occidentalis* recognises, we are making our own attempt to control the mystery and danger of the production of new human beings. The hospital will control the pollution, just as the hospital deals with the pollution of blood and death. The fearful blurring of the edges between one life and the next, between blood and faeces, between soundness and mutilation, will be pared away by the surgeon's knife. The episiotomy routinely practised in American obstetrics is a ritual mutilation rather than a necessary medical procedure: it is a sign that the woman herself is incapable of giving birth.

It would be clearly absurd to maintain that traditional childbirth is more efficient than modern obstetric techniques in keeping perinatal mortality to a minimum. Some of the procedures appear instead to be calculated to cull the newborn, such as cutting the umbilical cord with a dirty sickle or branding the infant with a hot iron. People living at subsistence level or below know that there are worse fates than death; slow starvation is a more painful end than extinction on the threshold of life. Traditional societies are aware of a wider range of anguish than we of the cushioned West. At the same time that the child confronts artificial hazards at birth, care is taken to see that nothing threatens the establishment of suckling and lactation. Thus the newborn is not separated from its mother, not "monitored" for twenty-four hours to see that all its systems are functioning and no intervention is required. If such intervention is in fact required, the infant will die. Having given itself so great an illusion of control and so great a power of interference, Western medicine has to confront a series of dilemmas which are resolved before traditional practitioners become aware of them. At Johns Hopkins Hospital in Baltimore, a mongoloid child with intestinal atresia was born to a nurse and her husband. Perhaps because she was a member of the confraternity which is allowed to exercise a measure of control they were asked if they wished to refuse permission for the operation to correct the intestinal atresia, which they were legally permitted to do. They took the opportunity; the child starved to death for fifteen days in a corner of the same nursery where dedicated nurses were battling night and day to save the lives of premature babies. The moral chaos of our pseudo-rational society is vividly illustrated by this case; no law was broken but nobody behaved well.[22] Nobody had the courage to give the child an opium pellet or push its face into the pillow and nobody snatched it up and mended its bowel so that it might live. If the child had been born in a dirty hut in some poor and backward country, and placed upon his mother's belly to suckle when he was ready, he would have aspirated the milk and died.

Clearly infant and mother mortality is greater in traditional births, but in our anxiety to avoid death we may have destroyed the significance of the experience for the vast majority who live.

No one would deny that each infant and particularly every maternal death is a tragedy to be prevented if at all possible, nor that modern obstetric care, which has developed in the hospital setting, has been at least partly responsible for the dramatic decrease in both maternal and perinatal mortality over the past half century. But it is not necessarily perverse to question whether our present priority should be to reach minimum figures for perinatal mortality at any price when this includes giving up things which free human beings have often felt to be more important than their own survival – such as freedom to live their own lives their own way and to make individual choices in line with their own sense of values.[23]

Childbirth has been transformed from an awesome personal and social event into a medical phenomenon, from a heroic ordeal into a meaningless and chaotic one; physical pain which we can bear has been transformed into mental stress, which we are less well geared for. The management of pregnancy, childbed and child raising was the principal expression of the familial and societal network of women, itself one of the essential cohesive elements in any society and a necessary leaven to the competitive hierarchies of men. The institutionalisation of child production has destroyed this alternative structure. It is largely as an unconscious reaction to this diminution of women's role that women are now exerting such pressure to be allowed into the competitive male hierarchy. It is probably inevitable that such women, who have the considerable advantages of literacy and articulacy, should see in the lives of women still living in the web of fertility and continuity the meaninglessness and bewilderment that they themselves would experience in such roles in a society that sets no store by them. The women who are active in international organisations are likely to assume that no one who had a choice would go through childbirth more than once or twice and at a relatively advanced age; the women who compile the Knowledge–Attitude–Practice studies, beloved of family planning organisations, noting the correlation between education level and decline in fertility, may be convinced that their "own-society" values are valid for all times and places. The women they are seeking to help might feel sorrier for them than they can well imagine. The majority of the world's women have not simply been entrapped into motherhood: in societies which have not undergone demographic transition, where children are a priceless resource, the role of mother is not a marginal one but central to social life and organisation.

In many societies women still go forth from their mothers' houses at marriage to live with a mother-in-law and the wives of their husbands' brothers. It is a truism of anthropology that such women do not become members of their new family until they have borne a child. If we consider that in such societies the marriage was quite likely to have been arranged, it is understandable that the bride too longs for the child who will stand in the same intimate relationship to her as she with her own mother. The Western interpretation of such mores is that they are backward, cruel and wrong; it is assumed that the sexual relations between the spouses are perfunctory and exploitative and that all mothers-in-law are unjust and vindictive. At a conference to mark International Women's Day at the UN Secretariat in Vienna in 1981, two members of an organisation called Amnesty for Women provided the assembled women with a description of typical Muslim marriage which was no more than a coarse ethnocentric libel. The one Muslim woman on the panel, who may have been virtually the only Muslim present, looked up in astonishment to hear the domestic life of her people described in terms of the utmost squalor, but, less willing than the speakers to divide the consensus, she decided to hold her tongue. One of the greatest difficulties in the way of feminists who are not chauvinistic and want to learn from women who still live within a female society is the tendency of those women to withdraw into silent opposition when participating in international fora conducted in languages which they cannot speak with fluency; women officials of the Sudanese government told me that they had given up going to international conferences, even though the trips were a tremendous treat, because they were tired of being told about their own lives instead of being consulted.

Thus we in the West would regard it as outrageous that a woman could lose her own name and become known as the mother of her first-born, once she has borne it – although of course most of us do not protest against the sinking of the woman's lineage under her husband's name at marriage. In many traditional societies the relationship between mother and child is more important than the relationship between husband and wife: in some, indeed, the child's relationship with the rest of his family is as important or even more important than either.

> ... a number of social usages may stress the child's relationship with the rest of his kin-group at the expense of that with his parents. His aunts and uncles may be permitted greater physical intimacy with him in public than his parents. In many traditional societies in Africa and India the biological family is deliberately weakened, by enforced abstinence or actual separation of parents, in order to strengthen the extended family – thus children are not born at the whim of the parents, but in response to a broader pressure from the whole group.[24]

Among the fierce Rajputs, a bridegroom leaving to collect his bride "sucks his mother's breast to signify that the highest duty of a Rajput is to uphold the dignity of his mother's milk."[25]

The woman who satisfies the longings of her peers by producing the child they are all anxious to see, finds her achievement celebrated in ways that dramatise her success. Among the few first-person accounts of how this works in practice is this one from a young Sylheti woman:

If a girl is lucky, and her parents are alive, she goes to her mother's house for the last few months of her pregnancy and about the first three months of the baby's life. There she gets a lot of love and care. She is asked, "What would you like to eat? What do you fancy?" All the time she is looked after. The whole matter of pregnancy is one of celebration. When the baby is born it is an occasion of joy for the whole family. The naming ceremony is lovely. It is held when the baby is seven days old. A new dress is bought for it and a new sari for the mother. There is feasting and singing until late at night. The women and girls gather and sing songs. Garlands of turmeric and garlic are worn to ward off evil spirits. That's when the name is chosen ... The ceremony is held for the birth of a boy or a girl. Of course it is considered better to have a boy, but the birth of a girl is celebrated with the same joy by the women in the family. We sit together eating *pan* and singing. Some of us might be young unmarried girls, others aged ladies of forty or fifty. There are so many jokes, so much laughter. People look so funny eating *pan* and singing. The men don't take much part. They may come and have a look at the baby, but the singing, the gathering together at night – it is all women. The songs are simple songs which are rarely written down. They are about the lives of women in Bengal.[26]

Among the rewards of pregnancy in this case, as in many others, is that the woman gets to go home to visit her mother and sisters; the nostalgic tone of the description, which is clearly tinged with rose, may be the product of the contrast that this young woman finds in England. Another of the Asian women who found a voice in Amrit Wilson's book gives a similarly rosy picture of rearing a child in Bangladesh:

In Bangladesh children under the age of five or six are looked after by the whole family. All the children of the joint family are looked after together. They are taken to the pond for a bath perhaps by one daughter-in-law, and she baths them all. Then they all come in and sit down to eat. Perhaps the youngest daughter-in-law has cooked the meal. Another woman feeds them. As for playing, the children play out of doors with natural objects. Here people say that Asian children don't play with toys. In Bangladesh they don't need toys. They make their own simple things ... In the afternoon they love to hear Rupthoka (fairy tales). Maybe there is a favourite aunt, she tells them these stories. But at night when they get sleepy they always go to their mothers and sleep in her embrace. But other women do help a lot, in fact they have such strong relationships with the child that it is not uncommon for them to be called Big Mother or Small Mother ...[27]

The system does not always work as well as it does in this account from Hashmat Ara Begum but it is the ideal that lies behind the common sight of children carrying children in the sub-continent. In the tone of her explanation of the fact that Asian children do not have toys, the strain of confrontation with industrialised lifestyle can be sensed; deprived of the real Bangladeshi world, children have yet to develop a taste for the expensive surrogate objects with which we placate our children for their lack of human contact. The Asian lifestyle seems austere to consumerist society; to the immigrants the British lifestyle seems inhuman. Transplanted from their villages to the decaying inner suburbs of dull industrial towns, these women suffer greatly, despite the fact that they have a better chance of bearing healthy children than they had at home. Their misery is not simply explained by their ignorance of the language or the thinly disguised racist hostility they encounter. Their entire support system has vanished; from never being alone they have moved into a situation of utter solitude for which their relative affluence cannot compensate. The crisis of childbirth, faced as it is for all women in the West without psychological support and involving severe outrage to Muslim modesty, frequently precipitates them into depressed states. (The attitude of medical personnel to these women, based as it is in utter incomprehension of their terror and despair, is a contributory factor.) Amrit Wilson went to visit one such woman, forced into emotional dependence upon a husband who was working long hours to give the family the good life they had come to England to find.

> Late, late at night my husband comes home. He loves the babies. He is a good husband, but what can he do? And what can I do? How can I live, sister, how can I live?[28]

Children in the West then are a far greater burden than they are in the countries these women came from; not only are women more likely to be dealing with the children alone but the children themselves are more demanding than they are in non-consumer society. In the Egyptian village, for example:

> there are invariably at least two grown-up women attending to the rearing of the child. As the newborn baby, or even any child, has no special cradle, cot or bed, it always sleeps by its mother or sits on her lap.[29]

The Egyptian baby is not trained in consumer behaviour any more than the Bangladeshi baby. In the last hundred years the consumerism of Western babies has gone ahead by leaps and bounds.[30] The baby-carriage, a relatively modern invention, is the most expensive item, and, significantly the one that is paraded before the public; to it are added the baby's layette, crib, cot, napkins and the like, all clearly designed for baby's use and therefore instantly obsolescent. Some of the impedimenta, such as bootees and talcum powder, are completely useless, but most is designed to keep baby dry, tidy and out of contact, hemmed in from the real world by bassinet walls or perambulator covers or, most bizarre of all, the bars of the play-pen. The child who has no pram, no crib, and certainly no room of its own cannot be escaped, especially if it cannot be put down on the floor because it is made of dirt or because precious water cannot be spared to wash it very often. Children who are constantly attached to adults obviously cannot be segregated; they must come into the workplace and into the sleeping place and the patterns of both must be modified to receive them. Often drudgery separates adults from children, if they are working on road gangs or construction sites, for example, but the separation is seen as another of the trials of poverty.

The child's socialisation will be carried out in the midst of his kin-group; it is not easy to drive the wedge of professional care into traditional families. There is no need of a play-group, because the play-group is right there, no need for that matter of the nursery school. The noise of children is a constant accompaniment to daily life, and probably a good deal less fraying to the nerves than the cacophony of consumer society. Mothers are not so vulnerable to infantile ill-temper because they do not have to take sole responsibility for it. Reward and punishment are doled out according to family practice; mothers don't have to rush to Dr Spock to find out how to deal with some particularly antisocial manifestation. The family ethos prevails, as it has prevailed for generations, without anxious soul-searching, which is not to say that it is always humane or just, but simply that it is not a cause of internalised tension. The extended family is in many ways a boring and oppressive environment, but it does offer a sense and a context to mothering which two-bedroomed villas in the suburbs do not. The children may be grubby, they may be less well-nourished than Western children, but they have a clear sense of the group they belong to, and their own role within it. They will not be found screaming for all the goods displayed in the supermarket (and to make them so scream is the point of the display) until their frantic mothers lose control and bash them, and then compound the injury by poking sweets into their mouths.

The closeness of adults and children in traditional societies is partly a result of the exclusion of women from the public sphere and their generally low levels of literacy, but these disabilities are in part compensated for by the centrality of the household in daily life. There is little in the way of public or commercial amusement; entertainments and celebrations take place in the household and children are included. Men may go to the coffee-house or the *mudhif* for their entertainment but their freedom to do so is not regarded with envy, for women and children are capable of having riotous good fun on their own. Perhaps the most important difference between mothering in traditional societies and mothering in our own is that the traditional mother's role increases in complexity and importance as she grows older. If she is skilful and fortunate enough to keep her sons and her sons' wives as members of her household, she will enjoy their service and companionship as she grows older. She will have time to play with her grandchildren; her flagging pace will match their unsteady steps. As she sinks into feebleness, her sons' wives will assume her responsibilities and care for her until the last. The ideal situation is not inevitable; dispossessed old women can be found begging and dying on the streets of India, but success is possible. The role of matriarch is a positive one which can be worked towards by an intelligent and determined woman. Mistreating daughters-in-law is unlikely to further her aims, because discontented wives are a principal cause of the fissioning of the extended family. Because the household is an essential unit in the production of goods and services, her role as its manager is a challenging one beside which the role of the Western housewife seems downright impoverished. Even her absent daughters, whose departure for their husbands' dwellingplaces caused her such grief, keep close to her in feeling. One of the most remarkable aspects of Elizabeth Warnock Fernea's life as the veiled wife of an American anthropologist in an Iraqi village was the utter certainty of the Iraqi women that she must have been as attached to her mother as they were.

> "Where is your mother?" Kulthum asked. I told her she was in America far away . . . the woman clucked in sympathy.
> "Poor girl," they said, "poor child . . ."
> "When you have children, you will not feel so alone without your mother," prophesied Kulthum.

When she announced her impending return to America, the women saw only one reason for her going:

> "Ask Mr Bob to bring your mother, and then you'll never have to leave us and go back to America."[31]

Mrs Fernea did not volunteer to reveal the truth about the status of mothers in Western society. Eventually the Iraqi women confronted her with it:

> "And is it true," asked Basima, "that in America they put all the old women in houses by themselves, away from their families?"
> I admitted that this was sometimes true and tried to explain but my words were drowned in the general murmur of disapproval.
> "What a terrible place that must be!"
> "How awful!"
> "And their children let them go?"
> . . . It had never occurred to me before, but the idea of old people's homes must have been particularly reprehensible to these women whose world lay within the family unit and whose lives of toil and childbearing were rewarded in old age, when they enjoyed repose and respect as members of their children's households.[32]

This discussion of the difference in the role of mother in highly industrialised bureaucratic communities and in traditional agricultural communities is not meant as a panegyric for the disappearing world, but simply to indicate something of the context in which the birthrate in the developed world has fallen. There is little point in feeling sorry for Western mothers who are most often as anxious to be freed of their children as their children are to be freed of them. The inhabitants of old people's homes and retirement villages do not sit sobbing and railing against destiny, although they do compete with each other in displaying the rather exiguous proofs of their children's affection. As the recession bites deeper and unemployment rises, more and more adult children are having to remain dependent on their parents, who are lamenting loudly and wondering more vociferously than usual why they let themselves in for such a thankless task as parenting. The point of the contrast is simply to caution the people of the highly industrialised countries which wield such massive economic and cultural sway over the developing world against assuming that one of the things they must rescue the rest of the world from is parenting. That motherhood is virtually meaningless in our society is no ground for supposing that the fact that women are still defined by their mothering function in other societies is simply an index of their oppression. We have at least to consider the possibility that a successful matriarch might well pity Western feminists for having been duped into futile competition with men in exchange for the companionship and love of children and other women.

There is no possibility of return to the family-centred world. Groups of individuals may attempt to live in the electronic age by the values of an earlier time: they may go back to the land, live in artificial extended families, and give birth at home according to rituals they have learned from anthropology books or from Lamaze and Leboyer, but their freedom to do so is itself dependent upon the wealth created by the workers who live in the mobile nuclear families which the communards despise. If they fail in their chosen lifestyle, the safety net of consumer society will catch them: if their home birth goes wrong, they can load the suffering woman into a car and speed down the tarmac road to the nearest hospital. The women giving birth in African or Asian villages cannot telephone for emergency squads to speed to their aid, supposing there existed a road suitable for travelling on at speed. Yet the chances are that women in traditional societies will cling to their own methods, for such methods are among the ways that peoples define themselves. Humane and intelligent planning could devise ways of decreasing perinatal morbidity without destroying the character and significance of the experience, but international aid does not come in such forms. There are too many indications that the impact of our medical technology on traditional mothering has been disastrous, to the point of raising the question whether it has not been our subconscious intention to discourage parenting among foreigners even more effectively than we have discouraged it among ourselves.

If there are few accounts of traditional childbirth management, there are even fewer of traditional childbirth management transplanted into hospitals. One such has been written by Ian Young, a medical student who took his midwifery training in Kabylia. He called his book *The Private Life of Islam* although it deals with no such thing; in all the time he was working in Algeria Young never mentions a normal birth, which would have been conducted far from his eyes. Instead he saw the women who had laboured and lost, who had tried folk medicine and, despairing, had undertaken the long hard journey in filthy trucks over barely existing roads. He found women with foetuses long dead *in utero* and women who had retained placenta or incomplete miscarriages, who had bled their lives away before the East European doctors could begin their savage ministrations, in filthy conditions, lacking the most basic equipment, administering drugs which had long since fallen from favour in the countries of their manufacture. Young's rage is principally directed at Islam and ignorance; he never doubts the superiority of the system which he, as a British-trained doctor, represented. He raged that the women arrived in filthy garments stiff with blood and faeces, and insisted on washing the women himself. He begged and bullied husbands not to drag their sick wives back to their duties on their mountain farms, not understanding that for them it was a question of the life or death of the whole group.[33] There was even the possibility, which Young does not mention, that care among the family would have been superior to the squalor and agony (and danger) of the hospital. He did not see that the stunned passivity of the women who suffered and died in silence at the hands of his callous colleagues was the outward expression of their belief that the disaster had already happened. That these men should touch and reach inside them was a humiliation beside which the agony of procedures carried out without pain relief of any kind paled into insignificance. Pain was something they had learned to cope with; destruction of their psychic integrity was not. Young saw them as brutalised cows, not understanding that the Islam that he was seeing was Islam in disarray, disrupted and turned upon itself by a civil war. Perhaps he would be pleased to hear that fewer and fewer women dice with death by giving birth in isolated settlements because more and more the struggling poor are drawn to live in the *bidonvilles*, where if life offers fewer opportunities it also presents fewer dangers.

Even where traditional kinship systems still prevail, the authorities are providing clinics and hospitals for the institutionalisation of childbirth. In 1961 E. R. Leach recorded that most pregnant women in the Sinhalese village of Pul Eliya "regularly make the seven-mile journey to Medwach-chiya to attend the government ante-natal clinic." He does not explain why the clinic could not come to the women. While hospitalisation had clearly reduced perinatal mortality, Leach did log a small but significant disadvantage of the situation:

Now that all the women had their babies in hospital the rewards of the ritual office of washerwoman were no longer worthwhile ... Formerly attendance at birth was the most regular and the most lucrative of the washerwoman's various caste obligations ...[34]

In terms of the delicate orchestration of relations between the various castes in a village with an extremely complex kinship system, the significance of the washerwoman's displacement may extend far beyond her loss of livelihood and function. It is another sign that the pattern that Leach logged so patiently twenty years ago was on the verge of dissolution. The institutionalisation of childbirth is not simply undertaken as a way of making the demanding lives of peasants a little easier and a little longer: a system which immobilises the populace and confines the economy to mere subsistence is incompatible with the aims of a modern nation state. Complete hospitalisation of birth is beyond the resources of most third-world governments, but as most ruling elites in ex-colonies have accepted the value system of the imperialist hegemony under which they came to power, Western methods of health care are seen as the standard. The development of hospital facilities in such countries is usually haphazard: foreign aid builds hospitals glittering with chromium and stuffed with expensive equipment which stand empty because the people cannot leave their fields for the days and days it takes to get to them on foot or by ox-cart. Exasperated foreigners lament the corruption and stupidity of local officials, the essential supplies that are lacking, the broken equipment that is not mended. As the light of perception dawns on the administrators of aid schemes they begin discussing the possibility of ox-cart medical care in lieu of the Rolls-Royce system which is so conspicuously maladapted to the needs of peasant society, but the illusion of control cannot be forgone.

The humane method of lowering the mortality associated with traditional childbirth methods would have been to have consulted with the women who were dealing with the problem and accepted their definition of the shortcomings of their methods. Instead, governments half-train young women and send them to live among the peasants and take over from the traditional midwife. The Auxiliary Nurse Midwives, or whatever version of some such name they are called, are usually not trained to perform any kinds of surgical procedures and not given any useful drugs, and they may well lack the special skills of the traditional practitioners which are almost invariably assumed not to exist: for example, Brigitte Jordan frequently observed the Yucatecan midwife with whom she worked turning the foetus *in utero* by massage in order to avoid a breech birth.[35] Oscar Lewis, whose detailed account of childbed procedures in Tepoztlan is probably based on information collected by his female assistants, simply writes that "Midwives say they can change the position of the fetus if necessary by means of massage."[36] His whole account reeks of scepticism and distaste; most of the practices described seem to have no rhyme or reason, perhaps because the information was collected by interrogation and not by observation. Most peasant peoples are bad at explanations and disoriented by questions asking why they do what they do. In fact Lewis and Redfield, who studied Tepoztlan before him, got very different impressions of childbirth procedures, probably because they asked different questions in a different manner.[37] Scepticism and contempt are attitudes which prevail in the day-to-day treatment of traditional birth attendants by trained medical personnel, even those with a special responsibility toward them. When I asked a woman doctor in Karnataka who was taking a class of midwives through their paces whether she had ever asked the women what they used to do and why, she sneered, "Do, they don't do anything!" threw her pink chiffon palu over her shoulder and sailed out. The women had walked for miles in shimmering heat to visit the class and get new supplies of carbolic soap and their other meagre requisites. They had not been offered so much as a poppadum and a glass of water and had squatted crushed together on the floor of the tiny classroom for hours waiting for the lady doctor to make her film-star entrance and flourish her nasty plastic model of the pudenda, which the women hardly seemed to recognise. It being bright pink, matching the doctor's rubies and chiffon, they probably thought it was some esoteric accessory worn by very high-caste Brahmins.[38]

The replacements sent by government for these hard-working women who share the hardships of the communities in which they live found themselves in an extremely unenviable situation; compelled to live as peasants, to drink filthy water and live in whatever accommodation could be spared, they were exposed to the curiosity and distrust of the villagers who had no experience of kinless women.[39] The village women feared that their presence would be disruptive, and so it was; in the village I have mentioned the sarpanch's son had fallen in love with the ANM who had been sent away; her lover had run away to be with her and eventually his family was prevailed upon to accept a marriage. Scandal and tragedy dogged the unhappy ANMs in India while the peasant women continued to prefer the ministrations of their traditional assistants who spoke their dialect, who knew them well, who respected their modesty and who helped with household chores during the period of confinement and pollution. Nowadays governments are increasingly accepting the idea that they cannot push the traditional midwives aside, but they mostly train them in schoolroom situations and simply confuse and bewilder them.[40] The hostility built up by the generations of struggle between modern technicians and traditional attendants is not easily neutralised; many midwife training programmes are as perfunctory as the one I have described.

Government-trained midwives were expected also to recruit patients for the shiny hospitals; they were representatives of state control and as such deeply distrusted by people for whom the state exists only as a tax-gatherer and maker of idiotic laws which prevent hard-working people from earning a living. Once separated from their kin and exposed to severe psychic stress in hospital, women can easily be pressured to accept other people's ideas of what is best for them. Hospitals do not welcome the children of the poor, but they do promote sterilisations, especially if the government has given them a quota to fill. There are too many discussions of the effectiveness of offering sterilisation during and after childbirth for us to ignore their significance. If the trauma of childbirth inclines women to accept sterilisation, especially in the immediate post-natal period, why reduce the trauma? Why not enhance it, indeed? Public servants have accepted the idea of a common good and with it these days the idea that there are too many children around, particularly too many poor children. I have never encountered a doctor who was consciously genocidal, but there are hundreds of thousands who truly believe that sterility is good for people, whether they want it or not. The kinder, the gentler, the more expert they are, the more power they can wield.

All technological change causes social problems; the impact of Western medicine in traditional societies is one of the most problematic areas of modernisation. The prestige of the white-coats is enormous, the respect for their miraculous hypodermics total. The pressure of expectation makes for aggressive and dramatic procedures even when the health status of the patients is too poor to withstand them. Allopathic doctors in peasant communities are dependent upon expensive drugs, sparkling equipment and lots of electricity, most of which they have not got in sufficient quantity. Where foreign aid has established that temple of our religion, the hospital, it must make a ritual display of its power with horrible results: Sheila Kitzinger visited an enormous modern hospital for "Bantu patients" in South Africa, and this is what she saw:

> The delivery ward was full of groaning, writhing women – the majority labouring alone. Oxytocin drips and pumps were in widespread use. This was the meeting-place of the old Africa and the new technology of the West. Pools of blood lay on the floor like sacrificial out-pourings, and Bantu nurses were happy to leave them there as a witness of the blessings of the earth, while they busied themselves with technologically sophisticated modern equipment and ignored the labouring women as far as possible, which it was not so difficult to do as they did not speak the same languages anyway ... Birth was very far from normal here and it was conducted in such a way that I had seen before in American hospitals catering for black "clinic" patients from large urban ghettos: impersonal conveyor-belt obstetrics accompanied by a plethora of technical innovations and machinery.[41]

If we turn birth from a climactic personal experience into a personal disaster, it matters little that the result is more likely to be a live child. Women will not long continue to offer up their bodies and minds to such brutality, especially if there is no one at home to welcome the child, to praise the mother for her courage and to help her raise it. In fact peasant communities are more level-headed and sceptical of us and our methods than we realise and they have resisted the intrusion of our chromium-plated technology more successfully than we like to think. They know that death attends too frequently in the traditional birthplace, but they also know that there are worse fates than death. Nevertheless, all that stops our technology from reaching into every hut and hovel is poverty: the cultural hegemony of Western technology is total.

The voices of a few women raised in warning cannot be heard over the humming and throbbing of our machines, which is probably just as well, for if we succeed in crushing all pride and dignity out of child bearing, the population explosion will take care of itself.

Chapter Two

The Importance of Fertility

The disruptive powers of excessive national fecundity may have played a greater part in bursting the bonds of convention than either the power of ideas or the errors of autocracy.

John Maynard Keynes

In February 1980, in Orléans, a police inspector was sentenced to seven years imprisonment for the murder of an unarmed man called Paul Laurent whom he shot with his police pistol in front of three witnesses. The sentence is a light one, but even so the populace was shocked by its severity. The murderer, Louis Castalas, had joined the French Resistance as a boy of 17 in 1941; he was captured and subjected to torture and medical experiments in Buchenwald. For his heroism with the Resistance he won the Légion d'Honneur, for his endurance in Buchenwald the Croix de Guerre and later in Indochina the Médaille Militaire. As a result of what the Nazi doctors had done to him, he was sterile.

"That was the reason," summed up David Raymond, Paris correspondent of the *Sunday Express*, "for his first two wives divorcing him." He married a third wife, only twenty-six years old (to his forty-three) and when she presented him with a son, Hervé, he was overjoyed and made them the centre of his existence. The man he killed was the child's real father. Afterwards he drove his wife home and telephoned the police. "That was the last time he saw Hervé. From the day of his arrest to the day of his trial, Castalas never once asked to see the boy he called son," and had called son for more than seven years.[1]

In what sense were Castalas' Nazi torturers responsible for what followed? We do not know whether Castalas' wives left him simply because he could not give them children. Perhaps because his sterility rendered them also sterile, they left merely to seek a fertiliser for their ova, or perhaps because he was so obsessed with the problem of his sterility, his behaviour was unbearable, or, mid-way between these two very possible alternatives, he would not allow them to be impregnated by artificial insemination. It is significant that he chose to murder the man whose genes had been passed on through his wife, a man evidently bound to him by no special ties of trust, rather than the woman who had played upon his susceptibility, or the child who had enjoyed his devoted love by innocent false pretences, or himself, gross and credulous cuckold that he had been for years. Despite the irrationality of his behaviour – he killed the person who had been least responsible, who had not claimed his son, or stolen Castalas' wife, or enjoyed any advantage from the deception except the rather intangible one of passing on his genes – he was given a mere seven years in prison.

The sentence represents the survival of archaic concepts of shame and the vindication of honour. The woman was not killed because she was not an equal. Castalas was a warrior, who had left the army for the next best thing, the police. His life had been one of old-fashioned segregation concerned entirely with the affairs of men, aware of women only as sex objects and vessels for his posterity, and this factor may have been more decisive in his earlier divorces than his sterility. To the people of France represented in the courtroom in Orléans, his sterility seemed adequate justification for his antisocial behaviour. In this moral system, women have no honour as such, for honour is intimately connected with the potential for paternity. The community of males must uphold each other's honour against the duplicity and licentiousness of women. The idea of the untrustworthiness of women may stem directly from the fact that women cannot be deceived as Castalas was. They are always sure that their children are really theirs, whereas men can never be so sure. Men must *trust*, until such time as paternity can be positively demonstrated. Meanwhile, in terms of genetic morality, women have every reason to vary their partners because this gives them a chance of breeding with the most vigorous and virile strain.

When the systems of which Castalas' morality is a garbled survivor actually prevailed, his kinsmen would have aided him in taking vengeance on the invading male, much as the legal system purports to punish severely any male involved in rape for reasons entirely unconnected with the injury done to the woman. There would have been no punishment as such; either the killing of the adulterer, if a member of the group, would have been accepted as right, because his behaviour was potentially destructive of the commonalty, or it would have been avenged by the adulterer's kinsmen, if he came from outside the group. How the group is defined is not important: the Nazis destroyed Castalas' fertility in the interests of their group, the master-race, otherwise known as the Germans, otherwise known as the NSDAP, and they conceived their enemies as the French and in particular the Resistance. Poor Castalas had no group to support him when he destroyed the outsider male, and disowned the child who was no child of his. His tiny nuclear unit, itself only the last surviving fragment of ruined groups, had never existed.

Nevertheless, the crowds in the courtroom in Orléans and the people who read the newspapers felt that he ought to have been *let go free*. As a convicted murderer he had to be stripped of his decorations, and this too was felt to be wrong for a man so sorely tried. It was as if his occult castration by the Nazis was being repeated in public by his own countrymen and they were embarrassed by their unwilling complicity. The judge was implacable in his resistance, for the logic of the case was clear, the man had confessed to murder and murderers may not wear the Légion d'Honneur; the irony is doubled by the derivation of the very name of the distinction, for if you had asked Castalas why he killed Laurent he would have said that his honour demanded it, just as it demanded that he hold out under Nazi torture and resist the invaders.

Another word for *honour*, and one which anthropologists have found in close association with it, is *integrity* or *wholeness*. Animals which have not been castrated are called *entire*. Whole systems of stratification, precedence and patronage are based upon the idea of honour, which does not simply relate to sexual transactions, but in Mediterranean societies (and beyond) to all interaction. The basis of the notion is fundamentally that of manhood.

> The ideal of the honourable man is expressed by the word *hombria*, "manliness" ... it is a term which is constantly heard in the *pueblo*, and the concept is expressed as the physical sexual quintessence of the male (*cojones*). The contrary notion is conveyed by the adjective *manso* which means both tame and also castrated.[2]

Julian Pitt-Rivers is here describing a small town in the Sierra de Cadiz, but the point could be made about most Mediterranean societies.[3] Castalas may be of Spanish derivation, but the sympathy for his plight extends from Orléans to England. Manliness or *andrismos* may be demonstrated by sexual activity or by abstention from it, but it is completely incompatible with castration even if not resulting in impotence, for it has an essential connection with patriliny and patrimony.

> *Nif*, the cardinal virtue, the basis of the whole patrilineal system, is indeed essentially a respect for one's lineage, of which one is proud and of which one intends to be worthy.
> *Nif* is therefore the love of the honour of the family, a love of *h'urma* in the sense of respectability and esteem, a love for the good name and renown of one's ancestors, a love of the ancestral lineage, which must remain pure and unsullied, and must be protected from offence as much as from misalliance. It is *nif* that impelled the Kabyle to avenge pitilessly and intransigently the murder of a blood-relation, as well as any attack on the weakest point of the family, namely on his wife or on those women to whom he is allied through

women. Thus, *nif* is above all *amour-propre*, that is to say, in a society in which
the individual exists only through the group, the respect and love of the group.[4]

In many societies the notion of human accountability to posterity is
at the heart of the entire moral system. The group must be advanced
by one's participation, in material terms, in spiritual terms and in terms
of growing larger and more powerful, be it the family, the tribe or the
nation. It is no accident that valour is at the heart of the system, and
intimately connected with manhood, for the family, tribe, or nation will
survive if necessary at the expense of other groups. It will either protect
itself from miscegenation by endogamy or increase its dominion by
exogamy, but it is not advanced at all by childlessness. The extreme
version of acting in the tribal interest is the killing of rival men and the
taking of their wives and children, thus increasing the reproductive opportunity of the victors and the dominance of the group both numerically and
genetically. All polygynous societies reward successful males with increased reproductive opportunity, and insofar as "successful" equals
"fitter" in evolutionary terms, the system makes as much sense as the
behaviour of those does who are only receptive to the dominant male,
proved by fighting. In most such societies it is assumed that men are
fertile unless they have been castrated, and their fertility is called by many
names, as "blood" or "energy" or "mana" or "baraka". The reason why
male sterility is seldom recognised is precisely because the recognition
would strike at the heart of morality: all order and coherence would be
put in jeopardy. In societies whose morality is based upon this concept,
it is not uncommon to find severe prohibitions upon fornication and
adultery, although not on polygyny, and a measure of puritanism in
regulating the exposure of both sexes to supra-normal stimuli through
the mass media and in social activity. The pleasure principle is obliterated
by the demands of fertility, even within an established and duly conse-
crated relationship.

The management of fertility is one of the most important functions
of adulthood: in traditional societies puberty rites dramatise this new
responsibility. Often the passage through initiation indicates an end to
sexual experimentation which has not been discouraged among the sterile
young. After the ritual, sex is no longer a form of infantile amusement.
Nowadays anthropologists are deeply uninterested in the psychological
and moral importance of fertility, which is a pity, for now more than
ever do we need to know just what reproductive behaviour is and
what are the likely results of attempts to manipulate it. Anthropologists are notoriously unwilling to involve themselves with emotive
issues: at the very time when race hatred looked as if it might plunge
the United States into civil war, the subject of race, which had fascinated
ethnologists and anthropologists for a hundred years, was no longer being
studied by anyone. There might be cause to be grateful that no crackpot

theory of fertility is sweeping the globe with the sanction of expert opinion passing for knowledge, but it is nevertheless curious to find anthropologists immersed in the statistical studies of marriage and kinship which have "made their works so many monuments of dreary uninterest" without manifesting the slightest interest in the prevailing concepts of fertility. The relative status of the sexes may be discussed, the transmission of power, and the division of labour, but the spiritual importance of their progeny is nowhere broached. This incuriosity is partly a consequence of the scientific method which anthropologists feel they must adopt if they are not to be swept away on a tide of impressionism. How people explain their behaviour is simply rationalisation, ideology and humbug produced to entertain the intruder; what they do may be observed and recorded. Insofar as sexual behaviour may not be observed, it may not be recorded and sexual fantasy, the major component of sexual activity for many people, may not be observed under any circumstances, *pace* Nancy Friday who has collected material from those people for whom being tape-recorded was not inimical to the fantasy, none of whom ever fantasised about pregnancy or impregnation.[5]

Before the Golden Bough broke, letting fall baby and cradle and all, anthropologists were deeply interested in the cult of fertility. Frazer believed that "the sexual instinct has moulded the religious consciousness,"

> His work constitutes a fertile matrix and mirror of ideas, observations, beliefs and images central to the age. Both in *The Golden Bough* and the age the movements of these ideas were charted by a compass whose cardinal compass points were the concepts of rationality, fertility, irrationality and sterility. The major topics explored were sex, superstition and survival.[6]

The importance of his work is not denied even by modern social anthropologists:

> He showed how universal was the concern of religion with the fertility of men, their herds and their land; and his theory of 'sympathetic magic' drew attention to the symbolism whereby magical rites imitate the effect they are intended to produce,[7]

wrote Lucy Mair in her *Introduction to Social Anthropology*, which is still in use as a basic text for students. Frazer himself had no doubt that his work was of enduring and universal importance:

> To them (ancient peoples) the principle of life and fertility, whether animal or vegetable, was one and indivisible. To live and to cause to live, to eat food and to beget children, these were the primary wants of men in the past, and they will be the primary wants of men in the future, and so long as the world lasts. Other things may be added to enrich and beautify human life, but unless these wants are first satisfied, humanity itself must cease to exist. These two things, therefore, food and children, were what men chiefly sought to procure by the performance of magical rites for the regulation of the seasons.[8]

The compatibility of Frazer's scheme with the ideas of Freud added to its acceptability. Westermarck, Crawley, Hartland, Malinowski and Briffault all developed and diversified the basic notion, but the more they worked in the field the more they realised that Frazer's armchair scholarship was not adequate to describe the varieties of human experience. The aridity and specialisation of today's computer-driven numerical anthropology is largely a reaction to the high-handedness of the cultural anthropologists and the tendency of their speculations to reveal more about themselves than about the people whose lives were no more than grist to their academic mill.

The enduring influence of Frazer was not in the field of the pseudoscience which he founded, but in the imaginative writing of the twentieth century. The semantic connection between creation, procreation, rebirth and immortality is essential to our language. When Shakespeare wrote to the actual begetter of his sonnets:

> Then let not winter's ragged hand deface
> In thee thy summer ere thou be distill'd:
> Make sweet some vial; treasure thou some place
> With beauty's treasure ere it be self-kill'd:
> That use is not forbidden usury
> Which happies those that pay the willing loan;
> That's for thyself to breed an other thee,
> Or ten times happier be it ten for one;
> Ten times thy self were happier than thou art
> If ten of thine ten times refigur'd thee,
> Then what could death do if thou shouldst depart
> Leaving thee living in posterity?
> Be not self-will'd for thou art much too fair
> To be death's conquest and make worms thine heir.
>
> (VI)

he spelt out the relationship between the human career and the seasons, so dear to Frazer, and begged Mr W.H. (or whoever) to pay his debt to nature with generous interest. In the course of his sonnet sequence, he took over the function of conferring immortality and defeating death, in a kind of transference which Jung would have understood, as if he, Shakespeare, were the womb in which he, Mr W.H., was to beget immortal poetry.

> Libido is natural energy which first and foremost serves the purposes of life, but a certain amount in excess of what is needed for instinctive ends can be converted into productive work and used for cultural purposes. This direction of energy becomes initially possible by transferring it to something similar in nature to the object of instinctive interest.... After a period of gestation in the unconscious a symbol is produced which can attract the libido, and also serve as a channel diverting its natural flow.[9]

The persistence of pelvic imagery in this only apparently rational account is its own best demonstration. Whether this kind of thinking is actually comprehensible or not, contemporary Europeans thought they understood it, and the race for the generative myths of the machine age was on. Fertility of mind and body was exalted as the conqueror of entropy; dream imagery of the womb and impregnation sloshed wonderfully about the printed page:

> Astraddle on the dolphin's mire and blood,
> Spirit after spirit! The smithies break the flood,
> The golden smithies of the Emperor!
> Marbles of the dancing floor
> Break bitter furies of complexity,
> Those images that yet
> Fresh images beget,
> That dolphin-torn, that gong-tormented sea.[10]

When T. S. Eliot wrote *The Waste Land*, which was to be the most influential poem in the English tongue for thirty years, he was expounding the same moral system that he had learned from Yeats and Lawrence and their reading of Frazer, in which the highest value, to be rendered by F. R. Leavis as "life", was fecundity. Fecundity was the underlying principle of which productivity and creativity were the metaphors. Industrialised society was seen as a barren landscape inhabited by Hollow Men, impotent debased creatures performing meaningless tasks in rented accommodation, with only the barest recollection of a virile time when they fought at the hot gates. Writers as unlike as Joyce, Conrad, E. M. Forster, Edith Sitwell, Arnold Toynbee, Jessie L. Weston, Gilbert Murray and Robert Graves all responded to the notion of fertility as the governing content in their imagery: all symbols were phallic or vaginal and all artifice imitative of generation. The rice thrown at weddings was not mere rice, nor was it the wealth the union might bring, it was the seed that would impregnate the bride. Christ on the Cross was not so much the Son of God as he was a dying king upon a sacred tree, a corn-doll to rise again at Easter.

> Now the green blade riseth from the buried grain,
> Wheat that in dark earth many days has lain.
> Love lives again that with the dead has been,
> Love has come again like wheat that springeth green,

sang the neo pagans in 1928.[11]

This kind of thing may still be current in Cambridge Humanities teaching, at least in the English school, for Clive James, proud of the otherwise indubitable hardness of his head, had this to say of Jane Austen no longer ago than February, 1980.

In those days women had to choose between sex and art. She chose art and put all her fructive energy into it .... The force she shapes to her symmetrical designs is the same vitality that populates the world.[12]

The concept at the heart of Frazer's theory, which struck his followers with the shock of recognition, is actually completely mysterious. Called variously "the sex instinct" or "the principle of life and fertility" or a "primary want . . . to cause to live . . . to beget children", it was the product of thinking as vague and arbitrary as that which devised sympathetic magic in the first place. The use of the term *instinct* ought itself to have concerned those who had already observed that human females are receptive when not fertile, even, in fact, when pregnant – to Jonathan Swift's great horror – because it revealed the human race as licentious beyond the capacity of beasts. The urge towards orgastic release is much more evident than a primary want to beget children: in the jargon of modern institutionalised sex research:

> we believe that there is a basic physiological 'drive', an internal stimulus situation, which produces a state of tension normally relieved by the physiological and psychological changes produced by sexual arousal and especially orgasm.[13]

No goal beyond release is postulated for this "drive"; someone who has a weak sex drive is not assumed to be infertile, but rather to require infrequent release. Wilhelm Reich postulated that the orgasm was of overriding psychological importance in releasing tension which would otherwise be the cause of aberrant behaviour and neurosis; insofar as fear of pregnancy was an inhibiting factor in this process, fertility was seen as inimical to it. Although there are few adherents to the position as stated in Reich's *The Function of the Orgasm*, his basic point is now widely accepted. Most people believe that regular, orgastic sexual activity is essential to mental health, some even consider sexual abuse of others to be justifiable in the search for the healing orgasm.

In a mammoth work relating all the research so far done on the functioning of the urge to copulate in hundreds of species who reproduce by that means, and finding that the urge survived when fertility was absent and that fertility could be found where potency and orgasm were lacking, Frank Beach came to the following conclusion:

> This differentiation between the secretory and psychic aspects of orgasm leads us directly into a consideration of the fact that libido, potency and fertility are three independent functions, any one of which may exist in the absence of the other two.[14]

It is nowadays assumed that sex must be rescued from its primary reproductive function of which the repeated exercise is anti-social, and exploited instead for its other functions, some seen by Desmond Morris as positive, pair formation, and pair maintenance, physiological release, exploration, and self-reward. Other functions, such as mere pastime in situations of sensory deprivation (when it is compared to nail-biting) or as tranquillising displacement activity, or commercial as in prostitution, or as male status-seeking and display, are seen as negative. Although the separation of sex from its procreational aspect seems to Morris both necessary and good, he is appalled at the consequences of the separation of sex from its function in pair bonding, which litters the world with broken hearts. Human beings, he asserts, are incapable of casual sex or promiscuity. The evidence for this claim, which would see as its optimum situation one of universal, faithful and practically sterile coupledom, is far from scientific.

> The human animal is basically and biologically a pair-forming species. The pair-formation function of sexual behaviour is so important for our species that nowhere outside the pairing phase do sexual activities regularly reach such a high intensity ... only when the pair-bonding mechanism has been equally damaged or is equally suppressed in both partners can a casual human copulation be performed without due risk.[15]

The undeniable fact that sexual intercourse becomes less important in established pairs seems to Morris to be adequately explained in that the intense experiences of the initial phase cement the couple, which is then maintained by a more manageable form of interaction. Unfortunately for Morris, the literature of the Western world abounds in examples of extremely intense sexual behaviour outside the pair bond, to such an extent that it was considered that violent, obsessive sexual passion was essentially adulterous. Morris would say that this occurred in situations where pair-bonding was damaged by arranged marriage or where the original pair-bond was defective in some other way, but he has still to explain the fact that bonded pairs are in constant jeopardy from the prevalence of pair-formation intensity in adulterous relationships. The pair-bonding species which Morris observed, be they herring gulls or foxes, are not subject to this common threat and, as a result, do not exhibit a pattern of serial monogamy. The insecurity of his basic position is well attested by the scandalous *ad hominem* argument he used to refute in advance anyone who might challenge his position:

> Individuals whose pair-bonding mechanism has run into some sort of trouble have occasionally found it convenient to argue that there is no such thing as a biological pairing urge in the human species.[16]

Possessiveness and jealousy are certainly prevalent in human beings, but whether they are to be justified as proceeding from a biological urge is another matter. The miseries caused by rejection after intimacy have myriad observable causes rather than a single occult one, namely the frustration of a biological urge. The oddest aspect of Morris's argument is that while he is convinced that human beings are programmed for pair-bonding, as are numerous other species, very few of them primates, he assumes equally dogmatically that they are not programmed for reproduction and may defy this biological imperative with absolute impunity, although he can produce no examples of species where pair-bonding survives infertility.

Doubtless, human beings insofar as they are animals have biological urges, but their status as determinants of behaviour is extremely hard to gauge because the simpler biological programming is overlaid by extraordinarily complex cultural patterning. Although reflexes exist and produce involuntary actions sometimes called instinctive, there is no instinctual behaviour as such. All creatures may be diverted from a normal instinctual pattern by supra-normal stimuli, and such stimuli are man's normal environment. While the shrill hypotheses of Ardrey and Morris are unhelpful in deciding what sensible human behaviour is, and perhaps even misleading (for example in the assumption that man is a natural carnivore) the more modest caveat of Niko Tinbergen, upon whose careful work much of the fashionable human ethology depends, must be weighed:

> The motivation of human behaviour is a matter of much discussion. Here again, introspection is a hindrance to understanding: it reveals to us only the conscious subjective phenomena, though we have learnt from Freud that non-conscious phenomena of a quite different nature are at work as well ... Mating behaviour in man, not in the form of the accomplishment of the consummatory act, but in the preparatory appetitive stage of 'love-making' proves, when studied ethologically, to be basically dependent on sex hormones and on external stimuli and it is on these agents that our rational powers exert a regulating influence.[17]

What we learnt from Freud was not what the ethologists want to learn from them. While Freud rejected verbal explanations of behaviour as rationalisations, he still looked into the mind for his own account of the causality of the symptoms and actions that he witnessed. The ethologist goes beyond the unconscious and the sub-conscious to posit his own version of Jung's *Rassensinn*. The basic axiom of the ethological account is that "species characteristic behaviour can most fruitfully be viewed in an evolutionary perspective." Genetic programming is the way in which the experience of all the past generations is summed up and transmitted to the individual in the form of occult *motivations* – the word *instinct* having been rejected as too circular to describe behaviour in any but a tautological way.[18]

> From the teleological point of view it is not enough for an animal to remember all of its past experiences. The adaptive advances made possible by behaviour which is wired-in genetically is that learned behaviour is more finely tuned to the anticipated vicissitudes of the individual's experience, while that which is genetically endowed can only be an abstract of millions of years of experience of the species ... it is probable that we are endowed genetically with a system for evaluating current experience in terms of its survival value.[19]

Survival then is one of these occult motivations, and when our hormones gush in response to external stimuli which become more effective because the hormones are a-gush, the ancient, inveterate will of the species is being done, for the nadir of unfitness to survive is "inability or unwillingness to breed".[20] The argument from the computer model is more sophisticated than the old "reproductive instinct" talk, and its premises are the synergistic compounds which drive the human body in ways of which we are completely unconscious, in directions which we then explain to ourselves in terms of more or less irrelevant considerations. When we are actually drawn to someone willy-nilly by his smell, we become convinced that he is a good chap. "Mammalian residues still persist in human sexuality, and we may underrate them."[21]

Tinbergen believes, and there is a mass of evidence to support him, that man is at present in a phase of disadaptation, of loss of viability, brought about in part by his failure to modify his reproductive behaviour to compensate for his meddling in the scheme of things by keeping the unfit alive. His ambivalence can be sensed quite strongly in his description of our great achievement:

> Medical technologies have been highly successful in reducing to a minimum the massive weeding-out of comparative failures that occurs in every generation of animal and plant, and *which alone has ensured continued adaptedness*, i.e., viability.[22]

The concerted moral pressure of our age forces him to utter his support for population control as a symptomatic treatment of our ailment, even though he must be aware that this is an even greater interference in the process of natural selection. He defies the obvious strain to utter his *fiat*:

> Ethology is well-placed to play a part in re-shaping the environment and our own society because, after a phase in which it stressed mainly the genetic aspect of behaviour programming it is now moving to a position where it begins to map the interplay between our genetic blueprint and phenotype flexibility, and to spot the pressures which overstretch even our exceptional flexibility.[23]

Let us then, as the ethologists would do, attack a "problem of behaviour in terms of the sequences for the survival of the species."[24] It is a well-known fact that people do not carry out their stated intentions in the matter of contraception, in the words of the statisticians, "contraceptive attitudes are not related to practice."[25] Most people have tended to have more children than their stated ideal. The 1967–8 Population Investigation Committee National Survey found that 17% of all pregnancies for the marriage cohorts 1941–5 to 1961–5 were accidental, the proportion generally rising with the order of pregnancy.[26] The ideal contraceptive, we are told, must have "no temporal connection with intercourse" because we cannot rely upon the continuity and consistency of the motivation. Each year, 780,000 teenagers are pregnant premaritally in the United States, 680,000 fewer than would be if no contraception was being used, but if all the teenagers who did not want to have a baby had been consistent users of contraception there would have been only about 467,000 pregnancies.[27] This phenomenon might well be evidence of the "interplay between our genetic blueprint and phenotypic flexibility." It is not surprising to learn that "ambivalence . . . and conflict are recurring themes in the psychological literature on contraception." The results are fear, humiliation, distress and pain. Traditional psychologists describe in-efficient users of contraception as "immature", "neurotic", "dependent" and having "low self-esteem": it might be more profitable to take a leaf from the ethologists' book and tell these youngsters, and the older women who get into the same muddle, that their genetic programming presents a real hazard which will require all their vigilance to circumvent.

Traditional Freudians have no need of the ethologists' construct of genetic programming to explain contraceptive failure: guilt will suffice to explain the violence of the self-inflicted punishment of abortion for sexual activity, or masochism (but it must not be forgotten that female masochism itself is postulated as a consequence of the female's role as servant of the species). It may be another form of attention-getting para-suicide, a way of wounding others or blackmailing them.[28] The Freudians would agree with the ethologists about only one aspect of the problem: in these matters there are no accidents, and, like Tinbergen, they would reject the introspective explanation.

Twenty years ago a curious gynaecologist set about studying sixty-one cases of highly motivated, intelligent women, familiar with contraceptive techniques, who reported to him after exposure to the risk of pregnancy. Forty of them were indeed pregnant, only seventeen carried their babies to term; there were twenty-three abortions, of which twenty were induced (with the horrifying complication rate of 50%). He inquired into the circumstances as far as he might, and found that,

> At least twenty women, or their partners, were under severe stress caused by marital infidelity, severe illness, death, fear of sterility, pre-menopausal panic, protracted engagement period, religious conflicts concerning contraception, fear of remaining single, impotence or immaturity in one or both parties.[29]

The function of the pregnancy in such circumstances seemed clear, so he coined the term Wilful Exposure to Unwanted Pregnancy to explain what the women represented to him as an inexplicable accident. Their acceptance of abortion showed that they did not, even subconsciously, desire to have a child; rather it was important to them to assert their fertility in the face of the negative forces that were pressing in on them. Freudian analysis could explain the whole phenomenon, except for one part. Judging from the very incomplete notes, for this was in no sense a controlled experiment, many of the women had reported before their menstrual period was significantly delayed; some reported, and were believed, that they had failed to use their diaphragms on one occasion only, and yet, even after they had been given a hormonal emmenagogue, two-thirds of the women remained pregnant. If one looks for a period of oestrus in women corresponding to that observed in animals, it cannot be found. Women trying to get pregnant have to struggle to have intercourse on the right days, fiddling with thermometers and mucous examinations, but two out of three of Lehfeldt's sample hit the nail right on the head. We can only wonder how many of the 113,000 American teenagers who used contraception inconsistently in 1976 might have shown a similar pattern, i.e., of using contraception when they were sterile, and having unprotected intercourse when they were fertile.[29A] Certainly, my own unsystematic inquiries have come across it as a common pattern. "The minute he ejaculated I knew, and there was my diaphragm sitting on the bedside table"; the syndrome is not rare by any means. What is needed is some non-judgmental examination of contraceptive failure: the biological trip-wire across the path of family planning might be less effective if we know that it is there, and on the other hand it might not.

If we are to posit a mammalian residue lurking in our own fertility-regulating behaviour, it might also be fitting to suspect its presence in other contexts, especially when it comes to attempting to regulate the fertility of others. Irenaus Eibl-Eibesfeldt has said that "Cultures behave like species and can be compared as if they were":[30] even without taking so extreme a position, we perhaps ought to consider the possibility that we are in competition with other groups for the opportunity to pass on our genes. Perhaps what we really fear from the exploding populations of the world is that they will challenge the superiority of our own sub-group and compromise our survival as the biggest, richest, greediest and most numerous group on earth. Certainly, this is how the negroid minority could well see 1,757,000,000 caucasoids in contrast to its own 217,000,000. While we have been less than meticulous in implementing ways of inducing sterility in our own group, we have been positively cavalier in dealing with racial minorities at home, and in dealing with foreign populations. It was shocking, but not surprising, to learn that doctors injecting Depo-Provera post-partum in London hospitals were doing it almost exclusively to Asian women, unasked. Their explanations ought perhaps to be regarded in the same light as rationalisations of contraceptive failure.

If we are, as Wilson suggested in his *Sociobiology*, only our genes' way of producing more genes,

> blends designed not to promote the happiness and survival of the individual but to favour the maximum transmission of the controlling genes.[31]

then altruism towards our own genetic group and egotism towards others come into play. If, as Eibl-Eibesfeldt said, cultures in the human sphere relate to each other like species in the animal world, then we can expect human groups to be in evolutionary competition with one another. Certainly in tribal societies there is great reluctance on the part of any one tribe to accept family planning because of the fear of being supplanted by another group. Attempts to sway their intransigence by appeals to the common good have little force. The notion of a world-wide common good is far too nebulous and involves an exercise of altruism far beyond the range of the group protected by genetic identity, which can extend little further, it seems, than the family, the tribe, the race and occasionally the nationality. The evidence seems to suggest that human beings will spontaneously regulate their fertility in the service of the survival of perceptible groups to which they feel they belong, but that as the group becomes more conceptual than actual the motivation weakens. Within single cultures different classes may challenge each other's right to survival, whether it be because they are "educationally subnormal" or "chinless wonders" or "welfare scroungers" or "feckless".

It seems obvious that fertility regulation can effectively be promoted only by members of the culture which is being urged to adopt it. It must be seen to be carried out in the service of that group, in order to increase its survival capacity, and to be connected to visible consequences rather than demographers' projections. As long as "family planning" consists entirely of pressure to accept sterility or to limit fertility and is presented by strangers, it will be suspect, and not only in tribal societies with a history of mutual antagonism. Indeed, the promulgation of fertility control by outsiders could well have the effect of disrupting endogenous fertility regulation and even discrediting family limitation altogether simply because it comes from outside.

Most depressingly, the ethological account of human behaviour seems to imply that racial antagonism is an ineradicable aspect of it. When African and Asian politicians accuse the apostles of family planning of genocidal intentions, they are usually regarded as unscrupulous humbugs unmoved by the plight of their growing populations enmeshed in a vicious circle of poor nutrition, scant educational opportunity and unemployment. Their inertia in implementing the programmes set up by international agencies and their lip-service to the idea of population limitation are furiously resented, with a considerable degree of justification, but it must also be remembered that all small and struggling nations have an ideal of growth and expansion which is not easily discredited by the richest and hitherto the most expansionist group in the world. Teilhard de Chardin, one of the subtlest and most original thinkers of our age, considered that man is an exploding and accretive phenomenon:

> Ever since the paleolithic era, and even more since the Neolithic, man has lived in a condition of expansion; to progress and to multiply were for him one and the same thing.[32]

We cannot be surprised if minority races harbour a desire to expand beyond the limits that the majority would set upon them: they may even be taking our phenomenal success as a model.

The proponents of views like Wilson's must conclude, as Tinbergen hinted, that the dominant race had interfered with the process of natural selection to such an extent that it has severely compromised its own viability. By keeping the unfit alive, allowing them to breed if only to replace themselves, and allowing the fit to breed only in the same proportion, we have blocked the possibility of genetic improvement and instituted instead a kind of biological stasis. Because our own exponential expansion has come to a halt, for reasons inherent in our own lifestyles and not as a result of global altruism, we have an urgent need to impose stasis on other groups for whom the same considerations do not prevail. In fact we are at the mercy of philoprogenitive groups whose avowed expansionism we can only threaten with our death-dealing technology. There is a definite possibility that they will call our bluff.

Our own declining fertility and the frequency of aberrant behaviours like displacement eating, the "compulsive diversion" of sexual behaviour "into non-reproductive and apparently inappropriate channels",[33] and the intensification of stress resulting from our preferred, hyperstimulated urban lifestyle could be seen, say, by a Muslim ethologist as terminal disadaptation for survival. What strikes us as the unrealistic, medieval economic programme of the Ayatollah Khomeini may instead be a blueprint for genetic survival. Puritanism (in the banning of all super-normal stimuli) ruralism, and philoprogeniture adjusted by the *jehad*, however distasteful to us, make sense in ethological terms. The fact that most of us would rather be dead than live under such a regime simply bears out the point.

It is clearly absurd to postulate that all principled human behaviour is mere hypocrisy masking genetic imperatives; human beings are not merely transmitters of genetic information from generation to generation, and stasis is not foreign to human groups. Human beings have always striven for a balance between themselves and their environment; the difficulty in our own time is to form any clear concept of an environment which changes so fast, and then to orchestrate human responses so that they may be in tune with it. We are not a society composed entirely of sedentary eaters of protein and starch, banjaxed by the combination of stress diseases and obesity, any more than we are all self-absorbed thrill-seekers interested in sex only as entertainment. The universal two-child family will never be a reality if only because our sterility is rising, showing that the forces of natural selection are still at work. Obesity and stress both have an injurious effect on fertility.

We can and do learn from our mistakes, which is why ethologists bother to voice their concern in the first place. Although the emphasis upon repro-ductivity has been lop-sidedly in favour of severe limitation for the past twenty years, our veneration for it survives. Even though we have made motherhood such a deeply disadvantaged and conflict-ridden condition, women still endure it. Those who praise its special rewards still far outnumber those who denigrate it. At the same time as we recognise our own indifference to the involuntary sterility of other peoples and its possible basis in genetic egotism, we show every willingness to struggle against the involuntary sterility which occurs in our own society, even though most of it is much more intractable than that found in less evolved societies.

The vitality of the continuing desire to reproduce even in technocratic societies is evinced by our extreme reluctance to tolerate involuntary sterility. An ever-growing number of doctors specialise in treating infertility, performing all kinds of delicate interventions to correct blockages and abnormalities of the uterus, often in circumstances which pediatricians might consider counter-indicative. Fertility specialists draw up criteria for the evaluation of their patients, but in the face of the woman's desperate insistence these criteria often go by the board. The cynical explanation might be that the doctors are not trying as hard as they might to talk patients out of costly and interesting operations, but there is much more to it than that. The doctors themselves want to be associated with a triumph over infertility, and until more work is done on the medical history of women who undergo these operations, we cannot be sure that a doctor who refused on medical grounds to abet a woman in her desire to undergo a long and complicated operation which would leave her with a small chance of conceiving would not simply be abandoned in favour of the doctor who gave a more encouraging prognosis. The inescapable fact remains that aged nulliparae, whose fertility would be low were there no treatable abnormality present, willingly undergo tubal surgery of four and five hours' duration, and myomectomies rather than the hysterectomies which would make more sense in their circumstances and at their time of life, in order to maximise their chances of conception – which will remain low. It was no surprise to be told by a surgeon that one of his patients who succeeded after years of treatment in getting pregnant had an abortion. These elaborate rituals must be seen as the sophisticated version of the fertility observances which women all over the world have carried out since time immemorial. Indian women of high educational status, who have borne their children and may be practising birth control, still wear an open steel coil twisted around the second toe of each foot, said to be directly connected to the uterus. To remove the toe-rings would be to defy the expectations of kin in a gratuitous act of rudeness and to court the worst kind of bad luck. Millions of Indian women wear a mangal sutra to indicate their married status: the necklace is also a priapic symbol. If it should break, the woman should take to her bed until it is mended, a custom nowadays more honoured in the breach than the observance. The many forms of wedding ritual which prevail in India are replete with the imagery of fruitfulness, coconuts wrapped in blousepieces and placed beneath the bride's palu, banana palms over the doorway, sprinkling with water and stepping over fire, and so forth and so on.[34] Before we speak against such practices, we ought to consider why brides in registry offices still carry flowers.

The unwillingness of men to undergo vasectomy and of women to accept irreversible sterilisation may have something to do with the importance of notional fertility even to those who have decided that they do not want children. When deliberately childless people are asked why they are not sterilised, but still struggle with contraception, they make feeble response of the "Well, you never know" kind, which, when the respondents are already in their forties, is odd to say the least. It is as if their fertility left them a stake in the future, offered them a chance of defeating dissolution and decay, if only in theory. However, to say that human attachment to notional fertility is irrational is simply to open the possibility of its being confused or neurotic; if it is also biological, we may expect it to persist despite all incentives to childlessness. It is not incompatible with abortion, for pregnancy performs the function primarily of ratifying fertility; the decision to continue with a pregnancy depends upon more complex factors. It may indeed be profitable to consider the possibility that the high incidence of unwanted teenage pregnancy has to do with an unconscious need to verify fertility before taking measures to suppress it.

Margaret Mead saw the power to breed as more important for women than for men, although she expressed it in terms of wanting to bear and rear children, which is not the same thing. Male sexuality seemed to have no goal "beyond immediate discharge":

> Men have to learn as children to want to beget and cherish children, and to maintain a society in which children are provided for as well as simply protected against enemies. Women, on the other hand, have to learn to want children only under socially prescribed conditions ... Girls can certainly learn not to want children, but such learning seems always to be socially imposed.[35]

If we accept the tripartite description offered by Beach of sexuality as libido, potency and fertility, we might say rather that men's sexuality centred on libido and potency and women's on fertility, if it were not for the fact that men are less willing than women are to consider the possibility that they may not be fertile. The division in men seems rather to fall between the desire to beget children and the willingness to take part of the responsibility for rearing them. Thus it could be said rather that men have got to deny themselves the antisocial satisfaction of seeing how many children they can sire, and cultivate instead a desire to be actively involved in the rearing of the few they may sire. What Margaret Mead said of girls may also be true of males.

> ... we do not have the material to insist that those roles in which women have been contented although childless must be roles that may be interpreted as

sublimating the desire for children. We still do not know how completely any given girl-child or any group of girl-children, may learn *not* to want children.[36]

The most threatened group in human societies, as in animal societies, is the unmated male: the unmated male is more likely to wind up in prison or in an asylum or dead than his mated counterpart.[37] He is less likely to be promoted at work and he is considered a poor credit risk. It might be suggested that his fragility is the result of sexual frustration, but in reality he is unlikely to suffer it and it can apparently be borne by most who conscientiously adopt a celibate life without similar ill-effects. What the unmated male does not have is reproductive opportunity – that he is aware – and it could be that this is a more disturbing situation. An English doctor who discovered that he was totally aspermic imagined that he could take the discovery in his stride, but his failure to face the fact and to mourn it resulted in a complete and disastrous breakdown.

We cannot exactly calculate the importance of the idea of fertility to highly sophisticated people, whose culture has inculcated them with the notion that a healthy sex-life is a recreational one, liberated from masochistic desires and guilt and focused on tenderness and pleasure, yet it seems that it is not totally irrelevant. Extrapolating from our own attitudes, we tend to assume that peasants, like us, are principally desirous of having a good time in bed with their partners and that their many children are an unwanted by-product of their romping; but for many peasant societies the idea of fertility is much more important than that of sexual pleasure. In societies where wives are chosen by their husband's family and given by their own, where no courtship has taken place and strict segregation pertains, the purpose of cohabitation is not pleasure but impregnation. The Etoro of New Guinea believe that

> ... excessive copulation and sexual relations which are not productive of offspring deplete a man to no end. A woman who encourages, entices or demands her husband to engage in needless copulation – from which he alone will suffer – thereby approaches the purely negative role of witch. She sates her sexual appetite selfishly, knowingly causing harm, and perhaps with malicious intent.[38]

Margaret Mead ends her discussion of human reproductivity with a caveat which this discussion is meant to reinforce:

> ... to pattern and discipline this potentiality for mating, to balance the children we can learn to want with the children we can afford to have, so that no section of the population need be reared to psychological childlessness, so that no lives need be begun only to be flung beneath the feet of blind gods – this requires more knowledge and a more finely wrought pattern of human relationships than mankind has yet conceived.[39]

Margaret Mead wrote those words in 1948, before panic over the rise in the rate of population growth had caused otherwise compassionate people to suggest that compulsory sterilisation would have to be practised, or that licences for reproduction would eventually have to be issued. The criterion for adulthood has always been the ability to bear children, and authority has always been connected with having borne them or acting as a parent. The struggle to regulate the power of parenthood has been one of the ways in which peoples have developed and exercised their moral sense, wrestling with decisions of life and death which human beings still find perplexing, taking courses of action which were enormously costly in terms of mental and physical pain. For the struggle to be institutionalised so that the individual may merely carry out the moral prerogative of others is to degrade human beings even more than did throwing their girl children under the feet of blindfolded bullocks, because it denies their free will.

The importance of fertility cannot be gauged in the course of such a brief discussion, but some suggestions have been made. The first suggestion is that the notion of fertility underlies many human ethical systems, including our own, although in a residual and fragmentary form. The management of fertility is an essential aspect of maturity and a principal expression of our altruism towards our own groups: if such management, which is fallible and must be if human beings are to continue to exercise the essential human characteristic of free will, is to be taken over by instituted authority, the consequence will be the infantilisation and degradation of our species. If we must survive only at such cost, it may be better that we do not survive at all. It has also been suggested that human beings have deeply questionable motives for interfering in the reproductive behaviour of alien groups and, moreover, that the hidden biological imperative which prompts our hostility to the increase of others also prompts our own failures of rational control. If we allow the fertility of strangers to be destroyed by radiation or chemical pollution or untreated venereal disease or by surgical procedures carried out in the name of the common good, we cannot plead innocence. The sin may be one of omission in that we are simply inattentive to the evidence of their anguish, or one of commission in that we actively promote the programmes of which they are the victims, especially by paying for them. The actual existence of a state of emergency would not justify the destruction of an individual's power to reproduce if he has not positively willed it; the superstition that such a state exists is clearly no justification for the exploitation of poverty and ignorance in persuading the needy to accept the destruction of their fertility. Such destruction may be the result of ignorance or negligence or clumsiness, but none of these constitutes a justification.

Chapter Three
The Curse of Sterility

O wind of Tizoula, O wind of Amsoud!
Blow over the plains and over the sea,
Carry, oh, carry my thoughts
To him who is so far, so far,
And who has left me without a little child.
O wind! remind him I have no child.

O wind of Tizoula, O wind of Amsoud!
Blow away that desire for riches
That sends our young men away
And makes them forget the girls they've married, their mothers,
And the old ones left in the village.
O wind! remind him that I have no child.

Berber woman's song[1]

"Give me sons!" cried Rachel to Jacob, "Give me sons or I shall die."[2] Jacob had worked fourteen years for Rachel, and had always loved her more dearly than her elder sister who had given him four sons, but his love could not compensate Rachel for her failure. Even though the senior wife was her own sister, and her husband her father's sister's son, she was jealous and alienated in her own home, to the point of despair.

Millions of women in Asia and Africa find themselves in a far worse situation than Rachel. They come to their husbands as strangers, moving into the household run by their husbands' mothers, torn by the deep conflict between their desire to be accepted as a kinswoman in the new family and their attachment to their own mothers and the house where they grew up. Mothers watching their daughters set off on their bridal journey scream and tear their hair and pray that they will be kindly treated, that their pregnancies will be easy and not follow too hard upon each other's heels. The most unthinkable disaster would be a daughter's failure to conceive at all, for that is quite likely to lead to her husband's taking another wife or to divorce and her return in disgrace either to find another, less advantageous match or to live out her life as a subordinate member of her mother's household.[3] Barrenness is by many peoples associated with sin, and particularly sexual sin. If children are the gift of God, the lack of them is God's punishment.

In many societies, lechery is associated with barrenness, with some justification, as we shall see. The most extreme form of the syndrome can be seen in groups like the Hamadsha, who regard women with moist vaginas with disgust, possibly because they have confused the signs of female arousal with those of infection, which, untreated, commonly results in barrenness.

> Certain women in *jidba* (frenetic trance) are compelled to imitate pigs. They begin to squeal and grunt and grovel on the ground ... Such a woman is looked on with disgust by both male and female members of the audience. She is often said to be *marja* (lit. bog or swamp), to have a wet vagina possibly from leucorrhoea ... It is impossible to determine whether the moisture referred to is the normal moisture of the vagina during intercourse or a pathological condition. Given the fact that most of my male informants preferred to ejaculate as rapidly as possible after penetration and did not stimulate their women first, it is possible they were referring to the vaginal secretions of an aroused woman.[4]

It is more than possible that in groups such as the Hamadsha, who are only untypical of many Arab groups in that they are more extreme, the presence of disease has itself influenced the development of puritanical attitudes to intercourse; gonorrhoea for example "is said to be caused by semen backing up to the kidneys, if a man is not careful to urinate after making love" (if indeed that is what their intercourse may be called), which seems to indicate that urination is practised as a rough and ready prophylaxis. In sexually segregated societies where wives are outsiders and a good deal of affection is expressed in more or less genital homosexual intimacies, husbands consort with their wives principally for issue. The failure of a woman to conceive means that her relationship with her husband and his family is never stabilised, whereas once she is pregnant she may very well be allowed to go home to her mother and her kinfolk for the birth, thereby enjoying the best of both worlds.

Where lechery is associated with barrenness, virginity and modesty are associated with fruitfulness. Women who flaunt their sexuality, driving men to squander their precious seed in barren wombs, are the personifications of death, disease and evil the world over. Among the Balinese,

> The beauty of infertile women may become so meaningful to a whole people that the witch is defined as the woman whose daughter is rejected in marriage ... and who then in revenge trains beautiful, sexless little girls to spread death over the land.[5]

The misery of the childless woman in most pre-industrial societies can hardly be exaggerated. Hamed Ammar, speaking of the Egyptian village of Silwa in the province of Aswan, conveys a well of unhappiness in a few words:

... there were ten childless women in the village, and they were known by everybody ... two were living with husbands who had taken a second wife.

The fact that childless women retained their looks was considered in itself sinister: the villagers said:

A childless woman is usually like a she-camel who does not conceive, puts on more flesh and gets younger every day – but not fruitful, she can never "lengthen her husband's neck" among the menfolk. She is an eyesore to her family.[6]

In India "a childless woman is an inauspicious guest at a wedding or a *chauk* (infant-blessing) ceremony."

Nothing that a childless wife may do can counter-balance her gross failure in her most important role. Elizabeth Warnock Fernea was struck by the misery of Fadhila:

Fadhila was vigorous and attractive, with strong arms and bright eyes; she laughed from deep inside, a loud healthy laugh which infected even the dourest old ladies ... Her great sorrow was that she had no children ... Fadhila, despite her health and energy, was judged inadequate as a woman and as a wife.[7]

At the women's Kraya at Ramadan, the female mullah deliberately humiliated Fadhila by asking if she was pregnant?

"Why not?" demanded the Mullah.
Fadhila, obviously stricken, murmured, "God knows best?," in a low voice.
I thought it a cruel question, for Fadhila had been married for seven years, and everyone in the village knew she was barren.
At the American's leavetaking, Fadhila had a request: "Send me a charm from America, so I can have a child."[8]

If only she had known it, the charms from America are after all no better than the old sorceries; they can sterilise the fruitful. Children to the childless international aid has never brought except for a brief period when the Ford Foundation, embarrassed by the transparent hypocrisy of the euphemism "family planning", ran an infertility clinic in Maharashtra and couples came on foot from hundreds of miles around.

One of the more unthinking expressions of Caucasian contempt for other peoples is the assumption that they are all hyper-fertile and "breed like rabbits." The truth is that there are millions of women in Fadhila's situation.

Among social workers the awareness of the suffering caused by infertility is very low. An Indian health worker involved in setting up a programme in the Laldoghar slum at Chembur near Bombay was astonished to find that all the women wanted to hear about was a cure for their infertility. Her street-level meetings resounded to the urgent plea, "Take us to doctor, *bai*, so we can have children." Although they were all suffering from the usual galaxy of health problems which beset the poor, they did not respond to her offers of health care for eyes and teeth and feet, but simply repeated

their demand for infertility treatment. She had come into the field all
prepared to teach them contraceptive techniques and motivate sterilisation
acceptors and could not understand why they were so insistent until they
explained that their husbands either had taken or were threatening to
take other wives. The women all came from the same area in Maharashtra,
and there was a strong likelihood of some pathology affecting them as
a group. The Family Planning Association of India would have helped
her to establish an infertility clinic at the slum, but when I left India
two months after talking to her she had not yet made contact.[9]

The hundreds of millions of dollars spent every year on family limitation
programmes have got to be justified by a decrease in population growth; no
one is about to compromise their already extremely dubious cost-
effectiveness by earmarking any significant fund for the investigation and
combat of sterility and sub-fertility. Yet our failure to do so may adversely
affect the outcome of our attempts to persuade the same groups to accept
our notions of control. Where childlessness causes conspicuous humiliation and grief (while "population pressure" if it exists at all is not perceptible in anything like the same vivid and immediate way) it would seem
obvious that we must purchase respectability for our claims by attempting
to deal with infertility. One much desired child to a barren woman could
win more confidence than a thousand cute posters of the ecstatically happy
two-child family.

Dr Indumati Parikh, founder of a women's group in the slums of Dadar,
Bombay, began with a healthy set of priorities, in that she undertook
family-planning work "to enable women in backward areas to live a healthy
life". The belief that God was responsible for the birth of unwanted
children as he was for infertility

> had to be changed by giving women knowledge about reproduction and also
> by successfully treating at least some cases of infertility among them. We intro-
> duced IUD in 1965, and oral pills in 1968 in our programme and we started
> treating cases of sterility. Some successfully treated cases of sterility in the clinic
> gave us a permanent *locus standi* in the locality and made propagation of family
> planning easier.[10]

Put in Dr Parikh's typically no-nonsense manner, the connection of
ideas seems obvious, but it is not at all obvious to the agencies that fund
programmes like hers who can find masses of evidence to prove that money
and time spent on hearts and minds is money thrown away.

The Barma of Chad provide a typical example of a group caught in
a vicious infertility cycle. In 1970, they numbered only 34,500 souls. In
two villages studied, twenty-five percent of the women of child-bearing
age were classified as infertile.

> Barma are painfully aware of their infertility, and observe that "a woman with-
> out children is like a tree without leaves."[11]

Their society approves of sexual activity for adult males, but the requirements of bride-wealth mean that few young men may marry. Because of irregular sexual contacts, many of them contract gonorrhea before taking a wife, whom their disease renders infertile, in which case she is divorced, and must seek another mate, thus passing on the infection and perpetuating the infertility cycle. Sterility causes divorce and divorce causes further sterility. In societies with intricate kinship systems, the inroads of sterility can cause complete collapse of the cultural group and its subsequent submergence.

In 1951, 49% of the women of the Murut tribe in North Borneo were sterile. The Muruts had numbered more than 30,000 in 1921; by 1951 there were fewer than 19,000. Their general health and nutrition were poor; to the effects of malaria and hookworm and endemic goitre were added those of gonorrhoea, possibly resulting from the system of outwork which took the menfolk to work on distant rubber plantations. Similar conditions have brought hundreds of groups around the colonised world to the threshold of extinction. Pygmies, Bushmen, Hottentots, the Nzakara, the Bedik, the Todas, the Bubis, the Tasaday tribe, the Kaingang, the Arhuacos, the Cauca, the Ache are just some of the peoples who could tell a similar story.[12]

The story could be amplified if family-planning and other social workers were aware of the extent of infertility and of the suffering caused by it. Their capacity for ignoring it seems to indicate a peculiar and unpleasant kind of investigator bias. For example, a doctor and an anthropologist visited villages in the Banjar district of Himalchal Pradesh in 1976 to report on the extent of their practice of contraception. They reported that the families of twenty-seven of their hundred female respondents were "incomplete", i.e. childless. Of the two hundred and eight-two children ever born to the hundred women, eighty-six were dead, and among the Brahmins child mortality was as high as 35%; 61.5% of the women had families smaller than they wanted. Yet Dr Kaul and Miss Kala felt no urge to investigate the misery underlying their statistics or to ascertain its root cause: instead they stoically completed their original mission, claiming that an astonishing 16% of their informants were using contraception, a figure for which they felt bound to apologise.[13] Such blindness among professionals must have the effect of minimising the problem: the reluctance of childless women to come forward matches the lack of interest that investigators feel.

Doctors working in the Ludhiana district of the Punjab between 1954 and 1965 recorded an extremely low incidence of infertility, of the order of 3%. The figure may be partly explained by their lack of interest in infertility and in women not sexually active – no divorced women are mentioned in their sample, for example. Other Indian studies have come up with very different figures: in 1963, Andrew Collver reported that about 22% of families had no male heir; of that proportion 18% had a daughter, and the rest were childless.[14] This accords with the sample of people who had never practised "family planning" studied by Ranajit Dutta in 1976, where 57.3% were fertile, 25.6% sub-fertile with only one live birth, and 17.1% childless.[15] Even so, the incidence of infertility in a settled, ordered agricultural community of the Punjab, where extra-marital intercourse was to all intents non-existent, may well have been much lower than it is in India as a whole or in sophisticated Western societies, where the number of involuntarily childless couples is variously computed as between ten and fifteen percent of the total and rising.

Speaking of the United States in 1978 S. J. Behrman pointed out

> For every eighty-five married couples producing off-spring there are fifteen couples in this country who are unable to conceive.[16]

Marriage is far from universal in Western society: the fifteen couples unable to conceive are to be added to the twenty percent who never marry in the first place to get a picture of the prevalence of childlessness in the West. Nevertheless it is only in the West that infertility is taken seriously

> Millions of involuntarily sterile couples present an important and acute social problem. Infertility has an important impact on a couple's personal relations and consequently on their mental and physical health and may influence their social and economic status.[17]

People who have made the conquering of infertility their life's work are unlikely to consider the possibility that, in a society where children have no socio-economic function as heirs and parenthood brings no special privileges, people who cannot accept their own childlessness are neurotic. This muddle in turn affects their ability to assess the importance of psycho-genic factors in sterility.

> Eisner found that infertile women showed more disturbance in the Rorschach test. Carr found more neurosis, neurotic dependency and anxiety in infertile women. Grimm reported the increased presence of emotional instability, overt dependency, tension, hostile feelings and guilt in chronic aborters as opposed to non-aborters. Platt and his co-workers noticed that couples with infertility perceived the locus of control over events in their lives as being exterior to themselves.[18]

And so forth. Whether the successful outcome of pregnancy would relieve all or any of these symptoms is extremely doubtful; where infertility causes actual hardship, there would seem to be greater justification for the expenditure of considerable effort to reverse it. As it is, Western women may spend a fortune and masochistically undergo repeated surgical procedures in an attempt to bear a child, while the peasant-farmer must resign herself to misery. International agencies spend a fortune trying to convince fertile people that the "locus of control over events in their lives" is "interior" to themselves, without concerning themselves with the blindingly obvious fact that the sterile neighbours of the people they are trying to influence are powerless to alter their unenviable destiny. If we are to convince people that our methods of control are more efficient and responsive to individual need than their own, we must address ourselves to both sides of the problem.

Demographers desperate to reduce the number of variables in their multitudinously variable subject traditionally treat natural human fertility as a constant. In fact natural human fertility fluctuates, and in some circumstances fluctuates wildly.

Few people are born sterile. Congenital sterility may well become more common, however. Both sons and daughters of women who took diethyl-stilboestrol during pregnancy were born with impaired fertility. A recent study in North Carolina of the daughters of the five to seven million women who took the drug (for no good reason) found that only 45% of those who attempted pregnancy in their sample were able to bear living children. Other groups of DES children had serious defects in the reproductive system and some have developed malignant conditions of the genital tract. It has long been suspected that the fertility of men who have been in contact with defoliants, whether used in war or in peacetime, has been impaired; it is still too early to tell whether the fertility of their children has suffered too. The consequences of the explosion of the atomic bomb in Hiroshima and Nagasaki are well-documented, but not so well documented is the fertility outlook for the Alaskan Eskimos:

> Radiation surveys of seven Alaskan villages have shown that the Eskimos have far more radioactive Cesium 137 in their bodies than the rest of the American population . . . More than 700 Eskimos were examined by portable body counter. In the village of Anaktuvuk Pass, the average adult was found to have 450 nanocuries of Cesium 137 in his body and one individual had as much as 790 nanocuries . . . the substance which is chemically similar to Potassium, accumulates in the muscles where in sufficient quantity it can present a genetic hazard.[19]

Nuclear fall-out gathers in unusual concentrations on the lichens on which the caribou feed, and the unfortunate Eskimos live off the caribou.

Radioactivity is only one kind of genetic hazard; the rising levels of lead in the atmosphere may well constitute another. We know that benzene, carbon disulphide, chloroprene, anaesthetic gases, perchlorethylene, epoxy resins, radio frequencies and microwave and other kinds of radiation are all hazards to which the pregnant woman should not be exposed, but the consequences of prolonged exposure to them in non-pregnant individuals who then go on to parent is not so clear. Mercury workers show abnormally low sperm counts: we have yet to diagnose mercury mutations in their children. Only so far is it true to say that congenital sterility represents a very small proportion of the sterility spectrum. Most sterility is caused by disease, malnutrition, addiction, incompatibility and social and cultural practices.[20] It can be primary, in which case no conception has ever been possible, but is more often secondary.

Beginning at the beginning of the female reproductive process, with the ovary, we find that ovulation can be suspended by a number of factors; it can be halted by extreme hunger and its hysterical counterpart, anorexia, perhaps by mimicking the natural process by which immature women are prevented from conceiving, namely that a necessary proportion of body-fat must be built up before ovulation occurs. Psychological stress may result in suspension of ovulation; indeed, one of the reasons why we cannot be sure of the precise role of starvation in inhibiting ovarian function is that starvation is never present without stress.[21] Where people had got more used to hunger, amenorrhoea was not as likely to result from paucity of diet. As failure to conceive is often a cause of extreme stress, "management" of the infertile woman can be a problem:

> The physician should be aware that many people look on failure to conceive as their own personal failure, their failure as a sexual being, and they bring these feelings of inadequacy to their first medical interview. By the time the physician sees the man or woman, the patient may also be experiencing anger, depression, guilt, or obsession with his or her plight ...[22]

The evidence most often cited as proof of the psychogenic nature of much infertility is that childless women frequently manage to conceive after they have decided to adopt. The infertility specialist is faced with the conundrum that his very work-up intensifies stress as couples struggle to have intercourse in the right way on the right days or collect semen and rush it to laboratories or undergo repeated examinations. Ovarian function can also be suppressed, deranged or destroyed by radiation, by drugs legal and illegal, medical and other, by trauma, emotional and physical, and by aging. Ovarian function can sometimes be restored by the administration of substances like clomiphene, a synthetic analogue of the follicle-stimulating hormone, or by delicate and difficult surgery to remove adhesions or to bring displaced ovaries into the right relation with the Fallopian tubes. If the ovaries have failed to develop or are atrophied, for example, as a result of radiation, the condition is irreversible.

The most vulnerable part of the female reproductive system is probably the oviduct; the relatively poor ratio of success in dealing with tubal dysfunction or non-function is in part due to our ignorance as to the exact role of the oviduct in human reproduction:

> Processes essential to reproduction known to occur in Eutherian mammals include sperm transport, capacitation, ovum pick-up and transport, fertilisation and embryo transport and nourishment. Our knowledge of these processes in our own species, man, is incomplete. The reasons underlying our lack of in-

formation concerning the physiology of the human Fallopian tube are ethical, philosophical and technical. Although some of our failure to obtain definitive data in women has been due to ethical constraints, we have also been limited philosophically by our inability to formulate the critical questions and pragmatically by the lack of technology with which to accurately measure many biological phenomena. After more than a half century of clinical interest in female infertility, we are unable to assess accurately a single physiological function of the Fallopian tube. Our clinical armentarium is limited to appraisals of the patency of the tube to gas or liquid and to examination of the external appearance and texture of the tubes.[23]

In other words, all we can know about the competence of the Fallopian tubes in a woman being treated for infertility is whether gas or oil can be forced through under pressure in the wrong direction, which is what is done at insufflation. If it cannot, we may be practically sure that egg and sperm will never meet; if it can, we do not know whether they ever will.

The function of the Fallopian tubes can be impaired by any pelvic disease or trauma, including surgery. Any abdominal bleeding can cause adhesions. Childbirth, miscarriage, curettage all involve a risk of infection, which is greater the more unsanitary the conditions and the worse the woman's general health. The commonest bacterial culprits were usually considered to be the gonococcus, streptococcus, staphylococcus, and the tubercle bacillus. The whole history of *Neisseria gonorrhoeae* will probably never be told. Until the nineteenth century it was not well understood that syphilis and gonorrhoea were separate and dissimilar diseases: epidemiologists have always found syphilis, and its relatives, yaws, *pinta* and *bejel*, fascinating, but gonorrhoea, never directly fatal and not so much spectacular as dirty and commonplace, has commanded relatively little attention. The bacillus is uncommonly well adapted for dwelling in humans, and seems not to be viable in any other host. Close relatives are found in healthy mucous membrane, where they cause no problems, and human beings develop only a slight antibody reaction to *Neisseria gonorrhoeae*, not sufficient to guarantee any degree of immunity or to open the possibility of immunisation, although some individuals seem more resistant to infection than others. In women, gonorrhoea is at first asymptomatic, and may remain so in two-thirds of cases. As long as the infection is localised in the lower genitary tract it does little lasting harm, but if it ascends to the uterus and Fallopian tubes it causes an endosalpingitis which rapidly blocks the tubes altogether. It used to be thought that the infection ascends at menstruation; currently attempts are being made to isolate the strains of the gonococcus which are more likely to invade the Fallopian tubes.

The discovery of the efficacy of penicillin in treating venereal disease caused a degree of complacency, which was shattered in the 1960s by the mounting evidence that gonorrhoea was on the increase world-wide. The World Health Organisation reported in 1964 that the number of new cases per year around the world numbered sixty-five million. In the United States 800,000 cases were notified in 1974, while the actual incidence of the disease was estimated to be in the vicinity of two and a half million cases; between 1% and 5% of the population between the ages of fifteen and thirty was or had been infected, and it was thought that the proportion would rise to at least 6% and possibly 10%. Twelve to twenty percent of male sufferers had no detectable symptoms, sixty to seventy percent of women. The epidemic was not only recorded in the industrialised world; all the twenty-nine countries returning information about venereal disease incidence reported a steep rise. They included Bolivia, Chad, Colombia, El Salvador, Ecuador, Gabon, Iran, Iraq, Mali, Philippines, Rwanda, Swaziland and Venezuela, where perhaps the rise in the reported number of cases did not mean a rise in the actual number of cases but improvement in reporting. The World Health Organisation devoted its twenty-eighth conference to the subject and as a result governments stepped up the financing and development of venereal disease programmes.[24]

The incidence of gonorrhoea has settled at an extremely high level, second only to that of the common cold, and will probably stay there. The explanations are various; there are more young people and they are more mobile than ever before, populations are becoming more urbanised and the urban environment is more promiscuous. All these contributing factors are exacerbated by the supplanting of the prophylactic condom by the oral contraceptives and the IUD. In England only two percent of cases are caused by resort to prostitutes.

It used to be common practice for doctors treating rock stars to equip them with medical supplies before they set out on tour; conspicuous among them were massive single doses of broad-spectrum antibiotics. When I complained that this practice simply meant that the gentlemen in question would be disseminating a more resistant brand of gonorrhoea along the concert circuit, it was pointed out that no multi-million-dollar operation could be abandoned because the lead-singer had a purulent greenish-yellow discharge leaking through his tight white satin trousers. The fact that they were on the move meant that any infections they might pick up could not be treated methodically, and the same is true for all the youngsters who set off on the hippy trail every summer. Many a young woman returns from her adventure sterile, and when ten years later she sits tense and miserable with the doctor who is doing her infertility work-up she can no longer remember that dreadful stomach-ache and fever that she treated with erythromycin she found lying around and some herbal stuff and then it sort of faded into the general spectrum of abdominal discomfort somewhere between Agra and Benares. Or for that matter the names of the people she passed the disease on to.

In street markets in third-world countries one can usually find anti-biotics at a price; the vendor has no idea of the right dosage and the customer takes them until the symptoms go away. Resistant strains of gonorrhoea have been traced to specific locations because of these practices. One such strain from Ghana caused a particularly virulent out-break in Liverpool.[25]

Ten to fifteen percent of female cases of gonorrhoea will result in acute pelvic inflammatory disease in the first month. By the time the acute symptoms, pelvic pain and localised tenderness, with palpable adnexal masses, appear, it is too late to save the Fallopian tubes, which may become huge inflated sacs of pus. If untreated, the acute symptoms may subside to a low-grade inflammation until eventually the organism dies out, leaving the tubes blocked by scar tissue. Pelvic abcesses may develop and even cause death. There is a high incidence of recidivism in gonorrhoea patients, and some tubal occlusion is thought to be the result of repeated sub-acute infection. In some countries improved techniques of contact tracing have resulted in a decline in the number of cases of gonorrhoeal pelvic inflammatory disease, but the total number of cases of pelvic inflammatory disease has itself gone up, for newly identified organisms have been found to play an even more important part than *Neisseria gonorrhoeae*.[26]

Nowadays more numerous than new cases of gonorrhoea among the sexually transmitted diseases, are the non-specific genital infections. Among the organisms associated with NSU are the versatile *Chlamydiae* which often accompany and are masked by gonorrhoea just as gonorrhoea for thousands of years accompanied and was masked by syphilis. It is possible that *Chlamydiae* have always been more significant in salpingitis than was *Neisseria*, and it seems also that *Chlamydiae* may cause chronic, sub-acute salpingitis, which also results in scarred tubes and sterility.[27] Actinomycosis, a fungal infection, has also been inculpated in salpingitis, as have *Trichomonas vaginalis* and *Candida albicans*.[28] The role of the IUD in increasing the likelihood of these devastating infections is not well understood, but it is thought to increase the risk of spread after exposure to infection by a factor of three or four. Actinomycosis, for example, is associated with the presence of foreign bodies in the human organism and would be feared in the case of installation of a foreign body anywhere but in the long-suffering uterus. Whereas pelvic infection in IUD wearers used to be automatic indication of removal, it is more commonly treated nowadays by antibiotic therapy leaving the device *in situ*. The long-term consequences for the fertility of the patient have not been quantified. In one horrifying case in the USA a woman who had suffered repeated episodes of pelvic inflammatory disease caused by Actinomycosis but refused to abandon her IUD, died when a massive pelvic abcess released 1,500 cc of free pus into the abdominal cavity; she was found to have multiple adhesions and was probably sterile long before her death ensued.[29]

Acute pelvic inflammatory disease is always a medical emergency. It is said to cost the United States Government $200,000,000 a year, but perhaps the sum so cynically computed should be offset by the savings represented by the woman's subsequent infertility. Sub-acute pelvic inflammatory disease may cost very little in cash terms but it can also lead to medical emergencies. Tubal damage greatly increases the risk of ectopic pregnancy, in which the fertilised ovum remains in the tiny Fallopian tube which it eventually ruptures, putting the woman in imminent danger of death from shock, haemorrhage or peritonitis. The sperm, being much tinier than the ovum, can find their way through a tube down which the ovum cannot pass. Being motile they may not depend upon the peristaltic action of the tube, whereas the ovum does, or the ovum may simply snag on a furrow of scar tissue. Whatever the actual immediate cause, ectopic pregnancy is a likelier outcome in the case of tubal abnormality, whether it be caused by disease or surgery. Diagnosis is difficult, even when the diagnostician has been warned to suspect ectopic pregnancy, which he seldom is.

By no means all the women who find that when they wish to have a child they cannot, because of tubal blockage, can remember an episode of acute pelvic pain and fever. Commoner even than infertility resulting from acute pelvic inflammatory disease may be fertility impairment as a consequence of chronic sub-acute infection, or from a series of insults to the reproductive system: abdominal surgery for any cause, including appendectomy in childhood, an abortion or two, induced or spontaneous, legal or illegal, a curettage or two, a couple of minor infections, insertion, rejection or removal of an IUD. To the consequences of these unremarkable events must be added those of alcohol intake, of smoking, radiation and medication, of stress and of aging on the fertility of women who for cultural reasons tend to delay their child-bearing, to give a full picture of the commonest kind of infertility which causes disappointed women to besiege their doctors in the developed world.

The reproductive potential of women in the highly developed countries is greater than that of their sisters in the poorer countries. Because of superior nutrition and better hygiene they become fertile earlier and, barring the kind of syndrome described above, remain fertile longer. Both childbirth and abortion are less likely to result in infertility among Western women than they are in countries which are short of hospital beds and trained attendants, and where the majority of people are constantly menaced by polluted water and *ad hoc* methods of disposing of human waste. However, external cleanliness is not the whole story. A doctor teaching sterilisation by laparoscopy in Khatmandu told me in 1971, that in his practice at a famous east coast hospital he had never seen such healthy pelves as those of the Nepalese women. "American vaginas may smell of peppermint," he said, "but their pelves are sewers." Like most medical practitioners, he was quick to draw the moral that monogamy is good for health, but he might have been less enthusiastic if he had known just how different was the degree of exposure of the Nepalese cervix to the penis of even one man from what is considered normal in the United States.

There can be no doubt that the high frequency of pelvic disease in Western society is related to the degree of sexual activity and the number of partners that most people expect to enjoy, especially in adolescence and early adulthood. To point out that this is so is not the same as to say that increased and freer sexual activity is wrong, but it might suggest that the people who seek to suppress the expression of erotic desire because it conflicts with fertility are not simply irrationally puritanical in that their practice is justified by an actual connection between increased sexual activity and decreased fertility. Restrictive sexual mores could well be a response to the ever-present threat of extinction which many tribal societies have witnessed, if not in themselves then in neighbouring childless communities.

Infertility may be said to be a risk that the Western woman agrees to take when she opts for later child-bearing; the factors that erode her fertility are all aspects of her chosen lifestyle, although she may well object that no one ever spelt out to her with any clarity what their cumulative effect upon her child-bearing potential would eventually be. The same cannot be said of the childless woman in traditional societies; she does not choose between children and a career – children are her career. If she fails to produce them, there is no alternative lifestyle that she may adopt. From birth her fertility is menaced by factors completely beyond her control: malnutrition, hard work and disease. Poor diet means retarded growth, and retarded growth means later onset of the menses, and even after adolescence, sterility may last until the completion of physical growth, in the early twenties. This is a danger period, for conceptions are more likely to be problematic at the beginning and end of the menarche. Miscarriage and stillbirth are both more likely with poorly developed mothers, and their likelihood is increased in those women who suffer from relapsing fever, malaria, rickets, toxoplasmosis, syphilis, thyroid disease and goitre. Women who have been infested by parasites, as in filiariasis and schistosomiasis, or suffered from genital tuberculosis, may never conceive, but their lot is in some ways better than that of the women who conceive only to miscarry. Miscarriage without medical treatment can be problematic; retained placental matter can cause haemorrhage, trauma can cause infection, and miscarriage itself can be painful and shocking. Immature women bringing their babies to term may be killed by the delivery; without expert assistance the babies that are struggling to escape from immature pelves must die. Cervical tears, unless repaired, will result in scarring and relaxation, so that the woman becomes a habitual aborter. The story of many infertile women in the third world is one of reproductive disaster resulting in eventual inability to conceive, altogether a grimmer picture than that which pertains for the infertile Western woman, even without considering the different effect that childlessness has upon the life of the woman in traditional society.

There are no traditional societies in the world which are not subject to stress. None is beyond the reach of the mega-media pounding out their message of alternative lifestyle, even if only from the packaging of goods in the local store. The dwindling nuclei of once great bands of hunter-gatherers retreating before the colonisation of the deserts are under constant threat of dissolution and have for generations been exposed to diseases against which they have little resistance.

It is no longer fashionable to chart the progress of depopulation as was done in the 1920s by Malinowski, Rivers and Pitt-Rivers.

> The workers of this period analysed the relationships of the various institutions and their reactions on one another. They studied single cultures with the object of discovering how the different aspects interlock. It is significant that this is the era of depopulation theories. Tampering with any part of a culture led to the collapse of the whole, various writers insisted – Malinowski again among them – and the natives were then doomed to extinction through boredom. A vague psychological malaise overcame them, and they lost the will to live. We now know that a more probable explanation of the high death rate during the initial years of contact is to be sought in imported firearms, introduced diseases to which the people had no immunity, and poor diet. In point of fact the only native groups that did die out were those killed off by gunfire and poison, as in south-east Australia and parts of North America and those located in isolated areas – Ontong Java is an example – too far away for regular patrolling. Elsewhere, now that adequate medical services are available, numbers are starting to increase.[30]

Hogbin quite understandably rejects the notions of race suicide held by earlier workers, but he is a little too sanguine about the availability and effectiveness of medical care. He was unfortunate in the example of Ontong Java, which despite its isolation and the ravages of disease did recover, and probably because of the psychological factor which he is seeking to minimise. Groups less isolated, no worse affected by disease than their neighbours, once they have lost the will to reproduce will decline while their neighbours multiply. The more elaborate and cherished their life-style, the more vulnerable it is in this regard. However, even people living in the simplest fashion, like the Andaman Islanders, can be destroyed if sterilising disease enters the picture. On the island of Arioto in 1901 there were 625 people; in 1955, there were 23, among whom there were only two fertile couples, one of which was mixed. There was no young female of pure stock. The islanders adore children, but appear to be sterile.[31]

Numbers may be increasing but within the spectrum of growing national populations, many groups have been submerged and obliterated. Time and again we find the marker of tiny cultures consisting of bewildered and humiliated men without women. Throughout Melanesia, depopulation had produced these pockets of "high masculinity." In 1953 when A. P. Elkin submitted a report to the South Pacific Commission he asked for urgent intervention in Netherlands New Guinea, now Irian Jaya, especially among the Marind-anim, in Papua among the Koiari and the Suau, in the upper Waria, Biaru and Biangai in the Australian protectorate, in eastern Sena, Chimbu and on Fergusson Island, in Choiseul and Ysabel, in the Solomons and on eastern Santo and Epi in the New Hebrides. In other areas he opined that help would come too late.[32] Presumably excess masculinity such as that which prevailed in the Transfly area, where 3,725 men had to make do with 2,147 women, is partly caused by the persistence of female infanticide after the suppression of the tribal wars and raiding which kept the numbers in balance. In one area where the adult population was more or less in balance, there was a severe dearth of females in the 10–16 age group, which seems to indicate some such factor.[33]

Once depopulation is as severe as it was in 1953 on the islands of Evomanga and Aneityum in the New Hebrides, there is no way of compiling a diagnosis of the causes. One early observer, Dempwolff, was convinced that what he was seeing was race suicide. It seems more likely that a major disruption of an ancient and successful reproductive strategy, together with the discrediting of the value system which accompanied it, has resulted in intolerable levels of stress and confusion. One reaction to this is to reproduce in a haphazard fashion, but the higher the level of stress the more likely it is to lead to functional infertility and total impotence. This seems to be happening to some groups of Amazon Indians.

The masculinisation of societies in decline is often caused by the loss of women to dominant foreign males, either by outright capture, or because the invader's qualifications as breadwinner and sire are obviously superior. It is in the women's interest, sociobiologically speaking, to unite their genes with those of the more successful males. They and their children have a better chance of surviving, even as prostitutes and menials in the intruder's community, than of coping with his diseases in the bush. Men are more fragile and less practical. All societies on the verge of death are masculine. A society can survive with only one man; no society will survive a shortage of women.

We simply do not know how many kin-groups with their own language have actually died out, or by what stages their extinction was accomplished.

As we did not know how many of them existed at the time of contact or for some centuries after, most of the evidence is impressionistic. It seems likely that groups living on the edge of extinction were relatively often decimated by some concatenation of catastrophes or another and were consequently merged into other expansionist groups. It is probably simply sentimental to mourn the passing of peoples like the Amazon Indians, although not more sentimental than to weep for the embattled orang-utan, but the physical and mental suffering of this slow death cannot be tolerated by a "civilised" world.

> There were perhaps 10 million Indians living in the Amazon basin five centuries ago. Today there are scarcely 200,000. (During this same period the world's population has gone from less than 500 million to more than three billion.) In Brazil, the Indians numbered 3 million in 1500; less than a tenth of that number were living there by the turn of this century. There are still about 78,000 living in Brazil today. The Bororos were still a people 5000 strong in 1900; victims of contagious diseases, they are now down to less than 150.[34]

Lewis Cotlow, who visited the Bororo in 1968, explains in part how human groups like these die out:

> The Bororos were unlucky enough to have been in the path of intensive Brazilian penetration of the interior. They were partly victims of civilisation's diseases, partly of their own loss of confidence. Their tribal traditions, centring largely on their warrior pride, fell to pieces. Many individual members of the tribe left their villages and lived as beggars and outcasts on the run-down fringes of towns in the surrounding areas.
>
> I saw much evidence that the Bororos were committing racial suicide. There were few children in the villages. Like many other primitive peoples the Bororos kill all children who do not appear healthy at birth. I couldn't help wondering whether the Bororos were not unconsciously applying increasingly stringent standards to their infants. Moreover, I have heard Bororo parents maintain that they have no wish to bring children into the world as it is now, echoing a sentiment that is often heard in our culture.[35]

To find out just what was happening, we would need to do intensive demographic and medical-anthropological research on the Bororos, but if they are dying out there is no point. Among the "diseases of civilisation" which afflict people like the Bororos are those which prevent them from rebuilding their societies after epidemics and systematic genocide. Genocide in Bangladesh in the early seventies did not "solve the population problem" there because the people did not lose their fertility or their desire for children.

> In two centuries the Carajas of Brazil have declined from 500,000 to 1,200 ... The Guarani of Parana were reduced by slavery and torture. In ten years they have declined from 5,000 to about 300 ...[36]

Those words were written more than ten years ago, long before Karl Ludwig began turning three million acres of the Mato Grosso into the world's largest paper pulp manufactury, which has now been taken over by Tiny Rowland, presiding genius of the aggressive multi-national development conglomerate, Lonrho. At the time of Cotlow's writing,

> Indians, according to the *Jornal do Brasil*, had been clubbed to death, inoculated with smallpox, shot down and even massacred by explosives dropped from airplanes.[37]

The powers of recuperation from these onslaughts have long since been exhausted:

> It is possible to encounter natives living in still-unexplored parts of the Mato Grosso as they have lived since the stone-age; or to see Indians working on ranches or operating farm machinery, going to mission schools and wearing the first true garments in the history of their people. For the most part these people share the knowledge, or at least the intimation, that their end is approaching, that they are people without a future.[38]

People who feel they have no future are not likely to raise the necessary zeal for child-raising. We might consider that possibility that some of our own reluctance to reproduce might have something to do with the prevalence of the conviction that nuclear war is inevitable. Failure to reproduce is one side of the inculcated helplessness coin; the other is untrammelled reproduction. We cannot be surprised to find corralled peoples behaving like the great beasts in captivity, refusing to mate, failing to breed, and eating or killing their young. Overcrowded laboratory rats exhibit similar derangements.

The combined population of the Xingu National Park numbered an estimated 3,000 before the turn of the century.

> Today, fewer than 1,000 survive. There are less than 30 members of the Yawalpiti and Trumai peoples left ... In the sixties ... the Villas Boas brothers searched out the warlike and mistrustful Tchikaos, about 400 of whom has survived white invaders, their guns and their diseases. By the time they were located and brought to the Park, there were only fifty-three.[39]

Claude Lévi-Strauss knew the Nambikwara of the Mato Grosso when their numbers were already decimated by disease; even so he was horrified to read that only ten years later, the community he knew had shrunk to a mere eighteen individuals, reduced to hanging around the white settlement, scrounging or simply taking anything they could.

> Of the eight men, one had syphilis, another some kind of infection in his side, another was covered in some kind of scaly disease from head to foot and another was deaf and dumb ...[40]

It was impossible to trace the whole tribe, for groups collapsing in upon themselves had made alliances in their despair, as did the Sabane, who numbered only nineteen in 1938.[41] There are some signs that the Jivaro Indians are regrouping to demand their rights, but their claim is itself compromised because their lines of descent have been fouled. The same has happened to the Australian aborigines: the remnant of the tribals will not accept the urban militants, nearly all of mixed blood, who claim to represent them.

Settled groups who could not so easily be driven out of their habitat have suffered too; for centuries the depredations of slavers, and now the villainous system of outwork, have shaken the foundations of African tribal society. Doctors in the new African states struggle to reverse the die-back which has afflicted their peoples. It is not easy to build up a full picture of the reproductive failure of women in countries like Gabon, where 31.9% of the female population finishes its child-bearing years without a single live birth; among the Ogoone Lolo people that percentage is as high as 46.2%, nearly three times higher than that of the Nyanga people, who are still relatively infertile, with 17.8% of their women dying childless. In the Equateur province of Zaire, 40% of women have completed their childbearing years with no living child, followed closely by those of the Bas-Velé with 37.3%, and the Haut-Velé with 36.9%. In Tshuaapa 33% of women are childless at menopause and in Stanleyville and Nanié-Ma the figure is above 23%, shocking statistics otherwise submerged in an overall sterility rate of 17.6% in Zaire as a whole.

In South-east Cameroon, 28% of women aged twenty-five to twenty-nine are childless, compared to 23% among the older generation; wider disparities can be seen in the Central African Empire where 25.2% of women between twenty-five and twenty-nine have not given birth to a living child, compared to 13.6% of older women. What these figures represent is probably a laborious struggle to have a live child, a struggle complicated by maternal ill-health and perinatal mortality; the infertility rates are much higher among the child-bearing women of the Centre and River regions of the Central African Empire, 34.7% and 36.3% respectively, but the group worst hit is probably that of the Nzakara, with the astonishing crude birth rate of 20 per thousand. Among the Tuareg of Mali, more than a quarter of the women of childbearing age are infertile, a rate which contrasts interestingly with that of settled Tuareg populations. The general infertility rate in Sudan is not remarkably high in that 9.6% of women are childless at menopause, but that overall figure conceals extremes of only 2.3% in Upper Nile compared to 21.2% in Equatoria. In Central Equatoria, 42.4% of women are childless at menopause. Likewise in the Upper Volta, only 3.2% of women in Bissa die childless, but 17.6% of the Bobo people can expect that fate. In 1960, in two regions of Zanzibar, 25.1% and 37% of women over 46 years of age were childless.[42]

In Nigeria, infertility is responsible for half of all consultations at specialist gynaecological clinics. Doctors working in the field are anxious to convey to foreigners the particular suffering that accompanies the condition as well as their problems in trying to trace the kind of sterility and its origin. The patients are restless, desperate, the slow infertility work-up tortures them, and a high proportion abandon Western technology for magic and quackery.

> Reproductive failure in African society is a social stigma often associated with considerable emotional stress; the social implications are often as profound as the personal tragedies ... In two-thirds of our infertile patients, the fault can be attributed to tubal factor in the female secondary to pelvic inflammatory disease, while 35–50% of the males attending the clinic have pathological spermigram.[43]

Establishment of the exact cause of the pelvic inflammatory disease requires extensive examination of autopsy material and a controlled programme of biopsies taken from living patients during tubal surgery, both luxuries which the hospitals of Ibadan cannot afford. Drs Ladipo and Osoba were trying to establish the role of T-strain mycoplasma in the infections that they saw, both in the Fallopian tubes and because the organism attaches to spermatozoa; they were obliged to fall back on the likelihood that the sterility they see is multifactorial. Failing investigative surgery, they performed 576 hysterosalpingograms: of these patients only 155 had normal patency in the tubes, 357 suffered some blockage, and 165 had bi-lateral hydrosalpinx, that is, both tubes had become balloon-like sacs of liquid which persisted after the infecting organism had died out. Two-thirds of the women reported induced or spontaneous abortions; the chief causes of infection, the doctors opined, were post-abortal and puerperal sepsis.

In Enugu, Drs Chukudebelu, Esege and Megafu were coming to similar conclusions, and they too found it necessary to preface them with a plea for understanding:

> In Nigeria, reproductive failure has far-reaching social implications, because such a premium is placed on childbearing that childlessness is one of the worst fates that can befall a woman. In our traditional society, childlessness is invariably blamed on the woman, who passively accepts the verdict and spends the rest of her life seeking out one prospective healer after another, native and orthodox. If she is fortunate not to be thrown out of her marital home, she will eventually have to share it with a second or third woman.[44]

The doctors themselves were reeling slightly from their own surprising findings; whereas all things being equal, the female factor is more likely to be responsible for infertility, in Enugu all things were not equal. Like their colleagues in Ibadan, they found a high rate of male infertility, even though they used a low criterion for the concentration of sperm in the ejaculate. The men were chauvinistic and conceited, and unlikely to accept their own reproductive failure; the doctors on the other hand are not at all confident of their ability to reverse infertility of this kind. It was not caused by mumps or varicocele, and only a handful of men admitted to a brush with gonorrhoea. It is still possible that the men are contracting some infection from their women after a reproductive accident.

As well as finding a male factor in 48.2% of the cases they studied, Dr Chukudebelu and his colleagues found tubal occlusion in 51% of their female patients, most from pelvic inflammatory disease, a fifth as many from puerperal sepsis, two from septic abortions and nine of unknown etiology. They found no live agents of sexually transmitted disease, but still gonorrhoea seemed the most likely candidate for this devastation; the absence of live infection they put down to the habit of "commuting from one chemist to another", as well as self-medication with antibiotics.

Ectopic pregnancy is so common in parts of Nigeria that doctors are unusually quick to suspect it. Wilson Onuigbo examined fifty cases occurring among the Ibos, and of them five were recurrences; one was ascribed to tubercular salpingitis, thirty-seven to non-specific chronic salpingitis. Ten were seen before they ruptured. Most occurred in the ampulla, four were interstitial, and what was most interesting was that whereas most ectopic pregnancies result in rupture and the death of the foetus at six weeks' gestation, thirty-two of Oniugbo's cases were more advanced, and nearly all the women had not menstruated since the conception. He was obliged to come to the harrowing conclusion that in his group, ectopic pregnancies, manifest in younger women, are the first known pregnancy, and may recur. He could not say if post-abortal, gonococcal, puerperal, or other pelvic inflammatory disease was responsible. The fifty women Dr Onuigbo saw were lucky; they may have lost a Fallopian tube, but if they had been out of reach of the hospital they would have lost their lives.[45]

Now and then sociologists with a taste for pornoculture divert themselves (and sums of official money) by making "studies" of African towns-women, carefully logging numbers of sexual partners and kinds of living arrangements and places of resort without ever troubling themselves about the women's health or their eventual fate. Yet thirty percent of prostitutes in undeveloped countries have some sexually transmitted disease. Disease may have driven them to the towns in the first place – if they were divorced for childlessness – and disease will continue to recruit girls who will take over when disease forces the elders to leave off. The learned foreigners marvel at the matter-of-factness of their attitude to sex, little realising that their very insouciance is the only survival of a system that treated all healthy young people as potential lovers; what mattered to them more than sexual compatibility was the lineage. The kinship system shattered, and the men dispersed by the demands of outwork, the women dispense meaningless sex in a macabre kind of play. We may suspect the same factors at work among, for example, the prostitutes of Beirut. Samar Khalaf who generally corresponds to his quoted description of a sociologist "as one who spends forty thousand dollars to find a whorehouse"[46] administered questionnaires of 54 entries and pestered prostitutes for months to discover that they came from families in the lower income group, but quite failed to see the implications of the fact that they came from unusually small families and that only 52 of his group had ever given birth to a child, only two of them since they had been practising as prostitutes. The list of things they might be expected to dislike about their profession included "summer heat" and "ambivalent attitudes"; the "constant fear of venereal disease" was casually referred to among "occupational hazards". "Constant fear" has to be justified by frequent occurrence but Khalaf is not interested in anything as unromantic as disease, although he does make mention of the fact that a system of regulated brothels may have "the hygienic advantage of limiting the dissemination of venereal diseases". There is a strong possibility that disease caused the brothels to exist in the first place.[47]

African awareness of the risk of venereal diseases seems to have been high in the past and possibly is so still. Schapera in his classic work on the Kgatla of Botswana quotes one of his respondents as saying:

> When I began to understand things my mother said to me: Look, T— my child, this world is standing on its own two feet, this world does not want you to act carelessly. Don't mix too much with boys. If you love one boy, let it be that boy alone. And be careful of the boys with whom you sleep, for sometimes boys sleep with wrong girls, with girls who have syphilis or bad hips, and then the boy will come to you and put these sicknesses into you and when you are grown up you will not be able to bear children.[48]

Schapera explains too how the Kgatla attribute sterility to promiscuity, and to induced abortion which "spoils the blood."[49] In 1940, there was already a prevailing impression that women were "less fertile than formerly":

> This is variously ascribed to promiscuity before marriage and to the effects of labour migration.[50]

It is too late now for anyone to chart the process whereby *Neisseria gonorrhoeae* conquered the world. The assumption is that the bacillus is *ubiquitous*. There are some reasons for disbelieving that this was always so; for one thing, societies in which gonorrhoea has caused sterility on the scale of 30–40% would seem to be suffering the kind of virulent attack which comes earlier in the life of an endemic infection: as gonorrhoea so efficiently sterilises people in whom it is untreated, and relatively swiftly, it would seem in the organism's own interest to allow its hosts to reproduce to at least a limited extent by slowing down the speed of its operation. Where the degree of susceptibility is high, we may suspect a fairly recent exposure; in other cases, for example, in North African societies, a *modus vivendi* which includes the threat of sterilising disease, seems to have developed over the centuries. There is evidence of another kind, whose significance is not easy to assess, for the recent spread of venereal diseases to regions formerly free of them.

The African people classify diseases into two major groups: (1) Bantu diseases – a few examples of which are *Isifuba* (disease of the chest started by eating bewitched food); *Umeqo* (disease caused by having walked over bewitchment placed in one's way); *Umbulelo* (a condition of the eyes caused by bewitchment); and *Iqondo* (affecting the reproductive organs, and most prevalent among young adolescents). The next big group is (2) that called European diseases – the most common being syphilis and gonorrhoea.[51]

There is nothing new in giving the name of a hated invader to disease and assuming that he brought it with him, and there may be no more in this distinction than there was in the English tendency to call the Great Pox (syphilis) the French Pox. Venereal diseases usually accompany itinerants of any kind, be they soldiers or merchants, because of the forced promiscuity of their sexual contacts; Arab traders seem to have been responsible for venereal diseases in the slaving areas and among the Nilotic peoples. The African view of the mechanism is important, though, in that it recognises more than one kind of genital affliction, the old, familiar, and the new. These may be no more than different strains of gonococci; on the other hand they could be completely distinct, or some new combination could result in a bacterial symbiosis in which the gonorrhoeal infection is rendered more devastating by other vectors or by the sequelae of other disease.

Despite the great gonorrhoea scare in the early seventies, virtually no work has been done on nature's method of tubal ligation; we still understand little of the epidemiology of gonorrhoea and probably never will until we begin to feel the effects of its activities on our own race and class, by which time it may be too late. The Vietnam war reaped 40,000 cases of gonorrhoea a week; some of them came home to small mid-western towns where permissiveness was making its first impact. The mechanism was so apparent that the possibility of germ warfare was discussed and even became a kind of myth of Asiatic revenge. Actually, the rich Caucasians of the developed world are the most mobile people ever known on earth; we have already given more than we shall ever get in the way of exterminating disease. Whether it is half-treated in the American ghetto or untreated as among the Maria Gonds, gonorrhoea has been an agent of genocide.[52]

Those who suppose that the West has charms or technology to cure infertility will be disappointed. To be sure, gonorrhoea and syphilis can be cured by penicillin, and if the case proves resistant, with other antibiotics, but it is important in the case of gonorrhoea that the medication be given no later than a month after infection, if the possibility of sterilising disease is to be averted. As two-thirds of the cases recurring in women are asymptomatic, prompt medication depends upon efficient tracing, which depends upon staff and facilities available only in rich countries and central locations. The more disrupted a society, the more uneven the distribution of medical beds and trained personnel, the less likely it is to be able to contain the spread of venereal disease. Even in England and the United States a concerted campaign has only barely succeeded in holding the sexually transmitted diseases at a high level of prevalence; there is every reason to believe that even if poor countries could mount the same sort of campaign against syphilis and gonorrhea, the other sexually transmitted diseases which result in pelvic inflammatory disease would take their place. More sophisticated testing takes time, space, equipment and staff, all of which are at a premium. In the presence of high incidence of life-threatening disease, fertility-threatening disease must take second place. Hysterical fear of population explosion means that second place is a long way behind.

Some kinds of infertility, those resulting from congenital defects in the reproductive system, are impossible to treat. Others, resulting from pituitary and hypothalamic malfunction, may respond to sophisticated hormone therapy. Some require simple adjustments of timing, or of the vaginal environment, or position at intercourse. Infertility specialists usually test for all such simple impediments in the course of a long fertility work-up, itself a costly procedure in terms of personnel, time and testing equipment, before coming to test the tubal factor. Many of their patients become pregnant during the work-up, accounting for the highest proportion of their successes, and this is usually explained as the effect of the fact of consultation upon psychogenic factors in infertility.

Tubal occlusion, the commonest cause of infertility in women, may be detected in various ways. Liquid may be pumped into the uterus and the pelvis X-rayed to show its penetration (insufflation); the lumen and tubes are shown in silhouette and half moon-like shadows show where the liquid has (if it has) escaped through the fimbriae at the end of the Fallopian tubes. A more difficult and dangerous test involves the insertion of a laparoscope into the pelvis to see the relative position of tubes and ovaries and the extent of adhesions and distortions. The test requires deep anaesthesia, as the pelvis must be inflated with gas and the patient's body tilted steeply to allow the intestines to fall away from the reproductive organs, while the surgeon struggles to get a clear view, sometimes having to make an extra incision to get a new angle for the laparoscope.[53]

Once tubal occlusion is established there are several possible ways of treating it, all of limited efficacy, and all requiring surgical expertise of a high order. Salpingolysis, in which the tubes are delicately freed from adhesions or endometriosis, is the simplest and has the best prognosis for successful pregnancy. Thirty to forty percent of tubal incompetence is caused by external adhesions and endometriosis; forty to fifty percent of women thus afflicted will conceive after a salpingolysis and half of them will bring the pregnancy to a successful conclusion, accounting for 7% of women suffering from tubal occlusion. Where the fimbriae have closed over, blocking the tube in a hydrosalpinx, they may be resected by a longer and more delicate operation which has a success rate variously computed as from five to forty percent in terms of pregnancies, of which half will come to term. This operation, as do the succeeding ones, increases the risk of ectopic pregnancy. Salpingoplasty is the operation to reverse the effects of tubal ligation or cautery, or scarring which has a similar effect of blocking the mid-tube; often a silastic prosthesis is used to prevent the formation of new adhesions and must be removed by another operation. When the tube is blocked at the uterine junction or isthmus, a technique of re-implantation which utilises the "good" end of the tube is adopted; a tubular prosthesis keeps the tubes from closing again and is later removed via the cervix. All these operations require the more sophisticated anaesthesia and the elimination of all bleeding; steroids control inflammation and scarring.

None of these is an operation carried out by "every cross-roads hospital"; the wide fluctuations in the success rate include a considerable element of variation in the dexterity of the surgeon and his experience with microsurgery. As the techniques become better known, the degree of success could improve. In theory, doctors evaluate the individual cases very carefully, in terms of the patient's ability to survive the operation and the pregnancy and the outlook in terms of health and happiness of any child she might bear. In some cases, surgeons may even decide to carry out a second tubal operation, for which the prognosis is no better or worse than it was for the first, but even then they acknowledge that they are often forced to capitulate to a woman's insistence rather than their own evaluation.[54] In cynical terms, the fact is that any woman who is prepared to spend the money on tubal reconstruction will find a surgeon to do it. The surgeon may temporise, demand that she give up smoking, or drinking, or her job, take to her bed for a year, and she will do it. And then she may confound him after all by having an abortion.

The surgeon's motivation for devoting time and concentrated energy to defeating sterility is not simply a desire for fame and money; the satisfaction in causing a barren woman to bear is much more profound than can be supplied by either. It is the most seductive extension of his regard for his own power to father, and not in the least contemptible for that. The successful fertility specialist is the technological version of the polygynous patriarch, and a good deal easier to understand than the career abortionist. Both are a thousand times more likely to be male than female. The grossest example of personal philoprogenitiveness in medicine are those men who use their own semen to impregnate patients whose husbands are infertile, which is what the use of "fresh" semen can commonly be taken to mean: indeed, why the wives of sterile husbands should not be impregnated by their husbands' brothers, or why sterile wives would not be better advised to have their sisters breed for them, instead of undergoing tedious and costly surgery, can only be explained by the modern neurosis which makes child-bearing a self-centred activity, relating principally to the narcissism of the individuals involved. The paradox remains: the people who have least need of issue (in the absence of land which must be worked by the younger members of the family or kinship systems to advance), who have unlimited possibilities of satisfaction in the fields of commerce, political power and intellectual activity, are the only people who have access to the technological means of reversing their infertility. Patrick Steptoe chose to circumvent all the struggles to maximise, by tubal surgery, the potential of infertile women bypassing the Fallopian tube altogether and fertilising a human ovum with human sperm in the laboratory. His patients were not millionaires, but his experiments were the outcome of millions spent on luxury research. It is truly amusing to read the outraged reactions of the other scientists who worked with him at Cambridge on the fertilisation of animal ova in a petri dish, while he went off to Royston to try their techniques on human patients.[55]

However, the much publicised successes of men like Steptoe ought not to conceal a fundamental fact: our generation will not be remembered for infertility reversal but for mass sterilisations on an unprecedented scale. Like any native midwife with a pointed stick, we can destroy fertility. Our methods of tubal occlusion are more efficient and speedier than those of the gonococcus, but they are fundamentally the same, and we are as inefficient in reversing the one as we are the other. We are not as cavalier as the gonococcus in destroying the fertility of the young and childless, but we are moving in the same direction. Like the gonococcus we choose the poor and disadvantaged and would extend the scope of our sterilising activities further in their direction if we could. What we have offered the third world as contraception has turned out to be sterilisation in too many cases, when ectopic pregnancy and pelvic inflammatory disease have accompanied the IUD. To the people whose children are most at risk, we offer sterilisation; time after time, projects of law have come before state parliaments suggesting the compulsory sterilisation of welfare mothers. Time after time, cases come before the courts of women sterilised against their will, sometimes without their knowledge. Enthusiastic young doctors, unable to see why the poor should want their children, suggest tubal ligation to women in painful labour or undergoing abortion, stressing the convenience of mopping up the whole problem at once to disguise their own misgivings about the patient's motivation. What they ought to know is that the risk of abortion is increased enormously by its combination with tubal ligation, in a way that has been observed but is not yet fully understood.[56]

Sterilisation is now the most popular form of family limitation in the United States. More than 600,000 sterilisations are performed annually. At first, doctors were wary of sterilising any but women who had already borne many children, but their ideas of "many" were gradually eroded under the pressure of popular demand which intensified as women gained first-hand acquaintance with the problems of oral contraception and the IUD. Although doctors insist that patients are counselled that the procedure is irreversible and are given time to make a sensible decision, there are too many demands for reversal which cannot be turned away simply because the woman has changed her mind or misunderstood the doctor who sterilised her. In fact, fertility limitation is now so popular an idea that doctors have become blasé about offering it to all kinds of people in all kinds of states of mind. In India "family planners" have seriously considered suggesting vasectomy to men whose wives are pregnant on the grounds that their reproductive urge would be for the moment sated and their motivation would be "better." Even in the elite of the consumer society, sterilisation can be suggested in circumstances of great confusion and stress. A woman whose cervix had failed to dilate in a Cambridge hospital found herself unable to distinguish between two statements, one beneath the other, on the consent form that she was required to sign for the Caesarian section that she was then obliged to undergo. One statement was of her willingness to undergo anaesthesia, the other to undergo a sterilisation; exhausted after a day of aggressive mismanagement of her labour and in pain, she almost signed both parts. Nancy, born to her that night, subsequently died in her cot. Of a hundred patients requesting reversal in British Columbia in 1977, 47 had been sterilised post-partum, and 9 during induced abortions, both times of great stress when important decisions affecting the rest of one's life ought not to be taken; 52 were under the age of 26, 89 were under the age of 30. Seventeen had lost children in crib death, four had lost their children in accidents. Fifty-three had not been members of a stable sexual relationship at the time of the sterilisation, and sixty-three had "undergone a change in marital status."[57] Some of these situations are unusual; most of them are not. Instability in sexual relationships is the rule rather than the exception, especially if we are dealing with people who have most of their reproductive life still before them.

Voluntary sterilisation implies that no fundamental changes will be allowed to take place – life's die has been cast. It is the abandonment of management of one's own fertility and a regression to child status. Sterilisation is not a substitute for contraception because it is the destruction of fertility: it makes as much sense as blinding a man who needs glasses. Dr Rochelle Shain, at the University of Texas Health Center at

San Antonio, spent a great deal of time finding out whether people would prefer reversible to irreversible sterilisation, and found, to nobody's amazement, that if reversible sterilisation were as cheap and accessible as irreversible sterilisation, more people would want it, and they would want it more wholeheartedly.[58] The desire to be fertile and infertile at will is normal in any sane human being; the desire to destroy fertility irrevocably is a response forced by circumstances beyond the individual's control. The question arises whether we ever have the right to destroy fertility rather than suspend it. When we come to the bribing and enticing of individuals to undergo sterilisation, the utilisation of times of stress and confusion to extort a meaningless consent, and finally the sterilisation of those unable to give consent or to withhold it, we have abandoned all scruple.

As is normal in "family planning", sterilisation began to be practised on a large scale before anyone was certain of the right way of doing it. Between 1973 and 1977, each surgeon performing sterilisations at a clinic in suburban Washington, DC, changed his techniques three times "on the basis of his judgment as advances in technology occurred." They began with destructive methods. "Two-point electrocoagulation followed by the avulsion of the intervening segment," which may be relied upon to result in a well-wrecked Fallopian tube as well as the highest number of sequelae, was adopted in preference to one-point electrocoagulation followed by division, which seemed to cause both more PID (pelvic inflammatory disease) and more adhesions and to have a higher failure rate. Eventually they settled for the occlusion of the tube by a silastic ring, which seemed to cause fewer "real" symptoms, which are those symptoms whose existence the surgeons can verify by objective criteria, and not simply by taking the woman's word. Not the least of their problems in assessing the desirability of one technique as compared to another was that 81 of their 226 patients had "altered pelvic pathophysiology" as a result either of their contraceptive practice, or their contraceptive failures. One thing was certain about the insertion of the silastic ring in preference to the fizzing electric cautery; it was a way of avoiding the accidental burning of surrounding organs and tissues and subsequent malpractice suits. It is to be remembered that the surgeons changed the methods; the patients did not get to pick and choose, and as a matter of fact, those who came along late enough to get the rings also got the best chance of successful reversal.[59]

From the beginning of 1976 to the end of 1977, the Reproductive Endocrinology Division of the Department of Obstetrics and Gynaecology at the University of Florida ran an evaluation scheme for women requesting reversal of tubal ligation. Thirteen were screened out almost immediately, one because her husband was azoospermic, four for medical reasons and eight because they "were financially unable to pursue surgical reversal", in other words, they did not have the money. Six others had

had their tubes virtually burned away with less than 3 cm remaining; one had even lost the fimbriae. Eight patients went forward for tubal reconstruction; less than a year later one patient was pregnant and two had given birth. One of the eight had been sterilised at the age of thirteen. The conclusion of the study was that the women who were sterilised by mini-laporotomy "with resection of a small portion of the isthmic segment via the Pomeroy technique" have the best prospects for reversal.[60] As long as reversal must be done by microsurgery the chance of reversal for the sterilised peasant is nil in any event. Dr Rajnikant Arole, accepting that reversal is out of the question, removes the whole fimbrial end in his sterilisations, and yet he is a merciful man, who cares passionately about his rural health programme and has had phenomenal success in training illiterate women in self-help.

Female sterilisation is not a trivial matter. Whether or not a sterilised woman suffers after-effects of the operation depends on what technique was used and how skilfully it was carried out. She runs an elevated risk of ectopic pregnancy with some methods, an elevated risk of abdominal adhesions with others. If blood supply to the ovary is disrupted she may suffer abdominal pain and menstrual irregularities. In rare cases a tube will recanalise and a normal pregnancy may ensue. Doctors should investigate patients thoroughly to make sure that there is little likelihood of a sterilisation acceptor's needing further surgery, for example, a hysterectomy, for reasons unconnected with sterilisation, but evidence of the frequency of post-sterilisation hysterectomy shows that this is not being done.[61]

The whole world is involved in an orgy of cutting and burning human reproductive tissue. More than 75,000,000 women have been sterilised, 9,000,000 in the United States. In 1970 only 20% of contracepting women had been sterilised; by 1975 the proportion had risen to 51%. In 1973, the median age of sterilisation acceptors was 28; fewer than half of the total were over thirty. In Fiji 22% of couples, and in Sri Lanka, 13%, have one sterilised member. In Panama 26% of married women are sterilised, and in Costa Rica 15%.[62] Mass sterilisation projects are carried out by electrocoagulation and laparoscopy; if the complication rate were no higher than that observed in the United States, it would be unacceptable; chances are that it is higher. The number of women who regret their decision is unknown, but as infant death is commoner in the third world than in the USA we may assume that it as often provides a desperate desire for reversal. The other reasons, religious and psychological, could be assumed to be at least as powerful, if not more so.

If we believe, and most of us would say we do, that coercion has no place in birth control schemes, we must consider whether it can be eliminated if sterilisation is the only option. The choice of sterilisation is itself dictated by the paucity of other options. It cannot be a free choice because the acceptors' knowledge of what they are choosing is inadequate. For that matter the sterilisers' understanding of their activity is less than adequate; for example, it is not known whether the formation of spermatic granulomas at the site of the vasectomy is a good prognosis for reversal, or neutral and unimportant, or possibly agonising and debilitating. Nearly a third of vasectomised men will have a granuloma, and ten percent of those will suffer pain during sexual excitement, perhaps steady from the beginning of sexual excitement, becoming severe at ejaculation or as post-coital ache; some will develop fistulae, or moist spots or severe scrotal scarring. The tendency to minimise post-vasectomy symptoms was finally reversed when a doctor himself reported that he had never experienced more agonising pain and had to be given 15 mg of morphine on five occasions in less than two hours.[63] If he had not been a doctor he probably would have got no morphine at all. If he had been an Indian farmer he would have got no morphine at all, and no other man in his village would have dreamt of undergoing similar agony, and pretty soon the news would have travelled to all parts of his district.

If the incidence of symptomatic spermatic granuloma is of the order of three or four per hundred, it is clearly too high. The decline in acceptance of vasectomy in India is probably connected with such experiences rather than with the political campaign run by Mrs Gandhi's opponents; nowadays Indian sterilisation programmes are predominantly addressed to women. A peasant population would not know, although in its own sceptical way it might suspect, that the long-term sequelae of vasectomy are more problematic still. The oldest surviving vasectomy patient is an ape, who is far from well. Because of the leakage of sperm, an "alien" protein, into the bloodstream, the vasectomised male could develop auto-immune disease; in the case of the monkeys, the disease is athero-sclerosis.[64] Unmoved by the monkeys' sufferings, the sterilisers continue their destructive labours. In a study of a thousand men sterilised in London, the mean age at the time of sterilisation was found to be no more than 26. As one gynaecologist put it, "the world has gone sterilisation-mad". International fertility conferences are dominated by elaborate discussions of techniques for reversal of surgical sterilisations. Meanwhile help for the childless poor is as far off as ever it was.[65]

The spectrum of sterility in our world then has three aspects, all of them menacing. The first is the involuntary sterility that has been spread by disease throughout the developed world and throughout its colonies and dependencies, with which we have not begun to deal; whether the rich spend fortunes in trying to reverse it or the poor simply suffer it, it carries out its inexorable work. The second is the sterility we choose for ourselves in preference to continuing the struggle to regulate our own fertility. The third is the sterility we persuade others to accept because we doubt their capacity to regulate their own fertility or because we do not trust them to do it. Among the dubious achievements of the twentieth century, along with total war and the neutron bomb, will go our character as the sterilising civilisation.

We cannot guess how superstitious we will seem to future generations, if there are any, for they will know if the threat which we tried to avert by our blood sacrifices and burnt offerings was ever likely to come to pass. The white protestant materialist regards all those religious people whose faith he does not understand as backward and superstitious or simply hypocritical. Posterity may have worse to say of him when it contemplates the crimes against human autonomy that he was willing to countenance in order to avert that theoretical catastrophe, the death of the world through over-population. The most savage irony is that sterilisation is poor birth control and unlikely to produce the chain reaction that those who fear the population explosion need, for it denies the human dignity which was our reason for undertaking to control births in the first place.

Chapter Four
Chastity is a Form of Birth Control

Oh these illegitimate babies!
Oh girls, girls,
Silly little valuable things,
You should have said, No, I am valuable,
And again, It is because I am valuable
I say, No.

Nobody teaches anybody they are valuable nowadays.
                                                Stevie Smith

The most straightforward and unambiguous way of keeping human population in balance with resources is the denial of reproductive opportunity by the imposition of restrictions upon sexual activity. No human society exists in which human beings may copulate at will; no human community has ever been organised around the principle of free love, or could be, as long as reproduction and sexual activity were inextricably connected. Marriage is a licence to reproduce. Even in societies where sexual experimentation among young people is encouraged, illegitimate birth is rare and regarded as disgraceful. The pattern in such societies seems to be that youngsters may copulate irresponsibly during the period of adolescent sterility, the existence and extent of which has only recently been understood.[1] In some groups, play sex must cease when the menses appear and the fecundable woman is secluded until marriage.

Chastity is not primarily a way of limiting fertility, or rather, it is not presented to people bound by its laws primarily as such, for it would fail of its effect if it were. The unmasking of chastity as merely a way of limiting reproductive opportunity would stimulate each individual's reproductive egotism is a completely unacceptable way. Instead, chastity is magnificently shrouded in myth. Christians are taught that both Christ and his mother were virgin all their lives, an incredible situation but one in which millions have firmly believed, and struggled to control their own carnal desires in imitation of divine example. Virgins could expect to be placed higher in heaven even than spouses who lived in perfect married chastity. Protection of bodily purity in some individuals became such an obsession that they refused to allow doctors to touch their bodies when their lives depended upon it. The Catholic god is pleased by sexual abstinence even when it deprives a lawfully married spouse of his or her rights. In the unmarried, sexual lapses are on a par with robbery and murder, mortal sins of the blackest dye.[2]

The very elaboration of the Catholic cult of virginity probably affected the efficacy of its social function, for most ordinary mortals rejected virginity as too difficult for them, but expiated their own lapses by undergoing childbirth, since sex was only permissible as God's way of peopling heaven. In vain the Church fathers denigrated the married state and hedged the married couple about with restrictions on sexual activity, holding out the example of their own celibacy as the highest form of human life. Except in cases of body-hating cults like the Skoptsi and the Cathars, most people continued to marry. It is now impossible to assess the effects of the monastic movement on the population of Europe; even if the proportion of celibates in the population was at times as high as 5% of males, the proportion of women living in convents was very much lower.[3] It was partly the laxity of the large celibate populations which led to the Protestant reaction against celibacy as a worthy way of life for anybody, even the clergy. Even in these post-Counter Reformation times, people in Catholic countries with a large celibate population often accuse the priests of adding to the population, jokingly referring to them as the comforters of widows and wives separated from their husbands. Nevertheless, it would be a mistake to underestimate the effects of the Catholic church's control of primary education in many countries upon the sexual competence of many Catholics, who are taught from babyhood to repress their natural desires and chastise themselves even for involuntary lapses. The existence of the confessional, in which probing questions of the most intimate type can be asked under divine sanction, while the penalties for lying, a sin against the Holy Ghost, are expulsion from the sight of God and eternal torment, has a profound effect upon the capacity of the individual for sexual response.

The effects of Catholic teaching upon the sexual activity of the individual vary according to the other pressures exerted upon him by custom and his socio-economic situation. Because of the difficulty of incorporating the influence of the Church (itself variable) in the spectrum of other variables, most demographers simply omit it from their considerations, beyond remarking darkly that Catholic countries have more rather than fewer abortions than others, or that the Belgian birth rate fell below replacement despite the Church. For Catholics, however, if not for demographers, the Church is enormously important. The Catholic morality of individual salvation is often in conflict with the higher morality of altruism toward members of one's own group. Because Catholics have difficulty accepting sexuality as a part of the personality and deploying it sensibly, and therefore have special difficulties in planning reproductive behaviour, they are especially exposed to the danger of unwanted pregnancy and guilt-ridden abortion. Catholic insistence upon purity might not affect the demographers' figures, except paradoxically to increase the totals, but it enormously increases the amount of stress contained in those figures.

Burma may represent a case where anti-sexual religion has kept population increase low, if religion is the deciding factor in the remarkable sparsity of the Burmese population, and not, for example, successful resistance by the hill tribes, whose ferocity and personal courage are still proverbial, to the expansionism of the immigrants who peopled the Irrawaddy and its delta only two thousand years ago. The mere prevalence of anti-sexual belief is clearly not sufficient in itself to explain the phenomenon, but neither can the phenomenon be explained without it. The most remarkable aspect of Buddhism in Burma is the degree to which it had penetrated the daily life of every inhabitant. Every village had a monastery and every male child was educated free of charge in the monastery, by monks who, although they took no vow of poverty or chastity as such, had renounced the society of women along with their right to have a home. The Burmese Buddhist monk's rejection of worldly pleasures is total; he may not look more than six feet before him, but must walk with downcast eyes. He may not preach more than five or six words to a woman without a man present, and in public must shade his eyes with a fan so as not to feast his eyes on women.

> The daily life of the monk teacher who had hitched his wagon to the supernal star leaves an enduring impression on the mind of the pupil. The living example of a life of poverty, chastity and self-abnegation imparts added strength to the early moral training he received at home. Indeed, the early impregnation of the religious spirit together with the influence of the parents in childhood and the precept reinforced by the monk-teacher are the dynamic forces which have given the Burmese their natural character.[4]

When the Burmese boy shows signs of the restlessness of adolescence he is sent to the monastery to live; after a ceremony known as *shinbyu* he is admitted to the monastery as a neophyte. At the age of twenty he may leave the monastery or be ordained and remain. The function of such a system is primarily to ensure its own continuity. Burmese monasticism exists to further monasticism by constant indoctrination and recruiting and the success of both functions is due to the absolute sincerity with which they are carried out, for there is no way to hide hypocrisy in such a system, which is as unlike the secular priesthood of Catholicism as it could be. The Burmese boy's role-models are all champions of self-abnegation; when he decides to leave the monastery self-abnegation is more natural to him than the spontaneous expression of physical desire. There are some signs, for example the extreme touchiness of Burmese and the high rate of violent crime in Burma,[5] that this self-repression is not without a huge cost, but even under the new regime of revolutionary socialism the usefulness of self-abnegation must have grown rather than diminished.

Women used to be excluded from the monastery schools and the secular schools set up for them hardly fulfilled a fraction of the same function. As is common in Buddhist Asia, the women performed the lion's share of physical work, which fell to them since childhood when their brothers were contemplating higher things, and the importance of their physical labour militated against their child-bearing function. In 1914, J. Stuart reflected upon the oddness of the under-population of Burma; he could find no evidence of population pressure in the past or present, the Burmese had developed no sea-power.[6] Their failure to fill their land could not be explained by war or despotism or by physical infertility, so Stuart was obliged to put the phenomenon down to Buddhism, comparing the Burmese to the Buddhists who could not hold their own against the expanding Tamil population in Sri Lanka, but he limited his comments upon the influence of Buddhism to noticing the disparagement of marriage by the Buddhists for whom it is not a sacrament and the religious unimportance of leaving male issue. A rather tart answer from a Burmese would have given a further clue to Burmese psychology if Stuart had cared to interpret it:

> The one reason why Burma is so sparsely populated is that there is no desire for numerous progeny among the Burmans. The second reason is that the average Burman is not lustful (I hope my readers will pardon me for using that word) as his brother the Jew, or any other person of any nation.[7]

Those people who fear that over-population will bring revolution ought to ponder the result of under-population in Burma. The necessity of importing foreign labour was a direct cause of the Burmese revolution, and the training of the "average Burman" in self-denial prepared the perfect medium for the reception of the ideology of collectivism. The other relatively sparsely peopled, Buddhist countries, Thailand, Laos, Cambodia and Vietnam, have all been devastated by revolution and revolutionary war.

The campaign to limit population growth in China in the sixties and seventies was largely a campaign against sexual activity in itself. The Chinese authorities, and all those with the duty of explaining official policy to interested observers, insisted that there was no homosexuality and no prostitution in China, despite the fact that marriage was delayed, often until the spouses were relatively elderly. Young people in China were not expected to have sexual activity of any kind, regardless of adolescent sexual impulses, for a low sex drive was considered normal. Signs on factory walls proclaimed, "Sex is a mental disease." Young Chinese women asked if they "had a boyfriend" by puzzled Westerners who could not readily credit such stoical self-denial were upset and angered by the question, which they took as a reflection on their characters. The merest imputation of hypocrisy in the observation of sexual restrictions was regarded as an inexplicable insult. Inability to control sexual impulses was evidence of degeneracy: the Chinese were proud to distinguish themselves from the lecherous Westerners. Relatively sophisticated Chinese girls visiting the West, even after the expulsion of the Gang of Four, shrink from unsupervised contact with males. Self-denial is not only easier in an anti-coital society, it is actually easier than recognising sexual desire for what it is, especially when there is virtually no privacy, and self-restraint is reinforced by the supervision of others. Bemused Western women dealing with Chinese girls abroad find that they are called upon to play the part of chaperone, thus buttressing a degree of prudishness of which they actually disapprove.

Historical studies of European populations have revealed that in all the countries of Western Europe, a unique pattern of late marriage prevailed with a large proportion remaining unmarried. The famous study by J. Hajnal revealed that in sixteen countries around 1900, the proportion of never-married people ranged between six per cent and twenty per cent of men and ten per cent and twenty-nine per cent of women. The mean rate for men was 12.75% and for women 15.6%. The highest proportion of marriages took place in the late twenties for both men and women. Hajnal traces this phenomenon as far back as the seventeenth century, comparing data from Venice in the eighteenth century, from the Netherlands in the late sixteenth century, from Bavaria in the eighteenth century, Norfolk and Somerset in the sixteenth and seventeenth centuries, Parma from the seventeenth to the nineteenth century, Crulai in Normandy in the seventeenth and eighteenth centuries, and finds sufficient similarity to permit him to define a "European marriage pattern" which has never been challenged.[8] The effects of late marriage upon fertility are difficult to quantify, especially if we take into account the longer period of adolescent sterility which would have prevailed in societies less well-nourished than they are today, but one fact is obvious: there must have been considerable and effective restriction of the sexual activity of young people. That there is more than absolute segregation involved in such a system may be inferred from the fact that the women were not more than a few years younger than their husbands at most. In many cases marriage was preceded by long periods of courtship, infomal and formal betrothal, and a surprisingly high number of brides were pregnant at the time of solemnisation of marriage.[9] The full implications of this phenomenon are discussed elsewhere.

Certain occupational groups in European society were unable to marry, and they are, not surprisingly, the groups in which young adults were most likely to be found. One of the most numerous of such groups is that of domestic servants, who formed 13.4% of the population of England judging from a sample of a hundred English communities from 1574 to 1821. The greater proportion of these were males, and it seems likely that they were more labourers than domestic servants in the nineteenth-century sense. Men in service had a slightly better chance of marrying, but only if their wages were high enough to permit their running a household, for their dependents would not have been welcome at their employers' tables. Women in service could not marry, for their employers would not submit to the claims of pregnancy and babies upon their health and time. Many of them lived out their lives as unmarried servants; others went home and married their childhood sweethearts – if they had not been debauched and turned out by their employers, *bien entendu*. The role of servant shades into that of hired hand, dairymaid or shepherdess and it also shades into kinship, for it was not uncommon for the children of poor relations to be sent into the service of more affluent members of the family. All such servants came under the authority of the head of the household, which could extend to the right of corporal punishment, and certainly did extend to the right of dismissal or turning away without references. Quite young children were sent into service before they had time to make contacts amongst their own peer-group, and grew up entirely dependent, emotionally and physically, upon their masters' families. Apprentices were traditionally a more unruly lot, given to terrorising the staider townsfolk on high days and holy days, and they were privileged among other dependents in that although they might be employed in hard menial labour and physically ill-treated, their employers were in some degree responsible to their parents and to their guildsmen or fellow tradesmen. Apprentices could not marry, nor could they when they reached the next rank of journeyman.[10]

The notion behind these prohibitions is that he who cannot set up an independent household may not marry. They applied also to students and scholars dependent upon the accommodation of their colleges; although tradition has it that Cambridge scholars kept mistresses and whores in Bishop's Stortford, it seems probable that there was more celibacy to be met with in the college community than active whoremongering. Soldiers might not marry without the consent of their commanding officers, which, although it nowadays seems relatively easy to come by, was by no means so in earlier times. The prohibition survives in that, for example, Italian *carabinieri* may not marry until the age of twenty-six; if a marriage should be contracted for urgent reasons before that time, the soldier is not entitled to a married man's allowance or to married quarters.

Some of the factors here discussed make for a life without marriage, and others for late marriage, but there was a further condition to marriage even for those who escaped from servant status into independence. The European marriage pattern is predominantly one of a household centring on one married couple with unmarried members of the same and other generations, related and unrelated. Marriage necessitated the setting up of an independent household. This pattern itself may have developed out of population pressure upon available land resources. Its inhibiting effect upon population growth can hardly be doubted; even in the case of the mastercraftsman whose connection with food production may be more tenuous, ability to raise a family depended upon the productivity of the land from which the surplus would be generated to buy his manufactured goods. His own trade organisations meanwhile exerted themselves to ensure that the number of qualified craftsmen nowhere jeopardised their individual chance of survival.

The European pattern was the unique product of specific population density, life expectancy and patterns of inheritance and land use. The effect of the Industrial Revolution was to shatter it and gradually to replace it with the pattern of early propertyless marriage and high birth rate which has now become that of early propertyless marriage with prolonged contraception. Such a summary is absurdly over-simplified, but what it ought to suggest is that when we come to study the population-regulation systems of other countries we might remember the four hundred years or so when we achieved a satisfactory balance between population growth and predominantly agrarian economy without any intergalactic planning agency to tell us how to do it. Casual devaluation and contempt for cultural patterns of chastity and self-discipline are not only arrogant, they actually discredit our activities in the eyes of people who are supposed to be impressed by them.

While other societies never enjoined lifelong celibacy upon so many or delayed marriage as long as the Western European countries, there are hundreds of groups which observe strict and sometimes lengthy restrictions upon the sexual intercourse of spouses. The most abstemious society ever studied anywhere are the Dani of Irian Jaya, Indonesia. Anthropologists still have difficulty in accepting Karl Heider's five statements about them:

> The Grand Valley Dani have a four-to-six year post-partum sexual abstinence.
> The period of abstinence is invariably observed.
> The norm of a long post-partum sexual abstinence is neither supported by powerful explanations nor enforced by strong sanctions.
> Most people have no alternative sexual outlets.
> No one shows signs of unhappiness or stress during their abstinence.[11]

Heider observed the Grand Valley Dani for thirty months; in that time Dani men told him of their custom of abstaining from sexual intercourse after the birth of a child, and among all the scurrilities they occasionally told him about each other, never did they mention an infringement of this code. Moreover, siblings seemed to be the right distance apart in age and he could find no evidence of contraception, abortion, infanticide or sexual intercourse of any kind but that which sooner or later results in conception. What most puzzled Heider was that this extraordinary low level of sexual activity was not enforced by any powerful system of threats, natural or supernatural, or other controls. Men with a number of wives did not resort to the compounds of receptive wives, but tended to stay in the compound with the infant for the first year or so of its life. Of a hundred and seventy women, eighty-six had borne only one child, fifty-seven only two. Weddings take place only on the major pig feasts which occur every four to six years, and couples do not begin to have sexual intercourse until after a special ceremony two years after that. Most nights the men sleep in the loft of the men's house, the women in their own compounds. Heider's conclusion from the observation of the serene, healthy Dani was that the Freudian assumption of normal levels of libido for all people, regardless of enculturation, is wrong; rather sexual activity is learned in response to patterns of stimulus which are absent in the Dani from infancy, when there is little erotic play even between mother and child. The Dani are a strange case in that their sexuality is not repressed but rather undeveloped, so that no form of compensation or sublimation in art or warfare or intellectual activity can be found to take place. Oddly enough it may be the very health of the Dani and the easiness of life in the Dugum neighbourhood which has prevented the development of the cultural forms which stimulate sexual fantasy and desire. Perhaps pro-coital societies have developed in conditions of weakened libido as a result of malnutrition and disease along with a high degree of pregnancy wastage, so that continued reproductive activity needed all the cultural help it could get. Living in Shangri-la, protected by the terrain from marauders and their diseases, with an equable climate and productive land, the Dani did not have to struggle with the forces of death: in their condition we may glimpse what population homeostasis might really mean.

So extraordinary did Heider's observations seem to his colleagues that some of them believe to this day that he invented the whole story. There are indications however, that low-energy systems may be commoner than used to be thought, especially in societies which have settled into a mutual accommodation with limited terrain and a circumscribed food supply, and are prevented from forcing their territories to support agriculture because of climate and soil conditions, such as the Amazon Indians. Cotlow gives an insight into the kind of sexuality that prevailed in the Xingu area:

Orlando's Xinguanos are deeply disturbed by *civilizados* who are sexually frustrated; they cannot understand how a man can become aroused at the sight of a nude woman. In his twenty-five years of daily life with Indians, Orlando told me, he had never seen an Indian with an erection. It would be absurd to them. Nor has Orlando seen or heard of any instances of sexual deviation among the Indians. They did not know what masturbation was until they saw a *civilizado* telegraph operator doing it.

From then on the telegraph operator was a problem to Orlando and his colleagues at the Park. The Indians despised him because, in their eyes, he had done something reprehensible. There was nothing to do but remove him from the Park.[12]

Other traditional New Guinea societies have much in common with the Dani. Men and women are commonly segregated, men sleeping together in men's quarters and women and children in other quarters or in individual compounds, therefore coitus is not simply a result of propinquity but must be deliberately sought. Among the Maring, who see women as those whose wombs bring forth replacements for slain warriors, women are expressly excluded from certain areas and certain activities. At certain times men and women may have no contact of any kind.

> Men and women sleep in separate houses. Women may not enter men's houses, for doing so would injure the health of those residing there ... While a man may enter the front room of a woman's house, he exposes himself to harm by entering the little sleeping room in the rear ...[13]

Sex segregation, especially of sleeping quarters, is not in the least a rare phenomenon. While segregation itself does not necessarily mean sexual abstinence, for couples may be encouraged to consort by stealth, as Lycurgus ruled in Sparta, it allows a considerable degree of supervision of sexual activity and especially of reinforcement of ceremonial abstinence. Moreover, in such groups, the nuptial bond is very much less important than the social bonds between men; competition for reproductive opportunity would jeopardise the community of interest which should prevail between males, so often abstinence is more likely to be practised faithfully by the whole group than hypocritically with routine infringements. It is hard for uxorious Westerners to realise that conjugal relationships may take a second or lower place in a man's social life, when Western society has practically demolished all groups except the mobile consumer unit of the nuclear family: but there is a wealth of evidence to prove that in Islamic groups, among the Micronesian and Melanesian people and even among Hindu groups, segregation is the preferred way of life, although the Western media machine is fast dismantling it, not only loosening the societal bonds between males, but shattering the substructure of self-contained cooperative female society, so that women actually suffer a decline in status with modernisation. The result of the dismantling of such structures may very well be a bulge in the birthrate, and some such bulge may already be hidden in world population figures, especially where those relate to the reproductive behaviour of recent migrants to the city from traditional societies. The nuclear family often shows higher fertility than the traditional family.

It must be made clear at this point that abstinence has a two-fold function; not only does it keep the birthrate lower than it might otherwise be, it actually protects fertility by placing a high value on the activity which must be forgone. The man who is enjoined to abstinence is being both encouraged and discouraged at the same time; sexual tension is being augmented by giving to sex an enhanced psychic value. Thus coitus is not a routine activity, but a risky and sometimes truly perilous exploit. The commonest belief is that sperm is a precious substance directly related to energy or power, the wanton expenditure of which will cause weakening of mind and body. The phenomenon of detumescence itself is thought to be a direct manifestation of the way in which sexual gratification unstrings a man. One of the commoner kinds of symbolisation of male potency in horticultural societies involves the transference of the man's own sexual potency to plants that he is growing, which will not thrive if he indulges in sexual intercourse. The Western Abelam people in New Guinea grow ceremonial yams, *Dioscorea alata*:

> Male status is largely dependent upon the number and size of the tubers grown. As a result great effort is put into various forms of magic used to ensure successful yam growth. To further ensure the success of their yam crop men who grow long yams observe a series of taboos, the most important of which is a prohibition against sex for the six-month growing season. There is also curtailment of sexually related behaviour such as sexual joking, and menstruating women are particularly avoided by yam growers.[14]

As far as this anthropologist could tell, the seasonality of births corresponded to a period of abstinence lasting from August to January; meanwhile, presumably, the yams were as the yams of ten, because the hearts of their growers, like that of Galahad himself, were pure.

Even such a long period of abstinence as six months need not lower the birthrate very much; women who conceived at the beginning of the period of sexual activity might well be ready to conceive again at some time during the next. However, as sexual abstinence helps yams to grow, it also helps babies to grow in the womb. The number of traditional societies where sexual intercourse is automatically suspended as soon as a pregnancy is verified is far greater than the number of those where intercourse during pregnancy is encouraged. Sheila Kitzinger has quoted evidence of men rendered practically impotent by the feeling that there was "someone else in there" even in our pro-coital society. Generally, it seems likely that abstinence during pregnancy is the direct result of the parents' deep desire for a healthy child. The connection is not a logical one, derived from physiology of pregnancy although sexual intercourse does in fact slightly increase the risk of spontaneous abortion it is, rather, a religious one. The parents hope to *deserve* a healthy child by their self-denial.

The same societies that practise abstinence during pregnancy often continue to practise it after the child is born.

> ... once the child is born, the responsibility for its future lies almost entirely in the father's hands. By the food taboos and sexual restraint ... he steers the child safely through the post partum period.[15]

This description comes from the Fore of New Guinea. Many other peoples too have considered the period between birth and weaning a particularly dangerous one for the child, whose chances of being carried off by common ailments may be greater than his chances of survival to weaning point. Obviously sexual abstinence cannot directly affect the child's chances, but it does have a psychoprophylactic function in that it helps the parents to deal with their anxiety. If the worst happens their grief will not be complicated by guilt. The idea that everything possible has been done has great consoling power.

The most methodically studied example of post-partum abstinence is that of the Yoruba people of Nigeria. Even though the Yoruba have been undergoing rapid social change, so that by 1963 fewer than half the Yoruba labour force described its occupation as farming, and by 1975 a majority of the adult population had received some schooling, and almost half are city-dwellers, "long periods of post-natal lactation and abstinence were still prevalent."

> It was generally agreed that lactation and periods of abstinence had traditionally been sanctioned in Yoruba society and frequently grandmothers or other old women were quoted as authorities. But the range of periods quoted suggests that change has been under way a long time, or that there have always been local differences, or, more probably that there has never been exact agreement. Three years has been reported as the traditional period of post-natal abstinence, but, even now, seven per cent of illiterate women in the city of Ibadan observe longer periods as do eight per cent of all rural women. One-seventh of women in their fifties advocate periods exceeding three years, as do one-eighth of farmers' wives.[16]

At any given period, only a minority of women under 45 years of age are likely to be engaging in sexual activity, even if they are city-dwellers. Needless to say, many modern young Yoruba are abandoning traditional cultural values and practices, which placed the kinship group above the marriage pair. Where modernity means acceptance of Western technology, conventional contraceptive techniques are replacing abstinence, and the evidence is that such change may actually be responsible for an *increase* in conceptions. Obviously, the system which the agriculturalist Yoruba developed thousands of years ago cannot be carried into the twentieth century unchanged, but it is ironic that energetic promotion of foreign family planning should be a factor in the disruption of a tried and proven method of local family planning. It is to be hoped perhaps that the Yoruba will not experience the selfishness, instability and impermanence of the nuclear family along with its higher fertility.

Among the Yoruba, the most important reason for refraining from intercourse during lactation is the health of the child; which is the reason why prolonged lactation takes place in the first instance. Weaning a young child because another is on the way is widely considered to be the cause of the nutritional deficiency called by an old Ghanaian name, *kwashiorkor*, literally "one-two", a syndrome associated with too-early deprivation of mother's milk. Moreover, lactation is a strain upon the mother's health, a strain which would be unduly intensified by a new pregnancy. Generally, abstinence outlasts lactation by about six months while the woman regains her strength. As might be expected, the elite define themselves by their ability to depart from practices which have grown up in the context of food staples with low nutritional value, and pride themselves on being able to wean their babies earlier and forgo abstinence; either they can afford the higher number of children, and can ensure that they will survive, or they can master the arts of modern contraception. Unfortunately this is one of the few cases in which the trickle-down theory is likely to work; people less able to defy traditional sanctions will also take up modern practices, especially when the Nestlé company advertisements on every street corner give the impression that prepared baby formula turns an ordinary baby into a sleek, well-fed baby genius.

Delicately adjusted social mechanisms like Yoruba marriage and parenthood, which are fundamentally different from anything the ethnocentric West would call normal or natural by extrapolation from its own historically unprecedented behaviour, are extremely fragile. Ways of life which have proved their usefulness and practicality over thousands of years can be obliterated in two or three generations. The dislocation of any one segment of these complex patterns will completely unbalance them, as has happened in the case of the Bantu-speaking Tiriki of Western Kenya. The rationalisation of post-partum abstinence in their case is that the drool of a suckling infant is dangerous and causes a skin rash.

> In recent years however the notion has developed that a good washing with Lifebuoy soap, widely sold locally, effectively prevents skin itch in all such cases. Men nowadays often start to have intercourse with their wives after a wait of only two or three months following childbirth, taking a Lifebuoy bath the next morning as a safe and easy decontamination procedure.[17]

The rash – if any such had ever been observed – was probably the

somatic expression of guilt and anxiety about the infringement of the prohibition. It is startling evidence of the power of the white man's manipula-
tions of fantasy that this link was broken. The result of Western marketing
know-how, in this and other cases, is that lactating mothers are conceiving,
with dire consequences for themselves and their families.

We may expect similar disruption of control mechanisms as extended
kin-groups are broken down by urbanisation and the demands of employment. Among the Fulani, for example, pregnant women go to their
mothers' homes for their confinement and stay there two and a half years,
thus imposing a post-partum sexual abstinence which neither Nestlé nor
Lifebuoy can undermine, but how long this group, scattered as it is over
thirteen African states, can preserve its way of life is a moot question,
for along with baby formula and deodorant soap the Western media
promote the notion of romantic love; the modern African woman may
soon end up as dependent upon the sexual love of her husband as the
Western woman, and like her, may have to be sexually accessible at all
times.

In many agricultural societies, it is considered extreme for parents to
continue sexual activity after the eldest child has reached puberty, and in
even more it is considered unseemly for a grandmother to bear a child.[18]
In societies like the Yoruba, a woman is likely to bear her first child fairly
soon after puberty, so the distinction between the two kinds of prohibition is not absolute. The reasons for ceasing sexual activity may never
be discussed, because loss of interest in coitus is considered to be normal
and unworthy of remark, while "old" people known to be still copulating
may be butts of ridicule. When I joked with a young Tuscan grandmother recently that the papers were predicting a baby boom because
power cuts had curtailed evening television, she was deeply affronted at
the suggestion that she might conceive at her age. "Mi divido da mio
marito," she said firmly. She was a strong, healthy, good-looking woman,
who had enjoyed sex, on her own admission, but as her daughters had
embarked upon their sexual life she had abandoned hers without regret.
If anything, she and her husband had grown closer in their advancing
years, although they would have never dreamed of exchanging the sorts
of public caresses which American Darby and Joan couples take a rather
suspect delight in displaying.[18]

Among the Yoruba, the decision to cease sexual activity is actually discussed. A younger wife may find that her husband has taken the decision
because he wants to concentrate on a new wife or that he considers her
too old, but twice as often it is the woman who decides "because she
has become a grandmother or believes she is infecund, or feels too old
or resents the presence of a new wife or believes that she had demonstrably
borne enough surviving children". When it comes to the substitution of
other forms of contraception for abstinence it is vital to consider whether

such a substitution would improve the lives of these women in their own eyes. It cannot be simply assumed that women resent sexual deprivation and will benefit by being more accessible to their husbands, and the readiness with which such assumptions are made leads to more than a suspicion that it is male convenience which would be best served by such an arrangement.

Only 15% of wives claim to miss intercourse at all during post-natal abstinence and half of these say that they did not miss it much or experienced such feelings only occasionally. The same low proportion claim to feel any sexual deprivation at all during terminal abstinence, although three-quarters of this group do state they feel real loss. Among the better educated members of the urban elite the proportion feeling deprivation is somewhat higher even though their post-natal abstinence period is usually shorter.[19]

The degree of deprivation felt does not seem surprisingly low when we learn that Yoruba women rarely eat with their husbands and forty-eight per cent *never* do, and only 30 per cent join their husbands at festivals and parties. Hardly any husbands and wives sleep in the same bed, and only twenty-seven per cent in the same room. Obviously, the women's principal emotional satisfaction does not come from their relationship with their husbands, and may very well have much more to do with their relationships with their children. Yoruba grandmothers, for example, take a very active part in the rearing of their grandchildren. Moreover, the actual physical pleasure that women experience in sexual intercourse, apart from the receiving of attention and affection and the reassurance of attractiveness, can be severely curtailed by quite trivial factors. The Yoruba do practise clitoridectomy upon young women – in a fairly off-hand way.[20] Accidents and diseases of the puerperium are also likely to interfere with their capacity to enjoy intromission, as do a multitude of other infections both trivial and serious. Even in Tuscany, an astonishing number of women plead *infiammazione* as an excuse for refraining from intercourse, but as far as this observer could ascertain, few seek medical advice, and when they are forced to, usually by pregnancy, the doctors have no advice to give. If the promotion of chemical and mechanical contraception to groups such as these is not to result in a worsening of the quality of their lives, such problems have got to be dealt with. As it is, fear of pregnancy is a legitimate reason for refusing to allow intromission, and may result in a form of lovemaking which the woman finds more pleasant and more gratifying than the missionary position. The threat of pregnancy is not only a way in which a woman's enjoyment of intromission may be hampered, it is also a way in which she may influence the specificity and immediacy of the male sexual urge to conform to the slower pace and more generalised pattern of her response.

No aspect of human socialisation is more difficult to characterise than the nature of the relationship between spouses, and in particular the nature of their sexual interaction. While external decorum is fairly easy to observe and record, the nature of the intimate relationship between spouses cannot be extrapolated from such evidence, and most anthropologists assume a measure of hidden libidinousness in puritanical societies, based, one suspects, upon their own experience of a social morality in process of radical change. Nevertheless the suspicion occasionally strikes them, that publicly expressed modesty and reticence prevail "in the boudoir" as well. Even Western women of a generation or two ago can recall being warned by their mothers that sexual intercourse was an unpleasant duty which they owed to their husbands, and that they were "to lie still and think of England". It is perhaps because of such associations that we are so ready to assume that the sexual morality of other peoples is backward. A Canadian anthropologist observing the Ghegs of North Albania was puzzled by the degree of reserve manifested by spouses in their behaviour toward each other:

> It is impossible for an outsider to make any authoritative judgments about the depth of romantic attachments between marital partners in a culture different from his own, but certainly the Ghegs seem to be highly restrained in the overt expression of sexual emotion ... The essential element in marriage was the virginity of the bride ... Indeed chastity provides one of the key concepts in the chain of rights which makes up the ideal of family honour ...[21]

Doubtless the Ghegs would find Canadian spouses mawkish and un-dignified, their togetherness effeminising and their notion of "falling in love" an unsubstantiated myth. The work of Perestiany among Mediter-ranean societies has revealed the existence of many such value-systems of which our much-quoted double standard is a deformed survival.

> The consequences of sensuality destroy the integrity and honour of the family. Sensuality is a condition which constantly threatens to undermine this institu-tion from within. It must therefore be disciplined by all the strength and will of each man and woman. Even in marriage sexual activity is something "out of alignment" (*anapodo*). In some way it pollutes. After sleeping with his wife a shepherd ought to wash his hands before milking a ewe, a sacred animal. Intercourse must occur in darkness, without speech, and the woman must remain motionless and passive. Conversely, virginity is a quality which provokes the deepest respect and a sense almost of awe. It is obligatory for maidens and preferred in youths. The noble *pallikari*, the self-disciplines warrior youth, as yet innocent of sexual experience with women, presents the Sarakatsan ideal.[22]

The Sarakatsani are transhumant shepherds of Greece, grazing their goats and sheep in the Zagori mountains in the summer, and in the winter on the Epirote coastal plain. J. K. Campbell observed that their kind of sexual discipline was fundamentally different from that of northern European countries, where sex is assumed to be well within the individuals power to control. Instead the Sarakatsani see sex as an omnipresent power against which to struggle is heroic, thus promoting the importance of sexuality and increasing human susceptibility to it at the same time as they impose restrictions upon sexual behaviour.

In the summer of 1967 I arrived at the small town of Rossano Calabro with the first draft of my PhD thesis on Shakespeare under my arm: an unforeseen collapse in my arrangements meant that I was a woman alone, a phenomenon unknown in Magna Grecia. I found two rooms in a *frabb'ca* near Capo Trionto where I set about rewriting the thesis. My neighbours were peasants working for the Marquis whose empty rose-pink villa dominated the skyline. I acquired a bicycle to ride to market, and was not at all surprised when the old women spat on my bare legs as I whizzed past, for I knew this kind of behaviour from a recent sojourn in Sicily and was determined to defy it. This time, however, I was not the privileged guest of a modern family, but had to depend upon my neighbours for my survival. My confidant, or informant, as anthropologists say, was a sixteen-year-old girl called Rosetta who would come down to the deserted pebbly beach with me along with all the children who were too restless to sleep with the rest of the family in their one stuffy bedroom with its tightly shuttered windows. Rosetta expected to marry; one day someone would come to her father to *chiedere amore*. If her father approved, he would ask her if she wanted him. She thought she probably would, especially if she had seen him before, or rather, looked into his eyes, *guardato amore*, she said. He would be her kinsman, probably, for nearly all the boys in the district were. "Don't you want to get to know him first, go out with him?" I asked, but even as I asked I knew how silly the question was. All that needed to be known, the boy's reputation, would be known. Rosetta laughed, and said what she always said, "Da noi si fa cosi". I did not realise how far the possibility of sexual incompatibility was from anybody's reckoning until, one afternoon as we chatted on the beach, a terrific clattering of cobbles announced the arrival of a half-naked young man on a huge grey horse. We both bent our heads under his insolent gaze, but Rosetta kept looking under her spiky brows. "Avete visto?" she said, digging her stiff finger so far into my thigh that the mark remained for days, "Avete visto? Avete visto?" At first I misunderstood, then I realised that she was referring to a specific part of the young man's anatomy. I, a veteran of ten years' campaigning for sexual freedom, found myself blushing. Then I realised that sex was in the air that Rosetta breathed: she was ripe and the ripeness was all. I never again tried to wheedle her into putting on my spare bikini and swimming like me. The virgin Rosetta, with her sturdy, hairy legs, and her faded print dress, and the dark tan that ended at her elbows and knees, had more confidence in her female sexual power than I would ever have.

Rosetta's family knew all about the alternative value system of Milan and Turin, for they watched it on television every night, but they watched in much the same spirit as we might watch spiders copulating on television. I stopped trying to shock the peasantry and sued instead for acceptance by the other women. I gave the bicycle away to a little boy, and I took another little boy as my chaperone whenever I went out. I lengthened my skirts and kept my eyes down if a man came towards me and wore an old bathrobe down to the beach. The women let me write their letters to husbands working in Germany, "Caro sposo," they all began, "la mamma sta bene . . ." Not a breath of sexual desire or sentimentality disturbed their perfect formality. When I was leaving, at four on a chill autumn morning, *la mamma* came out to bless me. For all my money and my education and my freedom, she pitied me. Through her eyes my life seemed shapeless, improvised and squalid. Living with those proud and lawless people, whose morality was so much sterner than anything the fat priest preached in the Marquis's rose-pink chapel, I at last understood how the Greeks could imagine that Artemis sprang forth fully armed from the head of Zeus. Sexuality was not a resource of the individual personality in this part of Magna Grecia; it was a universal power palpable in the air itself.

The typical thumbnail description of such a society goes something like this: speaking of the origins of the story of Don Juan, William Mann writes:

> Spain in the sixteenth century claimed the credit for the creation of this modern libertine, significantly a country where family honour and female virginity were protected hardly less stringently than the cult of the Virgin and the Crucifixion. The wife was relegated to a pedestal, says Marañon, the bedroom was a monastic chamber, marriages were arranged by parents, and matrimonial couples met on the day of betrothal, in the presence of their assembled families. Young men sowed their wild oats in brothels; any girl who was not a prostitute was protected, as with a chastity belt, by family restrictions.[23]

Anthropologists have been fascinated by the figure of Don Giovanni, but if you were to take a sixteenth-century Spaniard's eye view of him, or the view of a peasant from Capo Trionto, you would see that the crime of El Burlador de Sevilla is the trivialisation of the great forces of life, sex and death, in much the same way as lies beneath Mann's contemptuous summary of the Spanish morality of honour and shame. Such value-systems are all under enormous pressure. Family loyalties cut across legally constituted powers and defy them. The requirements of honour break the laws which delegate the responsibility for punishment of crime to the state. Poverty and *latifundismo* force the migration of many mediterranean groups to the polyglot towns with their improvised hand-to-mouth morality of individualism and immediate gratification. Perhaps when the time came, the boy who was to have *chiesto amore* of Rosetta's father was spending his German wages in a Munich strip club. Some of the husbands I wrote to will never be seen again.

In case my description of the power of the chaste woman in Calabrian peasant society seems fanciful, I hasten to point out that it pales into mundanity next to the spiritual power of the chastely married women, the *cumankali*, in Tamil culture.

> At the most abstract metaphysical level, Hindu thought links the male principle with coolness, forms and transcendence, while the female principle is linked to heat, energy (*cakti*) and worldly action. The male and female aspects of the universe should theoretically operate as a balanced unity, but there is nevertheless a widespread and androcentric preoccupation in South Asia with containing and controlling female energy.[24]

The monthly flow of menstruation reduces a woman's excess heat and energy, which otherwise goes to make new human beings and the milk to nourish them. The arrival of the menses is celebrated with as much public ceremony as a wedding, which is inevitable and ought not to be delayed. The woman's modesty is absolute; her breasts and vagina are too sacred to be seen, but her contribution to intercourse and impregnation is both active and indispensable. Female orgasm is thought of not as an end in itself but as an essential part of the fecundation process. The fact that women are not free to follow their own inclinations and preferences in sexual matters may not be experienced by the woman as a restriction, for she is not encouraged to internalise the repressive mechanism or to cultivate an image of herself as powerless or passive:

> Clearly the status of women in South Asia is related to Hindu belief. Women, who like the goddess are feared, must, like the goddess, be kept under male control. Through male control and her own chastity, the Hindu woman controls her dangerous powers and is able to use them for the benefit of her family. Further, there is strong evidence that the attribution of sacred powers to women derives from the indigenous beliefs and practices of the people of India and images of sacred femaleness are prevalent in the earliest Tamil literature. Even today the Dravidian-speaking sections of southern India give evidence – through puberty rites, menstrual taboos, and widow restrictions – of greater concern for controlling and containing female powers than do the Indo-Aryan linguistic regions of the north.[25]

In societies like peasant Calabria and south India, a woman does not have to be sexually capacitated by falling in love: she is already aflame and the dazzled male must approach her gingerly, under the protection of sacred sanction.

Chastity may be seen, then, to have two contrasting functions. On the one hand, it endows sexual activity with added importance by limiting its enjoyment to special persons and special times. This may be no more than husbanding of the limited resources of human sexual energy by institutionalising the period of detumescence, which amounts to no more than natural chastity as defined by A. E. Crawley. This kind of chastity may actually serve to stabilise marriage unions by maintaining a constant level of sexual interest in a wife who is often unattainable. The fiction which underlies and gives point to the restriction is that the potency of the male is limitless; the stronger the prohibition and the more dire the punishments, real or imaginary, of infringement, the greater the assumed potency and the more effective the flattery of the male ego, which will bear fruit in actually increased potency and a higher level of sexual interest at those times when intercourse is allowed. The result of natural chastity is not primarily to reduce fertility; in fact it may be said to maintain optimum fertility by spacing sexual activity and sustaining sexual interest over a long period rather than allowing it to burn out in a shorter period of unbridled indulgence. Such regulation is found in many forms and in many societies; among the Kafa of south-western Ethiopia, for example,

> ... it is felt that coitus interferes with good farming practices because it drains a man's energies. This is especially true for the plowing season ... and when preparing the fields for maize planting. Men fear that if a man has intercourse frequently he will become a "weak man" not only in the physical sense but mentally as well. Frequency of intercourse is connected also with the amount of sperm a man can generate. Men believe that the greater the amount of sperm in an ejaculation the more likely that a woman will conceive a son, therefore, because men want sons, a more moderate frequency of intercourse is considered to have definite advantages.[26]

The idea that sperm is the distillation of the individual's energy which is thus drawn away from other activities has been elaborated into whole systems of religious belief and has provided justification for a degree of sexual abstinence which greatly exceeds anything Crawley would call "natural". The requirement of lifelong celibacy in the priesthood of ancient Mexico, of Zoroastrianism, of Buddhism and the Jains, derives from the notion of energy diverted from sex to spiritual activities in the same way that abstinence husbanded energy for other important activities like hunting, planting, fishing, travelling and military enterprises among pre-literate peoples. The notion is primarily religious rather than scientific, but despite the lack of empirical evidence, prohibitions of the same kind are still uttered by those training sportsmen for special efforts. If self-control is to be practised with dedication and seriousness, it follows that it must be shown to have a positive function, and there are millions of people in the world who are convinced that it has. In order to challenge this belief, its opponents need better evidence than they have so far been able to marshall. Discipline and self-denial have obvious social functions, if only the simple ones of refraining from enjoyment of leisure activities until work is done, something the restless schoolchild finds as difficult as an adult might find sexual abstinence. Faced with a country enslaved not only to a foreign ruler, but to self-indulgence, inertia, ignorance and disease, Mahatma Gandhi sought to apply an indigenous remedy drawn from the Hindu scriptures. The student of the Vedas must practise continence as part of *brahmacharya*, the conquest of self and purification from earthly desires. The psychic force generated in the man who conquers his desires for personal gratification is so great that he may challenge the gods, and Hindu legend is full of *rishis* to whom the gods sent supernatural spouses in recognition of their supernatural powers.

The unifying symbol of this power is *bindu*, a drop or globule, represented as a circle or a dot, and emblem of the universe. It is that metaphysical point outside the spatio-temporal continuum where *samadhi* is experienced, the heart of life. This energy, the quintessence of manhood, is present throughout the body, but it is distilled in the drop of semen; it is composed of two elements, the seed which represents the male principle, Shiva, and the blood, which represents the female who gives actuality to its potential power, Shakti. Behind Gandhi's simple asceticism lay an enormous body of Hindu mysticism, present in its most ritualised form in the disciplines of the yogis and the tantrics.

Gandhi saw in the acceptance of *brahmacharya* the only way of turning the weaknesses of India into strengths. He turned to the poorest of the poor as his allies and strove to teach them to regard their poverty as a blessed state which would enable them to transcend the worldly desires that kept the educated elite divided and torpid. They were to cease being victims by becoming victors over themselves, and that involved the renunciation of the only thing most of them had left to renounce, sexual pleasure. Foreigners who besought him to take pity on the people and permit them the recourse to artificial methods of birth control could not understand how fundamental sexual abstinence was to his doctrine of *brahmacharya*; it was by such abstinence that Indians were to grow spiritually strong enough to practise the rule of *ahimsa* and vanquish injustice by altruism. The weakest were the guardians of spiritual power, and so he appealed to women to turn away their demanding husbands by quiet resistance; time and again he reiterated his belief:

> ... to regard the control of the sex urge as impossible or unnecessary or harmful is to my mind a denial of dharma, for self-control is the basis of dharma ...[27]

> This is a question of women's true dharma ... Draupadi has shown what a woman's true dharma is.[28]

It was because the woman was passive and suffered unwanted pregnancy that the process started with her; in her weakness lay her majesty. Gandhi besought husbands to undertake the chaste life through love of their wives, and it was on this point that he weakened so far as to consider male sterilisation briefly in the thirties, when Hitler's example was held up to him, but he eventually abandoned the idea even in the case of lepers, for he saw over-reproduction as a symptom of spiritual malaise, not as its cause. He considered the rhythm method as a kind of relative self-control,[29] but rejected that too, returning to the *smriti* texts which clearly said that love was only not lust when sexual intercourse was performed for issue.[30] As his whole philosophy turned on the abnegation of self, absolute chastity was the only feasible ideal. Any partial abandonment of the principle meant total abandonment of the ideal and a rejection of the spiritual rewards which accrued from its pursuit. As for the theory that sexual abstinence was harmful, he himself was the best refutation of that:

> ... it is not proved to my satisfaction that sexual union in marriage is itself good and beneficial to the unionists ... momentary excitement and satisfaction there certainly was. But it was invariably followed by exhaustion. And the desire for union returned immediately the effect of exhaustion had worn out. Although I have always been a conscientious worker, I can clearly recall the fact that this indulgence interfered with my work. It was the consciousness of this limitation that put me on the track of self-restraint and I have no manner of doubt that the self-restraint is responsible for the comparative freedom from illness that I have enjoyed for long periods and for my output of energy and work both physical and mental which eyewitnesses have described as phenomenal.[31]

Gandhiji did not succeed in turning India into a nation of semi-celibate mystics, perhaps because he himself was too extraordinary, and in any case he fitted in too well with the Hindu notion of the man who has completed first his reproductive life then his public duty and who goes away from his house and family to wander as a *sannyasin*, passing his days in prayer and contemplation, whose behaviour is irrelevant to his children who are in another stage of life altogether. We shall never know what he would have thought of a world which as he predicted became a "quagmire of contraception on a scale hitherto unknown", where we may be said to have experienced the wisdom of his advice: "Remember that there is always a limit to self-indulgence, but none to self-restraint."[32]

Gandhi's doctrine of *vairāgya* was very close to the cultivation of dispassion which is at the very heart of the Hindu character, but in his exaltation of sexual abstinence he defied the Hindu sense of dignity and proportion by exposing himself to risk and thereby mocking the Hindu reverence for the body as a sacred and powerful thing in itself. By sleeping with his daughters and grand-daughters, Gandhi isolated himself from the common man, while his own candid disclosures about his life before he made his vow of sexual abstinence revealed him to other Hindu Mystics as a sexual barbarian, and to the common people as a man without modesty.

If Gandhi had been less of a fundamentalist and had remembered more of the "superstitious" lore he had grown up with, at the time when he wore the top-lock which is the sign of the body's divinity before it was shaven off and he went to England to re-learn Hinduism from a Puritan viewpoint, he might have arrived at a concept of sexual regulation which was closer to popular attitudes. The physical concomitant of the emotional restraint which foreigners often confuse with apathy is the modesty which accompanies a lifestyle in which privacy is both impossible and unsought by the vast majority of Indians. The story of Queen Draupadi is the story of a woman married to seven princely brothers who lost her to a neighbouring ruler by gambling her away. Draupadi prayed to Shiva to be spared the humiliation of having her nakedness uncovered by a stranger. When the man who had won her grasped at her sari to pull it off in full sight of her humiliated subjects, he found to his astonishment that it unwound forever; on it were embroidered the stories of the great Hindu legend of the Mahabharata. The sari, and to a lesser extent, the dhoti, are the outward signs of bodily integrity, and it is reverence for that principle which still dictates that Hindu film stars may not so much as kiss on the screen. The conjunction of man and woman is sacramental, not casual; the great erotic sculptures of Khajuraho are not depictions of daily life, but emblems of the union of Shiv and his Shakti which result in the creation of all that is. The tourist is titillated by the linga that he sees around the temples; his guide, who is likely to be a divinity student, tirelessly repeats that they are emblems of universality, but his earnest insistence falls on deaf ears. The tourist assumes that the Hindus are as lecherous as he is.

Indians are very ready to admit that they trivialise sex, but what the foreigner is not apt to realise is that when they make such admissions they are using a much higher standard than the Westerner would do. The vast majority of women in India sleep with children and other women and wear their saris in bed. They even bathe in a sari. Men are voyeurs, but they see little and feel great guilt. To institutionalise sex and make a Westernised parlour game of it is to perpetuate what is seen as a failure which most try constantly to transcend. The helpless gestures Indians make when asked by outsiders why they have so many children are the expression of their humility in this defeat in a struggle which is humanly impossible, although by their own standards of reticence and modesty they have done their best. The teaching of contraception, even when not undertaken by a member of the wrong sex and a stranger, involves a demystification of the body which is in itself insulting. An aristocratic lady tells a story against herself as a family-planning worker which goes like this: for teaching purposes she used a model of the female reproductive system, an ugly thing made of plastic with movable parts on which the flies would sit and which had one way and another become rather travel-stained. One evening, after she had done her stuff and been patiently and courteously heard out by a group of village women with their veils drawn half across their faces, they quietly rose to thank her and take their leave. "Highness," said one of the elder women kindly, "You may be made like that, but we are not."

The old lady was right. No woman is made of hard puce plastic with movable parts down which the "egg" rattles like a marble in a child's toy. The processes of ovulation, fertilisation and implantation are still only partially understood, and have more to do with rhythm, movement, secretion and timing than with mechanical contiguity. In reaffirming the wonder and mystery of her body and tacitly refusing the mechanical forms of interference with its processes which were all that this family planner had to offer, the spokeswoman was making a typically modest statement of the dignity of their lives, however squalid and chaotic they may have seemed to an observer. In his conviction that to set this at nought would be to accomplish the enslavement of the Indian people in a way that Moghuls and Christians had never managed to do, Gandhiji was absolutely right, but his way of explaining it to foreign birth-control enthusiasts was flippant and wrong. He conceded far too much to their view of Hindus as "breeding like rabbits" because he was tainted with a view of sex which he had learned from his protestant oppressors.

It is truly ironic that representatives of societies where breaches of privacy are punishable in law, even if they consist in no more than the photographing of a couple in a public place or the revelations of an individual's sources of income, should have no scruple about interposing themselves between man and woman in their sexual relation. Western concern with privacy seems to have grown up as modesty decayed, so that the young woman who displays clitoris, labia minora and vaginal introitus in a double spread in a girlie magazine suffers less injury thereby than she would if her telephone were tapped, but most other societies have not brought the despiritualisation of the body to anything approaching such a level. In ignoring or flouting the fear and reverence which other people feel for the body and its sacred orifices, because we feel that such feelings are irrational and a bar to progress (to our own blessed condition) we do not thereby save those people, but rather inflict upon them a new kind of stress which may be socially ruinous.

> The social body constrains the way the physical body is perceived. The physical experience of the body, always modified through the social categories through which it is known, sustains a particular view of society. There is a continual exchange of meanings between the two kinds of experience so that each reinforces the categories of the other.[33]

Professor Douglas refers to the essay of Marcel Mauss in which he "boldly asserted that there can be no such thing as natural behaviour ... Nothing is more essentially transmitted by a social process of learning than sexual behaviour ..." yet those people who suffer guilt and anxiety about their frustration of "god's will" or their submission to the penetration of their bodies by foreign objects, are dismissed as neurotics. Anthropologists may have accepted the blazing truth of Mauss's thesis, but sexologists have not. They are still tending forwards in their sequent toil to the formulation of a theory of sexual health, in which frequent orgasm performs a therapeutic function (interpreted by some unquiet souls as displacement activity from the struggle for social justice) necessarily liberated from the "threat" of pregnancy which interferes with orgastic release. The people actually involved in the delivery of health care to the world's poor are the least likely to understand the tremendous psychic stress which afflicts those people who feel that they are purchasing the magic of modern medicine at the price of the wrath of their native gods. The woman who climbs on to the table and places her feet in the stirrups under the brightest lamp she has ever seen, while the speculum opens her vagina to the light and the air and the doctor's eye, may be destroying her own concept of her personality by so doing. Even if she has persuaded herself that the invasion does not matter because it was only witnessed by a foreigner, her relatives and neighbours may very well not feel the same way, so that her IUD remains a guilty secret. If she expiates its presence by heavy blood loss and pain she may see these as punishments or as a necessary price to pay, and not seek help to have the device removed because she thinks it is evil in the first place and has reconciled herself to weakness and seclusion for giving in to it. If on the other hand, she has accepted the IUD as the badge of allegiance to a new religion, infinitely superior with its gleaming instruments and dazzling lights to the old, she will wear the IUD about her neck when she spontaneously rejects it, and feel purged by pain.

Even when modesty is carried to such lengths that women are shocked by menstruation, and then by intercourse, and approach childbirth in a state of ignorant dread, it cannot be taken as read that the situation does not have its unique compensations, which to deny is to deny the fundamental nature of the culture. Faced with such a situation in the case of the women of San Pedro la Laguna, a village on the shores of Lake Atitlan in Guatemala, Lois Paul asked herself the obvious question:

> What purposes does it serve to mystify menstruation, pregnancy and childbirth? The mystery surrounding these phenomena can appear to support the ascendancy of men over women, of older women over younger, of parents over children. But in terms of the Pedrano world view, the mystification of biological processes contributes, not to a sense of powerlessness on the part of women, but rather to a sense of participation in the mystic powers of the universe ... Because of the miraculous nature of their biological processes, women are more attuned than men to cosmic rhythms.

The demystification of biological processes, which has been greatly exaggerated by the rationalistic West, has resulted in the aggressive management of childbirth which has meant that for many women a climactic life-experience has been transmogrified into a institutionalised medical ordeal, deprived of spiritual or emotional satisfactions. Childbirth for the Pedrana is celebrated by a priest-like midwife:

A girl's first experience with menstruation and intercourse generates fear and a sense of helplessness. But this feeling is transmuted into an attitude of awe and wonder at the birth of a baby, an attitude heightened by the ministrations of the midwife and her sacred connection with supernaturals who can confer the gift of life or withold it. With the birth of her first child, the young woman is no longer estranged from her own body; she is now aware that her body is the seat of magical powers.[34]

The Pedranas distinguish themselves from women of the neighbouring village of Totonicapan who sleep with their skirts off, because they *never* do. Similar distinctions may be found all over the world, even among naked peoples, who distinguish themselves from others who disgracefully do not practise female circumcision, or equally disgracefully cry out during sexual intercourse, or walk abroad with their faces unveiled, even with heads and arms uncovered, or, worst of all, legs. Such distinctions are important, for they contribute to notions of prestige or independence; discipline of one sort leads into disciplines of other sorts which are necessary for survival. Purity becomes a value in the fight against pollution, whether it be by one's own excretions or by the excretions of others, and that value is symbolised by all kinds of reticence and formality which far exceed any function of the avoidance of pollution as reduction of the risk of disease. One of the most insidious forms of pollution is the destruction of the integrity of one's culture by that of another, dominant, outsider group, and it is under such conditions of cultural resistance that adherence to cultural standards of purity become most important; it is part of taking the line of most resistance, whether it be to lipstick, Coca-Cola, opium or oral contraceptives. Defending the Jewish religion against Simone Weil's attack, Mary Douglas has this to say:

> It would be impossible for the leaders of an occupied but still resisting nation to adopt an effervescent form of religion. To expect them to stop preaching a stern sexual morality, vigilant control of bodily boundaries, and a corresponding religious cult, would be asking them to give up the political struggle.[35]

One of the reasons for the success of Islam as a proselytising religion is that it treated the lowest and least prestigious groups as deserving of the same respect as the highest; it covered their nakedness and veiled their women, conferring upon them a new kind of value and hence, self-respect. When the Shah of Persia outlawed the veil in 1937, he did not so much liberate his people as announce their dependency upon the West. Older women, humiliated by the possibility that soldiers might tear off their veils in the street, made themselves prisoners in their own houses. Gradually a version of the veil re-established itself; peasant women marked the rise in their status when their husbands gained work in the cities by assuming a lighter and more coquettish version of the *chador*, nowadays replaced in revolutionary Iran by the old heavy *chador* or the unbecoming uniform of Islamic Marxism, which confers upon young women the aspect of military nuns. No longer does the passer-by glimpse nylon-clad legs in a swirl of black nylon held with one hand, these young women bind up their heads and necks, so that their hands are free to carry weapons. The veil is now a symbol of liberation through self-discipline.

The defiance of such codes of reticence by outsiders does not automatically render them invalid; rather it covers the infidel himself with opprobrium and is apt to undermine his credibility – or at any rate the applicability of what he has to say to the people whose behaviour he might be seeking to influence. Besides, the sophistication of such systems ought not to be underrated; Western journalists questioning Iranian women about their predilection for the veil after a period of relaxed public morality during which, presumably, they had become used to a measure of social and physical freedom, were puzzled at the earnestness with which unattractive women announced that by wearing the veil they were protected from the uncontrollable lusts of men. "Squinting, moustached, pockmarked" women firmly assured the foreigners that only by covering themselves did they eliminate the ever-present possibility of ravishment. A new and potent mythology had arisen to feed the revolutionary masses: on the one hand, women were all beautiful and desirable and on the other, men were all super-potent. Their belief will be self-validating because it will be reinforced by the inevitable effects of repression. The Western journalists ought to have sensed in their own sneering connoisseurship the evidence of jaded appetite.

It is fatally easy for Western folk, who have discarded chastity as a value for themselves, to suppose that it can have no value for anyone else. At the same time as Californians try to re-invent "celibacy", by which they seem to mean perverse restraint, the rest of us call societies which place a high value on chastity "backward." It is as well not to forget that, in the words of R. V. Short,

> Throughout the world as a whole, more births are prevented by lactation than all other forms of contraception put together ... The more unfavourable the environment, the more infant survival and birth spacing both become dependent on breast feeding.[36]

Short does not point out how often lactation is accompanied by restrictions on sexual behaviour,[37] or how necessary it is that a mother give suck at regular, short intervals for the depression of ovulatory activity to continue.[38] As industrialisation takes hold, women are less and less free to suckle their infants on demand. As Western notions of glamour and the role of the wife as sex object take over, the effects of prolonged lactation on the breast are found to be unacceptable. As Western marketing pushes the idea of superbabes fed on superhuman formulae, breast-feeding falls into disuse. As husbands learn from the west that a husband takes precedence over his children in enjoying access to his wife's body, the practice of post-partum abstinence is seen as primitive.

If we had begun gently we might have found that contraceptive measures involving periods of abstinence were more acceptable to traditional societies than they were to ours. Instead, women who explained that they did not become pregnant because they were breast-feeding were simply disbelieved. Few people thought to ask whether the breast-feeding involved the observation of marital abstinence: the more natural and inevitable the practice, the less likely it was to be mentioned. Now that we have sabotaged it, it may be too late to reinvent it.

The chief objection to the rhythm method that I hear in my travels around university campuses is that it does not work. What this generally means is that my respondents could not work it. They did not know when they were fertile and they were not motivated sufficiently strongly to find out. The perennial attempts to teach ways of telling become more elaborate and more sophisticated each year. The Billings method is one of the many descendants of Ogino and Knaus, via John Marshall, deviser of the muco-thermic method. [39] It would be as well perhaps to start with girls in school, in their biology classes, to teach them the cycle as subjectively perceived, and have them keep practical books of readings and so forth, so that they could learn the structure of their endocrine rhythm before there was anxiety attached to the possibility of making a mistake. If the Catholic Church was really serious about taking a stand on the issue of artificial family limitation this would already be done in Catholic girls' schools, but it is not. Only by extended observation can woman distinguish the flare of Mittelschmerz, or the changes in mucous viscosity, but once they have tuned in to these processes, they will be no easier to forget than ice-skating, provided the women learn young enough. In the same classes the girls could learn the other aspects of self-help, such as breast examination. (The knowledge will be of more use to them than elementary botany.) Other religions have far more complicated seasonal observances than periodic abstinence under the rhythm method, and it ought not to be impossible to fit the rhythm method into them. It would be relatively easy to inculcate respect for the female reproductive cycle and acceptable as long as the emphasis remained positive.

It is ironic to reflect how effective a cult would be which limited intercourse to certain weeks and days in order to safeguard a child's life, which, if it lengthened the birth intervals, it would probably succeed in doing. Instead of teaching reverence for the body we chose to teach callousness; instead of exploiting concern for children and the passionate desire for them to survive, we assumed that too many were surviving already. The chance to develop the human propensity for sexual restraint in the interests of the congested world has been missed.

Chapter Five
Polymorphous Perversity

... even in its most simplified and rudimentary form, human
sexuality involves the development of motivation through a lengthy
and complex process: the positioning, the looks and gestures, the
movements and responses; all these are necessary before orgasm
occurs. It is all a far cry from the insertion of turgid penises and the
depositing of seminal fluid, like squirting jam in a doughnut.

Brian J. Ford Patterns of Sex

We know, from sources other than those recognised by the historians
of population, that the European pattern of late marriage existed side-by-
side with prolonged courtship, and that in many countries courtship was
not conducted under the watchful eye of a chaperone. Parish records,
a kind of evidence which is extensively used by demographic historians,
tell us that marriages often preceded christenings by too few months for
the conception of the child to have been the result of marital intercourse.
A similar pattern prevails in parts of present-day rural Tuscany, and an
examination of what it actually entails may prove illuminating for those
who are perplexed by the seventeenth- and eighteenth-century English
pattern.

In some parts of Tuscany (and in many other parts of rural Italy from
Asti to Agrigento) a young man begins to keep company with a young
woman while he is still in his teens, with the full knowledge of both his
and her family. Once the courtship has proceeded beyond a certain point,
not in itself easy to define, but related to the amount of time which they
have spent in no other company but their own and the extent to which
their relationship is public knowledge, the young woman cannot be set
aside without serious consequences for her future and the friendship of
the two families. The young woman will be known as *fidanzata* although
no announcement will be made, no ceremony undergone, and she will
wear no ring. The degree of sexual intimacy will gradually increase by
dint of wearing the young woman's resistance down with caresses and
entreaties, a kind of intense foreplay which may be carried on over years,

until eventually coitus takes place; however, because the young man has no intention of compromising his future by setting up house before he can afford it, he practices *coitus interruptus*. In Tuscany this period is simply referred to as "quando si faceva all'amore" a fairly explicit reference to the accepted practice of *coitus interruptus*, which is what makes engagements of twelve or sixteen years possible.

Often it is the *fidanzata* who is the first to tire of courtship because she wishes to escape from her parents' household and become head of her own, or because she considers that people have begun to laugh at the long delay in her marriage, or because she begins to fear that she is growing too old to bear a family. She begins to use all her blandishments to disrupt the *fidanzato*'s control until she is pregnant and unblushing proceeds to the altar, dressed in white as a testimony of the chastity of her relationship with the only man with whom she has ever been intimate. Provided it has been correctly timed and neither of the parties is too young, the illegitimate conception is not regarded as a disgrace, but as a blessing upon their union and evidence of its rightness. After the birth of the child, *coitus interruptus* will be resumed again until a second pregnancy is desired or accidentally results. When unwanted pregnancies occur, husbands who have always practised *coitus interruptus* are apt to insist that their wives take drastic action. The desperate women have recourse to abortion, which is very common. None of this behaviour has the sanction of the church, which regards *coitus interruptus* and abortion as grave sins.

The characteristic pattern which results is one of relatively aged spouses, with no great age difference, a birth soon after marriage, and limited births thereafter – the European pattern in short. Obviously, such a pattern is very easily disrupted. The benign supervision of both families is an essential part of it, for it ensures the young man's continuing responsibility and precludes the possibility of his absconding, while any really unsuitable conjunction can be headed off while the lovers are still young enough to obey their parents. The young man learns what to do from his peer group, and quickly learns to mock pityingly those who cannot master the art of *coitus interruptus* and marry *disgraziatamente* to live in misery with their resentful inlaws. The system cannot exist along with any intemperate consumption of alcohol. If the young men wish to get drunk they do so in exclusively male company, and that very rarely.

It must not be thought that *coitus interruptus* is unwillingly practised as an undesirable substitute for other, unavailable forms of contraception. My evidence, which is admittedly of the kind called impressionistic, is that other kinds of contraception are used only as a last resort in the case of an inconsiderate or maladroit lover. Rather, a specific ideology of *coitus interruptus* dignifies the practice, for men call themselves *servitori delle donne* and frequently express their belief that women gain much more pleasure from sex than they do themselves. The men value their capacity to prolong intercourse "all night" if they wish, and seem more attached to the increased potency which results from postponement of release or partial release than to unfettered intercourse and complete detumescence, which they call *sgonfiamento*, deflation, an expression which also means disappointment or being put off. The male character which typically results is sometimes called in Italy, *gallismo*, and it seems to this writer at least that a similar notion may underlie notions of *machismo* as well. In such societies we need not be surprised to find that a male contraceptive is more acceptable than a female contraceptive, for the men value the illusion that they are controlling the fertility of their womenfolk and suffer a concomitant anxiety that women who do not have to rely upon their love and altruism to avoid unwanted pregnancy will be debauched by other, less considerate, men.

No scientific study of the effects of *coitus interruptus* either as a method of fertility regulation or as a kind of sexual release has ever been made; nevertheless a firm conviction has grown up that it is ineffective as birth control and positively dangerous to the mental and physical health of both the people involved. Most of the adults who have experienced *coitus interruptus* are not likely to be affected by the emphatic promulgation of such views, but as they are not responsible for passing on this illicit sexual morality to their children, who ought to find out from their peers, it seems likely that *coitus interruptus* will continue to lose ground for no very good reason. Those who might otherwise have practised it will have resort to mechanical and chemical contraception instead, replacing the long court-ship pattern with the commoner Western one of juvenile promiscuity and unstable marriage. The advantages of this transition are not obvious, to say the least, unless, of course, *coitus interruptus* is as inefficient and harmful as many sexologists believe.

The attack on *coitus interruptus* as a contraceptive method was mounted on several fronts in the last years of the nineteenth century. The early pro-ponents of birth control, Richard Carlile, Robert Dale Owen and Charles Knowlton, had all been for it, in preference to douching and the sponge.[1] One aspect of the campaign against it which has never been examined is that a large contraceptive-manufacturing industry had grown up in the second half of the nineteenth century, selling a fantastic array of occlusive devices, spermicidal creams, quinine pessaries, douches, rubber sheets, syringes, condoms, abortifacient pills and early intra-uterine devices, at huge profits considering the cheapness of the materials that went into them. One of the side effects of British imperialism was a plentiful supply of cheap rubber, which became expensive rubber when it was formed into sheaths and cervical caps. The flood of literature instructing gullible buyers in contraceptive methods which began in the 1870s was largely subsidised by the manufacturers of contraceptive hardware, and we cannot be surprised to find that it had little to say for a method which used no hardware at all.

One of the earliest to speak out against *coitus interruptus* was the Scottish doctor George Drysdale in *Physical, Sexual and Natural Religion* which later went through many editions in an expanded version under the title *The Elements of Social Science*. He denounced *coitus interruptus* as physically injurious, "apt to produce nervous disorder and sexual enfeeblement and congestion".[2] He spoke out against all male methods, in fact, thus beginning the long tradition of leaving contraception to women. Mrs Eliza Bisbee Duffy attacked *coitus interruptus* too, in *What Women Should Know*, in 1873, on the completely invented ground that it caused inflammation, tumours and ulcers of the uterus.[3] Dr Alice Stockham, who dreamed up the Karezza method of *coitus reservatus* was passionately opposed to *coitus interruptus* which she claimed led to neurasthenia, impotence, sterility and diseases of the uterus;[4] from this point *coitus reservatus* and *coitus interruptus* are treated in the literature as if they were contrasting opposites. The pseudo-scientific language in which the objections to withdrawal are couched seems after all to cloak a fairly silly aesthetic objection – namely an aversion to seeing the ejaculate. Stockham's completely fantastic theory of the copulating male's ability to reabsorb his semen by holding it back and never allowing it to emit at all is an outrageous case of rationalisation but very few people knew enough to call her bluff.

Freud considered that *coitus interruptus* was a direct cause of symptom formation[5] and his followers in the various societies for the study of sexual psychology soon took the point as an orthodox tenet, which it remains to this day. Withdrawal in order to ejaculate elsewhere than in the vagina is thought to result in incomplete release, which gives rise to pathological conditions. Much is made of the non-fact that withdrawal must take place at the moment just before the involuntary reflex takes over. Clearly, if *coitus interruptus* is practised as an unsatisfactory substitute for "normal sex" and masquerades as "normal sex" until the last minute or so, it will be a cause of anxiety and disappointment. If a man brings his partner to orgasm and then sets about achieving his own outside the vagina, this unsatisfactory scenario will not be acted out. What the tendency of modern sexologists to denigrate *coitus interruptus* really indicates is their own lack of sexual imagination or, as some might prefer, their own lack of creativity and tenderness. It is truly astonishing to find Clive Wood and Beryl Suitters in 1970 maintaining half-seriously that brothers who refused the duty of the levirate by the method adopted by Onan, of spilling his seed upon the ground, were not struck by a thunderbolt, "they died of heart attacks brought on by the strain of their contraceptive practices."[6] They seem to be concurring in the judgment of the fanatic Routh, that "conjugal onanism" leads to "general nervous prostration, mental decay, loss of memory, intense cardiac palpitations, mania and conditions which lead to suicide".[7] By 1922, when Frances Mabel Huxley gave evidence to the International Neo-Malthusian Conference, she felt confident in remarking, "*Coitus interruptus* is recognised on all hands as undesirable." Norman Haire and W. H. B. Stoddart took the same view.[8] The people went on practising it regardless.

C. V. Ford, of the Department of Psychiatry at the UCLA Medical School wrote in 1978, that the psychological ill effects of *coitus interruptus* "include potential failure of orgasm in women who reach a plateau level of general sexual excitement and are then frustrated, with a concomitant build-up of psychic tension."[9] It might with justice be remarked that every instance of sexual intercourse, whether interrupted or not, includes a "potential failure" of this kind for women, and whether or not the potential failure to reach orgasm becomes actual has very little to do with where the man ejaculates and a great deal to do with what he does before he ejaculates, and even after. It would seem that the old fantasy of simultaneous orgasm dies hard, even with people who ought to know better.

Coitus interruptus can be as bad as bad sex can always be, if it is nothing but a rapid episode of intromission, unpreceded by foreplay, but if it has been resorted to out of consideration for the woman in the first place, it is not likely to take such a barbarous form. Most intelligent sex contains an element of *coitus reservatus* in that the male attempts to prolong his erection by avoiding orgasm, thereby enhancing his own and his partner's pleasure. A great deal of the work done by sex therapists consists in teaching this control and one of the methods resorted to very often is a form of *coitus reservatus*, known as the Semans stop-start method, used especially in cases of premature ejaculation and other anxiety-related dysfunctions.[10] It is almost as if the best treatment for anxiety about potency is to transfer the anxiety to another focus; the man who is concerned not to ejaculate in the vagina will not be able simultaneously to worry about his erection, while the man who concentrates on his partner's needs has a good chance of escaping worry about either. However, sex therapy does tend to be reductive and mechanistic: the situation as described here is by no means unproblematic for a sensitive woman:

> The belief that masculine endurance rather than feminine responsivity limits a woman's coital responses is confirmed by another remarkable set of Masters-Johnson findings. Five of the men seen in their clinic for infertile couples, they report, were fully potent sexually in all other ways, but were unable to ejaculate into a vagina. As a result, these five men "can and do maintain coital connection for 30 to 60 minutes at any given opportunity." In three of the five cases, the wives reap the full benefit. They "are multiorgasmic as a result of the constant opportunity for long-maintained coition". As in the case of other women in

self-stimulatory episodes, these women have one orgasm after another until "coition is terminated by the female partner's admission of sexual satiation."[11]

In these cases evidently ejaculation within the vagina was not a necessary concomitant of female bliss. If it is merely the duration of intromission which is in question a man must bow to a vibrator every time; actually, retrograde ejaculation is a sexual dysfunction, just as premature ejaculation is, and there is no point in carrying *coitus reservatus* to such lengths simply to serve as the tool of a woman's pleasure, which is every bit as degrading as a woman's consent to serve her lover with no hope of pleasure for herself. The example is cited merely to show how specious the condemnation of *coitus interruptus* is. Orgasm is not the only pleasure in sexual intercourse; many men are intensely excited by their lovers' response both mentally and physically and would rather forgo their own orgasm than that excitement; it may happen that orgasm becomes less likely for a man the longer he defers it, but there is no law which says that episodes of lovemaking should be uniform. The most valuable fact that Masters and Johnson have taught is that sexuality is not an excretory function which needs to be regular, healthy, normal and relatively unconscious; it is rather learned behaviour, multifarious, intricate, protean and minutely responsive to changing demands and circumstances. Considered against the whole spectrum of human sexual polymorphousness, the reaching of male orgasm outside the vagina is as normal and may indeed be more frequent than the reaching of orgasm inside it. Weird pathologies extrapolated from any assumption of unnaturalness are nothing but obscurantist scare tactics.

Coitus interruptus, if correctly performed, will not result in pregnancy; there is no truth in the supposition that the few spermatozoa which may be found in the pre-ejaculatory secretion will cause pregnancy, but actual ejaculation must not take place in contact with the vaginal membrane. Indeed, the procedure is often called in dialect (although it more often has no specific name at all) *belly-painting*, which is a fairly accurate indication of the most effective and commonest way of carrying it out. Sterility experts are still not sure of the least concentration of spermatozoa which will result in pregnancy or the least volume of seminal fluid which will not be overwhelmed by the vaginal pH, but a man who could summon nothing more than the secretory drop which heralds ejaculation would be considered functionally infertile.

One of the very few studies done on the efficacy of *coitus interruptus* as a fertility inhibitor has come up with the very favourable ratio of eight pregnancies per hundred years of exposure, another with seventeen pregnancies per HWY (hundred women-years) compared with fourteen for the condom and thirty-eight for the safe period. The difference in the two results may be partly accounted for by the fact that the first study was carried out in England, where a greater degree of experience and acceptance might be assumed for the practice, and the second in America, where *coitus interruptus* is rarely used systematically. However, an Indianapolis study came up with a rate of ten pregnancies per HWY for *coitus interruptus* compared with twelve as a mean rate for all other methods; among those in the higher income bracket who chose this method, *coitus interruptus* produced only three pregnancies per hundred woman-years.[12]

A survey made for the Royal Commission on Population of 3,300 marriages in 1947 showed that 43% of the sample had used no other method in regulating their birth rate, and in Social Class V, the figure went up to 61%. In Jamaica 60% of couples were said to have used it; in Puerto Rico, 47% and in Hungary, 67%.[13] There is also some evidence that *coitus interruptus* is a preferred method when other methods are available; of 91% of patients in a Birmingham clinic who abandoned the diaphragm, 58% had reverted to *coitus interruptus*. A story told by Dr Shirley Emerson indicates just such a choice and the circumstances in which it was made:

> ... a contraceptively elderly lady came to my clinic for a Dutch cap. She seemed so sure and knowledgeable, that I went ahead and fitted her, with the instruction to reappear next week with the cap in place. One week later she did return "cap in hand" or should I say handbag and started to apologise for her uselessness, "but doctor I couldn't get on with it." On delving into the situation I found that she and her husband had been using withdrawal for twenty years; during this time she had had two planned pregnancies and had been very happy. Unfortunately she got talking with a knowledgable neighbour who had proceeded to scare the wits out of her about the damage to her health, her husband's health, the family health and had sent her off hot-foot to the "family planning". I stongly reassured her and told her to carry on ..."[14]

The observer in the Birmingham study was mildly surprised to notice that

> Dependence on *coitus interruptus* is so widespread that many women think of it not as contraception but rather as a normal part of sexual intercourse. In a number of instances the husband himself had become so accustomed to withdrawing that he was unable to give up the practice when the wife wore a cap.[15]

Marie Stopes' mailbag contains some interesting glimpses of the practice of withdrawal in the 1920s. A farmer's wife from Lincolnshire wrote to her in January 1921 saying:

> Before we were married he told me he did not intend to have any damned kids who would spoil our amusements and cost us a lot of money which we could use better to enjoy ourselves. When once married he put into practice what he intended. He told me he intended always to "pull back" – what you call *coitus interruptus*. He did this on our first night together and has done so ever since and he has never spared himself any connexion with myself ... you will know whether or not this is an abnormal experience ...[16]

Few people were less likely to know whether or not this routine practice of *coitus interruptus* was abnormal than the virgin Stopes. Although Constance Lytton wrote to her in 1923 that withdrawal had "been practised in our family and by their numerous friends for generations", Stopes never ceased counselling her correspondents to desist from it. A schoolmaster from Eton attempted to remonstrate with her, saying the *onus probandi* was on her, but she disregarded him.

In *The Practice of Birth Control*, one of the earliest systematic attempts to chart actual fertility regulation practice, Enid Charles found that most of her sample of nearly a thousand women used "male methods", the condom and withdrawal; only 204 had ever used caps, of them only 81 the cervical cap.[17] The evidence for the practicability of withdrawal as a contraceptive method could with some ingenuity be assembled, but it is a question of reading rather carefully between the lines, for it is almost always described by some mildly witty metaphor. It is not the kind of perversion which excites literary libertines for it is typical of a loving husband or, at any rate, keeping in mind the Lincolnshire farmer's wife's experience, of a husband. Professional family planners have now repented their hastiness in attacking a settled and reasonably effective contraceptive practice and now go to some lengths to include *coitus interruptus* in the cafeteria of methods.

In the *Family Planning Handbook for Doctors* issued by the International Planned Parenthood Federation in 1974, a concerted attempt was made to reinstate withdrawal as a contraceptive method:

> *Coitus interruptus* or male withdrawal is certainly the oldest method of reversible contraception and probably remains the most widely used on a global scale. It is the majority method in Continental Europe and has been partially responsible for the decline in fertility, measurable from the 17th and 18th centuries in countries such as France. In contemporary Europe its use is associated with some of the lowest birth-rates ever recorded for human communities. In Britain it is the third most common method, only being exceeded by oral contraceptives and condoms ... In 1970, 38% of British users of *coitus interruptus* claimed they were completely satisfied with the method and 41% fairly satisfied. Approximately twice as many couples who had tried *coitus interruptus* persisted in its use compared with those who had tried a vaginal diaphragm.[18]

The mythology of ineffectiveness is taken by the IPPF Central Medical Committee to have resulted from the fact that doctors would never have been consulted by satisfied users and have based their impressions on the reports of people who had been unsuccessful.

> Psychologically the method has been credited as the cause of numerous possible neurotic symptoms, but again there is no objective evidence linking the use of *coitus interruptus* with any adverse emotional effects. Indeed, the widespread use of the method suggests that it is unassociated with serious side-effects while,

conversely, its commonness makes it likely that people complaining of any neurotic symptoms may have adopted the method simply by coincidence.[19]

Nevertheless, of six hundred and one doctors who answered a questionnaire in 1971, only five per cent said that they would encourage patients practising *coitus interruptus* to continue doing so, and 78% said they would advise them to discontinue it.[20] Where the method is successfully practised, it is men who are the instigators of *coitus interruptus*, and it is in no way demanded of them by women, who do not suffer the fear of pregnancy or abortion, which would characterise the situation in which a woman who did not want to get pregnant demanded *coitus interruptus* of an inexperienced and unwilling male. In the Italian example the woman is allowed to imagine that she wants children and is ready to have them, and it is the man who is imposing a discipline upon himself. His achievement of the sexual relationship has been a long process of winning his *fidanzata*'s trust, and in this he is supported by the tacit connivance of their two families. Nothing could be more different from the situation in which Mr and Mrs G found themselves when they sought help from a sex therapist:

> The wife was able to reach orgasm only by herself with a vibrator. The therapist met fierce resistance from Mrs G, a dedicated feminist, when he tried to suggest to her that *coitus interruptus*, upon which she had insisted, was a poor method of contraception and that the use of a condom, her alternative, also interfered with the couple's sexual enjoyment. The wife was also enraged by the male therapist's advice that sex would be more enjoyable if she took some responsibility for contraception and chose an alternative method which she regarded as an expression of male chauvinism. In addition she was very humiliated at having to admit to two men (the therapist and her husband) that the most exciting erotic imagery consisted of a bondage fantasy that she was tied and overwhelmed by a strong man. Not surprisingly, therapy became blocked at this point.[21]

Therapy was unblocked by the addition of a female therapist to the gang working on this unfortunate woman's case. Rather than deal with her distrust of her husband's ability and willingness to perform *coitus interruptus* adequately, they decided (and she submitted) that she should have an IUD. Why she *had* to admit to masochistic fantasies is never made clear, but she accepted them along with her contraceptive hardware, and became more orgastic, we are told, and presumably as happy as any sterile, acting-out lark, and never "fierce" or "enraged" again.

Mrs G might well have envied a woman who came up to me on a Sydney Street the morning after I had participated in a debate on women's right to abortion in the Sydney Town Hall and began by roundly saying, "You are very stupid. You think you are very clever, but you are really very stupid." "Very likely," I replied, "but why do you say so?"

"You stupid feminists," she went on, "don't know what it is to have a good man's love." (Well, I had heard that one before but she would brook no demurral.) "My husband loves me. He doesn't make me take dangerous medicines or have gadgets put inside me. He takes care of me. For twenty-five years he has taken care of me, because he loves me." Like the lady in Dr Emerson's case she had two children and no abortions, nor had she ever been afraid that she might fall pregnant and never had she been inorgastic with her husband, who was a skilled and attentive lover still. She was Hungarian. My naïve dismissal of *coitus interruptus* on the Town Hall stage has never been repeated. Instead I have often asked men if they have ever performed *coitus interruptus* over extended periods, and whether they found it frustrating or difficult if they have. One respondent told me that he had experienced great tenderness and a positive pleasure in taking the responsibility, which was the last thing I expected to hear. The clock can probably not be turned back, but it is truly ironic in these days of female emancipation that the young women in my college audiences in the United States do not feel that they could ask their lovers to do as much for them as the husband of that middle-aged Hungarian woman, even though many of them have had horrible and dangerous experiences with contraceptive hardware and steroids.

We shall never know to what extent *coitus interruptus* has been responsible for limiting population growth. Evidence that the procedure is known to most people is regularly gathered from sources as ancient as Genesis, where the crime of Onan is not masturbation, but performing *coitus interruptus* so that he does not give children to his dead brother's wife. It seems more likely that the crime consists in refusing to perform the levirate rather than in the manner of failing to carry it out; Al-Ghazali, Rhazes and Avicenna all described the procedure and its contraceptive effect, but such sources may be taken as much to indicate that literate people did not know about it as that they did. The brevity of some of the descriptions implies a lack of need to go into the details of *azl*, as it was called. More importantly, *coitus interruptus* is so obvious a way of reducing the possibility of conception, and especially obvious to herdsmen and agriculturalists who must sometimes supervise the intercourse of valuable animals and hold the female still in order to facilitate a strike, that there is no point in belabouring the matter in learned writings. There is every reason to suspect, on the other hand, that literate people were less likely to encourage young people, overtly or covertly, to amuse themselves in stereotyped intercourse or to observe the same regulation of family growth that herdsmen and farmers would have seen as desirable.

In colder climes and colder seasons, where young folk might not walk out together, and early nightfall curtailed work and left long, dark hours before bedtime, the custom known as bundling was tolerated by parents of couples who were regarded as betrothed, and it seems likely that what actually occurred began as what the teenagers of the 1950s called *petting* or *necking* and progressed through various stages of limited intercourse to *coitus interruptus*, with the young woman's bedroom performing the function taken over in the fifties by the family automobile. Neither church nor secular authorities sanctioned the practice, and the actual degree of acceptance might vary from the family simply turning a blind eye to an open window in a daughter's bedroom to public betrothal ceremonies with limited visiting rights understood as attaching to them, in much the same way as working-class families used to tolerate an affianced daughter sitting alone with her sweetheart in the parlour while they entertained themselves elsewhere. Such stereotyped sex play performed a valuable social function, in that it cemented the partnership between the spouses-to-be and safeguarded a relationship which could not come to fruition for many years. Also it early instilled the pattern of control and consideration which would typify the married life of the couple, for the effects of late marriage upon fertility may all be nullified by failure to control fertility within marriage.

It is because of consideration of patterns of this kind that some demographers have come to challenge the prevailing conception of birth control as a new idea which is first adopted by the advanced or literate urban class and spreads by deliberate propaganda or by trickle-down from the town to the rural classes. The work of E. A. Wrigley in reconstructing the population of the town of Colyton in Devon showed that fertility was extremely sensitive to changes in the economic situation and responded in an immediate way which could not be explained by any gross environmental factor; the only explanation was control of fertility within marriage, for nuptiality itself could not explain the phenomenon.[22] The possible methods of control include total abstinence, which is difficult, and partial abstinence which is unlikely to be effective given ignorance of a safe period. The most likely explanation is the practice of *coitus interruptus*. *Coitus interruptus* is also taken to be the mechanism by which the French and Swedes began the decline of their birth-rate long before efficient modern chemical or rubber contraception was available, and independently of industrialisation.[23]

Coitus interruptus is such an obvious way of separating the making of love from the making of babies that we cannot be surprised to find it appearing in different circumstances all over the world. Among the Tikopia *coitus interruptus* was actually institutionalised in a public ceremony:

The recognised method of avoiding unwanted pregnancies is *coitus interruptus*. This is used by both married and unmarried couples. Married couples do so when they do not desire to enlarge their families. In olden times there was a ritual called *fono*, in which the heads of families were exhorted to limit the number of their children by *coitus interruptus* and the reason given was the prevention of infanticide and other social disorder.[24]

As we have come to expect, the young men were not taught by their elders how to fulfil these expectations, but by their peers. Doubtless the missionaries disrupted this practice as they did most of the sexual hygiene that they encountered.

The rarity of illegitimate births in many pre-literate societies is partly the result of limitations upon the kind of sexual intercourse permitted to the unmarriageable. Among African groups it is often not withdrawal but *coitus inter crura*, in which orgasm is reached by the friction of the penis against the partner's upper thighs which is permitted among the unmarried, sometimes quite promiscuously. Among the Swazi of Swaziland, for example:

> After puberty boys and girls are expected to find lovers with whom to indulge in a stereotyped sex play, stopping short of full intercourse. Formerly a girl who became pregnant before marriage was mocked and the boy was beaten and fined but the occurrence has become too frequent to evoke strong reactions.[25]

Hilda Kuper's observation goes to show how fragile such mechanisms of social control can be; they are always the first systems to be unbalanced by the disruption of the life of the group, and may vanish before anyone has thought fit to record them. Among the Masai the initiated bachelors were permitted to engage in this kind of sex play in which avoidance of pregnancy was a part of the chivalric function. Among the Tswana, withdrawal protected lactating women and the unmarried from unwanted pregnancy.[26]

The fact that withdrawal has been and is still successfully practised by millions does not in itself constitute a reason for using it if more convenient, easier and healthier methods are available. In the sense that no equipment is needed, beyond those which nature has supplied, there is no more convenient technique. It is not dependent upon the efficiency of the pharmaceutical industry, does not require a bathroom in close proximity, does not presuppose a bedroom – all distinct advantages in circumstances like those which prevailed in the Ludhiana district of the Punjab when a Harvard study team went there in 1959 to conduct an introductory birth-control programme. At that time IUDs and oral contraceptives were not available, so the field workers had equipped themselves with two kinds of foaming tablets, one of which was almost immediately withdrawn as a suspected carcinogen. They had decided against condoms and diaphragms as too expensive and too liable to perish in the climatic conditions which prevailed. Besides, condoms were illegal. Of

course, three years after the programme had got under way, they discovered that the village shop sold condoms. The villagers were not motivated to use them on their wives, but rather for other contacts which
might result in disease. The known efficacy of the suppositories was hardly
better than fifty per cent. The husbands of most of the women who did
not want to get pregnant were already practising withdrawal, a far more
efficient method in any case, but the field workers were convinced that
coitus interruptus did not work, and exhorted people to use foam as well.
They even asked the women to carry little bags filled with pieces of cotton
which they were to soak in a saline solution, a contraceptive method of
no proven efficacy whatever, and which actually entailed a greatly increased risk of trauma and infection, so little was their faith in what they
called a "folk method". In vain the Punjabi women may have attempted
to explain their own system of birth regulation by prolonged lactation,
abstinence and *coitus interruptus*; the field workers would not have recognised their terminology and were convinced that they must have been
having unwanted children. The villagers, out of politeness one suspects,
accepted their suppositories, may or may not have tried them out (and
discovered that they sting and burn and definitely interfere with pleasure)
and abandoned them.

> During the first year of the definitive study, and despite a strong effort to en-
> courage couples to accept contraception, the number accepting began to decline.
> Investigation revealed that a number of couples who accepted contraceptive
> materials were not using them and that reports of contraceptive use did not
> always tally with the number of contraceptives provided.

During 1957–9 the birthrate actually went up, perhaps because couples
were believing the official line about contraceptive foam and disbelieving
in their own more efficient method. Eventually the observers came to
a rather disheartening conclusion:

> During the study some five hundred couples practised contraception for varying
> lengths of time and more or less consistently. No change appeared in birth-
> rates, although a small effect was evident as delayed conception. A possible
> explanation is that the introduced contraceptives replaced an earlier practice
> of folk methods, perhaps equally effective.[27]

Examination of their own data reveals that the people they were dealing
with were more level-headed than they supposed; most had never
abandoned their methods of choice in the first place and some even used
foam as well as *coitus interruptus*, an outcome which is even more likely
when we reflect that in the traditional Western manner, contraception
was mainly discussed (i.e. urged upon) the women, while their husbands
were quite likely to have ignored this woman business and to have clung to
methods they knew and trusted.

In 1969 a follow-up study was conducted. Contrary to the diagnosis of population pressure, for the initial study had been applied as therapy to a disease of this name, the villagers had actually prospered; there were tube wells and tractors, better housing, better marriage prospects for the children the farmers had continued to have (and lose, for the study had not included any interference with the infant death rate). Most crushing of all was the discovery that the practice of birth control was exactly as it had been in 1959; most women were not using contraception, nobody was using foam, and only seven per cent were using modern methods, compared to nine per cent in the control village, where no attempt to promote birth control had ever been made. For the birth-controllers this result was very disappointing, but for other students of human nature it provides an encouraging example of the power of illiterate peoples to resist interference and indoctrination, to retain faith in their own capacity to order their lives as they think fit.

For the Ludhiana farmers and their wives whose homes did not have electric light and hot and cold water, withdrawal was much more manageable than anything the birth-controllers could suggest, especially as husbands and wives did not sleep together in private rooms and mothers-in-law were apt to take a dim view of spermicidal tablets hanging about. The objection could still be made that for people whose sex lives are not subject to these restraints *coitus interruptus* is a difficult and inconvenient method. In fact, even for men who have become used to unrestrained intercourse, it is easy to master the art of withdrawal; even for inexperienced and very young men with equally inexperienced partners, it can be mastered, especially if it forms part of the great traditional love story, the seduction of a young wife by an eager but gentle husband. The very emphasis placed by Hindu culture (for example) upon the woman's pleasure in sex encourages the development of the idea that sexual intercourse is not a gross, evacuatory procedure but a restrained, considerate and artful business, which, if properly managed, leads to bliss for both partners. The violence of the prejudice against *coitus interruptus* springs at least in part from an erroneous idea that sexual intercourse is a spontaneous, natural, uncalculated function which is frustrated by any measure of deliberate control.

Obviously, withdrawal cannot be demanded of an unwilling participant in any spirit of hostility or challenge. It will only be satisfactory if it is an expression of love offered and received in trust; this may have been what Gandhi meant when he said that the problem of unwanted pregnancy could be solved if men would but love their wives. Indian erotic mysticism, with its celebration of the energising properties of semen, places great value upon the prolongation of coition and the highest value upon *coitus reservatus*; the great yogis who are depicted pleasuring several women at once are actually absorbing the women's vital power instead of expending their own, for the women's secretions are thought of as their *bindu* which the yogi draws from them. Jaundiced observers, who doubt the capacity of yogis to withold ejaculation (which to this writer seems a good deal easier than some of the other things they do) assume that they make use of the dangerous practice known as *coitus saxonicus*, which requires firm pressure on the base of the urethra at the moment of ejaculation, so that the ejaculate is forced back up and into the bladder. The results of this practice include traumatisation and infection of the seminal ducts and the epididymus, with eventual incontinence and prostate problems. As detumescence immediately follows the deviated ejaculation, it cannot accomplish the yogi's primary aim of greatly prolonged intercourse, and as it requires help from the female partner, it would appear to place the myth of the yogi's superhuman control in disrepute; it is more likely that the yogi finds that orgasm becomes easier to forgo the longer he continues.

A variation of *coitus obstructus* which involves pressure on the urethra just above the scrotum is suggested by Kokkoka in the thirteenth-century *Secret of Sexual Desire*. Chinese texts celebrate as Immortal the man who can absorb the *yin* of women without expending his own *yang*, prescribing the same feats of sexual athleticism ascribed to the yogis:

> If a man engages once in the act without emitting semen, then his vital essence will be strong. If he does this twice, his hearing and vision will be acute. If thrice, all diseases will disappear. If four times, his soul will be at peace. If five times, his blood circulation will be improved. If six times, his loins will become strong. If seven times, his buttocks and thighs will increase in power. If eight times, his body will become glossy. If ten times he will be like an Immortal.[28]

It may be some association of the idea of superhuman health and strength resulting from the husbanding of vital essence which lies behind the acceptance of voluntary male sterilisation in India. If the procedure is explained to the acceptor as the blocking of the seed from the genitals, so that it must continue to circulate in its generalised form as "the body's essence", it could well appear to him in the same light as the sexual feats of the yogis, and not as a form of castration, which is how many Westerners see it. To describe the procedure in such terms is no more incorrect than the usual schematic explanations which are offered to lay people. Spermatogenesis does continue, though at a reduced rate because of the blockage of the feed-back mechanism, and some sperm does leak into the bloodstream, while the fact that the rate of spermatogenesis is greatly slowed down could well mean that a poorly nourished man could convert more protein into energy for other tasks. The unexplained phenomenon of the change in attitude which brought thousands of men to sterilisation camps of their own accord (before the atrocities of the Emergency) might have been the result of some such reasoning which the villagers and their elders arrived at independently of official promotion.

In the mid-1970s Chinese family-planning workers included a version of *coitus reservatus* among the methods of birth control that they were recommending.

> When the male is about to ejaculate, he uses the tips of his fingers to press tightly on the spot between the anus and the scrotum, pressing against the pubic bone for about one minute until the spot against which the fingers are pressing has completely stopped pulsating ... This method is simple, and when the timing is controlled and the pressure is in the right spot, the effectiveness is comparatively good ... In order to raise the effectiveness of contraception when using this kind of method, it is best first to try it while using the condom ...[29]

There is no suggestion that there are any problems associated with this method which is generally thought by Western doctors to contribute to inflammation and infection by forcing the seminal fluid back up into the bladder. Peter Fryer refers to the method, as *coitus obstructus* or *coitus saxonicus* without differentiation and tells us not only that Sanskrit writers knew of it, but also that the *International Journal of Sexology* published an account of thirteen years' successful use of the method in 1953.[30] Uncritical as the Chinese account is, the method seems unlikely to catch on, except perhaps in a country where illicit pregnancy could lead to forced abortion. A minute after all, is quite a long time, and involuntary wrist flexion is not unknown in the circumstances.

An even more effective way of exploiting human polymorphous potential in making love rather than babies is the resort to homosexuality. In societies which practise rigorous sexual segregation, a degree of juvenile and adult homosexuality with a more or less overt genital component may be assumed. Among the Etoro of New Guinea, homosexual release for men has been incorporated into a complete ethical system. Like most New Guinea peoples, the Etoro practise strict segregation of men in order to protect them from dangerous contact with women which may result in *hame hah hah*, or shortwindedness. They believe that sexual intercourse with women represents the greatest depletion of a man's life force:

> Every male possesses a limited quantity of life-force which resides in his body as a whole but especially in his semen. A portion of this is expended in each act of sexual intercourse so that a man's reservoir of life-force is gradually depleted over his life-time ...

Many literate peoples have assumed that a man's spermatic reserve was limited, and the Etoro cannot be regarded as unusual in that idea, nor in their idea that if a man who has had sexual intercourse gives food or smoke to another on the same day, he too will be afflicted with *hame hah hah*.

> A man must avoid seeing or coming into contact with a new-born child for seventeen days. If he fails to do so he will suffer especially severe *hame hah hah* and may die as a consequence.[31]

As is usual in societies with highly developed notions of the depletion of bodily power and energy by sexual intercourse, the Etoro practise long periods of abstinence:

> Men are protected from undue depletion ... by prolonged periods of enjoined abstinence. Heterosexual relations are narrowly circumscribed with respect to permitted times (and places) of occurrence. In all, copulation is prohibited (*tobi*) for an estimated 205 to 260 days a year ... The prohibitions are linked to virtually all aspects of the productive economy ... Moreover these activities tend to be segregated in time so that there is relatively little overlap between one proscribed period and another. This imposes substantial limitations on the frequency of heterosexual relations, and there is moreover indirect evidence of general adherence to the prohibitions. Eight of ten births which occurred within the tribe during a 15-month period took place over a short span of 3 months ... Heterosexual intercourse should take place only in the forest, never within a house, in a garden dwelling, in the longhouse or the general vicinity of the longhouse ... Violation of the prohibition on copulation in and around the longhouse is a serious offence which may provoke public rebuke and expulsion from the community.[32]

All these prohibitions relate to heterosexual intercourse; the rather austere picture thus presented is utterly transformed by the discovery the mature men help boys to develop manly characteristics by "inseminating them", which is a rather prudish way of saying that they have the boys swallow their semen:

> A youth is continually inseminated from about age ten until he reaches his early to mid-twenties.

There are no prohibitions of any kind upon this altruistic form of intercourse which has clearly beneficial effects, for the beardless boy of ten becomes bigger and stronger, as long as he continues to consume the semen of his elders.

> Men and boys may properly engage in sexual relations in the men's section of the longhouse (and in gardens) on any day of the year.[33]

The logic is incontrovertible; if semen makes babies it stands to reason that it must also strengthen a baby; the long debates conducted in the columns of sex magazines about the benefits of swallowing semen are evidence that for all our technology we have no clearer idea of the nutrient value of sperm than the Etoro. What is not clear from Raymond Kelly's account is whether the practice of insemination is carried out in a perfunctory way or whether there is any erotic context or any celebration of intimacy or homosexual incest prohibitions or any attachment to one boy in particular, but what emerges with great clarity is that what underlies the Etoro practice of insemination is their own great respect for masculinity. For the Etoro it is heterosexual contact which effeminises, homosexual contact which masculinises; the literate West makes the opposite assumption, on no better ground. In both cases, the argument is self-validating.

There are indications that similar notions persist in other military castes of Asia and Europe: there may be good reason to assume that the relics of a belief in the masculinising power of homosexual society (if not homosexual genital contact) underlies the attachment of armies to their traditional sexual segregation. British soldiers were puzzled by the suspicion that their most valiant Sikhs and Gurkhas were performing vile acts with their subordinates.

Ever since Marie Stopes wrote her rhapsodic descriptions of marital sex in 1918, there has been an enthusiastic and lucrative campaign to introduce variety, imagination and innovation into the sexual commerce of spouses. Many of her readers had difficulty in imagining what the "beautiful subtleties of wooing" might be. Forel advised his "eager and intelligent couples fully to probe themselves" figuratively at any rate, and eventually in the concrete understanding of the vulgar, physically, "to discover the extent and meaning of the immensely profound and spiritual results of marriage".

> Each couple, after marriage, must study themselves, and the lover and the beloved must do what best serves them both and gives them the highest degree of mutual joy and power.[34]

This solemn injunction could be understood as permitting all kinds of sexual intercourse, but still Stopes' readers had difficulty in knowing quite what she meant. As the Reverend C—D— of Nottinghamshire wrote to her on 2 November, 1920:

> ... the third point is how best to arouse. I have had no instruction in what you call the Art of Love ... This Art of Love is so often referred to, p. 42, "romantic advances", p. 50, "charming love play", p. 100 "the love play", p. 82, "ardently to woo her", p. 84, "a passionate return" – these and other passages seem beyond me. They raise pictures I long for, but do not know how to attain to ...[35]

Poor Reverend C—D— ought perhaps to study the visual content of his pictures rather than invite the poetic palaeobotanist to provide more of the same. We may contrast his clerkly ineptitude, which will not be adjusted by book-learning, with the way in which sexual competence is actually learned in Italy, where little boys are busy wooing little girls with flowers and entreaties when they are only four or five years old. Their parents will describe in detail how they came home from school despairing because some little minx had refused to smile and how they set off next morning determined to win her over. The children learn the vocabulary of love as they learn to speak. It is impossible to imagine anyone who has grown up in an anti-sensual environment, reading a book, however detailed, and knowing what to do and how to do it. The proliferation of sex manuals in the English-speaking world in the 1920s is usually interpreted as a sign that connubial intercourse was becoming more pleasurable and intelligent; the enormous demand for this kind of literature is more likely to indicate the opposite. The demand came from the middle, professional classes. The poor and the rich both had other sources of information which were probably more effective. The entry of sex into the domain of print was one edge of a movement out of the body. This is the era of sex-in-the-head, so hated by D. H. Lawrence who became its high priest.

What the manuals taught was tamer than what the working classes and the depraved aristos were doing. By way of sexual variety, Stopes could suggest changing the position from the missionary to lying on one's side; by way of delicious stimulation she suggested a kiss upon the bosom. The wilder shores of fellatio and cunnilingus, of rear entry, belong in the spheres of the lecherous which should never encroach to sully the romantic. Gradually the manuals of wedded bliss began to increase the repertory of sexual practices permitted to the chastely married pair so that they drew a little closer to the range of activities which some of the people who did not buy the books already permitted themselves. The anonymous author of *My Secret Life*, although living in the approved style of the repressed middle classes, with a wife who was totally estranged from her own sexuality, approached his extra-marital encounters with more than adequate enthusiasm, imagination and tenderness, giving and getting enormous pleasure – admittedly by his own account, but in the manner of recounting we can readily see that he did not need any kind of officially sanctioned instruction. His companions and his own urgings appear to have been quite adequate. There was a difficulty, insuperable for most, of approaching one's wife with the same gusto that drew one into the willing and resourceful arms of the prostitute, but pious manuals of sex practice were not likely to resolve it. The sex religion of the East was based upon the necessity of introducing a shy and modest wife to physical pleasure, but the Northern European religious inheritance could not be called upon to serve the same function, even when Dr Stopes claimed to have had a vision.

Gradually, the notion that husbands and wives may do anything that "gives them the highest degree of mutual joy and power" has come to include all the variations and fetishes, gadgetry, pornography, adultery – everything, in short, except anal intercourse.

In theory anal intercourse is acceptable between spouses, if in many areas still against the law, as long as it is not forced upon an unwilling partner and is not carried out in such a way as to cause damage to the rectum. However there is a curious and enduring reluctance on the part of any heterosexual group to admit that it practises anal intercourse. (Homosexuals, on the other hand, might be accused of exaggerating the extent to which they practise it.) In these days of enlightenment, we have all had to accept the idea of consenting adults of the same sex celebrating their togetherness *in anum*; even homosexual women have demanded the suspension of our more squeamish feelings about anal communion of various kinds.

> Only the sight of her below me, such kindness I feel for these cheeks such greed feeding upon her given and open defenseless vulnerable, but I shall never cause her harm careful to relish our abandon to savor each thrust as she does and my hand ever so slowly deliberate moving her closing on my finger's steady in and out, feeling her in my own anus contracting as hers does the secret joy of it found out at last.[36]

Dr Stopes could hardly write more rhapsodically about the marital embrace than does Dr Millett about rectal massage. The ano-rectal area is, we are told, an erogenous zone, if dormant in a large number of individuals. In *Sexual Inversion* Havelock Ellis describes Florrie as extremely excitable in the anal region and notes that this trait is often found in conjunction with abnormal gluteal development; the pseudo-scientific argument is actually asinine, but a footnote points out that:

> A correspondent remarks on "the fact, patent to all observers, that simple folk not infrequently display no greater disgust for the abnormalities of sexual appetite than they do for its normal manifestations." In further illustration of this I have been told that among the common people there is often no feeling against connection with a woman *per anum*.[37]

The sages of the British Society for the Study of Sexual Psychology issued a translation of the German text published by the Wissenschaftlich-humanitären Komitee in 1903, which stoutly averred that:

> according to authoritative testimony, the employment for sexual purposes of parts of the body not designed for such purposes is comparatively rare in homosexual intercourse and certainly not more common than among the normally sexed.[38]

The gentlemen of both organisations knew more about homosexual practice than they did about the other, but although the argument is *a priori* unlikely, for male homosexuals could hardly be expected to limit their activities to entangling the organs "designed" for sex, it does supply some evidence for the prevalence of polymorphous practices at least in commericial sexual transactions. Allen Clifford writing on "Perversions, sexual" in Ellis and Abarbanel's *Encyclopaedia of Sex* tells us that 20% of male homosexuals and fewer than 1% of heterosexuals "use anal intercourse regularly".

> This invalidates the theory that it is used as a substitute for vaginal intercourse and supports Freud's views. When heterosexual analism is used as an occasional variation from other forms of coitus, it is not a perversion, but is within the normal range of sex behaviour.[39]

Curiously perhaps, the learned gentleman does not consider its use as a contraceptive measure, which would probably be occasional enough to pass as normal. Although most of us would defend to the death the right of homosexuals to bugger each other *ad libitum*, we are strangely reluctant to claim any such right on our own behalf. The commonness of references to buggery in popular parlance, such as the French *vas te faire enculer* (which does not mean *get fucked*) or the Bolognese fixation with the trials of being *cul rotto*, indicates the persistence of a strong taboo and concomitant anxiety on the point. The cult of heterosexual anal intercourse, is, as we might expect, limited to the writings of those individuals who delighted in scandalising a fundamentally pious and repressive society, but they too were not alone. There was a vigorous subculture which supplied them with their raw material. Thus when Aretino writes *"chi non fotte in cul, dio gl'el perdoni"* because *"questa fottitura é la piú ghiotta, che piacque a donne a cui ben piacque il cazzo,"* he is reflecting actual practice among courtesans.[40] They may have pretended to appreciate anal intercourse for reasons of self-interest, such as the avoidance of pregnancy, but the evidence seems to point to something more inventive and joyous. An eighteenth-century source calls the two orifices of the female *"l'uno e l'altro sesso"*; the same source refers to the contraceptive function with the judgment that the practitioner *"molto ben fece"*.

The Marquis de Sade was a passionate advocate of anal intercourse; although he cherished the inevitable sadistic fantasies of its ruinous effects, which are the principal ground for his own exquisite pleasure in contemplating it, he also called it "la plus délicieuse" of the ways of cheating nature.[41]

Certainly, the fathers of the church knew about anal coitus, and included it among the sins to be sought out in confessional interrogations. I have been told by non-Italians that Italians practise it, and by Italians that American girls insist on it. It is claimed by non-Greeks that Greeks have a weakness for it. Among the extraordinary variety of cultural practices for the maintenance of the balance between population and resources it appears always to have played a very minor role: few if any groups, even those which have accepted sodomy among young men, claim to regulate their numbers by anal intercourse within marriage. When the claim is made by outsiders, it is usually an indication of libellous intent. Yet, we learn, it is a practice which can be associated with intense pleasure for both parties. It is tempting to speculate upon the reasons for this strange and almost universal reluctance, but any attempt at explanation can be no more than speculative.

It is clearly understood in our own society that intromission is not essential for either partner to enjoy intercourse, and there has been a concerted attempt in our time to remove all vestiges of guilt from the enjoyment of less orthodox methods, yet no one has attempted to exploit human sexual creativity as an alternative to mechanical or pharmaceutical population control. Oral sex is preached, as a tender, satisfying version of love-making, but not as a contraceptive method. The assumption on the part of those who recommend the rhythm method is that abstinence, rather than restraint from intra-vaginal ejaculation, will be practised on the fertile days. In the case of Catholics, who believe that ejaculation should not be deliberately induced outside the vagina, such an assumption is only to be expected; but other groups – feminists who refuse to use potentially damaging forms of birth control, for example – also assume that no alternative to ejaculation in the vagina can be seriously proposed. The common morality seems to reject any notion of deliberately selecting kinds of love-making in order to avoid pregnancy, at the same time as it ordains the maximum use of creativity and versatility in sex. We might ask what the point of all the versatility is if not to avoid unwanted pregnancy; the answer seems to be that it is an end in itself and ought not to be debased by ulterior considerations. This attitude is not so much realistic, for sexual intercourse is a part of ordinary conscious human relations, as religious. Sex may be debased by using extraneous aids to stimulate flagging desire, by inviting third parties, by substituting instruments and other limbs for the flagging penis, but not by reverence for the power of sperm and ovary. Couples may dress up, play roles, manipulate and abuse each other, but they may not treat the vagina as dangerous. Our culture obliges us to abandon all attempts to control our own fertility by using our polymorphous potential for pleasure, and to give that control up to external agencies on the grounds that they are both more efficient and less harmful. The harmfulness of traditional methods of stereotyped intercourse has often been asserted but never shown. The efficacy of traditional methods has never been studied because they were invariably assumed not to exist.

Our preference for mechanical and pharmacological agents of birth-control is irrational. Our position with regard to the function of sex is absurdly confused. The other systems which have occasionally been referred to so far have had a certain internal consistency, outlandish though some of them may have seemed. There is no logic in a conceptual system which holds that orgasm is always and everywhere good for you, that vaginal orgasm is impossible, that no moral opprobrium attaches to expenditure of semen wherever it occurs, that considerable opprobrium attaches to the bearing of unwanted children, *and* at the same time insists that "normal" heterosexual intercourse should always culminate in ejaculation within the vagina. These are the suppositions which underlie our eagerness to extend the use of modern contraceptives into every society on earth, regardless of its own set of cultural and moral priorities. As the basic premises of the position are incoherent, the position itself is absurd.

Another name for this kind of mental chaos is *evil*.

Chapter Six

The Short History of Contraception

(We) would gladly accept (family planning) provided it:
- not interfere with our working;
- not do us permanent harm;
- not be against our religion;
- be free or nearly so;
- have a woman to examine us and to teach us what to do and how to do it;
- remain a secret between her and us.

Women's Meeting, Central Javan Village, 1977

(The source is Barbara Rogers, *The Domestication of Women: Discrimination in Developing Societies* (London, 1980) quoting Sam Keeny, "View from the Village", *Populi*, Vol. 4, No. 1, 1977, pp. 7–13)

If people insist on making love in the way which normally results in the making of babies, and yet find that the possibility of making a baby causes them worry and dread, thus spoiling the pleasure they take in the activity, they may resort to contraception. It might seem more logical to resort to other forms of love-making, especially during the fertile period, but for reasons discussed elsewhere, most Westerners now prefer to pay a largely unknown price for their sexual preference, namely the imposition of temporary or permanent sterility on one of the partners. Before reliable methods of doing this had become commonly available, various kinds of barriers were used, which interposed themselves between the sperm and the cervix. The most venerable method of doing this was by sheathing the penis.

Gabriele Fallopio is thought to have been the first to use linen sheaths as prophylactics; in many countries condoms are called prophylactics still. Protection against the *lues venerea* continued to be the main motive for the adoption of the condom, as it came to be called – why, nobody knows. As prostitutes were usually sterile because of disease, the connection with pregnancy was unimportant and no gentleman would have dreamt of using such "armour" with his wife, although it seems to have been well understood that what prevented infection prevented conception too. The greatest advance was the manufacture of condoms out of sheeps' gut, which was as impermeable as modern rubber and a good deal finer, only half the thickness of a modern English fine rubber sheath, which is very much thinner than an American rubber sheath.

The condom has never recovered from its early association with promiscuity, bought sex and disease, even though there is an ancient precedent for the augmentation of the effectiveness of the penis by the addition of caps, rings and thick sheaths made of gold, silver, copper, ivory, wood, tin, lead, leather, horn and tortoiseshell. The idea of using the condom to enhance intercourse has always been around; the French in the early twentieth century made novelty condoms with names like the Porcupine, Tickler, Cockadoodledoo, Bibi Tickler and so forth. The Japanese, who had a tradition of penis enhancement before condom use as contraception, have always had a positive attitude towards them; they made the first condoms in pastel colours, and another called

MORE BIG, OR RUBBER BAND. This may be used by men who have small tools in order to increase sexual pleasure which give unexplainable feeling to women.[1]

Nowadays sex shops sell fantastically decorated condoms which seem to be mainly conversation pieces in all shapes, sizes and colours, but even the superfine, lubricated-both-sides condoms have attained new heights of glamour and sophistication. German condoms are often marketed as ways to prolong sexual intercourse, although it is doubtful whether this description actually complies with the Trades Descriptions Act. It is just conceivable that interference with sensation does retard orgasm, but whether it ought to or not is another matter. Condoms might be lubricated with sensitising compounds which could more effectively counterbalance the loss of direct contact with the vaginal membrane. In America the FDA has virtually destroyed the condom's potential attraction as a method of fertility control by insisting on a minimum thickness which is the highest anywhere in the world, and a standard of length which is longer than the longest permitted in other countries.[2] However, until *Love Story* is remade with moving episodes of condom-related sex play, the rubber sheath will continue to be associated with casual sex and fear of disease.

Failure to glamourise the condom may have serious consequences. The menarche begins earlier among the well nourished women of the West nowadays than it ever has done before; meanwhile marriage is retarded for social reasons, as long as ten years after the onset of sexual maturity and sexual activity. The result, whether we like it or not, is inevitably a prolonged period of sexual experimentation which occurs not when the female is sterile, as used to be the case when adolescent sterility did not fade out until the girl was nearly twenty and long married in most parts of the world, but when she is both socially immature and fully fertile. In the United States in 1979, 17% of all births were illegitimate, most of them to teenagers. Teenage pregnancy is a social crisis with severely disruptive consequences, which may involve three generations, the parents,

the pregnant child and the child of a child. Leaving aside for the moment
the vexed question of teenage abortion, the consideration of the problems
involved in teenage contraception leads irresistibly to the condom or the
diaphragm as the only solution, for the insertion of IUDs in such young
women is inadvisable, and few intelligent physicians would feel that the
administration of contraceptive steroids to developing women was a good
idea. Moreover, the adoption of systematic birth control involves the
development of a stable and committed attitude to sex which the average
thirteen-year-old is unlikely to achieve without a good deal of trial and
error. The wonder and excitement of the discovery of sex would be greatly
diminished by the teaching of sexual hygiene as a branch of good citizenship in high schools, and children would as strenuously resist it as they
do the other branches of good citizenship. It would be truly frightful
to provoke the sexual equivalent of soccer hooliganism or punk squalor
by endeavouring to commit children to a kind of dreary genital discipline
which they felt bound to challenge.

The epidemic of sterilising disease among juveniles is a reality, just
as teenage pregnancy is, and the tragic results are already making themselves felt. The only country to report any degree of success in reducing
the incidence of gonorrhoea in teenagers is Sweden, where a condom
programme produced heartening results, although, oddly enough, the
same decline was not observed in the incidence of *Chlamydia*
infections.[3] The possibility that *Chlamydia* is a sterilising disease
of the genital tract which is not solely spread by genital contact is too
awful to contemplate. Given the present state of our knowledge, the
condom seems the best kind of protection of children against both
unwanted pregnancy and sterilising disease; it is now vitally important
that we find a way of making the condom a cult object of youth, which
is by no means the same thing as advertising condoms in steamy small ads
or putting condom dispensers in public lavatories. We need to see the
Fonz dropping a packet on the floor now and then, if the idea is not
already *passé*.[4]

It must have cost Carl Djerassi, the man who gave us the contraceptive
pill, a great deal to state unequivocally in *The Politics of Contraception*:

> I do wish to emphasise that on safety grounds the diaphragm is clearly the
> best contraceptive ...[5]

The women who abandoned the diaphragm so willingly in the early
1960s had good reasons for doing so. They may not look so good now,
because the Pill is not the magic thing we thought it was, but that does
not mean that women should be satisfied with the present state of
diaphragm technology, which has not altered in any significant respect
for fifty years. If that were all it were enough, but there is good reason
to think that there was at least one superior form of female barrier contra-

ceptive which has fallen into disuse, fallen so far, in fact, that few people now remember that it ever existed.

The first cap, which fitted snugly onto the cervix to be removed only for the passage of the menses, whereafter it was re-inserted either by a doctor or by the lady herself, was devised in 1838 by a German, Frederick Adolphe Wilde. He took a mould of the cervix in wax and made the cap out of latex.[6] Various other kinds of cap were made, of ivory, gold, platinum, silver, rubber, lucite or polythene; we have no way of knowing how extensively they were used, for they were once-in-a-lifetime acquisitions, never the subject of public advertisement or discussion. Many women who were shown how to use them by their mothers do not even realise that the modern diaphragm is not the same at all, but a much cruder and more uncomfortable thing altogether. The cap went in on a fingertip and was pushed snugly over the cervix so that all the air was pushed out and it adhered by suction. Getting it out was more difficult, for a finger had to be hooked under the rim, to give a good tug and break the suction.

The diaphragm, called the Dutch cap after the country where the first birth-control clinic, offering principally the diaphragm, was opened in 1882, is a rubber dinghy for spermicide. The fit is crude, being merely the largest circumference which can be got to stay taut inside the vagina after it has been inserted by pressing it between finger and thumb and making sure that it is pushed up well behind the pelvic bone. What is wrongly called a cap is actually a rubber partition, a diaphragm. Once this large, springy object is thickly piled with spermicide it is remarkably difficult to keep the circular spring compressed between finger and thumb. The loaded diaphragm is quite likely to shoot out of the inserter's tentative grasp and to fly through the air, splattering glop in all directions. The spermicide is usually cold and dense, with a slithery consistency; it is meant to coat the cervix, but succeeds in coating everything else as well with chilly sludge. If intercourse continues so long that this sludge is dissipated, it is a sign that a fresh injection is required, so that a night of love becomes a kind of spermicidal bath. Oro-genital contact is definitely counterindicated, especially as the spermicides are about as toxic as if sperm were mice.

Why the diaphragm and all that sails within it should be so gross is unimaginable; if toothpaste tasted as disgusting as spermicide, the teeth of the nation would have fallen out years ago. Because the diaphragm is made of obscenely pallid rubber, the least thing stains it, and putting it away damp makes it perish, so the bathroom taps are forever garnished with a drying diaphragm – to the immense interest of casual visitors. For years I and my fellow fighters for sexual freedom strove to like our diaphragms, to the extent of wearing the springs from worn-out ones as ceremonial jewelry and marks of caste. Long before its uses as a contraceptive

was officially authorised, we were wheedling the oestrogen pill out of
our doctors. No one who has ever forced herself to carry her dilly-bag
with spermicide and diaphragm at all times and gamely tried to squirt
and insert in the woods and on the beach, who has not cudgelled her
brains to know when one occasion of sexual intercourse ended and
another began so that she could decide whether or not to squeeze more
cold glop into herself (a procedure which necessitated the carrying of a
plastic applicator – never totally clean – as well as all the other impedimenta
in the dilly-bag) has not longed to do away with the whole kit and caboodle.
If we had known that there was a small, discreet little cap which could
stay in for days or weeks at a time, which a man could not detect (as
he often definitely can the diaphragm in its wallow) which needed no
spermicide – or at most a dab – which could be made of gold, which
would last a lifetime, neither Gregory Pincus nor Jove himself could have
got us to give it up.

Tracking what happened to the cervical cap is not easy. The matter
is fuddled from the beginning by the number of names under which the
cervical cap passed. It was probably a cervical cap that Margaret Sanger
showed to Marie Stopes in 1915 as a "French pessary". The device
advertised by Lambert and Son in 1886 is clearly a cervical cap, but it
is called a *check pessary*.

IMPROVED CHECK PESSARY
Is a simply devised instrument of pure soft medicated rubber, to be worn by
the female (during coition) as a protection against conception. It is constructed
on a common-sense principle, and strictly in accordance with the female organisation; can be worn any length of time with ease and comfort; is easily adjusted
and removed, adapts itself perfectly, and no apprehension of it going too far
or doing the slightest harm need be felt, and with care will last for years. Post
free with directions for use, 2s. 3d. each.[7]

So much for modern freedom; the reader of *The Wife's Handbook* had
simply to send off her money and she obtained a perfectly practical form
of contraceptive protection. No ban on advertising applied and no prudery
was expressed in what was a commonsense approach to the solution of
an unremarkable problem.

In the early twentieth century two women, on opposite sides of the
world, not themselves very familiar with the ways in which more discreet
women managed their reproductive affairs, seized upon the idea of family
limitation as an innovative cause to be publicly campaigned for. From
being a private matter solved between middle-class mother and daughter,
often ineptly no doubt, contraception became a public rallying-point in
circumstances which must have alienated both the people who needed
help the most and the people most able to supply it. Sanger and Stopes
saw the possibilities of the acceptance of birth control by the poor, which
they translated into a rhetoric of glorified motherhood and racial hygiene.

Women who had managed their affairs with less clamour may well have been revolted by the specious arguments and vulgar publicity-hunting of the zealots. Certainly, they did not come forward to explain their own practice. Stopes and Sanger were permitted by this reticence to continue believing themselves the inventors of married love. Stopes certainly received more than enough evidence in the way of loony letters from middle-class husbands, onanist clerics and horribly knocked-about mothers-of-ten-six-dead, to reinforce her conception of herself as the sexual messiah. Both Sanger and Stopes were tireless self-promoters, unintelligent and insensitive observers of human nature and wildly overoptimistic about the methods they chose to promote. Each was constitutionally incapable of respecting the opinions of the people she ostensibly desired to help.

The heir of the self-same Lambert and Son supplied Stopes with her first gross of check pessaries when she opened the Mothers' Clinic for Constructive Birth Control in 1920. It is doubtful whether the existence of the clinic made very much difference to their sales, which were already considerable: eventually the cervical cap was to lose out to the diaphragm, and it is an interesting fact that Lambert wrote to Stopes in 1932 telling her this was bound to happen. Stopes, who took advice from no one, ignored him. When she decided to see for herself, she ordered her first supply of diaphragms in secret.[8]

Even Ruth Hall, Marie Stopes' biographer, perpetuates the confusion between the cervical cap and the diaphragm. Speaking of Stopes' *Wise Parenthood*, Hall mistakenly asserts:

> What doctors could more easily quarrel with was her advocacy of the cervical cap – not so much in itself but because she makes the mistake of saying that it could be left in place for several days, or even weeks, without removal.[9]

The vast mass of Stopes' papers to which Hall had access is crammed with material of great interest to the historian of fertility control, but Hall does not concern herself with the actual contraceptive hardware offered in the early clinics. She notes that the rubber check pessary was the preferred method in the first clinics, but quite irrelevantly includes an account of the invention of the diaphragm by a German called Hesse, who adopted the pseudonym "Mensinga" in 1882. In fact Hesse invented two occlusive devices, the large and the small Mensinga Pessary which eventually evolved into the diaphragm and the cervical cap, respectively.

> The term "Dutch cap" is significant. Holland was for many years the only country in the world where birth control was officially approved. In 1882, the year after Mensinga's invention, Dr Aletta Jacobs opened in Amsterdam the world's first birth-control clinic. Within a few years Holland had thirty such clinics in operation.[10]

Margaret Sanger began by prescribing the small pessary, but eventually elected to follow Dutch practice, without informing her clients or anyone else about the reasons for the change, which was perhaps because the effectiveness of the diaphragm had been demonstrated in the controlled use of them by clinic attenders, whereas use of the cervical cap had never been institutionalised. It may well be that the casualness of the Lambert approach was their downfall. The popularisation of the term "Dutch cap" for what was not a cap at all meanwhile obscured the existence of a genuine cap.

How it happened that the diaphragm replaced the cap in English clinics is not at all clear. The Malthusian League opened a clinic eight months after Marie Stopes under the direction of Norman Haire who was experienced in the prescription of the diaphragm, which Marie Stopes opposed on rather sketchy grounds, preferring "the small check pessary she had designed herself, after French models, and christened the 'Pro-Race' cap."[11] Why Lambert's home-grown product had fallen from favour is not obvious; perhaps Dr Stopes had simply recommended improvements on the basic model, which now comes in two models and three sizes, as well as in two alternative versions for women who have suffered cervical or vaginal damage in childbirth or have other abnormalities. All these can still be had from Lamberts Ltd who are still doing business at the old address.

It is possible that the cervical cap suffered from the way it was catapulted into the limelight by Marie Stopes' unsuccessful libel action against Halliday Sutherland in 1923, when all kinds of vague assertions, including that women could not fit it on and that it occluded discharges from the womb, were uttered with all the power of deluded authority – as they are still.[12] However, Stopes herself must bear some of the blame for her rejection of other methods of contraception was hasty, prejudiced and downright irrational. When Dr Helena Wright, the medical missionary and pioneer of family planning in Britain, asked Stopes if no other cap but the small "Pro-Race" that she advocated and inserted would do, Stopes replied that all other sorts caused cancer, an opinion for which she had no evidence whatsoever.[13]

In 1930 a number of rival birth-control clinics banded together to form the National Birth Control Association (later the Family Planning Association) and in their clinics the diaphragm was the preferred method.

> Marie clung doggedly to the small, high-domed pessary. Her exaggerated claims for its success, based as they were on inadequate follow-up procedures, made her something of a laughing-stock in medical circles.[14]

Adequate follow-up procedures, it must be realised, were the exception rather than the rule, and the failure of other clinics to find the same low rates that Stopes claimed is not simply explained by the fact that if a patient did not return to report a failure. Stopes assumed that no failure had occurred. Diaphragm failures are chiefly caused by inefficient or irregular use, as well as the tendency of the diaphragm to become displaced during protracted or violent or intermittent intercourse. Also the diaphragm must be regularly renewed. It is in the nature of the cervical cap which was used by many women for a lifetime that the users rarely returned to the clinic, for they did not need new prescriptions. Among the scores of women who have recounted their effective use of the cervical cap to me there are many who went to family-planning clinics for replacements after loss or accidental damage and only then discovered that they could not find a replacement; when they were directed to use the diaphragm they all found it inferior, some disgustingly so. Because it is not inserted in anticipation of intercourse, the cap is in fact less likely to be associated with contraceptive failure than the diaphragm; this important difference may cancel out any difference in mechanical efficiency, which, in any case, has never been demonstrated. Many diaphragm users are continually uncertain as to whether they have inserted the device correctly; in the case of the cap the correct fit can be positively demonstrated because it is quite difficult to dislodge the device once it is in place, that is, the cap fits positively in a way that the diaphragm which simply exerts pressure on the mobile vaginal walls cannot.

By the nineteen-fifties the cap was past history. A woman embarking upon sexual activity who desired contraceptive protection found that her choice was limited to pessaries of one sort or another, all relatively unpleasant and ineffective, the condom, unpleasant but effective, and the diaphragm, which by now was being used in conjunction with spermicidal creams and gels which were also designed to be effective if used independently of their rubber raft. Some gynaecologists recommended smearing the spermicide all over the diaphragm, some agreed that a teaspoonful in the centre, which might coincide with the cervix, would suffice while the hapless user was only too well aware that the more spermicide was lathered about, the more slippery the diaphragm and the less her vaginal sensation. There had to be a better way. The Pill was anxiously expected long before it came.

The British Family Planning Association still lists the cervical cap as an approved and preferred method, provided it is manufactured by Lamberts of Dalston, whose quality-control methods have been found satisfactory. In practice, clinic attendants are loth to fit them and tend to discourage acceptors. In a recent case of which I have personal knowledge, the client was obliged to insist that she wanted a cervical cap, was told she did not know what it was, insisted that she did, was told that she would be unable to learn how to insert it or get it out. The nurse had great difficulty in doing either, and communicated her ineptitude to the client, who went home with a diaphragm which she eventually threw away. In the USA the FDA insists that current statistics on the cap's effectiveness must be gathered before distribution will be approved: a 1978 shipment of caps was seized on the grounds that it was "mislabelled and lacks caution"; they were considered acceptable for "investigational use only" but the period of grace expired in 1981. In October 1980, the cervical cap was available from the New Hampshire Feminist Health Center; 30,000 to 40,000 American women were estimated to be using the cap at that time. Michelle Harrison at Princeton has also been studying the cap. The results of a study in Brookline, Massachusetts, have been disappointing but research in caps and related barrier methods continues.[15]

The story of Russell Marker's extraction of Diosgenin from yams began as the search for a commercial way to produce progesterone. In 1948 Marker left the company he had set up in order to exploit his discovery, leaving his successor, Dr George Rosencrantz, to rediscover his method, and to go a step further in discovering how to synthesise the male hormone, testosterone, from the same yams. Dr Carl Djerassi was invited by Syntex, as the yam-collecting enterprise was called, to find a way to synthesise the miracle steroid, cortisone, from the same source. He used the resources and the opportunity to work on his own pet project, the finding of a more cost-effective way of producing the female sex hormone, oestradiol, than deriving it from the urine of pregnant mares. He has recounted the story of the experimental route that he took in his book, *The Politics of Contraception*.[16] Suffice it to say that on 15 October 1951, Luis Miramontes, working in the Syntex laboratories under the direction of Djerassi and Rosencrantz, succeeded in synthesising 19-nor-17α-ethynyltestosterone, generically known as *norethisterone* or *norethindrone*. Djerassi notes proudly, "it is the only patent for a drug listed in the National Inventors Hall of Fame in Washington."[17] At the same time, chemists at Searle were working on the same problem, and in August 1953, well over a year after Djerassi had sent a sample of his product to Gregory Pincus at the Worcester Foundation in Shrewsbury, Searle patented a very similar compound known as *norethynodrel*. It was Pincus, working now for Searle, who saw the possibility of using the synthetic oestrogen as a fertility inhibitor. Although Djerassi's account reveals his own dissatisfaction at the relative unimportance given to his own work and that of his fellow chemists at Syntex, he admits:

> Not in our wildest dreams did we imagine that eventually this substance would become the active progestational ingredient of over 50 percent of currently used oral contraceptives.[18]

Pincus, on the other hand, had been looking for a safe, reliable, convenient contraceptive since 1945. The work, based on a successful 1937 experiment to suppress ovulation in rabbits by administration of progesterone, was stepped up in 1953. Progesterone was the drug of choice, because the carcinogenic properties of oestrogens had been noticed in 1939, and so it was that Pincus, whose early years had been spent at the Worcester Foundation for Experimental Biology in the edifying pastime of trying to transplant rabbit foetuses, teamed up for respectability with John Rock, the Catholic chief of Obstetrics and Gynaecology at Harvard and ran the first tests to see if progesterone would suppress ovulation in humans at the Reproductive Study Centre at Boston's Free Hospital. For Rock, who was trying to use the hormone as a way of combating infertility, the results were encouraging; four of his patients conceived after completing the treatment. Pincus was not so happy.

> For one thing, about one in five of the women had begun to bleed before the end of their monthly cycles. Also it had still been necessary for the women to swallow massive daily doses of progesterone: the dose was still 300 milligrammes. And worst of all, as an ovulation-preventer the progesterone was far from one hundred percent efficient.[19]

Then Pincus's colleague, Dr Min-chueh Chang, began to test the efficiency of the synthetic oestrogens produced by Syntex and Searle; both were efficient ovulation-suppressants, with the Searle compound requiring only half the dosage of the Syntex version. It was Pincus, with the help of Margaret Sanger and the patroness she found for him, Mrs Stanley McCormick, who presented the idea of "hormonal" contraception, with Rock and Chang, at the fifth Conference of the IPPF in Tokyo. Their research was presented diffidently, and the scientific observers were unimpressed.[20] The use of steroids to suppress ovulation was nothing new: the only novelty was the method of administration – by mouth. Everyone with any knowledge of human biochemistry could see at once that suppression of ovulation was a serious business which involved the disruption of the entire endocrine system; the desirability of the daily gulping of millions of steroid pills by millions of women for decades was practically invisible at that stage, although Pincus's motives for choosing to unveil the idea at an international conference seem pretty obvious. (Ironically, Japan is the one place in the world where the steroid pill is illegal to this day.)

Further tests were needed. Pincus and Rock got together a group of student volunteers and female psychotics and – just for good measure – a group of male psychotics, and administered norethynedrol to all of them, for five and a half months. They knew that the progestin would suppress ovulation, and they expected no side-effects, and found none. Pincus moved immediately to the area for which an oral contraceptive had always been intended, women in poor countries "where the population problem was at its worst". Like Stopes and Sanger and Mrs McCormick and all the birth controllers in history, Pincus was convinced that the poor were multiplying too fast. On America's doorstep there was a whole colony of C3 parents, in Stopesian terminology: Puerto Rico.

Dr Chang was uncomfortably aware that the administration of large amounts of synthetic progesterone, which turned out to be adulterated with initially unwanted oestrogen, by mouth in daily doses was an extraordinarily inefficient way of inducing temporary sterility. As Pincus had said in his paper at the Tokyo conference:

> The delicately balanced sequential processes involved in normal mammalian reproduction are clearly attackable. Our object is to disrupt them in such a way that no physiological cost to the organism is involved.[21]

They succeeded in disrupting the sequential processes, but at terrific cost to the organism. The inducement of a state of mock-pregnancy which upset the whole endocrine system by the use of synthetic analogues of natural secretions, not themselves identical with the natural substances and therefore requiring administration in high doses to achieve the same effect, is rather like using a steamroller to crush a frog. Pincus was a good endocrinologist, as endocrinologists went, but he simply did not know enough about the interlocking patterns of sequential processes which make up the female cycle to justify his optimism that throwing his pharmacological spanner into the works would not eventually harm the organism. We have since learned that there are no wonder-drugs, that every decision to use a potent medication must be weighed carefully with its advantages seen in relation to its disadvantages – there is no point in yelling for a perfect pill or in complaining that we wuz robbed by Searle and Upjohn. The present state of our ignorance about the Pill has been summed up by a biochemist who has no axe to grind:

> Steroidal contraceptives have now been administered for more than twenty years and world usage was recently estimated at over eighty million women ... one would expect our understanding of the clinical pharmacology of contraceptive steroids to be comprehensive and sound. Yet, rather the opposite appears to be true ... At present relatively little is known about the exact influence of a multitude of factors governing the bio-availability and metabolic rate of synthetic steroids, e.g., drug formulation, route of administration, absorption processes, entero-hepatic recycling, binding to plasma proteins, catabolic events, modes of excretion, etc. Even less data are available on the relationship between steroidal pharmokinetics and such variables as ethnic background, nutrition, climate, disease states, simultaneous administration of non-contraceptive drugs, etc.[22]

What this adds up to is that we do not know what the processes are by which the body is affected by the powerful chemicals or where they end up; oral administration has actually had the effect of disseminating the steroids' activity far more widely in the body, and may also produce different compounds through the processes of digestion and absorption.

If the right biological pathway could be found, contraceptive steroids could be administered in such a way that they acted directly on one of the processes necessary for fecundation, instead of acting on the whole system. The fact that "intravaginal rather than oral administration leads to an increase in bioavailability"[23] probably means that most of the steroid we take by mouth is at best wasted and at worst does mischief unrelated to its intended function. After all, this is no more than commonsense – if you want something to work on the reproductive system, why would you think it best to put it in the mouth? Mysteriously, it was the very distance between the act of swallowing a pill and the freedom to enjoy sexual intercourse at will which was its main attraction. A progesterone pessary would never have conquered the world.

The great red herring in discussions of the pill's side-effects is cancer. A classic example of the use of the spectre of cancer to sidestep all the rest of the evidence against the pill is Carl Djerassi's chapter on it in *The Politics of Contraception*, which quite justly points that tests on cancer-prone beagles are useless in determining carcinogenicity in humans, that huge numbers of carefully matched women would have to take the pill over long periods if any rise in cancer incidence were to be noted, that the pill may have more to do with the inhibition of cancer than causing it, while he admits with crystalline scrupulousness that there does seem to be a connection between the ingestion of contraceptive steroids and liver tumour.[24] If the argument against the pill were to be expressed solely in terms of increased risk of death, it would be obvious that taking the pill every day is some thousands of times safer than getting into a car every day, or lighting a cigarette every day. The car and the cigarette both carry a risk of death, and both are tolerable notwithstanding, because of the contribution that they make to life and because the damage they might cause is not transmitted to posterity. No woman yet born is willing to sacrifice the future of her children and their children to her desire for aesthetic and unhampered sexual activity. The problem with the pill is that we simply do not know what the deal is. What are we risking for what?

The fearful responsibility that a woman feels for generations yet unborn is not felt only by sophisticated women – indeed, it may be a greater source of anxiety to women with a stronger sense of the continuum between their own behaviour and that of generations to come.

A woman who uses the pill is afraid she will bear a sterile child: from her mother's milk comes the baby's blood and from his blood originates his semen. And in his blood will remain the chemical made for the prevention of pregnancy. Boys and girls alike, the Pill will make them sterile. And sterility is considered by us a punishment of God.[25]

In our present state of ignorance of the biological pathways travelled by the contraceptive pill and the mode of eventual secretion of the steroids, we cannot smile at the anxiety of this Arab woman. The DES nightmare is only now approaching its dreadful climax as the sons and daughters of the women who were exposed try to cope with their fate. Diethylstil-bestrol is a non-steroid sex hormone which was mistakenly administered to "nearly six million women between 1943 and 1959" in the drive for bigger and better babies; even without considering the four in each thousand DES daughters who will have vaginal or cervical cancer before the age of thirty, the consequences for their sons are disastrous, just as the Arab woman feared.

> Of the first 42 DES sons who were examined and compared to other young men of the same age, 10 had genital abnormalities, including undersized penises (2 cases), varicocele (or enlargement of a vein in the testicle) (1 case), abnormally small testes (2 cases), testicular mass (1 case) and the same cysts of the epididymus that had long since been demonstrated in mice. By contrast only one genital abnormality, a varicocele, was observed in any of the 37 controls.[26]

Both daughters and sons of DES takers are four times more likely to be infertile than others. Birth defects in the children of oral contraceptive users seem only to result if contraceptive steroids are still circulating in the body at the time of conception, although there is some evidence that children of women who have *ever* used oral contraceptives may be less bright than others. Gross visible defects such as limb reductions and triploidy do occur. Three doctors from the Vanderbilt University School of Medicine in Nashville, Tennessee, have suggested that there may be an Embryo-fetal Exogenous Sex Steroid Exposure Syndrome. In a paper presented to the twenty-eighth annual meeting of the American Society of Human Genetics in 1977 they described a group of children whose mothers had taken some form of sex steroid in pregnancy:

> Seven of the nine children were males, and six of them had hypospadias or even more severe genital ambiguity. Six of the nine were also mentally delayed. On physical re-evaluation their faces were suggestively alike. There were facial elongation with frontal bossing, primary telecanthis, and downward slanting palpebral fissures. A broad, flat, nose bridge with pouting lower lip and blunt, square chin were frequently noted.[27]

The published paper was illustrated with photographs of deformed baby bottoms with a deep sacral trench, minute genitals, and bewildered or affectionate or worried or innocently smiling baby faces, quite unaware of the mark of norgestrel, or ethinylestradiol, medroxyprogesterone, clomiphene or premarin, 6-Dehydroxyprogesterone or simply don't-remember-what-steroid written across their bulging foreheads.

There are various ways in which an embryo or a foetus can be exposed to sex steroids *in utero*, if the mother has just come off the pill, if she takes them as part of a pregnancy test or as a morning after "contraceptive" (i.e. abortifacient), or if they are erroneously administered during pregnancy. There is reason to believe that the earlier the exposure, the worse its effects. Such a connection is not in the least far-fetched; one wonders indeed if the marketing of high doses of sex hormones as pregnancy tests was not a disguised way of selling do-it-yourself abortion kits. The instructions for the use of Primodos are simply too good to be true.

> 1 tablet on each of two consecutive days. Bleeding follows in 3–6 (rarely as long as ten) days, if there is no pregnancy. An existing pregnancy is unaffected by Primodos.[28]

In 1967 Dr Isobel Gal, a research worker at Queen Mary's Hospital for Children at Carshalton in England, found that the mothers of children with spina bifida were twice as likely as other mothers to have used a hormone pregnancy test. The British research director of Schering, the makers of Primodos, asked a mathematician to study the occurrence of birth defects and sales of Primodos to see if he could find a correlation. He did. The German parent company refused to take any action, despite the concern of their British employees, a concern well founded, for four out of ten women who thought they might be pregnant were using the homone tests. The tests performed no useful function, because there were already more practical urine tests available, but although a survey for the Royal College of General Practitioners came up with more evidence of the damage done by the hormone tests in 1969, Schering refused to withdraw them, despite considerable pressure from their English staff. The French Company, Roussel, which also marketed a hormone pregnancy test, had withdrawn it and were using the steroid only for treatment of amenorrhea, but Schering still resisted. In 1970 the Swedes banned hormone pregnancy testing, followed by the Finns in 1971. In 1978 two hormone pregnancy tests, Primodos and British Drug Houses' Secodryl were still available although a survey carried out at the Hebrew University of Jerusalem on 16,000 mothers from 1974–6 had confirmed that exposure to sex steroids *in utero* causes birth defects. The survey recommends that women cease taking the pill two or three months before trying to conceive and use some other method of contraception until they are "de-toxed" and cautions that women over thirty-five or who are underweight seem to have more difficulty in eliminating the steroids – another indication of the ramifications of the biological pathways travelled by steroids ingested orally.[29]

It is relatively easy to make the connection between medications taken immediately prior to and during a pregnancy and a birth defect but the example of DES seems to suggest that we must take a very much longer view, for the sequelae of DES lay dormant for ten years. The FDA banned the use of hormone pregnancy tests in 1976, but it has not banned the administration of oral contraceptives to lactating women. What their embryos escaped may be lying in wait for them later on as they take in mothers' milk laced with synthetic steroids.

It is at least a possibility that such exposure could compromise the protective effect of antibodies in mother's milk and the development of the immune system. Nothing about the present situation is reassuring, neither our ignorance of the way that sex steroids work, nor the vast masses of information which do not add up to anything like a clear picture of pros or cons, nor the strange reluctance of drug companies to act on the findings of their own researchers. The unthinkable possibility remains that within the murk of our incomprehension some monstrous plague is waiting to make its appearance in the bodies of our children. No individual woman can hope to shake this mass of floating material into a clear view. She must make her decision whether or not to contracept by the oral route according to her own observations and her gut feelings. When an Italian neighbour was asking me if I could advise her daughter who had got pregnant twice in two years of married life, and whose husband was therefore considered maladroit, I suggested the pill. She shook her head slowly. *"Non é genuina."* I was about to remonstrate, when I remembered what she had last said that about, the defoliant, 245T. For twenty years she and her fellow peasants resisted DDT, and still have birds and butterflies as a consequence.

The individual woman must make what she can of the remote chance of catastrophe to herself and her children if she takes the pill, and she must then address herself to the much more relevant problem of how she feels while taking it. The commonest effect of steroid munching is depression, from mild to clinical.[30] Depression is one symptom which utterly destroys the quality of life (and with it, sex) so it would appear that the thirty per cent of pill-takers who are depressed should throw away their pills and abstain periodically instead. The fact that they usually do not throw away their pills is further evidence of the malaise which underlies much oral contraceptive practice. For far too many women the oral contraceptive is just another version of the line of least resistance. They do not make love when they feel like it, and cannot exert any influence on the frequency of sexual relations or the form they take. For them oral contraception does not open any vistas of new freedom, but simply removes one of the inconveniences of their enforced receptivity. For other women the threat of unwanted pregnancy is so paralysing that it destroys their sexual pleasure even when they are not depressed; throwing away the Pill would only work for them if they were sure that other techniques of birth control were both available and equally effective. Barbara Seaman's brilliant analysis of the effects of progestins on nutrition and the way to combat them might also stop many women from throwing away their pills. It is worth remarking, too, that the incidence of birth defects in children conceived by women coming off the pill may have more to do with the vitamin deficiencies listed by the Doctors Briggs, "involving vitamin C, riboflavine, thiamine; vitamin B6, vitamin B12 and E", than the direct action of the steroids themselves. So for the woman who is willing to monitor her own nutritional status and supplement the Pill with a flotilla of other pills, the deal may still be a deal.[31]

Other common side-effects, in Djerassi's terse formulation, "thrombo-embolic complications, hypertension, and reported carbohydrate, protein and lipid metabolic changes" are less easy to assess.[32] Women suffering from the first two would be taking an intolerable risk if they continued the use of oral contraception. The meaning of the metabolic changes is less clear; fifteen percent of women on the pill become diabetic or peridiabetic and a pill-user should be tested for glucose tolerance once a year. Many women suffering metabolic change have to struggle to keep their weight down while they are on the pill, and find at the same time that they feel bloated and sluggish.

Conclusive evidence of the effect of oral contraception on the sex drive is practically impossible to find. Many new pill-users are also in the new phase of a relationship, and in any case revel in their new freedom from fear, so evidence about enhancement of sex is not significant; while all long-time users can probably all remember a time when they "got more out of it". Libido is far too complex an entity and far too sensitive to myriad factors to be quantifiable in the experimental situation. If we limit ourselves to the kinds of facts which can be observed and measured, we come up with some which have an obvious effect on sexual activity.

> Our research on 100 users of an estroprogestative minipill, in coded questionnaire form, which identified symptoms the women thought they had, indicated the following: 10 consider that they now have more satisfying sexual intercourse; 14 find that their relations are less satisfying ... In our opinion the latter cases seem to prove an indirect, organic effect on the sexual compatibility between partners, as well as on mycosis, vaginal dryness, etc., that we encounter frequently.[33]

Mycosis is considered an unimportant side-effect of changes in the vaginal environment produced by the action of the contraceptive pill, whereas it is common and persistent and extremely damaging to the activity which the pill ought to enhance, sexual intercourse. Fungal infections can plague women, causing discomfort, pain and disgust, costing time and money as they search for effective treatments, inflict the treatments on their unfortunate partners as well as themselves, and eventually manage to clear up the discharge and the smell only to find it returning at the first sign of unusual sexual activity or tiredness – or without apparent rhyme or reason. Impoverishment of vaginal secretion impoverishes sexual response, and may even have subtle and far-reaching effects upon sexual attraction. It certainly increases the risk of trauma to the vagina and the incidence of painful intercourse and post-coital irritations. The risk of local infection is much higher, for the vagina is no longer the healthy self-cleansing organ which it must be to fulfil its sexual function adequately.[34] The risk of exposure of the cervix to carcinogens and other organisms associated with the penis must be increased by the destruction of these natural defence mechanisms, and thus the pill may be an accomplice in the rising incidence of cervical cancer in many areas. This is Jean Cohen's review of the evidence which is almost unanimous on these points, as on few others.

> A number of direct effects, although varying with the products and the dosage employed, can be identified; the mucus of the vagina has a luteal, slightly congestive, sometimes atrophic appearance, occasionally accompanied by a decrease in the amount of secretion; cervical mucus is poor, coagulated and not very ropy, except when sequential pills are used; there is bleeding and spotting between periods; finally the appearance of recurrent vaginal mycoses was mentioned by a great many authors.[35]

He summarises the whole picture of the effects of oral contraceptives on sexual behaviour thus:

> Present information does not allow definite conclusions about the frequency of positive or negative effects oral contraception might have on sexual behaviour. The existence of ill-effects is beyond doubt, although the predominance of the biochemical or the psychological mechanism is not understood.[36]

The pill is usually only negatively inculpated in the epidemic of venereal disease because it does not function as a barrier between cervix and penis, but in at least one case it played a far more active role. *Candida albicans* existed as a member of the flora of a healthy vagina, but the changes in the sugar balance of the vagina consequent on pill-taking transformed it into a destructive pathogen causing painful inflammations in both men and women and completely changing the nature of sexually transmitted diseases, for *Candida* can become a pathogen in totally monogamous people. Recently candidiasis has been isolated as the cause of episodes of acute pelvic inflammation.[37] Researchers have found a positive correlation between the use of sex steroids and chlamydial infection as well.[38] It seems possible that the action of the sex steroids affects the body's immune system, impairing the formation of antigens, as has been the case in long-term use of other steroids. At this stage the evidence is largely impressionistic. Dr Ellen C. Grant of the Neurology Department of Charing Cross Hospital wrote to *The Lancet* in September, 1978:

> The evidence is accumulating that oral contraceptive use is more toxic than smoking and oral contraceptive use seems to produce severe migraine and multiple food allergies in a much shorter time. This effect may be related to alterations in liver function.

For many years there has been some concern about the pill's effect upon subsequent reproductive performance, but as the pill is seldom, if ever, the only insult delivered to the reproductive system of its user the evidence is bound to be inconclusive, not least because fertility is not established definitively before the oral contraceptive is prescribed – there being no way of ascertaining fertility except by a pregnancy. Barbara Seaman gives a figure of 5% sterility in women ceasing pill use, which is rather lower than it is in the general population; sexually active people are at greater risk of sterilising disease than inactive people who are unlikely to be using the pill, so all things considered incidence of secondary infertility in pill-users could well be higher than that of the general population without the pill itself being inculpated as a fertility destroyer. However, it would be very surprising if administration of sex steroids to women who were yet to arrive at physiological maturity, that is, at the stage in their development when they ovulated regularly, had no effect upon the maturation of the complex sequence of biochemical processes which assures fecundability and implantation. While it is painfully obvious that our youngest women need contraceptive protection, it seems hardly less obvious that sex steroids are the wrong protection. We cannot afford to trivialise a medication as mysterious and powerful as the contraceptive steroid; if some delayed consequence of its action should make its appearance sometime in the next twenty or thirty years we want to have some chance of tracking down those of our children who are at risk. Even when doctors have to keep records such tracing can be extremely difficult, as researchers found when they went looking first for the DES daughters and then for the DES sons. If we were to put oral contraceptives on sale in supermarkets, we would lose all chance of monitoring their effects. By putting them on sale in supermarkets we would be making them available to the teenagers who are not yet committed to sexual activity, who are likely to use them haphazardly, to begin using them in mid-cycle and to take them in large doses as a post-coital measure, and to use them in conjunction with other drugs.

Yet, contraceptive pills can be bought from shopkeepers in Antigua, Bangladesh, Chile, Fiji, Hong Kong, South Korea, Pakistan, Panama and the Philippines, and in Sri Lanka and Thailand from nurses and midwives. It might be argued that over-the-counter sales are less problematic where unmarried people do not engage in sexual activity, but in so far as this may be true it is counterbalanced by the much more serious health problems that accompany pill use in poor countries. Dosage of steroids is critical; doses which are correctly calculated for women on a good diet with a certain body-weight can produce the symptoms of hyper-oestrogenism in a tiny emaciated woman; the drug disperses more inefficiently in the metabolism of an undernourished person. It used to be thought that high blood pressure and the disposition to thrombo-embolic disorders were rare in skinny, hard-working, vegetarian populations, but such is apparently not the case; some groups have a higher genetic pre-disposition to these disorders. Moreover the tendency seems to be, apart from the contemptible and unscrupulous practice of dumping of dis-continued high-oestrogen pills in public programmes in poor countries, to prescribe ovulation suppressants rather than mini-pills because of the likelihood of break-through bleeding and disruption of the cycle if a few mini-pills are missed.

Community-based distribution of oral contraceptives is one way to avoid the waste of the small family-planning aid budget in the administration of unwieldy, badly designed and very costly experimental programmes, but it may prove to be a short cut to nowhere. Dr Henry Moseley of Johns Hopkins noted that 90% of pill-users in Bangladesh were lactating mothers and 80% of them reject the pill within three months; their average body weight is 92 lb and the depletion of essential vitamins induced by the pill is simply intolerable. The paradoxical result of this pattern of pill use is an increase in pregnancies and a shortening of the inter-birth interval, a potentially disastrous situation.[39] To reflect that the pushing of unsuitable pharmacological contraception has probably disrupted a practice of abstinence during lactation which is now considered old-fashioned and unnecessary is extremely depressing, to say the least.

Population Services International "presents" Maya contraceptive pills in Bangladesh, advertising it in newspapers thus:

> From dreams to reality ... A reality that could remain as sweet as dreams once you make Maya part of your way of life. Maya the highly reliable imported birth-control pill will help keep the woman in you alive and young. Maya also ensures menstrual regularity, relieves you from cramps and discomforts and improves your complexion. Maya, the choice of millions. Now in this New Petite Pack. Buy a pack today.[40]

The pills contain 1 mg of norethindrone and 0.05 mg of mestranol; the Chinese low-dose pill contains 0.635 mg of norethindrone and 0.35 of mestranol; low-dose pills in England make do with 0.5 mg of norethisterone. Medium doses, approved but not preferred by the FPA, may range from 1 mg to 4 mg of norethisterone. It is a fair bet that there are more metabolic effects than the mythical "live woman in you" and that the effects on the complexion are of the order of a muddy mark around eye-sockets and mouth. In 1979 Stephen Minkin, Chief of UNICEF's Nutri-tion Programme in Bangladesh, attacked USAID which distributes pills through PSI in thirty countries to the tune of 130,000,000 cycles, all acquired from Syntex with the taxpayers' money, in an article for *Health Right* magazine. The dust has not settled yet.

There can be no doubt that health care will have to be administered in poor countries by paramedics, if only because so much of the care is routine hygiene and because so much of the intervention is in the nature of first aid. There is much to be said for involving midwives and other villagers in counselling for family planning and in distribution of birth-control equipment. Of course pan-sellers and door-to-door salesmen can sell condoms, the more publicly the better. They can offer prizes for the chief condom buyers, if they choose. But it is wrong to give them oral contraceptives to sell, because there is absolutely no chance that they will monitor the buyers, who are more likely to be husbands than the women who will have to eat them. Pan-sellers are poor men too; every sale helps them to stay at subsistence level. It is inhuman to expect them to refuse a potential customer, or even not to make absurd claims for the product – after all, even PSI succumbed to that temptation. It is idiotic to expect them to conduct interrogations intended to reveal a wife's health status. The contraceptive pill is far too potent and enigmatic in its operation to be so casually treated but not so unmanageable that it could not be made available more consistently to poor acceptors. It should not be beyond our ingenuity to devise dosage systems that can be tailored to fit the recipients, instead of prescribing a one-size pill as if steroid dosage were as elastic as pantyhose, and to devise a monitoring system which an illiterate midwife could handle. Whether we scatter them broadcast by distributing them free to people who don't want them, or exploit the greed of middlemen to sell them to people who could find another way, or have expensively trained and massively discontented allopaths prescribing them with all due pomp, makes very little difference if they are the wrong pills to begin with.

The story of hormonal contraception is not complete until the chapter of errors with regard to the injectables has been added.

In 1953 Karl Junkmann discovered that by esterifying progestogen alcohol a long-acting injectable could be produced. Junkmann *et al.* synthesised norethindrone esters and Upjohn and Co. synthesised medroxyprogesterone acetate. Initial studies of the injectables were first conducted in Peru, Egypt and Europe. Depo-provera was first introduced as a treatment for threatened and habitual abortions and for endometriosis in 1960. In 1963, clinical trials started on the use of Depo-provera for conception control.[41]

The drawbacks with Depo-Provera (DMPA) are the same as the drawbacks which attend all continued administration of progestogens, namely, irregular bleeding and "spotting" in about 20% of users in the first year diminishing to 10% in the second year, but this disadvantage is aggravated by the fact that a slow-release injection cannot be withdrawn if the injectee suffers adverse reactions. The progestogens have a considerable advantage in that they are free of the side-effects caused by the oestrogens. They prevent conception by suppressing ovulation in some cases, by causing changes in the uterine lining which render implantation impossible and by causing changes in the cervical mucus. Weight gain, raised blood-glucose levels, nausea, dizziness, headache, skin pigmentation changes, painful menstruation and loss of interest in sex have all been reported by users of Depo-Provera. For these reasons, Depo has been considered unsuitable for the British or the American market, although it may be used in Britain to inhibit the development of endometrial carcinomas, and on women who have been vaccinated for rubella or whose husbands have been vasectomised. Opposition to the drug was stimulated in Britain by the disclosure that it was being selectively used at doctors' own discretion upon unwitting patients, mostly Asian. Some suggestion of carcinogenicity was found, in that over 15,000 women/years of use, 35 cases of carcinoma-in-situ of the cervix were found – and beagles on Depo developed lumpy breasts. Another progestogen preparation, the chlormadinone acetate mini-pill, was withdrawn from testing on the sole grounds that it caused changes in the mammary tissue of beagles.[42] Ironically perhaps, Depo had already been widely used before the results of these tests brought it under suspicion, and not solely in the less-developed countries. Doctors in New Zealand were routinely prescribing it in the late sixties. First-hand user reports I gathered in 1970 were good and great things were expected for it.[43]

In 1978 two rhesus monkeys who had been given high doses of DMPA for ten years developed endometrial cancer. The tests had been carried out by Upjohn at the instance of WHO but surprisingly perhaps after considering the data and the histopathology specimens WHO recommended that the drug be used without "undue concern" in studies and national family programmes. Dr Colin McCord, Chief Technical Adviser on Mother and Child Health and Family Planning to UNFPA in Dacca, was dissatisfied with the conflicting accounts of the significance of the monkey study: he wrote to his colleague Bernard Kervin in April 1980 summarising his reasons for concern, namely, that DMPA is secreted in mothers' milk and no one knows how that will affect the baby's development, that the drug can be administered in error during pregnancy, that WHO should not have ordered the screening test on the monkeys if there was no intention of heeding its findings, especially as cancer of the uterus in monkeys had never been reported before, and the etiology of the cancer in the stimulation of atrophic endometrium by the action of the steroid is not in itself surprising. His recommendations were three:

Do not start any new patients on the drug. Continue old patients but follow them closely.[44] Do not let anyone take the drug for more than three years.

But DMPA had been used widely for more than ten years. An obvious place to undertake epidemiological studies was Thailand, but the only existing study produced fewer cases of endometrial cancer than would have been expected even in an Asian population not using Depo-provera;

instead of setting aside the study as inconclusive and misleading, the conclusions were published over the signatures of three reputable scientists. While Dr McCord was struggling to give the best advice he could to the Bangladesh government:

> ... I don't think that the small increment in fertility control which will result from use of this drug justifies the possibility that we might be responsible for an epidemic of uterine cancer ten to twenty years from now. Such an epidemic would be a disaster, not only for the women involved, but also for the credibility of population-control programmes,[45]

other workers distressed at the fumblings of Upjohn and WHO, and the reverberations of feminist campaigning against the drug in the developed world, stopped giving their clients Depo, even at their request.

In 1980 workers for the Bangladeshi organisation, Gonoshastaya Kendra, described their dilemma regarding DMPA in these terms:

> Since beginning use of Depo-Provera at GK in 1974, we have had 7,358 acceptors. This was to test the suitability of the drug for Bangladeshi women. During this period of use our findings were consistent with the observations reported in the *British Medical Journal* of "menstrual chaos," and in just the past eight months we had eleven cases of severe P/V bleeding which actually required hospitalisation.
>
> We became worried by some of the questions raised by Steve Minkin regarding immuno-suppression and effects on child-growth in Depo-Provera users. Also to date there have been no scientific studies done measuring the prolactin to decide the issue of increased/decreased lactation.
>
> With no clear answers on these and other questions and in view of Bangladesh's government's decision to start a national programme, (as a result of international aid pressure) in which there are bound to be abuses, a meeting of our health workers in mid-November 1979 decided to stop Depo-Provera.
>
> By withdrawing this method we don't know if we have helped our women or not. Despite the various side-effects they still prefer Depo-Provera to the Pill or the IUD whose complications they must now face. Because of past misuse and no follow-up care with the IUD there is tremendous resistance to this method.[46]

The threat of annihilation of the Khmer population was still on the front pages of Western newspapers when in March 1980, ICRC report No. 6 on "Medical and public health surveillance, Sa-Kaew, Kamput, Khao-I-Dang and 'the Border'," published its finding that 20 to 30% of all married Khmer women of reproductive age living in refugee camps in Thailand were pregnant. The Thai government had expressed its unwillingness to support an exploding population of idle refugees; the Khmers, after five years of high infant mortality in Kampuchea and the separation of husbands and wives under the Pol Pot regime, were anxious to rebuild their families, as soon as the women recovered from the stress, diseases

and malnutrition that had accompanied them on their exodus from their
homeland.

> Uncontrolled fertility amongst refugees in Thailand can be a sensitive political
> and emotional issue, evoking radical rhetoric, and sometimes actions, from
> influential Thai leaders. The most recent occurrences in Kamput bear
> testimony to this fact, where a rigorous family planning programme is reported
> to have surfaced, following the arrival of startlingly high numbers of pregnant
> women from Kao-I-Dang.[47]

In April, the Kamput medical coordinator, S. Rye, made a strangely
twisted attempt to describe what was going on:

> A further series of 96 injections of Depo-provera have been given this week.
> The impression maintained by the Khmer refugees is that these injections are
> compulsory. The Thai Marine Officer in charge of the garrison has stated
> firmly that these injections are not compulsory. However, it is in my view
> from observing the proceedings that these injections are compulsory, in fact,
> even though the Thai authorities maintain that this is no longer the case. The
> women are summoned to attend for the injection; any defaulters are chased
> up by the Thai authorities and given the injection. In any case, there is great
> need for the Khmer women to receive information and instruction concerning
> contraception.[48]

At a meeting of all the concerned "volags" (voluntary agencies) in
August, 1980, some rather less compromised information was forthcoming.

> It appears that the Thai military (according to information Dr Tom D'Agnes
> received from a concerned CONCERN nurse and Khmers on the spot) has
> begun "injecting all women, single, pregnant etc." "rounding them up with
> sticks" to receive an injection, reportedly a contraceptive. Even children
> received the injection and experienced the same symptoms as the women: "hot
> flushes." This has not been investigated with the local military authorities
> (who apparently would resent the interest) and no VOLAGS actually witnessed
> the events. But a related event a week earlier in Meirut may be ominously
> related: a physician from COERR Italy was quickly dismissed from the country
> following some disagreements about family planning. CBERS expressed grave
> concern that the military is prepared to implement involuntary population
> control given the high fertility of the Khmer population in Thailand. In some
> centers pregnancy rates are very high, and it is implied that some VOLAG
> groups have been deliberately sabotaging the efforts of CBERS to implement
> voluntary family planning.[49]

The point of the meeting was to get it across to the volags that indulging
in the DMPA controversy was inappropriate. The injections had been
widely used on Thais for ten years; the last thing the Thai authorities
wanted to hear was that it was not safe to use on Khmers. The attempt
to alert the Khmers to the dangers of indiscriminate use of DMPA was

seen by both the Thai authorities and the old hands as both misguided and mischievous. A leaflet in the Khmer language which said:

> You will receive 1 chicken if you come to get a contraceptive injection. If you are pregnant this injection will kill your baby and cause the excessive bleeding which will be very dangerous. If you are a breast-feeding mother and receive contraceptive injection it will stop your milk flow. You may receive this shot if you are pregnant or having a small baby but it may be very dangerous.[50]

had been circulating for some months. Acceptance of DMPA had declined.

To complicate matters further some of the volags were religious groups which did not support birth control of any kind, voluntary or involuntary. The other volags found themselves forced to mediate between authorities who wanted no Khmer babies born on Thai soil, and Khmer women who wanted their babies. Their leaders wanted them to protect the women from "involuntary family planning," but all they could really do was alert the Khmer women to the danger, and beg them to take pills and condoms instead of Depo. The compulsion was still there, but second-hand and inefficient. Dr A. G. Rangaraj, Senior Health Coordinator at the UN High Commission for Refugees Regional Office in Bangkok, described the forcible injection of DMPA in terms which indicate a hardening of attitude, warning that the military authorities might employ "techniques that family planning purists might consider "heavy-handed." Family planning purists thus are people who find the rounding up of single and pregnant women and children for contraceptive injections "heavy-handed."[51] Evidently Dr Rangaraj is not himself a purist. The Thai refugee camps offer the most dramatic example of the problems attached to the injectable contraceptives; a potential for abuse exists in every kind of clinical situation, abuse endangering a woman not only by administering the drug, but by failing to administer it.

Depo's high acceptance rate among poor people is due to many factors. First it is an injection, with all the kudos attaching to a method of administration which has been seen to work wonders. Second, it requires no bathroom and does not have to be stored away from rats and the children. It cannot be detected or destroyed or removed by a mother-in-law or a husband or anyone else. It is certainly true that the relative risks of side-effects and cancer are unlikely to have been explained properly, but as they are infinitesimal in real terms and even more minute in comparison with the hazards of pregnancy and childbirth, the Bengali acceptor of Depo may feel at least as inclined to take her chances as a Western smoker feels in ignoring warnings about lung cancer. In any case her chances of living long enough to die of cancer are slim, or, to put it more crudely, she would like the chance to die of cancer rather than one of the diseases associated with pregnancy and childbirth. On the one hand the opponent of Depo will argue that what is not good for

Western women is not good for any woman anywhere, and on the other the African peasant may argue that it is racist to suppose that she is not the best judge of her own situation.

If Depo-provera is to be campaigned against as a hazardous drug then all sex steroids will have to be given the same attention; again the problem seems very much to be one of dosage. The delays in return of fertility after a course of DMPA injections seem likely to be caused by systematic overdosing, especially as a delay of "a few weeks" in repeat injections apparently makes no difference to the cover. We must know more about the systematic administration of steroids, for such hit-and-miss treatment is simply not good enough. The problem is exacerbated by poor diet, irregular food supply and the depleting effects of lactation. The high rate of oral contraceptive discontinuation by lactating mothers suggests that there would be a parallel reaction to DMPA but the women cannot stop using it. However, there can be no doubt that many women ask for DMPA and many doctors working in the field ask for DMPA, in India, for example, where its use is not permitted. There seem to be as many arguments for smuggling DMPA as there are for banning it. However, the effects of synthetic progestogens in breast milk on suckling infants are utterly unknown and doctors I have spoken to in India and Colombia had given no thought to the matter. Women do not like "not to see" their periods; the amenorrhoea induced by DMPA in about half the long term users is frightening, because they cannot tell whether they are pregnant or not.

Women who are bleeding irregularly or "spotting" almost every day can be seriously upset by this fairly trivial symptom if they believe themselves to be polluted by a discharge of blood. In countries where survival has been protected for aeons by the constant struggle against impurity in diet and personal habits, the constant presence of even tiny amounts of "filth" can cause severe stress. Women who are supposed to be segregated during menstruation may be totally confused about their status while stop-start bleeding is going on. It is not often realised that menstrual segregation has a positive side; it can be a longed-for rest from preparing food and other chores, a time to chinwag with other women. A general rule can be elicited in a very various spectrum of female society: where the menstrual cycle has been institutionalised in forms of segregation and prohibition it is an important ordering principle of women's lives and its disruption will have undesirable consequences. The crassness of the attempts of the population lobby to deal with women's reluctance to disrupt the cycle reaches its nadir in a "study" (admittedly a cheap study) mounted in Egypt under the auspices of the Program for the Introduction and Adaptation of Contraceptive Technology (PIACT).

This study by the University of Alexandria represented an attempt to improve the continuation rate in a group of subjects using DMPA who would otherwise have dropped out due to the absence of menses. An IUD is temporarily inserted to establish a cyclical pattern of menses.[52]

The results of this brainstorm have yet to be published.

Administration of the steroid DMPA is potentially more disastrous than hormone pregnancy testing ever was; amneorrhoea induced by DMPA may merge into the amenorrhoea of pregnancy before a follow-up dose is available. The slow elimination rate of the drug raises the possibility that circulating levels may still be dangerous when a conception occurs after a period of DMPA use.

While it is undeniable that the champions of DMPA use in developing countries have been and will continue to be cavalier in their attitude to the integrity of the individual poor women who come within their purview, and that it is foolhardy to place the guardianship of civil rights in their care, the singling out of DMPA for condemnation in the general spectrum of drug abuse in developing countries is downright crackpot. DMPA does what it claims to do, prevents pregnancy; the in-built problems of the method are inconveniences rather than major health hazards, and many of them are subjectively discernible and will cease eventually upon cessation of use of the drug. The energy spent on creating a great deal of heat and very little light on the matter of DMPA would be better spent hounding Ciba-Geigy to withdraw Cibalgin from markets in Sierra Leone and Malaysia; Cibalgin is a dangerous drug because it contains amidopyrine which was shown sixty years ago to cause a precipitous drop in the number of white blood cells, and therefore to leave the taker without bodily defences against a host of ruinous infections. People in Sierra Leone and Malaysia take it for headaches and some of them die as a result. Sandoz and Hoechst market preparations containing amidopyrine in poor countries too. Parke-Davis encourages the use of chloramphenicol for all kinds of ailments, rendering it useless in treating typhoid as well as producing a crop of cases of aplastic anaemia. If we are to attack potential abuse of Depo-Provera, perhaps we ought to make sure that the aggressive marketing of anabolic steroids as promotors of children's growth, of phenylbutazone as a routine medication for "pain and fever," of indomethacin for toothache, of chlorpromazine for dysmenorrhoea, of diphenoxylate for diarrhoea have all been denounced and the perpetrators brought to book.[53] These are all much graver cases of abuse both because the consequences are statistically disastrous, being fatal in a significant proportion of cases and in relatively short order, and because the preparations are no more effective in the cases mentioned than any one of a number of cheaper, less powerful agents.

Depo-Provera continues to be used in 70 developing countries and in 10 developed ones by about 1.25 million women. It has been aggressively promoted in Thailand for the last ten years; one of the most recent studies on the restoration of fertility after using DMPA was carried out at the McCormick Hospital at Chang Mai. The Cambodian women at Kao-i-Dang and other refugee camps who were forced to accept DMPA were not part of the study. The very aspect of DMPA which makes it so useful in the context of traditional societies is what makes it so susceptible to abuse. We should be able to design a distribution strategy which would make the clandestine administration of Depo impossible, coded ampoules, uniquely coloured contents, something must be possible. So far nothing of the kind has even been tried. When the rich world releases a drug for distribution in the poor world, it is abandoned to its fate. In a cruel and exploitative world, the drugs are used in a cruel and exploitative manner. There are doctors working in primary health centres in Bangladesh who could be trusted with Depo and millionaire gynaecologists in Harley Street who could not.

The agitation about Depo-Provera may prove useful in one respect. It may convince the drug companies that they must find an alternative to systemic dosing with steroids whether by mouth or by injection. Alongside research into a group of long-acting injectables based on levonorgestrel, and into subdermal implants of progestogens or levonorgestrel in silastic pellets, a concerted attempt is being made to perfect vaginal rings which will slowly release steroids so as to act directly on the uterine system and bypass many of the problems associated with oral administration. It is futile to repine at the manifest defects of current steroid contraception and to oppose the experimental use of new compounds, new dosages and new delivery systems at the same time. If we do not want all the dirty work to be done in China where the injured have no redress, so that we can have the benefit of it, then we had better offer ourselves as experimental animals − if anyone will have us, suspicious as we are, and so inconsistent as to scream blue murder if one person in a hundred thousand falls seriously ill on our contraceptive regimen while we dice with death by smoking, not wearing seat belts, using drugs for recreation and making love to *herpes* and *chlamydiae* with gay insouciance.

Before we leave the vexed question of hormonal contraception, it might be profitable to consider the points raised by R. V. Short in a discussion meeting at the Royal Society in 1976. He pointed out that women living now represent the first generations to ovulate thirteen times a year for most of their adult life. Our ancestors spent more time pregnant and lactating than they did otherwise. Between pregnancy and prolonged lactational amenorrhea a hunter-gatherer might not see her menses again after the original puberty ritual and marriage. The difficulties that many women have with menstruation may indicate that we are doing too much of it; the fact that they can be alleviated with natural progesterone, the hormone that sustains pregnancy, seems to bear out Short's hypothesis. There are signs that the menstrual cycle is a stress upon the organism, and particularly upon certain parts of it, such as the breast, which may go through massive changes associated with the cycle for more than ten, and often nearer twenty years, before it can complete its function and become a secretory organ. Short suggests that some of the diseases associated with our low birthrate, for example, breast cancer, might be caused by some such mechanism...

> Other gynaecological disorders, such as carcinoma of the ovary, carcinoma of the endometrium, fibroids and endometriosis also seem to be increased in nulliparous women, presumably as a result of the increased ovarian activity associated with nulliparity.
>
> All these facts surely highlight the importance of developing a non-steroidal contraceptive that would allow a woman to return to the reproductive state that was the norm of our ancestors – amenorrhoea ...... if we devoted more thought to the development of new contraceptives for the future, we might be able to reduce the incidence of those killing diseases and debilitating disorders that at the moment appear to be an unfortunate by-product of the low birthrate in developed countries.[54]

The breast could perhaps be protected by artificially triggered lactation in young women, if there were any chance of them standing for it. (Those who have just buried their forty-year-old mothers might.) Short's argument actually goes further, and indicates a certain conceptual limitation in current thinking about contraception. If we approached hormonal contraception with the positive attitude of protecting women's health rather than preventing birth, which can be done in other ways, we would not have begun by overdosing them with oestrogens. We would not be in the mess that we are in now, with the best-informed women in the world abandoning the pill while the poor women increasingly take it up.

We are still a long way from achieving satisfactory contraception; the enormous rise in the acceptability of irreversible sterilisation is the best evidence of that. If we are very strongly motivated to find a way to control fertility without destroying foetuses and without pre-empting the individual's life choices by sterilisation, we are going to have to put more imagination and more passion into the refinement of methods that already exist and into the development of new ones. It is too important a matter to be left to the drug houses whose control of the patents for new drugs does not protect their rights for as long as it will take them to get their money back, let alone make a profit. We will have to demand that some of our taxes are used to support research in fertility limitation. We will have to amass our own user-oriented data. We will have to make the simpler barrier methods work by hook or by crook. We will have to find anti-spermatic agents that feel good, smell good and taste good as they persuade the sperms to give up the ghost.

Every woman must make her own decision regarding the pill and the alternatives, for only she can assess the indications and counter-indications in relation to her own sense of values. The decision to use the pill because less passive methods are too difficult may in itself be suspect, but only the individual knows whether she is at all likely to go to bed tipsy or leave her toilet bag in the car on a snowy night. A woman who can take abortion in her stride will make fundamentally different decisions from a woman who is terrified or digusted by it. A woman who has less menstrual discomfort and no acne when on the pill has a positive reason for using it which may well outweigh the possible hazards, but the woman who feels sluggish and bad-tempered and has a dirty-looking pregnancy mask around her mouth and eyes may feel that cancer in beagles is just the last straw. We women who seized on the pill before it was ever released for routine use as a contraceptive, fought to gain access to it, convinced that institutionalised sexual repression would keep it from general distribution for years. Those were the high-dose oestrogen pills, but when our heads ached, our ankles swelled, our breasts grew tender, and we had bouts of morning sickness, we put it down to everything but the oral contraceptive. One day, after bursting into tears five times at work for no reason, I decided that the pill was the only possible cause. "Oh, no," said my doctor, "there's no evidence for that sort of effect." There is now. I took a sequential pill too, and those have been withdrawn. I think I can remember its name. Perhaps the most frightening thing about this whole mess is that women who are hyper-critical of the pill but are still taking the pill, could not tell you the name of the principal ingredient. They certainly cannot tell you why they are taking that pill and no other. Students in a social anthropology class carried out a practical exercise examining garbage cans; of all the discarded steroid pill packs they found, almost none had been properly used. If we are not vigilant for ourselves, nobody can be vigilant on our behalf. If we are not vigilant for ourselves, it is absurd to thrust our vigilance on others. Others will rather profit by more rigour exercised on our own behalf. The alternative possibility is that the age of the sophisticated chemical contraceptive is over. The fertility control of the future may be all abortion and sterilisation – and a few billion condoms a year.

Chapter Seven

Abortion and Infanticide

O sleep, my babe, hear not the rippling wave.
Nor feel the breeze that round thee ling'ring strays
    To drink thy balmy breath,
    And sigh one long farewell.
Soon shall it mourn above thy wat'ry bed,
And whisper to me, on the wave-beat shore,
    Deep murm'ring to reproach,
    Thy sad untimely fate.
Ere those dear eyes had open'd to the light,
In vain to plead, thy coming life was sold,
    O waken'd but to sleep,
    Whence it can wake no more.

Sara Coleridge

Human reproduction, like most natural processes, is a wasteful business. A human male generates millions of sperm every day. Each one should be capable of capacitation, of moving on its own account and living independently of its creator for days after it has been ejaculated. As by far the greater number of ejaculations occur far from an ovum in space and time, billions of sperm are doomed to struggle and die completely pointlessly. The problem of sperm wastage would not be solved if some superhuman power decreed that all ejaculations could only occur in the right place and at the right time from a reproductive point of view. In theory it would be possible to produce any individual's full complement of issue from a single ejaculation so absurdly extravagant is nature in her supply of this precious substance – extravagant and inefficient, for a purpose, it would appear.

> Up to 15 or 20 per cent of the sperm production of a normal healthy man is abnormal and one way of regarding the female reproductive tract is as a series of hurdles designed to eliminate unhealthy sperm. The cervix hangs down into the top of the vagina – the opposite design to the one that any intelligent plumber would make – and the tubes leave the uterine cavity by the smallest of openings; so of the hundreds of millions of sperm deposited in the vagina, only a few hundred make it as far as the egg. It is reasonable to believe that the abnormal sperm are screened out in the process.[1]

No voice is raised to question the justice of a world bathed in dying sperm although sperm are more obviously alive in some ways than the torpid and passive blastocyst which is the beginning of a pregnancy. The short life-cycle of the spermatozoon moves us less than the fate of the supernumerary young of the stickleback, who is no relative of ours, and carries infinitely less interesting genetic information than each of the tiny creatures which men create and waste so carelessly. Some future generation may decide to husband this powerful protein more responsibly; present thinking regards sperm as completely expendable.

Ova, although they are far less numerous than sperm, are not given any more importance. Each female is born with her undeveloped ova lurking inside their immature follicles waiting for the endocrine signal which will bring them to fecundability when the time and the environment are more or less right. She is not taught to safeguard this genetic treasure, because it is assumed, so far more or less correctly, that she has enough ova to cope with daily accidents such as irradiation and medication and drug use, and to spare. Indeed, it seems very likely that a woman living the kind of life in which she is always either pregnant or lactating will reach menopause and die with most of her follicles and their microscopic treasure intact.

It seems, what is more, that ova may have the same in-built non-viability factor as sperm; many a winner sperm takes the lead in the obstacle race through the female reproductive tract only to fertilise a dud egg – just how many we will probably never know for sure:

> Probably many eggs are also abnormal when first ovulated, although a study of this is more difficult than in the case of sperm. What is certain is that many of the products of conception are lost at varying stages of pregnancy. Of the eggs fertilised, up to half prove abnormal and are lost before the first week or ten days of pregnancy ... It is a reasonable speculation that many women conceive during every cycle of unprotected intercourse, although pregnancy diagnosed by menstrual delay takes an average of several cycles of coitus.[2]

Neither the active sperm nor the relatively huge and passive ovum excites much concern until the one fortunate sperm, aided and supported by millions of siblings, has encountered the mature, receptive ovum and fought its way through the outer membrane to the nucleus and fertilised it. The process is very simple and unremarkable; it has been observed with quite incomprehensible wonderment in a petri dish, wherein it looks just like the fertilisation of any ovum by any sperm, whether of mouse or crocodile. The difference is that there is a human life in the petri dish, and the attendant biologists genuflect before it; the fertility experts are less starry-eyed. The contents of the petri dish might as well be served scrambled on toast unless they can be maintained and nourished in a benign environment. Fertilisation may be the beginning of a human life, but it is an extremely conditional beginning. Many more pregnancies are begun than ever come to fruition. Abortion is as natural, and possibly more prevalent, than birth.

There are millions of people who believe that the immortal human soul comes into being at the moment that the sperm fights through to the nucleus of the ovum; what happens in the petri dish is as wonderful as the Transubstantiation when unregarded bread and wine becomes divine, and therefore they argue passionately that such an event ought not to take place at a biologist's whim. It would be consistent to learn from the example, to concern themselves with the circumstances in which conception often takes place only to be aborted, all unknown to the parents, who would be horrified and contrite if the fact was brought to their attention. A Catholic biologist may baptise the contents of his petri dish before he washes them down the drain. A Catholic woman losing her blastocyst at menstruation has never been told of the possibility that a human life has just ended. It may seem very complicated to keep a jug of holy water beside the lavatory bowl to baptise sanitary napkins with, but it is no more elaborate than many of the rituals which believing people all over the world practise several times every day of their lives. It would certainly dramatise the fact that Catholics take life before birth very seriously. The fact that they do not carry out rituals of this kind suggests that in fact they do not really believe what they maintain in polemic. There is after all nothing intrinsically improbable in the idea that the soul comes into existence at the moment of fertilisation, but if such a view is to be held, it must be held rigorously as a matter of personal conviction and not simply brandished in arguments with unbelievers. Catholics have to be interested enough to master the complex biology of reproduction. They should be aware of the facts as pointed out by Alberman and Creasy.

> There is circumstantial evidence to attest that we do suffer from an extremely high incidence of early embryonic mortality. Thus Hertig (1975) examined the uteri of 210 fertile, married women who were having hysterectomies ... he recovered 34 embryos aged 1–17 days of which only 21 were adjudged to be normal, giving an embryonic mortality rate of 38% by the time of the first missed menstual period. French and Bierman (1962) were able to follow 3084 presumed pregnancies on the Hawaiian island of Kanai from the time of the first missed menstrual period and they showed that 23.7% of them failed to result in a live birth ... Chromosome studies of spontaneous abortions show that the abnormality rate is highest, approaching 50%, at eight weeks gestational age and declining to 5% by the end of the twentieth week.[3]

Thus the ethical problems posed by abortion go far beyond the relatively few cases of deliberate interruption of pregnancy, which are in themselves so variable and so subject to factors beyond the individual's control that each case must be taken on its merits, which cannot themselves be understood without an understanding of the whole spectrum of abortion. A genuine attempt to disentangle the complex ethical questions involved in pregnancy termination would benefit us all, for individual women are struggling, with very little help from their spiritual mentors, to confront a genuine problem. Catholic opponents of reproductive freedom for women remain fixated on the minority of cases of induced abortion, incurious about the vast majority of cases, and unable or unwilling to understand the morality of actions taken because the individual came to the conclusion that she had no choice. Their interest is predominantly legalistic, for they concentrate on preventing the existence of adequate facilities for pregnancy termination, and not on the souls of those trying to live in the most responsible and conscientious way. The problem with the machinations of the Catholic lobby against abortion is not that they are bigoted or fanatical, but that they are frivolous.

We do not know and we may never know how many conceptions are wasted (or, in Catholic terms, how crowded Limbo is). Some ovarian cysts, we do not know what proportion, are caused by the fertilisation of ova which have failed to escape from the follicle. Until the microscopic examination of ovaries removed at surgery is undertaken as a matter of course we shall continue to have no idea how common an event this is. Many ovarian cysts balloon up only to subside, possibly indicating the reabsorption of such pregnancies.[4] Other kinds of early pregnancy wastage occur because the fertilised ovum fails to be gathered into the Fallopian tube and wanders off into the peritoneal cavity to be eventually reabsorbed. In the case of the fertilised ovum which is blocked by a fold of scar tissue or otherwise snagged in the Fallopian tube, the abortion which results is a medical emergency and therefore well-documented, although there has been little discussion of the surgeon's dilemma. Any good surgeon would remove the tube before it ruptured and be very glad that he had caught it in time, but he would be greatly surprised to be called an abortionist for so doing. A commoner and much more mysterious kind of early pregnancy wastage is caused by a "shortened luteal phase". In a normal pregnancy the ruptured follicle changes into the *corpus luteum* which secretes the progesterone needed for the maintenance of pregnancy and the suppression of further ovulation; if conception does not occur the *corpus luteum* is shed at menstruation. If the luteal phase is accelerated, the process of sloughing begins before the fertilised ovum has a chance to implant in the uterine wall. Women who suffer from this kind of infertility are, in fact, habitual aborters.

Nowadays the biggest hazard in the way of the blastocyst in search of a home is the Intrauterine Device, falsely called an intrauterine *contraceptive* device when it is no such thing. The IUD is any object placed inside the uterus to guarantee the free flow of the menses, and as such, it has been around for a very long time. Hippocrates speaks of a hollow lead tube filled with mutton fat to be inserted through the cervix and, together with most of his successors describes the device as promoting fertility, although the descriptions of its function are sufficiently ambiguous to include its possible use as a fertility regulator, in that they protected a woman for whom a pregnancy was counter-indicated, and could be worn and removed without mishap. The nineteenth-century stem pessary was frankly used to "prevent conception" although it was still masquerading in different disguises as a treatment for various uterine disorders, principally "obstruction of the menses". It is difficult now to estimate just how general the understanding of its actual function was. The contraceptive pill is available in Italy only as a treatment for menstrual disorders, and produced by a firm in which the Vatican is a major shareholder; those with wit to invent the right story for the doctors may use it as a contraceptive. It is probable that the function of the stem pessary was just as open a secret.

In 1909 a German doctor invented a thread pessary which was meant to be placed inside the uterus, and another the Graefenburg Ring in the 1920s. The Graefenburg Ring was still being fitted by discreet doctors in a hand-picked clientele as far afield as Victoria, Australia in the 1950s. The chief requirement of an intrauterine device is that it stay put; its design is largely a matter of engineering, and since the collar-stud shapes of the early pessaries and the simple ring of Graefenberg we have had the Margulies Spiral, the Lippes Loop, the Birnberg Bow, the Copper Seven and the Copper T, the Dalkon Shield (modelled on a crab-louse), the Majzlin Spring, Progestatert, the Saf-T-Coil (a ram's horn), and so forth, all with radio-opaque nylon threads so they can be tracked if they wander off.

The IPPF and the Population Council began to test new intrauterine devices in the 1960s and there is no doubt that population panic lay behind this surge of interest. The IUD is the cheapest form of birth control and is beyond the individual's power to control from month to month. Because it is *in situ* continually, it is not immediately obvious that it is not a contraceptive at all. A device inserted in the uterus prevents intrauterine pregnancy, and intrauterine pregnancy only, by transforming the welcoming environment for the blastocyst into a toxic sink.[5] Some IUDs are called "inert" because they include no specific pharmacologic agents but the description is as misleading as calling them "contraceptive" for the metals and plastics of which they are made are chemically active, copper extremely so. The circulating levels of copper in the bloodstreams of women with copper IUDs has never been measured. The womb is also active and responds to the presence of the foreign body, by secreting abnormally and perhaps also by deranged spasmodic reactions to normal changes in the endometrium. The dissected womb of a woman who has had an IUD in for several years shows the pattern of the device clearly worn into the layers of tissue which are distorted by the pressure; some areas over-grow, others are eroded, others dead and dying.

The literature on IUDs is vast, but completely inconclusive; like

Limbo-dancers the devices always slide under the wire of scientific proof, for there are too many variables in establishing the single cause of a pathological syndrome in which the IUD is a factor, but one thing is certain: the IUD prevents implantation, not conception. The muddled thinking which refuses to observe this distinction is one of the reasons the role of the IUD in the incidence of ovarian and ectopic pregnancies cannot be estimated; if we had any idea how many non-ectopic pregnancies are yearly aborted by IUD wearers we would be able to establish whether the incidence of ectopic pregnancies in IUD wearers is normal or elevated.[6] It is unlikely that the IUD actually causes pregnancies to be ectopic, but the IUD promoters prefer to remain silent: for to defend themselves is to emphasise the unpalatable fact that their preferred method of contraception actually causes an increased number of conceptions.

If all that the IUD supplies is a twenty-eighth day abortion several times a year, it supplies it at a high cost, the first being the wearer's ignorance of what is going on in her body, which may be to her completely unacceptable. There is a story often told among family planners about peasant women who were fitted with IUDs only to be found wearing them as amulets the next time the field workers came by for their follow-up, but the real point of the story has never been grasped. As long as the IUD is presented to women as a kind of amulet which magically wards off pregnancy by hovering in the womb rather than as the fierce disruption of normal processes that it is, their credulity is being abused in the most callous manner. On the one hand women are told that the device is a boon to millions of women who have never had any problems with it and on the other every intern knows that the first question to ask a woman reporting to emergency with severe abdominal pain is whether or not she has an IUD. Doctors are well aware that the installation of any foreign body in the human organism is a risky business, but optimistic supporters of population limitation thought fit at one time to wear IUD coils as earrings by way of increasing their acceptability. For the individual woman to pick her way through this tangle of suspicion and misplaced optimism is practically impossible. Usually the decision to accept an IUD is a forced one, brought about by the paucity of alternatives and the pressure of circumstances: by now few Western women will not have heard of some IUD disaster but those who accept it will hope to be among the lucky ones for whom the device quietly, secretly, solves the problem of fertility regulation: after all, some ostriches with their heads in the sand do not come to grief.

For many women the IUD experience does not go much further than the insertion of the device, subsequent infection or pain, rejection or removal.[7] The percentages of women suffering abortive insertion vary greatly with the kind of device, the skill of the inserter and the health and fertility experience of the women involved. Perforation and infection are both most likely in the initial stages: something of the order of a third of all women receiving IUDs will be without them two years later, and have no pleasant memories of the experience. Insertion is particularly problematic with women who have had no children or with women who have just aborted or given birth and the search goes on to find a device which will be tolerated by young, tense nulliparous uteri, and by the relaxed enlarged post-partum uterus. In 1977, an experiment was carried out in Chile using a pleated membrane which was inserted within three days "of treatment for incomplete or inevitable abortion", i.e., one supposes, after curettage. The results were considered encouraging; of 154 insertions, two pregnancies resulted, twelve women expelled the device, and six had it removed for pain and/or bleeding.[8] The interest in an IUD which can be inserted at the same time or soon after the termination of a pregnancy is easily explained. Many poorly motivated women only seek gynaecological help when childbirth looms or when they are pressured into seeking abortion. Insertion of an IUD at such a time would function as pre-emptive birth-control in that most intractable of groups, the feckless, unlettered, confused poor. The almost inevitable corollary is that they will be lost to follow-up so the known complication rates of the IUM, as the membrane is called, may be very much more sinister than they appear.

Because they are not dependent upon the day-to-day motivation of the user, as is the pill, the IUDs were for some time the preferred method of birth control pushed in the Third World. Even now family planners discuss the desirability of supplying ignorant women with IUDs without strings so that neither they, nor their husbands, nor the village midwives can remove the devices. This concept they justify by saying that it postively necessitates the woman's return to a modern clinic for pre-natal and general health care, but much more obvious than this benevolent coercion is the element of fertility control over and above the individual's power and will to choose. In recent years the IUD has faded out of Third World Family Planning Programmes. The reasons have in large measure to be hypothetical, precisely because follow-up was so inadequate. The immediate priority was to get as many IUDs inserted as possible; it would be truly astonishing if personnel and equipment which could have been pushing ahead inserting more and more devices had been diverted to careful monitoring of the effects they had upon their recipients. Nowadays dark references to the IUD experience may be found in the literature, but no one has yet put together the story of the suffering caused by Western gadgetry to trusting women all over the world.

Dr Indumati Parikh was involved in a successful pioneering study of the IUD for the Pathfinder Fund in 1964, but "by the end of 1966, IUD was in complete disrepute" because of the drive to insert hundreds of thousands of the devices in Indian women.[9] Dr Parikh, who has patients in her Bombay clinic who have worn the IUD for twenty years without mishap, has this to say about what went wrong with the mass programme:

> The tempo of Government IUD programme reached its apex as soon as it began. Hopes were raised sky-high and hundreds of camps were organised all over the country without any previous groundwork. IUD is one contraceptive device which needs maximum cooperation from the medical profession. Government programme undertook the gigantic task of popularising IUD without bothering to take into confidence the medical profession at large, without taking care to introduce IUD at centres where the cases could be followed up strictly and meticulously. Ancillary trained staff was made to do the work which was practically beyond their capacity. The selection of cases according to the menstrual history of each woman and her general health was nowhere done ... loops were inserted indiscriminately almost on demand and women were lured to accept the device with monetary incentives. Side effects and complications were never mentioned nor were any arrangements made to do the insertions in proper cases and arrange the follow-up work and treat acceptors who suffered from one or the other effects of IUD insertion.[10]

Given the high rates of rejection and removal for pain and bleeding even in well-equipped and well-staffed Western clinics, we may safely assume an even higher rate of spontaneous rejection and pain and bleeding, together with infection concomitant upon insertion, in more primitive circumstances. It seems not unreasonable to suppose that the pelvic musculature of labouring women would be less tolerant of the insulting presence of an IUD than the slack pelves of sedentary Western women.[11] If higher rates of complication are simply surmise, it is however obvious that the increased blood loss caused by the IUD would be much more damaging to the general health of a hard-working woman on a poor diet than it is to well-nourished women.

> One of the most common side effects of the IUDs is an increased loss of blood during menstruation. Increased and prolonged menstrual bleedings have been found with all types of IUDs. The increased fibrinolytic activity in the endometrium of patients using IUDs appears to account for the increased bleeding. The only exception to this rule appears to be the progesterone or gestagen medicated IUDs, which reduce the total blood loss but not the number of days of bleeding.[12]

A woman who accepts an IUD may expect to have her blood loss doubled as a consequence. If she has a meat-rich diet and plenty of eggs and fresh vegetables, this drain may not affect her general health, but even among the well-nourished women of Sweden, iron-deficiencies were found in group of women who lost more than 80 ml of blood at each menstruation. What such figures might mean when applied to women living on a diet of cereal and low-grade protein, who must carry out hard manual labour all day every day in order to ensure the survival of themselves and their families is a matter for genuine concern. However, all accounts of IUD programmes seem to ignore the real questions raised by their experience, as does for example, this account of what happened in Fiji.

> In 1965 a campaign was begun under the family planning programme to encourage the use of the intrauterine device. A trial had been held in 1964 at the main family planning clinic in Suva, and this had been successful enough to warrant a Colony-wide effort to promote this *inexpensive* method of birth control. Staff were trained and facilities were arranged at all major medical centres during 1965. In that year 2,579 loops were fitted by the Department. The loop campaign was well advertised by the Family Planning Association ... and was accompanied by a great amount of "fanfare" designed to encourage acceptance. However, as the problem of side-effects of the loop affected increasing numbers of women, *rumours* about the dangers of the device began to spread and the removal rates rose rapidly (my italics)[13]

If women observe the effects that an intrauterine device has on other women and therefore decide to have nothing to do with it, they can hardly be said to be being affected by anything as insubstantial as a rumour. The trial run at Suva in the preceding year cannot in itself have justified the setting up of a national campaign accompanied by "fanfare"; rather than the women showing a degree of irrationality in rejecting the loop, it seems that the authorities themselves acted hastily and on insufficient evidence in promoting it:

> A study undertaken at the Lautoka Hospital Family Planning Clinic between 1965 and 1969 concluded that the over-enthusiasm of the initial stages of the campaign, coupled with unsatisfactory follow-up care, in large measure accounted for the poor retention rates which were being registered.[14]

About 40% of the Indian women and ten to twenty per cent of the women of other races who had had IUDs *who returned for follow-up care* still had their devices after three years. We shall never know what happened to those whose first encounter with family planning was so traumatic that they were lost to follow-up.

David Nowlan is rather unusual among family planners in that he publicly takes some of the blame for the discrediting of the IUD – in this case, in Jamaica, where he was a Government Medical Officer in the mid-1960s:

> A massive batch of Lippes Loops had arrived on the island and the medical officers were to make them available to the population. This we duly did, our confidence founded on total ignorance of the nature and effects of the devices. Given the high prevalence of pelvic inflammatory disease in the country, it was hardly surprising (alas, only in retrospect) that we were soon removing more IUDs than we were inserting and many women had come to associate contraception with pain and anxiety rather than with relief and liberation. Our

ignorance and incompetence must have set back by several years the cause of
family planning in Jamaica.[15]

Dr Nowlan is a little hard on himself; all he and his colleagues got
with their massive shipment of loops (paid for by foreign taxpayers) was
a half-day's "training" which was carefully organised to produce just the
unreasoning enthusiasm that Nowlan experienced. No one who had pulled
off the entrepreneurial coup of promoting a gadget like the Lippes Loop,
and has finessed AID into paying for millions of them, is going to
jeopardise the whole operation by expressing scepticism at the distribution
level. Dr Nowlan is Irish and is used to obscurantist opposition to family
planning but he had had little experience of the obscurantism and blind
faith that promotes family planning practice. The bitterness of the tragedy
can be better understood when you stand in the gynaecological ward of
almost any Jamaican hospital and realise how many of the women are
there because of septic illegal abortions.

Adequate follow-up for IUD wearers is not an easy thing to arrange.
The device does not become safer or more effective the longer it is left
in.[16] The unluckiest women of all are those whose initial tolerance of the
device encourages them to rely upon it so that eventually they take it for
granted; their misplaced confidence is paralleled by that of the doctors
who have decided to treat cases of pelvic inflammatory disease with an
IUD *in situ* with antibiotics and without removing the device, or even,
in cases where the device has become misplaced, to insert another without
removing the first! One unfortunate woman in Atlanta, who had had
repeated episodes of pelvic inflammatory disease, but was determined to
keep her IUD on which she had evidently come to rely, died of pelvic
actinomycosis. This is the first case in which the IUD and only the IUD
was the cause of death. Actinomycosis is the body's reaction to the
presence of a foreign body.[17]

The continuing risks associated with the IUD have been well
summarised by Vessey and Doll.

> Of these the most important are uterine perforation and pelvic inflammatory
> disease. In addition, unplanned pregnancies occurring in women using an
> intrauterine device are much more likely to be ectopic or to end in spontaneous
> abortion than usual and there is some evidence that such abortions are
> particularly likely to be septic, occasionally with fatal results for the mother.[18]

The increased risk of pelvic inflammatory disease is now so generally
recognised as attaching to the IUD that the FDA now insists that each
device carry a warning to the consumer on the packet.[19]

It would be misleading not to point out that intrauterine devices have
been improved and can now be tolerated by a wider range of patients

than formerly, but the very variety of devices should mean that the insertion of an IUD is carefully considered by the health worker in question who ought to weigh all the counter-indications, such as recurrent vaginal or pelvic infection, cervical erosion, small uterus, presence of tumours, anaemia, menstrual disorders and the like, and then choose the device which seems most appropriate or reject the idea altogether. Nothing could be further from the notion of mass insertion of a single type of device as happened in Fiji. In the first weeks follow-up should be intensive, for most perforations happen on insertion as do the majority of pelvic infections. If the device settles down and bleeding is manageable, the patient should still be examined regularly, blood counts should be taken and the device should be checked to see if it is still in the correct position. To demand such medical care for a peasant population is to cry for the moon, but without it no IUDs should be inserted. The nett result of careless IUD programmes is to discredit modern methods of birth control altogether. At the overall rate of two or three pregnancies per hundred woman-years in IUD acceptors, every village community will have direct experience of a pregnancy with an IUD *in situ*, which can have hideous results ranging all the way from birth with an IUD embedded in the fontanelle to septic abortion and death.

The IUD is successfully used among high-density urban populations living within easy reach of emergency services where there is a high index of suspicion for IUD malfunction. There can be no doubt that some populations tolerate them better than others, but so far no comparative account of IUD programmes has ever been published.

The great IUD success story has always been Taiwan, a compact island of 361 townships and an intensive family-planning programme organised round locally resident paramedics called pre-pregnancy health workers. The T'ai-chung experiment which instituted the programme in 1962 revealed that for the Taiwanese the IUD was the method of choice, perhaps because the people had heard of a Japanese version, the Ota ring, in use (although illegally and with many abuses) since the 1930s. In two years, out of 6,285 couples accepting contraception, 5,000 had chosen the IUD. By 1970, half a million loops had been inserted, and Taiwan remains the statistical paradigm of the intensive IUD campaign, but in 1969, Health Commissioner T. C. Hsu was already saying to a rather obtuse interviewer:

Too many loops are coming out. The rate of retention has been as low as fifty per cent. If it goes on, they'll be coming out just as fast as we can put them in ... The problem is that the women simply want the IUD removed. Three times out of four it's the same doctor who takes it out as put it in. Part of the trouble seems to be that the doctors and PPH workers have not been able to spend enough time warning women about possible side-effects. Bleeding, cramps, that kind of thing. One woman tells another and the bad news travels as fast as bicycles can travel downhill.[20]

One may feel sorry for Dr Hsu, but one feels a good deal sorrier for the women whose experiences caused the falling off; the blurs in Dr Hsu's statement cover serious rifts in its sense. Women who have IUDs do not take them out because of someone *else*'s side-effects, although women who are thinking of accepting one might be so influenced. Women with IUDs tend to try to get on with them; either the side-effects are completely unmanageable or they hear of or witness the kind of IUD disaster which makes them afraid. Dr Hsu's interviewer did not see behind his factitious explanation, and when faced with the obvious fact of the IUDs fading from the population control limelight, could only opine, on the evidence from Hong Kong:

> ... there has been worrying evidence that the IUD is well past its peak of popularity. Not only have new insertions fallen off markedly from the annual rate of twenty thousand which was reached in 1965 and 1966; there has also been a large number of terminations. The [family planning] association needs to mount a major program to determine why termination rates are so high. (In part, it seems to be the old rumor about ectopic pregnancies resulting from the IUD.) It needs to increase retention rates by effective publicity programs and by raising the level of the service offered.[21]

It is probably unfair to expect Stanley Johnson, a novelist on a public relations exercise for the population lobby, to investigate the scientific evidence of the increased exposure to risk of ectopic pregnancy in IUD-wearers, but he could show more respect for the people who have actually experienced the IUD and were disappointed. The IUD was not a fad which passed away, but a method tried and rejected; not rumour, but hard empiricism brought about its downfall. Johnson's own grasp of the IUD and its function is a good deal hazier than that of the people he speaks of with such easy contempt. In Singapore, wandering around the Fourth Asian Congress on Obstetrics and Gynaecology, he fails to hoist in the significance of another IUD programme failure, and embarks instead on a fantasy about the IUD:

> As I looked around the exhibition, I at first wondered why the IUD did not receive the same promotion as the Pill. On reflection, the reason was rather clear. There's no money in the IUD. This little piece of plastic, spiral, bow-shaped, U-shaped or what you will, cannot – as far as the profit motive is concerned – compare with the Pill. It costs cents to make; it lasts a lifetime.[22]

There has been money in the coils and spirals too – money for insertions, money for rejections, money for surgical repairs, money for royalties in designs and patents, and money for damages. IUDs may last a lifetime, but the women who have died with them *in situ* have had no joy of the fact.

When even the most conservative descriptions of the action of intrauterine devices cannot fail to convey the idea that they are abortifacient rather than contraceptive, the inescapable question arises: why has the IUD achieved acceptance when other forms of non-traumatic early pregnancy termination have not? It might be argued that vacuum aspiration of the contents of the uterus of an amenorrheic woman involves a deliberate act, whereas the abortions caused by the intrauterine device are involuntary, but this fact ought to make the IUD *less* acceptable rather than more so. The woman is an unwitting accomplice in what she may well consider to be a crime and as such she ought to be considered a victim of the callousness and lack of scruple of those who ought to have known better. Insofar as her ignorance is the result of her own carelessness, lack of curiosity, credulity or servility, she may be considered to bear some part of the blame. The extent to which many women refuse to take responsibility for their own health and avoid the unpleasant necessity of considering exactly what they are allowing to be done to them and the risks involved is even more striking evidence of their oppressed condition in the literate, informed, sophisticated Western woman than in the illiterate farm worker, whose suspicions and superstitions may have more to do with an abiding self-esteem than the silly passivity of more privileged women.

Clearly, the commonest kind of IUD abortion, the twenty-eighth day termination, is, apart from increased blood loss and perhaps some pain, completely non-traumatic. No theologians, bishops, pro-life groups, psychiatrists or jurists sit on the case of the IUD acceptor, and the manufacturers and promoters of the devices are not at all anxious to attract their attention. It is to be hoped that the multi-million-dollar suits pending against the Dalkon Corporation will bring up the question of whether the device failed as a contraceptive in the cases of fatal septic abortion associated with its use or whether it was criminally wrong to have distributed it as a contraceptive in the first place.[23] The incidence of infection with an IUD *in situ*, ought to be compared with the risk of infection in early abortion, in which case its showing might not look too bad. Ironically, once the abortifacient action of IUDs was recognised in law, they would become illegal in most countries, for however liberal the abortion laws, there are no legal codes which permit uncontrolled abortions to be carried out without the knowledge or consent of the woman, which is what happens in the case of IUDs. Once again the IUD may slide under the rope; but the space is narrowing. This is a precis of the current description by the US Food and Drug Administration of the way in which the IUD works.

An inflammatory response to the presence of the IUD always develops in the endometrium. Numerous polymorphonuclear leukocytes are seen in the human endometrium and uterine cells shortly after insertion of an IUD; then foreign body giant cells, mononuclear cells, plasma cells and macrophages appear. It is now believed that it is these cells that are responsible for the contraceptive effects of IUDs, either by phagocytosis of the spermatozoa and/or blastocyst, or by the prevention of implantation by the blastocyst as a result of chemical alterations in the endometrium induced by the IUD. In support of this theory it has been shown that the degeneration product of neutrophils, macrophages and other intrauterine cells are toxic to blastocysts.[24]

The FDA is keeping the contraceptive possibility open, but there is not much conviction in it; four hundred million racing spermatozoa are a very different proposition from one lumbering blastocyst in search of a home; the very fact that IUD are ineffective if they slip into the cervix instead of maintaining contact with the endometrium seems to indicate that their successful function has much more to do with the frustration of implantation than with killing sperm.

A clearer statement of the probable mode of functioning of the IUD by Malcolm Potts, whose dismissal of possible objections is typical of committed family-planners, gives an unexpected insight into one of the causes of the distrust which has effected the IUD's international career.

Like the Pill, IUDs *may* have a number of anti-fertility effects. They may interfere with the passage of sperm, but it is also clear that fertilisation can occur with an IUD in place and yet pregnancy is usually prevented. If an IUD is inserted after unprotected coitus it prevents pregnancy occurring. The post-coital use of IUDs is much more acceptable than the post-coital use of hormones and is likely to become more common. Conversely, if a device is removed in the middle of a cycle, even if a woman takes contraceptive precautions afterwards, an already fertilised egg may still implant. Biologically, intrauterine devices may work partially as abortifacients. No doctor is going to stop using them because of this possibility and no reasonable woman is going to be disturbed by this fact, both of which observations emphasise the very genuine difference between the destruction of a newly fertilised egg and an abortion later in pregnancy.[25]

What is biologically true is also logically true; Dr Potts might as well have said that IUDs *are* abortifacients. The slipperiness of the IUD discussion can be seen in the slide from possibility for doctors to fact for women, and (the classic trick of special pleading) the tranquil assertion that no right-minded person is going to take exception to what is said. People whose religious faith prevents them from regarding the IUD's function with equanimity are, by definition, unreasonable. People who might be exasperated by the humbug of disguising the real nature of IUDs, suspicious of the blurring of logic in such arguments, more respectful of their own bodies than to bury abortionist's tools in them, are also unreasonable and to be ridden over, smooth-shod.

Chinese family planners appear to be rather less specious than the Anglo-Saxon variety, for they present the IUD quite uncompromisingly in their literature as an abortifacient, preventing the implantation of the fertilised egg. It is conceivable that the advice given to acceptors, to avoid "bathing in the tub" and sexual intercourse, for two weeks after the insertion or removal of an IUD, is a sensible way of trying to reduce the incidence of PID.[26]

The fact that "if an IUD is inserted after unprotected coitus it prevents pregnancy occurring", or translated from Family Planningese it "prevents pregnancy continuing" or "prevents implantation", seems proof positive that it does not work principally by preventing the encounter of live sperm and live egg. IUD insertion as pre-emptive abortion is now routinely practised at the Marie Stopes Memorial clinic and at Pregnancy Advisory Services clinics in London. The earlier technique of "post-coital contraception" as it used to be called is the administration of high doses of oestrogens, usually in the form of Diethystilboestrol. Although the history of DES is well-known, it is still routine in campus clinics in the United States to inject it as a "morning-after contraceptive" i.e. early abortifacient. The worry of this is that while the early administration may masquerade as afterthought contraception, it does not always work and a woman who could not accept deliberate abortion once she was assured of the fact that she was pregnant would run a completely unacceptable risk of bearing a damaged child. Nevertheless, many doctors can be found who are untroubled by this fact and incurious to know whether their patient has been in the habit of bombarding herself with high doses of oestrogens. Professor John Newton of Birmingham University thought fit to inform "all women" via the *Observer* newspaper that the simplest morning-after "cure" for unprotected intercourse was two double doses, twelve hours apart, of the oral contraceptives Ovran or Eugynon 50, that is, 2 mg of DL-norgestrel in a twelve-hour period.[27] As these substances are not yet available on supermarket shelves, this advice cannot have been very useful, except to people who were already using the pills in the first place – or perhaps to their daughters, who shouldn't be old enough to need it. Such abortifacient use as Professor Newton suggests would very likely be the commonest kind of use among teenagers.

In England, the confusion over the morality of such interception is reflected in the medico-legal ponderings on the matter. The Department of Health and Social Services holds that post-coital contraception by bombardment with oestrogens or insertion of an IUD is legal as long as it occurs within 72 hours of sexual intercourse taking place. Translated into practical terms, this means that clients should say that they had intercourse less than 72 hours before they came to the clinic. There is no earthly way that the staff at the clinic is going to know whether that was *the* episode for which the pre-emptive abortion is required, unless the client is silly enough to say very much the wrong thing about how long ago the last period was. (It is a simple matter to teach teenagers to say "Fourteen days and I'm never regular anyway.") Dissatisfied with this proviso, the Pregnancy Advisory Service asked for expert counsel from Ian Kennedy, Reader in Law at King's College London, whose decision was even more fuddled:

> The morning-after pill and other methods of post-coital contraception are legal, provided they are used as an emergency measure ...

This we can interpret as an instruction to arrive wild-eyed and, if possible, with semen in the vaginal vault.

> Mr Kennedy says that provided the pill or other methods are used before a fertilised egg is implanted in the womb their use is legal.

He might as well have put it the other way round, as nobody can be sure whether an egg has been fertilised or whether implantation is going to ensue.

> Post-coital birth control will be lawful and judged by the court as contraception rather than abortion, up to the maximum period of implantation ... seven to ten days ...

The anti-abortion organisation, Life, argues that pre-emptive abortion or interception comes under the definition of abortion in the Offences Against the Person Act of 1861. Kennedy argues that a miscarriage cannot be procured unless there is a "carriage", i.e. an implantation. If his interpretation does not become the accepted one, not only post-coital pills and insertions, but the IUD itself could be declared illegal. Even the mini-pill could find itself an outlaw, the only true contraceptive being those which suppress ovulation.[28] At least those people who elect to be sterilised avoid all these brain-teasers, and, what might be more important, they hurt no one but themselves.

Potts prefers IUD insertion as post-coital contraception over large doses of steroids because he admits that large doses of steroid can damage a developing foetus. Unfortunately, he states quite categorically that "normal doses" of steroid do not present a hazard to the foetus:

> Fortunately, there is no evidence whatever that the pill in normal doses, even if taken by pregnant women in error, will damage the embryo.[29]

There is no such thing as a "normal" dose of synthetic steroids; Potts simply means "usual" in this case, but the word "normal" is more soothing. Because steroid dosages tend to be uniform and not calculated in relation to the bodyweight of the user, some oral contraceptive users are routinely over-dosed. The question of correct levels of dosing is far from solved, but Potts implies the contrary, with an avuncular disregard for the responsibilities of women both to themselves and to their progeny. The soothing is ineffectual anyway, for the pregnant women most likely to use steroids will use elevated doses of them, as Professor Newton suggests. In fact, the work of Aarskog, Levy, Cohen and Fraser, of Janerich, Piper and Glebatis, of Nora and Nora, of Harlap, Prywes and Davies, of Ambani, Joshi, Vaidya and Devi, of Heinnonen, Slone, Monson, Hook and Shapiro, and of Lorber, Cassidy and Engel, clearly implicates steroids as teratogens and gives no reassurances that dose levels make any difference. It seems much more likely, that, as with teratogens like alcohol, it is not the amount of the drug which is crucial but the timing of its impact.[30]

To anyone who finds the idea of a womb ready equipped with a permanent abortionist's tool disgusting, the desirability of a safe, clean, controllable early pregnancy-termination method must suggest itself. Only in the context of birth control do physicians uncritically accept the idea of a powerful remedy which the patient must take constantly even if he has not been exposed to the disease. In weighing the advantages and disadvantages of the IUD a woman must consider not only whether the intensity and pleasurability of her sex life is such that the risks and inconveniences of the IUD pale into insignificance but also whether the likelihood of her conceiving justifies the transformation of her uterus into a poisonous abattoir. If a safe, simple, twenty-eight day abortion method should be found, it would have many advantages over the messy, uncontrollable and mysterious function of the IUD. It would not be necessary to put young women through the agonies of IUD insertion at a time when they might well be experiencing a majority of non-ovulatory cycles, as happened in a rather ghastly experiment in Uppsala, when the Copper T-200 or the Copper 7 was installed in 243 young women aged from 13 to 20, with a mean age of 16.4. A fifth of them expelled the device, a quarter had it removed, there were five intrauterine pregnancies. The incidence of Pelvic Inflammatory Disease is higher in young women and seven of this sample had the device removed for this cause. The Swedish researchers had no option but to counsel against the IUD as "contraception" for young nulliparae. Some of their subjects paid dearly for the truth of their conclusion.[31]

Adolescent pregnancy is one of the most serious problems confronting family planners. In 1978 the House of Representatives Select Committee on Population devoted a whole week of hearings to this problem, because, in the chairman's words:

> Over 1,000,000 teenagers became pregnant last year. At least 30,000 of them were under the age of 15. Twenty per cent of our 14- and 15-year-old girls are sexually active ... One-third of all births to teenagers, ages 14 to 19 are illegitimate. Furthermore five-sixths of all infants born to girls 14 and younger are born out of wedlock ... You may be as astonished as I was to find out that adolescent pregnancy in the United States is substantially higher than in any of the developing countries.[32]

One of the points that expert witnesses made over and over again was that the sexual behaviour of the teenager was very different from that of an adult and that the most effective forms of contraception, namely the pill and the IUD, were not suitable in the context of irregular sexual activity. Frequent reference was made to the possibility of a "morning-after" pill, which simply means, an abortifacient pill, rather than constant medication to prevent conception. Particular concern was caused by the possibility that federal funding might be withdrawn from abortion as it was in 1979, so that the penniless young whose only hope lay through Medicaid would be saddled with the unwanted consequences of their own hastiness. The six hundred pages of evidence collected during that week all point to an obvious conclusion, which was not well-taken, that the factor of cost and dependence upon hospital resources must be removed from abortion, as must pain and guilt and fear, if our lip-service to the ideal of sexual freedom is to become the real thing. There is no contraceptive which is appropriate to the turbulent and dazzling time of the discovery of love and sex, in which the realisation of the immediate and personal possibility of pregnancy plays an important part.

Curiously enough those representatives of anti-abortion groups who appeared before the committee had no objection to the insertion of IUDs in teenage women, although abortion itself was so touchy a topic that no one was game to come clean and state that what was needed to solve the problem was a free, fast and non-traumatic abortion service. The acceptance of the IUD while rejecting no-nonsense deliberate pregnancy termination is simple hypocrisy, which is a common phenomenon, but what is uncommon about this moral sloppiness is its utter callousness when it comes to the life and health of the young women who are expected to endure such diabolical gadgetry. Throughout the hearings, the fiction that adequate contraceptive technology existed and that the problem was simply one of delivery and KAP (Knowledge-Attitude-Practice) among the young was repeated *ad nauseam*, although one young mother-to-be had had her say about the mess in no uncertain terms:

> I was having so many problems with different kinds of birth control that it was getting on my nerves, so I stopped ... I had an IUD and it fell out. It twisted and moved and then fell out. After that I waited for a while and then went on the pill. I had bleeding for seventeen days and I went to Howard University Hospital and they gave me a shot and some pills because I was losing too much blood ... A lot of people don't realise and, I guess, men don't, that women are human. (Laughter.) We are just tired of putting all this stuff in our bodies. It is really hectic.[33]

The idea that young people should use abortion as a primary method of birth control causes the most extreme disgust, while the phenomenon of a very young woman struggling with powerful and potentially very destructive medications leaves most people unmoved. The attitude seems to be a punitive one; if young people wish to be sexually active they must put their own health in jeopardy or suffer unwanted childbirth and forced marriage. It was notable that the chairman of the committee was very much less troubled by the tragic phenomenon of teenage marriage than he was by the rising rate of illegitimacy.

The commonest idea of abortion is still that of dilation and curettage involving hospitalisation and anaesthesia; if that was still the principal and virtually the only mode of pregnancy termination, the rejection of abortion as a form of birth control would be understandable. In dozens of debates and public discussions of abortion it has been obvious to me, as one of the speakers, that we were quite unable to discuss abortion in principle, or ideal abortion, because speakers and audience included had absolutely no idea of how much techniques of pregnancy termination had improved.[34] The universal conviction is that abortions should be carried out at great expense by highly qualified personnel in hospital, while the only alternative is "back-street" abortion carried out by wicked old crones in filthy conditions with bent knitting-needles. Laws and regulations made to control the number of abortions carried out have the ostensible purpose of controlling profiteering by highly qualified personnel, and those who fight for the liberalisation of abortion law generally justify their activities by reference to the scourge of "back-street" abortion. The only way to deal with both sides of the problem is to develop low-cost, easy-access abortion services which can respond sensitively to the pressure of demand, so that abortions are not unnecessarily delayed and women are not forced to have recourse to private or illegal agencies. Such a course of action involves a positive commitment to abortion which very few public authorities are prepared to countenance, so women languish in the present absurdly confused situation where public hospitals have nine-month waiting lists for abortion beds, where private clinics are crowded with foreign women undergoing delayed terminations, where simple intervention becomes an increasingly serious operation and the complication rate is criminally elevated, where organised crime runs abortion clinics and thousands of gynaecological beds all over the world are continually occupied by women who have been butchered or have butchered themselves in their desperate determination not to bear a child. If it were possible to deliver to women a safe, early-intervention abortifacient instead of sending them pleading and plotting round the private and public delivery services growing ever "more pregnant" as their bodies adjust to the demands of a growing foetus, and the foetus proceeds inexorably towards viability, it would seem mad and perverse to refuse to make it available. In effect, through humbug and compromise, this is exactly what has happened.

The most likely development in "contraception" after the steroid pill is some form of luteolytic agent, a once-a-month pill which will act directly on the *corpus luteum* so that it ceases to secrete the progesterone necessary for the maintenance of a pregnancy. The advantages of such an abortifacient pill over the contraceptive steroids which he did so much to develop have been summarised by Professor Carl Djerassi:

> Such a once-a-month pill would have at least four advantages over presently used oral contraceptives. First, ingesting a single pill once a month is more convenient than daily pill taking. Second, periodic short-term administration of a drug (once a month) would be expected to give rise to fewer long-term side-effects, primarily because the agent is intended to act at a specific time on a well-defined biological process rather than interfere for long periods with the entire hormonal balance. Third, a luteolytic agent would be effective as a contraceptive irrespective of whether fertilisation has occurred – it would be a menses inducer in the non-pregnant woman and an early abortifacient in a pregnant subject. Fourth, such a luteolytic agent might be active any time during the first eight weeks after fertilisation; it could then be taken bi-monthly.[35]

Professor Djerassi's use of the term *contraceptive* in this inappropriate context is typical of the doublethink which seeks to keep the action of mini-pills and IUDs out of the troubled field of abortion polemic. It must be obvious to any scientist that if it is better to take a medication only when it is necessary, it must be better to use the luteolytic pill only when a period is delayed and a pregnancy is suspected, nevertheless Djerassi insists upon a ritualistic usage on a regular basis, whether it be once a month or once every two months. This squeamishness extends further into the field of early abortion in the case of what is euphemistic-ally known as Menstrual Regulation.

Menstrual Regulation was given that name because it was thought initially that it would escape classification as a method of abortion if it were to be practised on the twenty-eighth day of every cycle and not simply when bleeding was delayed. The technique used is simple, being the extraction of the contents of the uterus by inserting a narrow cannula (c. 4 mm) and exerting negative pressure while turning the cannula so that the nicks at the head of it pass over the whole of the uterine wall. The method requires asepsis and dexterity and very little else, besides the cannula and the pump, which may even be a hand syringe. Oddly enough, Djerassi, who thought that the luteolytic pill should be taken regularly, is of a very different opinion when it comes to menstrual extraction:

> Though it is frequently done without a pregnancy test (especially in developing countries), this is definitely undesirable since less than 10 per cent of missed menses are due to pregnancy. As newer and more accurate pregnancy tests are introduced (those currently available are already reliable within one week of fertilisation, that is, before the first missed menstrual period), menstrual extraction should be performed only after a positive pregnancy test is obtained.[36]

The woman who applies for menstrual extraction may not wish to wait until a pregnancy is confirmed in her case – for one thing, if she lives in crowded circumstances, her mother-in-law might notice and thereafter an abortion could well be impossible.[37] Whether or not she was pregnant could always be ascertained afterwards by proper examination of the material removed from the uterus. Such examination would also reveal abnormalities which might be disrupting her cycle and ought to be dealt with whenever she did desire to become pregnant. For many women, repeated visits to a clinic are simply not possible; they require decisive help at once, without ceremony or excessive consultation, for the difficult decision is already taken.

In October 1977, a village-based maternal and child health care programme was introduced in 70 villages in Matlab *thana*, in Bangladesh. The services were carried out by trained women who lived in the villages themselves, paramedics, in fact; or in other words, back-street practitioners, properly trained and equipped for once, rather than vilified. In four clinics at the periphery and one in Matlab bazaar, six Lady Family Planning Visitors carried out Menstrual Regulation.

> The procedure, equivalent to an induced abortion early during the pregnancy, is being offered in a setting in which induced abortion is prohibited culturally and on religious grounds and is socially associated with illicit relationships. There is, however, no doubt that many women who want to terminate their pregnancies seek help from traditional herbalists and other healers as well as from village *dais* (traditional birth attendants). One-tenth of the cases in the gynaecology ward of the Dacca Medical Hospital in 1979 were admitted because of complications (mainly acute damage to the uterus) following induced abortion by such persons.[38]

The procedure is not equivalent to an induced abortion – it *is* an induced abortion by another name – but the researchers insist upon their superiority to the herbalists and midwives although one might well wonder whether the comparatively low figure of ten per cent of cases in the gynaecologic ward does not point to an unusual degree of competence rather than the opposite. Rather higher proportions of abortion damage cases are to be found in other countries in hospitals where a higher proportion of normal births are routinely carried out; until we know more about the case load of Dacca Medical Hospital in 1976 we cannot assess the significance of the ten per cent. The implied contempt for "such persons" who are responsible for supplying cheap and accessible pregnancy termination services had cost the women of the world very dear.

In 1975 the *Journal of Pharmaceutical Sciences* published an extraordinary article in which the results of a computerised digest of information on 3000 plants said to have direct effects upon the human reproductive system were set out schematically. Proceeding from "folkloric" information, pharmacologists all over the world have been trying for the last twenty years to isolate the active agents in plants and to establish the mechanisms by which they function. In the last ten years the work has intensified, culminating in the programme set up by the World Health Organisation Special Programme of Research, Development and Research Training in Human Reproduction at six centres, the Chinese University of Hong Kong, the Natural Products Research Institute at the National University of Seoul, the University of Pernambuco in Brazil, the University of Sri Lanka, the City University in London, and the College of Pharmacy at the University of Illinois, headed by the Professor of Pharmacognosy from Illinois, Norman Farmsworth.[39] Thus history has come full circle, for the story of women's loss of control of their fertility is at least in part the story of the suppression and disappearance of local herbal lore and practice, which was supplanted by modern professional medicine.

The story of how

America's regular physicians committed to the forward-looking tenets of what would become scientific medicine, began a concerted, self-conscious and eventually successful drive designed to improve, professionalise and ultimately control the practice of medicine in the United States

has been partly told in James C. Mohr's *Abortion in America*.[40] It must be added, however, that the commercialisation of herbal lore coincided with its debasement and a great decrease in its effectiveness. The vegetable preparations which included black hellebore, aloes, oil of juniper, jalap, scammony, seneca snakeroot, black cohosh, pennyroyal, as well as other herbs of no likely effectiveness, were sold at ridiculous prices by unscrupulous people without concern for the niceties of timing, dose calculation and the synergistic action of other compounds. As Professor Farmsworth and his colleagues are only too well aware, it is no easy matter to ensure that the right part of the plant is used, that it is gathered at the right stage of the plant's development, that the active agent is not destroyed by preparation or the manner of keeping, that it is administered to the patient at the right stage in the cycle or in the pregnancy, and that the administration is continued for the right length of time. Mistaking the dose of purgatives and poisons can lead to uncontrollable results, ranging all the way from total ineffectiveness to adequate function and beyond to drastic uterine damage and death.

Plant substances have been found which influence the reproductive cycle at all stages, from the suppression of ovulation to the creation of a vaginal or cervical environment hostile to sperm, and through all the stages of pregnancy. The most obvious aspect of the work of Farmsworth and his colleagues was that abortifacients outnumbered contraceptives – including substances which prevented implantation rather than fertilisation – by six to one. The difference *may* mean that there are simply more substances which act upon the uterus than act upon the hypothalamus, but it *must* mean that there has always and everywhere been a higher demand for botanicals to restore missed menses than to suppress fertility, with the result that there is a far higher index of awareness of botanicals as interceptors when other means have failed. In other words, people have preferred, historically, to regulate fertility by non-medical means, resorting to medical means in times of immediate need only. Even in Farnsworth's list of fertility-inhibiting plants, which include many which by the criteria used by this writer are actually early abortifacients, the majority of plants used have been shown to have little or no unpredictable effects, in that they reduce fertility rather than suppressing it altogether for distinct periods.

J. F. Dastur, in his "concise work describing plants used for drugs and remedies according to Ayurvedic, Unani, Tibbi systems", does not even include the locution, "contraceptives". The one plant he refers to in the text as having contraceptive properties, noting simply that women eat the seeds to prevent conception, was repeatedly tested by Indian pharmacologists in the late sixties and was found to have anti-oestrogenic properties but to be too toxic for regular use. The twenty-eight abortifacients he lists, on the other hand, are almost all of scientifically proven effectiveness while being accessible to all who can recognise the plants (most of which are very common and very well-known) and have the elementary knowledge necessary to prepare the active compounds.[41]

It must not be thought that every patch of waste ground contains a multitude of miraculous vegetables which have only to be popped into the mouth or some other orifice to restore missed menses. Most herbal abortifacients, if taken by mouth, exert a double action, on the one hand simply toxic and on the other uterine stimulant. The woman makes herself so sick that the life of the foetus is jeopardised and the direct action of the drug on the uterine muscle expels the dead or dying foetus. Women undergoing these crude abortions need constant care, for in the course of the operation of the drug, which may be built up over days, they will become deathly sick and their vital functions may be severely impaired, while the violent contractions of the uterus, coupled with changes in temperature, heart rate and blood pressure, may cause severe haemorrhage.[42] Successful abortion by folk means depends upon the tremendous courage of the patient and the skill and resource of her attendant. The masculine culture may proscribe abortion and deny that it ever happens, but this privileged optimism is bought at the expense of women's guilt. Not only must women risk their lives to serve the common good, but they are repaid with a secret and sometimes heartrending burden of shame instead of the honour they deserve. The women who share the risk, who struggle to accomplish the necessary act with inadequate means and in insalubrious circumstances, are often outcasts, resorted to by stealth and regarded with fear and disgust.

In Europe, the most commonly used plant extracts were the volatile oils of tansy, pennyroyal, rue, parsley (apiol) and juniper (savin). They were usually employed in conjunction with plant alkaloids and other substances having catalytic properties. The identification of the mode of their operation and the degree of their effectiveness is nowadays almost impossible, for the exact procedures are forgotten. Extracts and compounds prepared in laboratory conditions may lack certain essential properties, in much the same way that say, pharmaceutical vitamin C is less efficiently absorbed by the human organism than the vitamin C in fresh oranges. Moreover, the oral dosing of the patient can seldom have been the whole story of folk abortion. Highly irritant and uterine stimulant pessaries were often placed in the vagina and even pushed through the mouth of the womb. One of the commonest kinds of abortion practised in the Indian subcontinent was the insertion of a blunt twig or root or bark into the cervix, which it gradually dilated by absorbing fluid from the surrounding membranes, while its own volatile or aromatic properties both stimulated the uterus and helped to prevent infection. In the West and her colonies, a *sonda* or urethral catheter is a less efficient substitute. Infusions of uterine tonics taken by mouth helped to speed the process of expulsion. The procedure was hardly comfortable, but in comparison with the other kinds of medi al and surgical treatment which people had to undergo in the age before anaesthesia, it was a breeze. There were and are attendant dangers, but these are very much lessened by the competence and dexterity of the practitioner. In circumstances where such alternative medicine is alive and well and respected, rather than cringing along in the shadow of white-coated professional allopathy, abortion is likely to be much safer than childbirth, and that fact alone would explain why so many women had recourse to it. The tragic end of this female self-determination can be seen, in England at any rate in the working-class resort to gin (itself a feeble memory of oil of juniper, for gin is flavoured with juniper berries) castor oil, boiling-hot baths and, if you were lucky enough to find any, quinine, ergot and strychnine. If you boiled yourself alive, drank yourself into a seizure and gulped down the quinine bolus until your ears rang, you might lose your baby. You were slightly more likely to lose your life.

The general rule is that abortions are more likely to result in complications the more advanced the pregnancy.[43] There is some evidence that dilation of the cervix and removal of its contents in very early pregnancy has a worse effect upon subsequent fertility in that it affects the future capacity of the womb to carry a foetus to term, although the champions of menstrual extraction give little weight to it. The search for a reliable luteolytic agent goes on, and the results are very encouraging, but even more work is being done on the group of complex and powerful human proteins known as prostaglandins. Fifty years ago researchers noticed that there was something in human semen which caused the uterus to contract; in 1935 the Nobel prize-winner Ulf von Euler gave the substance the name *prostaglandin* in the mistaken belief that it was produced by the prostate. In fact there are numerous prostaglandins produced in many tissues throughout the body and they have been found to effect great advances in the treatment of blood-clotting disorders, stomach ulceration, high blood pressure and rheumatism. The first clinical use of prostaglandin was carried out by Dr S. S. Karim in his native Uganda. He used them to induce labour in childbirth and then, noticing their efficacy in inducing uterine contractions, in 1970 he began to use them to terminate pregnancy.[44]

At first, the greatest problem was posed by the route of administration. Instillation into a vein had to be undertaken gradually, and although the abortions which resulted were complete, the side-effects were unacceptable, because of the prostaglandin's effect on vital processes. Administration by mouth was far too upsetting to the stomach, so Karim decided to try placing lactose tablets containing 20 milligrams of prostaglandin in the vagina. Of the twelve patients in his original sample only one failed to abort, and the side effects, nausea, abdominal cramps and heavy bleeding, seemed manageable. Injecting prostaglandin under the skin or into a muscle had unacceptable systemic effects, and research into this kind of administration was abandoned. Gradually, Karim and the other researchers in the field worked out that the best way was to bombard the uterus with frequent doses at high concentrations, but the side-effects, "diarrhoea, feeling cold or shivering, headaches, coughs, cramps and dizziness" had to be controlled by further medication and the patient had to be kept under observation in hospital because of the possibility of collapse. Nevertheless, the researchers were jubilant; the do-it-yourself abortion kit was just around the corner. In 1975 M. Bygdeman reported that the prostaglandin suppository

> eliminates the need for hospitalisation, personnel and anaesthesia; is almost 100% effective in terminating pregnancies if administered in the first 4 weeks after the missed menses; is suitable as an outpatient method; may reduce the risks associated with surgical intervention in the uterus; causes only minimal side-effects that are easily controlled; seems to be harmless to the non-pregnant individual; can be self-administered.[45]

G. M. Filshie, however, who has been associated with the prostaglandin programme in Uganda under Professor Karim since the early days, is more cautious about the feasibility of prostaglandins for regular household use in the case of missed periods. On the one hand he is concerned that women themselves are too feckless and ignorant of their own body processes to use the medication responsibly and he doubts the ability of many health workers to establish the stage of gestation. Self-administration of prostaglandins in late pregnancy will result in abortion but the procedure is much more dangerous and any patient who overdosed herself would be in immediate danger of uterine damage, haemorrhage and death. On the other hand, delivery of prostaglandin interception at an early stage in pregnancy is jeopardised by the state of public awareness, and by the inadequacy of medical services. Moreover, he reiterates the strange red herring that prostaglandin's side-effects would deter most women from taking it every month as if it were a contraceptive.[46] Like almost all the other workers in the field, Filshie perpetuates the muddle about contraception and interception by disguising abortifacients as contraceptives. More cynical observers might see in the whole rigmarole a curious lack of interest in a medication which might never need to be used at all (as hundreds of thousands of infertile women take the pill regularly in the mistaken fear that they might fall pregnant) and would at most be needed two or three times a year. For women whose sex lives are less than intensive – the majority, one might guess – a pack of three prostaglandin suppositories in the medicine cabinet might be all they would need for years on end. The relative unpleasantness of using it might reinforce other kinds of fertility regulation while removing the weight of anxiety which makes them such a burden. Nowadays prostaglandins are regularly used in hospital terminations, when they are either instilled into the uterus or placed inside the uterus in a silastic pellet in much the same way as IUDs are, with an applicator. Prostaglandin gels are the safest way of inducing second trimester abortions.

The prostaglandins have been successfully synthesised, and are no longer the extremely expensive derivatives of human bodily fluids which once they were. Many of the patents are held by the pharmaceutical multinationals, who are in no hurry to knock the bottom out of their own huge oral contraceptive market by supplanting three-hundred odd pills per woman-year by six or nine at most. Meanwhile the population controllers tear their hair, for in countries where women regularly undergo abortions much more frightful in every way than the nauseated, purging, chilled and sweaty episode with prostaglandin, the availability of prostaglandins would be a tremendous boon. Dr Reimert Ravenholt, who has been passionately interested in prostaglandins ever since Karim's original experiments, openly stated to me that he intended to use AID money to supply prostaglandins to less-developed countries in his capacity as director of AID population services, and he would have them manufactured in Italy or some other country which did not respect drug copyrights.[47] Unfortunately perhaps, he was relieved of his post before he could bring this to pass. Some women's lives may have been saved as a result, but many more have been lost.

So far, the discussion has concerned itself exclusively with very early pregnancy termination, which is sometimes quite inexcusably confused with contraception, and at other times is distinguished both from contraception and from abortion by being called *interception*. From the technical point of view interception, whether by vacuum aspiration, luteolytic medication or by prostaglandin suppositories, is quite possible but in practical terms interception is not a viable option. The obscurantism and sluggishness of the medical establishment in this matter have the effect of making interception a mere pipe-dream, thereby procuring unequivocal abortion in its place. For those people who see an essential difference between interception and abortion, the promotion of interceptive methods might be seen as part of an anti-abortion campaign. For those who prefer to call a spade a spade, interception has only the considerable advantages that it does not torment the woman by unnecessary delay. It is a minor operation with an extremely low complication rate, it costs less than surgical abortion, it makes less demand upon the practitioner, and it can be carried out in privacy or in neighbourhood clinics or health centres. If the viability of the foetus is a fundamental consideration, as in the view of this author it ought to be, interception has the further advantage that the incipient life is not brought nearer realisation than is absolutely unavoidable.

We hear of pregnancy tests which are cheap to carry out and accurate although carried out within a few days of the missed menses, but in fact, even in Harley Street, pregnancy testers prefer to wait until the 42nd day since the last period or later, and they take their time about the results which may take another week or ten days. Women in experimental programmes may have different experiences, but for the woman trying to cope with the problem of a missed period the keynote of her experience is humbug and delay. The effect of all controls on the number of abortions carried out, whether by the *ad hoc* method of licensing a certain number of beds and allowing only as many abortions per twenty-four hour period as there are licensed beds, or by demanding the consent of other doctors or psychiatrists, or by maintaining inadequate services in public hospitals so that there is a nine-month waiting-list for abortion, is to lengthen unwanted pregnancies and to make their termination more problematic than it need be. There are few diseases which have as precipitous a career as unwanted pregnancy which runs its whole gamut in nine months; in any other case the muddle and delay which result in second-trimester terminations would be considered highly unethical, whether from the point of view that any practitioner who refuses a minor operation in the full knowledge that a few weeks later a major operation with general anaesthesia will be necessary if the minor operation was not performed, is not acting in the best interests of his patient. Nor is he behaving responsibly toward the foetus, whose capacity for suffering increases as its capacity for independent life develops.[48]

Even the most enlightened champions of women's right to choose work from a curiously limited viewpoint, which has little relevance to the world's women and their history of struggle with life and death. Thomas Szasz is a man of vision, but even he sets the problem out in an ethnocentric and institutionalised form:

> Abortion is a moral, not a medical problem. To be sure the procedure is surgical; but this makes abortion no more a medical problem than the use of the electric chair makes capital punishment a problem of electrical engineering ...[49]

To use his own analogy against him, we might say that surgical abortion stands in the same relation to the whole picture of abortion as judicial electrocution does to death. Abortions may be spontaneous, as the vast majority of them are, or IUD-induced, induced by drugs, by disease or even by massage. "Fully eighty per cent of abortions" in Thailand are estimated to be performed by a technique which has no reference to the experts who, Szasz rather disingenuously contends, must perform the bidding of women who have made up their minds, and is also widely used in Malaysia and the Philippines.

> Twenty-year-old Chun is a village abortionist who took over this role from her mother when she died. Each of her clients – she usually sees about seven each month – lies on her back on the floor with her legs spread apart and a pillow or rolled cloth is placed under her back to raise the lower abdomen. Chun locates the foetal mass using external palpation and raises the uterus by pushing with her bare heel just below the pubic bone.
> The mass is dislodged by a pressing and pulling motion of the fingertips from the pubic bone to the navel, and the area of the abdomen above the embryo is then massaged with the thumb or base of the palm. The whole procedure may extend over 20–30 minutes or more since Chun will pause if the client complains of intolerable pain; if necessary the procedure is repeated next day ...
> The Thai caseloads are very mixed, with both single and married women and a whole range of occupations from farmers to students and civil servants. Most abortions are carried out in the first trimester, although it is occasionally carried out as late as seven or eight months and is sometimes performed even before a period is missed ... Rural abortionists charge from a minimum of 170 *baht* (US $8.50) to about 660 *baht* (US $30) – only a few charge very exploitative prices.[50]

The village abortionist in Thailand is an expert; in Harley Street her hands would be worth a fortune and instead of seven patients a week she would take seventy. Her job, on the other hand might be more difficult, as her patients would come long distances in fear and trembling, oppressed by the hardship of finding the exploitative price which pretends to be no more than the expert's due and a guarantee that there will be no complications. Massage abortion does produce complications, in about the same measure as spontaneous abortion after the first few weeks necessitating curettage to remove retained material and to stop bleeding.

Its greatest advantage is that it occurs completely outside the institutional framework, in the ambience of the neighbourhood, responding only to the pressure of demand. Thai women who have no access to the village network must rely upon institutional abortion, legal only in case of severe threat to maternal life and health, or in cases of rape or incest, or with the consent of two doctors; in 1975 only 1,200 of these kinds of abortions were carried out. Now that Thai hospitals deal with the complications of abortion, spontaneous and induced, the element of danger is further removed from the village abortion: among the 3,530 cases of septic, incomplete or threatened abortion treated in one Bangkok hospital there must have been a certain proportion of women treated by village practitioners, as well as a certain number who had used the herbal preparations sold in most village stores.

> The question is not one of medical and psychiatric justification for abortion, but of ethical judgment and social policy. If we truly believe that in a free society the expert should be on tap, not on top – we must place the power to decide when an abortion may be performed (legally) in the hands of the pregnant women, and not in the hands of the Church, the State, the American Medical Association, or the American Law Institute.[51]

So runs the rest of Szasz's argument. The struggle for control of the uncontrollable, of which his argument forms a part, is itself a legacy of the thousands of years of history in which human society has been ruled and has been publicly constituted by the sex that does not menstruate.

It is clearly wrong for the pregnant woman's wish to override the "experts'" own convictions of the correct course to follow, whether from a professional or a personal point of view. To use a practitioner's skill, intelligence and industry against his will is to reduce him to the status of a machine. The struggle for free abortion is undertaken precisely because we see that to reduce any person to that status is wrong, whether it be as a baby-producing machine or a baby-killing machine.[52] Szasz's attempt to drag abortion into the public arena as a sort of super-value which overrides the individual's right to withhold his labour is a product of his own faith in the power of institutions, but women have always lived and died outside legality, religion, established morality and righteous ideology – this is what is meant when they are described as practical, primitive and so forth. The only sensible course to follow in cases like the Thai example is to supply the village practitioner with what she lacks, emergency health care in the case of complications, hygienic surroundings in which to carry out her work, healthy women to work with, and freedom from the fear of prosecution.

Even in countries like Italy, the legalisation of abortion may be as irrelevant as it is in Thailand. The vast majority of Italian abortions are carried out by the midwives, who use no criterion beyond the client's need and charge modest sums. The new Italian abortion law simply means that the luxury clinics can operate without fear of closure; the midwives, who provide a necessary service as best they can, are still outside the law.

In the old days of dilation and curettage, surgeons preferred to wait until the last two weeks of the first trimester because dilation was easier, and the products of conception were more easily detached from the uterine wall. Other crude forms of traumatic abortion also were carried out in the second trimester rather than the first; they range from the damaging of the foetus and rupture of the amnion by massage by the methods known to wise women in Asia, to appallingly brutal methods such as that practised by the Yanomamö Indians, among whom the pregnant woman would simply lie on her back "and have a friend jump on her belly to rupture the amnion." Among other peoples a board was placed over the pregnant woman's belly, and two other people trod up and down on it. In lesser degrees of brutal effectiveness we have the whole gamut of insertions of pointed objects in the uterus together with the instillation of all kinds of fluids, in cruder forms of the usual method of second-trimester termination, which proceeds in two stages, instillation and evacuation.

A modern woman can only marvel at the heroic determination of women who underwent these appalling tortures and at the strength of motivation that such courage implies. The Yanomamö Indians practised infanticide as well as abortion, and it would seem obvious that the sacrifice of a new-born child whose grip on life was weak at best was far preferable to jeopardising the life and health of a grown food-gatherer with other mouths to feed, but women underwent this ordeal to avoid infanticide, which was not, and probably never has been, taken lightly.[53] Others were forced to abort by husbands who feared that the child was not theirs. Sometimes women crushed their bodies in this way because they could not wean their living child too early, or because their fixed and limited food supply was already inadequate. It was tantamount to martyrdom, for the complication rate must have been colossal. Uterine damage, cervical tearing, retained material and haemorrhage may well have been more likely than the successful expulsion of the whole contents of the uterus. The point of the historical fact is clear; women would risk death rather than bear an unwanted child.

Sentimentalised notions of motherhood have blurred the real nature of the maternal function as it has been carried out since prehistory. In reality motherhood is a bloody business, from the first menstruations through pregnancies, births, miscarriages, infant deaths and the frequent deaths of mothers themselves. Besides the virtues of tenderness, patience, and self-forgetfulness, a mother had to exercise courage, determination and decisiveness. It was not only her duty to bring children into the world in the service of her people, but her duty to see that the number of children remained in the right balance with the adult population and the potential food supply. It was she who instructed her attendant not to wash the child that she had brought forth with pain, or to see that it did not draw its first breath. She herself may have bashed its brains out with a rock, or thrown it on the ground or against a tree, or strangled it with a vine or stood upon a stick laid across its neck or poured sand into its mouth. Such violent acts were the more merciful; the fate of children thrown into ditches or cess-pits or left on hillsides to die of exposure was more cruel, as the people who gathered up the children of American soldiers from Vietnamese ditches can testify. The cruellest fate of all is that suffered by millions of female children who gradually succumb to infantile diseases rendered fatal by the consequences of years of chronic malnutrition. Where sons are an asset and daughters a liability condemned to a life of toil and misery in the houses of strangers, when food is scarce the boys eat and the girls do not. When boys are ill, poor parents trudge for hundreds of miles to find help while girls simply turn their faces to the wall. When well-meaning missionaries moved heavenly and earthly authorities to stamp out the evil of infanticide, they succeeded both in unbalancing the population and condemning female children to slow death rather than immediate annihilation by a merciful opiate.[54] The lesson is clear, *if you will not feed them, do not condemn them to life*, but it was never taken.

The observed practice of infanticide amongst hunter-gatherer peoples like the Bushmen of the Kalahari, Australian Aborigines, Eskimos and the Yanomamö Indians is gradually leading to the reluctant acceptance of the idea that infanticide was the chief mechanism by which stone-age man regulated his own numbers and maintained the optimum relationship with his environment.[55] While many anthropologists exclaim angrily against the modishness of infanticide as an explanation of the astonishingly slow rate of increase of pre-agricultural populations, others, like Marvin Harris, have erected whole theories of history upon this basis. Harris states quite unequivocally:

> Actually, the most widely used method of population control during much of human history was probably some form of female infanticide. Although the psychological costs of killing or starving one's infant daughters can be dulled by culturally defining them as non-persons (just as modern pro-abortionists ... define foetuses as non-infants), the material costs of nine months of pregnancy are not so easily written off. It is safe to assume that most people who practice infanticide would rather not see their infants die. But the alternatives – drastically lowering the nutritional, sexual and health standards of the entire group – have usually been judged to be even more undesirable, at least in pre-state societies.[56]

There are some aspects of Harris's thesis which are, as he would readily admit, a little too schematic and generalised. His insistence on a standard of sexual life which involves free access to sexual pleasure is a modernistic extrapolation, especially when, as we have seen, ritual and spontaneous homosexuality are not unusual in so-called primitive societies. Sexual abstinence does not terrify the illiterate anywhere near as much as it appals the post-Reichian generations. Nevertheless, it is obvious that when techniques of abortion are crude and dangerous, infanticide makes more sense. Even in terms of Christian morality, the calculation must be made: abortion kills one and places the life of another in jeopardy, while infanticide kills one only. Harris does not take into account the slenderness of the hold that the new-born have upon life in many societies, a slenderness which is eroded by apparently senseless practices which have a further effect of culling the new-born, whether it be cutting the umbilical cord with a dirty sickle, so that children die of easily avoided *Tetanus neonatorum* or sending women to give birth in dangerous and filthy conditions, as is still done in traditional Hindu societies.[57]

The element of individual decision and guilt in infanticide can be reduced by haphazard culling by virtual invitation of disease, or, say, by having the child trampled by blindfolded animals, or by the superstitious seizing of all kinds of reasons for eliminating a new-born child: for example, the Tswana of Botswana are said to have killed infants born feet-first. All hunter-gatherer peoples would have to kill one of twins, because gathering women cannot deal with more than one child who cannot travel for long periods at her own pace: the birth of children too closely one after the other was partly obviated by lactational sterility and by abstinence, but when such methods failed infanticide had to be used. A child whose mother died in childbirth was condemned to death because there was no mother to feed it; sometimes a child whose father was dead would not be allowed to live. Deformed children, whose care would have have been an intolerable burden, were killed. Children whose mothers' milk failed starved to death. Where there was a taboo on intercourse during lactation, the birth of a girl child might postpone the arrival of a desired boy for years, and so she must die.

In almost all such cases, some kind of supernatural reason is produced by way of showing that such actions were not wanted but were prescribed, so that the parent responsible could carry them out in grief and deep reluctance, while feeling that she had fulfilled an onerous and agonising responsibility in the only way possible. The element of stress was reduced by the acceptance of a higher, inscrutable will. The executed infant would be characterised as some kind of a criminal or blighted thing or as a non-human entering upon human life only after the performance of some ritual of acceptance of which modern baptism, which cleanses the stain of original sin, may be some pallid recollection. When the frequency of infant death, to which parents had perforce to inure themselves, is taken into account, the great affection of infanticidal peoples for their surviving children is quite understandable. Paradoxically, infanticide is typical of cultures in which the maternal relationship is the most important; the loss of a grown child will distress those parents more who killed other children so that the child might have a chance. Sometimes, dead brothers and sisters were buried beneath the threshold or the floor of the house, so that they would still be members of the family, collectively realised as it were in the children who survived. An odd survival of the continuity concept uniting siblings is the habit of calling successive children whose elder siblings are dead by the same name, as if children replace one another.

Primitive man could not afford to devote any significant proportion of his resources to the preservation of the lives of sickly children; modern man, whose chances of bearing genetically incompetent children are probably greater, is morally bound to keep children alive as long as is humanly possible, even if the unfortunate children have got to live in isolation in sterile chambers. The killing of a new-born child is deeply repugnant to modern sensibility, or is thought to be.[58] We assume that we have this reverence for human life because our moral sensibility is more elevated, whereas we simply lack the concept of a collective good to be served by our difficult choices in such matters. We accept only a sort of abstract good which has very arbitrary and often quite destructive requirements. Our concepts could more correctly be described as legalistic rather than moral, in that "morally" specifically refers to our responsibilities to others rather than to the letter of the law. Given our behaviour in cases like that of the mongoloid child described in Chapter I, we are not entitled to claim moral superiority over the people who might have taken the mongoloidism for the mark of the devil and killed the child, or who might innocently have given it the breast and asphyxiated it.

It is difficult nowadays to discern any clear-cut moral good to serve, for we do not live in distinct communities with stable food supplies, but in the exploding capitalist economy where there is virtually no demonstrable relationship between the numbers of people and the supply of resources. The invention of agriculture is thought to have been spurred on by the necessity of intensive food production, which may itself have been forced by the increasing reluctance of people to live by infanticide, and warfare. Many religions, among them Islam and Buddhism, made their appeal at least partly as an escape from infanticide while the ideology of production spawned its own ideology of reproduction. Families became imperialistic while those deprived of reproductive rights, the fornicators and adulterers, killed their offspring.

"Disguised infanticide" was a further limiting device prevalent throughout Western Europe in the late eighteenth and early nineteenth centuries (Darwin,

1871, Vol, I, p. 129; von Öttingen, 1882, pp. 236ff.). Langer (1972, pp. 6–8) provides vivid documentation of this widespread practice as it was systematically carried out in England and France. The London Foundling Hospital, which after open admissions in 1756 was to accept some 15,000 children over the next four years, was called by one of its governors a "slaughterhouse of infants" because the mortality there was nearly equal to its admissions. There were always, of course, the more common, direct physical means of ridding oneself of an unwanted child. Legal sanctions against it were light and ineffectual. The physician W. B. Ryan wrote in 1862 that not only is infanticide not considered by the general public "in the same light" as other murders, but there is no other crime that "meets with so much sympathy." And infanticide was equally prevalent on the continent. Between 1824 and 1833, a single decade, 336,297 infants were consigned to the French hospices, there to meet the same fate as their opposite numbers in England. It would appear that late in the eighteenth century and early in the nineteenth, fully 80% of the foundlings died within a year after birth.[59]

The angel-makers of Europe in the late eighteenth and early nineteenth century may have had earlier counterparts, but their existence seems dependent upon that of an urban proletariat. Before the Factory Acts women were preferred as mill-workers, because they were steadier than men and had not usually the male predilection for strong drink. The survival of their families depended upon their keeping in work, so the frequent pregnancies which resulted from deracination, helplessness and gin which undermined the old forms of regulation practised by agrarian workers, were simply ignored. Many women miscarried on the factory floor, others brought their babies to term and immediately returned to work their twelve- or sixteen-hour days, while the milk ran down their bodices. The hungry babies were given into the hands of a nurse who silenced their screaming with laudanum, and so died tens of thousands of babies every year in European manufacturing towns. The crimes of the angel-makers were hardly recognisable as infanticide.[60] Mothers had to work, children had to wait and laudanum was merciful. Besides, there is a good deal of evidence that infanticide was not rigorously prosecuted by law, unless it was the subject of some sort of scandal. The grim fate of so many children of poor working women went virtually without comment, or else it was assumed that the high rate of wastage among the children of the labouring poor was due to ignorance and fecklessness. In 1903 a quarter of the children born in mill towns died every year.[61] The possibility that mothers of families in which one child died of starvation (including Marx's own family) were practising some *ad hoc* form of triage is a horrifying one; it opens up vistas of mental anguish beyond human endurance, but behind the terrible apathy in the eyes of many of the thousands of women who are sitting with dying children in their laps as I type this, lies not blankness but the exhaustion of intolerable decisions protracted through fear and uncertainty and the hope that a solution might be found.[62] There are many handouts but no solutions; peace workers might be horrified to know how often the stronger children get all the food and the starving ones none. Motherhood, like nature herself, is red in tooth and claw.

Demographers may develop amazing statistical skills to demonstrate how long it takes a bereaved family to replace a dead child, but their statistics can hardly make sense of the different circumstances surrounding the death of a wanted child and the death of an unwanted child, the death of a boy or the death of a girl.[63] There are so many fine shades between resignation to unavoidable infant death and the deliberate killing of a child, that we cannot be sure what infant death in any one case actually signifies; for example, mother's milk may have failed but while for a son an alternative source of nutrition might have been found, for a daughter death is the better fate, partly that she might be spared her mother's present anguish.

Infanticide is not then simply a matter of dishonoured girls throwing their new-born infants into water-closets in ecstasies of post-partum derangement; it is a dark, secret side of motherhood itself. By characterising women as in some sense inhuman, or sub-human, men have been able to create dazzling superstructures of ideology in which women have no place, but their deluded idealism is constructed over the stark reality of women's struggle with the forces of life and death, abandoned in their custody.[64] Thus women in many cultures regard men as children, who sit all day smoking and discussing morality and politics with their friends, arguing the pros and cons of abortion, possibly, while a hundred yards away in the women's *souk*, a dozen abortifacient poisons can be bought, and round the corner lives a lady who knows the use of a root-bark and if that fails, there's another who'll massage it out for you. And if those same men cannot find the money to buy food for the children who are the proof of their manhood, it is the women who will conduct them as gently as possible out of the world into which they should never have come. Such women do not envy the world of men; they see it as a dream-world and more than slightly absurd. As for their own sufferings, they are tough enough to confront them and to endure all kinds of atrocities and mental torture, even death, without begging for mercy. But if mercy is at hand we, the privileged, have no right to deny it out of some fancied allegiance to our own much softer, even cushiony, but arbitrary and confused moral code.

The pushing of contraception involves an intrusion into the privacy of people whose defensive space is very small, reduced perhaps to genital modesty alone. It involves crass assumptions about the frequency of intercourse, about where it takes place, about beds and baths and rooms and running water and a "healthy" sex life. The problem is too desperate for so dandified a solution, and it is not the problem of overpopulation which as the statisticians created it, they may also solve. The problem is the birth of unwanted children, the failure of endogenous systems of control after hundreds of years of mischievous interference. The ancient checks on population growth will probably never reassert themselves; in the meantime Western technology ought to exert itself to fill the gaps in systems which are by no means utterly obsolete. The most immediately useful and effective measure would be to establish the kinds of abortion services which can masquerade as contraception at every lane's end. Mothers themselves and traditional birth attendants should deliver the treatments and there should be none of the drama and the noble reluctance which characterise abortion as seen by its supporters even now, when vacuum aspiration has been continually practised for ten years and the IUD has been haphazardly aborting anything that happened along.

The great bugaboo of the anti-abortion campaign has always been that of the late termination, when babies cry before being tossed into the incinerator. Feminists impale themselves on the insistence that women should have the right to kill the foetus at any stage in the pregnancy while anti-abortionists speak of all pregnancy termination as if it was third-trimester abortion. There is something ghoulish in this fixation on abortion after quickening and something downright absurd in the pretension that all foetuses, whether ten days old or ten weeks old or twenty weeks old, are the same sort of thing. There are few absolutes left in the age after Einstein and the case of abortion like almost everything else is a case of relative goods and ills to be evaluated one against the other. When an abortion is so late as to be very much more dangerous than childbirth, it is bad medicine, and anti-feminist to boot, to insist upon carrying it out, yet every month some unfortunate sixteen-year-old undergoes a third-trimester abortion by hysterotomy, the marks of which she will carry all her life. The friends of the foetus may concern themselves entirely with the rather intangible sufferings of the child in such a case, but the misery, uncertainty, confusion and fear which have tormented the mother since its conception are equally intolerable. Rather than legalistically insisting upon the right to have abortions as late as possible, the emphasis should be on attacking the obscurantism and arrogance that make late terminations too common. In virtually every abortion that is induced there is an unacceptable element of delay caused by the inaccessibility of advice, the caprice of doctors and competition with other forms of health care as well as sheer humbug, cant and callousness. This delay adds as much as five or six weeks to an unwanted pregnancy, adding mental, emotional and medical complications as the mother is uselessly readied for childbirth and the foetus hurtles through its evolutionary phases towards human capability.[65]

Great play is made of the emotional sequelae of abortion, as if they were generated by abortion *per se*, which they clearly are not, or all women with IUDs and all other habitual aborters would be in padded cells. The most glaring evidence that the brouhaha about abortion counselling is itself part of the hypocritical muddle is the failure of health facilities to provide adequate psychiatric care for the women who lose wanted babies late in pregnancy. The exhaustion and depression which follow spontaneous abortion are immeasurably greater than the unhappiness which follows an unwanted and terminated pregnancy but women usually get no more sensitive treatment than being told to run off home and try again, something which most of them are too frightened and humiliated to do.[66]

To be sure, abortion counselling is necessary, as is counselling before any surgical procedure, from the pulling of teeth and removal of warts to open-heart surgery, or any medical procedure from the ingestion of vitamins to cytotoxics. Women aborting ought to know what they are doing, but abortion counselling seldom goes so far as to tell them that the bones of the foetus must be broken for a twelve-week termination, that later it is dismembered and the skull crushed. Such information might do more than pious exhortations to shock women into avoiding late termination. Foetuses are not presented to women as drawn teeth are, and it is as well, for it is not the women's fault that what has been drawn from the uterus is so much more shocking than what is sloughed every month. A ten-week foetus is not pink jelly, but only the woman who loses her baby spontaneously is likely to know how human the tiny creature was and to grieve for it for the rest of her life. Women presenting for abortion, (except of course those who go to illegal abortionists to have soapy water instilled into the uterus and sit over a bucket until expulsion occurs) are shielded from grief, which would be appropriate, and from guilt, which is not. The only guilt to be borne is that which relates to the clumsiness and the tardiness of the measures taken to free her from pregnancy: the woman is doing the only possible thing, but those who should help are making the business more painful, more traumatic, more dangerous and more costly than it need be. The real guilt is theirs, for the only acceptable medical care is the best possible, but the medical profession does not deliver it and never can until it is wholly committed to immediate abortion on demand.

So far it has been assumed that the only pregnancies which are aborted are accidental ones and the only foetuses destroyed those whose mothers could not bear the thought of their becoming children. In a just world this would be the case, but the world is far from just. Too many women are forced to abort by poverty, by their menfolk, by their parents. Poverty has many faces; it may be the poverty of the young, the unmarried, the student, the unemployed, the female or a combination of these. When Sir Keith Joseph noted with puzzlement that illegitimate babies seemed to be born almost entirely in social groups 5 and 6, he was smartly reminded by Barbara Castle that unmarried mothers all inhabit social

classes 5 and 6, no matter what class they were born into. Victoria Greenwood and Jock Young stated the postion succinctly;

> Abortion out of economic necessity is a tragedy. It must be demanded from
> government not as a dispensation to women but as a consequence of the
> government's own failure to provide facilities for children and support for the
> mother. Abortion out of choice, where no overriding economic pressures occur,
> is a fundamental right of women to control their own fertility, it is a comment
> on the inadequacy of contraceptive technology and it is a pre-requisite for
> women's social equality.[67]

Abortion is an extension of contraceptive technology and the most
promising extension of it at that. It is not an alternative standing in
dichotomous relation to contraception, for contraception is too often
abortion in disguise. Moreover, if we take women's right to life into
consideration, the cruder forms of contraception, the condom and the
diaphragm, coupled with early abortion, are the safest ways of conducting
one's reproductive affairs, in terms of life expectancy. Abortion is not
a stop-gap between here and some future perfect contraceptive; it can
very well be the chosen method of birth control for more and more women.

It may be true that in countries like Bulgaria and Hungary which have
extremely high abortion rates, 98.5 per 100 live births and 122.8
respectively, this rate would fall if satisfactory contraception were
available.[68] What is obviously true is that in the circumstances women are
choosing abortion, and rather than lamenting that choice, the sensible
course of action would seem to be to provide the best possible abortion
service. Abortion may relate to a method of choice, for example, it may
be the method chosen to cope with *coitus interruptus* failures, and this
fact itself may relate to the complex fabric of values and preferences which
constitutes the cultural personality of human groups. Yet time and again
we find family planners who seem to consider that part of their role is
to reduce the number of abortions in any community, rather than to make
them the best that can be provided, and moreover they delude themselves
that they can do so by promoting contraception methods which may be
no more reliable than those already practised. This is as irrelevant to the
problems of the women in such areas as was the missionaries' supposition
that chastity would solve their problem.

Most Third-World governments are cast in the mould of the erstwhile
colonial authorities: their enactments *re* abortion therefore have nothing
to do with local practice, and so the birth controllers find themselves
ludicrously bound by hypocritical local laws as well as by their own
superiors who do not wish to see tax dollars spent in the construction
of abortion factories. Only some such radical therapy can really help the
women whose ravaged bodies are the battleground on which the
pro-life/pro-abortion debate is fought out. The senseless irony of the situation is that both sides ought to be the same side.

Chapter Eight

Changing Concepts of Sexuality

Give me the old salty way of love. How nauseated I am with sentiment
and nobility, the macaroni slithery-slobbery mess of modern adorations.

D. H. Lawrence, Sea and Sardinia

Emancipated modern man acknowledges no great design of which he
is a part, and bends his knee before no image. He congratulates himself
upon transcending fear and superstition and assumes that he has entered
into the bright calms of rationalism. He regards with half-amused dismay
the frantic activities of the fanatics and devotees who are so easily
mobilised to attack his cherished liberties, but he is too indolent to defend
them with as much fervour or tenacity. Nevertheless the liberties survive,
because they are not liberties at all but rather decoys which draw him
safely away from political activity and the forming of groups which might
disrupt the inert continuation of established power. He, never suspecting
that he is himself a pawn, assumes that his liberties survive because they
are the product of rational thought, and therefore right. The rightness
removes from them the property of mere contingency so he regards
countries and cultures where these same rights do not prevail as backward,
superstitious and inhumane. The modern liberal is a bigot and his bigotry
may be heard in the corridors of all the international organisations, the
NGOS, the charitable cartels which seek to extend the cultural hegemony
of the West with every tittle of "aid".

It has been argued many times that *homo occidentalis* has far too much
faith in reason and his own power to deploy it, and therefore is as arrogant
and evangelical as any other who considers himself endowed with
ultimate wisdom through revelation or holy writ. The other side of the
religion of rationalism is not so often descried. Modern man is profoundly
religious, but his religion is no longer centred upon the propitiation of

heavenly or infernal powers, rather it concentrates on his propitiation of himself. There can be no doubt that Michel Foucault is right: what we have all along taken as the breaking-through of a silence and the long-delayed giving of due attention to human sexuality was in fact the promotion of human sexuality, indeed, the creation of an internal focus for the individual's preoccupations.[1] Freud's statement that all neuroses are accompanied by a disturbance of genitality must be interpreted at the vulgar level as implying a duty to keep genitality in order in the service of the status quo. Reich's elaboration of Freud's idea into his own concept of the individual as a closed energy system needing to discharge accumulated sexual energy efficiently and regularly in order to function properly is inimical to his notions of revolution.[2] In removing the focus of attention from the body politic to the body erotic, the motivation of political action is destroyed. Because the promotion of genitality requires fealty to the pleasure principle, it actively interferes with the building up of political power by controls and delays in accordance with the reality principle. Reich himself understood this perfectly, and described how every successful social revolution instantly betrayed the sexual revolution, but what he did not understand was how far his concept of sexual revolution played into the hands of the consumer economy and the monopoly state. He eventually rejected all politics, and turned his attention more and more to the physical mechanism of orgasm, continuing as the dupe of commercial sex even while he was horrified at its visible manifestation. As Paul Robinson summarised in *The Sexual Radicals*, an utterly orthodox text in terms of late twentieth-century sex religion:

> He was haunted by the thought that men with dirty minds would misuse his authority to unleash a "free-for-all fucking epidemic". Once again he revamped his terminology in the hope of heading off the pornographic exploitation of his discoveries. The word "sex", "abused and smutted into a horrible nightmare, into a rubbing of cold penises within stale vaginas" was abandoned altogether, and for "sexual intercourse" he substituted "the genital embrace".[3]

Reich's ideas were taken up by the avant-garde of the late fifties and became the unacknowledged morality of the late sixties. Their exponents had no political power, although they were extremely visible. Their ideas affected legislation and custom, not because they were in some sense correct but because they were eminently compatible with the perpetuation of the mechanisms of power in consumer society. Sex is the lubricant of the consumer economy, but in order to fulfil that function the very character of human sexuality itself must undergo special conditioning. Its connection with reproduction, which is potentially disruptive, must be severed. Its anti-social aspects, human susceptibility to passion, obsession, jealousy, guilt must be purged. Sexuality which is a feature of the whole personality must be localised and controlled. Fantasy, on the other hand, must be expanded, elaborated and exploited. The promotion of sex which had begun with De Sade has reached its apogee in a civilisation which gives tangible expression to every form of human sexuality, every perversion, every paraphilia – except passion. The proper arena for these expressions is the bedroom of the sub-fertile monogamous couple: insofar as they prolong the survival of the consumer unit any elaborations of sexual congress are acceptable, even the mutual sin of condoned or shared adultery.

> The deployment of sexuality has its reason for being, not in reproducing itself, but in proliferating, innovating, annexing, creating, and penetrating bodies in an increasingly detailed way, and in controlling populations in an increasingly comprehensive way ... sexuality is tied to recent devices of power; it has been expanding at an increasing rate since the seventeenth century; the arrangement that has sustained it is not governed by reproduction; it has been linked at the outset with an intensification of the body – with its exploitation as an object of knowledge and an element in relations of power.[4]

The new opiate of the people, like all religions, has its ritual observance. The discipline imposed is the discipline of the orgasm, not just any orgasm, but the perfect orgasm, regular, spontaneous, potent and reliable. The cathartic function of sex has replaced all other rituals of purification. The blessed are laid-back, into their bodies, in touch with themselves. They shrink from no penetration, they feel no invasion of self, they fear nothing and regret nothing, they defy jealousy. The regular recurrence of orgasm provides the proof that they are in the state of grace. To object that orgasm is itself inadequate to this high purpose is to expose oneself as orgastically impotent, for sex religion, like all others, relies upon self-fulfilling prophecies. To the faithful, who believe that orgasm will release tension, make all potentialities accessible, dissipate discontent and aggression and stabilise the ego in its right relation to the world, all these are achieved when the sacred duty is discharged. Those who rise from orgasm sad or angry, disappointed or bored, are themselves at fault. They have held something back, harboured deep scepticism: they are the self-destructive.

Not everyone who holds these notions has read Reich, and many would disagree with him if they did. The popular religion of sexuality has spread insidiously despite its prophets whose works are seldom read, and even when they are not contradictory are not understood. Everybody imagines that he understands what is meant by the word *sex*, when in fact he simply responds to it with a feeling of recognition. Sex is actually a magical, suggestive and utterly indefinable idea. It includes gender, eroticism, genitality, mystery, prurience, fertility, virility, titillation, neurology, psychopathology, hygiene, pornography and sin, all hovering about actual experiences of the most intractable subjectivity, and therefore an ideal focus for religion. Some sexologists, exhausted by wrestling with such

clouds, spend much time and devise extraordinary equipment in order
to discover how the machine works. Reich spent three years measuring
the bio-electric charge in excited genitalia: Masters and Johnson have
attached cameras, electrodes and other paraphernalia in an attempt to find
what physical evidence identifies the perfect orgasm, so that faking it will
become a ploy of the past. They did not succeed, which is just as well,
for orgasmism, true to its character as a religion, relies to a large extent
upon lip-service. However, all of the sexologists have played their part
in the intensification of the body. Where once lovers may have inflamed
each other with words, spoken, written and sung, now they know which
tags of flesh to manipulate and how and for what result. They may also
have recourse to electrical aids, drugs, and commercial pornographic
stimuli without disgust or shame.

We now sneer at those people who believe that to come was to spend
some vital substance which ought to have been treasured and husbanded
like a savings bank balance, whether they be our own forebears or members
of an alien culture; even though many of our culture heroes tell us that
sexual abstinence enhances their performance, we assume that such a rule
cannot apply to us. We no longer believe that psychic energy discharged
as orgasm is withdrawn from some other activity. Rather we hold firmly
that physical fitness and spiritual power depend upon keeping the circuits
unjammed so that the bio-currents flow freely. None of these ideas is
susceptible of empirical proof precisely because each relates to a self-
validating self-image. When we believed that masturbation was debilitating, it probably debilitated, and guilt and fear of exposure contributed
the neurasthenic indications considered to be symptoms of the activity.
The attitude of doctors who prescribe masturbation as bedtime
tranquillisation or to restore uterine tone is no less irrational than that
of the doctors who remove clitorides to abolish masturbatory mania:
the patients of both are equally likely to report satisfactory results.

Sexual activity, and by this is largely understood genital sexual activity,
should begin early and ought to continue for the whole inordinately long
lifetime of modern consumer man. The mass media are cooperating in
a campaign to promote sexual intercourse among geriatrics who now feel
that they ought to be interested, just as definitely as old people in peasant
civilisations believe that to be interested in sex past the age of reproduction
is comical. When there are no grandchildren to be involved in tender
contact with, and no administrative powers to wield in the family, sex
is the decoy which will mask the economic marginality and the powerless-
ness of the old. If genital activity should lapse or tail off, steps should
be taken to re-jig the circumstances so that the rhythm can be re-
established; generally the recommended changes involve an increase in
consumerism, whether they be bedroom ecdysiasm (requiring G-strings,
pasties etc.), belly-dancing, dressing up and other role-playing, electrical

appliances, mutual enjoyment of pornography, watching blue films, co-opting strangers, or wife-swapping, as well as the cheaper spices of sado-masochism (which sometimes requires elaborate specialist equipment), buggery, bestiality and pederasty. The sex-mystics shrink from no ordeal which the sacred duty of orgasm might impose.

The seeker after corporeal blessedness should not be deterred by any considerations of taste, emotional consequences, the family or the law. Those marriages deemed "dead" because they are not dignified by frequent and superlative orgasms must either be rejuvenated with the help of sex aids, sex therapists, marital guidance and stimulants of various kinds, or abandoned, for to be inorgastic is to be as if in the state of sin, muddied, defective and defiled. To continue amiably in a state of friendly sexual inactivity is to "live a lie" and divorcees tend to look back on that state with a shudder. Adultery, if carried out as hygienically as marital sex itself, is perfectly acceptable, but adultery with a partner who is difficult of access, in circumstances of guilt and secrecy, will not accomplish the desired purgation. As far as modern man is concerned, Tristan and Isolde were simply neurotic. Anxiety undermines orgasm and must be avoided, despite the unregenerate tendency of some to seek rough trade in slum alleyways when smooth trade lies on a silken bed at home surrounded by gleaming sex aids, spiced with amyl nitrate and cocaine. Because orgasm is everybody's right and bounden duty, progressive couples commend each other to adultery and freely discuss whether or not these adulteries restore them to blessedness, each acting as the other's lay therapist. This is called "being up front" and usually acts to the disadvantage of the unwitting third parties, who have no notion that their most private behaviours are being anatomised by the cannibalistic couple, who need the input in much the same way as a painted warrior needs to eat the heart or liver of his opponent.

The state of being inorgastic is sometimes described as being *out of touch with oneself*, a revealing phrase, for it gives away the basic self-centredness of the whole cult, or *not into one's body*, which in turn reveals the drawing away of the individual's attention from the external world of politics and social activity. Women in this contemptible state feel as much guilt as once they felt for experiencing spontaneous sexual desire. If women are to escape blame, usually expressed as a kind of corrosive pity, they must achieve orgasm, and with it orgastic release. The woman who insists upon all kinds of bizarre and tiring activities in order to achieve orgasm is admirable, even though she regards her human partner as no more than an inadequate substitute for a vibrator. The woman who feels no disappointment and drifts serenely off to sleep "unsatisfied" is incorrigible. As long as women were relatively inaccessible, the fiction of male potency was unchallenged: now that women are always and everywhere accessible, men can no longer glory in the fiction that their libido is far superior to any demands which may be made of it. As nobody knows what frequency of orgasm is required by the unwritten ordinance, men are baffled to know whether or not their own capacity is normal. Where once men were troubled by unwanted tumescence, now they are as likely to be troubled by inconvenient and intractable detumescence. None of their advisers will say that the patients ought to stop peering into their underpants and get on with some other activity. Instead they will be laboriously treated for dysfunction. The regimen for men is even more demanding than for women, for the man is in some degree responsible for the orgasm of his partner. Now that sex is a social duty, in large measure replacing conversation and flirtation, so that the long build-up of psychic foreplay is lacking, much of the excitement has ebbed. Sex as a kind of callisthenics minutely instructed by the ubiquitous manuals of fucking is more and more mechanical. In promulgating universal, regular ecstasy, the sex religionists have driven the transcendental sexual experience even further out of reach.

In March 1982, the Science Correspondent of the London *Observer* reported that "Sex researchers have fallen out over the causes of declining sexual activity in marriages." It is to be noted that they did not fall out over whether sexual activity declined in marriage or not; the phenomenon was assumed to exist. Dr William James of University College London was quoted as saying that he had a recent survey to prove it.

> We found that on average couples have sex about 20 times during their first month of marriage. A year later it was down to 10 and from there on it slowly declined each year.[5]

Dr James works at the mammalian development unit at University College. He might have come across an interesting study of rhesus monkeys which could shed some light on the problem, for Dr James rejects the theory expounded by his peers at the University of North Carolina that a decline in the woman's hormonal activity is to be blamed. Richard P. Michael and Doris Zumpe at the Emory School of Medicine Psychiatry Department found that

> Ejaculations decreased and mount latencies increased when intact males were paired regularly over a 3.5 year period (3180 tests) with ovarectomised females made constantly receptive by daily injections of oestradiol. The deterioration in potency was abruptly and completely reversed by substituting a group of new but similarly treated females for the original ones.[6]

Our monkey cousins were confronted with perpetually receptive females, as modern husbands are. Evidently they suffered from boredom: the only remedy was adultery. It does seem rather close to our pattern of sterile marriage and serial monogamy. Perhaps certain pheromones were missing in the females, and the frustrated sires eventually registered on one or other of their receptors the impossibility of fecundation. Perhaps divorce for sterility is built into monkey society; the whole experiment makes Desmond Morris's position about the anthropoid Man being a pair-bonding even if sterile species more unlikely than ever.

> One can speculate that in societies with institutionalised monogamy, the uninterrupted sexual life of modern man – insulated as it is from exteroceptive seasonal factors – might provide conditions in which similar phenomena would be observed. Were this so, one would expect (i) a tendency to break and remake consort bonds (with new partners), (ii) the use of cultural means for periodically changing one's stimulus properties (clothing, adornment, coiffure and odor) and (iii) an imposition of periodicity on sexual activity (menstrual and pregnancy taboos, Lent, safe periods and so forth). Many of the prohibitions and customs surrounding sex in human societies are traditionally thought of as protecting the sexes from each other and protecting the female from the constant sexual demands of the male. An alternative view is that they also function to maintain male potency. The rhesus data, though perhaps irrelevant for man, suggest the hypothesis that if the factors responsible for sexual rhythmicity and periodicity are absent, male potency is not fully maintained.[7]

It will not do to make this one monkey experiment the clue to human sexuality in all times and places but somehow the scenario fulfils our expectations. We would have been amazed if the monkeys had mounted their receptive females day in day out and ejaculated as readily as they did the first time around every subsequent time. Of course the latency period grew longer (that is, the monkeys took a great deal longer to get excited and to reach orgasm). Nothing is said of the unfortunate lady monkeys whose veins are full of oestradiol. Rhesus monkeys get endometrial cancer from high doses of DMPA, rhesus monkeys cannot learn to striptease or belly-dance. If the tepid embraces of the laboratory beasts are a figure of modern marriage, then what they tell us about it is pretty grim. In some cultures marriage begins slowly; the groom does not leap on to his wife as soon as the law permits, but approaches her by degrees. He never arrives at a stage where his wife is his convenience. Both would be humiliated by the suggestion that she strip for him, or he read pornography with her. They connive in the myth of his limitless potency which her reserve maintains.

It is now heresy to preach that sexual repression primarily enhances sex, i.e. that a basically banal experience is made more attractive by being cloaked in mystery and danger. It is now universally assumed, in the secular West at any rate, that any form of sexual repression is *sui generis* bad. Most Westerners believe, for example, that the degree of deprivation required by the rhythm method of contraception makes it impossible. Refraining from sexual intercourse during menstruation is deemed fainthearted. Men in their middle thirties sincerely believe that they would be incapable of more than two days of celibacy because of the sheer pressure of sperm production, which would force them into some form of sexual gratification. It is assumed, with some justification, that the rule of celibacy is imposed upon members of certain groups as a measure of control, and that they spend all their time struggling to master their own urges. In fact the duty of chastity is one of the easiest duties of the religious: it does not shake the faith of the orgasmist one iota to point out that total celibates are not more deranged, inefficient, unhappy or unhealthy than any other segment of the population. Many people simply believe that celibates are not celibate; that priests have liaisons with nuns and so forth, just as the protestants of the sixteenth century believed that convent fishponds were full of the skeletons of aborted foetuses.[8] Modern sex religion believes that sex is the most potent force in the world, and its power is ineluctable.

Behind sex-religion lies its own form of repression, namely, a tremendous sexual orthodoxy. All cultures which do not exalt sex are wicked and the members of such groups must be caught up in some neurotic syndrome which ought not to be perpetuated. It is assumed, following Freud, that all human beings have a high level of innate sexual energy which their civilisations see as disruptive and struggle to repress: the rich oppress the feckless poor, the elders crush the joyous activity of the young and religion hangs about an innocent act a fearsome set of phobias and shibboleths. John H. Gagnon and William Simon found from their studies of prison populations, that the levels of sexual activity were very different in one institution and another, and they advanced the revolutionary theory that the level of sexual activity itself was determined by social and cultural circumstances.[9] We have for long understood that different cultures express sexual activity differently; while some have "high affect" (that is, they are obsessed by sex in thought and word) they have low activity (that is, infrequent genital contact); others have low affect (that is, they take a very casual attitude to sex) and a very high level of activity. Donald S. Marshall and Robert C. Suggs in 1971 edited an interesting collection of essays on *Human Sexual Behaviour* in which some of these variations and their possible causes were discussed, but in all of the essays, it was assumed that the sum total of sexual energy available for expression was uniform across all cultures.[10] Gagnon and Simon's work, together with Heider's work on the Grand Valley Dani, who have low affect and low activity and no evidence of sexual energy sublimated in war or artistic activity, suggests that the truth is that the sexual energy of the human animal is not a pan-cultural constant but rather developed in response to complex cultural stimuli to varying levels in various cultures.[11] Freud's image of man as a highly sexual creature may in fact derive from his own experience of the victims of a culture of extremely high affect, principally expressed in detailed prohibitions and a vigorous pornographic subculture as well as medical fascination with the subject, and low activity.

Anthropologists are very wary of making value-judgments about the emotional and sexual life of alien peoples because they are aware that the tangible expression of feeling is not always what it seems to be. Confronted, for example, by a society in which men and women are strictly segregated, where spouses never speak to each other before strangers or before their elders, where no expression of sexual affection is ever witnessed by an outsider, no good anthropologist would assume that affection and passion were absent from the connubial partnership. In many cultures, intimacy between spouses is too sacred to be exposed to public comment. In others, a man always speaks ill of his wife as a way of appearing modest himself or in order to indicate the opposite feelings, much as Australians fondly dub their dearest friends buggers and bastards. Men may be more thrillingly aware of women swathed from head to foot in floods of drapery than they are of the firm-muscled thighs of a woman in tennis dress. The high degree of affect in puritanical societies is understood even by the crassest observers, who will tell you that Moslems, for example, are obsessed by sex and will follow a scantily clad Western girl for miles, but the general occidental attitude to such a phenomenon is to regard it as evidence of backwardness and deprivation, not as a sign of a different economy of sex. When the aroused foreigner reaches for the flesh, it is assumed to be the expression of pure sexual desire, hitherto unaroused or frustrated. It is just as likely to be an insult or a challenge. In exposing her body, the foreign woman has defied cherished notions of male potency, for the veils and the harems also function as elements in the aggrandisement of male libido. To spurn modesty is to dare fictive male potency to do its worst.

To many visitors, the kind of public fondling which can be seen on any English tube train is deeply shocking, because it is assumed to lead to intromission, and in relatively short order. Mediterranean males might wonder why the display is not more obscene than it is, in view of the fact that the British male does not exhibit signs of genital arousal. What they might very well see in such casual sucking and rubbing and licking is evidence of the relative impotence of Anglo-Saxons, of which they are generally already convinced. Sexual organisation is a fundamental part of any culture; even groups living in the same place, governed by the same economic and climatic influences, will develop sharply contrasting modes of sexuality and will define themselves by these modes, always, of course, to their own credit. Masai women who had had their clitorides cut off considered themselves superior to the women of another tribe living in a neighbouring village, because they did not groan and cry out during intercourse. Veiled women generally consider themselves to be superior to the unveiled, who are often members of the labouring classes.

The tearing-off of the veil does not liberate them, if they feel that they cannot walk in the streets without it. After the banning of the veil in Iran in 1937, many older women refused to leave their houses because their self-image depended upon being screened from the eyes of strangers. Even now, after years of punctilious sexual revolution, no woman likes to be thought *cheap*, and serious personality disorders can result from haphazard sexual experimentation. The ways in which sexual exposure leads to personality destruction and fears of worthlessness are intimately bound up with systems of prestige and privilege. In some ways modern woman has a harder row to hoe than the woman who knows that her integrity is safeguarded as long as she throws her veil around her whenever she goes out of the house, for the modern woman must be sexually active, must be prepared to take the initiative and yet is only too open to cold-blooded exploitation and public humiliation, which cannot be righted by her brothers' chastisement of the offender(s).

The younger generation always imagines that it has invented sex; traditionally sex is not a subject discussed between generations, but between peers, and is often indulged in by adolescents and young adults as a harmless way of asserting themselves against their superiors, as their superiors are very well aware. Even today, after endless fossicking in the sex lives of "patients" we have a very hazy idea of what sex meant to our parents and grandparents. We have even lost the key to many of the hints given in the popular culture which they absorbed: sexual references appeared in censored forms in the films and books and songs which they enjoyed, and were powerfully responded to. Nowadays, instead of the vaporous passion of *Waterloo Bridge*, we have the literal depiction of sexual congress, in which we may count the number of thrusts and check the erogenous zones. The remake of *The Postman Always Rings Twice* is typical of our documentary attitude to sex: the subliminal imagery was neglected for explicit depiction, the stars were without charisma or suggestion. Too many zippers, too much stubble and stale cigarette breath effectively destroyed the sensual appeal of the photography, so that the audiences trudged home unmoved to their own zippers, their own stubble and stale cigarette breath. Like *Tristan und Isolde*, *The Postman Always Rings Twice* is a story of fatal passion but the tradition of heroic passion is dead. The union of Eros and Thanatos has been dissolved: the music of the love-death is now only an ironic comment on the coupling of so many Woody Allens with so many Shelley Duvals. In the journey from high affect and low activity to low affect and high activity which we took for our better health, we have lost the possibility of occasional transcendence. What the reformers wanted was transcendence for everyone; what they got was demotic sex.

And now sexuality has become a major commodity. The sex merchants have a huge market among sexually repressed and starved people. While in earlier periods this market was restricted by Christian inhibitions, now that the sexual revolution has released us from the compulsions of secrecy, sexual commodities are flooding the market and are becoming the most profitable area of capitalism next to the market of aggression – the armaments industry.[12]

As a devout Freudian and Reichian, who found that "even the internal organs have a sexual cathexis"[13] George Frankl is personally disappointed at what became of the bright dreams of destruction of the authoritarian personality by the liberation of libido, but he is not moved to question his basic hypothesis. A certain deliberate myopia can be detected in this short quotation. The sex merchants are not only the purveyors of pornography, as Frankl must know from his claim that sex is the biggest earner after aggression, they are also the advertisers, the publishers, the merchandisers of everything that is sold. Frankl might argue that all buyers of pornography are sexually repressed by definition, but the facts do not tally with his assumption that the sexually deprived are exploited by the sex market. The people who buy vibrators, for example, are acting out. The chief market for sex aids is the sexually active who wish to expand their activities. The largest and most recherché collections of pornography are owned by the sexually privileged, not the sexually denied. Sex has always been a commodity, since young men vied with the elder to collect a bride-price and acquire a young and juicy wife who was not a hand-me-down, and a struggle has always gone on for the powerful in any group to arrogate the most effective sexual stimuli for themselves. Prostitution is the oldest profession; the selling of sexual services is the paradigm for all tertiary industry. Nothing about the present situation is new, except its scope and intensity. Sex-based traffic has proliferated as the bureaucratic state has elaborated itself into the most far-reaching, most penetrating mechanism for control ever devised.

Post-Freudian sexual radicalism takes as one of its basic premises the proposition that the authoritarian state is formed on the model of the patriarchal family and exhibits at the national level the same character structures that are fostered by the family, thus the freeing of the libido from pleasure-anxiety is a prerequisite of the shattering of patriarchal structures and their replacement by a cooperative mode. This has so long been a truism for sexual radicals that challenging it causes a certain vertigo; however, unless it is challenged, the obvious phenomenon of the cooption of the sexual revolution cannot be understood. Let us suppose rather that the bureaucratic state is not formed as analogous to the family, which is rooted to land, embedded in alliance and incapable of the rapid adjustments which entrepreneurial activities require, but by imitation of two ancient bureaucracies which both found it essential to exist outside and in conflict with the family, namely, the army and the church. Both the army and the church forbade their members to found families by refusing permission to marry; instead, they encouraged polymorphous permissiveness mostly (but not always) tacitly. "Better that a priest should have a hundred whores than one wife" was the judgment, and priests actually enjoyed sex without responsibility in much the same way as the sub-fertile acting-out spouses of monopoly capitalism are encouraged to do. Many priests had (and still have) a working knowledge of contraception; most were content to let their children sit by other men's fires. As all intercourse was mortal sin for them, it mattered little what kind of sexual release they found, whether natural or unnatural. The army, similarly, condones the inevitable accompaniment of troops on the move by camp-followers and accepts venereal disease as an occupational risk; buggery, rape and the taking of concubines have always been privileges of fighting men. Both priests and soldiers were deliberately moved away from the region where they had ties of alliance; like the modern executive, they had to be prepared to up stakes and move their households at the whim of their superiors. No loyalties could be allowed to conflict with their duty to their employer.

The church, the army and the bureaucratic state in their different ways all deploy sexuality as a means of control and it is particularly interesting in this context that Foucault sees in the confessional, which demands endless verbalisation of sexual behaviour, the true antecedent of twentieth-century intensification of the body.[14] The family, on the other hand, seeks to harness rather than to dissipate sexual energy in the deployment of alliance. Its extension is the tribe, not the nation-state with which it is often at variance. The family is inextricably committed to the idea of patrimony, usually in the form of land, and exists far beyond the individual both in time and in power. The will of the family is performed willy-nilly by its members who have no personal accountability, so that they are immune to the techniques of manipulation that capitalism employs. As a consumer unit, the multi-generational family is unsatisfactory because of its economic efficiency. Whatever is acquired is used to maximum capacity: keeping up with the Jones's is not a matter of acquiring and scrapping more and more consumer durables, but of becoming more numerous than the Jones's and eventually absorbing them. Modern cooperative movements try to imitate the ways in which the stem family foils capitalist enterprise, but find that they cannot insist upon the long hours of unpaid work put in by familial labour, because familial labour works, as it were, for the collective self. The stem family is more oppressive than the bureaucratic state in terms of the discipline which is accepted by its members and some, often the most enterprising, of its members are all too ready to flee to the cities and escape its toils. The most powerful of the blandishments offered by the urban environment is the possibility of unlimited sexual enjoyment, whether it be with one's spouse in the privacy of a flat, or in the multitudinous brothels which spawn in every shanty town.

Such generalisation is dangerous, for forms of family organisation are as various as capitalist republics are similar: the only point that should emerge from this attempt to contrast them is that there is a fundamental opposition between the ethos of the family and the consumer economy. To have rejected patriarchal authority within and without the self, however desirable in itself, is to have become vulnerable to much more insidious and degrading forms of control. The basic family structure assumed by the Freudians is a triad – father, mother, child.

> In the typical conservative family, the influencing of sexuality takes on a specific form which lays the basis for a "marriage and family" mentality. That is, by an overemphasis on the functions of eating and excretion, the child is arrested in the stages of pregenital eroticism, while genital activity is strictly prohibited (prohibition of masturbation). Pregenital fixation and genital inhibition cause a displacement of the sexual interest in the direction of sadism. The sexual curiosity of the child is actively suppressed.[15]

This is Reich's description of the sentimental education of the executive class. However, in his presumptions about family structure, he reveals himself as duped in large measure by contingency posing as inevitability. He notices that in working-class families the way to genitality is less efficiently blocked than in middle-class ones, but he still assumes that localised and concentrated sexuality, intromission with orgasm as practised by the heterosexual unit which the child cannot enter, is the ultimate goal of emotional development. In fact the phenomenon can be interpreted in a different way, and again the suggestion is offered diffidently. The "overemphasis on the functions of eating and excretion" begins as an attack on the mutal eroticism of mother and child. If we take the Kalahari bushmen as an indication of how hunter-gatherer man managed these matters, we see at once that the mother keeps her (naked) baby by her (naked) self all the time, even when she sleeps, and the breast is never denied.[16] Although mammary pleasure has been under attack for centuries, it is still a relatively common phenomenon. The touching and stroking by baby hands during feeding is a kind of caress; the child's hand moves slowly, rhythmically back and forwards across the mother's skin. Babies often look directly into their mothers' eyes at feeding. If the primary couple is viewed in this way then it is the father who is the supernumerary. Where women sleep with their babies, either in their own quarters or in compounds or in long-houses, men are graphically excluded from a child world of mutual gratification which although it is not genital – or rather, although it places no particular emphasis on genitality – is enormously erotic. The first suppression of this whole-body eroticism is the refusal of the breast, either at certain times or totally at weaning. Weaning is always a trauma, and one which pyschology has done little to explain or alleviate: it is often made worse by irrational practices which might have something to do with father's revenge.

In modern consumer society the attack on mother-child eroticism took its total form; breast feeding was proscribed and the breasts reserved for the husband's fetishistic delectation. At the same time babies were segregated, put into cold beds alone and not picked up if they cried. On the other side of the world Indian mothers continued to massage their babies' naked bodies (including their genitals) with oil and some New Guinea women plucked at their daughters' labia to help them grow long and increase their eventual pleasure in sex. Even in the Western hemisphere, some Mediterranean mothers took their boy babies' penises in their mouths to stop them crying.

At the same time as the child was denied pleasure in the maternal body, toilet training became a gigantic problem. Why the northern Europeans should have decided that defecation and urination should take place on a throne is impossible to imagine, for the position is neither comfortable nor anatomically efficient. It is almost as if they wanted to reduce infants to humiliating dependency upon adults, as they are helped on to the porcelain pedestal and off again. To make matters worse, they are dressed in complicated clothing which has to be taken off by others. The nett result of such irrational procedures is that the child must announce every episode of excretion in advance, well in advance – too far in advance in terms of baby sphincters. In saner societies all children need to do is squat so that they do not soil themselves, then they learn to squat in the right place, i.e. where others will not tread in it and then they learn to squat at the right times. Mediterranean mothers still dress children in panties with a slit, so that squatting removes clothing from the area of soiling. The lavatory is at ground level and as children like to see a place for everything and everything in its place, they quickly learn to use it without consulting anyone. Others trot out to the fields at dawn, for where there is no sewerage only sick people and old people soil in their own houses. Even given the obvious commonsense of such arrangements, it is possible to create an atmosphere of great anxiety around excretion and many primitive societies clearly do: the point is that given Western logistics it impossible *not* to. Those radical mammas who applaud when their children present unwary visitors with a box containing turd of their own manufacture (and expect the visitors to applaud with them, excrement being the child's achievement as is well-known) would do better to remodel the lavatory, take off the child's clothes and let him get on with it.

At the same time that we have schooled ourselves not to make a fuss about little girls hiding beads and pebbles in their vaginas and little boys hanging on to their penes for days on end, we have done very little about ensuring the gratification of infantile erotic needs, both oral and whole-body. It is as if we were forcing genitality on children by allowing them only genital gratification; it is very doubtful, to this observer anyway, whether genital attention is gratifying to small children and genital handling is not itself a displacement activity deriving from other frustrations. Little boys who hang on to their penes hang on to them in the same way that they suck their thumbs, compulsively. The only little girl whose intense masturbation behaviour I witnessed over a long time never seemed to achieve release of any kind. Her masturbatory behaviour seemed to be born out of intense loneliness and rather heartless exposure to the primal scene, repeatedly, at an important stage in her infant development: the most remarkable aspect of her chosen method was that she mimed being both partners. The *ad hoc* therapy, for this compulsive behaviour had become a problem, of replacing the fetish objects that she used in her rituals with real people, never leaving her awake in bed alone, and treating her as an infant with lots of kissing and cuddling and skin contact, worked.

Obviously, complete submission to the demands of infant eroticism is impossible, for most mothers are not Kung bushwomen. They do not live in an environment where food may be had for a minimum of effort but in a society where the only way of acquiring food is by earning money to pay for it, which requires participation in industry. Agricultural workers may work with their children on their backs and the children may reach for the breast whenever they wish, as long as the women are working laboriously and inefficiently with a simple hoe, but the woman who goes to work in a factory cannot be at the beck and call of her child. Commercial baby foods are selling throughout the world not only because Western notions of attractiveness are changing traditional values but because women must find paid work outside the home. Where once the mother-child relationship was more important than the sexual relationship between spouses, and women went to the maternal home for as long as two years after the birth of a child so that they could enjoy to the full this engulfing tenderness, the wife now prefers to cling to her husband. Instead of surrendering to the peremptory demands of her child and enjoying the vestiges of her own infantile eroticism, the woman concentrates upon the needs of her husband, who is no longer bound to her by the system of alliance, but kept solely by sexual attachment. Where once she played a dynastic role and could exploit the enduring and passionate attachment of her children, she is now totally dependent upon her success as her husband's *geisha*. The cross-generational tie which is the distinguishing characteristic of the family has withered away and only the couple, united by a fragile sexual bond, remains. To compensate the child for the loss of gratification from closeness to his mother, he is placated with consumer goods and social advantages – and he is allowed the free expression of his genitality.

The mother-child relationship will not function if it is the unwilling submission of a bored and rebellious woman: in order to participate in

it, the woman must retain a large measure of body-eroticism. She must
be susceptible to her baby's advances. She must find the episodes of em-
bracing and playing and falling asleep together completely satisfying even
though they are not accompanied by orgasm. She must also know what
to do when breast feeding produces genital stimulation, which ought to
be part of a generalised response but, given the sexual conditioning to
which women are increasingly exposed, may not be. Strangely enough
there is evidence from two unlikely quarters that the most sophisticated
Western women still retain a significant measure of physical pleasure from
contact with their babies, their daughters in these cases. One is the actress,
Diana Rigg, who was completely intoxicated by her daughter and rhapso-
dised about how she simply had to bite her bottom from time to time
– and the other, the superstar, Viva, who found it impossible to wean
her little girl and kept on giving her the breast for years after everyone
around them thought the child had been weaned, mother and child resorting to each other by stealth, like guilty lovers.[17]

It has been assumed that the path to genitality lay through the infantile
stages of oral and anal eroticism and culminated in genitality; to be fixated
at any pre-genital stage is bad and to have arrived at genitality is good.
What is not so often understood is that genitality is the culminating development of sexuality which completes its elaboration in the adult. It
does not replace the earlier forms of sexuality but complements them.
The techniques of control that have grown up have made of man, as it
were, a one-crop economy: sexuality in the adult male is localised and
concentrated in a motor function, the trivial spasm accompanying ejaculation. The tendency to localisation has bedevilled Freudianism from the
first, perhaps because the study of sexuality grew out of allopathic
medicine with its ingrained tendency to isolate functions and dysfunctions.
If the machine was functioning correctly, then it produced a tangible event
which could be measured, graded, quantified. While insisting on the
psychic element, and even making claims for a spiritual and moral element,
the sex prophets looked for a sign. Their version of the pillar of cloud
by day and pillar of fire by night, was the perceptible part of orgasm
in the external organ. The female, it seemed, was simply a less efficient
orgasm producer. Whereas simple manipulation would produce the
tangible result in the male, the female required mental stimulation by
words and ideas, generalised caressing, together the subtlest of manipula-
tions and the most patient and sensitive.

It has been argued that women are not genetically programmed for
orgasm, simply because the male orgasm was necessary for the propagation
of the species and the female orgasm was not.[18] On the other hand, it
might be thought that sustained pleasure in suckling is a biological
necessity and women are programmed to respond erotically to non-genital
caress in a way that the male cannot afford. If the attachment of the female

to her mothering function is to be severed it would seem obvious that she must discover another source of satisfaction.

> Most workers have been greatly impressed with the overwhelming role of conditioning, learning, and experience in determining female erotic responsiveness.[19]

Daniel G. Brown is here summarising forty years of research into the female orgasm, from before the First World War when "it was shameful for a woman to admit to experiencing pleasure in intercourse" to the present day when "many women feel ashamed to admit they do not experience orgasm".[20] The words are Eustace Chesser's, and the most interesting aspect of them is that the idea of "pleasure in intercourse" is assumed to be identical with experiencing orgasm. Brown and his fellow sexologists tend to assume that the object of their study is some kind of a given, as it were, a branch of anatomy, when actually sexuality is so dynamic that it is being affected by the very fact of being studied. If a woman (and many women are exhibitionistic) is the subject of the attention of a gang of experts who wish to observe her orgasm, the achievement of her orgasm becomes a highly gratifying experience replete with rewards. It is not to be expected that what Masters and Johnson observed will be always and everywhere true of human females, nevertheless although they were intent on observing the orgastic response itself they were obliged to record that clitoral and vaginal stimulation could both lead to orgasm, and in some women stimulation of the breasts alone would suffice. Moreover, Masters and Johnson provided objective proof of what masculine sexologists had angrily denied, namely, the capacity of the female to achieve multiple orgasm. Some evidence would appear to exist for the argument that female sexuality is fundamentally different from the male cycle of tension and release, that it is more diffuse and more continuous, as these vestiges show, even in women who are striving for orgasm as defined by others.

Women will not hit the streets and march for the right to have diffuse, vague, continuous and unrealisable sexual pleasure, and even if they did it would be of no avail, for every youth who reads his manual of sexual etiquette now knows that he must belabour the tiny clitoris with his well-meaning attentions, if he is to be considered an experienced lover. Besides, manipulation of the clitoris will effectively disguise any ineptitude in the phallic department. Whether women like it or not, current sexual mores are conditioning them to become clitorally centred: their sexuality is being conditioned into the likeness and the counterpart of masculine response. The process has everything to recommend it, for it renders men and women compatible. It leaves no irritating surplus of orgastic potency or inscrutability in woman. Once female sexuality has been tamed, concessions may be made without fear of abuse. There is now no reason why a woman can't be more like a man. Female sexuality has been tailored to fit male inadequacy. One-dimensional man has been joined by his one-dimensional woman.

Sexology has grown since Masters and Johnson first began publishing their work on human sexual response in learned journals in the 1960s until it is now a vast and respectable field of human endeavour. The World Health Organisation sponsors international conferences on education and treatment in human sexuality. In 1964 The Sex Information and Education Council of the United States (SIECUS) was set up with the aim of securing for sexology a permanent place in public health education programmes in the United States. By 1976 no fewer than fifty-eight institutions in the United States were offering post-graduate summer workshops in human sexuality and sex education.

> In the University of Minnesota, twelve sex-related courses were listed apart from the Medical School's seven for the Department of Family Social Science, two for the Department of Sociology, one each for the Divisions of School Health Education, of Home Economics Education, and for adult, higher and teacher education.[21]

The Université du Québec à Montréal went somewhat further than the University of Minnesota in seeing that sexology penetrated into the syllabus. From 1969 the university has run a sexology programme "to train educators in sexology to intervene, inform, teach, animate, educate or help through research, the different social or school groups affected by sexual problems." Graduates could boast a BSc in Sexology after taking thirty courses from a total of thirty-seven course options including Personal Maturation I & II (which require experiments with sensitisation, non-verbal interaction, bioenergetics, and transcendental meditation), Sexo-pathology, Ethnosexology, Sex and Civilisations, in all a wonderful brew of biology, psychiatry, psychology, psychoanalysis, sociology, criminology, anthropology, education and philosophy.[22]

As might be expected, the most highly evolved expressions of secular sex religion will be found in California. An interesting and typical case of the twentieth-century religious festival was the weekend conference entitled "Human Loving: Sexuality and Intimacy; A Multidisciplinary Holistic Approach" organised by the modestly entitled Institute for the Advancement of Human Behaviour, "a non-profit educational corporation ... founded for the purpose of making a contribution to the evolution of the human condition," based in Portola Valley, California. Pilgrims to the Cabana Hyatt in Palo Alto could have heard Masters and Johnson, or either of two other heterosexual couples discoursing upon sexuality, or a pair of bearded young PhDs on biofeedback and meditation; they could have homed in on "Enhancing Sexuality throughout Life", on "Sex and Aggression" or a body-therapy approach or hypnosis, and all for a mere $75, or $85 if you registered late. The fee did not cover accommodation or drinks at the cash bar during the social period with faculty. The high point of the weekend was a $12.50 dinner with Assemblyman John Vasconcellos whose Assembly Bill 4178 requires mental health professionals to have had "training in human sexuality", and (here was the best part) the conference was "designed to fulfill the requirements of Assembly Bill 4178 as a course in human sexuality to meet the licensing requirements for health professionals". The conference was repeated the very next weekend at the Sheraton Universal in North Hollywood.[23]

Most sexologists are still taken up with a battle against the forces of darkness. Mary S. Calderone, one of the founders of SIECUS after eleven years as medical director of Planned Parenthood–World Population, sees her opponent very clearly:

> Historically, the prime contender for control of the sexuality of a person by an outside agency is, and continues to be, religion. Although human sexuality has been a dominant theme in the art and literature of most cultures, control (meaning repression) of this alleged "rampant" and "uncontrollable" yet universal factor in human life has been held by most religions to be necessary in order to restrict its use to its so-called primary or even sole, function, procreation.[24]

Why religions should see procreation as in their interest is nowhere discussed. Indeed, there are many religions which do not exalt procreation above celibacy – Buddhism and Catholicism, for instances – and some thought ought to be given to the possibility that one of the functions of religion in the past was to maximise human reproductive potential given the huge wastage of mothers and children and the extremely effective deterrents to survival of the group that such experiences could provide. To survive and grow, a religion must fulfil a useful social purpose. The social function of religion has been supplanted by a secular mechanism for behaviour control and Dr Calderone and her cohorts are given public office, paid stipends and sent hither and yon to complain about its enemies in the name of freedom and love.

Dr Calderone is doubtless right in protesting against the sexual repression exercised by parents and institutions but when she speaks of control of sexuality, she immediately raises the disturbing possibility that a better way of controlling is not to drive underground and out of sight by repression but to draw out and manipulate in the guise of education, first, and then, treatment. The authority of teachers and doctors is in our time as sacrosanct as ever religious dogma was. Doubtless the sex educators are all honourable men and women and insofar as the present state of sexual *mores* may seem to them freer than the one they grew up with, they may be champions of freedom, but to some young people growing up in the morality of sexual health, this freedom is already felt as servitude.

The point may be illustrated by a sad (but true) story. A progressive young mother of my acquaintance decided to take the opportunity of a moment when her fourteen-year-old daughter was being unusually friendly and communicative to give her a little peptalk about sex, the importance of tenderness, no need for guilt or fear, contraception is easy and so forth. She began by extolling the loveliness of first sex – if properly handled. "I thought it was a bore," said the child coldly, and walked out of the room. Her mother was dreadfully upset and one must sympathise with her: she had done all the right things; the child had no reason to keep her in the dark, no reason to be experimenting coldly with sex; her parents' marriage was a model; she was probably going to get pregnant ... the mother's tears were all too understandable and doubtless the child would have got very bad marks in her sex-education class if she had exhibited the same behaviour. However, the child's rebelliousness is not untypical of her age and social group. If sex is to be preached at them and if they are to be taught how to do it as they are taught how to dissect rabbits and compose nourishing meals, correct fucking becomes an extension of orthodoxy. Their sexuality is given up to the scrutiny of the elder generation and the excitement is lost. To be sure the secret discovery of sex with one's peers is a rocky road with many wrong turnings, but it is a thrilling road down which to venture by fits and starts, retreating to the safety of childhood and innocence with one's unknowing parents. The child of my story saw her escape cut off on the one hand and the secret road illuminated by the searchlight of her mother's superior knowledge and experience at the same time. Her cutting short of her mother's exordium was another version of the adolescent's never-to-be-heeded prayer, "Leave me alone."

When the perennial figures announcing the rise in teenage pregnancy in the most advanced countries make their appearance, the sex educationists leap to the podium and urge acceptance of sex classes in schools so that children may avoid the perils of haphazard lust. They are doubtless well-furnished with statistics to show that where there is sex education there are fewer juvenile pregnancies, if only because where there is sex education there are usually middle-class parents who whisk their pregnant daughters off to be vacuumed out before they can become statistics. (Astonishingly, in the United States there was until recently no uniform legal requirement to register pregnancy terminations or to return pathology reports on the conceptus.) For every embittered child like the one in my story there must be good children who take to sex as mental hygiene as they brush their teeth and use their dental floss each day, and when they come up against problems, such as loss of interest, they will attend sex clinics and get the trouble put right with the same confidence with which they will accept IUDs and hysterectomies. There will also be, there is already, rebellion, rebellion against the earnest teacher who tries to defuse magic dirty words by using them in his classroom, who tries to dispel anxiety about penis size and body odour, who encourages children to experiment with non-verbal contact and so forth. At present the rebellion, which may take any form from truculent celibacy to sadistic ritual, is buttressed by the sexual jealousy of the elders and the blind outrage of punitive religions, but it is doomed to failure.[25] Regardless of the superficial religiosity of political leaders, religion is a spent force. The pervasiveness of commodity sex is so absolute that even religion has had to accommodate it. The gigantic phenomenon of video-religion in the United States learned its techniques from the subliminal soliciting of advertising. Its dogmatic content is minimal: its gospel is merely another version of the principle of gratification.

Such an attack upon the ideology of sexual freedom, usually, and quite correctly, called permissiveness, must seem shocking coming from a sexual radical, as the present writer professes to be. It is galling to find oneself lined up with bigots and body-haters as it were circumstantially when the point of opposition to contemporary sex religion is that it is based in a dreary, circumscribed and thoroughly predictable version of human libido. Human libido is the only force which could renew the world. In allowing it to be drawn off, regularly tapped in domestic ritual, we are preparing the scene of our own annihilation, stupefied by myriad petty gratifications, dead to agony and to ecstasy. If our own annihilation were all that was in question, it would be a matter of small moment, but the gospel of consumer gratification spreads wherever our marketing machine may go, which is everywhere on the planet. Young grinning couples grace hoardings among the intricate polycellular structures of villages full of families and their message is intensely seductive to the young and rest-less. The lineaments of gratified desire they see there will be theirs if they abandon the land, abandon the old, earn their own money and have fun. Having fun means having recreational sex: recreational sex means no fear of pregnancy, a wife who is always available and who is content with orgasms in place of land, family and children – orgasms and consumer durables.

Most of the pleasure in the world is still provided by children and not by genital dabbling. Most of the women in the world still spend long hours in close body-contact with their babies and many men can be seen with their sons or daughters standing between their legs as they gossip on their charpoys or under the trees or squatting by the house wall. There is an unshaven guerilla leader who was found by a journalist who came to interview him, with a baby on his knee, letting little fingers stretch his lips while he uttered the words that strike fear into the heart of nations. The eroticism of most of the world still includes the vast store of sensuality that radiates from children, whose deliciousness is more obvious to people grown old and gnarled prematurely by a life of bitter toil and hard rations than it is to our smooth-skinned, overfed selves, but the attack has been mounted.

> "Who will you love more when you get married, your mother or your wife?" Most of the adolescent males in the class respond with conviction, "My mother, of course." The group leader then asks the teenage girls in the class, "And who will you love more, your child or your husband?" The children will always be loved more than anyone else, reply these very young women. "No wonder couples don't stay together in Panama!" thunders the group leader, and the adolescents in San Miguelito, an over-crowded town of 180,000 on the outskirts of Panama city, are startled to learn that sex education is more than just the facts of life.[26]

Clearly, this kind of education does not deal with fact at all, for the fact is that the parental relationship is more important than the sexual relationship in this community.

The group-leader, he who thundered in imitation of the deity, is the one who is not prepared to accept the fact as stated. Clearly this Boanerges is about to preach the gospel of coupledom. He is justified, at least in his own eyes, because the traditional values of Panama have decayed so far that one in every five of the 50,000 babies born in Panama every year has a mother under nineteen years of age, and teenagers account for the same proportion of abortions. The traditional restraints on juvenile sexual activity having broken down, something must be supplied in their place to complete the process of cultural colonisation. The words of the thunderer have less force than the economic circumstances which will wear down the ties that bind mothers and children without his help. In the *bidonvilles* and industrial suburbs of third-world cities we may see harassed young people who have no joy of their children. Mothers working long hours in factories spend a high proportion of their meagre wages on commercial baby foods: from its conception the factory-worker's child has been nothing but a burden. There have been no privileges connected to pregnancy and no pleasures connected with motherhood. There is a Family Planning Clinic on many a corner and possibly a sex clinic as well, so that the poor woman who has every cause to be wretched can have access to the panacea. Orgasms, not babies, is the slogan. If all pleasure in babies has been destroyed, orgasm is the only alternative. Actually the whole set-up seems ludicrously inappropriate: the Bombay woman who attends the weekly sex clinic is likely to be young, middle-class, progressive and privileged. The factory workers are too stressed by long hours, inadequate housing, rising prices and pathetic wages to respond awfully well to treatment. They would prefer an unbroken night's sleep to all the orgasms in Masters and Johnson. As it is, sex is over pretty quickly, and that is the next best thing. It is a sad and a dreadful situation, but it would be no less sad and dreadful if mechanical orgasm made these people resigned to it. Where in the crowded slum dwelling can the sacrosanct couple find time and space to do their tinkering? In such circumstances it is very easy to see the connection of the gospel of sex hygiene with consumerism. The Bombay couple is denied sexual satisfaction because it cannot afford it. And so the hoardings continue to preach their version of blessedness, sari-clad wife and Western-suited husband gazing lasciviously at their latest material acquisition. In turning their backs on the ikon the recalcitrant poor confirm their own backwardness and inadequacy.

It is surely retrogressive to argue against the dissemination of sex knowledge among people whose lives are generally so short on pleasure, but my objection is that the sex knowledge so-called is actually sex belief and includes a system of values which are appropriate only to a bureaucratic, consumer society. In promulgating those values as scientific facts, we are actually promoting the methods of manipulation and control which maintain our own pseudo-democracies and we are doing it principally at the level of the executive class who are the representatives of Western monoculture in traditional societies. The onslaught on cultural identity, resting in traditional values which have no institutional expression, is deadly, even in countries like India, which have made a concerted attempt to preserve ways of life which are deemed contemptible and incomprehensible by the ruling class of the world. The sex reformers, who exhibit no respect for traditional values and address themselves to sexuality without interest in or comprehension of the whole personality, are the bawds of capitalism.

The occidental certainty has been succinctly and quite unconsciously summed up by Paul A. Robinson:

> In the popular mind . . . the orgasm is the sugar coating with which the Creator (or Nature) has disguised the bitter pill of reproduction.[27]

In view of the fact that orgasms may be had by masturbation and homosexual contact (and, indeed, involuntarily) nature or the creator would seem to have been rather careless in condemning man to reproduce and to have left rather too many loopholes. The unexamined assumption here is that reproduction is a bitter pill. To be sure, it is a pill which was, and for many peoples still is, relatively dangerous, but is reproduction actually simply a way to orgasm and are children nothing but a by-product? The suspicion that the pop psychologists may have got it all wrong would never have been born if I had not had opportunities to live with people for whom the babies were the fun. In fact, the suspicion was first implanted by the behaviour of my female cats, who wept piteously when it was time to undergo the gang rape which is feline intercourse, and purred continuously while in labour, even when the labour was obviously painful, and purred all through their suckling, not stopping till the kittens were weaned. The triumphant tom-cat may have enjoyed his brief ejaculation, but the females purred for eight weeks. My association with Italian peasants and with South Indian women and aborigines offered endless examples of the undemanding pleasure which children give to non-materialistic peoples, for whom they are the only entertainment and the reason for undergoing all the hardships which are their daily life. Evidence that once we of the West were alike in this came from an unexpected source. In Emmanuel Le Roy Ladurie's analysis of *Le Régistre d'Inquisition de Jacques Fournier, évêque de Pamiers* (1318–25) which has recreated the life of the peasants of Montaillou in the early fourteenth century, the heretic Jacques Authier explains to the peasants how Satan tempted them to leave paradise and come upon the earth.

> Satan entered into the Kingdom of the Father, and told the Spirits of the Kingdom that he, the Devil, owned a much better Paradise ... "Spirits, I will bring you into my world," said Satan, "and I shall give you oxen, cows, riches and a wife for company, and you will have your own ostals, and you will have children ... and you will rejoice more for a child, when you have one, than for all the rest which you enjoy here in Paradise."[28]

The greatest temptation to the blessed in heaven, which caused them to frustrate God's plan, was not sexual pleasure or the pleasures of riches, but the possibility of reproduction. The Cathars of Montaillou would not have understood Mr Robinson and his notion of a bitter pill. As befits the greatest pleasure, child-bearing was the worst sin in the Cathar book, only to be expiated by refusing the new-born food and drink, to let it die *in endura*. Like modern sexologists the Cathars thought that any form of sexual activity was permissible as long as it did not lead to reproduction, not because they thought of the body as good, but because they thought it essentially bad. It is one of the ironies of history that modern permissiveness and mediaeval Catharism should be so similar in effect. The pain and bewilderment of women who protested against the heretical ordinance that they must not give their babies the breast must have been similar to the feelings of those poor women who are offered free abortions rather than the food supplements and the opportunity to rest which might make childbirth less dangerous and the outcome more joyful. Much of the world still has more in common with the Pyrennean peasants of the thirteenth century than it has with our goodselves. Like the Cathars, we seek to make their pleasure in their children a sin.

Chapter Nine

The Fate of the Family

If we could grasp we might shatter and remould, but our human grasp is limited, and our remoulding should be accordingly cautious, with due care not to shatter what we cannot mend.

Nafis Sadik[1]

On the eve of the referendum which voted No to the abrogation of the Italian divorce law, I found myself on a train between Rome and Terontola. Opposite me sat a sleek woman in her forties. Because we were in Italy, where politics and philosophy may be discussed between total strangers, we were discussing the referendum.

"*Signorina*," said the lady, after the inevitable glance at my ring-finger, "I understand the referendum only too well. I am a divorced woman." She sighed.

"Surely it is better," said I, voicing at a venture the conventional wisdom on the subject, "to be divorced, rather than to live separated *a vincolo* according to the law of the church?"

"*Lei dice* . . . we were *divisi* just after the birth of our second son. We've lived separated for fifteen years. You can't tell me that it's better to be divorced. When we were separated I was still a member of the family. My sons were members of his family. If I had problems, I called them. When we were deciding where the boy should go to school, all that sort of thing, we took the decisions together. The family invited us to parties, saints' days, weddings, to stay with them each summer in *villeggiatura* . . ." Her eyes suddenly filled with tears. "I had no reason to consider myself a failure."

There was silence for a few minutes as she stared out into the darkness. "And now?" I prompted.

"Nothing. The *alimenti* come regularly, every fortnight. If I need anything I must ask through the lawyers. They have paid me off. Since the divorce we haven't spoken. Not once. I've got my own family, of course, but there's bad feeling ... I married against their wishes – for love. My husband's family was much better off than *i miei*." She laughed ironically, without bitterness. "We thought we were so modern, my husband and I. What did we care for parents' consent? We were in love."

"Why has your husband's family taken this attitude?" For a few moments I was genuinely puzzled.

She spread her hands palms up in the classic gesture of helplessness. "My husband has a new wife. My sons and I no longer exist. Our names are not mentioned in that house."

"So how will you vote?" I asked after a little while.

"Oh, I shall vote no, like everyone else. *Ormai e troppo tardi.*"

She was right, as it turned out. The Italians voted massively to keep their divorce law and newly divorced women like my friend on the train probably voted with them.

What this story is meant to illustrate is the struggle going on within the family, or perhaps we might say between two kinds of family. Almost all discussions of the family founder because of the difficulty in deciding what the family is, as distinct from what it was or will be, because families are always building up and breaking down, acquiring new members by marriage and procreation and losing them by estrangement and death. Obviously, a man and a woman must get together for a child to be conceived, and we might concede without too much irritability that such a link constitutes the basic unit in a system of links we may call the family. We might indeed, as we are describing something like the dynamic associations which make up living bodies call the procreating couple the nucleus of the cell in the family structure. I will only describe a family as nuclear when the relationship takes precedence over all others, and involves more time and more attention than are given to any blood relationship; for the purposes of my discussion I will not exclude even the relationship with the children of the nuclear unit, who are given less time in the nuclear family than the spouses give to each other and are compensated in other ways. The children of the nuclear family become infrequent visitors to their parents' household, and the least courteous and communicative visitors at that, as soon as they feel that they are grown-up. Where adult children willingly seek their parents' company the family, according to this definition, is not nuclear. It must not be thought however that because the nuclear family gives more energy and attention to the relationship between spouses, it gives more time to conjugal interaction than anything else. The relationship with the employer takes precedence over all in terms of time, energy, concentration and loyalty. This clearly cannot be the case for an unemployed partner, but even for the increasingly rare stay-at-home housewife, the relationship with the children is secondary to her relationship with her husband (and with her husband's employer). The woman in a nuclear family who puts her children before her husband is "asking for trouble": all the advice systems that have been set up to keep her on the right track will warn her that she is heading for disaster. The majority of women in the world do put children before husband, and are encouraged by their own families and their husbands' families to do so, and the majority of women in the world do not live in nuclear families by my definition. Thus, while it may be true that the copulating couple is the nucleus of the family and families may be composed of cells all produced around some such nucleus it is absurd to maintain that everyone lives in a nuclear family. The family becomes nuclear when it is stripped down to this function, all other relations of blood and affinity having atrophied and fallen away.

If we return for a moment to the case of my friend on the train, we can best understand her position as the result of a capitulation by the larger Family, which I will identify by a capital F, to the claims of the nuclear family. The idea has gradually become accepted that every man is entitled to romantic sexual gratification with the wife of his choice. In our own time some such notion has been given the status of a civil right. In this case the Family has succumbed to its own feelings of guilt and anachronism and has cut adrift one of its affines and two of its blood relations as a penance. Now, in developing the notion of the Family with a capital F I am striving for a description of an organic structure which can be shown in law, in genetic examination, in patterns of land ownership and parish records, but has its realm principally in hearts and minds. Historians who have tried to describe the family as *mentalité* have been sneered at for excessive abstraction, nevertheless it is precisely in kinds of awareness, patterns of feeling, concepts of self, that the Family has its existence. Where Family is strong, individuals take first their friends, and then their lovers from inside its sphere of influence. Where Family is supreme, individuals define themselves as junior or senior members of a hierarchy of blood.

The Family that insisted on maintaining its ties with my friend on the train was strong, but not strong enough. When she and her husband agreed to live separately, fifteen years before, it was still a Family in which the conjugal bond was secondary to blood bonds between siblings and generations. In such families, if the conjugal bond should slacken because of incompatibility of one kind or another, it can be allowed to decay until it becomes little more than a formality in that the spouses live together in estrangement or agree to separate. Such a withering away is not regarded as disastrous, because the conjugal bond is not the prop of the household which is buttressed by other forms of support. These may exist principally as networks of responsibility and expectation outside the actual dwelling without being actively represented by members of the wider kin-group cohabiting with spouses and their children. My friend on the train remained a member of her husband's Family in this sense long after her relationship with her husband had dwindled into mere toleration: at any time her parents-in-law would have known what she was living on and how, what age her boys were, how they were doing in school and what measures were likely to be necessary in the future to help her to maintain a standard of living appropriate to their kinswoman and their grand-children. If she had lived in a polygamous society her husband's remarriage would not have caused embarrassment and rupture. We dis-cussed how she would have felt if she had simply become her husband's senior wife but she thought, probably correctly, that it was the new wife who could not have dealt with any retention of her and her sons within the family circle. Possibly out of anxiety that their son's second marriage should prove no more successful than his first, his parents had given up their friendship with their older daughter-in-law altogether. She for her part felt that she had no redress and did not wish to become a whining voice on the telephone.

What the Family had decided to do was to respect the claims of the new conjugal bond to the detriment of its own structural relationships. Historians of the family might claim that Families have always done this sort of thing, that they are continually hacking off limbs here and there in a sort of pruning which keeps the central growth strong. One of the principal defects in the kind of demographic history which now occupies hundreds of statisticians in accreting honeycombs of cells of unusable information, is their tendency to treat the Family as a static structure rather than a process. Their methods demand that their evidence be of the quantifiable kind. So far they have not found any way of quantify-ing the difference between the soulscape of a young man who says that he is Doug's boy and another who says he is a Piscean. The superficial difference corresponds to a radical distinction.

In the case of my friend on the train, the impossibility of divorce kept the sexual demands of marriage partners secondary to their bond as parents. No matter how hostile they became to each other, or how many other sexual partners either of them took, in law they were simply the parents of the children they had had together. They were not obliged to make each other happy. They were not to expect happiness as their marriage portion. Divorce was not accepted by the majority of Italians until they had accepted the idea that marriage was a bower of bliss and the Family a system of irksome shackles. Once they had imbibed this idea, the efforts of the church and the *Democristiani* to turn the clock back were all in vain. Even the sacred feelings of a mother were not sufficient to convince my friend on the train that she should resist the radical change which had convulsed Italian family life in the lightning flash of a single human lifetime, or, as in her case, in rather less than fifteen years. It might be argued that the change in attitudes had long been prepared for, by the irresistible force of industrialisation pulling people away from the land which gives coherence to the notion of the family as a longitudinal structure linking generations, by the ideology of sexual love, by the charisma and visibility of certain apostles of liberalism or even by the horror of two world wars and the threat of annihilation which make nonsense of the idea of human life as a continuum. Some such cause or concatenation of causes has left aging peasants in Europe clinging to patches of unproductive earth – unproductive because there are no sons and daughters-in-law to work it – afraid of dying alone and unblessed, as some neighbour does each year. The body of Angiolina, the best story-teller in the Tuscan valley where I grow medicinals, was not discovered until the postman noticed her hens dying of thirst. She had been felled by a stroke as she undressed for bed, but although death was long in coming she could not make anyone hear. The police swept what was left of her into a plastic bag and the shocked neighbours sluiced the wet parts away, wondering how they could hide the bloody scratch-marks on the walls before her son arrived from Turin. The children who whiled away rainy afternoons listening to Angiolina's *fiabe* are dispersed to the four corners of the earth. When they used to sit spellbound all the people in the valley were kin: now their houses belong to pleasure-seeking foreigners in exile.

Yet, despite the overwhelming certainty that great changes are sweeping from the Western world across every traditional community, demographic historians insist that this is merely an impression, and an erroneous impression at that. The Family has always been as it is now, we are told, the holy family, of father, mother and 2.1 children living under one roof. Any wider kinship system or more complex social organisation has been composed of the copulating couple as its basic unit. To say all this may be to say a great deal less than the truth, but we are so hypnotised by our exclusive concern with what goes on between marital sheets, that we cannot see that the mere existence of double beds in separate apartments or separate houses does not constitute clinching evidence about the nature of the family. (Actually, it must also be said that facts about the distribution of double beds would be better indicators than most of the ones that are used.) Let me give an example of a household which is these days constituted of a man and his wife, a single generation, for their daughters are married and gone. The one who lives nearer eats with her parents at least once a week and stays over in her old room, and neither of the daughters would dream of spending the holidays anywhere but in their parents' tiny cottage. Just a nucleus, you might say, with a slightly stronger than usual bond with the nuclei that are descended from it, a bond strengthened by modern communications, for any new development can be instantly signalled by the new telephone, if only the wife were less afraid of using it. Every time it rings, she picks up the receiver with a trembling hand, for its use is associated in her mind with serious emergencies, not

least with the serious emergency of the bill. Let us agree that this family
falls within some parameters of variability, which demographic historians
might accept as the nuclear norm, so far as their descriptive criteria which
rely on the number of people eating out of the same cooking pot and sleeping under the same roof may be expected to carry them. They will have
missed the whole point. This family is a Family, made out of Marisa (we
will call the wife Marisa) and her daughters. Because her sons-in-law and
her grandchildren are firmly bound to her household rather than to her
in-laws, Marisa is one of the most unequivocally successful women I have
ever met.

The demographic historians will not let us consider meaningless scraps
of data of the impressionistic kind. They would not wish to hear how
Marisa reacted when her eldest brother and his wife ran away from the
house of her parents, leaving the old people who had outlived their usefulness as child-minders and domestic help to fend for themselves. Marisa's
mother had been disabled by a stroke. Now Marisa calls her sister-in-law
"*la budella*", best translated as "pig's gut." Marisa's mother went to her
next son, but Marisa was uneasy about the situation, for her mother needed
a woman's care and a daughter-in-law who was no blood of hers would
be unlikely to comb her hair the right way, or to put up with her wetting
herself for the fourth time in a day, and could not know her favourite
flowers. So Marisa struggled to find ways to bring her mother home,
not just to her two-roomed house, but to her bed, which her husband
willingly gave up for the duration. There she slept with her mother, waking
often during the night to check whether the slowly dying older woman's
feet had got any colder. It was her dearest wish that her mother would
die in her arms. The wish was eventually denied her, but her mother
came home to our valley to be buried next to her first-born son who was
shot in the head by the Nazis in front of his terrified family, suspected
of collaboration with the partisans. They had been too poor to work land
of their own, and had lived up and down our hills as tenant farmers until
Marisa disgraced herself by marrying a mere charcoal burner, the poorest
of the poor. Her mother had sold eggs and cheated her husband out of
her earnings so that Marisa would have sheets to her bed.

Yet Ferdinand Mount, the latest in Pangloss historians who wish to
tell us that the family has always been exactly as it is now, tells, us categorically that Marisa's is an extremely unusual attitude.

> ... there might exist a tradition that married couples with children ought also
> to look after their parents by taking them into their homes as honoured guests;
> but in most societies, this was a tradition more honoured in the breach than
> the observance, for the simple reason that most married couples in traditional
> society could not afford to feed their parents. Most old people died alone in
> the workhouse or in wretched poverty.[2]

There have been few inhabitants of Europe poorer than Marisa's family growing up in the famine and disorganisation which was post-war Tuscany but where there are no workhouses no one can die in them, and where there are few blankets a crowded bed may be warmer than a roomy one. When people are living off chestnuts and acorns and wild sallets, more hands make better collecting. We still use Marisa's mother's herbal remedies in my house to this day, although we are now *mutuati* and can go to the hospital. Mr Mount has little acquaintance with poverty, it seems, and his idea of "most societies" seems to be based on the kinds of distinctions made by *The Tatler*.

There are few people poorer than the inhabitants of the worst slums in Bombay, yet even there, in rooms which Mr Mount would consider too small for even one adult of Indian dimensions, space is found for the husband's mother or father, or both, if need be. Need only is, if the old ones are too feeble to be left or if the Family home in the village is gone. The pattern of comings and goings from city to village and back again may continue over generations. Demographic historians are in danger of underestimating both the degree of mobility that human beings may exhibit and the degree of tenacity to their heartland and their inheritance. Moreover, where knowledge is accumulated by experience (rather than by going to school), the older people are indispensable in the household, as indispensable as Mr Mount would consider gas and electricity. People in traditional societies, especially poor people in traditional societies (and that means practically all people still living in traditional societies today) can trust only their own kin, for they have been exploited by all their other contacts. They are, alas, often exploited by their own kin, without redress. Brothers do steal each other's savings. Families are as full of bad blood as good, but the struggle is on a human scale.

The Family remains the poor man's last resort: it will give him power and authority when no one else will. It will extend to him the palm of success, when no sign of even basic respect is forthcoming from any other quarter. Only the Family can make sense of growing old: only the Family can give shape and coherence to all the phases of human life. For these services the Family exacts a price, a price which some pay gladly and others begrudge every hour of every day. At some stages in the career of any individual the pressure seems unbearable, relentless or vicious. The Family has its casualties, the stranger brides immolated at their cooking stoves, the runaways, the prostitutes, the unpaid labourers for tyrannical kinsmen, the runts, the ill-matched, the childless. Everybody who has ever lived under the yoke of Family has at some time longed to escape from it: the most passionate hatreds have been hatched within it as well as the most enduring love. But Family is a slow-growing thing, its roots sunk in a time beyond the individual's remembrance. Where the doctrine of instant gratification is preached it must wither. If the Family pits itself against the power of the preachers of instant gratification, it presents itself as a stumbling-block to the establishment of the consumer society, which has resources which can sweep the whole tenacious structure into the void. Among those resources are intelligentsia of every shade of red, pink and blue, who have mounted attacks on the Family from every side.

The best known attack upon the family and the most influential in recent times is that mounted by Engels, who carried out the execution of Marx's bequest by presenting the world with his own collation of Marx's commentaries upon Lewis H. Morgan's "researches in the lines of human progress from savagery through barbarism to civilisation", as *The Origin of the Family, Private Property and the State* in 1884. The basic premises, and the logical inferences, of Engels's arguments are wrong, but what is even more interesting about his discussion of the family, is that like all the other participants in the debate about the origin, nature and history of the family, he is actually discussing marriage and the sexual relationship of spouses, and not the family at all. The great apostle of the brotherhood of man is not at all interested in brotherhood itself, let alone sisterhood or maternity. Like all his fellow familiographers, Engels would defend himself by saying that he is not interested in kinship which is a different study. If it is, then ethnocentricity has made it so, for what distinguished the Family from nuclear families is precisely that it is a working network of kin and not a dormitory full of double beds. Whatever he might maintain about the phases through which the family has passed, Engels actually sees it as husband/wife/issue, paradigmatically employer/employee/product, or owner/means of production/commodity. His unconscious sexism is quite striking; women are passive, men are jealous, women are desirable, men are rapacious, all four are unconscious assumptions underlying his entire discourse. The received idea of the ultra-left is that Soviet moves to weaken the family, by the institution of state nurseries, the facilitation of divorce, the ideology of free love, and the legalisation of birth control and abortion, were modified because the family was found to be the necessary training ground for the submissive citizen, and so it is, but not in quite the way that revolutionary Marxist orthodoxy sees it. What state capitalism realised was that the nuclear family is the most malleable social unit; houses were built for it, social services catered to it, and its descendants were drawn off into training institutions and its parents into state care. State capitalism and monopoly capitalism necessitate the same patterns of consumption, mobility and aspiration. The idea is simple and irrefutable; if all men are to be brothers, then nobody can be anybody else's brother. It is as true for Western Europe and America as it is for those parts of the Soviet Union where Family has been shattered. The operation of the process in the Soviets may be cruder, more brutal than in, say, Australia, but it is only therefore slightly less likely to succeed.

The ideal of universal brotherhood is a high one; just as every reformer yearns to establish harmony and abolish pain, he yearns to extend altruism from the kin group to the society at large (as defined by him). Engels quoted the ideas of Fourier, who called monogamy and private property "a war of the rich against the poor".

> We also find with him the deep perception that the individual families (*les familles incohérentes*) are the economic units of all faulty societies divided by opposing interests.[3]

The Family always has its own enrichment and aggrandisement in mind; it constitutes a pressure-group in conflict with other pressure-groups, but the amount of pressure it can exert is in direct correlation to its size and its tightness of organisation. If we whittle Family down to nuclear families, the nuclei will continue to act in their own interest, but by division the quotient of self-interest will be reduced to a manageable level. If we concentrate on the copulating couple, and convince it that frequent and prolonged copulation is its chief good, then we have little or nothing to fear from its self-interest which has all been neatly channelled off into the double bed with its attendant consumer goods ranged lovingly about it.

The heads of all the Utopians since Sir Thomas More who have wanted to make us into one big happy family, are too soft to contain the unpleasant thought that human kind cannot bear very much harmony. We cannot all slosh about in a soup of mutual wish-fulfilment, but we can be persuaded to concentrate upon our own gratification while somebody else decides what would be best for us all. Rooted in territoriality, self-defensive, disciplined in aggression, the Family is resistant to any authority but its own, while the biddable nuclear family propitiates its children, unable to check their insistent demands for gratification without experiencing guilt, because self-indulgence is the creed on which their fragile social micro-organism is built. The Marxist-Leninist attack on the Family was inevitable but its attack on the nuclear family was half-hearted and was soon abandoned.

It has often been observed that Christianity is anti-family, which is true enough, but what is less often understood is that Christianity is above all anti-Family: that champion of the nuclear family, Ferdinand Mount, notices quite correctly that Jesus Christ was not married, thereby showing quite clearly where he stands *vis-à-vis* the Family, for a more remarkable thing about Christ is that he had no brothers or sisters, and his mother had no brothers or sisters.[4] No uncle or cousin of Christ is ever mentioned, although some of the older sources indicate that Jesus' kin was just another aspect of him that was suppressed during the bureaucratisation of the Catholic church. The Holy Family is the nuclear family; Mr Mount is so hypnotised by the unpalatable fact that Joseph and Mary did not have simultaneous orgasms (or indeed any orgasms if the scriptures are any guide), that he sees only the Christian attack on sexuality and interprets that as an attack upon the family. The power of the icon of the Holy Family during the rise of capitalism can hardly be exaggerated: the only emblem more powerful is that of Madonna and Child, in which the Madonna is always nubile, the child always male, and the Oedipal fixations of the faithful cunningly gratified. Looked at across an ocean or two this sanctification of the nuclear family seems blindingly obvious: within the Anglo–Saxon sphere of influence it seems right, natural, inevitable, and completely invisible

> ... I am come to set a man at variance against his father, and the daughter against her mother, and the daughter in law against her mother in law. And man's foes shall be they of his own household. He that loveth father or mother more than me is not worthy of me: and he that loveth son or daughter more than me is not worthy of me.
>
> Matthew, X, 35–39.

Mr Mount does not choose to point out that neither wife nor husband is included in this list of inferior relations, nor does he notice that this is the part of Christ's injunction which has been fulfilled utterly; however it is not Christ who is loved at the expense of kin, it is the Spouse. Nevertheless although Christ's first miracle was performed at a wedding, Mr Mount is not satisfied with him as a champion of the nuclear family, accusing him of being half-hearted about it.[5] He quite fails to see that Jesus is the architect of the nuclear family, for his description of the married relationship must have seemed very odd to his first audiences:

> For this cause shall a man leave his father and mother and cleave to his wife; And they twain shall be one flesh: so then they are no more twain, but one flesh. What therefore God hath joined together, let not man put asunder.
>
> Matthew, XIX, 5–6

(Mr Mount is not happy with this because it does not allow divorce, so that our couple, although amputated from all other connections, might not be a truly copulating couple.[6]) The Epistles bear out the message, reiterating the duty of the spouses to each other, and failing utterly to mention any duties they might have to anyone else. All of which is perfectly understandable, if we recall the way in which converts are made, and the kind of implacable opposition they were likely to have met from their kin. Christianity survived because it was correctly adjusted to the socio-economic systems which developed in pre-medieval and medieval Europe, but with the rise of capitalism the weakness of marriage which the medieval church had always considered an inferior state became its strength ...

> ... he that is married careth for the things that are of the world, how he may please his wife ...
>
> I Corinthians, vii, 32–33.

The ideological battle to prove marriage the highest state open to human aspiration was joined in the sixteenth century, at the same time as modern capitalism was evolving. Despite the literary and other evidence of dislocation and confusion occasioning the polemic, it is generally thought that evidence for a change in family structure in northern Europe in this period is lacking. Northern Europe may have always been unique in that marriage was late, between partners of roughly the same age, fertility was always low, and the household seldom harboured kin outside the nucleus and its offspring, but gave space to servants instead.[7] Perhaps we should see the Reformation with its fervent anti-celibacy pro-monogamy stance as the crack which became a fracture under pressure from the ill fit of the Church of Rome upon peoples of non-Mediterranean customs. The case is far from proven; the Irish refuse to fit into the picture and perhaps we need to posit a *Rassensinn* obstinately surviving among the descendants of raiding Germanic hordes famous for their lechery and conspicuous consumption in order to explain the peculiarity, which may not have been shared by the Celts and their relatives. This is an extraordinarily vast and impertinent hypothesis and there is absolutely no hope of proving it or disproving it in what remains of my lifetime. A suspicion has been voiced merely that the peoples of Northwestern Europe are unique in their aggressiveness, mobility and intolerance of any ties beyond those involved in sex and minimal parenting. If this is true, it would be no more than a curiosity to be remarked by Oriental anthropologists in much the same way that Robert Suggs tabulated the Marquesan personality and its socialisation processes[8] – if it were not for the fact that the phenomenal success of the Germanic peoples has created an irresistible precedent which is shaming the kin-based societies by the stunning contrast, so that they apologise for themselves as backward and their children yearn for a two-room apartment in an urban slum, with the darling wife of their choice who is adroit in satisfying every whim.

The thesis of the historical demographers is summed up by their doyen, Peter Laslett, in his Preface to the collection of studies called *Household and Family in Past Time*, a preface which proposes to be also an analytic introduction on "the history of the family".[9] Unfortunately, what the book is really about is household, and not family at all, except in the narrow sense of people living under one roof. The size and structure of "the co-resident domestic group" are its real subjects and no evidence is considered which does not relate to actual enumeration of inhabitants of single dwellings and their relationship to each other. Census information, as anybody knows who has ever supplied any, is curiously unreal, because it must provide for comparability among incomparables. Moreover peasants are seldom anxious to tell the whole truth to bureaucratic authorities, even when they think in terms which bureaucracies can grasp, which they seldom do. Nicknames are more real than the names on official

records; father's name more real than husband's name, and so on. Absent
children are not named, but may be supporting the family by their earnings
as migrant factory hands. Even the definition of addresses can be extremely
misleading: Italian authorities, completely baffled by the protean nature
of the accretive farm buildings in which Italian peasants live, finally hit
upon an *ad hoc* system of numbering every external door as a dwelling.
This they have done three times, have come up with completely different
sets of numbers, for doors can be blocked up, even when the municipal
authority forbids any building alterations without specific plans and
written permission. A census based upon evidence of this kind would
indicate at any time that most of the houses were abandoned. When we
actually examine the kind of evidence upon which Laslett and his colleagues base their assessments of household size we find that it is just
like census information, if anything even more numerical and abstract.[10]
It is not surprising then that the subject under discussion tends to disappear.

> A question might even be raised as to whether the form of the family has
> in fact played as important a role in human development as the social sciences
> have assigned to it. It is possible to wonder whether our ancestors did always
> care about the form of the families in which they lived, whether they were
> large or small, simple or complicated, and even whether they contained kin
> or servants or strangers.[11]

It is always possible to wonder, and even permissible, but the idea of
our ancestors, whoever they were (most of us knowing little and caring
less) working to maintain households composed any old how does not
appear any more credible than any of the large generalisations about the
effect of urbanisation and industrialisation on the family that Laslett is
anxious to refute. Laslett constantly protests that he is not talking about
kinship and then uses the word family so that it overlaps with the idea
of kinship; moreover he seems to have got the arguments of his opponents
upside down.

> To go as far as this is not necessarily to deny that the form of the family has
> a determining influence on the outlook of individuals and the structure of
> society. Yet this determining influence may have been in fact of restricted
> significance. This would be because so little real variation in familial organisa-
> tion can actually be found in human history that examples of societies changing
> their character in accordance with changes in the family are unlikely ever to
> be met with.[12]

What a fact of unrestricted significance might be cannot well be imagined. Granted that the form of the family (used here in any sense you
please, *pace* a rather hurried asterisk pleading that it is not used in the
sense of kin) has a determining influence, one might ask if Dr Laslett
would be so kind as to admit that the outlook of individuals and the

structure of society have an influence and perhaps even a determining influence upon the form of the family. It is not easy to decide what Dr Laslett would take as a variation; if he insists on seeing a distinct statistical kink in historical diagrams (especially after corrections according to moment coefficients of skewness and kurtosis) then he is probably correct in assuming little variation, but if he should mean difference rather than variation, the ways in which families are organised are not just different but contrasting. Nevertheless we always return to the kind of point made by Jack Goody, which he develops partly out of his reading of G. P. Murdock and Talcott Parsons, that

> the opposition between 'family' and 'kinship' (or small and large family systems) is quite inadequate unless it recognises explicitly that all societies with more inclusive patterns of kinship also have, at the turning centre of their world, smaller domestic groups that are involved in the processes of production, reproduction, consumption and socialisation.[13]

The centre of the turning world is, of course, *still* not *turning*, and once again we have the feeling that somehow the argument has got itself upside down. Professor Goody seems to think that in order to be described as an extended family, a group of people related by blood and marriage must live under one roof, sleep in one room, eat from one pot and answer in unison like Hewey, Dewey and Louie. For him the "family" is the nugget of the reproductive alliance, which he identifies with some contortion of his argument as the unit of production and consumption, even though he describes the wives in his African example as individually preparing food shared out from the central granaries. He notes dispassionately that some compounds numbered more than a hundred people, but seems anxious to claim that these are not different in kind from compounds holding less than twenty, for all the world as if he were describing the inhabitants of a North Kensington high-rise. In fact, the discovery that all the inhabitants of a high-rise (who are under the same roof with a vengeance) were related by blood and marriage would astound us if it were to be made anywhere in the protestant world. (We would instantly expect to discover evidence of criminal corruption to explain the phenomenon, and, what is more, we would be virtually certain that some foreigners had perverted the bureaucratic process.)

In the course of his delicate footwork about the terminological hazards of familiographic discourse Professor Goody inadvertently gives the whole game away. He describes the kin living around the private apartments of a man and his wives as the "larger cooperating group", "morphologically a unit" of rather the same kind of "extended family" as exists among "any small-scale community with a relatively stationary population."[14] Even though Professor Goody sees the "larger cooperating (kin) group" as only an extended family in inverted commas, he has described exactly what other commentators mean when they talk about the extended family, and he has made certain claims for it which are rather more overweening than those other observers have made, i.e. that it exists in *any* small-scale community, which can only be interpreted to mean that the extended family can be found *only* in small-scale communities and in all small-scale communities, "with a relatively stationary population". Other anthropologists may point out that transhumant pastoralists can hardly be described as stationary but often have huge kinship networks. Australian aborigines have patterns of seasonal migration which cover thousands of miles, but they are aware of ramifications of the family tree which go much further. As any civil servant dispensing aid to the aboriginal community is aware, even today the absolute duty of cooperation and mutuality extends to distant relatives meeting for the first time. In disarray, the mobility of the aboriginal population has increased rather than diminished, but forced miscegenation, abject poverty and humiliation have not destroyed the ethos of the aboriginal Family.

By his rather careless aside, Professor Goody inadvertently betrays the fact that the cat is no longer in his bag. Now that it is out, it is important to examine the creature. There are all kinds of ways of amassing information about the Family, and the numerative approach is one of the worst, for what is in question is a complex of attitudes with various concrete manifestations, housing, village structure, religion, ritual, rivalry, law written and unwritten – and statistics. What we are trying to establish is a quality, which, as jargon is the rule in such studies, we might call familiality. A society with a high degree of familiality will be one in which Families exercise more actual power and influence than bureaucracies, in which the power of the civil authority cannot intervene in matters occurring within the Family, in which Families may enrich themselves at the expense of each other and the public purse. As one extreme on our scale of familiality we might describe a society composed of large but closely knit groups, which marry and give in marriage according to the interests of the group as a whole, with a sexual ethos contoured to advance this procedure. The heads of such groups will be the members of the oldest generation not yet incapable of exercising authority, and the ultimate power is likely to be vested in one person, probably a male. The property of such a Family, however it is described in written records, is a functioning unity, kept together by a combination of skilful administration and tyranny, and maintained by the unpaid labour of familial workers who must keep the Family ahead of the forces of disintegration such as inflation, by a combination of economy and aggressiveness. Such a structure is extremely dynamic, constantly becoming something other than it was, as struggles for leadership among brothers, or struggles to overthrow a senile patriarch, disease, infertility, war or other disasters take their toll. The Families that grow must fission; the Families that stagnate must die.

Such Families support themselves by skilful deployment of manpower and resources; they are as unlikely to welcome a state subsidy as they are to rejoice in paying taxes, but if subsidies are offered they will grab them. The larger body politic and the broader notion of the common good are likely to mean very little: in fact in highly familial societies every public programme meant to aid the poor or raise general standards of living is likely to be perverted as the "larger cooperating group" figures out ways to increase its eligibility at no cost to itself. American missionaries in Haiti were shocked to find that the Food-for-work project set up by CARE had been completely co-opted:

In the village where we are living one family controls all the community and government offices including judge, mayor, community council president etc. Besides owning vast tracts of land, "the family" speculates in coffee and controls all the illegal tree-cutting in the area. When CARE entered the village with a Food-for-Work soil-conservation project (using US food aid) it came as no surprise that "the family" was the local administrator of the project. "The family", through the auspices of the community council president, is also responsible for seeing to the actual food distribution ...

The workers on the project were not the landless peasants for whom it had been set up, but instead of working their own land, they worked three days a week on the project, one on the road for the community council and one day in the garden of one of the community leaders (i.e. "the family") in return for food they could have produced themselves.[15]

The power of "the family" in this case is real: no project could have been set up in opposition to it. The missionaries are strangers in competition with "the family" for influence, and they see it as criminal. The peasantry, very likely, sees "the family" simply as successful and hopes to keep within its sphere of patronage and favour. Examples of the same kind could be culled from any familial society in Latin America, in the Muslim world, in Asia or in Africa. Governments are formed from powerful families and attempt to maintain power by crippling their rivals, fall and are replaced by others just as eager to milk the commonwealth for their own aggrandisement. The network may be so huge and so pervasive that the outsider is unaware of its existence.

Versatility is a necessary attribute of the successful extended family, but along with versatility must go loyalty and consistency, so that the family storm-troopers infiltrating bureaucracies and businesses are not themselves co-opted. In a highly familial society, a man who becomes, say, personnel officer for any firm or organisation, will give jobs to his relatives and no one will think any the worse of him for doing it, no one, that is, except his employer, and even he (if not a relative himself) will not complain as long as he does not get the dolts among them. In such societies the morality of the family is the only true morality. A politician's policies and trustworthiness are likely to matter less than his successful deployment of his kin-group and its alliances. In fact, we might enunciate a principle here: the more familial a society, the less effective its administration. In the training of any professional elite, be it military, religious or civil, familial loyalties must be specifically overridden. In the case of every successful movement to institute an effective bureaucratic instrument of control, the human components of the instrument have been decisively estranged, not from wives and children, but from kith and kin.

The attack on the Family comes at all stages and from all quarters, as each of its functions is taken over by institutions and its freedom to exclude the institutional presence is undermined by law. If we were to begin at the beginning of a human life, we might notice that in non-familial societies, birth itself has been institutionalised. It is not a family event, which relatives attend, and the child is not presented to the Family of which it is the newest member, but is subject to institutional scrutiny, and the charting of its life begun. If anyone besides professionals is allowed into the birth chamber, it is the sexual partner of the mother, who is eligible to attend on very slight evidence of relationship indeed. Her mother, her sisters and her other children are excluded. The care of the infant is likewise taken over by institutions, to the extent that the mother is subject to constant surveillance by health professionals; she will be likely to see more of her health visitor than of her own mother and sisters or of her mother-in-law and sisters-in-law. Even if she were to enjoy a measure of Family support, the decisions of the health professionals would be seen by them all as overriding any traditional wisdom they might have left.

The institutionalisation of birth is a newer phenomenon than the institution of systems of compulsory state education which first removes junior members of the family from their duty to contribute to its prosperity and then trains them in skills not shared with their elders, thus seriously compromising the authority by which the cooperation of family members is assured. Of course it does not always happen that literate children despise illiterate parents, but the disparity creates a further strain which will only be overcome by the more astute family heads. The strain would be lessened if the educational authorities praised the traditional skills and wisdom of the elders, but anyone who has observed who the state teachers are in traditional societies, how they are selected and how placed, will realise that this is seldom what they are concerned to do. Whether they are bright young children of the new bourgeoisie or bitter underpaid remnants of a dispossessed ruling class or downright foreigners, they are all unlikely to respect the culture which they are actively supplanting. In the Families ruled by love, the educated young may still gladly return and offer their new expertise to the service of the commonalty. The Family in its turn may decide whom to promote and subsidise in the pursuit of the new skills, and the new doctors and teachers and engineers may return to work within the family orbit, and marry the girl chosen for them while they were at school. Certainly highly familial societies have absorbed the new culture and turned it to their own profit, but those Families which could not manage without child labour and could not meet the costs of sending their children to school even with scholarships are likely to have suffered a crushing loss of status with its concomitant loss of influence even in their own "small-scale, relatively stationary" communities.

Supplanted as educator, the Family finds itself threatened also as employer. Where working the family land or carrying on the family trade or exercising the family skills are the only options, the able-bodied members of the Family have no choice but to work for the sustenance of their elders and their infant brothers and sisters and cousins. Once a choice is available a new source of tension arises; the young, by nature restless, are easily enticed by the promise of money in their pockets. The Family, meanwhile, is faced with a serious dilemma, whether to encourage some of its members to leave the traditional avocations in order to bring cash into the household or to attempt to make working for the Family more attractive than working for wages. Where Family bonds are strong, (which is not the same thing as authoritarian) the able-bodied may be allowed to go without their dependents facing the prospect of pauperisation, for the money will find its way back to the Family in one form or another. The situation causes a good deal of anxiety, for a wedge has been driven into the fragile web of mutual obligation which must somehow absorb and neutralise the threat of disintegration. The Families who surmount the difficulties, and must surmount them continually, stretch long tentacles after their absent sons; the village group meets for prayers with a priest of its own sect in the far-off industrial city. Caste members, peer groups, age sets try to cling together in the alien world of the large town, speaking their own dialect, wearing their traditional insignia, braving ridicule as ignorant provincials. As poverty grinds smaller, the distances that sons travel grow longer; the employer offers less and less, dormitories packed with men, beds slept in by turns, wages insufficient to keep the workers fed if they are still to send money back home. Servants from Uttar Pradesh with wives and children at home sleep on staircases and in broom cupboards, on kerbstones and park benches all over Bombay, so they can save up the five hundred rupees or so to build a pukka house back home. As long as the employers exploit the Family at home, by treating their workers as mindless chattels with neither chick nor child to call their own, the Family remains the haven of human values and the workers yearn to go back, although the way may grow longer and harder the more years they sweat in the dark satanic mills which are the legacy of the industrialised world to the developing world. If and when real wages enable a worker to bring his wife and children to stay with him permanently, an axe has been laid at the foot of the family tree.

As long as the city is merely drudgery among strangers its impact upon the Family is negligible, but however filthy, overcrowded, noisy and dangerous the city is, it is always much more than that. The city is stimulating as well as terrifying, and the most energetic and courageous of the country boys arriving in it will rise to its challenge. They are the ones who will skip their meals in order to buy a cinema ticket, who will gamble, who will go with prostitutes, who will dress sharply and pit themselves against the myriad entrepreneurs who make a living off the teeming streets. They will absorb the message of the consumer society, learn its language and its ways, and its values. The distant home becomes something to be ashamed of, an unsewered hole, full of ignorant people who revere their animals and think their children the most entertaining things anyone has ever seen. The hard-working shy wife is seen as graceless and plain and boring, her modesty as frigidity. Visits home become rarer and shorter; communication with the elders becomes more and more a matter of concealments and evasions. The Family watches, grieves and is silent. A spell in prison may save the situation; they may come to take him sadder and wiser home, or they may feel that he has disgraced them and disown him. There are many scenarios arising out of the outwork situation, most of them tragic, even when the worker returns worn out to his wife and his children and his parents and has not married a blonde and bought himself a bar in some suburb of Munich.

Families do survive even such strains as these. We may take as an example the Family of Karam Chand described by Jane Morton in her series on the British family for *The Times*; the first impression made by the story of Karam Chand and his wife Chint Kaur is that they are both remarkable people.[16] "The whole family" paid Karam Chand's fare to England where he lived and worked for ten years before he could bring his wife and five children to join him. Morton does not say who "the whole family" is, but we may be sure that they were not his wife and children, but those other members of his Family who also made sure that his wife and children were properly looked after and never lost sight of their ultimate destiny. Chint Kaur's experiences on leaving her Punjab home and running the gauntlet of the terrifying journey and the gratuitous humiliations arranged by British immigration officials for her and her daughters are not described in the piece, which features an extraordinary photograph of thirteen happy, open and sharply individual faces, who are not quite all of Karam Chand's Family. Morton does not say how strong the links with the Family home in Jullundur still are; what we actually see in the Chand case is an extended Family which has fissioned from another extended Family; it may have passed through a phase where it was nothing but husband and wife and their children, but that must have been short, for now Karam Chand is sixty-five, his wife fifty-nine and their eldest child only thirty-two. For fifteen years or so they lived in the Family at Jullundur, for ten separated, and now with their own adult children. Nor do we know if the principal spur behind Karam Chand's migration was need to find dowries for three daughters, one of whom, still only nineteen, is as yet unmarried. Ten people now live in Karam Chand's household; husband, wife, eldest son, eldest son's wife and only child, younger son, younger son's wife, unmarried daughter, widowed mother-in-law of younger son and her thirteen-year-old son. The children of their married daughters are frequent inmates of the household.

However, the strains on Karam Chand's household are mounting. Their three-bedroom terrace cottage is found to be much too small for all these people, and Morton stresses how Karam Chand misses the "spacious" Family home in Jullundur. I doubt very much whether she would actually find it spacious; it seems just as likely that different patterns of space usage prevailed in Jullundur which cannot prevail in Wolverhampton, for many reasons, not the least important among them being climatic, and that the expectations of the Chand Family are changing so that they now require rooms of their own and an un-Indian measure of privacy. Council by-laws about overcrowding also apply. So the Family has had to acquire another house, which unfortunately does not adjoin and cannot be converted into a Family home.

> Many families in the neighbourhood sustain an extended family lifestyle from several neighbouring houses. Sat Pal's family will still eat together most days. But Siso Pal is nervous. Even as she longs for more space, she is afraid of "being in a house by myself."[17]

Meanwhile the widowed mother-in-law has been registered for a council flat. Karam Chand is too old to work in the car components factory now, and the Family is supported by the earnings of the two sons, swollen by long overtime hours. How long they will continue to believe that this is the best arrangement is a matter for speculation, as in terms of taxes, rate rebates and other allowances, they are almost certainly losing money in their battle to remain independent and together. How they will feel when it is time to contribute to Krishanda's dowry is another matter; how Krishanda will feel about having to wait until they have done so is yet another. Many Punjabi girls in Wolverhampton no longer feel that their parents have any rights in their marriages at all: the wonder of it is that so many more smile at the British mania for true love and carry on regardless in the old ways. The eventual death of Karam Chand will also provide a new source of strain, for not only will the Family lose a remarkable individual whose personal endurance and loyalty has kept them together so far, and even attracted the in-laws into his orbit, but inheritance taxes could cost them dear.

> Sat Pal (elder son), who handles most of the paperwork, merely shakes his head with a smile at the idea of tangling with officialdom. For his father, how-ever, it is a matter of principle. "They would decide that this was my money and that was his," he exclaims. "We do not choose to think in this way – we know only family money."[18]

In a familial society there would be ways of dealing with officialdom; in Wolverhampton Indian expertise in money management may come to the rescue of Karam Chand's Family, but equally possibly it will not.

Karam Chand's Family may make light of the pressures building up against it, but they are relentless. Every extended Family must ride out Family crises, and it is at such moments of fragility and inner strain that the external pressure can produce a fissure. As long as the adult men can see that, even slaving in the factory for long hours, they are living at a higher standard than they would be enjoying if they had remained in Jullundur they may not begin to chafe or to feel that the Family is a parasitic organism, but their sons, who will be educated in England, will almost certainly feel very differently on the subject. Karam Chand's sons still feel that they function more efficiently as a commonalty. Family altruism must coincide with self-interest in order to continue to prevail, but it seems clear that Karam Chand's sons were counting a large number of intangibles among their benefits, intangibles which may well be imper-ceptible to their younger kin. Meanwhile, the tangible advantages of Family life have more and more been assumed as the state's duty to provide.

If laws are enacted which are meant to prevent property being con-centrated in the hands of family heads and necessitate division, the power base of the patriarch is destroyed, unless the Family agrees to connive in perverting the law, which it often does. If taxation favours the small household and penalises the large, by accepting only wife and progeny as dependents, say, it becomes uneconomic to live in an extended house-hold or to share the earnings out from a family kitty. Family duties will not be carried out if the money to carry them out has been claimed by the state on the grounds that it has assumed the responsibility; for example, there is little incentive to support the old if the state has already taken the money from their children to do it, however wastefully, inadequately and bureaucratically, on their behalf. If state subsidised housing schemes (which the Family has been forced to contribute to) build two-bedroomed villas and flats, the Family is going to have to carve itself up in order to take advantage of them. If the law is going to maintain that children have the right to marry without their parents' consent while the media blare out the message that an orgasm-laden double bed is every man's right, careful family building with suitable affines is out of the question.

When divorce muscles in to make the wife of one's youth expendable, and sexual excitement is considered the *sine qua non* of human happiness, the Family must find itself clawing to stay on the slippery slope. When polemicists of every shade of political opinion, from Ezra Pound to David Cooper, see the Family as a joyless, puritanical, grasping tyranny of the aged over the young, ignorant, conservative, reactionary and infinitely boring, the Family loses its last rag of prestige.

Such a view of the Family is actually based on attitudes which have developed within the nuclear family. Because very few of us who have been brought up in the unending parent-child confrontation still really like our parents, we imagine that the extended family is simply a proliferation of negative attitudes. If we see twenty Parsees taking up a table at a Chinese restaurant to fête some ancient female of their clan, we expect there to be an atmosphere of constraint and punctilio towards the old lady. We would not expect any glee to develop, and if it did, we would assume that it must be in spite of the presence of cranky female eld. In fact, the old lady is seated at the centre of the table, with her favourite grandchildren and great-grandchildren around her, and every joke and every piece of showing off is staged to her and for her. She is the pivot of the social group, surrounded by a circle of admiring faces, even though every time she is offered a new dish of Chinese food she is picky and hypercritical. There is never so much as a hint of boredom or annoyance; indeed the hilarity at the table makes the rest of us feel downright gloomy by contrast.

It may seem strange for a twentieth-century feminist to be among the few champions of the Family as a larger organisation than the suburban dyad, for most Families are headed by men and men play the decisive roles in them, or at any rate usually appear to, but there are reasons for such a paradoxical attitude. For one thing, if the family is to be a female sphere, then it is better for women's sanity and tranquillity that they not be isolated in it, as they are in the nuclear family. The Family offers the paradigm for the female collectivity; it shows us women cooperating to dignify their lives, to lighten each other's labour, and growing in real love and sisterhood, a word we use constantly without any idea of what it is. When I saw three little girls in a house near Bangalore, hurrying to finish their separate tasks so that they could join their mother in pounding rice with a long pole, each skipping over and taking up the work in synchrony with the others, barely stroking the pole, guiding it as it bounced with its own momentum by finger-tips only, all the time keeping up a flow of satiric commentary on their uncle the sarpanch's unfortunate guest (me) formally seated on a divan like an honorary man, I saw something I had never seen before, the dynamism of sisterhood in action. Their mother was the daughter of the master of the house, rather than his daughter-in-law. She had married a man who couldn't keep her, whose family had disintegrated, and so had brought him and her girls home to her parents. The littlest girl brought her sleeping mat into the entrance hall, where she slept next to her grandfather, fully clothed in her sari, as is the custom. The house was a grand pukka affair, built on the proceeds of manufacturing Gobar gas plants, but it was used as the old mud house and courtyard had been. There were apartments for the three married couples, but only one couple slept together. Sleeping, in India, is hardly a private activity.

Another reason for championing the Family is that it seems a better environment for children, and not simply because poverty means that children are not trained as wasteful consumers from an early age. Again to give an example, let me take a twelve-year-old's birthday party in Khartoum at which I was a guest. The others present in order of seniority were, besides the hostess, hostess's mother-in-law, hostess's sister and her four children, hostess's divorced sister and one daughter, and hostess's three children – not a recipe for a terrifically entertaining evening, you might think, especially as the birthday boy was the eldest of the children and might quite likely be bored and fractious. He was a little taken aback by his present, a wooden carving of a fish from Melville Island which was all I had, and apparently quite unconcerned whether anyone else had brought him a present or not, which might be because birthdays are a Western importation in Sudan, but might not. The eight children amused themselves without any problem; the birthday boy himself spent a great deal of time stringing up apples so that the children could play at eating them, a game they found side-splitting. At no time did any of them pester the adults for attention; instead the adults found themselves joining in the hilarity. The most remarkable sight which remains in my mind was the birthday boy taking an extra fifteen minutes to tie an apple with a very long string so that a three-year-old, who had been bumped and bounced by the bigger children without ever showing ill-temper, could join in and then teaching him how to do it. Another part of the time was spent in having the growing girls do the pigeon dance which they will perform at their weddings, with made-up songs of their own. The eldest girl was a natural comedienne and kept everyone roaring at the words of her songs and her elaborate suggestive gestures, but alas, I could not understand what she sang. The evening took on rather a bizarre character when the electric cables outside began to fizz and explode at intervals in showers of white sparks, which everyone but me thought added greatly to the fun.

It was all rather rough-and-tumble, I suppose. My hostess's daughter had a painful fungus infection of her right hand but she played along with everyone else although I saw her wince once or twice. The mothers did not propitiate their children, did not step in to see that everyone had a good time, were not anxious. Although we were in the house of a senior government functionary, the room was furnished very sparsely, and what furniture there was was shabby. The women spent some time choosing new *taubs* from a selection apparently bought in bulk by the larger Family who would have been invited if it had been a real family feast and not just a little get-together for a birthday. Indeed, within a few weeks eighty-six of them were due to go and meet a suggested fiancée for one of my hostess's cousins. What remains in my mind is a very happy evening spent with women and children, without drink, with simple food, the only sophistication a cigarette smoked by one of the old ladies, and a spate of laughter, love and good humour. When I left, the birthday boy made me an elegant little speech in English, which convinced me that the swimming fish was just the right present after all. Too good to be true, you may say, yet my Sudanese friends thought nothing of it. They are very proud of their Families though and their president, Gaffer al-Nemeiry, is so concerned to keep Sudanese family structure intact, that he is refusing the kinds of aid which will necessitate caring for the helpless and infirm outside their own families. Not that it is easy to get suffering individuals away from Families, for they tend to follow them for thousands of miles, even into the hallowed portals of the London Clinic, where the women-folk sit on the floor around the sufferers' beds while their children play around them, and the menfolk stand smoking in the corridors. As for what the nurses think of the situation, and the half-eaten home-cooked food scattered round the room, the Families could not care less. The London Clinic is just another of the myriad points where familial society and bureaucratic society meet and clash.

Women in the extended family are not at the mercy of their husbands; indeed, their relationships with the other women in the Family, especially with their husband's mother, may well be more important. What this means in effect can vary enormously. In the doctor's records at Jamkhed, for example, the commonest complaint recorded was "Anxiety". The term almost exclusively referred to the strain felt by young wives who were ill-at-ease with their mothers-in-law. The story of Ruth is a typical love story of the extended family, for the love of daughter-in-law for a good mother-in-law is a favourite theme of the literature of the Family. What is not often understood among sophisticated observers is that each role assigned within the Family is a career role in which it is possible to do well or badly, and one's capacity to do either is strictly related to one's personality and potential. Selfish people in the Family will be deeply unhappy and their fate is shared by the greedy, the miserly, the arrogant and the paranoid. The Family guarantees no one success and sheds no romantic veil over the situation, so that selfishness and vanity cannot masquerade as bliss and beauty has no commodity value. There is no element of competition in the marriage stakes, for the assignment of spouses is made according to immutable characteristics of family and social

standing and not according to power to entrap, thus one of the most divisive
aspects of growing up in the bureaucratic world is eliminated, or rather
has never existed. There is no dating dance, there is no most popular
girl, there is no campus queen. Cross-eyed, pockmarked, flat-chested,
good-natured, hardworking girls have happier lives than Southern Belles,
which could strike other plain, industrious women as fair enough. The
most valuable commodity in the Family is a loving heart whose happiness
consists in seeing others happy.

Woman in the extended Family is not an object but an agent; the
Family's prosperity and cohesiveness will be directly due to her. She does
not briefly blaze as her husband's paramour and decline into the whining
mother of one or two, until she becomes that most loathed of Western
species, a mother-in-law *cum* blue-rinse widow; she has the opportunity
to develop and to play an increasingly important role for an increasing
number of people, until infirmity deposes her. Even then, if she has been
successful, her daughters-in-law will keep her prestige intact. I once sat
for five hours on a bus in Maharashtra next to an old lady being taken
by her sons to a clinic to have spectacles fitted after a cataract operation.
She was supported by one of her daughters-in-law, a strong, merry-faced
woman, whose tanned cheeks told of work in the fields alongside the men
who sat ranged around their mother like a guard of honour. Although
we were all perched three to a seat and the bus was very crowded, the
first bench behind the driver had been completely taken up by one of
the driver's male relatives snoring away fast asleep. None of us individuals
had had the courage to rouse him, but the Family swept him off in a
trice and installed itself around the old lady, who needed to have the
windows open. Everyone dragged the windows open and sat in the stinging
dust, while the old lady bowed her head, shielded from the dust by her
dopatta. There was not a murmur of dissension at the old lady's imperious-
ness; indeed everyone sprang to do her bidding, inaudibly uttered to her
daughter-in-law. She could not sit Western-fashion with her legs dangling
down, but squatted on the convex bus seat, so that every lurch of the
bus threatened to shoot her on to the floor, but that her daughter-in-law's
strong arm was always there.

Some of the respect given by the bus passengers at large might have
been due to the fact that the Family, although dressed in the same cheap
green cotton saris and off-white khadi as the rest of us, with the same
grimy Congress caps, was clearly what passed for "rich", although the
distinction between their poverty and the poverty of the others would
have been largely imperceptible to a foreigner. Their hands were just
as cracked with toil, their bodies just as hard. Their riches was their
familiality and they were making a display of it, but even so, there was
no mistaking the younger woman's awareness of the older woman, which
never faltered. There was never a hint of impatience, although the way

was long and the bus was an oven and the old lady whimpered rather too much. She was handed off the bus like some infinitely rich and fragile thing, and the last I saw of her was her regal progress into the clinic, walking erect, completely veiled and very slowly, with her lady-in-waiting beside her, and her three sons walking at her pace in the vanguard.

John Demos, in an essay in the Laslett collection already cited, suggests that

> An "extended-family" household ... creates above all a radically different set of *emotional* arrangements. For example, it offers the strong likelihood of some type of "multiple mothering" (with broad consequences for child-rearing), and a considerably diluted relationship between spouses. These possibilities now seem to have been largely ruled out by my findings for Plymouth ...[19]

What the improbably named Demos found out about Plymouth was that it did not contain "extended-family" households; how this discovery should have ruled out the possibility that he would have found radically different personality structures in Plymouth if he *had* found "extended-family" households there seems to be another example of demographers arguing upside down. In the peasant family I observed on the bus, it is practically certain that the children of the daughter-in-law would have spent more time with her mother-in-law than with their own mother, if only because she was frequently obliged to work on the family land. Besides, even if she had not been, too much of her time would have been taken up in time-consuming tasks such as cleaning grain, which the old lady would have been freed from by age and seniority. Moreover, daughters-in-law begin their married life as strangers in the Family, and the disciplining of children in the Family way is best left to the elders, which is not to say that the relationship with the biological mother is obscured (because children almost certainly sleep with their biological mothers) nor can it be, because it in turn will become the lynch pin of the household. In fact children are the entertainment of the Family, and everybody is anxious to spend time with them, even older children. As well as a little granddaughter bringing her sleeping mat alongside her grandfather's, I have seen young uncles protecting sleeping nephews from flies as they themselves doze on charpoys in the noon heat, and exhausted little girls coming back from a morning at school to roll up in grandmama's *taub* and snooze with her on her day-bed. Among the Western families of my acquaintance, children generally sleep in their own beds alone; the difference between us and them is not just a matter of whom children have contact with, but also of the kind of contact they have. As for the results being a different personality structure, I should say that this is indubitable, although I should not like to be responsible for defining what the differences are, beyond remarking that they are what makes dealing with wily Oriental gentlemen so difficult for Westerners. Perhaps I can quote an extremely sophisticated oriental gentlewoman who lives half the year in Belgravia with publisher husband and one son at public school, and the other half in the family home in Delhi, to show the other side of the difference. "My dear," she said to me once, "none of the British are real to me. They are all so fly-by-night, you see. I've never met any of their parents."

Contact with a highly familial culture can be superficially charming and exhilarating, for affection within the extended family takes so many guiltless forms that a kind of innocent admiration and lovingness is easily forthcoming; the shock comes when the outsider realises that it is in no way connected to him "personally" as we say, and that what he may have thought of as a warm and intimate friendship has been totally forgotten. Indeed he must realise that most, if not all of the charm and generosity that his presence have called forth is what the Family sees as proper to itself and its self-image, and in no way a response to himself. It is partly because of these differing emotional structures, which make the members of familial societies so difficult for us to manipulate, that there is such a strong dislike for familiality on the part of non-familial man.

It would be intellectual hubris of the worst kind to suggest that perhaps the genus *Homo sapiens* comes in two species, familial and non-familial, and that never the twain shall meet, but the combined efforts of the demographers seem to be tending towards some such conclusion. In the words of Professor Goody:

> An examination of the figures for England reveals however, as Laslett points out, that mean household size . . . has been relatively constant from the sixteenth century to the beginning of the present century. Does this mean that special conditions obtained in Western Europe which assisted the emergence of industrial (i.e. non-familial) productive systems?
>
> The hypothesis is tempting, especially as interesting suggestions have been made as to the possible relationships between delayed marriage and capital accumulation . . . [20]

Professor Goody goes on to resist the temptation, but so far no independent school of oriental demography has arisen to apply the methods of the historical demographers to its own social history and as a result the discourse seems distinctly astigmatic. Even the basic terminology is a matter for debate. There are many missing links in the Laslett argument; for example, he does not concern himself at all with the crucial question of the interest of parents in the marriage of children, and the bitter question of the necessity of parents' consent to any match, which was passionately debated in England for more than a hundred years, nor does he or any of his disciples consider the question of actual sexual behaviour as distinct from recorded alliance, even though he is clearly excited and interested by the question of "illicit Love". "It is possible to wonder," as Laslett would say, whether he would get any different picture of Marquesan society or the Mae Enga by using such insensitive indicators. Nevertheless it is a shock to discover that Nicholas Bacon, the cooper of Clayworth, turned his mother, Joan, and his sister, Anne, out of the house when he became householder in 1688, so that they became inmates of the parish poorhouse. The parish records do not tell us whether Joan and Nicholas still spoke to each other.[21]

Still, while insisting upon the caveat that the historical description of the English family is fragmentary, and that we may be taking extraordinary cases for typical ones simply because they are the ones that appear in written records, we may agree that the case of anthropologists like Leach and Goode, that

> ... wherever the economic system expands through industrialisation, family patterns change. Extended kinship ties weaken, lineage patterns dissolve, and a trend towards some form of the conjugal system begins to appear ...[22]

has not been proved. The next step, agreeing that North-western Europe has been exclusively populated by conjugal or simple households since time immemorial, is too big a one to take on the present evidence, although we might have no difficulty in agreeing that it has been so since the beginning of the seventeenth century and perhaps even since the beginning of the sixteenth. If this should prove to have been the case when all the bids are in, it is very strange and odd that our spectacular elite, the British aristocracy, is a network of extended kinship systems which have so far managed, with some exceptions, to keep their hold on land and money, despite the concerted efforts of every administration for the last century to pry them loose. The old school network is, after all, just another version of the kinship system. It is all the more ironic then that the non-dynastic English should be so spellbound by the doings of the extended Royal Family, and that the Americans should be equally spellbound by Families – by the Mafia, by oil dynasts, by wine-growing matriarchs – *and* by the Royal Family. By the way, all of them, including the Royal Family, are more or less maverick, being laws unto themselves. The Queen must be among the most powerful big sisters in the world, for she is widely believed to have prevented her sister carrying for love because the man in question was a divorced commoner. The Royal Extended Family does not live under one roof, but it does live in properties belonging to the Crown which means that it lives in family properties, and its members cannot wander off and live where they choose. It does not educate its own any more, because it is anxious to democratise its image, but all its members know that they must work for the family firm, and they all learn how to do that within the family. It is its own entertainment, for all the public occasions that the Queen attends are business. Fun happens within the Family, and they are the traditional feasts of the extended family, christenings, engagements, weddings and funerals. The Royal Family, being a dynasty, must exercise a measure of control over the affinities that it acquires, but because the commons are sentimental, they must believe that when the Heir Apparent takes a woman to wife whose claim to the throne might be considered better than his own, that he has married for love, just as they did when his mother married her cousin. Heaven forbid that I should intimate that the royal spouses do not love each other devotedly: rather I would insist that if you love your Family and honour its achievements, you will love your Family's natural choice. Sexual love is much less hard to arrange than we have all been led to believe. Meanwhile the British press by tacit agreement has kept the names of Prince Charles's pre-marital sexual partners from the public at large, even though there is hardly a cub reporter who does not know who they are. It is a curious hypocrisy which sees that the riches of the country, together with power and the glories of the cultural heritage, are in the hands of an interrelated group of dynasties, and yet continues the fiction that the Royal Family is just a little old nuclear family such as you might find in any council home. In fact the Queen is only Queen because her uncle demanded the right to marry the woman of his choice and live in childless bliss outside the Family.

The Royal Family escapes the usual kind of prejudice against old-fashioned Families because it masquerades as a loose collection of nuclei and manages to keep its clannishness out of the limelight, although the lesser mortals who wander into its purlieux are often heard to complain of it. Like all other Families, the Royal Family is really only concerned with itself. Affines recruited from outside its circle of approved matrimonial contacts are expected to work hard for acceptance, which is by no means a foregone conclusion. Similarly, the Queen's functions as disciplinarian of the Family are not publicised; one version has it that these are usually deputed to the Prince Consort, to whom the Queen herself defers in domestic matters – all very subtle, very adroit, and very complicated.

There can be no doubt of the envy which makes the lives of rich dynasts compulsive viewing for American television audiences, but it is not as often realised that the American fascination with the Mafia, Cosa Nostra, Camorra, *l'onorevole fraternità*, Black Hand, *la'ndrangheta* under whatever sobriquet, is tinged with admiration. The Southern Italian kinship networks are assumed by many Americans to be co-extensive with organised crime, which is in fact not familial but bureaucratic in character and only makes use of the Mediterranean extended family with its code of *omertà* and death before dishonour for minor functions, for its unreliability is insurmountable. The Mafia functions upon the principle that "loyalties to kin supersede all other loyalties. For this reason alone kinship must be the enemy of bureaucracy." While the syndicate, like the rest of us, demands "that a man be loyal to his office before his kin." The usefulness of people who put family loyalties before all other considerations is limited; neither the organised crime, nor its close relative, the state, can risk such conditional alliances, while the Mafia has few alternatives, being virtually condemned to delinquency: for

> These unthinking, familistic, kinship-centred loyalties run in opposition to the laws of church and state and the demands of an industrial society.[23]

In the common American fantasy, the body politic, a loose agglomeration of disparate groups, is terrorised and manipulated by a close-knit group sharing genes, language, religion, and culture. The generalised claims of the common good, morality, decency, or freedom, cannot galvanise the polyglot citizenry into decisive action: they look on with fascinated horror as gangsters act out tribal warfare and *giustiziamento*, snuffing out colourful individuals like so many candles. The *famiglia* will never take over the vast territory controlled by bureaucratic crime, which steals, exploits, debauches, plunders, terrorises and kills by computer, but it will not be extirpated until the personality structure of the *mafioso* is fundamantally changed, and the discipline of the *famiglia* becomes more disgusting to him than the idea of working nine to five and paying his taxes. Its present criminality is a sad end for the organisation which began as an *onorevole fraternitá* cooperating to protect the interests of local power groups against the representatives of the various alien powers who conquered and controlled their homelands, the most recent being the centralised government of the new nation-state of Italy. The Mafia has always been passionately attached to its own values, scornful of less rigorous codes, and concerned to exercise real power rather than to enjoy the patronage of the legally instituted authority, so that the *de jure* power often had to come to terms with it. Only in the last sixty years or so has the Mafia become criminal and contemptible, preying on its own.

The Family without riches and power is much more contemptible than the Mafia which is assumed to have both. We are all familiar with the cliché of the hillbilly gang of brothers with foreheads villainous low riding into the neat settlement of protestant nuclear families and creating mayhem. The hero, celibate or sub-fertile, mows them down as they were born, like flies. He is Hercules, they are the Hydra, horribly unanimous but quite half-witted. What is so frightening about the "Whitehead boys" or whatever they are called in the instance, is their lack of individualism, their sinister mutualism and unreasoning togetherness. Typically they are involved in a territorial dispute in defiance of state and legal authority, to which they oppose their shared vigour, only to lose life and all. Among the latest versions of the cliché are some that have them driven well back into the badlands where they live like brutes, preying on strangers, whom in one famous case (*Deliverance*) they collectively bugger.

The stereotype of the Family in Western imagination is either very rich and powerful or very poor and backward; coincidentally, the reality may be fast approaching the same violent contrast, as rich and powerful Families continue to consolidate their power as oligarchies controlling the economies of new nation states hastily cobbled together out of divided, familial societies. One of the first necessities is to ensure that the Family stays at the top either by allying itself with potential rivals or by doing its best to see that no other faction achieves enough power and influence to challenge it. Families themselves are not likely to be promoters of familiality as a value. They are more likely to see themselves as magnificent exceptions and a group apart and to seek to use those from outside the group as pawns.

The Families who retain power during industrialisation may very well do so partly by creating a servant class of employees who, unlike the traditional servants in the caste system, do not bring their families at their backs and do not practise family trades. Thus Families may wreak as much havoc on other Families as any faceless bureaucracy, and they may use all the techniques developed by the bureaucracies to increase the scope and intensity of their control. Perhaps what we shall see in coming decades is the gradual concentration of the Family at either extreme of the economic scale, among the very rich and among the very poor, the very rich because the centrifugal pull of money and power keeps its members consolidated and the very poor because they have no alternative but to huddle together. Although Families can be shown to be surviving despite massive migration to urban slums, largely caused by the increase in landlessness, it seems impossible that they can long survive such strain, especially as the urban situation so often proves intractable. I can think of dozens of examples of families split up in high-rise apartments in Indian cities, where mother-in-law's bearer brings the yoghurt over at eight and takes back the ghee, while sister-in-law's bearer is sharing out the mangoes and cousin has come to use the telephone, but I can think of even more examples of professionally trained Indians living in nuclear isolation with their wives in Canada and Australia, convinced that it is a better way of life, even when their marriages were arranged. The very idea of development carries with it the idea of the adoption of Western standards of consumption, of space available to individual members of the family, of privacy. How long does it take before Families begin to fill the rooms of their new apartments with underutilised furniture, consumer durables, and stored possessions instead of keeping the floors clear for the bed-rolls, number constantly changing, which may have to be spread out any and every night? How long can babies keep tired people laughing when what they signify is not riches but a crushing series of responsibilities, not just schooling, which is usually nominally free, but recreation facilities, special foods and medicines, decent clothing fit to go to school in, a place to study, and adequate sleep, like cuckoos in a nest whose other inmates demanded much less. How long will peasants like Marisa continue to enjoy themselves at family festivals rather than public entertainments if the adored grand-children are roller-skating about cut off from all human intercourse by earphones clamped to their heads playing disco music? The Family's weakest point has always been its link with the young adults who are at the point of heaviest individual contribution and minimum return. Consumer society offers them its most glittering rewards. By the time they have realised that transient thrills are all it has to offer, it is too late.

A gradually increasing tendency to nuclearity in family building might actually increase the sum of human happiness; such, at any rate, is the belief of the numerous champions of one man, one wife (at a time) and as few children as can possibly be managed, under one roof and unen-cumbered by kin, as the natural way of life, only departed from in emergencies or as a result of the plotting of the old to keep the young and vital in their power. Now, if the multi-generational family were to be found flourishing in societies like our own where the elderly are an appreciable proportion of the total population, we might suspect that it was the product of some conspiracy among geriatrics, but in fact it is usually found in countries where the achievement of old age is relatively rare. Moreover, in order that the Family achieve its multi-generational character, it has been necessary to marry children at a very early age, sometimes committing them to marriage before puberty, and consum-mating the alliance as soon afterwards as possible, in case the elders should not survive. The champions of sexual bliss should see this as an attempt to gratify the natural urges at the right time, i.e. when they are at their strongest, rather than forcing young adults to delay the commencement of sexual activity until parents died or until capital was amassed. But this is not how they see it. All of them seem to identify with the not so young adult male tucked up with the bride of his choice, with no in-laws to listen to their groans of mutual bliss through the thin cottage walls. It seems more important for the couple to be alone than for its halves to be together. A cynical feminist might say that this gave the husband unlimited power to brutalise his wife, as well as to please her. Certainly there would be as little restraint on hostility as on tenderness.

There exists no literature of the extended family comparable to the lengthy shrieks of rage and hatred which the nuclear family has provoked. It would be very risky indeed to base a denunciation of the nuclear family upon the arguments of someone like David Cooper who produces hideous snatches of evidence against it, such as the tale of the young man who blew up a plane crammed with holidaymakers simply because his mother was one of the passengers. She was carrying his Mother's Day card, which said, "To someone who has been just like a mother to me."[24] Cooper, and his mentor, R. D. Laing, are convinced that the authoritarian family has dominated the formation of personality to such an extent that the sexual and spiritual independence of the individual has been destroyed. The solution that such theorists always posit is that we should have less family rather than more, and, as to have less than the nucleus is to have nothing, they are usually in favour of complete spontaneity and unstructured relationships though perish the children if any. When Sir Edmund Leach allows himself bitter invective against the family, we are up against evidence of a rather different kind:

> Far from being the basis of the good society, the family, with its narrow privacy and tawdry secrets, is the source of all discontents ...

The family that he was referring to is the narrowest, the most private, and allows its inmates the least privacy, peering into their bowels and their fantasies constantly, namely the nuclear family. When an anthropologist of the stature of Leach tells us that:

> History and ethnography provide very few examples of societies constructed around a loose assemblage of isolated groups of parents and children ...

he cannot be refuted by evidence from Parish registers or by statistical overviews of the size of British households over the last three hundred years, a mere blink in the anthropologist's time-scale.

If he asserts that the nuclear family is "a most unusual kind of organisation" and dares to "predict that it is only a transient phase in our society", he cannot be laughed out of court by the bland counter-assertion that families have always been a father and a mother in bed reading the Sunday supplements while their two carefully spaced children smashed their expensive toys in another room or if they were not it was just because they were too poor or illiterate or their land could not be cultivated by groups of less than four. I have only the most glancing acquaintance with the other systems with which Leach is familiar, but I think I would rather be a hungry twelve-year-old in Pul Eliya than an obese twelve-year-old in Tulsa, Oklahoma. I think he is right, and children do "need to grow up in larger more relaxed domestic groups centred on the community rather than mother's kitchen",[25] although I would not agree that a commune or a kibbutz will fill the bill, especially if constructed to David Cooper's model which requires utter self-absorption from all the inmates.

It seems clear to me that mothers need their children to grow up in larger more relaxed domestic groups too; Marisa asked me yesterday why it was that her granddaughter never cried when her mother was not around, never refused the food that everyone else was eating, never mooned around but chirped about alongside Marisa, helping to gather up the potatoes and rushing to show me a clutch of lizard's eggs. "She's a different person," said Marisa, and so she was. She was not trapped in being mother's daughter, mother's problem and the justification of mother's existence. There was no point in screaming when she fell down, for mother was not there to feel guilt and be punished. She was free without being abandoned, for the love of her kin was around her and she was open to it. When mother appears on the scene, the horizon closes in on the child and they are locked in their terrible battle of exhausted, possessive love. As David Cooper would say, mother is "the person who knows one 'inside out'", but only when she has been sucked into an obsessive relationship, principally by deprivation of other adult contacts, but also by being unable to escape her child even when she feels incapable of dealing with it, which produces tremendous tension and guilt.

To mother-guilt in the nuclear family must be added the other guilts and fears which build up because of the immense burdens placed upon parents who must "do their best" for the child, first by denying it brothers and sisters, then by struggling to give it a better life than they had, for the consumer society is never satisfied. More space is needed to play, to sleep; more medical attention, balanced nutrition; more stimulus is needed in the way of books, music, intelligent conversation, participation in schoolwork, outings, trips, development of special talents, sport, sports equipment, entertainment, electronic hardware and on and on. The losers are the parents of "poor children": their offspring fall below the subsistence line and become a statistic to be singled out for special treatment, for free lunches at school and uniform supplements and all the other petty humiliations. To keep these cuckoos in their nests mother and father must both go out to work, so the whole point of the parenting exercise is lost. No wonder couples concentrate more and more upon themselves and their orgasms while the European birth-rate, despite the best efforts of immigrant populations the majority of whom are in their childbearing years, gently declines and the sales figures for sex aids go up. In the end the modern nuclear parents get what they deserve, a long, barren and meaningless old age, made worse because of their inability to relate to their own peer group. The rich die drunk in retirement villages; the poor rot away in substandard housing in the decaying inner suburbs. It is to be hoped that this is the lifestyle adopted only by the pawns of the consumer society and that it cannot supplant more complex domestic organisms, but within the grudging arguments of the demographic historians there is evidence that even over the short period that they can study, nuclearity has intensified. If it were still possible to believe, as it was ten years ago, that capitalism was about to implode and nation-states and bureaucracies were bound to slide with it into the void, this tendency might mean nothing. As capitalism continues to prevail, its character is changing. It needs fewer and fewer pawns as workers, and so Ricardo's iron law is beginning to work in a peculiar way; the worker is being encouraged to spend more and more of his earnings on his own gratification so that he will reproduce less and less. The problem is how to keep up the supply of pawns as consumers: the answer is to proselytise the working masses of the non-industrial world in the manners and modes of consumerism.

The most effective medium of consumerism is the nuclear family: it is the only target our fabulous marketing machinery can reach, and therefore its first job is to create it. It is created out of restless young adults who slip the hobbles of kin: the electronic siren-song is being thumped and pumped out in every corner of the world.

Chapter Ten
Eugenics

Babies are the enemies of the human race.
Isaac Asimov

Within months of the publication of *The Descent of Man* in 1871, Darwin's supporters began to mis-apply his arguments to the races and classes of men. Just as religion had provided the justification for the oppression and extermination of alien groups during the earlier period of European expansion, the new religion of science was plundered for evidence to justify racial and class antagonism although no justification for treating man as a genus containing several species of higher and lower orders could be found in Darwin's work. The Reverend George Arthur Gaskell did not scruple to communicate his own ideas on the subject to Darwin himself in his invalid's retreat at Down. Darwin replied vaguely and formally, evidently hoping to put his correspondent off, but Gaskell, unembarrassed, sent him another letter in which he expressed himself more clearly:

> There is certainly a great danger in decreased fertility of some races, viz. that the pressure of other races on them might extinguish them. The lessened fertility commences in the races which are stronger socially; I trust they will endure. The nations guided by reason could not long submit to having their standard of comfort lowered or their means lessened by the influx of an inferior race.[1]

The year was 1878; Gaskell's letters were published by his friend and disciple, Jane Hume Clapperton, in her book *Scientific Meliorism* in 1885, evidently because she was impressed by their cogency. It certainly did not occur to her to question the basic assumption, that there are higher and lower orders of humanity, or that they are distinguished, as some of the evolutionary orders are, by their reproductive mechanisms. Although Gaskell failed to extort agreement for his view from Darwin, there seems to have been a strong current of contemporary opinion running in much the same direction, urged on by writers like Robert Knox, James Hunt and Thomas Huxley. Darwin's readers had no inkling that they were not entitled by nature itself to reap the profit accruing from the labour of others in order to live the higher life of the mind. They were convinced, on the other hand, that they, the European professional classes – or at least some of them – were distinct not only from the many-hued inhabitants of the rest of the world, but also from the working classes in their own countries whom they regarded as aliens, if anything less tractable and less educable than the aliens beyond their borders.

Before the British Empire had reached its zenith, the energy of the elite, at least of that part of it that stayed in the homeland, began to flag. While some busied themselves in trying to bring about obviously necessary reforms in education, sanitation, sewerage and health care, others contemplated from afar the squalor of the industrial slums and bethought them how much better it would be for the labouring poor if they had never been born. The beginnings of systematic taxation prompted a gush of self-pity as the affluent classes began to nurse the suspicion that they were being pillaged to support degenerate idlers. It comes as a shock to read the poet Matthew Arnold on the subject of the children of the poor:

> So long as these children are there in these festering masses, and so long as their multitude is perpetually swelling, charged with misery they must still be for us ... and the knowledge how to prevent their accumulating is necessary, even to give their moral life and growth a fair chance ... To bring people into the world, when one cannot afford to keep them and oneself decently and not too precariously is ... by no means an accomplishment of the divine will or a fulfilment of nature's simplest laws ... but contrary to reason and the will of God.[2]

There is an interesting confusion in this passage, for Arnold may well be talking about himself, one of nine children, obliged to undertake gruelling and ill-paid work as an inspector of schools in order to keep his own large family, when he felt himself called to higher things. Many people in Arnold's situation did feel that they needed the kind of knowledge of which he speaks, and many of them got it. Arnold's curious use of the words "perpetually swelling" might reveal his unconscious resentment of his wife's frequent pregnancies, especially as he moves in the course of a few paragraphs from the third person through the impersonal pronoun which English writers often use to denote themselves into the first person "we", abandoning the posture of humanitarian onlooker appropriate in the context of the whole essay. The key to differential fertility is to be found in the word "decently". Arnold's notions of what constituted decency could well have included servants, a large house, gardens and so forth, while for the labouring poor the word would have meant no more than clean, neat clothing, freedom from cold and hunger, and a roof that did not leak too badly. Both Gaskell and Arnold assumed that comfort and wealth were due to the professional class on no other ground than that they were born to that class. That most of their peers agreed with them seems *a priori* highly likely. In 1869, when Arnold published these remarks, there was no systematic way of investigating the reproductive behaviour of the various groups which composed British society; when statistical tools were developed, the impressions of observers like Gaskell and Arnold were borne out. The upper classes were having fewer and fewer children, *ergo* the coming generation was being recruited from the "lowest" classes of the population. Some might shrug it off, saying, like Havelock Ellis in an uncharacteristic moment, that society was a lamp that while it burned from the top was replenished from the bottom, but others saw in the higher fertility of the poor actual evidence of degeneracy, for higher fertility had to mean less responsibility, less forethought, more lust. The proposition, actually nonsensical, seemed to them self-evident. Miss Clapperton, who saw herself as the latest in a line of fearless female realists descended from Harriet Martineau, steeled herself to face the phenomenon in all its horror:

> The most rapid growth of our population is taking place in the great industrial centres ... and the type that there prevails is necessarily widely affecting the British race ... it is precisely in these centres that the greatest amount of poverty and destitution exists and the racial type is most degraded ... it is in the poorest localities that children most abound and prudence has *no control* over the multiplying of the lowest species of humanity.[3]

Clapperton's idea of the dysgenic effect of excess fertility in the slums is somewhat vague, for she leaves open the possibility that the inferiority of the slum-dweller is not innate. Others were careful to close that loophole. A. R. Wallace, the naturalist whose own discovery of the mechanism of natural selection had hurried Darwin into print, made a similar point in a more rigorous manner in his essay, "The Action of Natural Selection on Man", which Clapperton cites in support of her case:

> At the present day it does not seem possible for natural selection to act in any way so as to secure the permanent advancement of morality and intelligence, for it is indisputably the mediocre, if not the low, both as regards morality and intelligence, who succeed best in life and multiply fastest.[4]

When we find a scientist claiming that a point which has not been proved and probably cannot be proved is "indisputable", it is clear that we are dealing with matters of emotional conviction or faith rather than informed observation. Wallace and the other scientists who set about patiently studying the mechanisms of evolution did so in an atmosphere of surging impatience. The concept of race had been expounded unsystematically by Herbert Spencer; his disciples lost no time in devising systems of "dynamic sociology," which, they hoped, would bring about in their life-time the development of societies planned on rational principles, for the advancement of "the race." Clapperton's book trumpets one very new and radical instrumentality for bringing Utopia into existence.

> The racial blood shall not be poisoned by moral disease. The guardians of social life in the present dare not be careless of the happiness of coming genera-tions, therefore the criminal is forcibly restrained from perpetuating his vicious breed. Now mark the result ... The type will disappear; whilst evenly balanced natures, the gentle, the noble, the intellectual, will become parents of future generations; and the purified blood and unmixed good in the veins of the British will enable the race to rise *far above* its present level of natural morality.
>
> To promote the contentment of congenital criminals within their prison home, where they are detained for life, an alternative to celibacy might be offered, viz. a surgical operation rendering the male sex incapable of reproduction.[5]

In support of her suggestion, Clapperton refers her readers to the *British Medical Journal* for 2 May 1874. Her book is dedicated to George Eliot, who is credited with the coinage of the term "meliorist" although even she could not get it a permanent place in the language. It is possible that Clapperton first heard these ideas discussed in Eliot's drawing-room, al-though none of Eliot's biographers is aware of Clapperton's existence. Whatever the truth about the Eliot connection it seems clear that such ideas are already current. Clapperton evidently had less to fear from venturing into print with them than did Harriet Martineau when she dared to support Malthus in 1832. Clapperton claims that a mere fifty years later the idea that England was overpopulated was generally accepted, and with it, that it had become so by the increase of the wrong kinds of people. The way to a better future and more rational social organisation lay through "stirpiculture" or eugenics. The application of Darwinian principles to the social organism entailed the cutting-off of inferior strains and breeding only from the best. Humanitarian social legislation was con-sidered short-sighted, even suicidal. William Rathbone Greg is typical of those observers of humanity who thought that commonsense entailed some necessary interference with human reproductive behaviour as illuminated by the tenets of social Darwinism.

> Among savages the vigorous and sound alone survive, among us the diseased and enfeebled survive as well ... with us thousands with tainted constitutions, frames weakened by malady or waste, brains bearing subtle and hereditary mischief in their recesses, are suffered to transmit their terrible inheritance to other generations, or to spread it through a whole country.[6]

By the time that Francis Galton had begun his enquiries into human inheritance the reading public was eager to find its prejudices ratified, and Galton did not disappoint them. In 1865 *MacMillan's Magazine* published "Hereditary Talent and Character".

His evidence justified him in putting forward a proposal or scheme, one of the most audacious ever formulated by a sane man of science, that the State ought to select its most gifted young men and young women in order to breed for genius. He even went so far as to write the speech which the "Senior Trustee of the Endowment Fund" was to address to the "ten deeply blushing young men of 25" who had issued successfully from the public examination which proved that they had "in the highest degree those qualities of body and mind which do most honour and service to our race".[7]

Ten young women of 21 were to be mated with the young men in a ceremony in which they were given away by the monarch and endowed with £5,000 "to permit them to rear and educate their children." According to Arthur Keith, who delivered the Galton Lecture to the Eugenics Education Society in 1920, Galton "was never more in earnest in his life than when he placed this scheme before his fellow men as a practical project, one which he believed would place the people who adopted it in the vanguard of human progress." All his life Galton remained more excited by the possibilities of positive eugenics than convinced of the necessity of negative eugenics. The word "eugenics" was his coinage, and for years the Eugenics Education Society quoted his definition of it on the cover of the *Eugenics Review*:

> Eugenics is the study of agencies under social control that may improve or impair the racial qualities of future generations, whether physically or mentally.[8]

As long as eugenics is merely a study, it cannot presumably do very much harm, except to the much-studied agencies themselves, schoolboys, soldiers, and the inmates of gaols, hospitals and asylums, who were quizzed, measured, tested and tirelessly watched to provide evidence for all kinds of hypotheses. Galton had a veritable mania for mensuration and the collection of statistics; he was not in the least daunted by the dubiousness of his categories or the essentially subjective nature of his criteria. His faith in systems of public examination was touching in view of his own failure to achieve academic honours, just as his faith in selective breeding is touching in a man who, after choosing a wife with a distinguished pedigree, failed to father a child. Such inconsistency might have been after all expected from his pedigree, for he was the grandson of a Quaker who made a large fortune from the sale of small-arms. He had spent a year studying medicine at King's College, London, had read mathematics for a time at Cambridge, travelled in Egypt and Syria, and then devoted himself to sport. He took off for South-West Equatorial Africa and made a name for himself as an explorer, then became interested in meteorology and made some contributions to the development of that new science, most notably the idea (and the word) anti-cyclone.[9] When he happened upon the study of heredity, he found his life's work, which occupied him for more than forty years.

Galton could have been content simply to collect and codify data, but he himself had embarked upon his life's work from the feeling that something had to be done. We ought perhaps to be thankful that although he was a rich man, he was not in a position to bring about the implementation of eugenic schemes. He was particularly squeamish about the idea and practice of family limitation, and he ignored the question of sterilisation of criminals and defectives which, as we have seen, was already being discussed when he began his work. Instead he limited himself to advising celibacy for individuals bearing hereditary taints, hoping that a new religious sense of responsibility could be planted in the soul of modern, secularist, rational man.

> There are three stages to be passed through. Firstly, it (eugenics) must be made familiar as an academic question until its exact importance has been understood and accepted as a fact; secondly, it must be recognised as a subject whose practical development deserves serious consideration; and thirdly, it must be introduced into the national consciousness as a new religion.[10]

He did not give up the idea that the best and the brightest should be encouraged to breed; he thought that it would be a simple enough matter to persuade the authorities to issue eugenic certificates to the young people of greatest genetic worth, and even went so far as to design a sample certificate and send it to his disciple Havelock Ellis. Negative eugenics was entailed in this, of course, but Galton did not stoop to describe it in concrete terms.

> Natural selection rests upon excessive production and wholesale destruction; eugenics on bringing no more individuals into the world than can be properly cared for, and those only of the best stock.[11]

If natural selection is a natural law, then it cannot be overruled by any but a supernatural agency. Galton should have known that the only eugenical scheme which would succeed would have to be one which itself was a part of the process of natural selection. Ostensibly, he was claiming an ability to select the winners in the natural selection race before the race had been run, in order to eliminate the losers painlessly by seeing that they were never born. Yet he was clearly aware that the classes commonly taken to be superior were not holding their own in reproductive terms, for if he was not, there would seem to be little point in his incentive schemes for the generally well-endowed. For all Galton's much-praised brilliance he would seem after all to have been deficient in both common-sense and imagination, for he seemed on the one hand not to grasp how impractical his plans for running other people's lives actually were, and on the other to have no suspicion of the vastness and mystery of the genetic process. It is not altogether fair, perhaps, to take issue with Galton for his theorising, for by far the greater part of his time was taken up with the collection and interpretation of data, for which he devised schemes of mathematical analysis which were the basis of the modern science of statistics. He was responsible for the founding of the biometric laboratory at University College, and its journal *Biometrika*. In 1904 he founded a eugenics laboratory at University College and funded a research fellowship.

By the time of Galton's death in 1911 the relevance of eugenic considerations was accepted by all shades of liberal and radical opinion, as well as by conservatives like himself. In his will he left a bequest for the establishment of a chair at University College, and named his own candidate, the brilliant mathematician and biologist, Karl Pearson, who was duly elected.

Pearson prided himself on adopting a scrupulously scientific approach, and he was ruthless and insulting to anyone whose methods and reasoning he suspected. He was determined that eugenics should become an academic discipline but he was also responsible for investigations which rested upon curiously unquantifiable criteria, such as schoolteachers' impressions of the "vivacity, assertiveness, introspection, popularity, conscientiousness, temper, ability and handwriting" of their students. In the Huxley lecture of 1903, he pronounced on the subject of "national deterioration" which was to become the subject of a series of studies financed by the Worshipful Company of Drapers.

> The mentally better stock of the nation is not reproducing itself at the same rate as it did of old; the less able and the less energetic are more fertile than the better stocks. No scheme of wider or more thorough education will bring up in the scale of intelligence hereditary weakness to the level of hereditary strength. The only remedy, if one be possible at all, is to alter the relative fertility of the good and the bad stocks in the country.[12]

With his colleague and disciple David Heron, Pearson set about "proving" the negative correlation between fertility and social status and, in 1913 the negative "Correlation of Fertility with Social Value".[13] He subscribed to the doctrine of the plurality of man, and initiated studies in immigration which gave full rein to the most arrogant racism. "The Problem of Alien Immigration into Great Britain illustrated by an examination of Russian and Polish Jewish Children" was completed before the outbreak of the Great War. When it was finally published in 1925, its racist arguments fell on fertile ground.[14]

Pearson distrusted popularisers, and, although unconscious of his own prejudices, he was exasperated by the prejudices of others. The aims and ideals of the Eugenics Education Society, founded to spread the gospel of eugenics, were alien to his temper, and from the beginning he insisted on standing aloof. Because his own studies had convinced him that alcoholism was a behavioural result of innate mental defect, and he had drawn opposition from the members of the society who were equally convinced that alcohol was a "race poison", he quarrelled bitterly and publicly with them. More damagingly, he kept up a lifetime quarrel with Bateson and the Mendelians, from whom he had much to learn, as had they much to learn from him. Both sides lost valuable time and energy in fruitless and acrimonious confrontation.

Clearly the first duty of the Eugenics Laboratory was to prove the truth of the hereditarian hypothesis. There were two sharply contrasting avenues of enquiry. One, scientifically respectable, consisted in studying simple organisms with a short reproductive cycle in order to identify the actual mechanisms of genetic transfer. The other, presumptuous and disreputable, was the collection of human pedigrees, a pastime much enjoyed and promoted by Galton, but completely inconclusive. For thirty years students in Britain, America, Germany, France, Scandinavia and Switzerland stumped about the purlieux of the poor, the ignorant and the in-bred, collecting masses of evidence to prove not only that drunkenness, illegitimacy, insanity, tuberculosis, feeblemindedness and criminality ran in families, but also that all these manifestations derived from a single gene, i.e. that they were all part of a "unit character". The kind of evidence they were collecting could not possibly have led to such a conclusion, which was actually the result of a passionate desire to believe that social injustice had the sanction of the new divinity, science. The names of the families selected for examination became household words. Every researcher knew the dismal histories of families like the Jukeses, subject of a pioneering study by R. L. Dugdale, which proved that one mentally defective woman had caused 600 problem cases, criminals and/or idiots, to come into the world. The movement to segregate mentally defective persons was well established in America, where the idea had been mooted in 1848. By 1923, 40 states had set up asylums. Even so, the mere facts of segregation and supervision seemed inadequate. Some individuals were occasionally discharged from these institutions, and many others managed somehow not to get into them in the first place. Such was the inexplicable urgency felt by some professional men that they did not wait for a consensus on the desirability of cutting off defective strains or upon the method by which it should be done before they set about performing sterilisations with a will.

In 1898, the trustees of the Kansas State Institution for Feeble-minded children [approved] by resolution the work of Dr F. Hoyt Pilcher of that institution who had castrated 44 boys and 14 girls over a period of years. Public opinion took sides in the controversy that followed and the practice was stopped.[15]

In 1899 Dr Harry Sharp, member of the Purity Society of Indiana and medical officer at Jeffersonville Reformatory, decided to carry out vasectomies on his own initiative: in 1912 he wrote to the *Eugenics Review* in London, triumphantly describing his philanthropic activities:

As to the workings of this law in the State of Indiana, I must say they have been most satisfactory ... in many instances, we have operated on many against their will and over their vigorous protest ... Since October, 1899, I have been performing an operation known as vasectomy ... I do it without administering an anaesthetic either general or local ... I have two hundred and thirty-six cases that have afforded splendid opportunity for post-operative observation, and I have never seen an unfavourable symptom ... the patient becomes of a more sunny disposition, brighter of intellect, ceases excessive masturbation ...[16]

At the time Sharp embarked upon this course of action, there was no law permitting sterilisation; eight years later, in 1907, a law providing for compulsory sterilisation was passed in Indiana, but in 1911, the state governor threatened to cut off all appropriations to the institutions involved and the practice was stopped. By that time, 873 sterilisations had been carried out. The law was in fact unconstitutional, for all Dr Sharp's assurances of the immense gratification to be got by all parties from a little forced sterilisation.

The good doctor seems so far out of touch with reality that some of the eugenists who read his views ought to have wondered whether he were not himself a candidate for the miraculous operation. They should have been the first to point out that tying the vas cannot conceivably make a man more intelligent, and that if it does then the eugenic justification for the operation vanishes, since eugenic sterilisation is undertaken because intelligence is held to be innate. The first law providing for sterilisation of feeble-minded, insane, syphilitic, alcoholic, epileptic and criminal individuals had been passed in Connecticut in 1896. Kansas followed in 1903, Ohio, New Jersey and Michigan in 1905, but in Pennsylvania the governor refused his consent to the bill. In 1909, Washington adopted a sterilisation law, but in neighbouring Oregon a similar law was vetoed by the governor. In California a law was not only passed in 1909, but was energetically implemented; in seven years, 635 "partly eugenic, partly therapeutic, partly punitive" operations had been carried out. In other states, such as Nevada, North Dakota, New Jersey and Kansas, the laws were inoperative; in others, such as Michigan and Wisconsin, they were selectively applied. In all, twenty-two states had sterilisation laws on the books in 1918, when a Supreme Court decision found the New York act to be unconstitutional and invalid. This was the seventh time such a law had been challenged; this time, as on all previous occasions, the law was simply re-drafted and passed again.[17]

While valuable work in genetics was being carried out at the Station for Experimental Evolution of the Carnegie Institute in Washington, its director, C. B. Davenport, was not content to limit his activities to the observation of the reproductive patterns of the fruit-fly *Drosophila* and the other obliging organisms being bred there, perhaps because those observations did not bear out his own theories.[18] He lusted after power to bring about the brave new world of eugenics, and to this end he persuaded Mrs H. I. Harriman in 1910 to endow a Eugenics Record Office at Cold Spring Harbor in New York. There gangs of young people, mostly women, were trained in the collection of pedigrees which were duly classified and filed. The first report, published in 1913, was compiled by H. H. Laughlin, who later became head of the Psychopathic Laboratory of the Municipal Court of Chicago. Laughlin noted not only that the universities of Columbia, Cornell, Brown, Wisconsin and North-Western had set up courses wholly or partly devoted to eugenics, but also that eugenics had become a popular craze:

> Both facts and "near facts" readily become disseminated in America. Of late the subject of eugenics has become a popular one for newspaper topics ... Anything even remotely related to sex hygiene, infant mortality, birth marks, baby culture, sex control, pre-natal influence, or to care, "cure" or treatment of defectives is given a heading entitled "Eugenics" ...[19]

The public might have been forgiven for its confusion on the subject, for the eugenists themselves kept expanding the field of their operations, claiming all kinds of behaviours as genetically determined characteristics. Davenport included among the "feebly inhibited" vagrants (whom he preferred to call "nomads") and carried out self-validating studies of the inheritance of temperament, especially in twins and suicides. Both Davenport and Laughlin were convinced that racial intermarriage was genetically deleterious and that immigration should be severely limited; Laughlin's summary of the grounds for such beliefs is actually less virulent than much of what was published in support of such ideas:

> There is no nation whose lowest family stocks are biologically superior to the best stocks of other nations nor is there any nation or race whose blood cannot be improved by selection within its own seed-stocks. On the other hand, there is no nation whose race-integrity and characteristic value cannot be destroyed either by radical outcrossing with races that may be equally talented but which biologically are very different, or by absorbing inferior family stocks from the generally best and most talented foreign races, which in general are quite assimilable to it. Thus in the exercise of its own rights and in building up its own stocks, the receiving nation must exercise its sovereign right and select courageously and radically for the improvement of its own human values in future generations. Immigration is a long-time investment in human stocks. Each nation must look after its own interest in this field.[20]

Laughlin served as the eugenics expert on the Committee on Immigration and Naturalisation of the House of Representatives from 1921 to 1931. The American eugenics lobby was powerful, and it had the support of powerful and wealthy men. John D. Rockefeller provided funding for a research fellowship at the Eugenics Record Office as well as operating

capital out of the vast profits of Standard Oil of New Jersey. Alexander
Graham Bell delivered a paper on eugenics to the American Breeders'
Association in 1908, along with David Starr Jordan, distinguished ichthy-
ologist and first president of Stanford University. As a result the Plant
and Animal Sections of the Association were joined by a Eugenics Section,
with Jordan as chairman and Davenport as secretary. From its beginnings
the approach was activist; agitation for projects of law to provide for
sterilisation of idiots and criminals began at once. In 1913 the American
Breeders' Association changed its name to the American Genetic Association and its magazine assumed the new name *The Journal of Heredity*,
and as such both continue still. The name of the first editor of the journal,
Paul Popenoe, will be forever associated with the Human Betterment
Foundation of Pasadena, set up in 1927 by the philanthropist E. S. Gosney
to analyse the efficiency and efficacy of the Californian sterilisation programme in which 6000 individuals were deprived of their fertility. It must
not be thought that sterilisation mania was an exclusively American
disease. The Scandinavian countries had tougher laws: Sweden carried
out as many sterilisations in a year as were performed over the whole
period in America. The Danish law was frankly punitive. Switzerland
passed a eugenic sterlisation law in 1907.[21]

The chief historian of the eugenics movement is C. P. Blacker, whose
Eugenics Galton and After is a basic reference. As thirty years of his life
were devoted to the Eugenics Society, for he served as General Secretary
from 1931 to 1952 and as Secretary from 1952–1961, we cannot be
surprised to find him endeavouring to clear its reputation. The historic
fact is that while it is easy enough to prove that Hitler was not a follower
of Galton, many of the members of the Eugenics Society were closer in
spirit to Hitler than to Galton. The Royal Commission on Feeble-minded-
ness had alarmed many people who genuinely believed, and were
bombarded with evidence to show, that the racial type was deteriorating
because of the greater fertility of inferior strains. As early as 1904 we
find even a man as revered for commonsense as George Bernard Shaw
blandly asserting that the end of civilisation as he and his peers knew
it was at hand:

> There is no reasonable excuse for refusing to face the fact that nothing but ...
> eugenics can save our civilisation from the fate that has overtaken all previous
> civilisations.[22]

A good deal of breath and brainpower was expended on speculation
as to just what fate *had* overtaken previous civilisations, but the consensus
began to emerge that the classes whose superior abilities had built the
great empires of Greece and Rome had been overwhelmed by fecund
morons (a word invented by H. H. Goddard in 1912 to describe the
superior feeble-minded). Clearly the raving lunatics and drivelling idiots

were not the real problem, for they seldom reproduced. The real danger
to the race lay in the borderline cases. The more apparently able to cope
the high-grade moron was, the more fraught with reproductive peril to
the race:

> ... in Degeneracy healthy aspirations no longer exist, the struggle for survival
> the higher in the organism against the lower in the organism having ceased
> and the cells having conformed in mass to a lower grade of being ...
>   There is no greater menace to a race than is furnished by such sturdy
> degenerates.[23]

Such sturdy degenerates could in fact be flushed out only by systematic
application of that rather new instrument, the intelligence test, which is
only one of the eugenic tools which have survived. Galton was the first
person ever to carry out a systematic examination of a school population.
He chose Marlborough, and what he found was what he was looking for,
evidence of the superior talents of the sons of privileged parents. The
motives behind the IQ tests administered in the first decades of the
twentieth century were rather different; they proved that the children
of the poorer classes were not as bright as their upper-class counterparts,
and that they came from larger families. The evidence seemed irrefutable;
even people who knew and respected the working people of England were
daunted. Anna Martin, living and working in the working-class district
of Rotherhithe, resisted the influence of the eugenists for a time: she knew
that working women performed mathematical feats of considerable complexity when they managed to feed their families on their husbands' tiny
wages while leaving the breadwinner a couple of shillings for the beer
and tobacco which were the only indulgences permitted to anyone in the
family. She also knew that the logistics of running these households were
extremely complex and that in terms of practical intelligence, not to
mention wisdom and courage, working women could have run rings
around her own middle-class peers. In 1911 she published an article in
The Nineteenth Century and After in which she implicitly rejected all that
the eugenists were saying:

> The establishment of a living wage is the only reform which appeals to the
> hearts and minds of the women at No. 39 and their compeers. They do not
> want charity or rate aid, but they do claim that it shall be put within a man's
> power to keep his family. The standard of life would then rise automatically
> among the whole working class, and the dread of a degenerate nation would
> be a thing of the past.[24]

Two years later, after reading the report of the First International
Eugenics Congress and after the passing of the Mental Deficiency Act,
even Anna Martin had given ground to the eugenists, although she did
permit herself to wonder:

How far did experience gained in the actual homes of the masses tally with the conclusions of those eminent men who had come together from all parts of the world and whose years of patient toil had found expression in such elaborate statistical tables and with such ingenious diagrams?[25]

Neverthless, with all her scepticism, she went on to discuss unwanted pregnancies and the effects of alcohol on the working-class stock itself, pleading for a limitation on the hours in which liquor could be sold. The eugenists in England pleaded for taxes on liquor, which eventually they got – and that abundantly. Eugenists in the United States pleaded for Prohibition, which they also got. Socialists like to pretend that they remained aloof from eugenic paranoia and tirelessly worked towards the development of the welfare state, but such, historically, is not the case. The thesis of race suicide seemed proven; even Sidney Webb called himself a eugenist:

> What we as eugenists have got to do is to "scrap" the old Poor Law with its indiscriminate relief of the destitute as such and replace it by an intelligent policy of so altering the social environment as to discourage or prevent the multiplication of those irrevocably below the National Minimum of Fitness.[26]

The eugenists assumed that social control of the individual was absolutely essential and they pioneered the most intrusive forms of classification and tracking and record-keeping; nevertheless Bertrand Russell felt that he could accept their premises, although he used them to come to what they called mischievous conclusions:

> The present state of the law, of public opinion, and of our economic system is tending to degrade the quality of the race, by making the worst half of the population the parents of more than half of the next generation ... a new system is required, if the European nations are not to degenerate.[27]

When this was written Europe had already plunged into the barbarous and totally dysgenic stupidity of the Great War, but when the flower of European manhood had been effectively sterilised by death, a gaggle of foolish men and women were still bleating about the "best practical means for cutting off the defective germ-plasm in the human population". The evidence that the crude Galtonian version of heredity was mistaken was gradually being compiled, but the eugenists seemed unable to grasp its implications, which were, quite simply, that sterilising the manifestly defective would have very little effect upon the incidence of the defect in the next generation. Nevertheless eugenists like L. Burlingame were still arguing in 1940 that:

> The present situation is one in which it seems probable that no reproduction of all parents below I.Q. 90 would practically wipe out feeble-mindedness in a single generation.[28]

In 1926 C. P. Blacker published a tract pleading for eugenic legislation on the American model. If as he pointed out a thousand teachers have but 95 children, a thousand ministers of the Church of England 101, a thousand doctors 103 and a thousand labourers 231, the conclusion seems obvious. Besides, cited Blacker tranquilly (and incorrectly) "Mental defectives generally are very prolific." If Roosevelt believed in the possibility of race suicide, we can probably not be too hard on Blacker for pointing out that

> ... it would nowadays be very difficult for any individual, however worthless, to starve, and many people of defective stock and bad physique who in the ordinary course of nature would perish, are now artificially kept alive to perpetuate their kind.[29]

The concept of the worthless individual was part of the everyday intellectual currency at the Eugenics Society, and as the years passed its application became wider and the terms used to describe it coarser and more arrogant. The zoologist E. W. McBride was doubtless expert and scrupulous in his field, but when he allowed himself to animadvert on political economy he was hardly rational:

> ... all history proves that stock is all-important and to the qualities of each stock corresponds a certain grade of culture. Lower races can be made to adopt the customs of a higher civilisation so long as they are under the guidance and control of a higher race, but when left to themselves they steadily regress to the appropriate level, as the history of states like Hayti, Liberia and Mexico itself abundantly proves. Further if we distinguish strains within the same race the same fact stares us in the face. The researches on the inheritance of mental deficiency show that a large proportion of our prostitution, habitual drunkenness and crime is actually inherited. For vice and crime are both due in the last resort to want of self-control – the latest acquired of all the virtues and the most decisive in the struggle for existence. No permanent improvement can be effected in any society so long as such types are allowed to breed and money expended on their education is largely thrown away. Among ancient virile peoples they were ruthlessly eliminated.[30]

Although his followers are anxious to dissociate Galton from views of this kind, it must not be forgotten that he regarded modern man as no better than a mediocre Greek, presumably because such laudable eugenic activities as the exposure of infants and the keeping of slaves had ceased to prevail. Considering the primitive recourse of ruthless elimination McBride obviously found sterilisation positively merciful, and he seemed moreover to feel that no outcry would be heard in the Eugenics Society if he expressed such a view as though it were consensus.

> It seems to us that sooner or later society will be driven to adopt measures of compulsory sterilisation: this can now be harmlessly and painlessly done by means of X-rays ... it does not appear to have occurred to anyone that parents who produce children beyond their means of support are "unfit" in

the proper fundamental economic sense – and that the penalty for this should be sterilisation.[31]

Just so, we learn, the Spartans demanded the killing of infants born without a pre-allotted plot of land. Professor McBride's enlightened views were expressed in these terms in January, 1921. If we are to believe Dr Blacker, the Great Depression and the general acceptance of Mendelian theories obliterated this kind of thinking in England long before the Nazi eugenic programme was instituted in 1933. As far as a less partisan observer can tell, the tide of economic hardship rose and engulfed many hardworking and worthy souls, and no doubt, many of the eugenists' old schoolfellows, without the eugenists' learning anything from the experience. In 1936, we find McBride in business at the old stand, although it is fair to say that his uncontrollable paranoia and eloquent contempt for others had resulted in a rift with the Eugenics Society by this time. (Perhaps, in view of their lifelong anxiety state, we should not be surprised to find that eugenicists were a quarrelsome bunch.) For fifteen years McBride has continued in the belief that compulsory sterilisation would eventually become necessary, but now he has a new, even vaguer, demographic justification for it:

There is probably only one remedy for the over-production of children that we can see, and it is very unpopular, so it will probably be some time before the necessity of it forces itself upon the public mind. This is compulsory sterilisation as a punishment for parents who have to resort to public assistance in order to support their children.[32]

If sterilisation is a punishment for bearing children it is not likely to abolish poverty by preventing the poor from being born, but before we dismiss McBride as a lunatic, we ought to consider that today's recommendations of compulsory sterilisation programmes in countries with high birthrates and poverty problems suffer from the same defects of reasoning. In a world in which the numbers of landless peasants increase hourly, the idea that the poor are born rather than made is a dangerous delusion, but many hold it.

In 1930 the Eugenics Society, encouraged by the Report of the Joint Committee of the Board of Education and the Board of Control which found that "Mentally deficient parents create centres of degeneracy and disease which welfare work can never reach," began concerted lobbying and propaganda for a Eugenic Sterilisation Bill. The committee was presided over by Lady Askwith; C. P. Blacker served as Honorary Secretary. The bill was drafted by Major A. G. Church and the campaign was financed by Lord Riddell, the original Press baron. Lancelot Hogben and H. G. Wells, as well as Darwin's son, Major Leonard Darwin, who had served as President of the Eugenics Society from 1911 until 1929 and had initiated the campaign, all contributed signed statements of support to the Society's propaganda pamphlets. Professor Julian Huxley, a member of the committee, had this to say:

> I consider that the Bill introduced by Major Church embodies a valuable sugges-
> tion in a workmanlike way. The principle of supplementing the segregation
> of defectives by sterilisation in certain cases, is to my mind very important,
> and indeed essential, if we are to prevent the gradual deterioration of our racial
> stock. By making sterilisation voluntary in all cases, the Bill prevents any high-
> handed abuse of power by local or other authorities, and the rights of individuals
> and their relatives appear to be abundantly safeguarded.[33]

The concept of "voluntary" sterilisation is a curious one, considering that the primary targets of the bill are the feeble-minded, who, if they are in truth feeble-minded, can be got to agree to anything. Conversely, the more intelligent the inmate, the more likely he is to seek to please his gaolers by accepting sterilisation. In some countries, it was considered perfectly proper to offer sterilisation as an alternative to segregation. In the case of complete imbeciles, consent was to be got from their relatives, who, if the logic of the procedure was correct, should have been mentally defective too. In the circumstances (and it must not be forgotten that for those not being offered "voluntary" sterilisation the operation was illegal) the insistence on consent was a mere sophistry. As Dr F. Douglas Turner explained to Lionel Penrose:

> I venture to say I would not be fitted to hold my present office of medical
> superintendent of an institution for the care of mental defectives if I could
> not induce every one of my patients to be operated on or to refuse an operation
> just as I myself might wish.[34]

In 1934 the Eugenics Society's Committee for Legalising Eugenic Sterilisation merged with the Joint Committee on Voluntary Sterilisation to issue the Report of the Departmental Committee on Sterilisation. In 1935 one of the Darwin Research Fellowships offered by the Eugenics Society was awarded to R. B. Cattell, Director of the Schools Psychological Clinic in Leicester, "for the investigation by tests of the intelligence of a typical urban and a typical rural population of school children with a view to determining the average size of the family at each level of intelligence". He was a fervent supporter of the sterilisation campaign, which, by the time he published his conclusions, had been defeated. The Report of the Departmental Committee had been rejected by the London County Council after what Cattell described as "a fantastically irrespon-sible debate," by 63 votes to 44.[35] When Cattell published his polemic *The Fight for Our National Intelligence*, the King's physician, Lord Horder, was delighted to introduce it, because:

The level of the nation's intelligence is steadily falling. So much so that if matters continue as they are now our author reckons that in 300 years from now half the population will be mentally defective.[36]

If his royal patients were at all embarrassed that he volunteered to provide a foreword to a book in which Germany was given "the credit of being the first to adopt sterilisation together with a positive emphasis on racial improvement",[37] history does not record the fact, but then history does not recall the parts played by any of these eminent men in this disreputable campaign. In the history of the Eugenics Society which was published in the last number of the *Eugenics Review* (before its name was changed to *The Journal of Bio-Social Science*) no mention is made of its President's ten year campaign for an English eugenic sterilisation law.

Eugenic sterilisation had never been uncontroversial but opposition to it had not taken scientifically respectable form until the geneticists themselves entered the lists. One of the most brilliant, and perhaps the wisest, of these was J. B. S. Haldane, who entered the public fray in 1938.

In the last fifty years, we have learned something about human biology, and particularly human inheritance. This knowledge has so far found little application in Britain or America. But it has been used to support proposals for very drastic changes in the structure of society. And the stringent measures which have been taken in Germany, both for the expulsion of the Jews from many walks of life and for the compulsory sterilisation of many Germans, are said to be based on biological facts.

I do not believe that our present knowledge of human heredity justifies such steps.[38]

Haldane attacked not only Germany but also Cattell and even Blacker, who wanted to sterilise not just the feeble-minded but also the below-average. He pointed out that banning first-cousin marriage would be a more eugenic procedure than sterilisation, and went so far as to ask biologists to accept the proposition:

It is never possible from a knowledge of a person's parents to predict with certainty that he or she will be either a more adequate or a less adequate member of society than the majority.[39]

In a grim prophecy he quoted an article by Suchsland in the *Archiv fur Rassen- und Gesellschaftshygiene* on the eugenic effect of bombing crowded inner cities.[40]

In his historiography Blacker does not recall the historical battle with the geneticists but seeks instead to convince his readers that the discovery of the truth of the Mendelian hypothesis and the effects of the depression somehow painlessly smothered the old, cruel, bad eugenic thinking. The truth is that such thinking is still only stifled. So disheartened did both

Haldane and his colleague, Hermann Muller, become at the crass use made of staggering new knowledge, that they both rebelled. Haldane joined the communist party, Muller went all the way and took a post in the Soviet Union. Blacker himself had learnt so little in so long that he proposed his colleague, Cyril Burt, Cattell's teacher, to give evidence on intelligence and fertility to the Royal Commission on Population in 1946. Burt was then professor of Psychology at University College, London. He and Flügel, under William McDougall, a supporter of the eugenic sterilisation bill, had carried out the first systematic intelligence tests designed by Pearson. For 19 years he had served as consultant psychologist to the LCC for whom he designed the mental and scholastic tests used in schools; and he had not the slightest doubt that what he was measuring was "inborn, general, intellectual ability."

> During the past forty years work with standardised tests has conclusively established (i) that a general factor underlying all forms of mental efficiency may plausibly be assumed, (ii) that this factor can be assessed with reasonable accuracy by both group and individual testing, (iii) that the differences in intelligence as thus defined are due largely to the individual's inherited constitution.
>
> So far as the evidence goes, (*a*) it seems almost certain that there is in this country a negative correlation between innate intelligence and size of family and that the size of the correlation (about 0.20) is large enough to demand urgent practical attention; (*b*) it seems highly probable that the average level of intelligence among the general population may be declining at a rate which might produce serious cumulative effects if at all sustained.[41]

Clearly the old rhetoric of "race" could no longer be used but without it Sir Cyril's (for he was knighted for his services) argument is simply silly. The only kind of urgent practical attention that the negative correlation between family size and intelligence could expect is that people with one child could elect to have no more (which of course would not make the one they had any brighter innately) unless of course you treat fertility as a hereditary characteristic linked with low intelligence and take steps to limit fertility in the offspring of fertile people. In fact, fertility is not a markedly inheritable characteristic, contrary to the eugenists' convictions. If Burt had been a simple country clergyman his prejudices might have been unimportant; given his power in the London education system, they affected the careers of hundreds of thousands of young people whose aptitudes were defined by his criteria.

We now know that Burt's evidence was faked. He did not test the parents of his subjects but made his own subjective appraisal, thus begging his own question. His faith in the innate superiority of his own class was such that he believed that if the testing were done his conclusions would be found to be accurate. He died, full of honours, just before more scrupulous psychologists reluctantly exposed him.[42] The chief opposition to this right-wing religion came from the socialists who minimised the importance of the hereditary element. Their case was irrevocably damaged by Lysenko's frauds. Muller and Haldane, sadder and wiser, returned to the capitalist fold.

Even after the series of legal skirmishes which had resulted in the insertion of consent provisos in the American eugenic sterilisation laws it was evident that the spirit of such legislation was plain contrary to the Bill of Rights. The matter finally came before the Supreme Court of the United States in 1926, when Mr Justice Holmes uttered his now famous opinion:

> The judgment finds the facts that have been recited and that Carrie Buck "is the probable potential parent of socially inadequate offspring, likewise afflicted, that she may be sexually sterilised without detriment to her general health and that her welfare and that of society will be promoted by her sterilisation," and thereupon make the order ... We have seen more than once that the public welfare may call upon the best citizens for their lives. It would be strange if it could not call upon those who already sap the strength of the State for these lesser sacrifices, often not felt to be such by those concerned, in order to prevent our being swamped with incompetence. It is better for all the world, if instead of waiting to execute degenerate offspring for crime, or to let them starve for their imbecility society can prevent those who are manifestly unfit from continuing their kind. The principle that sustains compulsory vaccination is broad enough to cover cutting the Fallopian tubes ... Three generations of imbeciles are enough.[43]

Mr Justice Holmes had accepted the basic tenets of eugenic religion, that mental defect is inherited, and that the fertility of mental defectives is such that they may swamp society with incompetence, and that criminality is part of the same hereditable unit character. Judges in Kansas, Idaho, Nebraska, Oklahoma and Ohio agreed; similar verdicts were brought in Ohio and Nebraska as late as the sixties. In fact, Holmes's opinion in *Buck* vs *Bell* is still the prevailing view in American law, Mr Justice Whitehead's dissenting opinion notwithstanding.[44] Unavailing too was the dear-bought wisdom of the geneticists, and even of those who had been connected with eugenic sterilisation programmes. Gunnar Dahlberg had expressed the dilemma in unmistakable terms in 1943:

> Sterilisation of defectives can never bring about results of practical value. Meanwhile ill-considered handling of the problem may cause unnecessary suffering for a small section of individuals, but that is all it will do. If we sterilise a few we may avoid having to feed a trifling number of defective people. If we go too far, and particularly if we adopt compulsory sterilisation, we shall make an unnecessarily large number of people unhappy.[45]

Such a statement can hardly be condemned as sentimental, for Dahlberg deliberately speaks as baldly and brutally as possible. If American sterilisation fans were unwilling to accept such views from a foreigner, perhaps they might have paid attention to their home-grown vasectomy buff, Paul Popenoe, who after years of studying sterilisation under the auspices of the Human Betterment Foundation in Pasadena, was obliged to conclude that most of the effort was wasted:

> ... fecundity of the insane is cut down partly by hospital residence, partly by voluntary action on their part, partly because their lives are shortened by their diseases ... the constant stream of new admissions, so far as it is due to heredity, must be largely due to the matings of persons who are not themselves insane but who carry insanity in their germ plasm.[46]

Although Popenoe does not dare follow his own observations to their logical conclusion and question the notion of insanity infecting the germ plasm, he does nerve himself to tell the truth about misguided attempts to control the contagion. It is more frightening to read the impressions of an English psychiatric social worker who travelled to North Carolina in 1949.

> Seen in sociological perspective, the adoption of the eugenic sterilisation law in North Carolina nineteen years ago and the subsequent establishment of State-sponsored contraceptive services eight years later, have acted as powerful agents to accelerate the rate of social evolution and to crystallise otherwise unformulated conflicts.[47]

Moya Woodside carefully notes the higher birthrate of Negroes, and their higher illegitimacy rate, as well as the high incidence of mental deficiency, the highest in the United States:

> It is certainly true that the feeble-minded Negro woman, often with illegitimate children, is a familiar and recurrent problem to health and welfare agencies.[48]

She was, presumably also a frequent candidate for "voluntary" sterilisation. The eugenics package had always included racism of the most egregious kind, but as minorities became more vocal, the old arguments about the deleterious effects of intermarriage, the absolute necessity of limiting immigration and about the origins of the different "races" of man fell into disuse. When the United States was drawn into the war with Germany, eugenists like Leon F. Whitney had cause to be deeply embarrassed about statements like this:

> We cannot but admire the foresight of the [German] plan [of sterilising 400,000 people] and realise by this action Germany is going to make herself a stronger nation. American jewry is naturally suspecting that the German chancellor has had the law enacted for the specific purpose but I believe nothing to be further from the truth.[49]

Because such views were discredited, it was hardly possible to remark, as Whitney does, that "the negroes in Newhaven furnished six times as many subnormals as did the native-born whites."[50] We are not surprised to find Woodside avoiding racist statements, but we would be foolish to assume that neither she nor the authorities at the State Hospitals and Correctional Institutions whose duty it was to initiate sterilisation proceedings harboured racist feelings. North Carolina came late into the sterilisation business. Forty-nine persons had been sterilised under a law passed in 1929 before it was found unconstitutional in that it had no provision for notice of the hearing of the case for sterilisation and no right of appeal. The law, as had happened in other states, was simply redrafted and repassed in 1933.

> The Eugenics Board has jurisdiction only in cases of feeble-mindedness, leprosy (*sic*) or mental disease. It may not authorise the sterilisation on physical or social grounds of any normal person, and it is likewise precluded from dealing with cases of transmissible physical defect ... An intelligence quotient of 70 and below is taken as the definition of feeble-mindedness ... The duty to institute sterilisation proceedings is mandatory on the "responsible head of any State penal or charitable institution."[51]

The grounds for sterilisation were to be established by the presentation of a statement of the individual's physical and mental condition, a social history and a sworn consent, either from the sterilee or his or her parent or guardian. Woodside includes résumés of more or less typical cases, which are interesting not primarily because of the cases but because of her selection of significant details. As might be expected, Woodside is hardly aware of the genetic dimension of the situation.

> A married woman, 24 years of age, who is the mother of five children ranging in age from six years to four months. She has been in court several times for sexual promiscuity and has also been guilty of maltreatment and abandonment of her children.
>   Diagnosis: Epilepsy with frequent convulsions. Consent form signed by herself and her husband.[52]

In North Carolina, evidently, one is more likely to find oneself in court for sexual promiscuity than for maltreatment and abandonment of children. No evidence of hereditary defect is brought: epilepsy is a term which covers a variety of phenomena, some caused by trauma. Woodside is more aware of the woman's fertility and her sexual activity than of any other aspect of her behaviour. There is a strong suggestion that Woodside herself saw the procedure as punitive, something which the early missionary eugenists sought at all costs to avoid. A more cynical observer might suspect that in this case a man and woman who had completed their family size used the delusions of authority to secure for themselves a free and effective method of birth-control.

In another case, there is no comforting possibility that the victim herself desired the procedure.

> A married woman, 36 years of age, who is the mother of a 12-year-old son born illegitimately. She was admitted to the State Hospital with a history of psychosis developing three months previously, and had a former attack 18 years ago. She is neglectful of her personal appearance and habits, continually talked and quarrelled with her family and displayed hallucinations, delusions and destructive tendencies. She has poor judgment and insight is lacking.
>   Diagnosis: Dementia praecox – paranoid. Consent form signed by her husband who does not wish to have any more children.[53]

Again no eugenic function of the operation is adduced. If the woman has only one child 12 years old it seems that she is either sub-fertile or infertile, although there may be other children whom Woodside does not mention. In any event a man who desires no more children ought not to be allowed to arrange for an operation upon a woman, especially when vasectomy is less problematic than the salpingectomy of the 1940s. Attacks of psychosis eighteen years apart do not seem consistent with a diagnosis of *dementia praecox,* nor do they seem consistent with a diagnosis of paranoia, especially in a woman who is clearly being persecuted and may well have been very distressed. Presumably her husband, unless he is a rapist, will not have intercourse with her until she is returned to her senses. While she is so disturbed hospitalisation is the only recourse, in which case she should not be exposed to the likelihood of pregnancy. There is no way to interpret sterilisation in this case except as an outrage on the body of a person who seems to have suffered a good many outrages already. It seems highly unlikely that her recovery from this episode of disturbance will be as rapid as her recovery from the earlier one; the forced surgery can only have made matters worse. In this case, sterilisation is a gratuitous intrusion into an already confused and painful situation. Another, even more bizarre case, crops up among the spastics and post-partum psychotics in Woodside's samples:

> A single boy, 13 years of age, who was admitted to the training school because of delinquency and assault. He created a disturbance in school, had temper tantrums, struck his parents and could not be restrained or controlled due to an ungovernable temper. On a mental test, he received an IQ of 43.[54]

The semantic connections of *receiving* an intelligence quotient "on a mental test" would be funny if they were not so cruel and stupid. Woodside does not see fit to tell us which test it was. Given North Carolinian attachment to tradition it might have been the same test that had showed two-thirds of the American soldiers in World War I to have been morons.[55] We might wonder how such an uncontrollable individual was got to take the test in the first place: his low score might have more to do with his emotional state than with his innate intelligence. It is reassuring to know that at the age of thirteen he was unmarried, but the strong possibility is that he never will be, for if no method is found to subdue him he will end on Death Row, where few are impregnated. It is to be hoped that once sterilised he was not to be let loose while his intentions were still rapine and murder. If his condition was curable, or controllable, as it would be if caused by a disturbance in the biochemistry of the brain, there is no point in sterilising him in the first place. Again, Woodside makes no mention of a genetic element in the boy's condition. Moreover, by sterilising him, the authorities have made clear that they consider him irredeemable; there is no point in his trying to reclaim himself. He might as well act out his innate incorrigibility.

From July 1933 to June 1947, 1,901 "eugenic" sterilisations were performed in North Carolina, 407 men and boys, 1,494 females; more than half the females, 770, were under twenty, 169 of the males. Although only 27.5% of the state's population is black, and even though the Negro hospital at Goldsboro took no part in the sterilisation programme, as many black men were sterilised, both by vasectomy and castration, as white.[56] Woodside notes the fact without comment; in fact she regrets that the sterilisation provisions in North Carolina are not being fully implemented. To her mind too many heads of institutions were neglecting their duty in the case; the cause of such neglect was not that they saw how deluded and dangerous such attempts to cut the Gordian knot of social disease and disability were, but that sterilisations cost money, even when they are performed with minimum anaesthesia and post-operative care. There were too few crusading doctors who cared enough to master the procedures and carry them out for a pittance. If North Carolina had had an adequate tax-supported public health system the situation might well have been very different.

Meanwhile, the eugenics societies were finding themselves in difficulties. Genetics was too complicated a science to appeal to the general public, especially when the possibility of practical application of eugenic ideas had ceased to exist. The only way to mop up recessive defects in the human population would be to bar all heterozygotes from reproduction, and that would mean that only about 2% of human beings would be eligible to pass on their genes, and that 2% would not be co-extensive with the ruling elite, or even with the families of the geneticists themselves. The pressure groups fell apart.

Still, eugenics was a secular religion; it would take more than mere scientific fact to turn the faithful from the divine path of Galtonian revelation and more than false prophets like Hitler to put them to the blush. At its apogee in 1932, the British Eugenics Society had 768 members; despite two energetic recruiting campaigns, in 1956 membership had sunk to 456. The Secretary, Dr Blacker, suggested three possible lines of development for the future; the first was:

... That the Society should pursue eugenic ends by less obvious means, that is by a policy of crypto-eugenics, which was apparently proving successful in the US Eugenics Society ...[57]

The suggestion was not then taken up, but in 1960 four senior members of the committee presented a memorandum to the members inviting their consideration of a number of suggestions. The second clause, which was accepted in principle, read like this:

The Society's activities in crypto-eugenics should be pursued vigorously, and specifically that the Society should increase its monetary support of the FPA and the IPPF and should make contact with the Society for the Study of Human Biology, which already has a strong and active membership, to find out if any relevant projects are contemplated with which the Eugenics Society could assist.[58]

The Society gave up all idea of spreading the gospel and began to work in secret using "its influence at the centre by close liaison with cognate organisations". Thus Galton's own set of priorities was overturned. The Society gave up striving for practical "reforms" and got itself registered as a charity. In accordance with Blacker's suggestions, the Society also became a grant-giving and promotional organisation to further the cause of "biosocial science"; the new name for eugenics was only the old German name *Gesellschaftsbiologie*, but few people realised this. The ones who did were the least likely to object. In the same year the *American Eugenics Quarterly* changed its name to *Social Biology*.

It must not be forgotten that eugenists pioneered the study of populations; they were the first to deal with human society in a numerical way, completing the process of reification and control which had begun with the application of mathematics to other aspects of the physical world. The eugenists were the first to make human beings dots on a scatter-graph; as Galton walked down the street he used to make pin-pricks on a piece of paper in order to establish the incidence of prettiness in the girls he passed. The Population Investigation Committee which pioneered the mathematical science of demography was set up by the Council of the Eugenics Society in 1936, staffed by the Eugenics Society, housed in the Society's offices at Eccleston Square until 1946, when it moved to the London School of Economics, and financed entirely by "donations from interested individuals and organisations". And the eugenists were the first people ever to maintain that the world would be a better place if whole groups and classes of people had never been born. It matters little which classes or groups they chose, or that their selections were based on scientific errors. What matters is that they considered themselves entitled to make such a judgment at all. Man is not a rational animal, but only *rationis capax*; the very arguments of social biology itself should teach us not to trust ourselves when we are tempted to curtail the reproductive opportunity of people outside the groups to which we think we belong. The alliance with the family planners became inevitable as soon as the eugenists began to argue that sterilisation was good for people. We shall see in the next chapter how far the family planners gravitated towards the eugenists.

It was Hermann Muller's discovery of mutation in the early 1940s that destroyed the last vestiges of scientific respectability in arguments that the body politic could be tidied up by surgery. It would be reassuring to be able to say that all the energy spent preaching eugenic sterilisation was immediately invested in fighting the greatest enemy human germ plasm has ever had, namely the proliferation of mutagens in the environment, but this historically is not the case. Muller himself undertook an anti-radiation crusade, but it did not fire the imagination of the public in anything like the same way that the chance of operating on the genitalia of strangers did. An activity so cherished was hardly likely to be given up simply because it was discredited. No one now argues for eugenic sterilisations because no one has to. They are being carried out routinely all over the world. Medical students are taught very little about genetics and a great deal about destructive surgery. They have become the moral arbiters of the daily lives of our citizens and they do not scruple to decide who the clients for sterilisation are and how to sell it to them. To be sure, consent is legally required for any elective surgery, but consent is only possible when a procedure is offered and difficult to refuse when a procedure is urged. Where once doctors refused to hear a woman pleading for sterilisation even when they could see that her health was ruined by frequent pregnancies, they now accept minimal criteria and will sterilise teenagers and childless people without a qualm, especially if they are poor, unmarried, "promiscuous" and "subnormal".[59] I have heard doctors earnestly defending tubal ligations on teenagers presenting for repeat abortions, unembarrassed by the fact that their patients knew nothing about their radical intervention in their lives. The doctors also opined that the women were "educationally subnormal", the modern euphemism for "feeble-minded".

Negative eugenics now surfaces in the United States in the form of projects of law designed to provide for the sterilisation of welfare mothers with more than a certain (arbitrary) number of children. The hard truth that hid under the visionary claptrap of the eugenists and motivated much of their public support was that the infertile middle class resents having to shell out for the maintenance, however paltry and meagre, of the children of others. It cannot be placated by being shown that it shells out many times as much for the machinery to kill the children of others. So far the pressure for compulsory sterilisation legislation has failed, but it is constantly renewed and, given the changing climate of public opinion, could pass as soon as the right formulation is found. The mechanism will take the form of an ultimatum to the fecund pauper, of the order "cease reproduction or get off welfare"; the crux of the problem is the transformation of the ultimatum into surgery rather than the creation of a beggar class. In practical terms the problem does not arise. Doctors have great power, especially over individuals who are confused and in pain. It is routine to offer sterilisation to multiparous women undergoing repeat Caesarians; the tougher doctors do not deny that they do this for their own convenience, because the management of future pregnancies is their problem. Soft-headed ones, who are in the majority, will claim that they do so for the woman's own good; she will be saved a repeat visit to hospital and she doesn't want any more children anyway. As long as they apply these *ad hoc* methods indiscriminately we cannot claim to discern crypto-eugenic thinking, but statistics show that they do not. Of the women sterilised in federally funded population programmes, 43% are black; 20% of black married women are sterilised and only 6% of whites. Sterilisation is typically offered to the "feckless" patient who cannot be trusted to manage a contraceptive method. According to Dr Connie Uri more than 25% of native American women are sterilised. At Claremore Indian Hospital in Oklahoma, 132 women were sterilised in a single year.[60] Between 1963 and 1965 American money paid not only for the sterilisation of 40,000 women in Colombia, but also for lipstick, artificial pearls and small money payments to the acceptors. The Colombians were probably more interested in the promises of free health care that went with them.

In a historic opinion brought by Judge Gerhard A. Gesell at the instance of Joseph Levin, general counsel of the Southern Poverty Law Center, in the case of *Katie Relf and the National Welfare Rights Organisation et al.* vs. *Caspar W. Weinberger et al*, the situation is summarised thus:

> Few realise that over 16% of the married couples in between the ages of 20 and 39 have had a sterilisation operation. Over the last few years an estimated 100,000 to 150,000 low-income persons have been sterilised annually under federally funded programs ... there is uncontroverted evidence in the record that minors and other incompetents have been sterilised with federal funds, and that an indefinite number of poor people have been coerced into accepting a sterilisation operation under threat that various federal-supported welfare benefits would be withdrawn unless they submitted to irreversible sterilisation. Patients receiving Medicaid assistance at childbirth are evidently the most frequent targets of the pressure, as the experiences of the plaintiffs Brown and Walker illustrate ...
>
> The dividing line between family planning and eugenics is murky. And yet the Secretary through the regulations at issue seeks to sanction one of the most drastic methods of population control – the irreversible sterilisation of men and women – without any legislative guidance.[61]

The Health Research Group at Los Angeles County Hospital found in its "Study on Surgical Sterilisation" that the consent forms used were a "farce", that many women did not know that the procedure was irreversible, and that, despite Gesell's order, sterilisation was routinely offered at the time of Caesarian section at hospitals in Baltimore, Boston, New Orleans, Nashville, Chicago and Louisville – not the hospitals frequented by the fee-paying rich. The study quoted the President of the Association for Voluntary Sterilisation as saying:

> As physicians we have obligations to our individual patients, but we also have obligations to the society of which we are a part. The welfare mess, as it has been called, cries out for solutions, one of which is fertility control.[62]

The Association for Voluntary Sterilisation is the Human Betterment Foundation set up by E. S. Gosney, under a new name. Its president claimed that doctors had an obligation to *society* to pre-empt the individual's right to control his own fertility; if he had used the word "state" instead of society the semantic warning bell might have rung. The Nazi protocol that the Dutch doctors died in prison camps for refusing to sign simply asked them to agree that the care of the patient's health was "a public task".[63] Once such concepts become current in the thinking of medical technicians, because they are crammed with technical knowhow and intellectually dwarfed by poor education, overwork and fear, or for any reason, our civilisation will be well on the way to its last degradation. In 1972, the *Family Planning Digest* reported that 94% of gynaecologists interviewed thought that welfare mothers with three or more illegitimate children should be sterilised.[64]

The problems raised by crypto-eugenics in family planning programmes are inherent also in genetic counselling, sometimes called the "new eugenics". Clearly people who run the risk of bringing into the world children whose own suffering will be appalling, and who will cause grief and disaster to others, ought to know whatever medical science can tell them about their own predicament. The first eugenists thought that individuals should be made to supply pedigrees before being issued with marriage licences; in 1938 the Eugenics Education Society brought out a sample schedule of data which might be considered relevant when compiling a genetic profile. The candidates were expected to supply details of the health of father, mother, grandparents on both sides, siblings (including miscarriages and stillbirths) and uncles and aunts, and whether any of them had suffered from "nervousness, nervous breakdown, mental backwardness or defect, insanity, fainting spells, convulsions or fits, suicide, drug addiction, heavy drinking, tuberculosis, diabetes, asthma, blindness or deafness in early life, or any diseases thought to be hereditary". They themselves were asked, among a host of other intrusive demands, whether they suffered from backache, indigestion, gout, depression or fits of crying.

> Do you suffer from any morbid fears such as of traffic, heights, darkness, solitude, open or closed spaces, crossing bridges, animals, disease, insanity, death?[65]

Nowhere do the gatherers of this information suggest what they mean to do with it. Ideally, the state would have gathered it and refused marriage licences to people afflicted with too many of the above; in practice general practitioners simply failed to cooperate. It should have been obvious that nothing is to be gained by amassing a fund of incompatible subjective impressions, even supposing would-be spouses actually knew all about their mother's miscarriages and their aunts' fainting spells and their uncles' IQs. A genetic counsellor dealing with such stuff would simply have to wish the spouses good luck, which is what is usually done anyway. Somewhere between this case and the advising of parents carrying the genes for Tay-Sachs disease lies the proper sphere for genetic counselling, but nobody knows how to establish it. One solution would be to make mandatory the drawing up of genetic profiles of the whole population in order to identify the groups at risk and then make sure that they were fully apprised of their chances of having a defective child, either before they choose a mate, so that they will not choose from the group carrying the same gene, or before they conceive or after conception so that the defective child need not be born. Such a scheme has significant disadvantages; it would cost many times more to identify cases by such a method than it would take to treat them if they arose in the usual manner. An enormous bureaucracy would have to be set up to keep track of such a voluminous quantity of material, a bureaucracy so vast that any claim to preserving the confidentiality of this intimate information would be absurd. The current state of our knowledge of the etiology of congenital disease is imperfect,[66] and much of the information gathered would become obsolete even within the space of two or three years: Down's syndrome or mongolism is a case in point. It used to be thought that mongolism was a genetic defect until the relative age of the mothers of mongoloids was noticed. We are still unsure of the mechanism by which the chromosomal damage occurs, whether the ovum itself is damaged, or whether a defective blastocyst simply fails to be aborted, but it seems that mongolism is itself not a hereditary defect, although we may discover that certain strains are more likely to incur this kind of chromosomal damage than others. Genetic screening would not help us to target mongoloid foetuses before they were conceived. Notwithstanding, the Cytogenetics Unit of Adelaide Children's Hospital and Intellectually Retarded Services pleaded for compulsory registration of all cases.

As yet, there are no figures for risks of Down's syndrome by single-year maternal-age intervals from pre-natal diagnostic series based on large numbers for Australia. It is to be hoped that such figures will become available in the near future as figures derived from such data are useful for genetic counselling ...[67]

A plea is made for this disorder to be made notifiable, and for the data to be kept in a central registry. Pre-natal diagnosis is made by means of amniocentesis, which is not a routine part of pre-natal care except when the risk of abnormality appears to be elevated, because the rest is not itself without attendant risk. It is not easy to imagine just how detailed knowledge of fluctuating rates of incidence at different maternal ages would help genetic counselling. The most a counsellor can do is to suggest that a pregnant woman undergo amniocentesis, and she may either agree or refuse. The difficulties arise when we consider whose decision shall be paramount. A worried woman may ask for amniocentesis and be refused because it is not the policy of the health authorities to offer it to persons in her category. Moreover, she will not be automatically privy to all the information gained from the amniotic fluid, for example, in some cases the medical authorities keep the knowledge of the child's sex to themselves for fear that it should unduly influence the woman's decision whether or not to abort. As the procedure itself involves a risk to the foetus the hospital may wish to pre-empt that decision in order to escape liability for the problems of a child born after being damaged by hospital technicians *in utero*. If the cytogeneticists got their central registry of Down's syndrome cases they might be able to establish the categories of women who should be offered amniocentesis with a little more accuracy, but if their current figures show that over a period of 17 years 16- and 17-year-old mothers had a higher proportion of afflicted children than 29-year-olds who had less than mothers between the ages of 24 and 28 it is hard to see how they would accomplish even this.

By genetic counselling is usually, but not always, meant pre-natal investigation. In theory it is undertaken in the interests of parents and the unborn child, but the idea that parents should not burden the state with the cost of the care of their defective children also plays a part. The interest of the health authorities, who have to finance the setting-up of facilities, also has to be taken into account. An authority that has invested in the setting-up of a pre-natal screening programme has to justify it in terms of cost-effectiveness. Naturally women want to take the guesswork out of pregnancy and doctors are all too ready to pretend that their informed guesses are certainties. Some birth defects will not show up either in cytological examinations of amniotic fluid or in ultra-sound screening. Some mothers will not accept abortion even if they do. Both the patient and the professionals are struggling for control of the uncontrollable, and it seems as if the patient must lose, for she is one and they are legion. The bitterest irony is that the most severe birth defects are the outcome of direct mutation; we have given up all hope of controlling that. Meanwhile our level of tolerance for visible defect is subsiding: would we recommend abortion for foetuses with cleft palates or webbed toes or humped backs? We hear that infant pyloric stenosis, which used to be fatal because the infant's food could not pass into the bowel, is now on the increase because babies who would have died now grow up to give birth to more babies with the deformity. We should reply "So what?" but the obstetricians seem to be expecting a different answer. Will we start begging people whose lives were saved by abdominal surgery at birth to repay us by refraining from bringing any more such nuisances into the world? Or do we withold the life-saving procedure and let them starve to death? Once, when the child was a mongoloid we did exactly that.[68] Negative eugenics is not dead: it lingers in the corridors of the health establishment, emerging in swift guerilla raids on the Hippocratic tradition. It draws off blood from the foetal cord and assesses it for a multitude of rare disorders, some of which, like phenylketonuria, are much less damaging if treated in the newborn, and others, like sickle-cell trait, asymptomatic and untreatable. The baby's permission is not asked, nor is its parents'. What can it profit a child to know he is a sickle-cell carrier? Will his life be any more manageable if he only dates girls after they have had a blood test? The instrumentality for eugenic measures already exists under the statute that allows states to demand a blood-test as a condition for receiving a marriage licence. For that too we have the eugenists to thank. The blood was meant to be submitted to the Wasserman test for syphilis; in law it can be tested for anything at all and any use may be made of the information. This is the same statute that governed Oliver Wendell Holmes's decision in the Carrie Buck case. It is now less likely than ever that any move will be made to strike it down.

The gene pool is not only to be cleaned up, however; hope has not stopped springing in the hearts of those who think that its actual quality can be raised by breeding from the better strains and in Artificial Insemination by Donor, the eugenists believed that they had found the Way.

In 1910 the members of the Peithologian Society of Columbia University were privileged to hear the great biologist Hermann J. Muller on "The Revelations of Biology and their Significance"; part of what they heard was that artificial insemination would open up the possibility of exponentially increasing the progeny of transcendentally eminent men. The idea continued to fascinate Muller, who tried it on the public again in 1925 in a lecture at the University of Texas. In 1935 it resurfaced in *Out of the Night*; while the book was in press, Herbert Brewer's article "Eutelegenesis" appeared in the *Eugenics Review*.[69] Societies have often developed ways in which to give successful individuals increased reproductive opportunity, but they have never supposed that the beneficiary should not perform his own stud duty. Muller was probably trying to avoid accusations of immorality, and the kind of ridicule that greeted Von Ehrenfels when he argued, in an article in the *Archiv für Rassen- und Gesellschaftsbiologie* in 1907, that the best boys at school

> ... should be allowed to revert to the primitive conditions in which the best male qualities, courage, prowess and idealism, were stimulated to win the female, and a few such carefully selected youths should be ... allowed more than one mate of the other sex.[70]

Artificial insemination removed the suggestion of subversion of sexual morality as well as the practical difficulties which might beset an eminent gentleman attempting to impregnate a young stranger, allowing him to pass on his genes by remote control. Eutelegenesis was an idea that had found its time: it was no sooner mooted than, like eugenic sterilisation, it was put into practice by some hardy pioneers. In 1940 the national Research Foundation for the Eugenic Alleviation of Sterility carried out a survey under the direction of Drs F. I. Seymour and A. Koerner which was reported in the *Journal of the American Medical Association*, 21 June 1941. Clearly artificial insemination as practised was eugenic because sires are selected from specific populations, in most cases from among medical students. There was a little heartburning over whether or not they should be paid for their services, it being thought that the increased reproductive opportunity should be payment in itself. Talk about AID had become so widespread that in 1948 the Archibishop of Canterbury thought that he should set up a commission to study its moral implications. In 1958 the Eugenics Society set up an Investigation Council "to review the existing status and future possibilities of human artificial insemination genetically, medically, legally and socially." The Scientific Committee of the British Medical Association and the Church of England Moral Welfare Council were also investigating the subject. Just how fashionable the issue had become is indicated by the fact that in September of the same year the Government set up a Departmental Committee on Human Artificial Insemination. The chief result of their investigation was to show that AID was being practised on so small a scale that there was no way of collecting reliable evidence.

> What had emerged, however, was that the difficulties of AID would be much reduced and the efficiency much increased if some method of preserving human spermatozoa for long periods were available, that is, if a semen bank could be established.[71]

The possibilities opened up by accumulating donor sperm are enormous; here at last is a way of short-circuiting natural selection and placing the destiny of the human race under human control. If the constitution of the entire population of domestic cattle could be utterly changed by fully exploiting the reproductive potential of a handful of sires, so could the constitution of the human race. The handful of men who dominate political and cultural life in technocratic society could become the sole sires of coming generations. In 1962 twenty-seven distinguished men met at the CIBA Foundation in London to discuss the future of man. The opening address was given by that erstwhile advocate of eugenic sterilisation, Julian Huxley, now Sir Julian and well into his seventies.

> The population explosion is making us ask the fundamental question – so fundamental that it is usually not asked at all – what are people for? Whatever the answer, whether to achieve greater efficiency or power, or, as I am suggesting, to find greater fulfilment, it is clear that the general quality of the world's population is not very high, is beginning to deteriorate, and could and should be improved. It is defective, thanks to genetic defectives who would otherwise have died being kept alive, and thanks to the crop of new mutations due to fall-out. In modern man the direction of genetic evolution has started to change its sign from positive to negative, from advance to retreat: we must manage to put it back on its age-old course of positive improvement.[72]

It is possible to argue that all that is certain in evolution, as in human life, is change and that to dub such a change positive or negative is to confer a subjective value upon it. In rich societies the mechanism of natural selection may have altered, but natural selection itself is still functioning, and that means that the fittest are still surviving. If what that really means is that the poor nations which are still subjected to the weeding-out of the weak and handicapped by disease and food shortage will eventually overwhelm the rich ones, the result is still the survival of the fittest, the re-establishment of the norm. If technological man should annihilate his kind, leaving only "a [mutant] hare sitting up" in some post-nuclear version of D. H. Lawrence's vision, natural selection has accomplished this too. The norm may well not be "high" enough for Sir Julian, but then Sir Julian may well be too "high" for it. If the higher stocks are less prolific than the lower stocks, then they are less fit: this Sir Julian understood, therefore he proposed that the fertility of men like himself should be exponentially increased.

> The improvement of human genetic quality by eugenic methods would take a great load of suffering and frustration off the shoulders of evolving humanity, would increase both enjoyment and efficiency. Let me give one example. The general level of genetic intelligence could theoretically be raised by eugenic selection; and even a slight rise in its average level would give a marked increase in the number of the outstandingly intelligent and capable people needed to run our increasingly complex societies. Thus a 1.5 per cent increase in mean genetic intelligence quotient (IQ), from 100 to 101.5, would increase the production of those with an IQ of 160 and over by about 50 per cent.[73]

The only way that genetic IQ or innate intelligence could be raised would be by selective breeding, but as there exists no reliable way of measuring innate intelligence the only recourse would be to select as parents those individuals who had conspicuous success. This no one ever has who has not enjoyed considerable advantages in education and opportunity, both of which have more to do with politics and economics than they do with genetics. For all we know to the contrary it may take a Colombian *gamine* more raw intelligence to survive in the *barrio* than it takes to gain a double first at Oxford. Sir Julian continued:

> How to implement such a policy is another matter. The effects of merely encouraging potentially well-endowed people to have more children and *vice versa*, would be much too slow for modern psychosocial evolution. Eugenics will eventually have to have recourse to methods like multiple artificial insemination by preferred donors of high genetic quality, as Professor Muller emphasised a quarter of a century ago, and I emphasised in my recent Galton lecture. Such a policy would not be easy to execute. However I shall confidently look forward to a time when eugenic improvement will become one of the major aims of mankind.[74]

Professor Muller was at the symposium and welcomed the opportunity to restate his old idea about eutelegenesis. He was no longer the man who had put the explanation of why fertility is negatively correlated with social status in those terms before the rather unsympathetic audience of the New York Eugenics Society in 1937:

> In the first place it is undeniable that the profit system leaves little place for children. In general they are not profitable investments: their cost is excessive, the dividends from them uncertain, they are likely to depreciate in value, are practically non-transferable, and do not mature early enough ... For the great masses ... each extra child commonly means more intensified slavery for the parents ... And as the status of the middle class sinks, the parents hesitate to rear children with lesser privileges than they.
> How much can eugenic considerations weigh in determining the actions of people under these circumstances? Is it to be wondered that a census of geneticists themselves had disclosed an appalling failure to reproduce themselves despite the fact that they are maximally steeped in their own doctrines?[75]

If Muller had carried his argument a little further he might have got to the point of seeing that if a profit can be made from storing and supplying the semen of famous men, some American will find a way of doing it. His insistence that sperm be stored for at least twenty years before it is used is clearly meant to counteract the effects of publicity and popularity, but the cost would be prohibitive. If the extension of the reproductive opportunity of famous men is undertaken for the profit motive a whole generation descended from Henry Kissinger and Frank Sinatra would be a real possibility. The consequences for American genetic variability would be disastrous. In 1962, Muller indulged himself in the best Galtonian way, elaborating his idea for a repository for "Voluntarily Conducted Germinal Choice", and defining its operating conditions:

There are however several requirements to be met before germinal choice can be undertaken even on a pilot scale. A choice is not a real one unless it is a multiple choice, one carried out with maximum foreknowledge of the possibilities entailed and hampered as little as possible by material restrictions and by direct personal involvements. Moreover, to keep as far away as possible from dictation, the final decision regarding the selection to be made should be the prerogative of the couple concerned. These conditions can be fulfilled only after plentiful banks of germinal material have been established, representing those who have proved to be most outstanding in regard to valuable characteristics of mind, heart and body. In addition, such storage for a person's own germ cells should be a service supplied at cost for anyone wishing it. Catalogued records should be maintained, giving the results of diverse mental and physical tests and observations of all donors, together with relevant facts about their lives and their relatives.[76]

In order to achieve the same genetic result as that achieved without great technological know-how by systems of polygamy, namely, increased reproductive opportunity for successful males, Muller has to set up a formidable system of checks and controls, involving not only the putative sire, but his relatives and his scions. Muller, being a biologist, may have had little experience of the unreliability of mental tests, but from his own acquaintance with eminent men he ought to have been aware that a great many undesirable traits were often part of their genetic package. The dauntless eugenist, Sir Julian Huxley himself, had a very mixed genetic endowment. The Huxley family in some ways resembles one of the pedigrees assembled by the now discredited Lombroso, to show that genius, madness and criminality are all near allied. Good manners prevented any of the old gentlemen from challenging each other's pedigrees, but they might profitably have considered the demonstrated connection between myopia and intellectual ability as shown in intelligence tests. The vulgar stereotype of the bespectacled swot is derived from observation; commonsense tells us that many bookish children are so because they cannot play games and are shy with children who call them "four-eyes" and "gig-lamps" and so forth. A putative mother given the choice between a brilliant child who has to wear spectacles as soon as he starts to walk and a not very brilliant child who does not, might very well choose the latter. Besides, if she is being offered the sperm of a myopic genius, she is as likely to get the myopia without the genius as *vice versa*, and equally likely to get neither.

Muller's suggestion that anyone who wishes ought to be able to contribute his sperm to posterity "at cost" is an interesting one. It seems obvious that if we can conserve sperm at all, we should conserve the sperm of men who have been vasectomised, so that there is not the frequent and unavailing demand for reversal which has now become a principal preoccupation of fertility experts. The storage of ova from women undergoing tubal ligation would also seem mandatory, but no such protocol has ever been devised, a fact which underlines our deep unwillingness to put fertility within the individual's control once and for all. Muller's suggestion, a mere pipe-dream in 1962 and now completely practicable, has yet to be taken up.

The elderly geniuses listening to Muller liked nothing better than elaborate computation; even they might have been hard put to devise a scheme for estimating the cost of keeping semen for twenty years. Only by some such rule could the effects of popularity be neutralised. The reputations of men like Frank Sinatra and Henry Kissinger tend to adjust themselves in the course of twenty years (to say nothing of Elvis Presley). The chances of a scheme like Muller's being properly run either by private entities or by the state are extremely slim, yet it excited a good deal of enthusiasm. Francis Crick bounced up and cried, "I agree with practically everything Muller said," thus revealing that even the co-discoverer of the structure of DNA is capable of schoolboy silliness. The prospect of genetic control excited him so much that he went on:

> ... do people have the right to have children at all? ... in terms of humanist ethics I do not see that people should have the right to have children ... If one did have a licensing scheme, the first child might be admitted on rather easy terms. If the parents were genetically unfavourable, they might be allowed to have only one child or possibly two under special circumstances.[77]

The concept of genetic "unfavourability" is so vague as to be capable of almost any interpretation. Crick amused himself with formulating a plan for putting chemicals in the drinking-water which would sterilise the entire population, and then giving selected individuals a chemical to reverse its effects. The other learned gentlemen kicked this scheme around a bit, but they were more intrigued by the actual methodology of semen conservation than such Draconian fantasy. To the animal behaviourist their antics would have been crystalline in their transparency; of course all these sub-fertile old stags were vulnerable to the delicious notion of maintaining their control over the does from beyond the grave. The surprising thing is that they were so ingenuous as to allow their susceptibility to show. Haldane, on leave from the university in Orissa where he was then working, listened unsurprised. When he spoke, he repeated something he had said thirty years before; it had not been understood then, when his colleagues were agitating for eugenic sterilisation, and it was not understood now:

> I agree with Muller when he said that in most existing societies effective fertility is negatively associated with social rank. The same observation was made approximately 2,000 years ago in the statement, "Blessed are the meek, for they shall inherit the earth."[78]

In fact, Christ's words in the Sermon on the Mount are good genetics, as Penrose, who had succeeded Pearson as Galton Professor, pointed out, reminding his colleagues of what they already knew but longed to forget, that genetic homeostasis is based on the higher fertility of heterozygotes. Jacob Bronowski who, unlike many of his hearers, had learnt from experience, spoke in support of Haldane:

> If you are trying to upset violently the present gene frequencies in the population, then nothing Muller proposes could do this. Just as Haldane has shown long ago that sterilisation of the unfit would hardly have any influence on the proportion of recessive genes, so the multiplication of what we choose to call the fit can really have very little effect on the presence of recessives. (And no one who has known the children of accepted geniuses would suppose that the population would greatly benefit by their being several hundred of them.)[79]

None of what Bronowski and Haldane were saying was new to their audience. They knew that selective breeding for desirable characteristics in livestock was only successful after a long series of controlled matings accompanied by ruthless suppression of the duds, and that the achievement of improvement in one respect was often costly in terms of variability and adaptability. They also knew that the desirable characteristics in human beings, supposing they could arrive at a consensus on what actually constituted a desirable characteristic, would not be of the same order as increased body weight in steers or egg-laying capacity in hens. They knew that the most serious genetic diseases were the outcome of mutation and that the increased mutation rate of our time was a serious problem that should have been addressed, but they preferred, at a time when the future of man is seriously threatened, to indulge themselves in philoprogenitive fantasies at the same time that they seriously entertained notions of limiting the fertility of their inferiors. These men knew more about the mechanisms they were fooling with than any politician, more than any doctor, yet they clung to a seductive delusion in defiance of their own knowledge. If men accustomed to a lifetime of mental discipline and scrupulous testing of hypotheses can be so manipulated by their own egotistic genes, how can we expect wisdom in the application of genetic knowledge from lesser mortals? Most of the people who devote their lives to the delivery of health care are bred and trained in a different tradition from that which rules the hothouse where genius is forced, and few of them are likely to entertain such delusions of control – but then they are not the controllers. Politicians and millionaires do not function on the same or even similar principles as district nurses, nor do they examine their behaviour by the same moral criteria.

Let us take for example the case of Robert Klark Graham. (The reason for his middle name being spelt in that odd way may emerge as we proceed.) Mr Graham is the inventor of the plastic lenses which are now to be found in most of the eyeglasses worn in the world, therefore he is extremely rich and may do more or less as he pleases. In 1970 it pleased him to write a book with the same title as the Ciba symposium, *The Future of Man*. In it he argues that revolutionary movements develop when inferior stock, being more fertile, outnumbers the superior ruling classes and overwhelms them. The French Revolution was carried out by the educationally subnormal and in Russia "communist masses liquidate the intelligent", as they do in China. Moreover, Mr Graham goes on, "They plan it here too."

> Communism is based upon a fundamental biological phenomenon: it exploits the rapid increase of people with mediocre to poor intelligence which occurs because natural selection no longer keeps their numbers down. This is the source of inner confidence which gives to collectivist leaders the expectation of total world conquest.[80]

In this bald formulation, such an argument seems obviously deranged, but it can be found in more sophisticated forms closer to the centres of power than Mr Graham finds himself, which is, not surprisingly, in California, where another millionaire, E. S. Gosney, had approached college presidents with an offer to finance eugenic breeding schemes among their best students in the 1920s. Parallel to Gosney's Human Betterment Foundation set up in 1928 was the Foundation for the Advancement of Man where, Graham tells us, "an institution to store the germinal substance of our most creative men" was set up in 1966 and by 1970 is described as "in operation".[81] It is called the Hermann J. Muller Repository for Germinal Choice. At a secret site somewhere in the vicinity of San Diego, Graham has built an underground chamber lined with lead; there he stores the semen of exceptional donors, such as Dr William Shockley, winner, together with John Bardeen and Walter Brattain, of the Nobel Prize in 1956 for the development of the transistor under the auspices of Bell Telephone Company. Clearly, Dr Shockley is a very good electrical engineer, but the quality of his general intelligence might be questioned. He is evidently an enthusiastic amateur geneticist, with a marked attachment to old-fashioned hereditarian notions. In 1970 he managed to create a scandal by applying to the National Academy of Sciences for sponsorship of a study of black populations with a view to establishing relative IQ levels. Unfortunately, the National Academy, having its own protocols and its own daily ration of cranks whose privacy must be respected, did not make a loud and clear statement that it is not in the habit of funding well-heeled electrical engineers to undertake "studies" for which they are not qualified. Instead Shockley crashed into print, screaming that he had been discriminated against on political grounds, free speech was being muzzled by knee-jerk liberalism and so forth. His next exploit was to offer courses in eugenics at Stanford University in 1972; the offer was not taken up and Shockley found himself in the centre of another public controversy. Views which had been discredited thirty years before circulated through the popular press as though they were new "scientific" discoveries. A reporter from *The Times* sent to see him during the brouhaha was disconcerted to discover that Shockley records and files all telephone conversations and interviews and refuses to grant interviews unless he is allowed to vet the finished copy. So much for his attachment to free speech. His wife functions as amanuensis, producing file materials as Shockley calls for them by number to show the bemused representative of the public's right to know.

In 1973 the University of Leeds decided to award Shockley an honorary doctorate, presumably for his work in electrical engineering: the students, better informed than students usually are, doubtless because of the propagandist activities of their teachers, rebelled. The university authorities, startled and embarrassed, capitulated. The intellectual community was distressed that academic decisions could be reversed by mob rule and electrical engineers refused their honours because they believed in eugenic sterilisation of blacks. Shockley basked in the limelight.

It is an insult to the memory of Hermann Muller that so tawdry a personality should be the only known donor of sperm to Graham's establishment; the other four Nobel prize-winners who, Graham claims, have donated sperm, some repeatedly, have preferred to remain anonymous. The first woman artificially impregnated at Graham's establishment was very poorly selected as a dam for the master race, for she was a convicted felon with a history of child abuse. The setback was only temporary; in 1980 Graham announced that three "exceptionally intelligent women" had been impregnated. One of them, Afton Blake, PhD, had appeared on the Phil Donahue Show with her eugenic experiment gurgling in her arms.

Most eminent men are revolted and amused by Graham's advances; 11 Nobel prizewinners contacted by the *Los Angeles Times* in 1980 admitted that Graham had approached them and said that they had refused to serve. In 1981 the same newspaper announced that having exhausted the available sources of Nobel-prize-winning germinal material in the United States Graham was heading for London and Cambridge where the greatest concentrations of Nobel prizewinners were to be found. It matters little to men like Robert Klark Graham that the greatest concentration of Nobel prizewinners ever assembled worked together on that dysgenic catastrophe, the Manhattan Project. The birth of a handful of babies with half their genes donated by men of Shockley's ilk is hardly of cataclysmic importance, except for the babies themselves, who may well develop some severely anti-social behavioural symptoms in reaction to the pressure of curiosity and expectation which will hound them. If they eventually grow to understand something of genetics, they will know to expect the surfacing of any exceptional genes in their children rather than themselves, but they will have little chance of explaining the real situation to the cormorant public.

It is indeed a sinister astigmatism that can affect men of science so that looking hard at suffering mankind they see not the frustration of genetic potential but deficiency in the genetic potential itself. Whatever is written in the genetic instructions, which bids fair to be vaster and more intricate than all the conscious lucubration stored in our libraries, is obliterated by a series of devastating onslaughts emerging only in a dim and distorted fashion. The foetus *in utero*, if assailed by drugs like alcohol, nicotine and caffeine in its mother's bloodstream, or starved of essential vitamins and trace elements, or exposed to environmental poisons like lead and radiation or blinded by rubella, damaged by potent medications or de-sexed by steroids, loses some of its potential for development. More is destroyed if the infant struggles too long in the birth ordeal, or is poisoned by drugs or battered by the strong contractions of induced labour or is damaged by clumsy obstetric procedures. There are too many children in the world whose innate gifts wither because of infant malnutrition which affects the development of the brain in the growing child, who will not realise their potential because they die, or because they are blinded by infection or vitamin deficiency or because they struggle against resistant infections which weaken them. There are too many people whose available energy is exhausted in a losing battle with grinding poverty, who never have leisure to indulge in the life of the mind. Yet I dare wager that less cruel and stupid nonsense is talked by hungry farmers philosophising over a *bidi* after a day's brutalising toil than was heard when a gaggle of brilliant scientists met to kick around a few ideas in the luxurious halls of the Ciba Foundation.

The early eugenists did not know that it is only by exploiting the long, long memory of the gene that the wastage of human potential can be counteracted. It is folly to suppose that by selecting stocks for breeding we shall achieve lasting results which will justify the sacrifice of a vast quantity of unrealised potential in the groups selected for genetic death. The nature–nurture controversy is only useful if both sides are aware that the real issue is the reconciliation of nature's achievement, the genotype, with nurture's damaged product, the phenotype. Practical eugenics denies all the values which justify our civilisation. When we have a clearer idea of our own ignorance we shall see that eugenics is more barbarous than cannibalism and far more destructive. Such barbarism may well be part of our mammalian residue, but then so are our predilections for rapine and murder: we are who we are because we have decided not to give them expression. Every week we hear of a new species of creature whose survival is threatened because of man's phenomenal success and we bestir ourselves to save a few representatives of it, although it is of no use to us.

We do not ask what the tiger is for; we must not ask Sir Julian Huxley's question "What are people for?" We cannot contemplate the world's poor and ask what use they are, as they joy and sorrow, multiply and die.

Chapter Eleven
The Population Lobby

Dr R. T. Ravenholt proposed a programme known as "Advanced Fertility Management", whose objective was to sterilise a quarter of all Third World Women – a 9-year target. He was quoted as saying (in 1977): "Without our trying to help these countries with their economic and social developments, the world would rebel against strong US commercial presence. The self-interest thing is a compelling element. If population proceeds unchecked it will cause such terrible economic conditions abroad that revolution will ensue, and revolutions are scarcely ever beneficial to the interests of the United States."

> Dr Zafrullah Chowdhury,
> Savar Gonoshasthya Kendra
> Nayarhat via Dhamrai,
> Bangladesh

If we take it as a truism that every society struggles to keep its numbers in balance with its resources, and that the means by which that struggle is waged are intrinsic features of its culture, whether overtly expressed and explicable to outsiders or not, we have still to explain the rise of a powerful and vocal lobby pushing for public, bureaucratic forms of fertility regulation. The traditional way of telling the story has so far followed the pattern set by popular historiography, singling out conspicuous individuals and saluting them as pioneers. The assumption is that before Charles Bradlaugh and Annie Besant, or before Marie Stopes, there was unlimited reproduction, the "Rabbit" family, adjusted by appalling mortality rates. Such was certainly Stopes' assumption when she began her crusade; while she admitted that the middle classes had set about using artifical checks generations earlier she was convinced that the vast mass of the labouring poor would eventually canonise her for bringing light into their racial darkness. Her biographers have been equally convinced, uneasy though they may have been about the paranoid tendencies which were so obvious a feature of her personality. If we approach the whole story from a different angle, assuming that family limitation begins to be practised when there is endogenous recognition of the advantages to be gained by practising it and not because it is being preached or urged by outsiders, we might well begin to suspect that the "pioneers" were as much of a hindrance as a help to people seeking an acceptable form of fertility regulation for themselves.

If we assume that fertility regulation is an intrinsic part of cultural life, we must ask ourselves why there was an epidemic of excess fertility in the industrialised world in the nineteenth century. The usual explanation is that the deathrates fell very much faster than the birthrates, which is clearly true. We might argue that birthrates take a long time to adjust to such changes, which have first to become perceptible to the body politic and that some lag was inevitable. We shall not have understood the whole story however, until we have understood how the "masses" were created out of smaller communities dependent on agriculture and deeply provincial in outlook. The culture of the displaced agricultural labourer was effectively destroyed by industrialisation and urbanisation. He could form no concept of a good life or a better life because so much of each waking day was spent in securing the bare necessities for survival. While the economy itself was actually exploding and contracting in a highly volatile way, its character was perceived as one of continuous expansion – empire-building, in other words. The commercial and professional classes were quick to feel the pinch when rising expectations ran up against inflationary pressure on income. After a brief period of patriarchal hyperfecundity, when huge families were built by hard-working entrepreneurs, their descendants came to resent the expense involved in the management of large households. As the opportunities for gratification outside the household multiplied, the middle-class family became less satisfying to its members and less central in their lives. Its numbers began to diminish. The anti-birth controllers characterised birth prevention as frivolity and selfishness: the contraceiving couples saw it as commonsense health care and the exercise of social responsibility. Large families, they thought, crippled man and wife, preventing them from living the higher life. Smaller and smaller families began to qualify as large. The periodic depressions which afflicted industrial societies through the second half of the nineteenth century dragged on the aspiring professional classes and threatened to pull them under into the stinking squalor where lived the wage-earning poor; children in such a turbulent situation were as millstones around their parents' necks. The problem that remained to be solved for those who had already formed the clear intention of limiting their families was how to do it.

If societies have always had ways of managing their reproductive affairs, we must assume that in the industrialised world the emerging middle class and the struggling proletariat had somehow forgotten how their forefathers managed the matter. Given the massive changes in social organisation in Europe in the nineteenth century we cannot be surprised if they had, for concepts of what is normal and permissible in sexual behaviour are derived from custom and example in the immediate peer-group. People moving out of a settled society break this tenuous chain of information and can find no substitute. The old ways, if their existence is suspected at all, are seen as backward. Moreover, as literacy increased, the authority of the spoken word declined; information which could not be found in a book was considered no information at all. The users of traditional birth-control methods are aware of the sacrifices and difficulties involved in them and can be easily persuaded that there is something better. When a group of practices is expounded by printed authority and dubbed "modern", "scientific" and "medical", it is bound to replace older methods, and few will dream that they are actually less effective.

We can only guess at the degree of awareness of possible methods of birth-control in, for example, England in the mid-nineteenth century. Some people, perhaps a significant number of people, had never lost the knowledge of *coitus interruptus* and routinely practised it, thinking perhaps at the same time that it was a perversion and a shame. Others needed to be told; still others needed to be reassured. Because of the untrackable nature of the case, we are forced to rely on literary evidence like the fact that *Every Woman's Book; or What is Love? Containing Most Important Instructions for the Prudent Regulation of the Principle of Love and the Number of A Family* by the freethinker Richard Carlile, had gone through 10,000 copies by the beginning of 1828, whereupon Carlile wrote in his preface:

> It has become a standard work ... It is now stereotyped and no more will be said about the number of editions.[1]

We shall probably never know how many people saw Carlile's book, or how many of those people were totally unacquainted with the matters dealt with in it. They include two methods of abortion, one by introducing instruments such as knitting needles into the uterus and the other by ingesting "Ergot of Rye, Savine and violent purgatives".[2] Carlile quite correctly gauges that the latter are only effective if used in doses sufficient to endanger the mother's life. Abortion is so common, he claims, that "it is a little-thought-of matter of course." His purpose in publishing his book is to counteract this evil and the evil of infanticide which he claims to be as common in England as it has ever been in any other country in the world.

> The remedy has long been known to a few, and to the aristocracy.[3]

The remedy was contraception, to be effected by means of the sponge, as recommended by Francis Place, by the "baudruche or glove" (the condom), and by *coitus interruptus*, which he describes rather vaguely, although he is careful to state that

> Complete withdrawal before emission is certainly effectual in all cases; but not so easily to be observed by all persons.[4]

Of the three methods "this last is the more certain means",

> and some women, particularly those of the Continent, will make it part of the

contract for intercourse, and look upon the man as a dishonest brute, who does not attend to it.[5]

According to Carlile, birth-control propaganda among the working classes had already begun, in the form of "lectures to the working people by a benevolent gentleman of Leeds,"[6] whose name history does not vouchsafe. It is sobering to reflect that Carlile's advice remained the best that could be given for a hundred years after he gave it. He made no claims to scientific knowledge, although his knowledge of female anatomy was accurate and he had had experience as an apothecary's assistant and knew what substances married women and their attendants most often requested. He had a clear understanding of and respect for women's sexuality and their "erotic rights". He was not interested in speculating about new and advanced methods, but quite matter-of-factly set himself to describe current practice. He assumed that some form of fertility management would be adopted throughout married life, seeing the spacing of births as just as important as limiting the total number of children born. Carlile had invented nothing, was marketing nothing, and was not parading expertise. His successors were neither so disinterested nor so straightforward.

In 1832 a Boston doctor called Charles Knowlton published a treatise on human reproduction called *The Fruits of Philosophy*. It contained descriptions of four methods of contraception; withdrawal, which Knowlton describes correctly, the condom, "by no means calculated to come into general use", the sponge, which he sees as ineffectual unless impregnated with a spermicidal substance, and syringing, in which he had rather too much confidence.[7] He was twice prosecuted under Massachusetts State Law for *The Fruits of Philosophy*. The first time, in Taunton, he was fined £10 with costs, and the second, in Cambridge, he was sentenced to three months in prison. The proprieties thus successfully defended, the matter was dropped. Far from being a fleeting underground manifestation, as commentators like David Kennedy have assumed, Knowlton's book went through nine editions in seven years. Carlile's friend, the publisher James Watson, heard of the book and caused a copy to be sent to England, where for forty years it sold about 800 copies a year without harassment. After Watson's death in 1874 Charles Watts, publisher for the National Secularist League, took it over. In 1877 a Bristol bookseller decided to boost sales by interleaving it with obscene pictures. Both publisher and bookseller were arrested. Charles Bradlaugh, under the influence of Annie Besant, decided to make an issue of the matter in defence of free speech, but Watts disappointed him by pleading guilty. As a result Bradlaugh and Besant decided to become their own publishers, and not only included *The Fruits of Philosophy* in their first prospectus, but notified the Guildhall magistrates that they had done so. In twenty minutes their supporters bought five hundred copies. Bradlaugh and Besant were taken up, imprisoned and released on bail two and a half hours later.[8] The issue split the Freethought movement, but the trial was a propagandist triumph, even though the jury brought in such a garbled verdict that the defendants had to be declared guilty. They appealed, were released on bail, and the indictment was eventually quashed. In the three years that followed, 185,000 copies of *The Fruits of Philosophy* were sold.[9] Annie Besant saw that the demand was immense, and that Knowlton's information was out of date; her update, *The Law of Population*, sold half a million copies over fifteen years. Most of the book was given to an exposition of the Malthusian principle; Besant's descriptions of "marital prudence" are rather hampered by the prevailing misconceptions about the time of ovulation and the significance of menstruation, and by overconfidence in the efficacy of douching and the sponge without a spermicidal agent. It is to be hoped that none who were successful in practising *coitus interruptus* were misled by Besant's description of her preferences as scientific into abandoning a practice which she herself describes as "absolutely certain".[10]

The Bradlaugh-Besant trial set the precedent for future promotions of birth-control: by calculated indiscretion and taunting of authority, the proponents of family planning tricked the state into providing the best possible platform for the promulgation of their views. In Annie Besant the movement had an "interesting" spokeswoman, who thought very well on her feet and provided all the copy the competing newspapers could desire, being attractive, atheist, separated from her husband, eventually deprived of her children and suspected of an improper relationship with her co-defendant. Bradlaugh's career was virtually ended by the notoriety attendant on this prosecution but Annie Besant became one of the founders, with C. R. Drysdale, a medical witness at the trial, of the Malthusian League founded "to agitate for the abolition of all penalties on the public discussion of the population question" and "to spread among the people by all practical means a knowledge of the law of population, of its consequences, and its bearing on human conduct and morals."[11] Instead of recommending late marriage and abstinence as the check to population growth they recommended family limitation. Before long the League was receiving a thousand letters a month. Enthusiastic members, including our old friend George Gaskell, tramped for miles distributing pamphlets. Their official organ, *The Malthusian*, consisted principally of long-winded explications of Malthusian theory. It could hardly have been duller if their whole intention had been simply to provide evidence of their extreme worthiness and freedom from any whoremongering taint. Inside the back cover was a coupon which interested parties could clip and send, in order to have by return lists of recommended appliances and various handbooks of contraceptive practice. The coupon required the would-be client to affirm that he or she was married and over the age of twenty-one.

One of the instructive manuals made available to readers of *The Malthusian* was *The Wife's Handbook*, boldly published under his own name and full address by Dr H. A. Allbutt of 24 Park Square, Leeds, in 1887. As a result, he was stripped of his membership of the Royal College of Physicians of Edinburgh which objected that at the low price of 6d, his pamphlet was within the reach of everyone, to the detriment of public morals.[12] He was also struck off the register of the General Medical Council.[13] By 1916, the pamphlet had sold 430,000 copies. *The Wife's Handbook* was subsidised by the contraceptive industry, for it carried advertising giving full details of suppliers of "Preservatives, pessaries of all kinds, enema syringes", which were to be had over the counter at such prestigious establishments as W. Davies and Co. Park Lane Drug Stores. As the first method Allbutt suggested refraining from intercourse on the days immediately before and after menstruation, a practice which would actually have ensured that intercourse was more likely to occur when conception was possible than at any other time. He adds a completely bogus statistic by way of a caveat:

> I am bound however to point out that this method fails in about five cases in every hundred and therefore cannot always be relied on.[14]

What his bemused reader was supposed to understand by a "case" is nowhere explained; if Allbutt had meant that for every hundred occasions on which the safe period was relied upon, five would result in pregnancy, he was actually recognising the fact that this system has the effect of maximising the chance of fecundation. Even so the statistic is absurd, for a woman may well have a hundred exposures in a year but is not likely to be pregnant five times a year. The reader would probably assume that Allbutt meant that out of a hundred cases coming to him who had relied on the safe period, five would report a failure, which seems even more unlikely, for the other ninety-five, having already found a successful method would have no urgent reason for consulting him. The statistic is no more scientific than the surmise about the safe period, but as Allbutt himself appears oblivious of his own ignorance we can hardly expect his readers to be wiser. The second method he advises is *coitus interruptus*:

> The withdrawal of the penis (male organ) before the ejection takes place is largely practised in France. This method (if withdrawal is complete before discharge takes place) is always successful. I believe however that the practice of it is hurtful to the nervous system of many persons, therefore I cannot strongly recommend this means of preventing conception in every case. It is a method however advocated by many eminent physicians.[15]

He makes no attempt to estimate the degree of damage done to the nervous system by *coitus interruptus* or how often and to whom such damage is likely to occur. The fall in the French birthrate was well publicised; Matthew Arnold had written a pamphlet describing the idyllic life of the sub-fertile French peasantry, while news from France repeated that the government was trying every inducement to increase the birthrate without success. By citing the French example, Allbutt makes a very strong case for withdrawal, too strong perhaps to be entirely pleasing to the advertisers who subsidised the pamphlet. It is interesting to speculate just how many male readers of *The Wife's Handbook* would have pooh-poohed the idea that their nerves were not strong enough to cope with conjugal onanism. Thirdly, Allbutt lists a variety of methods of douching, all ineffective, messy and unwieldy, but he does include a last cheap alternative, which might have been more effective than the proprietary spermicides listed, namely vinegar. In fact not one of the proprietary preparations had undergone any kind of testing: if we consider the possibility that the use of them in douches or in Allbutt's fourth method, the sponge, may have been substituted for *coitus interruptus*, it must also be possible that a goodly number of infants had Dr Allbutt to thank for their conception. The fifth method, the condom or "letter" is described as "a very certain check", which it was if it had been reliably manu-factured, but Allbutt gave no indications of how reliability might be assured.[16] As the sixth method Allbutt included the diaphragm, which he called "a real preventive of conception", but he tells us also that he has improved on Mensinga's design.[17] The advertisers meanwhile name various pessaries, without clear indication of whether they are referring to soluble suppositories, cervical caps or diaphragms.

The Malthusian League proceeded discreetly, holding meetings in local halls, during which a doctor was often in attendance to give specific advice to individuals, speaking on platforms of other reforming organisations such as the Rational Dress Society and the Vegetarian Society as well as the various socialist and rationalist bodies, and building up links with sympathetic groups in other countries. A group of Dutchmen in-fluenced by *The Elements of Social Science* by Drysdale's father George, contacted the League with a view to investigating the possibility of organising a Dutch League and opening birth control clinics.[18] In 1879 the first was set up in Amsterdam under the direction of Dr Aletta Jacobs. By 1914 the Dutch League had 5,521 members and had issued 7,200 copies of its handbook. The birthrate in the cities, which had stood at 33.7 per 1000 in 1881 had shrunk to 25.3 per 1000 and was still falling. The infant mortality rate was a third of what it was in 1881, the overall deathrate had been halved. Moreover, the vital statistics of the Dutch recruits in 1914 were strikingly more impressive than anything produced by their European allies. Queen Wilhelmina declared that the Dutch League was an organisation of proven social value and eventually accepted the presidency. By 1922 there were four doctors and fifty-three trained women dispensing contraceptive advice and fitting diaphragms in nineteen Dutch towns.[19] The English Malthusian League relied heavily on the Dutch success story, but they were strangely loth to undertake any similar venture in England. The Dutch system was in practice quite informal. When Margaret Sanger visited Holland in January, 1915, she found many rubber shops where contraceptives were sold and where women were fitted with contraceptives by the saleswomen, alongside clinics operating without any central organising body or bureaucratic procedures, recruiting their clients by word of mouth.[20] Gertrude Sturges was rather shocked to find, on a visit to Holland in 1926, that the clinics were actually run by the women in charge and not by any central authority. Of the three she visited, one was run by a midwife, one by the wife of a street-car conductor and the other by a hairdresser. Although she visited them during the hours when they were supposed to be in operation, she found only one open and saw only one client fitted. The clinic was conducted in the home of the practitioner; the "patient" was asked no questions and no records were kept. The clinics were supported by the selling of the appliances at 200% or 300% profit.[21] What the Dutch actually pioneered is now called "community-based distribution" and it clearly worked very well. In England the same thing was tried and seems to have had some success in at least one case.

In 1917 or thereabouts, Dr Alice Vickery, half of the husband-and-wife team that ran the Malthusian League, visited the working women's centre run by Anna Martin at 74 Union Road in Rotherhithe to talk to them about contraception. There she found that some of the women had already adopted contraceptive methods and were willing to teach other women how to handle them, so she made them a present of money to buy a "supply of necessary appliances". Margaret Sanger, visiting the group in 1920, was impressed by what she found:

> One of the groups that is on the road to practical work on a large scale is that under the direction of Mrs (*sic*) Anna Martin at Rotherhithe. This is one of the most dilapidated and poverty-stricken districts of London. When I gave an address to Miss Martin's group there were present something over one hundred women from the neighbourhood. I was surprised to learn that these women had small families.[22]

As the rest of Mrs Sanger's account is a little awry, Martin wrote to *The Malthusian* to correct it, and to give credit where it was due, to Dr Vickery and the women themselves. She added:

> It is quite true however that since Dr Vickery's visit there has been a steady propaganda and demonstration of birth-control methods by the women she taught – and these in their turn have taught others. [23]

Margaret Sanger came to birth-control (the expression itself was her invention – or almost – and she came to lay a proprietary claim to it) via American revolutionary socialism, but it suited her in later years to conceal the connection. She never acknowledged her indebtedness to Emma Goldman, nor would she consider the possibility that family limitation was not her own solution to the world's ills, understood and accepted only because of her heroism in the battle with the authorities. The historical fact is that Sanger found birth-control almost by default. Her political understanding was rudimentary, her commitment to socialism nil, but her desire for notoriety and admiration was a passion. She was a feminist because it suited her egocentricity, not because she cared one whit about women who were less able to charm their way through life than she. Like all the family planners before her, she could spin a melting tale of female misery and she loved to see herself in the role of lady bountiful, like any prima donna. There are many to say that the family-planning movement needed a prima donna. Selfless socialists and feminists had accomplished very little before the greater performers, Stopes and Sanger, took the stage, but while I am uncomfortably aware that my case cannot be proved, I should like to suggest that Stopes and Sanger did not advance the cause of the individual's right to control his or own reproductive destiny. What they did do was create the precedent for the invasion of privacy which made reproductive behaviour a public matter and placed its regulation in the hands of the medical and pharmaceutical establishment. The facts that neither of them was aware of the process and both of them claimed not to have made a penny out of reproductive technology obscures the issue, as does the undeniable fact of the opposition of conservative elements during the early years of their "struggle". "Radical" they may have been, but their radicalism was not the radicalism which seeks to give reality to the notions of freedom and democracy. Stopes and Sanger were radicals of the extreme right: although they both fought the takeover of the birth-control movement by the establishment and tried to keep it as informal as possible, their motives were personal, not feminist.

Sanger's Pamphlet, *Family Limitation*, was written in 1914 and based on the material she had collected in France, "complete with formulas and drawings". It was written "for women of extremely circumscribed vocabularies".[24] From the outset Sanger's interest was to limit what she saw as the excess fertility of the poor. She learnt the association between fecundity and poverty very early in life: speaking of the town where she was born the sixth of eleven surviving children to a tubercular mother, she writes:

> Along the river flats lived the factory workers, chiefly Irish; on the heights above the rolling clouds of smoke that belched from the chimneys lived the owners and executives. The tiny gardens of the former were asprawl with

children; in the gardens on the hills only two or three played. This contrast made a track in my mind. Large families were associated with poverty, toil, unemployment, drunkenness, cruelty, fighting, jails; the small ones with cleanliness, leisure, freedom, light, space, sunshine.[25]

Her mind, having taken this track, never abandoned it, despite the socialist propaganda she was exposed to during the years when she lived in New York with her first husband. She continued to believe that high fertility was the cause of poverty and oppression and, moreover, that despite the fact that she herself came from a very large family tainted with tuberculosis, that the fertile strains were genetically inferior and should be cut off. In 1920 she published her most successful book, *Women and the New Race*, a thoroughly orthodox eugenist tract, and followed it by *The Pivot of Civilisation* in which she argued against the provision of social services in the approved eugenic manner:

> Looked at impartially, this compensatory generosity is in its final effect probably more dangerous, more dysgenic, more blighting than the initial practice of profiteering and the social injustice which makes some too rich and others too poor.[26]

In 1926 she wrote in the *Birth Control Review*:

> There is only one reply to a request for a higher birthrate among the intelligent and that is to ask the government first to take the burden of the insane and feeble-minded from their back. Sterilisation for these is the solution.[27]

By 1939 she was so far gone in this kind of false reasoning that she boasted in her "autobiography" (actually written at her instigation and under her supervision by Rackham Holt and Walter S. Hayward):

> The eugenists wanted to shift the emphasis from less children for the poor to more children for the rich. We went back of that and sought first to stop the multiplication of the unfit. This appeared the most important and greatest step toward race betterment.[28]

If Sanger's approach seems a little crude, it must be understood in the general context of philanthropic thought in New York, where, in 1915, the *Medical Review of Reviews*

> selected several men from the bottom strata of life, gave each a banner to carry, and directed them to parade in the crowded districts of the city. The banners which these human wrecks held aloft did not bear the inspiring device Excelsior, but these large-lettered warnings:
>
> I AM A BURDEN TO MYSELF AND THE STATE. SHOULD I BE ALLOWED TO PROPAGATE?
> I HAVE NO OPPORTUNITY TO EDUCATE OR FEED MY CHILDREN. THEY MAY BECOME CRIMINALS.
> WOULD THE PRISONS AND ASYLUMS BE FILLED IF MY KIND HAD NO CHILDREN?
> I CANNOT READ THIS SIGN. BY WHAT RIGHT HAVE I CHILDREN?
> ARE YOU WILLING TO HAVE ME BRING CHILDREN INTO THE WORLD?

I MUST DRINK ALCOHOL TO SUSTAIN LIFE. SHALL I TRANSFER THE CRAVING TO OTHERS?

Thus was the question of birth control placed in the path of society.[29]

It is well known that the modern population-control movement traces its lineage back to such exalted beginnings, but there is a tendency to shrug off this kind of brutality as a kind of down-home directness or simplicity. The arrogance and cruelty of the people who designed this propaganda exercise are not less repulsive because they are disguised as cuteness. Family-planning propaganda has continued in the same tradition, in cartoons showing endless comic versions of starving black children, bombs in black women's pregnant bellies and so forth. Although socialists and libertarians and radicals of all kinds have believed in birth-control and worked for it, the cause remains a cause not of the left, but of the radical, ultra right.

Sanger soon discovered that her natural allies were not the idealist socialists like Rose Witcop, with whom she visited Germany in 1920. (Witcop was prosecuted in 1922 for keeping copies of *Family Limitation* in the house she shared with Guy Aldred; she went on to publish and distribute more than a hundred editions of it and to run her own clinic in Shepherd's Bush.[30]) She conveniently forgot what she owed to communists and syndicalists and preferred to stress her connections with the Malthusian League in England and in Holland, for she realised that power and visibility were to be gained from enlisting the support of the rich, principally her suitor, millionaire oilman J. Noah H. Slee who dumped a Roosevelt when she agreed to marry him, and her crony, Juliet Rublee, and also Clarence Gamble, George Brush, Frances Ackerman, Mrs Walter Timme, Mrs Thomas Hepburn, Kermit Roosevelt, Mrs Otto Kahn, Henry Morgenthau, Jr, Adolf Lewisohn, Mrs Thomas Lamont and their pals. No sooner did she gain access to big money, than she was already seeing herself as a world leader. In 1922 she made a trip to Japan, Korea and China, to introduce the Asians to her panacea for all ills, birth control; to Russia and India in 1935; to China and Japan again in 1937. Meanwhile the people who were really interested in developing reliable methods of family limitation and making them available to the people who needed them found Margaret Sanger as much of an obstacle as a help. On the one hand she was publicising the issue and winning a kind of respectability for the idea, but on the other she was so proprietary about the movement and so dishonest about what her clinics were doing and her own qualifications to be speaking to the issue that she managed to alienate the people who should have been her allies. It is fair to say that she opposed the professionalisation of the birth-control movement and sought to keep the matter within the control of individual clinics and out of the hands of the medical establishment, but she also created the sort of centralised visible organisation which could be taken over. By her own lack of professionalism and constitutional inability to cooperate or give credit where it was due, she helped to make some such takeover inevitable.[31]

In July 1915 Sanger lectured at the Fabian Hall under the auspices of the Malthusian League. The following is her own account of the way a palaeobotanist became the personification of the British birth-control movement:

> Many came up and talked to me afterwards, among them Marie Stopes, a palaeontologist who had made a reputation with work on coal. Would I come to her home and discuss the book she was writing?
>
> Over the teacups I found her to have a frank, open manner that quite won me. She took me into her confidence at once, stating her marriage had been unconsummated, and for that reason she was securing an annulment. Her book, *Married Love*, was based largely on her own experience and the unhappiness that came to people from ignorance and lack of understanding in wedlock, and she hoped it would help others. She was extremely interested in the correlation of marital success to birth-control knowledge, although she admitted she knew nothing about the latter. Could I tell her exactly what methods were used and how? In spite of my belief that the Netherlands clinics could be improved upon, I was fired with fervour for the idea as such, and described them as I had seen them.[32]

Thus, adroitly, does Sanger take the credit for Stopes' contribution to the birth-control propaganda explosion upon herself.

Marie Stopes was neither a revolutionary nor a feminist; she knew nothing of the sufferings of women compelled to bear a child every year, but she knew a great deal about the sufferings of women of ardent and artistic temperament yoked to men of little imagination. Sanger is quite correct in pointing out that *Married Love* was the direct result of Stopes' unconsummated union with her first husband, Reginald Ruggles Gates, which prompted her subsequent researches into human sexuality and in particular the marriage relation. Incurably "romantic" and pretentious, she mixed with the sexual feminism of Ellen Key the sex idealism of Edward Carpenter, whom she visited in 1916 at Millthorpe where he lived with his lover, George Merrill. Carpenter convinced her of the "purity" of her endeavour, and wrote to her in May 1916 making a shrewd observation:

> You certainly get in a lot of important points – menstruation, positions, ejaculation without penetration, birth control, insemination – which will terrify Mrs Grundy; but she, poor thing, is in a very moribund condition already, so the book will only hasten her end.[33]

If Mrs Grundy was on her death-bed, Edward Carpenter might have prided himself in helping to drive her there, for his *Love's Coming of Age* (1896) was a seminal text of popular sex religion. Stopes was to bring the cult of a few into the ken of the many in a way that had been impossible for Carpenter, who had carefully shielded his Uranian lifestyle from the limelight. The strong streak of exhibitionism in her nature, together with the obvious facts that she was attractive and "normal" and female, fitted her uniquely for the calling of sex prophetess which she took to with a will, as soon as the phenomenal success of *Married Love*, which went through five editions in its first year, convinced her that she had a mission. If Carpenter knew nothing of heterosexual relations, Stopes, who was thirty-six years old and *virgo intacta* when she wrote the book, knew little more. Some mythology she took over directly from Carpenter, notably the totally fanciful idea that women derive an essential health benefit from the absorption of some elements of the male ejaculate through the walls of the vagina.[34] The idea would be no more than an intriguing speculation if only the early birth-controllers had not used it to condemn the use of the condom, which was one of the few reliable methods available.

In *Married Love* Stopes confined herself to very vague remarks about family limitation; indeed, of her conference with Sanger a mere paragraph was made:

> It should be realised that all the proper, medical methods of controlling pregnancy consist, not in destroying an already growing embryo, but in preventing the male sperm from reaching the unfertilised egg-cell. This may be done either by shutting the sperms away from the opening of the womb, or by securing the death of *all* (instead of the natural death of all but *one*) of the two to six hundred million sperms which enter the woman . . . To kill quickly the ejaculated sperms which would otherwise die and decompose naturally is a simple matter. Their minute and uncovered bodies are plasmolised in weak acid, such as vinegar and water, or by a solution of quinine, or by many other substances.[35]

The assumption that the "proper" methods of controlling fertility are "medical" is nicely calculated to fit in with Stopes' use of technical vocabulary in the midst of all the froth of her breathy celebration of human union, which sometimes obscures much that is purely speculative, such as Stopes' theory about periodicity in the female sex urge. The technical vocabulary shields her from the suspicion of coarseness while the embroidery with which she cloaks her exposition is as falsely genteel as a daintily crooked little finger: of female desire she writes:

> Welling up in her are the wonderful tides, scented and enriched by the myriad experiences of the human race from its ancient days of leisure and flower-wreathed love-making, urging her to transports and to self-expressions, were the man but ready to take the first step in the initiative or to recognise and welcome it in her. Seldom dare any woman, still more seldom dare a wife, risk the blow at her heart which would be given were she to offer charming love-play to which the man did not respond.[36]

Such stuff is clearly adjusted to middle-class taste: the general assumption was that upper-class women were more spiritual than their working-

class counterparts, and certainly ladies of leisure would have more
sympathy with Stopes' vision of the fiction of the Golden Age than less
dandified souls would feel. Over lusty human desires Stopes threw a veil
of rainbow-tinted aestheticism which was to become another problem for
those desirous of controlling fertility. On the one hand, manuals of contraceptive practice described absurd and unwieldy contraptions involving
rubber sheets and enema syringes, and on the other the sex religionists
demanded the pretence of utter spontaneity, helpless yielding to the overwhelming gush of the sex-tide. Moreover, Stopes set about adding to
the weight of prejudice building up against *coitus interruptus*:

> It oftens happens nowadays that, dreading the expense and the physical strain
> of child-bearing for his wife, the husband practises what is called *coitus inter-
> ruptus* – that is, he withdraws just before the ejaculation, but when he is already
> so stimulated that the ejaculation has become involuntary ... This practice,
> while it may have saved the woman from the anguish of bearing unwanted
> children, is yet very harmful to her, and is to be deprecated. It tends to leave
> the woman in "mid-air" as it were; to leave her stimulated and unsatisfied
> and therefore it has a very bad effect on her nerves and general health, par-
> ticularly if it is done frequently. The woman too, loses the advantage (*and I
> think it is difficult to overstate the physiological advantage*) of the partial absorption
> of the man's secretions, which *must* take place through the large tract of internal
> epithelium with which they come in contact.[37]

Difficult as it may be to overstate the importance of absorbing the male
secretions, Stopes may be said to have succeeded admirably. Her description of *coitus interruptus* is certainly correct, but her assumption that
it invariably involves leaving the woman unsatisfied is completely unjusti-
fied, especially as she endorses the method of *coitus reservatus* described
by Dr Alice Stockham in her book *Karezza* as an alternative for the man
whose virility is not up to furnishing regular ejaculations. Thus the notion
grew up and was generally accepted that *coitus interruptus* and *coitus
reservatus* were fundamentally contrasting kinds of sexual interaction, one
nasty, brutish and short, the other saintly, artful and long.[38] At the time
of writing Stopes had no experience of either, but she was not one to
learn from her own experience, or to consult the experience of others.
Letters from the sexually suffering flooded her life and fed her conviction
that she had a sacred mission. She assumed that they came from a cross-
section of the community, although such a conclusion is hardly justifiable,
and she attempted to flesh out the picture by issuing questionnaires to
members of various professional groups, including 2,000 protestant
ministers of religion. None of the small proportion who replied was living
in a state of satisfactory sexual adjustment; some, possibly exhibitionists,
laid claim to the most extraordinary activities, such as seeking manual
relief from an elderly female cook.

Six months after *Married Love* burst on to the literary scene, Stopes contributed a "practical sequel", *Wise Parenthood*, dedicated to "all who wish to see our race grow in strength and beauty. The sales of both were to amount to almost two million in thirty years. Already, in 1918, Stopes had adopted a distinctly eugenic stance, perhaps partly as an alternative system of morality which would make her more acceptable to the establishment than the socialist and Malthusian groups which had preceded her into the field of birth-control propaganda, but also out of deep personal conviction. In 1919, she contributed an article entitled "Mrs Jones Does Her Worst" to the *Daily Mail*. Its theme was the by-now familiar argument that society has no worse enemy that the hyperfertile C3 mother, but even the most fervent supporters of stringent eugenic measures could hardly have welcomed the intemperance of Stopes' language.

> Are these puny-faced, gaunt, blotchy, ill-balanced, feeble, ungainly, withered children the young of an imperial race? Why has Mrs Jones had nine children six died, one defective? Nor is it for Mrs Jones to take the initiative. Isn't it for the leisured, the wise, to go to her and tell her what are the facts of life, the meaning of what she is doing, and what she ought to do? ... *Mrs Jones is destroying the race!*[39]

In 1922 Stopes, whose delusions of grandeur had already become a problem, took it upon herself to canvas the House of Commons, asking them to sign the following statement:

> I agree that the present position of breeding chiefly from the C3 population and burdening and discouraging the A1 is nationally deplorable, and if I am elected to Parliament I will press the Ministry of Health to give such scientific information through the Ante-natal Clinics, Welfare Centres and other institutions in its control as will curtail the C3 and increase the A1.[40]

Some of the replies which were sent to the Society for Constructive Birth Control and Racial Progress at 61 Marlborough Road N.19, were very perceptive and amusing but they did not suffice to check Stopes' fanaticism. In 1924, having received a letter from the deaf father of deaf children, she wrote to the Superintendent of the school where he had been educated in brutal terms.

> I should be much obliged if you would tell me how it came about that two persons educated at [the Royal Association in Aid of the Deaf and Dumb] were permitted to marry and bring forth children, all of whom are still more imperfect and a burden on the country ... Do you think it advisable that two defectives, both brought up at public expense, should be permitted to produce four defectives to be brought up at public expense and where is this geometrical progression to stop?[41]

In his reply the Rev. Alfred Smith asked her if she would recommend

the installation of a lethal chamber. As the years passed Stopes' intolerance
of genetic defect became even more violent: the Joint Committee on
Voluntary Sterilisation rejected her uninvited offer of help in 1935, on
the ground that she was too extreme. A Jewish reporter from the *Australian
Women's Weekly* described her attitude to miscegenation with remarkable
restraint:

> Somehow we wandered on to sterilisation on which the Doctor has most interest-
> ing and ardent opinions. She believes that all half-castes should be sterilised
> at birth. Thus painlessly and in no way interfering with the individual's life,
> the unhappy fate of he (*sic*) who is neither black nor white is prevented from
> being passed on to the unborn babes.[42]

When her son went against his mother's firm intention to choose his
wife for him, and married Mary Barnes Wallis who wore spectacles, Stopes
refused to recognise her daughter-in-law.

> The essential is health in a potential mother and she has an inherited disease
> of the eyes which not only makes her wear hideous glasses so that it is horrid
> to look at her, but the awful curse will carry on and I have the horror of our
> line being so contaminated and little children with the misery of glasses ...
> Mary and Harry are quite callous about both the wrong to their children, the
> wrong to my family and the eugenic crime.[43]

When she died she left the freehold of the house at 108 Whitfield Street,
where she hoped her clinic would continue to be conducted, to the Eugenics
Society, which set up and administered the Marie Stopes Memorial
Foundation. The surplus income generated by the clinic practice is "made
available for the general purposes of the Eugenics Society". The Marie
Stopes Memorial Foundation, alias the Eugenics Society, pioneered the
training of "overseas nurses" in modern contraceptive methods, as well as
being the first to provide contraceptive advice to the unmarried, sex
counselling and vasectomy, as part of the Society's practice of "crypto-
eugenics".[44] In 1976 the clinic was taken over by Population Services
International to become, some thought, an abortion clinic on the same
assembly-line model as the PSI clinics in the United States. The new
director, Jan Bumstead, with a degree in social psychology, family, sex
and social roles from "Cambridge, Massachusetts", aimed to "reach out to
men and women who find it difficult to get appointments at family-
planning clinics ... new techniques of birth control will be investigated."
Among the matters investigated were post-coital "contraception" and
sterilisation. In protest over the all-comers approach to sterilisation, Lady
Brook, who had enthusiastically accepted the position of chairman of the
clinic under its new management, and Peter Huntingford, one of the
directors, both resigned.[45]

Marie Stopes' supremacist delusions hardly mattered as long as the
public was able to exploit them for its own ends. The fight to make
methods of family limitation both acceptable and reliable is worth fighting

even if some of the leaders of the campaign are paranoid. However, complacency about the ultimate effect of Stopery may be ill-founded. Her
high visibility, her blind dogmatism, her refusal to undertake systematic
analysis of her own practice, her palpable dishonesty and vulgarity and
her unscientific crankery, posed problems with which her colleagues in
the movement had to cope, without the consolation of personal adulation
and the income from perennial best-sellers. Given the relative success of the
Malthusian League and the spread of contraceptive information through
books like Besant's and Allbutt's, to which were soon added more matter-
of-fact discussions like those by Norman Haire and Courtenay Beale
among others, the public was in a fair way to gain access to birth-control
information long before Stopes pulled off her most spectacular self-
promotion stunt, the libel suit against Halliday Sutherland.[46] Her enemy
was a representative of a minority group which had always excited English
intolerance, namely, the Catholics. By representing herself as persecuted
by Romish might, Stopes won over the last unwilling Protestant opponents
of her rhapsodic sex religion. She had been quick to point out that Besant
and Bradlaugh had arranged their own persecution for political reasons;
her own motives were more complex. She was hypersensitive to criticism
and obsessional about self-vindication, as well as exhibitionistic to a
degree. An occult desire to cause a stir can be the only motive for including inflammatory material like the gratuitous discussion of artificial
insemination in *Married Love*, which she justified on the palpably absurd
ground that Marion Piddington, who wrote a book on the subject called
Scientific Motherhood, was the wife of an eminent Australian and her wish
to be included in Stopes' book could not be set aside.[47]

Stopes would have done less harm if she had confined herself to
panegyrical sermons on sex-love and left the delivery of contraceptive
services to more qualified agencies but in May 1918 she married
Humphrey Verdon Roe, a rich man who had already tried to finance a
birth-control clinic at St Mary's Hospital in Manchester. The marriage
settlement was handsome, £20,000 and "a further £10,000 for the further-
ance of birth control". Other matters, a pregnancy and a stillbirth, and
a pamphlet circulated among the Bishops at the Lambeth Conference,
which purported to be a divinely inspired message to them to accept birth-
control, supervened.[48] Meanwhile *The Malthusian* reconciled itself to the
necessity of providing practical assistance in birth planning. In 1920
Margaret Sanger, who had been arrested for opening a clinic in Brownsville, New York, in October 1916, reminded them that they had not got
Comstock Laws to contend with:

> What is the reason that clinics are not established here? At a meeting at
> Cambridge on May 20th, I was urged to begin preliminaries at once for a clinic
> in a large provincial town.[49]

Stopes was present at the meeting chaired by Edith How-Martyn; so were Alice Vickery and Stella Browne; the moment was ripe for a collaboration, but the Stopes–Roe combination was determined to go it alone. When the Mothers' Clinic was opened in March 1921, *The Malthusian* gave a generous account of the fact, printing its full address and the full list of its patrons; the next number carried a glowing account of the public meeting in the Queen's Hall, called to publicise the venture and to set up the Society for Constructive Birth Control. Margaret Sanger was back in London and *The Malthusian* announced:

> It is absolutely determined that we open a really model maternity and child welfare clinic early in October and in a district central to this winter's central practical campaign.[50]

Thus the good people of London were faced with a divided birth-control establishment preaching different methods of contraception; both sides lost no opportunity to attack the competition.

Stopes' opposition to the Malthusians was rendered more irrational and intransigent by her bitter hostility to their friend and champion, Margaret Sanger. At the time of Sanger's return to face prosecution for *Family Limitation* in 1915, Stopes had organised a letter of petition to President Wilson, signed by such luminaries as Arnold Bennett and H. G. Wells, for which Sanger, although she describes the letter in her second autobiography as "invaluable", strangely forgot to thank her – or, in her first autobiography, even to acknowledge her. Moreover, she had taken a copy of *Married Love* to be published in America, not, as she later claimed, by herself, but by Dr William J. Robinson, who, in an unsuccessful attempt to avoid prosecution, made certain changes in it. Furious at the mangling of her work Stopes published an unexpurgated version under the title *Man and Wife: A Study of Successful Marriage*. Legal proceedings against Robinson, President of the Medical Board of Bronx Hospital Dispensary, dragged on for two years; he was sentenced to a fine of $250 or thirty days' imprisonment; an appeal failed. Stopes refused any support, moral or financial. Thereafter neither she nor Sanger had anything good to say about each other, and missed no opportunity to hinder each other's work. The estrangement affected the American movement almost as much as the estrangement between Stopes and the Malthusians affected the English movement, for Mary Ware Dennett, Director of the Voluntary Parenthood League of New York, one of the organisations instrumental in getting pro-birth-control legislation passed in the United States, was a loyal supporter of Stopes, telling Robinson that she was "shocked at the contemptuous and abusive language" published in the *Birth Control Review* with regard to Dr Stopes. Robinson replied rather tartly that Stopes' "interest in birth control is not that of a humanitarian, but of a bourgeoise who is afraid that she will have to pay higher 'rates' if there are too many poor children in the country." He might have said the same thing with equal justice of Sanger herself.[51]

It was very important to Stopes, if rather less important to her clients, that her clinic was the first ever set up in the British Empire, as every number of *Birth Control News*, the monthly organ of the Society for Constructive Birth Control (usually referred to as the CBC) announced. Occasionally the great lady permitted herself to forget Sanger's doomed effort in Brownsville, and the fifty or so Dutch clinics, and Anna Martin's self-help scheme in Rotherhithe, and informed the unwary that hers was the first real birth-control clinic in the world. In fact the clinic was no more than Nurse Hebbes fitting Lambert's cervical caps; the first gross of them, donated free, went quite a long way, for by the end of 1921 the clinic had seen only 518 clients, 47 of whom were "looking for help in becoming pregnant."[52]

Stopes' ideal contraceptive, the small, all-rubber cap, was designed to fit snugly over the cervix when suction had been created by pressing it firmly into place. The fitting was necessarily done on the woman in the lithotomy position, but the woman had to be taught to insert the device "half-sitting on her heels and leaning forward" and the device had to be checked to see if she had inserted it correctly.[53] Such a procedure could be relatively laborious and especially difficult for a male physician who was not accustomed to patients who hopped about in embarrassing positions. Stopes, despite her own natural inclination to roughshod dictatorship, was very keen that the medical establishment should not take over a procedure which was so cheap and simple, but her own obscurantist tactics were a principal cause of the institutionalisation of birth-control and the creation of a vast money-spinning contraceptive drug empire. Cervical damage was so common in women who had borne several children that Stopes ought to have been aware that the small check pessary would not always provide protection; there were other kinds of pessaries – indeed, a multitude of them, with air rims, double ridges, with sponges attached, and some which approached the form of the diaphragm. Physicians themselves were confused; Sir James Barr, who gave evidence at the Stopes–Sutherland trial, was not sure if the cap was meant to fit snugly against the walls of the vagina or not (as in fact it was not).[54] An even more serious confusion concerned the length of time the check pessary should be left in. Medical men voiced their concern that the cervical cap would bottle up the secretions of a diseased womb, thus creating a serious health hazard.[55] Stopes was not interested in the diseased womb; neither she nor Nurse Hebbes had any way of diagnosing uterine infection apart from the obvious symptoms, but the gynaecologists she chose to follow were convinced, correctly it seems, that secretions from the womb would simply well up in the cap and break the suction, so the cap would fall out. They did not have the courage of their convictions however, and agreed that the cap should not be left in for longer then twenty-four hours, thus actually compromising its effectiveness as a contraceptive, for sperm can live in the vaginal tract for much longer than twenty-four hours. The women who trusted Stopes and her minions to find them a way out of this morass would have done better to trust other women who had used rubber occlusive devices effectively and follow their direct "non-scientific" instructions. Of all the substances which Stopes recommended as spermicides over the years, none was effective and some would have actually increased the motility of the sperms; by insisting on the use of soluble pessaries with the cervical cap she once again compromised their efficiency and shortened the life of the device, an important consideration for women for whom three shillings was a considerable expenditure in addition to the high cost of the soluble pessaries themselves. Stopes' mailbag brought a significant number of complaints from people who had followed instructions to the letter without success, but she always found some grounds for making the pregnancy her clients' fault and not the fault of the method.[56]

Once she had chosen her method she clung to it, in the face of all opposition, claiming that the records of her first 5,000 cases revealed the highest success rate of any form of birth-control ever devised.[57] In fact, the clinic kept very *ad hoc* records with no provision for follow-up. The service was free; women for whom the cap did not work could hardly come back to create a disturbance. Instead they visited qualified gynaecologists and abortionists who got a very different impression of the reliability of the cervical cap, or small Mensinga pessary, as a result. They preferred to fit the diaphragm or large Mensinga pessary. Stopes' exaggerated claims for the cap, which she claimed to have "improved" until accusations of experimentation on the poor prompted discretion, discredited her efforts in the eyes of those who should have been her comrades.

One such was Norman Haire; born Norman Zions in Australia or New Zealand, he had come to England in 1919 and set up practice as a gynaecologist with a professional interest in contraception. Haire was not distracted by any messianic complex; he meant to provide the best contraceptive advice possible to anyone who could pay for it, and to some who could not. He was never popular among the reformers, all of whom found something to dislike, his fleshy body, his Jewishness, his homosexuality, or his interest in money, but he became a respected figure in Harley Street and at international conferences. When the Malthusian League opened their model clinic at Walworth, Haire took the job of medical director, but in no time he had transformed it from a free clinic for the poor to the headquarters of his private practice. In Haire's clinic the examination of individuals requesting contraceptives was carried out by a doctor, the cases were properly worked up and analysed in something resembling the modern "cafeteria" approach, attempting to suit the method to the patient profile. He visited Stopes' clinic when it first opened and she asked him to investigate the gold pin pessary. He did as she asked, but found from his enquiries that the pin, which was an intrauterine device, could cause septic abortion and pelvic infection, and wrote to Stopes advising her of the fact. Either she did not read the letter or she did not heed the contents for on 8 June 1921 she sent him two patients in order to have the device inserted. He did not comply and wrote to her again, explaining why he would not do it. Stopes replied in a manner which makes clear her utter disregard for the rights of others and her total ignorance of the code of ethics which binds those doctors who deal with living human flesh instead of fossil plants.

> I should like very much for you, if you do not mind, to take on two or three cases, which you should watch carefully, and if these yielded unsatisfactory results we would then drop it.[58]

Haire was of a placatory disposition; he revealed these dealings only because he had no choice. He had been summoned *sub poena* to give evidence in the Stopes–Sutherland libel case. The more discriminating of Stopes' supporters were appalled at what the trial revealed and concerned when she went on to appeal against the verdict and then to take the matter to the House of Lords. The proceedings cost her a fortune which in terms of self-promotion might have been considered money well spent, but for her co-workers in the family planning movement Stopes' extreme visibility was to prove more of a problem than a blessing. Stopes lost no opportunity to vilify her colleagues and to announce that the methods they recommended were "criminally harmful, needlessly expensive or commercially pushed, but not one of them is physiologically sound."[59] The cervical cap is a better contraceptive than the diaphragm, according to the small sample of women I have been able to interview who have used both, but few who read Stopes on the subject would have been convinced. In the violence of her attack on the competition, Stopes quite forgot how much she owed to the Malthusian League. The Honorary Secretary, Dr Binnie Dunlop, had introduced her to Humphrey Verdon Roe as a potential backer for *Married Love*. He was best man at her wedding. Dr Alice Vickery had given her a considerable collection of birth-control literature. When the CBC began to issue its own monthly in 1922, it soon became obvious that almost all the items were either admiring accounts of Marie Stopes written by herself under pseudonyms or by her endlessly complaisant husband, or attacks on those who threatened her absolute sovereignty of the family-planning movement. As Samkins Browne she wrote in July 1922.

> An American controller writes, "it is amusing indeed to read that you have been told by one of Margaret Sanger's devoted admirers that Dr Stopes is the

source of all the trouble in the birth-control movement. Margaret has apparently gotten into the habit of saying that about anyone whose efforts annoy her by their success. It is one of her most frequent remarks in this country about some-one else. Let us not take her seriously." Right oh! – so long as the world shares with us a realisation that *it is only Mrs Sanger's little way!*[60]

The use of Society funds and the Society's name to publish such personal animosity under a pseudonym is actually quite shocking. Sanger's supporters, who included some of the most influential figures with any understanding of the issues, were disgusted.

When the CBC refused to support Sanger in the defence of her pamphlet *Family Limitation* in America, Bertrand Russell wrote sharply to Stopes:

> I learn that the CBC has decided not to support the defence of Margaret Sanger's pamphlet. I very much regret this decision as the pamphlet seems to me admirable. Under the circumstances I have reluctantly come to the decision that I must sever my connection with the CBC as by remaining I should seem to condone this inaction.[61]

Eventually Russell and H. G. Wells, two of the most influential vice-presidents of the CBC, did indeed resign. The office-bearers of the CBC were not meant to interest themselves actively in what Stopes was doing; still less were they expected to offer advice, and under no circumstances criticism. The medical men who were also vice-presidents, like Sir Arbuthnot Lane and Sir James Barr, had only the dimmest idea of how the clinic operated or what it did. Despite all Stopes' obscurantism and bellicosity, the other birth-controllers continued trying vainly to work with her. In 1923 the possibility of amalgamation of all the independent clinics under a single banner was discussed, but Stopes, while appearing to accept the initial proposal, eventually made it quite clear that the only role she would play would be that of unquestioned leader – if things were done her way. The job of assembling reliable information about contraceptives devolved on the National Birth Rate Commission set up by the National Council of Public Morals, which was actually opposed to artificial checks in principle, but almost by default its Medical Committee did a better job than could have been expected. Stopes, who had covered herself with ridicule from the scientific community by publishing totally unsystematic analyses of her first 5,000 cases, refused to give evidence.[62] The investigation revealed, among much that was interesting and important, that little progress could be made on the basis of so much opinion and so little evidence. Some kind of control was needed in order to establish investigative procedures of large samples of people using contraception. With 25,000 cases treated in his private practice the unpopular Norman Haire was the *de facto* expert; meanwhile the questioners discovered that the two clinics functioning in London "use different methods and both claim success ... and also point to the fallacy of the other method."[63] In the interests of the public something had to be done; the medical profession decided, as much in enlightened self-interest as for humanitarian motives, that it had to take control of family planning. Needless to say, Stopes, who became hysterical when she was excluded from medical panels at birth-control conferences because she had no medical training, opposed every attempt to systematise and analyse contraceptive use in the public interest. In too many cases her personal prestige and influence dissuaded eminently qualified individuals from cooperating in investigations. Opposition to her hardened; her paranoid delusions of jealous persecution began to be justified, as the people who had generously helped her one by one turned against her.

When the attitude of the Ministry of Health to family planning changed in 1930, the birth-control proponents saw their chance. At a meeting at the house of Lord Denman, Stopes proposed that a National Birth Control Council be established, the motion was duly seconded and the Council came into being under the presidency of the King's Physician, Lord Horder, with John Maynard Keynes, Wells and Russell among those serving.[64] Stopes soon found that the Council would not dance to her tune, for it included representatives of the Society for the Provision of Birth Control Clinics who ran three clinics in London, as well as others in Cambridge, Manchester, Glasgow, Aberdeen, Oxford and Wolverhampton, and of the Workers' Birth Control Group, for whom twenty Labour MPs as well as Wells, Russell, Stella Browne, Frida Laski and Ruth Dalton had been working for the past six years. The impetus to the Ministry decision had probably come from Labour member Ernest Thurtle's repeated attempts (despite Stopes' fervent discouragement)[65] to get a bill passed in the house, and the major conference held in the Central Hall Westminster on the subject of "Birth Control by Public Health Authorities" under the chairmanship of Eva Hubback. That Stopes was chosen to propose the motion to set up the National Birth Control Council was probably both a courtesy and an attempt to avoid her inevitable opposition: she lasted as a member of the Council, which became the National Birth Control Association in 1931, until November 1933. Thereafter she lost no opportunity to vilify it and its members.[66]

Actually, Stopes had never been more than a sideshow in the birth-control movement, an extremely visible and entertaining sideshow, but a sideshow nevertheless. Perhaps it was an unqualified good that so much media attention was focused on what spouses did in bed, but it was also a symptom of the diminishing privacy of the individual and the increasing interference in the family by bureaucratic entities, first the family-planning societies and then the health services. The creed as taught by Stopes, who had succeeded in reducing two husbands to impotence and guilt in remarkably short order,[67] was spurious, based on a fantasy of what human sexuality is and could be, but even those who were most hampered by her antics continued to aver that her propagandist activities brought more people happiness than any writing had ever done before. If this is indeed so, then human kind cannot demand very much reality or logic or elegance in its prescriptions. The Stopesian wife is a rapacious geisha, the Stopesian husband a catspaw. The verdict of history, which has been harsh on Havelock Ellis and has yet to deal with Edward Carpenter, must be to find the Stopes phenomenon embarrassing, if not downright disastrous. A correct re-evaluation would involve systematic follow-up of the women who attended the CBC clinics while Stopes was still running them; my own haphazard investigations have indicated that the CBC produced a great deal more than its fair share of expensive abortions and unwanted babies.

Among those who served on the Birth Control Council in 1930 are some familiar names; our old friends the eugenists, Major Darwin, C. P. Blacker and Julian Huxley were in at the beginning, which ought not to surprise us, for in 1935 Lord Horder became President of the Eugenics Society, a position he held for the next thirteen years.

The cooperation of the eugenists was essential to the development of institutionalised birth-control because they alone had the unique combination of statistical skills together with the basic assumptions which underlay the whole attempt. The object was not simply to lower the birth-rate, but to lower the birthrate of the lower classes. The groups run by socialists and liberals insisted that their motivation was first concern for the health of the child, second concern for the health of the mother, third happiness in marriage and fourth making available to the poor the means of control over their fertility already successfully deployed by the ruling class. The Malthusians were primarily concerned with numbers, believing in the Malthusian hypothesis as perpetually self-verifying. The eugenists had a clearer idea of what they wanted, for their interest was primarily in social control. They would eliminate the apparently haphazard in human affairs by trimming out differential fertility and protecting the higher orders of humanity from the inevitable consequences of their own sub-fecundity. The idealists would provide the rhetoric; the eugenists would concentrate on devising the means of control. There would be no more talk of killing sperms with vinegar and salad oil. Dr Blacker took it upon himself to persuade Dr John Baker, an Oxford biologist, to continue the work of the American Michael Guyer (an eugenist) in developing spermotoxins.

> Dr Blacker had to awaken Dr Baker's imagination and to show him that this particular piece of new enquiry was certain to have world-wide social consequences. ... The final choice was a salt of mercury-phenylmercuric acetate.

The mythology had evidently changed. Where once the vaginal walls were exquisitely sensitive to miraculous health-dealing substances in the male ejaculate and absorbed them for the benefit of the whole organism, they were now assumed to be impervious to the products of a decomposing mercuric salt. The altruistic doctors decided that no profit was to accrue to the NBCA from the manufacture and sale of "Volpar" as it was called, a contraction of "voluntary parenthood". The eugenists knew that it had to be sold cheaply for the target was, as it had always been, the fecund poor. The idealistic women who did the donkey-work of the association were the ones who persuaded British Drug Houses to sell the product at prices "the absolute lowest that would allow the firm to trade with the smallest trading profit that was practical." Even a modest profit from Volpar would have financed the NBCA, but there were other priorities. Well might the British Drug Houses' representative cry in disbelief, "Ladies, *ladies, do* you understand what you are doing?"[68] When capitalist society refrains from making profits, it is as well to inquire into its motives. Volpar was eventually withdrawn from the market for reasons which were never made public.

The same close identification between eugenics and birth control can be seen in the development of the American birth-control establishment, admirably summarised by Linda Gordon in *Woman's Body, Woman's Right: A Social History of Birth Control in America.* The eugenists Lothrop Stoddard and C. C. Little both served on the board of Sanger's American Birth Control League; Guy Irving Burch wrote for the *Birth Control Review.*

> In planning the First National Birth Control Conference in November, 1921, Sanger had made an active attempt to recruit support from academics and scientists in particular. He won endorsement from ... Irving Fisher, Edward A. Ross, Ellsworth Huntington, Warren Thompson, F. H. Giddings, Thomas Nixon Carver and Raymond Pearl – all eugenists.[69]

The step from promoting eugenics and crypto-eugenics at home to population planning on a global scale is a short one. The poor are all too often distinguished from the rich not only by levels of consumption, but also by colour, language and religion. The eugenists had all been interested in immigration, which showed all too plainly that the poor beyond the national frontier were likely to become the poor within it. The attempt to curtail their expansionism was the simplest extension of the domestic eugenic policy. In America the professional expertise of the eugenists who pioneered the keeping of statistics on human populations was stiffened by the financial support of the huge corporations which could not fail to be interested in accumulating the knowledge of how to make the world safe for their own kind.

It now seems strange that men who had been conspicuous in the eugenics movement were able to move quite painlessly into the population establishment at the highest level, but if we reflect that the paymasters – Ford, Mellon, DuPont, Standard Oil, Rockefeller and Shell – are still the same, we can only assume that people like Kingsley Davis, Frank W.

Notestein, C. C. Little, E. A. Ross, the Osborns Frederick and Fairfield, Philip M. Hauser, Alan Guttmacher and Sheldon Segal were being rewarded for past services. The Population Reference Bureau, which had begun life collecting data for the racist Guy Burch's campaign against Non-Aryan immigration, simply expanded its field of operations and began issuing the *Population Bulletin* which still keeps people up to date on the precise degree of US population increase caused by immigration, legal and illegal. Frederick Osborn need have feared no conflict of interests when he set up the Population Council "at the initiative of John D. Rockefeller III" in 1952.[70] The sterilisation campaign mounted by the Population Council in Colombia in the mid-sixties was as eugenic as he could have wished, for the incentives offered were such as would only have been effective with the very poor and unsuspecting. The Council has area offices in Mexico City, Bangkok and Cairo. The Population Association of America, founded to "promote the improvement, advancement and progress of the human race by means of research with respect to problems connected with human population *in both its quantitative and qualitative aspects*" (my italics) was run by eugenists.[71] The International Planned Parenthood Federation was dreamed up by Margaret Sanger, whose ambitions had always been to be the recognised world leader of birth control and financed initially by the Brush Foundation and the Osborns. Its headquarters were at the Eugenics Society offices in Eccleston Square. Lord Horder and C. P. Blacker served as directors.

As long as the mass of the population was unaware of the population question, the power wielded by these individuals was limited; in the 1960s the threat of over-population was thrust to the forefront of Western consciousness by the kind of propaganda campaign that had previously been used only to create massive fortunes by marketing inessentials. The campaign was largely the work of one man, whose name is not yet a household word.

The story of the institutionalisation of family planning and the concomitant development of the zillion-dollar anti-fecundity industry is too long and too complex to be more than sketched in this chapter of this book. The fecundity of the working class gradually declined to match that of the privileged classes as, gradually, the conviction that the right to control one's fertility was a fundamental human right grew in the minds of the public, but such control was not to be exercised by sexual restraint or by choosing certain kinds of sexual intercourse. It could only be done with the help of the medical and pharmaceutical establishment. If manufactured contraceptive drugs and appliances were to be reliable they had to be tested on wide samples of people and over long periods: only the biggest drug houses had the funds and facilities to do the work. The local family firms that had supplied the markets with pessaries and rubber goods were swallowed up or went under; the multinational chemical combines took over an expanding market with limitless possibilities. Once contraceptive use had saturated a stable population, new users had to be found: if enough money could be made from the home market, contraceptive supply to developing markets could be subsidised. If governments would accept the need for aggressive marketing of contraceptive hardware, more and better subsidies would be available. The piddling activities of the Stopeses and the Sangers and their radical, liberal, upper-class, do-gooder friends, together with the muddled altruism of the socialists and the earnestness of the Malthusians, needed to join forces with the prestige and power of the biochemical establishment. If a set of crypto-eugenic priorities came with the package, they would be relatively easy to ignore in the momentum created by a streamlined and determined lobby which in less than a decade created a vast and intricate population cartel which pushed hundreds of millions of dollars back and forth across the world map.

One December afternoon in 1909, Hugh M. Moore burst into the New York office of Edgar L. Marston of Blair and Company, investment brokers, and startled him as he raised his coffee cup to his lips by saying urgently, "Do you know that it is very dangerous to drink out of the common drinking-cup?" Having thus created a scare, he produced his tranquilliser, the disposable *paper* cup. Marston was quick to see the potential in the situation. With the health authorities on their side the manufacturers of disposable paper cups had a captive market. Perhaps it was not altogether coincidental that the medical officer in Moore's home state of Kansas had just informed the proprietors of the Pullman railroad that carried tubercular patients through Kansas on their way to sanatoria in Colorado that they had to discontinue providing common drinking glasses for thirsty passengers. Marston put up some of the initial capital of $200,000 himself, and secured some more from Graham of American Can Co. and the rest from Percy Rockefeller.[72] By the time 40,000,000 people were routinely using paper cups and littering them all over the United States, Moore was looking for new worlds to conquer; he set up a non-profit educational foundation called the Hugh Moore Fund for the promotion of peace, but its activities remained more or less intangible until Moore read *The Struggle for Survival* by William Vogt and suddenly saw his way clear before him. The truth of the Malthusian hypothesis struck him like a bombshell, propelling him, as his friend and co-director of the fund, Arnaud C. Marts, former president of Bucknell University, liked to say, "way ahead of the experts".[73]

The first step in curbing the growth of population was rather like the first step in creating a demand for paper cups: a scare had to be produced. The fund produced a pamphlet called *The Population Bomb* and began to circulate it among university campuses, high schools, radio stations and newspapers. When in 1968 a lepidopterist from Stanford clambered on to the bandwagon, he included opposite the title-page of his best-seller, this notice:

The words "The Population Bomb", selected as the title for this book, were first used in 1954 on the cover of a pamphlet issued by the Hugh Moore Fund. Annual editions of the pamphlet have been issued and widely distributed, totalling over two million copies. The terms "population bomb" and "population explosion" which are now in general circulation were first used in this pamphlet.[74]

What Dr Paul R. Ehrlich does not say is that the Hugh Moore Fund also aided the distribution of his book:[75] Moore's hagiographer, Lawrence Lader, does not explain how this was done or to what extent Ehrlich had Moore to thank for his book's rapid rise to the top of the best-seller lists.

The terminology of population panic was promoted by other means as well as by distribution of the pamphlet. Moore was quite candid about his intentions:

"Who among us," he liked to ask at meetings, "will start a CONFLAGRATION?"[76]

Arsonists are easy to find, especially for people with Moore's kind of money. By bringing selected individuals together, wining and dining them and pitching his sales talk, Moore built the population lobby. On 20 March 1960, at a banquet at the Princeton Inn in New Jersey, he launched the World Population Emergency Campaign. The seed money was provided by Moore and matched by Lamont DuPont Copeland. The campaign was to be run by Eugene R. Black, President of the World Bank, and the cotton magnate and former Under-Secretary of State, Will Clayton, Jr with General W. H. Draper, Jr and Marriner S. Eccles, former Secretary of the Treasury under Roosevelt (now of the Rockefeller Brothers' Fund), and Rockefeller Prentice. Such people were the architects of the pilot project which tested the oral contraceptive in Puerto Rico. They got the money for it from the mid-western tycoon, Joseph Sunnen.

General Draper was the chairman of the committee appointed by President Eisenhower to study the effectiveness of foreign aid. Moore worked on Draper to get his own man, Robert Cook, co-opted on to the committee and in 1959 the section of their report dealing with population was published, but Eisenhower was loth to bring such intimate personal concerns into the direct purview of the government and no official commitment to the idea of birthrate reduction was achieved during his administration. More public feeling had to be generated. On 9 June 1960 readers of the *New York Times* were mildly surprised to find a full-page advertisement, showing the US taxpayer struggling under a huge burden labelled "Foreign Aid": the *Readers' Digest* liked it so much that it was repeated as editorial. It is generally true to say that the buying of full-page advertisements sooner or later merits recognition in editorial and equally true to say that the advertisements are very unlikely to meet rebuttal in the same newspapers. It was a simple selling campaign and it took as its starting point the notion that we have encountered time and again as a motivation for the family-planning movement, the fantasy that the high fertility of the lower classes, in this case the poor beyond America's borders, is achieved at the cost of the sub-fertile hardworking affluent middle class. Nobody at the *New York Times* was about to point out that what was in the foreign aid bundle was mostly military aid, that little of what would be left if that was taken out was free, and that its general effect was to weaken recipient economies and perpetuate corrupt suzerainties. Moore's campaign worked on the paranoid delusion that the richest people in the world were being pillaged by the poor. Chuckleheaded generosity had to stop. It was time to get tough. Disaster, in one form or another, was imminent.

Moore's ballyhoo campaign courted disaster when it arranged a tribute for Margaret Sanger at the Waldorf-Astoria during the three-day emergency conference called by the Population Council in 1961. The guests of honour included, inevitably, Sir Julian Huxley, International Chairman of the conference, and Marriner Eccles and the Indian Ambassador. Far gone in Demerol dependency, the great lady nodded out during the introduction to her speech, and Alan Guttmacher, President of the Planned Parenthood Federation of America, was obliged to carry her upstairs and put her to bed.[77] She did not appear in public again, but the campaign went on acquiring momentum and respectability without her.

The June 9th advertisement was the first of a series, all featuring in the best traditions of the birth-control movement, the signatures of carefully selected influential and prestigious individuals, among them Frank W. Abrams, ex-chairman of Standard Oil, Henry Ittleson, Jr, chairman of CIT Financial Corporation and Nobel prizewinners Linus Pauling and William Shockley. That series was followed by another, featuring the signatures of Hermann Muller, Albert Sabin, Jonas Salk, Mark van Doren and Jacques Barzun. By 1966 the World Population Emergency Committee achieved its major goal, the securing of government support. President Johnson included a commitment to federal funding for birth control programmes at home and abroad in his State of the Union message:

> ... let us act on the fact that less than five dollars invested in population control is worth a hundred dollars invested in economic growth.

The wording was crude, the motivation embarrassingly clear, but consciences were less tender than they had been; the panic campaign had seen to that. In 1967 the provisions of the Social Security Act which apply to the administration of Aid to Families with Dependent Children in the United States were altered to

(1) require that at least six per cent of all funds available for maternal and child care to be earmarked for family planning; (2) direct all the states to offer family planning services to present, past and potential AFDC recipients in an effort to reduce illegitimate births and corral welfare expenses; (3) establish a ceiling over the proportion of children under 18 who could qualify for AFDC in any state; (4) authorise states to purchase family planning services from non-governmental providers; (5) provide matching federal grants to the states for family planning.[78]

The extent of the commitment to lowering the birthrate of the poor can be estimated from the fact that for each dollar the state governments came up with the Federal Government was pledged to provide $9 in matching funds. However, Moore and his cronies were not the only lobby to get the President's ear; war broke out between them and the Catholics, a public-relations battle which is always decided in favour of the "progressives" who are seen as the representatives of a reasonable majority against a bigoted minority. Moreover, news of the faster growth rate of the black American population was being fed to the media by another of Moore's signatories, the demographer Philip Hauser.[79] Planned Parenthood received a considerable injection of funds from the industrialist Arnold Maremont, as a result of his experience as chairman of the Illinois Public Aid Commission which convinced him that sterilisation should be offered to welfare recipients at state expense. There was little chance of gaining acceptance for the idea in a state controlled by Catholic interests but Mayor Daley himself suggested that Maremont practise crypto-eugenics by giving money to Planned Parenthood.

> Planned Parenthood representatives now toured the maternity wards routinely in quest of clients ... Partly as a result the number of births in the charity hospital declined from 20,000 in 1963 to 12,000 in 1969.[80]

While Moore was lobbying for funding for population programmes in the third world, legislators were arranging for population limitation among the poor, the Latin American and the black communities. Tax-supported birth control programmes had appeared in the South, in North Carolina for example as early as 1937, but in the late sixties they began to proliferate. A Moore man, Paul H. Todd, Jr, took over as chairman of Planned Parenthood/World Population: when Burch died, his place as chairman of the Population Reference Bureau was taken by a Moore man, Robert Cook, ex-editor of *The Journal of Heredity* and *Eugenical News*. He and his third wife, Annabel, parlayed the *Population Bulletin* into a chief source of newspaper scare stories about the population explosion. According to Lader, the job of Moore's old allies, Frank Abrams, Walter Bergman of the Lily-Tulip Cup Corporation, and Lawrence Wilkinson, Executive Vice-President of Continental Can Company, was to persuade the Ford Foundation and the Rockefeller Foundation to beef up the Population Council. From 1959, the budget was quadrupled. The Council opened its branch office in Bogotá where the first mass sterilisation campaign was mounted, and continues under the auspices of the Council to this day.

In 1964, Moore took over as President of the Human Betterment Association, and swiftly changed its name to the Association for Voluntary Sterilisation. He hired Brock Chisholm and H. Curtis Wood to give 110 lectures a year on the subject of sterilisation. At the end of 1966, the Departments of Health, Education and Welfare and Defense both announced their support for sterilisation as a method of family planning to be promoted in government programmes.

Bills were introduced in many state legislatures proposing mandatory sterilisation after a specified number of illegitimate pregnancies. Legislators in California, Connecticut, Delaware, Georgia, Illinois, Iowa, Louisiana, Maryland, Ohio, Tennessee, Mississippi, North Carolina and Virginia proposed a welfare cutoff unless mothers of two or more illegitimate children submitted to sterilisation. Other bills that were introduced but failed to pass would have provided cash incentives to welfare mothers who agreed to sterilisation ...[81]

Hugh Moore, through his ghost writer, Lawrence Lader, may well have overestimated his own role in motivating General Draper, who seems to have had pretty strong motivations and considerable resources of his own, but it would be very difficult to overestimate the importance of the change of orientation in the United States Agency for International Development.

In 1967 Congress added Title X, Programs Relating to Population Growth to the Foreign Assistance Act. Three individuals were particularly influential in facilitating this move: General Draper, who was ubiquitous on all matters relating to birth control; Reimert T. Ravenholt, the recently appointed director of AID's population activities; and Philander Claxton, the special assistant for population in the State Department. Together they formed a triangle linking the State Department, AID and the population control lobby, led by Draper. Not only did the bill pass and Congress authorise $35 million for population assistance, but the funds were earmarked for this sole purpose. The AID administrator objected to this decision, fearing that the agency could not properly spend $35 million on population in the time specified. But Draper prevailed then and later, and Ravenholt was given a secure base of funds that could not be diverted by the AID administration.[82]

"Ray" Ravenholt was an epidemiologist by training; he liked to say that he had been called in to deal with the "people epidemic". His conceptual apparatus was simple and striking; if US medical technology had caused the decline in the deathrate, thereby causing the population explosion then the same means would have to be used to redress the balance. The way to do that was by "inundation" with contraceptive and abortifacient technology, oral steroids, vacuum aspirator kits, condoms, to be bought with public funds and showered on the recipient countries for distribution by private enterprise at the village level, "Community Based Distribution" as it was known. Resources divided by population equalled well-being in Ravenholt's engagingly simple world, and he was "trying to lower the denominator in that equation". He was expert in persuading both Congress and the Agency administration that he needed more and more money; by 1973 the Office of Population of USAID had $125 million dollars to spend in a single year. One of the lines Ravenholt used to pitch was a version of the familiar threat that overpopulation leads to communism, but much more directly and crudely expressed. Population control was needed to maintain "the normal operation of US commercial interests around the world".[83] Many people who observed the spending spree had deep reservations about the effectiveness of the programs, but Ravenholt would produce a slew of graphs all showing what the population growth curve would have been without USAID and what in fact it was. Ravenholt was convinced that spreading family limitation was simply a matter of marketing; money spent on education was wasted, money spent on mother and child health programmes was misdirected because it was likely to cause a bulge in the survival rate. Obviously Ravenholt's insensitivity was massive; in fact he was so unaware of scepticism and distrust in his immediate environment that he would place his hand on the knee of women journalists who were out to shoot him down in flames every bit as blithely as he would arrange to ship aspiration cannulae to countries where abortion was illegal. Under Ravenholt's administration USAID began to deal with commercial suppliers of contraceptive technology and to take delivery of cut-price lines for use in the field. The accounts have yet to be cast in order to find out just how much human misery "Ray" Ravenholt bought for his $125 million dollars a year: in this observer's view, he and some of his colleagues and clients ought to be subjected to a peace crimes tribunal, but the compiling of the dossier and the framing of the charges would cost fortunes that are at the disposal only of the great cartels.

During Ravenholt's rule, the Office of Population of USAID contributed half the funds of IPPF and the UNFPA, more than 90% of the Pathfinder Fund and the most significant contributions to the Population Council, Church World Service, and the Association for Voluntary Sterilisation, Family Planning International Assistance and a host of other programmes. The 1981 budget was $190 million dollars, 52% of which was used to purchase "modern contraceptives for use in population programmes in over 100 countries". In financial year 1982, "the amount of budgeted assistance for population activities is $211 million."[84]

According to Lader, who was probably writing at the instance of Moore, it was Moore who co-opted and motivated Draper. His aim was to develop what he called "firepower" in Washington in the shape of the Population Crisis Committee. He chose as the committee's first national chairman the retired senator Kenneth Keating, who still had access to the senate dining-rooms. He resigned from Moore's payroll to serve as ambassador to India in 1965, and his place was taken by General Draper, who chose to finance himself and a series of important lunches in which legislators were worked on by people like Sheldon Segal of the Population Council, and Jack Lippes, inventor, distributor and part-owner of the Loop. While Draper was working on USAID Moore had embarked on another barnstorming campaign:

> He proposed that the Government set up a "Manhattan Project" for population control – an allusion to the giant crash project that developed the atomic Bomb so quickly during World War II.[85]

At the time no one seemed to find the association of ideas unfortunate, which says a good deal about the level of sensitivity they shared. A new advertising campaign was undertaken, with the help of Merson Foote and Henry C. Flower of J. Walter Thompson. An *ad hoc* committee of the Hugh Moore Fund spent half a million dollars on a Campaign to Check the Population Explosion, distributing a taped radio programme with Ehrlich and David Brower of Friends of the Earth free to more than three hundred campus radio stations, as well as free cartoons to college newspapers; the campus offered prizes for the best slogans relating to "popullution". In 1970 a bumper sticker appeared: "Trouble parking? Support Planned Parenthood"; by 1970 the $29,200,000 set aside for family-planning activities in 1967 had grown almost ten-fold to $218,300,000. Moore's marketing campaign had paid off: people waiting in cinema queues blamed the population explosion for their inconvenience. Instead of seeing poverty and starvation and overcrowding in the developing world, they saw overpopulation. The panic had been so successfully raised that the old talk of coercion began to be heard again, and not from a gaggle of half-educated provincial legislators, but from people who should have known better.

Clearly there is no more justification in giving Moore all the credit for the genesis of the population cartel than there is for claiming that Sanger and Stopes changed the sexual orientation of the Western world; nevertheless it must be understood that Moore and others like him used the techniques which are successful in persuading people that they need inessentials like paper cups (instead of drinking out of their hands or pouring liquids into their mouths without allowing the vessels to touch their lips, as Hindus do) to influence people not only to limit their families, for in that respect they may well have had little success, but to limit their families in the manner appropriate to Western culture, by government-subsidised IUDs, by chemical contraceptives, some of which were bought by government agencies from superseded stocks of the big drug houses, and by the Draconian methods of male and female sterilisation. The emotion that was stirred in the West was fear; very little lasting good is done by people who are motivated by fear, especially if the fear is whipped into panic by constant assertions that time is running out. Demographic transition, when it is genuine, is a lasting change which has never yet been reversed; haphazard manipulation of reproductive rates only delays it for as long as people remember the effects of whatever campaign it was that pushed Lippes Loops into half-comprehending people, or sterilised them in return for gifts of cosmetics, money or promises of free health care that never came. The population establishment is now embarrassed about Hugh Moore, just as it is embarrassed about Reimert Ravenholt, to whom the Hugh Moore Memorial Award was made in 1974 by the Population Crisis Committee. The great eye-opener for the international pressure groups was the International Conference of UN Population Year: the philanthropists were genuinely surprised to find greater scepticism about their motives and their aims than they had dreamed of. John D. Rockefeller III went so far as to make a speech of recantation, as delegation after delegation rose to its feet and insisted that the problem facing the world was not the proliferation of the poor but the astonishing capacity of the shrinking rich minority to consume an ever-growing proportion of the world's goods. Most of the money poured into foreign aid programmes mislabelled "population control" had simply been wasted; a good deal of it has come back to America as private profits, to the drug houses and to companies set up to distribute and merchandise contraception, abortion and sterilisation at home and abroad.

Chapter Twelve
Governments as Family Planners

If you want to adopt very extreme means of controlling fertility I can immediately think of some, such as breaking down the family system, for example, by not giving children the family name of the parents; in fact not letting them know who the parents are and vice versa. Soon the motivation for having children would be seriously reduced.

Kingsley Davis, distinguished professor of Sociology, University of Southern California, testifying before the U S Select Committee on Population, 9 February 1978

In the preceding chapters some account has been given of the way in which political notions and irrational prejudice perverted the development of "scientific" birth control in the industrialised world. The residue of eugenic thinking and fear of the poor is not burnt away yet, even in our own "democratic" societies. Not only was there considerable overlap in the cast of actors in the eugenic movement and the birth-control movement, there is evidence that population planners who were never personally connected with the earlier movement still carry some of the same intellectual baggage. In America where the establishment of publicly funded birth-control programmes was long delayed by the powerful Catholic lobby, targets were eventually found which were considered exempt from the usual considerations:

The first direct O E O grant for family planning services – a piddling $8,000 – went to Corpus Christi, Texas, in a state with a large population of low-income Mexican-American families.[1]

Presumably even Catholics can be persuaded to countenance the aggressive promotion of birth control in Catholic communities provided that they are composed of members of a different racial group. Xenophobia can be stimulated so as efficiently to override scruple. Thomas B. Littlewood gives great importance in the development of American national family planning policy to the awareness of the growth of the urban black population played upon by demographers like Philip Hauser in his National Academy of Sciences study and given dramatic verification by the ghetto riots of 1968. The inclusion of free family planning among the services offered in publicly funded health-care programmes at the same time as the distribution of elective fertility control devices among the general population is conspicuously hampered, is inevitably interpreted as intended genocide by the recipients of the undemanded favour. The poor reacted with suspicion, the rich nobly explained that all they believed they were doing was making available to the poor the liberties that they themselves had always enjoyed, out of the simple goodness of their hearts. The principle, that family planning was a basic civil right, began to be enunciated. As long as fertility had been regulated by non-commercial, non-technological means there had been no need to claim any such right. As often happens, the fact that the right was promulgated actually meant that it had been lost. The rich began reducing their family size in defiance of law and common morality; the result of the marketing of new "scientific" methods, among people who had forgotten or abandoned traditional methods, was a spate of unwanted pregnancies and criminal abortions. This in turn helped to create the climate for the professionalisation of obstetric and gynaecological services and the commercialisation of fertility control. The American paradigm, of reproductive chaos in the disintegration of traditional *mores*, followed by the adoption of fertility limitation by the privileged who then urge it on the underprivileged, has been exported internationally. The impact of commercial hedonistic culture, plus the economic onslaught of modern techniques of production and marketing, intensified by the social disruption caused by piecemeal industrialisation and outwork, overthrows traditional strategies of family building, often in the name of liberalisation and progress. The result is often a rise in the illegitimacy rate, a rise in the birthrate and a shortening of birth intervals. The overall survival rate of the children born may be higher, but in the general spectrum of moral disorientation it may have a less central part to play in the population explosion than the other factors associated with loss of control.

The rich nations are tossing in the same nightmare that obsessed the early proponents of population control, but on an immeasurably vaster scale. As long as the spectre of the fecundity of the poor was so remote that its vastness was diminished in our awareness, we were less hysterical about the fertility of the brown peoples than Marie Stopes was about Mrs Jones, but the propaganda campaign of the old millionaires brought the spectre of the teeming slums into the forefront of middle-class consciousness. It is this "awareness" which stalks the corridors of power and distorts the structure of all the health programmes which receive funding from the international community.

In the world as we know it(which may well be quite another thing from the world as it is) "governments should" accept a measure of responsibility for staving off the cataclysm which rushes upon us if the proliferation of the human species is not checked. The international community which constantly utters protocols and plans of action beginning "governments should" believes that "governments should" not only have policies about population but that they should voice such policies freely and honestly in international fora. It is simply not done to lie to the United Nations or to any other authority which sees itself in a "donor" role. This convention puts governments in tricky situations, for there is not one government in the world which has come to power on a population platform, and there would be quite a few which would topple if they introduced a population package which the electors were not minded to accept or that the opposition could use to whip up fear and loathing. The international community earnestly hopes and trusts that it is dealing with legitimate and democratically elected representatives of the people; at the same time pressure is exerted to bring these same representatives to support policies which they have not been elected to promote. Most governments, particularly democratically elected ones, last a very much shorter time than a human lifetime; the alliances that governments make are less durable than marriages, yet they are asked and confidently expected to make decisions which will affect the course of both lives and marriages irrevocably. Democratic governments will only survive if the policies that they implement happen to coincide with what the electors feel they want; in population matters this really means that governments can only promote policies that will come to pass whether they are promoted or not.

Unfortunately, many governments have not been democratically elected; practically no governments have been elected by a true consensus of the majority but represent one minority group or another or one uneasy coalition of minorities or another. Clearly such governments must both safeguard and reinforce their power base; the only groups they can afford to oppress are those whom they do not claim to represent: thus it is practically inevitable that the population policies urged on governments by the international community and apparently supported by them are selectively applied to the groups whom the government feels that it can bully with impunity. It is obvious that concrete moves to limit fertility will be addressed to unpopular and powerless groups, in other words, refugees, unskilled and disorganised workers, the unemployed, the landless, the tribal minorities. There is hardly a country in the world which does not harbour a group whose fertility the government could limit by draconian means and not only keep the support of its followers but earn added support into the bargain. It is the more surprising and significant then that so many countries refuse to agree that their population growth rate is too fast. Angola, Benin, Burundi, Cap Verde, Congo, Ethiopia, Guinea-Bissau, Malawi, Mali, Mauritania, Mozambique, Niger, Nigeria, Somalia, Sudan, Tanzania, Togo, Upper Volta, Zaire and Zambia in Africa, Brazil, Canada, Colombia, Cuba, Ecuador, Guyana, Honduras,

Panama, Paraguay, Peru, Surinam, the United States and Venezuela in the Americas, Bhutan, Burma, Japan, North Korea and Singapore in Asia, Kuwait, Lebanon, Oman, Qatar, Saudi Arabia, Syria, the United Arab Emirates and the two Yemens in the Middle East, Australia, New Zealand and the USSR, and Albania, Austria, Belgium, Czechoslovakia, Denmark, Finland, Hungary, Ireland, Italy, Malta, the Netherlands, Norway, Poland, Portugal, Rumania, Spain, Sweden, Switzerland, the United Kingdom and Yugoslavia all perceive their rates of population growth as "acceptable", although they vary from 4.8% per annum in Kuwait to −0.1% per annum in Austria and the United Kingdom. The only countries on the list which have not accepted international family-planning assistance are the highly developed countries and the countries within the Soviet sphere of influence, including Tanzania and Cuba.[2]

What is meant when governments fill in questionnaires stating that they find population growth rates acceptable is not at all obvious or uncomplicated. Some governments would claim to accept birthrates as given and to have no fixed ideas of what they should be, as a matter of principle. They are quite likely to be painfully aware of differentials in the birthrate within their borders, as for example, the Russians are as they ponder the fact that the European citizens of the USSR are reproducing much more slowly than the Asiatics. In every country inhabited by groups of differing religions or mother-tongues or racial stocks, with significant emigration or immigration or problems of urban drift and consequent proliferation of over-crowded slums, there is a great temptation to interpret these problems in terms of the birthrate.

Thus governments accept aid offered in the name of the global dilemma and apply it to target populations within their own borders, just as Margaret Sanger did when she opened her clinic in Brownsville. The international population cartel takes it for granted that clinics will be set up in the poorest and most crowded areas, just as they took for granted until very recently the fact that they would offer the most sophisticated contraceptive technology to people who stood in dire need of basic medical care for parasitic infestation, for vitamin or iodine deficiency, diaorrheal disease or anaemia, all of which they simply ignored, without any sense of the brutality of the contrast or the mockery they were making of their own stated humanitarian ideals. We now look back with embarrassment on the period in our own development when the urban slums threatened to overwhelm the neat villas of the professional classes and prefer to forget the sway which ideas of cutting the working class off at the roots held in the minds of otherwise brilliant and perceptive men and women. At the same time we are allowing the myth of overpopulation to provide the sanction for the acting out of similar phobias in countries with less experience of democracy and a shakier commitment to it than the European countries enjoyed on the eve of the heyday of fascism. It would be a wonderful augury for the human race if the countries which stated that their population growth rate was acceptable really meant that they rejected the notion of manipulation of reproductive rates in principle; but that is not what they mean.

The activities of the population establishment in countries where there is no explicit policy of attempting to alter existing trends are of various kinds. They may simply be laying the groundwork for more reliable and detailed demographic fact-gathering systems, but it is always assumed that the point of establishing statistical machinery is eventually to provide the basis for population-control strategy. In the process of educating demographers, the instructing body can also inculcate its own views of satisfactory population management; it is unlikely that a demographer trained by the Ford Foundation or the Population Council will agree with the Government of Somalia that a growth rate of 3.7% per annum is acceptable, or with Nigeria about an annual increase of 3.4%. International programmes may be training medical and health workers in new techniques of fertility control to replace the old ones, and thus strengthening the potentiality for bureaucratic control over fertility regulation. With this goes training in management of health-delivery systems. The ultimate effect of these forms of aid is to create an infrastructure which has close ties with the Western medical establishment and the multinational pharmaceutical firms. There are careers to be made in foreign-funded health and family-planning programmes which pay much better salaries than local authorities, and may even lead to a glittering sinecure in one of the glass towers in New York or Geneva or Paris. The cultural impact of the intervention of the foreign-aid establishment and the changes it brings about, necessary as we might perceive them to be, is enormous. What may seem to us to be simply rational organisation can become, in situations of intractable poverty and constant social improvisation, the most inhuman regimentation. For years the population establishment has warned against offering Rolls-Royce medical care in ox-cart economies, without seeing that the salary of a fledgeling demographer in a foreign programme may be equal to that of five doctors working long hours in the back blocks.[3]

Brazil is a country which claims that its explosive population growth has kept pace with economic development, yet Brazil has accepted multilateral assistance from the UNFPA, the UN, the ILO, the WHO, the Pan-American Health Organisation, and bilateral aid from the Canadian Development Agency, as well as hosting eight projects funded by the Association for Voluntary Sterilisation, another by the Family Life and Population Programme of the Church World Service, and eight small projects from Development Associates Incorporated. Brazil accepted three grants from FPIA, four grants from the Ford Foundation, one from General Service Foundation, two from the International Committee on Applied

Research in Population, three from the International Development Research Centre, one from the International Fertility Research Programme, one from JOICFP, three from OXFAM, seven from the Pathfinder Fund, eight from the Population Council, four from the Rockefeller Foundation, and three from World Neighbours. The IPPF supports the Sociedade Civil de Bem Estar Familiar no Brasil (BEMFAM) to the tune of $3.5 million a year: the annual value of the other assistance is somewhere in the region of $7 million a year. The projects are of all kinds, integrated family health services in Rio de Janeiro (UNFPA), strengthening regional planning capability in Maranhao state (UN), development of a demographic economic simulation model for medium- and long-term regional planning based on the BACHUE model (ILO).[4]

> In 1980–1981 the WHO supported research on the safety and effectiveness of
> current oral and injectable contraceptives and on intrauterine devices. It also
> supported research on the development of new intrauterine devices and vaginal
> rings, and the causes of infertility.[5]

Vaginal rings are being tested not only in Brazil, but also in Chile, Colombia, Cuba, the Dominican Republic, India, Mexico, South Korea, and in some developed countries. Vaginal rings are an alternative system of steroid delivery through a silastic ring placed in the vagina. The steroid should act directly on the uterine system, thus bypassing the route of oral ingestion and the undesirable build-up of the steroid in sites which have no bearing on the reproductive process. If the rings can be worn comfortably and have no undesirable effects on the vaginal structures, they are a decided improvement in systems of chemical contraception. The only way to test them is in use by human subjects. Feminists may feel dubious about clinical trials conducted among people who have very little chance of understanding what is going on, but the vaginal ring has one enormous advantage from the feminists' point of view: it can be taken out by the wearer whenever she wants. Anything which lowers the dose of steroids and obviates systemic medication is to be welcomed, but when we read that in some trials rings broke, caused lacerations and delivered unacceptably high levels of steroid, and that some of them release DMPA, we might have preferred that more of the testing had been done on privileged patients. One aspect of the vaginal ring is puzzling; the ring itself seems a cumbersome object, held in place by exerting outward pressure on the vaginal wall; slow-release implants would have much the same function (although they would probably have to be removed by a health worker) and be very much less noticeable. It seems unlikely that Dow-Corning really needs the extra outlet for their silastic. Other shapes could be tried; even a cervical cap with a steroid deposit could be considered. For some reason, not immediately obvious, the research establishment has lumbered itself with the ring.[6]

One country which states firmly that its rate of population growth is satisfactory and has no internationally funded programmes being carried out within its borders is Japan, with 118.1 million people and a growth rate of 0.6% per annum and 1.8 children per woman. Before the period of the Meiji restoration during which Japan modernised and industrialised and developed the expansionist policies which led to Japanese imperialism and defeat in the Second World War, the Japanese population was kept within the limits imposed upon it by the geography of the archipelago at least partly by infanticide, which was given a horticultural name, *mabiki*, or thinning out.[7] In the hundred years that passed between the first and the second census the population remained stable at 26 million. The persistence of knowledge of anti-natal measures was ensured by the periodic recurrence of Hinoeuma, the year of the Fire-horse, in which no children were to be born: the population pyramid of Japan shows a unique dent for 1966, the last year of the Fire-horse.[8] At the end of the war, birth control was still illegal in Japan. "Nobody could advocate contraception without the risk of a jailed life."[9] Given the desperate shortage of housing, jobs and food, births had to be avoided at all costs. Dr Ogino worked on establishing the precise time of ovulation so that periodic abstinence could be effectively observed and the Ota rings, IUDs of the thirties, might have been still in use by a minority. The struggling majority was forced to have recourse to abortion. The Eugenic Protection Law of 1948 recognised a number of grounds for legal abortion, including leprosy (!) but this limited official sanction had little relation to the prevalence of the practice, except to make it easier for medical students to be openly instructed in the best methods.

In 1947 the Japanese birthrate stood at 34.3 per thousand; ten years later it had been halved. The way it was halved was by illegal, unregistered, as well as legal, registered abortion. The medical profession connived in the illegal practice because they preferred not to declare all the income derived from abortion in order to avoid taxation. Nevertheless in 1967 1.17 million legal abortions were performed in Japan, and probably as many illegal ones. When Miyoshi Oba went to work in the village of Takaho as a registered nurse, the number of abortions carried out in a single year was two and a half times the number of children born. Some of her patients had as many as five abortions in a single year. Nurse Oba kept watch to see who visited the next village in her formal clothes and when she returned followed her home to take over her work in the house and in the fields to give her time to recover. Gradually she won the villagers' trust and managed to set up the Mandarin Duck Club, named after birds famed for their long and happy pairing. The purpose of the club was to disseminate information about contraception, as well as to combat the evil effects of alcoholism and repeated abortion. There Nurse Oba, herself unmarried, initiated the distribution of condoms at 50 yen a dozen. Perhaps it was partly exhibitionism before a young unmarried woman which prompted some couples to buy three dozen condoms at a time, but before long condom use was accepted by the villagers along with Nurse Oba's determined efforts to let light and air into their homes, to find them a decent water supply and to control parasite infestation. In 1954 there were 56 abortions; in 1955 the number dropped to 32; in 1960 there were only 9.[10]

One of the Japanese traditions which lent itself to community-based distribution of contraceptives was that of the visiting medicine salesman, who would come to the house and leave a box containing all the medicines likely to be needed in a six-month period; at the end of the six months he would return to replenish the box and to receive payment for the supplies used. The Japanese Family Planning Association set up in 1955 distributed condoms by means of Love Boxes which were passed from house to house in the villages. Couples took what they needed from the box and left money in payment; thus peer-group pressure was brought to bear in a subtle way, while privacy was apparently respected.[11] The condom is still the method of choice in Japan; more than 80% of couples still use it, making the Japanese users of one quarter of all the condoms in the world; although the IUD has been legal since 1974 only 8.3% of contraceiving women use it. Oral contraceptive steroids are not legal in Japan, although a small percentage of women have them prescribed as therapy for menstrual irregularities. The easiest explanation for this anomaly is that the medical establishment has so far succeeded in protecting the huge income to be derived from abortion by blocking legalisation of other methods, but there is little or no indication that the Japanese people find the present situation intolerable. Although most Japanese couples practise contraception after completing their family size, sterilisation acceptors are hardly more than 1%:[12] doctors control access to sterilisation, but there is no sign of a Japanese traffic to places where sterilisation would be available for the same price as they are already paying for each repeat abortion. Again, we must assume that a need which seems obvious to us is not felt. So while Japan exports contraceptive steroids to fifteen countries, 600,000 Japanese women annually undergo legal abortion, and as many more unregistered abortion. Many of them visit the temples of Jizo to pray for the soul of the unborn child. The Japanese establishment remains inscrutable, flippantly refusing to explain the phenomenon:

> In terms of our abortion experience and technique Japan is a developed country and the United States is still a developing country,[13]

said Dr Shiro Sugiyama in 1978, in rebuttal of the suspicion that the Japanese male needs to find proof of his virility in repeated female suffering.

No one is about to muscle in on Japan and force her to accept inter-

nationally funded programmes pushing oral contraceptives and sterilisations (although there are probably health grounds for doing both) first
because the Japanese are not going to stand for it, second because Japan is
too rich to be susceptible to bullying and bargaining, and third because
no one is sufficiently interested in the health status of Japanese women.
If the Japanese birthrate was high or rising there would be a pretence of
concern for the health of Japanese women; as it is low and falling
further, the subterfuge is not necessary.[14]

Although "it was the people and not the government who first took
steps to restrict family size" in Japan, the Japanese government is now
practising negative imperialism by interesting itself in family planning
elsewhere. The Japan International Cooperation Agency was established
in 1974, taking over from the defunct Overseas Technical Cooperation
Agency in "providing fellowships, sending experts to developing
countries, supplying materials, assisting in agricultural development, and
administering the youth corps as well as medical cooperation."

> The Japanese Government concluded its first bilateral assistance agreement in
> family planning with the Indonesian Government in 1969 to be carried out in
> the framework of Indonesia's five-year family-planning programme. The
> assistance was executed by the Medical Cooperation Department of OCTA and
> included the provision of bicycles, motorbikes, contraceptives, operating in-
> struments, audio-visual aids, etc. to the Indonesian Family Planning Co-
> ordinating Board. The primary focus of JICA is on Asian countries and
> on family-planning programmes associated with MCH programmes. In 1980,
> for example, the Japanese International Cooperation Agency was responsible
> for reinforcing and expanding Japanese assistance to Bangladesh, Indonesia,
> the Philippines and Thailand.

Two other government organisations attached to the Ministry of Health
and Welfare of the Government of Japan, the Institute of Population
Problems and the Institute of Public Health, are involved in population
projects in other Asian countries but the most significant Japanese source
of cooperation and assistance to family-planning and MCH programmes
in developing countries is the Japanese Organisation for International
Cooperation in Family Planning, Inc., founded in 1968 "by Japanese
family-planning experts and leaders in the political, business and academic
fields," and funded in 1982 by "Japanese business circles" to the tune of
$8.3 million.

> One of the major JOICFP activities is the Integrated Family Planning,
> Nutrition and Parasite Control Programme. It has been conducted in several
> countries in Asia and Latin America in collaboration with IPPF since 1976 on
> a pilot basis. In 1976, Indonesia, the Republic of Korea, the Philippines and
> Thailand were the first to initiate the programme; then Malaysia and Colombia
> in 1978, Nepal, Brazil, Mexico and Bangladesh in 1979, and Sri Lanka in
> 1980.[15]

JOICFP showed a better grasp of the psychology of developing countries than her predecessors in the international family-planning movement by coupling fertility limitation with the perceptible benefits to be obtained by relatively simple means, namely supplementary feeding of infants and chemical control of parasitic infestation. The three-pronged approach immediately became family-planning orthodoxy, but already fears are being voiced that it is being misinterpreted and misapplied. Like all the countries with a growth rate of less than 1%, Japan adopted the small family norm without official assistance or encouragement, and not so long ago that the Japanese have forgotten how or why. Like the Western family planners, JOICFP treats recipients of aid as if they shared the same system of values; the difference is that in this case, they are closer to being right.

If Japanese "business circles" are investing in family planning among Japan's less developed neighbours in the Pacific region, it is because they expect a return. People who are less involved in generating children ought to be able to generate more spending power. Sony, Hitachi and Mitsubishi are probably also convinced that life is much better with video games and stereo sound systems than it is without, and therefore see their activities in family planning as altruistic to a degree. The hypocritical version of this motivation is to claim that helping the poor to control their fertility (i.e. pressuring the poor to control their fertility) will limit the cost of aid in the future, as if the rich nations of the world kept the poor nations alive, when actually they keep them poor. It would be a great relief if capitalist-funded population projects came out and said that what they were after was a bigger market for their consumer durables, and the recipient nations might not resent it, as they would actually like to have modern toys to play with, but instead we are locked into the stale rhetoric of the early birth-control movement, relying on the idea that a million dollars invested in birth control does more to reduce the quantum of human misery than a hundred million dollars invested in humanitarian schemes.

The class of hereditary paupers of whom the early Malthusians were so afraid is still with us, although it has practically vanished from our own societies; as the world has shrunk it has simply retreated beyond our borders. When governments took a hand in population management in their own countries, they were insensitive enough. When the American Senate passed the Family Planning Services and Population Research Act of 1970, which established the Office of Population Affairs and the National Centre for Family Planning Services of the Department of Health, Education and Welfare and allocated $382 million to be spent in the following three years, it took evidence from the Planned Parenthood Federation of America, but not from a single representative of the identified target population of five million people – five million female people, obviously. It was simply irrelevant to consider whether poor women had formulated or felt a need for what they were to be offered. It was somebody else's problem to get them to accept it. The bill was signed into law by that well-known humanitarian and champion of women's rights, Richard M. Nixon.[16]

The hard-line Malthusians were not satisfied with Nixon's commitment even so. They wanted figures, a ceiling for America's optimum population and a positive commitment to respecting it. If governments under the sway of powerful lobbies can show such insensitivity with their own citizens, even when a moment's reflection would suffice to see that they are in a fair way to repel the people whose behaviour they most want to modify, it is inevitable that they will be just as insensitive with foreigners. As it happens the proponents of foreign aid for family planning were the same people who pushed for federal aid for family planning at home. The typical career is that of Oscar Harkavy, who, as head of the Ford Foundation, had been pressured by the trustees, especially John Cowles, to include population within the scope of the Foundation's activities. For twenty years Harkavy administered population programmes at home and abroad. He was one of the authors of the inter-departmental report which recommended the incorporation of a population office within the Department of Health, Education and Welfare in 1967, and at the same time he was spending $26 million on population work abroad. The primary target for such work was, as usual, India.

> Ford's India effort became a visible pilot project in foreign aid and a training ground for some of the more prominent figures in the population scene. But it also proved to be a bone of contention in India and eventually within the programme itself.[17]

The Ford Foundation had entered the Indian scene in 1951, but the projected programme assistance was never given as Nehru was loth to allow such a sensitive area to be trampled by foreigners, especially so soon after the Indians had rid themselves of the British. It was not as if birth control was a complete novelty to the Indian elite.

In 1930 the Maharaja of Mysore opened clinics in three hospitals, offering diaphragms, "Japan pessaries", jelly, "Cooper's Cream" foam powder to be used with an insufflator, the sponge and, free to the poorest patients, vinegar and water with a sterilised tampon. The first vasectomy was carried out by Dr D. N. Nadkarni, District Surgeon at the Sassoon hospital in Poona – on himself. Neither initiative started a trend. Later, 318 mobile clinics were sent from the UK.[18] During World War II and the agonies of partition family planning receded from the consciousness even of progressive Indians, but for Western champions of married felicity, India was a case deserving of treatment long before it had achieved independence. It would hardly have been proper for the British, who were glad of the assistance of the flower of Indian manhood in all their wars since the eighteen-nineties, to have been heard maintaining that there were too many Indians in the world, but Margaret Sanger, "fearless" campaigner for the rights of others, rushed in where the British did not dare or care to tread. She was invited by Lady Rama Rau to attend the All-India Women's Congress in 1935, and construed her invitation as a divine mandate to convert all-India women to the use of the rubber cap. She was surprised and chagrined to find that not even her fellow delegates wished to hear her on the subject. She set off to visit Gandhi and make him see the writing on the wall, but arrived on his day of silence; the next day she worked on him, but to her amazement and pique he seemed impervious and even uninterested. As she had absolutely no realistic suggestions to make, beyond pointing to cotton bolls in the fields and lemons on the trees to show that God has provided us with the means of contraception (ineffective as it happens) it was as well that Gandhiji was immune to her charisma. In fact, he found her strident, insensitive and ridiculous. It did not occur to Sanger that the Mahatma knew her culture very much better than she knew his, and that he had rejected it along with its sexual values.[19]

A Hindu gentleman who had made his millions out of gift shops in Hawaii, and married an American wife, shared Sanger's conviction that India was the flashpoint of population explosion. He and his wife had set up a foundation, called after themselves the Watumull Foundation, to carry on philanthropic work; after a visit to India Ellen Watumull approached Margaret Sanger and asked if she would be willing to organise an international conference on birth control, to be held in Bombay.

> She began immediately, back in her element. She dictated dozens of letters to Lady Rama Rau, the Indian woman most interested in birth control. She suggested names of speakers and delegates; she ordered special stationery headed, *India World Conference, Margaret Sanger, World President*. She raised travel money for delegates who couldn't provide it themselves and even arranged secretaries for Lady Rama Rau. As money was crucial, she wasn't above taking donations as small as five dollars, raising a total of sixteen thousand dollars from Tucson friends alone.[20]

However much Sanger finally raised, and however much the Watumulls spent, the initial budget of the International Planned Parenthood Federation was a mere $5,000: the pattern of expensive conferences and top-heavy management, research, and planning structures was early set. Nowadays the cost of the secretariat has settled at about one-quarter of the total budget; only a small proportion of what remains is actually invested in practical family planning. It might seem reasonable to argue that we cannot begin to reduce population before we know exactly how many people there are and how many children they are likely to have. When the methods of counting and tabulating and forecasting and correlating are themselves moot and subject to constant revision and elaboration, when the information that is gathered is almost always out of date because of the time taken to process it, and when it is of a kind which cannot be useful to workers in the field, it might seem more reasonable simply to get on with satisfying unmet needs wherever they are encountered before they have been precisely tabulated, and to leave the assessment of the effectiveness of the various methods to some other agency. Many international bodies undertake demographic studies and many of the areas of activity overlap; this has necessitated a proliferation of coordinating bodies which are obliged to have even more conferences at even more exotic locations. The results of all this activity have been spectacular careers for a chosen few who were in the right corridors of the right powers at the right time, a vast academic industry of population studies, and an unwieldy mass of irreconcilable evidence expressed in systems of incomprehensible rhetoric.[21]

One of the most influential people whom Sanger caused to be invited to the Bombay conference was her old eugenist comrade, C. P. Blacker, who suggested the division of the international federation into regions: Europe, Asia and the Americas. The head office of the International Planned Parenthood Federation, as it was called, was at the same Eccleston Square address as the headquarters of the Eugenics Society. While Sanger's public crusade was for married bliss and freedom from fear, the real *raison d'être* of the IPPF and the motivation for its funding was population control. As long as the people in the field, who were not so well paid that they could have been working for anything but the satisfaction of easing the suffering of man- and womankind, could safely ignore the bureaucratic insistence on results, the essential schizophrenia of the organisation did not obtrude. The old eugenics had addressed itself to immigrants and the indigenous pauper class; the new, crypto-eugenics simply took a longer step and aimed its "philanthropic" activities at foreign targets. The change in the rhetoric is slight:

> Nor need we question that a husband and wife living in squalor and ignorance who already have a number of children not being reared properly, might well be considered unfit to have additional children. Yet many parents of these various unfit types keep producing unduly large numbers of children, chiefly because through ignorance or indifference – and often against their will – they let Nature take its course.
>
> To combat this situation, eugenists favour the spread of birth-control information . . .[22]

Thus succinctly were expressed in 1956 the basic tenets of the international family-planning movement. Those who live in squalor (the poor) and ignorance (the illiterate) and have children being improperly reared (i.e. scantily fed, scantily clad, ill and unschooled) ought not to be parents, are parents because of ignorance or passivity, and are bearing unwanted children. This is the mentality that believes in the occult "unmet need"; thirty years of promoting birth-control information and spasmodic distribution of contraceptive supplies have failed to uncover even the tip of the iceberg of need; the new version of the old orthodoxy is that the unmet need resides in the bosoms of women who are prevented from articulating it by the tyranny of men. Thus, along with laparoscopes, IUDs, silastic implants and vaginal rings, we export sexism.

For ten years the IPPF remained an inconspicuous and largely ineffectual organisation. It was probably yet another result of the lobbying of Hugh Moore that when the big foundations were looking for agencies to implement international birth-control policies, they lit upon the IPPF. Tom Griessemer, director of the Hugh Moore Fund, was seconded to the IPPF, "played a role in drafting the Constitution . . . became Secretary of the Western Hemisphere Region, and was one of the driving forces of the movement."[23] Hugh Moore provided the staff of the IPPF Western Hemisphere Region, and served on the IPPF Governing Body from 1957 until 1967, from 1962 as a Vice-President. When the Population Crisis Committee became Planned Parenthood/World Population, General Draper and Lamo DuPont Copeland served as Co-Chairmen with Cass Canfield. Nowadays the lion's share of IPPF funding comes from the US Agency for International Development, as well as from contributions from the member organisations (the national family planning associations), the Ford and Rockefeller Foundations, and the World Bank, among others. On the board sit representatives of DuPont Chemical, the Chemical Bank of New York, the US Sugar Corporation, General Motors, the Chase Manhattan Bank, Newmont Mining, International Nickel, Marconi–RCA, Xerox, Gulf Oil.

> Contributions to IPPF's budget, currently around US $50 million a year, come from private citizens and foundations all over the world, as well as from governments. In 1980 its expenditure amounted to over $49 million. In 1980, 59 national family-planning associations received grants of more than $100,000 each to carry out a wide range of family, planning, population and related activities. Many other countries received smaller grants.[24]

The Family Planning Association of India is still a major recipient of IPPF support; the projected grant for 1982 was $2,782,600 but again the FPAI actually provided services to only 138,502 new acceptors and 218,104 continuing acceptors in 1980. Most of the money is spent not in running its clinics and mobile units and providing services at its 42 branches but in "focusing particularly on the development of new approaches and strategies for promoting and accelerating family planning and evolving models particularly in rural areas, for integrating family planning with other development activities in collaboration with other agencies, including the Government."[24] None of these seems to be a way of satisfying the unmet need. Family-planning agencies have found in India that they have to create the unmet need by changing the entire set of cultural priorities, turning, as it were, a population with a spending power of nil into the kinds of materialists who see nothing to like or desire in children as poor as themselves. Such things can be done: if people can be got to spend a significant proportion of their tiny cash income on Coca-Cola or to abandon breast-feeding for expensive baby foods, they can be got to accept condoms and steroids. The FPAI has one major advantage over many of the other bodies working to reduce India's rate of population growth: it is Indian. If more of the international aid organisations had chosen to work through the FPAI they might have avoided some of their more expensive mistakes. Also, the FPAI is to some extent independent of the Government of India and its policies. Having been formed at a time when Government refused to recognise the existence of a population problem, it is now capable of criticism and scepticism and even survived the Emergency with many of its priorities and a good deal of its prestige intact. Although some sections of the public see the FPAI as excessively brahmin – "even the drivers are brahmins" as one man said to me in Karnataka, and there at least it was true – it is one organisation which knows how to introduce projects in the most sensitive situations and how to win trust, affection and cooperation from people with nothing else to give. Trust, affection and cooperation might build you a latrine block or plant a vegetable garden round the health centre, but they do not necessarily bring down the birthrate.

The first international attempt at organised family planning in India was the ill-conceived Khanna experiment mounted by Harvard University, the United States Public Health Service and the Population Council, with the cooperation of the Government of India, the Christian Medical College of Ludhiana and the Indian Council of Medical Research. The objectives were

> To determine if the rural couples in India could practice a single contraceptive method effectively enough to reduce significantly the growth rate of the population, and to evaluate factors affecting fertility. The targets were to increase acceptance and the effectiveness of contraceptives in order to reduce the birthrate from 40 to 35 births a year per thousand population.[26]

The confusion in this statement is obvious; rather than finding out if "couples ... could", they ought to have asked if "couples ... would", and they should never have gone in without better contraceptives than those they had to offer. The development of better methods could not have been expected to take place during the study or to have somehow evolved out of the study. The area diagnosed as suffering from population pressure simply was not; the methods they used to convince people who were far more sophisticated and sceptical than they imagined were so ineffective that contraceptive use was higher in the control villages than in the experimental area after seven years work with an annual expenditure of Rs. 197,000.[27]

The Singur project run by the All-India Institute of Hygiene and Public Health from 1954 to 1965 was slightly more successful, for the birthrate in the experimental area fell almost twice as fast as it did in the control villages, even though the project was begun with no new or reliable methods to offer and conducted by outsiders.[27] At the time of the commencement of this study the commitment of the Government of India to family planning was nominal. The Registrar-General in his report on the 1951 census had pointed out that economic growth would be losing the race with population increase, but Nehru was unimpressed with the urgency of the problem and only a very small budget allocation was made for Family Planning under the Five-Year Plan, 1951–6. In brute fact the Government was not yet secure enough to enunciate a policy which would excite passionate opposition. No other country had a national policy of birthrate reduction; India with its legacy of intercommunal violence and civil disobedience was not well-adapted to pioneering mass birth-control projects, even if the lifestyle of its peoples, nearly all of whom lived without bathrooms and far from running water, had been adapted to caps, foams, jellies, insufflators, douches, and all the other impedimenta of the inefficient contraception of the fifties.[29] Still, pressure for a commitment to family planning began to build up within Nehru's government, particularly from the Minister of Food and Agriculture, Subramaniam, and Asoka Mehta, the Planning Commissioner.

In 1959 the Government of India initiated a scheme of recruiting canvassers to motivate vasectomy acceptors in Madras State for a fee of Rs10 for each client produced. Other incentive payments were made to the client or to the panchayat in his village. The system was highly criticised on the grounds that the canvassers misrepresented the nature of the operation, brought ineligible candidates and cheated acceptors out of their fees. Halfway through the scheme the incentive payments were discontinued and the number of acceptors fell, but the government now knew what was the most cost-effective way of averting births.[30] Madras was the pre-test for the great push of 1975–77.

The greatest problem facing the Indian family-planning programme was the "poor motivation of acceptors", or, in plain terms, the fact that the poor did not wish to limit their families. At best parents were ambivalent; if a contraceptive method involved pain or inconvenience or discomfort, or the least exercise of initiative, it simply fell by the way-side. This attitude was generally interpreted by outsiders as horrible Hindu fatalism or crushed passivity, when it was actually of more complex composition, including good parts of scepticism and resistance. It was the more unfortunate then that in the search for a pre-emptive method, the device of choice should have been the Lippes Loop. An IUD is well-adapted to Indian conditions in that it is invisible and *in situ* at all times, requires no bedtime ritual, cannot be removed or damaged by persons interested in the user's fertility, such as husbands and mothers-in-law, and does not have to be hygienically stored. In other respects the loop was conspicuously ill-adapted to Indian conditions, for it can cause health emergencies which can be fatal in the Indian setting, it does cause blood loss which is severely debilitating to a woman with low protein and iron intake, and it ought not to be inserted unless careful, prolonged and consistent follow-up is possible. The device was so confidently and urgently promoted in India that it is now totally discredited; some of the problems may have been caused by the device itself, for the Copper-T is very much better tolerated nowadays in India than the loop ever was.[31] As no systematic study of loop acceptors in India was ever done, we cannot be sure.

> A campaign promoting intrauterine contraceptive devices (IUDs) was launched in 1965. Due to inadequate planning and lack of medical follow-up much adverse publicity resulted in the survey area and the IUD programme was virtually discontinued ...[32]

For Carol Vlasoff, the chief problem with bad planning and neglect of follow-up seems to be that it results in bad publicity, not that it causes human suffering and shows the population planners' humanitarian motives to be fraudulent. Her article treats a disaster in terms simply as an operational handicap for birth-control careerists. Most family-planning literature exhibits a similar sensibility. Elsewhere Vlasoff gives a hint of the reality which provoked the inconvenient publicity:

> Of those who had tried the IUD almost half had discontinued use within the first year. Health problems were the main reason for this, bleeding being the most common complaint. One woman complained that the IUD had penetrated her stomach; another suffering woman had waited a year before the public health nurse extracted her device and as a result of concern at a possible, similar delay many otherwise satisfied users left the programme.[33]

What a peasant woman who suspects that her IUD has shifted is supposed to say, rather than that she thinks it has penetrated her "stomach" I don't know, especially when I have heard doctors use the word "tummy" to mean abdomen when speaking to women graduates in England. The tone of the report is fake-judicious; the blame is calmly apportioned to the patients in their ignorance, to the public health nurse (who was probably expected to serve 40,000 patients or so) and to the Maharashtrian authorities. We are not told who provided the loops, what claims were made for them, and how the funding of the programme was structured. If funds were available from a foreign aid agency for insertion but not for follow-up, and at the same time the case was made that the IUD provided an instant solution to problems of child-spacing with reduced necessity for follow-up, the Maharashtrian government cannot take all the blame for a screw-up so vast that eight years later Copper-T's have to be called "butterflies" to distinguish them both from the loop and the generic IUD.

Oral steroids were never as enthusiastically pushed as the IUD because the foreign suppliers of contraceptive technology thought the average Indian woman too dim-witted and disorganised to take them. In 1968 a programme to test the acceptability of oral contraceptives was run by the Humanity Association and the Pathfinder Fund, headed by the wealthy individualist, Clarence Gamble, described by his colleagues as "willing to go in and do any damn thing to get started", in the Howrah district of West Bengal. Although less than a third of the slum-dwelling women accepted the free pills even after two attempts at motivating them, and only a third of that third was still using them eighteen months later, the experiment was generally taken to have proved that illiterate women were capable of taking the pill and could be motivated to do so.[34]

In 1967 *Central Calling* announced a USAID-financed pilot project involving the distribution in each state of five to ten thousand cycles each of a contraceptive pill containing 1mg of Ethynodiol diacetate, a steroid developed by Searle, with mestranol. In view of the scale of the project it is surprising that so little is known about it. The dose seems extremely high for women of low body-weight; the timing might indicate an unexpected source of discontinued high-dosage pills.[35] By some such means the oral contraceptive was discredited in India soon after the Loop. The symptoms described by Karan Singh could be related to hyperoestrogenism:

> Till recently oral pills have been utilised in the family planning programme as an experimental measure ... the drop-outs were as high as 75% due to certain side-effects such as nausea and bleeding ...[36]

To have incurred the risk of discrediting steroidal contraception in India by simply failing to consider the possibility that dosages needed to be adjusted to body-weight and nutritional status seems criminally irresponsible, but there was probably some half-formed intention to compensate, by overcompensating, for some irregularity in the actual use of the pills.

As Donald Warwick points out,

> India has been the proving ground for birth control. Almost every policy innovation, from incentives to workers on tea estates to sterilisation booths in railroad stations has been tried, applauded and abandoned. The country has alternately been the darling and the downfall of the donors, a prototype to be emulated and an anti-type to be shunned ... Yet despite the enormous investment in birth control and the myriad policy experiments, family planning has not caught on in India.[37]

The incentives for workers on tea estates and in many other industries run by private enterprise go on. The women workers on Glendale, Bengorm and Parkside estates are paid the tiny sum of Rs5 for every month they are not pregnant; 90% of the eligible women enrolled in the scheme but 505 of the 919 did not avail themselves of any method of contraception known to the administrators of the scheme, who were also responsible for their health care. Three-quarters of the women who did accept a modern method chose sterilisation.[38]

The realisation that the motivated women on the South Indian tea estates did not need a modern method in order to undertake to limit their fertility and preferred to do without emphasises the point made by R. S. Dheer in *The Economic Weekly* in 1967, "In a group of willing people, any method will do the trick." In India there had always been an insistence on "cafeteria approach", in which a potential acceptor was offered, as she was in the earliest Madras clinics, a range of possible ways to attempt fertility control. Enormous effort and an important slice of the government budget had been spent on educational schemes which have penetrated every village. Every child knows that the correct answer to the question, "How many children will you have when you're grown up?" is "Two," but it remains to be seen whether rote learning has really changed attitudes. After centuries of foreign dominion Indians are experts in lip-service: not that the children are lying, they are simply telling me what they think I want to hear. They themselves have not yet formulated a want; when they do it will be merely one in a series of expectations held by the whole kin-group. If they accept the idea of child-spacing or sterilisation, the choice will have more to do with the family circumstances than government policy.

The intensified educational campaigns of the sixties gradually produced more acceptors, but the birthrate continued to climb and the cost of each putative birth averted was far too high. In too many cases the modern methods were simply substituting for traditional ones like post-partum abstinence and long lactation, both practically universal in India. In some cases the modern methods simply supplemented the old. In 1965, the Government of India set aside Rs65 million for family planning; in 1966, Rs120 million; under the fourth five-year plan the annual expenditure on family planning was to be of the order of Rs600 million, but the population continued to increase exponentially. Even modest "improvements" (falls in the birthrate) remained beyond the grasp of the 70,000 full-time workers in the Indian birth-control movement. The attitudes of the donors began to change. In 1967 Kingsley Davis pointed out, in a much quoted article in *Science*, that the dissemination of modern birth-control methods was not sufficient, and perhaps not even necessary to a programme of effective fertility control. The experience of a quarter-century had convinced him that some parents needed their children and that the need was a genuine one. The only way to avoid catastrophe would be to override their wishes and to disregard altogether their notions of happiness, fulfilment, security and other factors generally perceived as pertaining to the good life.

> What is rational in the light of a couple's situation may be totally irrational from the standpoint of society's welfare.[39]

Davis's point was elaborated by Bernard Berelson for the Population Council, in "Beyond Family Planning"; as he was President of the Council, his suggestions had the force of policy for the population apparatchiks in the organisation. The stepped-up programme was based on eight components, the extension of voluntary fertility-control services, the establishment of "involuntary" (population-ese for "forced") fertility control, intensified educational (ditto for "propaganda") campaigns, incentive programmes, tax and welfare benefits and penalties, changes of orientation in social and economic institutions, use of political channels and organisations in recruiting, with augmentation of research efforts trailing the field.[40] Clearly the climate of liberal opinion was changing under the barrage of population panic propaganda that continued to assail it. Medical sociologist Lyle Saunders, addressing the Second National Seminar on Population Growth in Kuala Lumpur in March 1970, drew a sharp distinction between private family planning which seeks "to help couples control the number and spacing of their children" and government programmes, in which "giving individual service is not an end but a means to reducing fertility in a population."[41] In Saunders' world, which is co-extensive with the Ford Foundation's world, for the Foundation continued to use the reprint of the address for years after it was delivered, there are no governments desirous of increasing fertility or even of maintaining it. Saunders, who was a programme adviser in the Foundation's Bangkok office, makes a case for voluntarism, at least initially, but the purpose of his address was to show that promotion of marital happiness was certainly not enough and possibly not even relevant.

> Responsible social scientists have expressed strong doubts that family planning alone can succeed in lowering fertility to a sufficient degree because couples almost everywhere, although expressing a desire for fewer children than they actually have, appear to want more than the number required for a stationary or slowly growing population.[42]

Thus Saunders has his cake and eats it too; although the notoriously insensitive KAP studies (Knowledge, Attitude, Practice) tell us of unmet needs for contraception there is still not enough to be gained by satisfying them, so we may as well move straight to the coercive measures; from not being able to have the control of their fertility that they desired, the poor will be transported to a condition of infertility, whether they like it or not. Just so John Lewis, head of the Indian office of USAID,

announced that he "would press [population] funds on the Indian government whether it wants them or not."[43] Saunders was conservative in his
suggestions, speaking in favour of incentives, suggesting some fairly mild
disincentives, and praising the Indian system of mass distribution of
condoms set up in 1968, the forerunner of the community-based distribution projects set up by USAID and the IPPF in 1973. Even an observer
as sensitive as Malcom Potts allows himself to catch the prevailing
callousness and to hold on to it long after the revolt of the South had
turned the Bucharest Population Year Conference on its ear:

> The political compromise produced by the Bucharest conference with its
> emphasis on 'integrated' development is the most recent diversion of funds from
> the obvious. It is a jargon, which in organisational terms is as relevant as
> attempting to assemble motors cars on a railway station because both happen
> to be means of transport.[44]

Family-planning workers in countries like India know only too well
that they must overcome the defensiveness of the people they are trying
to help by showing that they can help and that they will help where they
can. Potts is particularly severe on integrated maternal and child health
and family-planning projects, but in practical terms it is obvious that a
woman is less likely to try her chances in the pregnancy lottery over and
over again if her children look likely to survive, and more likely to respect
the opinions of someone who has rendered practical help to her, and even
more importantly, to her children. It takes the refined brutality of Western
aid to shove expensive contraceptive technology into a village whose
people would feel a good deal better and produce more food and get more
done generally, if a few pence were spent on eradicating the parasites which
infest them. It takes an Oriental like Chojiro Kunii to bypass all the
"beyond family planning" rhetoric:

> Traditionally – and even today in many countries – the approach to family
> planning is based upon concern about population growth, without questioning
> the people's psychology.
> People are very realistic. They understand only what they can touch and
> they can see. So that in developing strategy of persuasion it has to be under-
> stood that the people want only the things that are visible and touchable and
> profitable to them.
> In some countries in Asia family planning comes under special organisa-
> tion, not under the Ministry of Health. Health and family planning should not
> be separate. It is a mistake.[45]

Under Kunii's leadership the Japanese Organisation for International
Cooperation in Family Planning has set up Integrated Family Planning,
Nutrition and Parasite Control Programmes in Korea, Thailand, the
Philippines, Taiwan, Indonesia, Malaysia, Bangladesh, Nepal, Sri Lanka,
Brazil, Colombia and Mexico. Treatment for parasitic infestation usually

produces spectacular improvement in health in a very short time: it is as much a persuasion strategy as common humanity that justifies the JOICFP system. There are many workers in family planning who share Kunii's priorities, but few or none of them are in a similar position of power.

While the attitude of the international population cartel was hardening, the Government of India and a host of non-governmental bodies were struggling towards the aim of lowering the birthrate, an aim which constantly eluded them. On the one hand they were encumbered by unwieldy projects like the Narangwal Study,[46] which came to a timely end when the USAID office in Delhi was summarily closed by the Government of India in protest against US support to Pakistan during the war in 1972, expressed in such subtle ways as sailing the Sixth Fleet into the Bay of Bengal. The situation can hardly have been sweetened by the publication of a sneer from the former head of the USAID mission to India, John Lewis: in 1970 commenting on the UN evaluation of the Indian programme he wrote:

> Given its rather remarkable ambivalence with a system that was doing rather well within its own terms of reference, but was also in the process of missing its mark by a mile, the even more remarkable thing about the UN team is that it remained overwhelmingly congenial to the theory of the India programme.[47]

USAID was a major contributor to the Indian programme; Lewis's call for a policy change was not to be ignored. Some of the Rs3788 million from USAID was earmarked for sterilisation camps. In the study of a village near Meerut John Marshall points out that none of the government employees in the village, neither of the two schoolteachers, nor the tax collector, nor the village-level worker in the Community Development Programme, nor the poor Auxiliary Nurse Midwife, "an unmarried urban girl with profound distaste for and some fear of village life" nor the Family Welfare Worker was doing anything to motivate acceptance of vasectomy in the village. It was the unfortunate secretary of the Panchayat who, in 1967, "was obliged to recruit forty men for vasectomy from the five villages or possibly lose his job". From "Bunkipur" he came up with six men, five widowers over sixty and one who had painful after-effects, a 35-year-old from the low caste of Chamars.[48] All the dangers of the delegated motivation system are clearly demonstrated in this early example, but the pressure of demand and criticism left the Government little choice. After all it was not as if sterilisation was a disaster; the sterilees would live to thank the benevolent authorities who rescued them from the burden of their own fertility.

What stimulated confidence that there was a right way of doing mass sterilisations was the phenomenal success of the camps in the Ernakulam district of Kerala in 1970 and 1971. The district was divided into units, and a list drawn up of eligible men in each unit, which was assigned its own day to visit the month-long camp. Two weeks before each day, an intensive publicity and education campaign was mounted in the unit, peaking on the eve of sterilisation-day, when the villagers went off to glory. Unfortunately not all the doctors were expert, nor were the sanitary facilities adequate for those who had to wait, nor is walking all the way home very good for weakened scrota. Still, 15,005 vasectomies must mean some averted births, even if the mean age of the men is 38.9, but probably fewer than the two per man that the cost analysis of the programme assumed. The next year another push was mounted, this time during the monsoon, and 62,913 vasectomies and 505 "tubectomies" were performed. The next year the effort split up, and camps were held in seven sub-districts; Copper-Ts and condoms were added to the list of services offered.[49] Meanwhile, the much larger state of Gujarat, with 27 million people, was to steal Kerala's thunder by performing 150,000 vasectomies in 1,000 small camps around the state. Targets had been fixed for all the states of the union and sterilisations were available free in all public-health facilities. Small "incentive" payments, barely enough to cover the cost of travel and reimburse the acceptors for work lost, were paid. By setting up the camp system, the Government of Gujarat and the State Family Planning Bureau performed 160% of their annual quota in little more than two months.[50] It was a heroic effort, but the inevitable consequence of such success is that it must be repeated and bettered year after year, when it is in the nature of the case that first results are usually better than later results as it becomes progressively more difficult to recruit younger and less willing men and women of lower parity. The cost per sterilisation was rising steeply; the showy camps with their carnival atmosphere, their free food and entertainment and the saturation propaganda campaign could not be indefinitely continued. Only one aspect of the psychology of the situation proved durable: in Gujarat the newspapers had published a scoreboard to show which districts were leading in the motivation race: family planning became a sport. Doubtless, some there could be found to make book on it. The pace began to heat up; employers like the railways, associations like the Chambers of Commerce and Rotary, vied with each other to set up camps, manufacturers gave away free samples. As long as the euphoria continued, attitudes towards the operation were positive and the incidence of after effects fairly well tolerated, but in fact they were all walking a tightrope.

Mrs Gandhi's resistance to pressure for more draconian solutions to the population problem bore up unchanged, at least until 1972. The tone of this interview conducted by the then editor of the *Hindustan Times* gives a fairly exact impression of the attitude of the articulate "liberal" elite to population conservatism:

"Don't you think that our failure to control our population is the biggest black mark against us?" I asked her.

"No, I don't," she replied emphatically. "We have done quite a lot to limit the size of families: we could have done more, but I don't consider the population problem with grave anxiety."

I was dismayed that she like her father underrated the importance of controlling an explosive birthrate. I showed her a graph with the latest figures depicting how if things went on as they were going, by the turn of the century we would have overtaken China and become the poorest and most congested country in the world.

She was not impressed. "I do not underestimate the importance of family planning; but it is only one of the many problems we have to handle. During British days large areas of activity were left untouched. We are operating on a larger scale and on many more levels. I am not pessimistic nor unduly alarmed at the rate of progress made in this field."

I did not give up. "Don't you think a measure of coercion would be justified? Fire government servants who have more than three children, disenfranchise those . . ."

She cut me short: "Coercion? In a democracy?"

"Let's say legalised coercion, like raising the age of marriage by Act of Parliament."

"What's the use of passing legislation you cannot enforce? The Sarda Act was passed fifty years ago but child marriages continue to this day."[51]

Kushwant Singh (for it was he) is not averse to taking the credit for fathering the system of "compulsuasion" which developed out of the vasectomy camp experience. In fact his are the orthodox arguments of the "Beyond Family Planning" school; he shared such opinions with a significant number of civil servants, people who, as Nehru had pointed out, were ill-chosen to initiate social change in India because of their alien Anglo-Indian orientation and lack of sympathy for the poor. Their spiritual leader was Mrs Gandhi's son, Sanjay.

The Union Minister of Health and Family Planning, Karan Singh, poet, ex-regent of Jammu and Kashmir, student of Sri Aurobindo, passionately committed to democratic socialism, began his term of office by reducing to a realistic level the speed at which the population growth rate was expected to fall; the pay-off was that the new realistic levels had to be reached, and this was to be done by linking central government grants to state legislatures to their family planning performance.

Workers in the field must be imbued with missionary zeal, and an important aspect is our ability for effective supervision and imaginative adaptation of strategies to suit local needs.[52]

The state governments in their turn delegated the responsibility to the heads of blocks and districts and they in turn to the village administrations. The pattern had been set in Haryana when the paving of access roads to villages and connection to the rural electricity supply was made contingent on family-planning performance.[53] Such are the beginnings of coercion; it would seem almost reasonable that if the state does something for the citizens the citizens should do something for the state, but it must not be forgotten that the state is the servant of the people who already provide their taxes to run it. If the proposed policies are for the people's good, it should be possible to prove the fact; if they are not, they are not to be implemented. A man who desperately needs electricity to run his pump or mill ought not to have to undergo a vasectomy in order to have what he needs, especially as the enrichment of his family provides his motivation for the pumping and milling. In the absence of any system of social security he may well be being asked to forgo security in his old age in order to have his electricity. In fact, he will not be vasectomised in return for electricity, he will find a poorer man with even narrower options and present him for sterilisation in his stead.

A typical example of the perversion of the motivation system was described by Malini Khanduri in the *Indian Express*. The Deputy Commissioner of Madurai in Tamil Nadu was eager to win the award for family-planning performance. The responsibility was duly passed to his subordinates, who had to find candidates for sterilisation or lose their jobs. They in turn pressured the district officers, who in their turn pressured the village-level revenue officers, who passed the problem on to the village headman.

> In their villages each headman had summoned the men and asked for volunteers. None. Then the headman casually asked Bihari, "Oh, Bihari, that land dispute of yours, it hasn't been settled yet, has it?" Silence. After a while Bihari spoke, "If I ...?" "Ah, my good man, God will reward you for your wisdom; you are a man after my own heart."[54]

In the follow-up of sterilisation acceptors from Madurai, it was found that the mean time elapsed since the wife's last pregnancy was 5.7 years; in other words, sterilisation was unlikely to have any effect on the birthrate as most of the men had completed their family size and were already taking fairly successful measures, probably abstinence. Whether they took advantage of their surgically guaranteed sterility and whether their wives were grateful for their attentions, history does not relate. Sadly, a quarter of men reported adverse reactions to the operation. In Ramanathapuram, in the Madurai district, the effects of the programme were still being felt in 1979:

> The innovators of family planning from this village happen to be three vasectomised persons. Among them one suffered a swollen scrotum, weakness of body and difficulty to walk long distances besides a lowered capacity for hard manual work. This adverse experience of the vasectomy acceptor early in the programme period in this village led to vasectomy becoming unpopular

even to this day, to the extent that for about three years after the three persons underwent vasectomy no one from the village came forward to adopt a family-planning method.[55]

There were many who realised that delegating responsibility to the panchayats and other local organisations would result in widespread abuse and injustice. To them it seemed that if India was to use economic and social pressure to force sterilisation on unwilling people, the only solution possible in a democracy was universal, compulsory sterilisation after the birth of the third child. Even if the entire health budget was devoted to the task, such a massive effort was beyond the capacity of the Indian health-delivery system; moreover, in 1974 more than two and a half million cases of malaria had been reported.[56] A major battle was looming on that front; there could be no universal sterilisation while children died for lack of malaria control. Karan Singh rejected the possibility of the Government of India attempting to bring in universal sterilisation, but he pointed out that the state governments had the option of bringing in their own legislation if they had reason to believe that their health-delivery services were adequate.[57] What this meant was that the Union government refused all responsibility for the implementation of population control while remaining the architect and paymaster of the scheme. Karan Singh may have been in good faith when he explained to Walter Schwartz of the *Observer*, who was asking if the government had abandoned mass vasectomy camps:

> Individual states can still do those if they want but from the federal centre these have been dropped. I think they belonged to the old rather than the new approach to family planning. Vasectomy, sterilisation, abortion and other terminal methods must still be part of the programme but not mass camps ...
>
> In the context of this five-year plan the condom is going to be the basis ... We are stepping up production to 330 million in a year's time and more as the plan goes on.[58]

While the central government ostensibly retained its commitment to the cafeteria approach, the states were gripped by what appeared to be sterilisation mania. On their own initiative, state officials faced with the task of motivating large numbers called in their subordinates and asked how many of them had three children or more, one of whom was a boy five years old or older, and were therefore eligible for sterilisation. A member of the Maharashtra government explained to me in 1981 that he was proud of the fact that when he found eligible unsterilised men in his own department, he gave them three weeks to undergo the operation or accept suspension. "In all my years of service," he said, "I never felt I was getting anywhere. In 1975 we were getting something done. How could I send my officers out to motivate people to accept sterilisation if they were not willing to undergo it themselves?"

Within months of the discontinuation of mass high-incentive sterilisation camps by the central government, private enterprise and the state governments had stepped into the breach. A camp run by the Corporation of Madras in conjunction with the Rotary Club in December 1974 carried out 2,006 operations in two weeks; acceptors were given six days paid leave and gifts of cloth. At the time mini-camps were being run at five Primary Health Centres in Himachal Pradesh, which brought its yearly total to 153% of the target. In March 1975 the Indian Railways proudly announced:

> Due to collective performance of the Indian Railways in the family-planning programme, about 2.51 lakh [251,000] births have been prevented since 1952 ... It is estimated that this has resulted in financial savings of Rs 10 million to the Railways in terms of expenditure on health and welfare services to the employees and their families.[59]

By April sterilisation mania was at its height, whipped up by the organ of the newly formed Central Family Planning Institute, *Centre Calling*, which gave space to statements like those of Aurelio Peccei of the Club of Rome regarding the duties of "immature" nations, which appeared in the issue for March 1975.

> ... every individual will have responsibilities toward society. He cannot over-breed, he cannot overburden society with his offspring beyond certain limits fixed by law ... The right to give birth in that society will no longer be an unqualified birthright as many seem to consider it today. Regulations in this sense, dictated in the interest of the community will, however, look less and less like intolerable impediments in the sphere of personal freedom as they will reflect the general understanding of what is the common good and everybody's ethical obligation.[60]

The next number of *Centre Calling* announced that "Three states – Haryana, Gujarat and Maharashtra – are running a neck-and-neck race to turn out the best performances of the year."[61] Haryana was concentrating on contraceptives and IUDs and had achieved four times the rate of acceptance in Maharashtra and Gujarat. In a camp at Mehsana in Gujarat, more than 500 sterilisation acceptors had registered on the first day. The District Development Officer himself raised the extra money for 500 extra acceptors. Thus, a year before the promulgation of the new Population Policy, the great push was on. In Bihar, all employees of the Department of Health and Family Planning had to motivate a certain number of acceptors for sterilisation under pain of censure, docked pay or, if the short-fall was of the order of 50% or more, dismissal. All teachers in government schools had to provide six sterilees a year, as did all Panchayat employees, village-level workers, Anchal Inspectors, Extension Officers and Supply Inspectors. Other public employees had to motivate twice as many. All Government employees were to be given privileges such

as travel passes, educational allowances and reimbursements of medical
expenses for no more than three children, and all candidates for government jobs had to sign an undertaking to accept sterilisation after two
children or guarantee cessation of child-bearing by some other means.
Positive incentives included priority for sterilised couples in the allotment
of cars and scooters, building sites and home and business loans.[62]

In June, the Indian Supreme Court declared Mrs Gandhi's election
invalid. Instead of stepping down, she invoked extra-constitutional
powers by declaring a state of emergency, which provides for the suspension of civil liberties and detention without trial of subversive
elements. The tempo of the population-control programme quickened,
still without direct intervention from the Union government. The 1975–6
targets were published in July. There were to be 2,521,000 sterilisations,
904,400 IUD insertions, and 4,086,100 new users of contraception in
India. Maharashtra revised its 318,300 sterilisation quota upward to
568,000 and achieved 611,000. Assam more than doubled its quota.
Jammu and Kashmir, Kerala, Meghalaya, Orissa, Punjab, Tamil Nadu,
Tripura, West Bengal, the Andaman and Nicobar Islands, Delhi,
Lakshadweep, Mizoram and Pondicherry all exceeded their quotas. The
worst performances were registered by key states Bihar, Gujarat, Haryana,
Madhya Pradesh, Rajasthan, and Uttar Pradesh.[63] One way of explaining
the discrepancy was to point to the higher proportion of Muslims in these
states; statistical evidence had already been produced to show that
Muslims, at 11.2% of the population, were providing only 5.6% of the
sterilisations and 6.8% of the IUD insertions. Inter-communal hostility
is easily exacerbated; obviously the issue of vasectomy acceptance is highly
charged. Hindus practise no bodily mutilation of any kind and it might
be thought that vasectomy is an even greater trauma for them than for
people who practise ritual circumcision. The thought that Muslims might
increase their numerical strength by avoiding their social duty provoked
violent reactions. The Muslims prepared to defend themselves against
persecution and began, rashly, to speak out against Emergency. The only
parliamentary opposition to the New Population Policy, announced in
April 1976, came from a Muslim leader.

Among the sixteen measures to be taken were the providing of group
incentives to popular institutions, including cooperative societies and
trades unions, the freezing of electoral representation on the basis of the
1971 population distribution until 2001, the allocation of Centre funds
to maintain the 1971 proportions until 2001, eight per cent of Centre
funding for the States family planning performance, the raising of the
minimum age at marriage to eighteen years for women and twenty-one
for men, and the offer of relatively large cash incentives to sterilisation
acceptors of low parity – 150 rupees to those with two children only, and
100 to those with three. The new sterilisation targets were nearly twice

those of the preceding year, but even so many states revised them upwards. Andhra Pradesh, for example, which had managed little more than half its 1975–6 quota of 294,200 sterilisations, not only accepted a 1976–7 quota of 400,000 but raised it to 600,000 and actually carried out 741,713. Family planning was the first point of Sanjay Gandhi's Five-Point Programme, officially adopted along with his mother's Twenty-Point Economic Programme. The State governments that went overboard to show their allegiance to the Youth Congress Party may have imagined that they were feathering their nests; they were also caught up in the finger-snapping, sunglass-wearing movie-idol world in which they imagined that the men of Sanjay Gandhi would live, and were correspondingly contemptuous of their own village traditions. The "smooth" and "sophisticated" politicos, however, were passing on the responsibility for motivation to people they saw as yokels and showing them the callousness which they would avenge upon their inferiors in turn. There was no shortage of opposition parties to take up the cause of opposition to the population policy, but the emergency rules gave its proponents an unusual sense of security. By some such mechanism the state authorities turned the 4,255,500 sterilisations demanded by the GOI into 8,132,209.

When the Congress Party Government of Uttar Pradesh received its instructions to implement Sanjay Gandhi's crash programme, the Chief Secretary sent the following telegram to the Financial Commissioner, all the Administrative Secretaries, all Heads of Department, all Sub-divisional Officers, and all district and sessions judges:

> Government attaches highest importance to achievement of family planning targets. Presume you have already fixed targets for each district and divisional level officer. Inform everybody that failure to achieve targets will not only result in stoppage of salary but also suspension and severest penalties. Galvanise entire administrative machinery into action forthwith repeat forthwith and continue to report daily progress by crash wireless to me and the Secretary of the Chief Minister.[64]

In the frenzy that followed 837,000 sterilisations were performed, little more than half the target of 1.5 million; as a result of post-operative complications, 201 people died. In Rajasthan, with only 364,760 sterilisations, 217 people died. Throughout the Union, 1,774 people died as a direct consequence of the operation; the figure is well authenticated, for the government which replaced Mrs Gandhi in 1978 directed all states to verify complaints and make *ex gratia* payments of Rs. 5000 to all families losing a breadwinner through sterilisation. In fact the number may be rather low, for about twice as many claims were made as payments. Not all states reported the number of unmarried persons sterilised, but the total is somewhere near 548. In Andhra Pradesh, no fewer than 21,653 sterilised men had fewer than two children; in Orissa, 19,237; in Punjab,

19,838; in Gujurat, 7,834. In Maharashtra, 151 died, 6,958 had fewer than two children, 368 were over fifty-five; in Barsi and Sholapur, two lepers were forcibly sterilised, and eight men were "sterilised" for the second time.

The common Western perception of Emergency is that all over India young men were being held down by brute force and sterilised, that truck-loads of manacled people were brought into camps by day and night to depart sterilised. To be sure, in Haryana,

> Buses were diverted to camps and passengers sterilised. Persons were forcibly taken from villages, bus stands and railway stations for sterilisations to family planning camps.[65]

With only 222,000 sterilisations, the Haryana death rate of 132 is one of the highest; the proportion of unmarried (105) and elderly (179) men sterilised is probably the highest for any state. The Haryana story is a particularly sad one, for the State had invested considerable effort in an IUD programme which by 1977 had resulted in almost half a million insertions despite the setback of the earlier loop campaign; in 1976–77, 27,609 Copper-Ts had been inserted, twice as many as the previous year, and the state had asked for its sterilisation quota to be reduced accordingly. There were 3.51 million users of contraception in the state and a well-established Nirodh condom distribution programme. Mass sterilisation had never been a part of the Haryana effort and in the rush to fulfil the new requirements, there was no time to train divisional officers in motivational techniques or to learn the systems of management of mass sterilisation programmes.[66]

Early in the morning of 6 November 1976, the village of Uttawar in the Gurgaon district of Haryana was raided by 700 police who rounded up 550 men and took them away. The village, inhabited by 8,000 Muslims of the Meo community, had refused to allow any family-planning worker to enter. Its defiance was becoming something of a rallying-point for other Muslims in a sensitive area. On 12 October the authorities took the un-precedented and illegal step of disconnecting the electricity supply to the village; the line superintendent, upon being informed that what he had done was illegal, restored the supply, only to be beaten by the police and forced to disconnect it again. The Inspector-General of Police who authorised the raid claimed that it was necessary as a security measure, the villagers being suspected of maintaining links with Pakistan, but in fact he had been informed of the attitude of the villagers to sterilisation and told that men rounded up would be taken for forcible sterilisation. Local leaders had tried to persuade the villagers to take a less suicidal attitude and had secured some sort of an agreement to produce acceptors when they were not needed for the sowing season, but the police could not wait. The villagers were taken to Hathin for interrogation; a hundred of them were imprisoned for assaulting a patwari, and 180 were sent to family planning centres at Nuh and Mandkola where they were sterilised.

Shri Abdul Rehman *alias* Lelha, son of Shri Shai Khan, 25 years, has stated that after the raid on November 6th, 1976, he was taken to the Mandkola Primary Health Centre on November 7th, 1976, along with others and forcibly sterilised there, despite his plea that he had only one issue, a daughter. He has also stated that initially the doctor had refused to operate, but was later on pressurised by the police to undertake the operation.[67]

The doctor explained that he could not afford to annoy the executive authorities because the annual confidential reports on his performance by the Directors of the Health Service were routed through the Sub-divisional Officers and Deputy Commissioners. The incident is important, because it reveals that the doctor, although he could not withstand the pressure eventually, did exercise his own judgment and sought to reject this man on the grounds of ineligibility, even though the police had brought him in under restraint. In earlier sterilisation programmes, the rate of rejection for ineligibility had sometimes been as high as 50%; if doctors in the Emergency had been sterilising all comers, the incidence of sterilisation of ineligible men would have been many times higher than it was. Not only did most doctors continue to reject ineligible sterilands in the vast majority of cases, but the incident at Uttawar was unusual in its summary brutality. Throughout India the pattern was more the kind of inexorable manipulation which had developed over centuries. In another society it might have been seen as "peer-group pressure." However, we may also assume, given the patterns observed in other sterilisation programmes, that the selection of sterilands by the subject groups was made on the grounds of those who had the least to lose, the fathers of completed families, the abstinent, the impotent, the physically disadvantaged, the expendable. The figure of 8 million-plus sterilisations seems high until we remember that it is still only a tiny fraction of the total number of eligible individuals in a population of more than 711 million people. What is more depressing is the reflection that each of the villages where 1,774 men died of their wounds will continue to send out shock-waves of dread, dread of one of the safest and most reliable methods of birth control, as the result of the perversion of the beginnings of a mass movement by haste and fear. As well as the silent dead, we must postulate a certain number, a much higher number, of living men with painful after-effects who will continue denouncing vasectomy until the day they die.

There is some evidence, although the Shah Commission chose to discount it, that Central Government was becoming alarmed at the excesses of the state programmes. In October 1976 Karan Singh wrote to the Chief Ministers of the States congratulating them on their performance, but including a request to see that only eligible candidates were motivated and to see to post-operative care. An Intelligence Bureau assessment of the family-planning programme reported that "certain hostile reactions have come to notice in ... Uttar Pradesh and to a lesser extent in Bihar, West Bengal and Maharashtra. An analysis of the various factors leading to hostile reactions which had sometimes resulted in breaches of law and order shows that the governmental agencies as well as the obscurantist and communal elements were responsible for them." However, although many officials claimed after the defeat of the Congress Party at the 1978 elections that they too thought the state targets far too high, none of them actually dissuaded the states from their headlong career. Some of the unrest in Maharashtra was caused by the use of the sterilisation issue by the Shiv Sena Party; in Tamil Nadu the Hindu Temple Protection Committee held protest meetings where members of the Jana Sangh spoke against the New Population Policy. Intercommunal tension lay behind disturbances in Karnataka, Madhya Pradesh, at Faizabad in Uttar Pradesh and in Calcutta where a policeman was killed. In Uttar Pradesh a series of uprisings in Muslim villages, beginning in Sultanpur in August, 1976, led to police firing on the demonstrators at Gorakhpur and Muzzaffarnagar in October and at Pratabghar in December, resulting in 1544 arrests and twelve deaths. In Madhya Pradesh the protests were occasioned by the use of force at Bhanpuri, Barela and Amiliha. Tribals were particularly defenceless in the situation; of thirteen *adivasis* sterilised at the Primary Health Centre in Bijapur, two died of sepsis. In Rajasthan, where the programme had been spectacularly mismanaged, 283 arrests were made even before the riots at the Turkman Gate. The uproar could no longer be contained, even if it had been possible to prolong emergency rule indefinitely. Mrs Gandhi went to the people and was rejected.

At the height of sterilisation euphoria, Tara ali Baig, head of the Indian delegation to the UN Population Year Conference at Bucharest, Chairman of the Indian Council of Child Welfare, in an article entitled "Prevention is better than Care" allows herself to vent convictions which should have been discredited forty years before.

> Sterilisation of one partner has to be made imperative where a man or woman suffers from hereditary insanity, feeble-mindedness or congenital venereal disease: they must be barred by law from procreating children. This should have been done decades ago.
>
> If children's lives and future are to be protected, compulsory sterilisation is necessary for many reasons. There are literally thousands of men in and out of joint families who have never earned, yet who marry and produce children.
>
> After all, considering the crime against children committed by irresponsible parenthood, compulsory sterilisation in certain cases is hardly punitive ... Sterilisation of the unfit is long overdue.[68]

Those who cannot learn from history are compelled to repeat its mistakes; while 41% of vasectomised men reported some kind of physical complication as a result of the operation, and another 19% were stricken by the death of a child according to a study by a Research Analyst at the Delhi Institute of Economic Growth.[69] Dr A. S. Gupta was conducting his own study at the RNT Medical College in Udaipur to show that vasectomy "leads to virility" (whatever that may mean in scientific – or in any – terms) and "increases sexual desire."[70] The naivety and political illiteracy of the champions of mass vasectomy would eventually have discredited their campaign even if haste and ignorance had not caused it to collapse in ruins; and perhaps we should be relieved that the process was so swift. One section of Indian political opinion, however, seems to have learned the wrong lesson from the insanities of the Emergency. Kushwant Singh, raised to the Upper House after Mrs Gandhi's return to power, tabled a bill providing for sterilisation of citizens with more than two children. Under the bill, couples with more than three children would lose their voting rights.[71] There was little support for the bill in 1980, but this strain of thinking pre-dated the disasters of 1976–7, and is only biding its time. Like bills for amendments to acts liberalising abortion, it will reappear time and again.

When the country was still reeling from the revelation of what had gone on during Emergency, a group from the National Institute of Health and Family Welfare carried out a "Survey of Public Opinion on Methods of securing a Most Effective Implementation of the Family Welfare Policy." Of a sample of 7,000 people, 78% said that they were in favour of mandatory sterilisation by law and not by administrative pressure. The highest numbers of this opinion were registered in Bihar and Madhya Pradesh where the most widespread abuses were reported during Emergency. The British government continued to send £3,000,000 a year for the establishment of sterilisation facilities in 325 district hospitals and 1000 Primary Health Centres. Targets were set as before, but not at the dizzy levels of 1976–7. Compensation was still paid to acceptors and at a relatively high rate of between Rs70 and Rs175; motivators are still rewarded, to the tune of Rs15 for each vasectomy and Rs10 for tubectomy. Between April 1979 and February 1980, 532,375 Copper-Ts were inserted and more than one and a half million people were sterilized.

When the Janata party came to power in 1978 the Department of Family Planning in the Central Government was re-named the Department of Family Welfare; the chief commitment was to the building up and strengthening of the health-delivery system based upon the Primary Health Centres. A vast training programme for a million traditional birth attendants was undertaken. Government took the lead, as it ought to have done from the beginning, from the voluntary agencies. There was no more talk of population control officially, but of Maternal and Child Health services. Doubtless the population hawks were disgusted with such cowardice; "time is running out", they used to say, as if it were not the property of time to be continually running out, just as Mrs Gandhi liked to say that "We do not have all the time in the world." The people working in the field have always known that there can be no hurry in changing patterns of family-building, especially if the motivation for trying to do it in the first place is to reduce human suffering. No dedicated doctor, spending his life in an ill-equipped, remote health centre for a salary which will be inadequate to support his family at the same level that he enjoyed when he grew up, could survive unless he could see that things were better because of his presence. The question of whether there are as many people as there might have been, or as few, fades into insignificance.

Throughout the Emergency the work of improving the people's health and raising their standard of living had gone on. In Dehu, in the district of Pune, for example, Dr S. V. Mapuskar set out to make his Primary Health Centre the centre of the village and to see that the people were committed to it and confident that it operated in their interests. The best way of achieving those ends was to get the villagers to build the centre themselves. Working through youth and women's organisations, Dr Mapuskar not only got the centre built, but the people made a garden around it and maintained it. The centre built, they turned to supplying other necessities, tube wells for clean water supply, latrine blocks to reduce the danger of infection, a Gobar gas plant to provide clean fuel and light. To show his commitment to their real needs, Dr Mapuskar treated 1,910 couples for infertility.[72] After the Emergency, treatment for involuntary infertility became a necessary and very visible part of the Family Welfare programme, as it should always have been, but it is doubtful whether intervention was successful often enough to reduce the trauma and suffering in the few instances in which sufferers were prepared to go under the knife again.

When I visited Dehu in 1981, Dr Mapuskar's place had been taken by Dr Shete, who radiated something rather unusual among underpaid and overworked medics in the back blocks and far off the promotion trail, which was happiness. When he realised that I was not going to rate his performance by the number of births he had averted, he relaxed visibly and his happiness increased. Yes, he did sterilisations, using the modified Pomeroy technique with a local only, as he had no anaesthetist. Virtually all the eligible women in his area were covered and the complication rate was low. He explained that the trick of cutting tubes without a general anaesthetic was to move fast, yet he was well aware of the danger of disrupting the blood supply to the ovary and positioned his cut very carefully. (Dr Ambedkar, at the nearby Cantonment Hospital claimed a complication rate of 20%, often leading to hysterectomy). Dr Shete did not remove any part of the tube, but everted the cut ends to make sure that it did not reanastomose. No, he hadn't inserted any IUDs in two years because he had found mycosis as a pathogen causing leucorrhoea and cervicitis in his IUD acceptors. Moreover, he recommended the pill unwillingly and kept a close watch to see if women on it showed signs of oedema and facial mottling. Dr Shete's preferred contraceptive method was the noble Nirodh. There was no doubting Dr Shete's active and sincere interest in the health of poor women; the quality of the care he was giving could not have been bettered in Harley Street, even though he was perpetually short of essential drugs and vaccines. Unfortunately, the training institutions that produced Dr Shete also produce the unhappy doctors in unvisited clinics, bitterly lamenting their idle fate, temperamentally unable and professionally unprepared to go out into the streets and win the confidence of the people. The same institutions produce doctors who now practise in Europe and America, preferring to treat the elaborate disorders of the rich. Dr Shete took me into the village, to the temple raised in honour of Turkaram, the author of the Ramayana, and to the kitchen of a grand Brahmin lady who had hallowed the lowly marsh-gas gathered from the excrement of people and cows by allowing it into the most sacred place in her house. The changes in the lifestyle of Dehu are expressions of the people's own values. They have been accomplished for a very small capital investment and a very large emotional one. If the people become aware of excess fertility in the way that they were aware of squalor and disease, they will deal with it without being diminished in spirit as they are if someone else identifies the problem and makes them instruments of an imaginary solution.

Compared to the dusty plains of Dehu, the Nilgiri Hills are paradise. The hospital on the Craigmoor tea estate is a grander affair than the buildings at Dehu and rather bigger than I should have expected. "Oh, we need all the beds," smiled the young doctor. "In the summer there are epidemics, influenza, enteric fever . . . We have them lying all over, in the corridors, outside." The hospital was well equipped, although the bedding was, as usual in India, very stained. The only patients were two women who seemed barely out of their teens. The babies lying on the neighbouring beds were tiny. There was something terrible in the blank faces the women turned to me but the young doctor did not seem to notice. "Ah yes," he said, sure that I would applaud, "the growers give a very good incentive, a gold chain worth 2000 rupees." The women were still stupefied from the pre-medication but not all the atropine and morphia in the world could change the hopelessness of that look. Two thousand rupees is two hundred days' wages for a tea-plucker, but who wants the gold, she or her husband? Who dies in the yearly visitations of infectious disease guaranteed by the polluted water-supply and primitive hygiene in the estate-workers' village? Why, the babies of course. For the planters, two thousand rupees is an investment in continued productivity from the female worker and reduced health and educational expenses, but for her?

Her sons might have rescued her from picking two-leaves-and-a-bud, two-leaves-and-a-bud for the rest of her life. What happens to a sterilised wife whose babies die? Her husband casts her off. During the Emergency the less poor man oppressed the poorer man by pre-empting his control over his fertility; nowadays the poor man can oppress the poor woman by the same means and the authorities will rush to help him.

Actually, although female sterilisation is a more difficult and dangerous procedure than vasectomy and requires a hospital stay, there is a positive aspect of getting the women into hospital, which is that their general health can be more adequately investigated, and they can be helped with hygiene and child nutrition problems more efficiently in the hospital setting. Some of the health workers I met made a point of keeping the women in hospital until they thought that they were properly rested and their anaemias and so forth dealt with, remonstrating mothers-in-law notwithstanding. The procedure is not laid out in their instructions but they do it anyway. Unfortunately the people who make the most difference to the health of poor patients are not the people who can be heard at international conferences. They are not the people who decide how the money shall be spent. They are not the people who will get the chairs in the teaching hospitals and train another generation of frustrated allopaths who can see no drama and no interest in joining the battle against poverty and its preventable diseases.

In sharp contrast to the agonies and absurdities of the Indian struggle to curb population growth in the interests of health and prosperity stands the Chinese success. An inter-regional seminar on primary health care held in Yexian County, Shandon Province, in June 1982 postulated five reasons for the achievement of health for all, a goal which is not yet even in sight for the nations of India and Bangladesh. As family planning forms part of the health package the five reasons apply to the population programme also. The first reason given is that:

China has demonstrated a tremendous political will to change the quality of life for all people, and especially the rural population.

The phrase "political will" is part of the armoury of cliché to be encountered throughout the international aid establishment. It is usually interpreted as meaning a clear commitment from government, but in the Chinese example the meaning is rather different. The revolutionary struggle and its atrocities were only justified if the citizens of the People's Republic proved themselves capable of constructing a better life for themselves; their standards of living were so low that an initial improvement was relatively easy to detect, especially when all opposition had been effectively silenced and failures in the reconstruction programme would not come to public attention.

The re-organisation of the economic and social structure of society has resulted in a level of decentralisation that has made possible close integration of health with all aspects of development and has facilitated the people's involvement in the management of health care.

What is here called decentralisation we would probably call by some very different name. What seems to be meant is the system of delegation from the leading groups through the structure of brigades and communes to the grass-roots level. In the case of family planning, cadres had the duty of persuading the citizens to accept the idea of birth quotas and calculating who was eligible for a turn at child-bearing. The collectivity decided, but the decisions were local expressions of central policies. The reasons for including birth limitation among the ways of improving the quality of life were all good ones: to safeguard women's health, to facilitate the full participation of women in production, to allow for study, work and political progress. Feminism had been an important part of the revolutionary policy and of its strategy. While the men fought with the revolutionary army the women had carried on agriculture and instituted the first agrarian reforms. Unlike other male revolutionary leaders, Mao did not send the women back to their homes after the military phase of the struggle; many of them were more radicalised than their menfolk and more committed to self-improvement by study. The re-education of men to work alongside women on terms of complete equality was an important propaganda activity. The limitation of fertility was an integral part of the coming-of-age of the Chinese woman.

Concerted sections in many sectors, e.g. shelter, clothing and above all the availability of essential foods and family planning, have contributed to this improvement of health status.

The availability of essential foods to all was accomplished only by planning the economy in a way which was completely incompatible with any degree of private enterprise. We can only guess how effective such planning could be in the absence of necessary storage and distribution facilities, but clearly, the necessity for planning in a country which had been periodically stricken by famine for centuries was generally understood; if planning was to be possible, then the increase in the number of mouths to be fed must be planned too. What Mao Tse-Tung managed to do was to extend the peasant rationale of fertility management to comprehend a nation of 600 million or so as a community, an achievement astonishing in itself and totally out of reach of any society which is not prepared to clear the decks for the establishment of a monolithic political system. The will of the community was translated into the greater good of the cells which composed it; as the policies were communicated outward, they were eventually enacted as peer-group pressure.

People's participation in the provision of health services and in the management of the health system has perhaps been the most important factor for achieving development of the health care system.

This claim could have been expressed in other terms, if it were possible to admit the genius of Mao at this stage in China's history. The innovation was actually that no separate elite of health professionals in imitation of the Western model, which is proving so ill-adapted to evolving peasant communities, was allowed to develop. Instead, students were obliged to be workers and workers to study, so that the relation of health services to the people they were designed to serve remained close. Given the immense poverty of China, where calorie intake is still almost as low as it is in India and Bangladesh, there was no possibility of creating an immense officer corps of fully trained allopaths and so the system of "barefoot doctors" was devised. These community health workers had enough medical training to deal with the common ailments of labouring folk, and to recognise when their ministrations were inadequate. They were members of the community they served, on an equal footing with their patients, and in no way an intrusion representing the policies of an alien and possibly hostile central authority.

Appropriate technology utilised in the health care system made widespread availability feasible in spite of limited conventional resources.[73]

The Chinese system of combining traditional medicine and techniques such as acupuncture with modern surgery and drug therapy has been widely and justly admired. China's isolation made it possible for her to avoid the continuing disaster of aggressive marketing of inappropriate drugs which afflicts the rest of the developing world and to cling to systems of health care which would have been swept aside by medical programmes set up and funded from abroad. As far as fertility regulation is concerned, however, little in the nature of traditional methods has survived. When the first campaign to keep down population growth was mounted in 1954, there was nothing in the way of contraceptive hardware to distribute, so in 1957 all restrictions were removed from abortion as the chief method of achieving the elimination of unwanted pregnancy. Opportunity to marry was restricted: students were not allowed to marry; civil servants ran the risk of dismissal if they married without permission and young peasants were discouraged from marrying by registrars. It became very fashionable to postpone marriage in the interests of the state and many heroic examples were publicised to serve as role models. After the Great Leap Forward a campaign to limit births in the interests of women's health laid great stress on vasectomy as the preferred method, and minimised official support for abortion, as is only consistent with a concern for women's health, exacerbated perhaps by difficulties encountered in the earlier campaign. The ideology of late marriage and delayed birth was almost universally accepted, except among the tribal minorities, who, as their unaltered death rate prevented them from presenting a demographic problem, were ignored.

The most popular method of family limitation in the sixties in China was the condom, followed by the diaphragm and the IUD, rhythm and prolonged lactation. We do not know how much trial and error accompanied the development of the Chinese IUD and we will probably never be told; one advantage of not having a free press is that disturbing news cannot be fanned into a panic, although the Chinese are as adept as any other peasant population in the circulation of rumours. The number of abortions seems to have continued to grow during the sixties and some reports of coercion, withholding ration tickets for clothing for a third-born child and refusing to register marriages considered too early, have been recorded.

After the Cultural Revolution the push for family planning began again, and this time there was a determined effort to add oral contraceptives to the array of methods distributed throughout China. After a number of false starts, about which nothing is known, the Chinese succeeded in developing their own series of low-dose pills. By about 1968 oral contraceptives were ready for mass distribution by the barefoot doctors. By 1972 China was ready to exhibit her family-planning achievement to the world. The world was impressed. Julia Henderson and T. Katagiri held a press conference upon their return to Britain in May 1972, announcing that 85–90% of couples in China were using some form of family limitation with the help of one million barefoot doctors and their three million assistants.[74] A medical team from America which included Carl Djerassi and General Draper came back talking of prodigies, zero population growth in Shanghai, Nanking and Canton, oral contraceptives in sheets like stamps, abortions by acupuncture and the like.[75] Against the background of the other Asian countries the Chinese achievement was stupendous; the cleanliness of the streets, the obviously high morale of all the people they dealt with, had the visitors ready to believe anything and to hold firmly that they had seen it with their own eyes. Foreigners began to speculate on the size of the Chinese population. The Committee of Foreign Affairs of the United States House of Representatives asked the Congress Research Service to prepare a report because in the words of the report:

> After being ignored for many years there is now a widespread impression that China may have discovered the answer to the innumerable problems which have plagued family planning programmes in other developing countries ... and the conclusion, by and large, was that there is valid cause for China's pride and for foreign interest.[76]

For family-planning idealists, needing desperately to believe that fertility regulation is a natural right and not a right-wing plot, and that there is some point in struggling to bring birthrates down before a rise in the standard of living in order to make that rise possible, China was a necessary event. Unfortunately the Chinese refused to deal in the rhetoric of demographic projections and population control. They knew perfectly well that the rest of the world saw them as an undifferentiated horde and considered the fact that every fifth child was Chinese to be somehow shocking, and it was the more important for Chinese delegates at international conferences to repeat the party line on population.

> At the Bucharest Conference the leader of the Chinese delegation rejected "over-population" in itself as the cause of unemployment, poverty, starvation, high mortality, and war, but conceded without elaboration that rapid population growth poses serious obstacles to economic, social and cultural development.[77]

The pressure to reduce population growth continued in the years that followed and the birthrate steadily fell. In 1978 eight million fewer babies were born than in 1971; in Beijing, Shanghai and Tianjin the growth rate was well below 1%. In February 1978 Chairman Hua Guo Feng included a demographic statement in his address to the Fifth National People's Congress:

> To control the population growth in a planned manner is in the interest of the planned development of the national economy, and of the protection of maternal and child health. It must be grasped seriously and continuously. Strive to reduce the natural increase rate of the population of our country to 10 per thousand within three years.[78]

Birth planning was written into the constitution adopted at the same congress. What the Chairman's statement revealed was first that reproductive freedom was not among the changes to be expected after the fall of the Gang of Four, and second that priorities had changed. The demographic transition that had happened so swiftly since 1963 cannot have been as painless or as widely accepted as outsiders had been led to believe; the new emphasis on increased productivity from individual households and the increases in the amounts of land available for private use had produced an instant rise in the birthrate, which began to climb back again in 1979, not to anything like its pre-liberation levels but the upswing was ominous. The factor of which the new leadership was forced to take account was that given the age structure of the population a huge bulge in the birthrate, with corresponding pressure on weak sectors of the economy (education, employment and housing) was inevitable even if present low rates of increase were maintained. Some observers included faltering grain production among the causes of anxiety. The opening of China to Western influence produced instant changes in the dress and appearance of urban Chinese women; it was only a matter of time before a measure of sexual freedom was demanded along with brassieres and lipstick.

While the government officially warned against coercion, coercion in the form of Singapore-style incentives made its appearance. In Sichuan province parents with one child were to receive a 10% wage increment, the same housing as a family of four, and priority of admission to schools and factories, and an adult grain ration for the child.[79] In Yunnan economic penalties were imposed on parents of more than two children and in Guzhon sterilisation quotas were announced. Lanzhon Chemical Company announced awards for employees making pledges to have only one child.[80] In June, the Xinhua News Agency announced that the demographic target had been revised; now the aim was 0.5% population growth by 1985.[81] The demographer Ma Yinchu, who had warned against the possibility of a Chinese population explosion, was rehabilitated and with him the idea that China was already overpopulated.[82] The long-range goal was enunciated, to reduce the Chinese population to 650 or 700 million by the mid-twenty-first century. After refusing foreign aid for two decades, China, claiming a per capita income of $152 per year, entered the aid market to the consternation of India and Bangladesh.[83]

In July 1980 articles began to appear in the Chinese press advocating the prohibition of marriage to people with genetic defects, including the relatively common one of colour-blindness.[84] Requests were made for instruction and facilities for genetic screening. In February 1981 the Beijing Hospital opened a premarital, family, sex and eugenic counselling service.[85] In January 1981 a proposal for the mercy-killing of all mongoloids at birth was reported in the *Daily Telegraph*.[86]

By March 1980 five million couples had signed the one-child pledge.[87] In September Hua Guo Feng proposed a "crash drive" to reduce the rate of population growth in terms oddly reminiscent of Sanjay Gandhi's Five-Point Programme.[88] By January 1981 ten million couples had taken the one-child pledge but with 160 million people reaching marriageable age in the next five years, the proportion was still far too small.[89] In August the suggestion was aired that the one-child family should be made law but already opposition to the idea was making it practically unworkable.[90] The lightning reversals in Chinese policy during the short time the People's Republic had existed had made people deeply sceptical about the benefits of enthusiastic support for any extreme idea. Besides, there was still in China no substitute for the family: someone had to look after the old couples who were living longer and longer. For years the Chinese had pursued a policy of persuasion to reduce the disabilities of families with no son by persuading a son-in-law to live in his wife's family house. The people had yet to be convinced that a daughter actually was as good as a son; it is all too obvious to them that at least half of the parents of one-child families will be without support in their declining years.

Besides, one of the reasons why the commune system was successful in China is that Chinese are familial people, not rugged individualists; they bore years of extreme poverty and hardship because "the East was red"; to cut their interest in the future to one child is to undermine the better part of their motivation. In statistical terms demographic transition may have occurred in China but in real terms China is still a child-centred society.

Resistance, expressed in illicit pregnancy, provoked repression. Peasants began to protest that they were being forced to pay "baby deposits" of 200 yuan to be forfeited if a child was born.[91] Wian Liancheng, Deputy Secretary General of the newly formed Family Planning Association, claimed that the number of sterilisations carried out in 1979 was between six and seven million, and that five million abortions were performed, some "involuntary".[92] Illegal practitioners were carrying out sterilisations and IUD removals.[93] In provinces like Laoning the birth rate was "soaring". In Guandong, 47,000 women were pregnant illicitly. The birthrate for 1980 was estimated as 1.2, and in 1982 at 1.3, still much the lowest of any developing country. The fear is that while the one-child norm is easy to enforce in the cities, where the advantages of children's help and support are not so apparent, opposition in the countryside is so implacable that it will tear the whole programme apart. While the peasantry identified with the state and cheerfully enacted its policies in what it saw as its own interest, even when they involved hardship and submission, the People's Republic of China was the nearest thing to a functioning communist society ever to exist on earth. If the peasants persist in defying the Party's insistence on rigorous fertility limitation, it seems inevitable that there will be some kind of purging of the resistant elements in a Chinese version of the slaughter of the kulaks, a hideously ironic development from the liberalisation of agriculture. From being the success which gave the population doves faith in integrated services, China has, by accepting demographic projections and reversing its priorities to deal with numbers before people, become the most ominous precursor of the future.

"Of all things in the world, people are the most precious," Mao had said, and many of the delegates at the Bucharest Conference were glad to hear the principle repeated. After ten years of struggle to implement policies which had little relation to the client communities' perception of their own needs, the Chinese experience provided the blueprint for integrated services. The delegates from the poorer nations took courage and told the donors that they had done everything wrong: they had failed to integrate the people in their schemes, they had flouted ancient custom, they had ignored other basic needs such as infant nutrition and parasite control, they had thrown away many times the cost of China's vast programme and achieved nothing comparable. The Chinese opposed the very idea of a world plan; what was devised was more like a protocol limiting the ways in which foreign aid could be used for population planning. The structure of foreign aid programmes did undergo a change as a result of what happened at Bucharest. Schemes to train paramedics, to involve traditional birth attendants in family planning, to delegate some of the organising and motivation to local groups like women's and youth organisations, were all inspired by the Chinese success. It would be difficult however to describe the change in the organisational structure of family-planning programmes as a change for the better. The integrated schemes stimulated the proliferation of coordinating bodies with confused aims and ever more convoluted monitoring systems. The motives behind the funding of family-planning programmes meanwhile remained un-altered; the only justification for the inclusion of a family-planning component in development schemes was a decline in the number of births. If at the winding-up of a project there were more babies about than there would have been had infant-nutrition schemes and parasite control not been instituted, it really did not matter whether more women were accepting contraceptives or not. The population hawks abandoned all attempts to manipulate a bureaucracy more unwieldy and pious than ever before, wheeled aside and launched the community-based distribution projects. Starving people who had nothing else would have oral contraceptives and condoms. The temple beggars would be vasectomised. Ravenholt (a passionate admirer of the Chinese system, by the way) and his cohorts bypassed the do-gooders and went straight for the profit motive of the small tradesmen. It is doubtful whether they ever really expected the pan-sellers of Bangladesh to interrogate women about possible contra-indications for taking oral steroids. In Bangladesh men do the shopping in any case: even if a pan-seller asked his customer if ants were attracted to his wife's urine as a way of finding out whether she had diabetes, it is very unlikely that a Bangladeshi husband would have spent any amount of time contemplating his wife's urine, or even if he would have known where to find it. He could not even be sure that no one else had urinated in the same place. Ravenholt, Potts and company must have known that the screening procedures were a joke. The government of the United States has a vested interest in showing that private enterprise is the most efficient agent of social change, but not sufficient interest to investigate what has happened and continues to happen in the marketing of pharma-ceuticals in the Third World. Funding from Upjohn, Syntex and their ilk is not forthcoming for research into the deaths and diseases caused by their marketing strategies.

Generally speaking, and without losing sight of the Chinese exception, which in any case seems to be on the verge of becoming another proof of the rule, governments are very inefficient regulators of human fertility. Even the least democratic governments cannot force human fertility to conform to externally imposed norms, partly because of the difficulty of formulating population policy in terms which are compatible with the ruling ideology. China and India are both socialist nations, although few political systems are so sharply contrasting as the approaches adopted in these two countries. Both have invested enormous energy in population limitation, India with politically disastrous and economically and demographically negligible results, China with an impressive measure of success which was deemed totally inadequate and proved to be temporary at one and the same time. The countries of the Soviet bloc have even more serious demographic problems of the opposite kind, for the birthrate in all communist countries, except Albania, fell spectacularly in the postwar years. The Malthusian hypothesis is contradictory to the traditional Marxist analysis and no communist country has ever preached anything but pronatalism, yet birthrates fell and continue to fall. There is no encouragement to fertility limitation, contraceptives are not easily available, and yet the hoped-for births do not eventuate. When the fact that the two world wars, the civil war, the collectivisation programme, famine and the Great Purge cost the USSR something in the order of 80 million souls is taken into account, low birthrate among the Russian citizens means a failure to repopulate and a corresponding chronic manpower shortage, which in turn necessitates the participation of women in the labour force. No matter how poorly paid the work and how generous the incentives to childbearing however, the Russian woman, and the Hungarian, Bulgarian and Czech woman, prefer to undergo abortion – and abortion punitively administered, without anaesthetic – rather than bear a child. The rates of abortion in the Eastern bloc countries are often higher than the numbers of live births.

The vicissitudes of abortion law in the Eastern bloc countries provide a key to the grimness of the situation. In 1936, abortion was declared illegal in the USSR but by 1955 it was reinstated because of an "epidemic emergency".[94] There was no public discussion of the situation and no maverick opposition press to make a *cause célèbre* out of the number of criminal abortions being carried out, so we must assume that what was happening was undeniable and terrible and possibly more damaging to the population profile than the loss of births that the liberalisation of abortion always entails. Behind such deliberate and recalcitrant infertility must lie a crisis of morale. The combination of collectivisation, of grinding hard work in a stagnant economy, poor day-care facilities and bad housing conditions, would seem to have crushed the glee out of child-bearing with utter efficiency. Yet before World War I, the birthrates of the Eastern bloc countries were the highest in Europe. The low birthrates which now prevail have exacerbated the manpower shortage; in the case of the USSR the higher birthrate of the Muslim soviets and unemployment in the Caucasus and Central Asia raises the possibility that the Russian minority will be overwhelmed: no one knows how long they can continue to juggle overemployment in European Russia against unemployment and unrest in the Asian soviets.

The options open to governments faced with problems of this kind are few. Contraceptives may be withdrawn from sale, but central Europeans have traditionally practised *coitus interruptus*. Failures of the method are not tolerated; women seek abortion legal or illegal. What happened in Hungary is fairly typical of the fate of pro-natal policies wherever they are promulgated. Hungarian women workers cannot be refused employment because they are pregnant; they receive their full salary without loss of seniority during the confinement and for five months afterwards, plus a child-care allowance for the first three years of the child's life; there are subsidised facilities for day-care. The positive inducements to motherhood are significant: on the negative side access to abortion has been restricted to women who are single, widowed or divorced, or have suffered some pregnancy-related mishap in the past. As a result the number of abortions fell by about 40%, from 1.024 abortions for every live birth in 1973 to 0.514 in 1974, and the gross reproduction rate bounced from 0.94 in 1973 to 1.12 in 1974, but immediately the slide began again.[95] The crucial effect of restricted access to abortion leads to the disturbing conclusion that there is a considerable number of unwilling mothers in Hungary. In any event the rate of natural increase in Hungary today is no higher than it is in England, Belgium, Denmark and Switzerland – that is, at about replacement level. Austria, Luxembourg and both the Germanies are not even reaching this level, despite handsome cash inducements offered for childbearing in East Germany.

Not all the countries whose women are failing to produce the 2.1 children each necessary to ensure replacement are anxious about the situation. Most of the Western European countries are making no effort to raise their population growth rates, but in France, Greece and Luxembourg there is an avowed desire to raise the birthrate. A group of French demographers headed by Alfred Sauvy has been voicing despair over the French *refus de la vie* which began more than a hundred years ago.[96] Every one of the sub-fertile countries has to recruit its labour force from abroad; in the Federal Republic of Germany, which registered zero population growth in 1971, two million Austrians, Greeks, Italians, Portuguese, Spaniards, Turks, North Africans, and Yugoslavs, among others, provide essential services. Sociobiologists might regard this as successful colonisation, but the exploitation and oppression of these refugees from poverty gives no cause for complacency. Twenty-five per cent of Turkish children of school age living in West Germany suffer from malnutrition, which is unknown among their peers in Turkey.[97]

Governments cannot plan families. They cannot even influence family formation. They certainly cannot keep families together, for, although they might express a desire to do such a thing, their own bureaucratic structure makes it impossible. The more government interferes with family life the more it is weakened. Subsidising childbirth does not work as a pro-natal measure because governments can seldom afford to do it at a high enough level to attract any but the unemployed and nobody wants the children of the unemployed. Most people do not refuse to go home and bear children because there is no money in it but because there is little satisfaction in it, and governments cannot provide that. When it comes to limiting birth, governments are heavy-handed, misinformed and haphazard in their methods. When the methods are deployed by the collectivity they can work, and work relatively fast. When they are imposed by a central authority, incentive and disincentive schemes will work, but only in crowded city-states like Singapore. Given this ineptitude, it is a frightening thought that virtually every government in the world will soon have a population policy of some sort.

Chapter Thirteen
The Reproductive Future

I sometimes wonder why so many foreign advisers are in such an irritating and persistent hurry to push us into programmes which are supposed to erase time and bring instant success.

Ary Bordes[1]

Time is running out.

Malcolm Potts[2]

Prediction in population matters is at the best of times a risky business. It is first of all difficult to identify trends, for there are contradictory trends within trends, some of which indicate genuine changes in direction and some of which do not. Given a hypothetical trend it is no easy matter to plot its continuation, as the trend itself becomes one of the variables in a veritable sea of variables. The population explosion, as its name implies, is a very short-lived phenomenon, for humanity has allowed itself to multiply at the rate of three per cent or so per annum for only a very short time. If the general argument of this book is correct, and humanity has always made concerted attempts to control the balance of population and resources, then the explosion is a temporary phenomenon, a sort of bump on the world population graph, as long as human beings can be convinced that in the larger community of the small world there is a point in keeping numbers in balance with resources. Population planners frequently express the pious hope that global consciousness can somehow be instilled in the fertile poor, on the assumption that it already has been so instilled in their infertile selves. That assumption this book challenges: the decline in fertility in the developed world has nothing to do with consciousness of a global responsibility and everything to do with cultural disincentives to child-bearing. Numbers all over the world will fall as those disincentives make themselves felt, and not before.

No other society in history has ever achieved the level of death control that we have; we can only guess at the ultimate price to be paid for our success, but one thing is certain, that price will not be paid by us. As

Alva Myrdal pointed out, speaking of infertile Sweden in 1941:

> This present generation of productive age groups will go down in history as
> the most ravenous of all. It has increased its spending power per consumption
> unit by not bearing enough children to replace itself, and at the same time by
> self-insurance and social legislation it has usurped legal rights to a labor-free
> income in old age. The annuities then to be paid must as always be paid out
> of the income of the productive people, of which the consuming old will not
> have supplied a sufficient number ... That is the interpretation in human terms
> of the abstract fact that a temporarily increased level of living can be gained
> by individual families at the turning point from progressive to regressive popula-
> tion trends.[3]

Myrdal points out that the burden of the aged itself, expressed in
taxation in social democratic countries, makes it more and more difficult
for the productive people to reverse the trend and return to producing
children along with everything else. Under all the complex structures
which have taken over from the family lies the ancient verity: we must
depend upon our children. In the advanced bureaucracies, this means
depending on the surplus revenue they generate, which goes to maintain
an unwieldy and inefficient administration before it puts a single sausage
on the pensioner's plate. The family was more efficient as a provider,
apart from constituting a more congenial environment than the rotting
tenements that house our pensioners in expensive squalor and utter loneliness. Myrdal's blueprint relies upon continuing prosperity; in times of
recession an inefficient system works even less well. Moreover, Myrdal
does not realise, as very few then realised, that the pinnacle of capitalist
well-being has been achieved at the cost of the entire world. However
wretched the pensioner, every time she brews a cup of tea she exploits
our imperial relations with the client nations. If we are nobly cultivating
a global consciousness in the minds of the world's peasant millions in
order that they may produce fewer claimants to the resources we have
already depleted so wantonly, perhaps we had better endure the global
consciousness ourselves, and commit suicide.

Aged nations, wedded to their own comfort, fearful of change, clinging
to an ever-dwindling treasure, tend to commit suicide anyway. It seems
as if life is endurable as long as there are tiny improvements in the standard
of living, or perhaps the hope of such improvements is sufficient to keep
human beings struggling and striving. It seems as if the hope of such
improvements for their descendants is enough to keep people taking risks,
going forth to labour every day, bringing their babies into the world in
pain. On the other hand it seems as if minute declines in the standards
of consumption cause crises in morale which are expressed in reluctance
to breed. Such has been the fate of practically every elite that has ever
existed; as its demands upon the environment have mounted, its viability

has been threatened until it has been swept aside by tougher and more dynamic people. There have been countless examples of this process in history; one which is relatively close to us is the example of the Parsees in India.

The Parsees were the community chosen by the British as their agents in India: as the East India Company became the empire of Queen Victoria, the Parsees thrived and expanded along with it. Not only did they become the merchant elite of Bombay; in 1881 they had the highest birthrate in India. What this probably represents is a great increase in the excess of birthrates over deathrates, as the Parsees enjoyed the better food and accommodation that wealth brought with it together with the communal health and social-security systems for Parsees which produced an increase in the number of ever-born children, conceived in the optimism of an expanding economy. The decline began long before the British withdrew from India, for by 1951 a pattern of low fertility had already been established. From 1951 to 1961 the population of India grew 21.5% but the Parsee community shrank 9.9%. The steady decline of virtually 1% a year continued through the next ten years and continues still. Since 1955, the deathrate has continually surpassed the birthrate.

> ... it is not only the population decline which is causing apprehension, but the impoverishment of the middle class, its increasing dependence on Parsee relief organisations, unemployment, the alleged moral and physical decadence as well as the high, above-average number of suicides committed.[4]

This situation began as the desideratum of demographic transition: the Parsee lifestyle changed exactly the way that Bernard Berelson describes, encapsulating the common theory of demographic transition as we know it from the North European experience:

> How, in theory, can India cut its birthrate in half? – get a major proportion of the labor force into industry and thus sharply raise the standard of living and promote urbanisation, give every Indian including the girls at least 6–8 years of schooling, forbid child labor, cut infant mortality to below 25 (per thousand), raise the female age at marriage to 25 or so, establish the nuclear family with separate residence, get 35–40 percent of the women of reproductive age into the labor force, set up a functioning system of social security ...[5]

All these things in one way or another the Parsees did; their social insurance system created a welfare state within India which still endures; their education system is more than adequate, their families have been nuclear since the turn of the century. Marriage became later and later, for the necessary accommodation with the measure of light and space due to the scions of the merchant elite was not available in the crowded city of Bombay. Doubtless there are some who see the decline of the Parsees as being in part caused by the pressure of population in the city of Bombay, and that they will attribute to the rogue fecundity of the non-Parsees: others will say that the Parsees fell with their masters the British. Regardless of the politico-economic explanation, the phenomenon consists of an aged population, presenting all the health-management problems relative to longevity, such as osteoporosis in women, unknown in the rest of India where the women simply do not live long enough to incur it. The young people (youngish rather) are well aware of their decline but they do not appear to resent it. Highly educated, charming, they appear rather proud to belong to a dwindling and exclusive club. Parsee women who marry out are Parsees no longer; the Parsee men who marry are few enough. The ones who marry out may call their wives and children Parsees – if they do not fall victim to the rising tide of divorce which is always more likely in inter-community marriage. Their marriages are likely to be childless in any event. Of the gallant band of Zoroastrians who left Iran in the 9th century less than 80,000 are left. Monuments to the great Parsee families surround them on all sides, but soon these genes will be extinct.

The Parsee rise and fall embodies perhaps our own rise and prefigures our eventual fall. Our demographic decline is not yet at the point which the Parsees have reached because there are so many more of us, but it must not be forgotten that as populations expand exponentially, they also dwindle at an ever-accelerating rate. Aging populations require expensive and elaborate health care, and are able to make little or no return for the time and energy they consume. Longevity now poses for many people problems more frightening than those posed by death itself, but an increasing number of people in the developed world will have to confront the humiliation of helplessness, mental confusion, chronic ill-health, depression and instability of mood. We may not see an image of our society in the Parsee woman living with and through her bachelor son, but the image has simply been institutionalised. The problems of a society heavily weighted with dependent old are obvious: more insidious are the problems presented by able-bodied eld.

> The over-representation of the old will not only have direct economic effects. The psychological attitude of the people will be different. The whole expansionist psychology of the last half century may be lost. Old people are not the most enterprising investors or administrators. Still, they will have power over wealth and hold the key positions. This mastery of old people has already manifested itself, but it will grow to more oppressive importance with the increase in relative numbers of old as compared to young ... The total cultural atmosphere will tend to become static as the old gain in importance ... Problems are less likely to take care of themselves in a shrinking population than in an expanding one ... The conclusion can hardly be avoided that it will become more difficult to be young in a society that is controlled by the aged ...[6]

Myrdal's gloomy prognosis might lead us to speculate on the curious phenomenon of the apparent unchangeability of certain power structures in our world and the intensification of conservatism in our own time as having to do with the relative aging of Western populations. It may be that what we see as stability in our political systems is no more than loss of dynamism leading to stasis, a stasis represented in the birthrate. The opposite is certainly often enough argued – that "soaring" birthrates lead to revolution, often described as "bolshevism", a system more geronto-morphic than any other on earth.

The lack of energy in aging populations is nowhere more tellingly illustrated than in the failure of our aged to secure themselves collectively a better deal. A gerontocracy may control money and power, but it does not control them in the interests of the old, but rather with the individualistic egotism which typifies the sclerotic personality. Our societies are at present morally obliged to offer facilities for the care of the aged and have gradually accepted the view that the responsibility cannot rest on unmated individuals marooned within the sphere of parental influence. The bureaucracy has taken over most of this responsibility but it cannot be argued that it fulfils it very well. What is more significant for the future perhaps is that we cannot carry out services for the aged even as well as we do without the recruitment of immigrant labour, which enters the workforce at the lowest, least powerful level as the worst-off members of the perennially exploited group of health workers. While we waste enormous time and quantities of money in developing organ-transplant procedures for worn-out human beings we allow old people to die of hypo-thermia or because no one knew that someone had fallen and broken a hip. Historically the old deployed strategies to keep the young bound to them by love and self-interest; as the young grow old in the absence of these strategies, the old will not take care of the old. The sclerotic changes in the brain of the aging individual produce irrational irritabilities, suspicions, malignancy. The sclerotic society produces the neutron bomb.

Life expectancy in the developed world has probably reached its limit and could even begin to fall as the profile of disease changes with the deterioration of the environment. The astonishing proliferation of auto-immune diseases, patterns of drug use, both legal and illegal, the con-sequences of wide-ranging sexual promiscuity and the intensification of stress may all affect the deathrate to some extent so that it rises rather than falling farther. The recrudescence of malaria will also have demo-graphic consequences but mostly in countries which already have a relatively elevated deathrate. It is generally assumed by demographers that as the deathrate stabilises the birthrate stabilises with it. The grounds for believing this are rather like the grounds for believing that the sun will rise again tomorrow; persuasive but actually non-existent. If the deathrate is now relatively intractable, the birthrate is still capable of falling, and falling, and falling. The stability which characterised human societies in the past was rigorously selected for. While admitting that birth control was practised, indeed while insisting that birth control was practised by all the means that have been discussed, it must never be forgotten that birth promotion was also rigorously carried out: women were ineluctably drawn into the reproduction process to risk their lives in the service of the group time and again by all the social and ideological pressures that could be mustered to the task. If we have underestimated the deliberateness and thoroughness with which this was done, we may have misunderstood the dynamic of human reproduction in a fundamental way.

The position is stated with admirable clarity by Clellan Stearns Ford:

Human reproduction is effected by biological processes assisted by learned behaviour. The customs which are thus in adjustment to the imperfections of human biological processes of reproduction arise from a desire to bear children. This wish for offspring is not an innate component of human nature; it is not a basic drive. On the contrary, it is an acquired motive which is constantly being reinforced by social rewards and punishments. Promises of security, approval and prestige support the desire for children; threats of insecurity, punishment and ridicule block incipient wishes to escape the fears and pains of childbirth and parenthood.[7]

It has been my intention to flesh out this statement by showing how whole ideological systems have been built on the achievement of parenthood and how child-bearing has been motivated in traditional familial societies. I am very well aware that people in power now consider motivation for child-bearing to be counter-productive and therefore quite consciously aim to destroy that motivation by loading child-bearing with disincentives, even in societies where the failure to produce children who survive to adulthood will mean degradation and destitution. While I hope that their efforts are doomed, because subject peoples will still act in their own long-term interest if they possibly can, it also seems necessary to point out that the cultural mechanisms which ensure the survival of the group are more fragile than anyone at present seems to realise. Once they are shattered, they cannot be replaced with cash subsidies for child-bearing or better day care facilities, or by banning abortion and the distribution of contraceptives. Governments have tried both and have reaped their reward in the increase in the number of unhappy women and children, in personal terms crucial, in statistical terms practically negligible. Again in Stearns' formulation:

Conflicting with the desire for children are other motives. Childbirth is an unpleasant experience. The woman who becomes pregnant finds herself increasingly handicapped and frustrated. She fears that her labour will be painful, that her child will be deformed or still-born, and that she may die in childbirth. She knows that after her baby is born she must spend the greater proportion of her time, attending to its wants. From such frustration and wishes such as these comes the wish to avoid conception and its sequels of pregnancy and birth. If people are to reproduce, social life must offer enough rewards for bearing children to more than outweigh the punishments involved in reproduction.[8]

The ways in which societies have constructed the incentives for child-bearing are many and various; only a small and rather haphazardly chosen series of examples has been adduced in this book. Western society, by contrast, has encumbered parenthood with disabilities. While it is true that risk of death in childbirth is much diminished, that fact in itself cannot serve as an incentive to child-bearing. We have less objection to risking our lives than we have to allowing them to become burdensome. We will not conceive and bear children in thanksgiving to the people who took the pain and danger out of childbearing and replaced them with stress and confusion. The disabilities of pregnancy and motherhood are exacerbated in our society. The role of mother is socially marginal. The role of parent is all responsibilities and no rewards; the role of child is correspondingly difficult to play.

The question then arises, could *homo occidentalis* give up reproducing altogether? Some would say that instinct will keep us reproducing even against our conscious will; my own remarks about a biological mechanism resulting in contraceptive failure might give them hope, but I would point out that the mechanism is very weak; it results in pregnancy rather than birth, at least in the particular example. If we agree with Ashley Montagu that

> With the exception of the instinctoid reactions in infants to sudden withdrawals of support and to sudden loud noises, the human being is entirely instinctless,[9]

then there is no question of our surviving despite ourselves. If one accepts the Freudian hypothesis of a death wish there is no argument. Certainly we will have to learn to die more willingly than we do at present, it would seem, and perhaps it will be no great calamity if *homo occidentalis*, who is in many ways so conspicuously maladapted, were to go the way of the dinosaur. It seems obvious that people who do not care to reproduce do not actually care whether they die out or not, although they tend to react with mild indignation when they are called "genetically dead". Such reflections make nonsense of the dismay of the French demographers who wring their hands over the long, implacable decline in French numbers. Individuals die, groups die, species die, each in its own season. "Men must endure their going hence even as their coming hither." The tragedy of *King Lear* could profitably be construed as a sociobiological parable teaching us that we must learn when to let go.

Sir Charles Darwin outlined a demographic premise which leads to some such conclusion in his *Problems of Population* (1958).

Suppose, for example, that half the world opted for comfort and succeeded in limiting its numbers, and the other half did not. Within a generation or two the proportions would no longer be half, but one-third and two-thirds; within a couple of centuries the comfort-lovers would be insignificant in numbers compared to the rest. Nature has automatically found a stabilising means of tremendous power, and nothing but an equally tremendous power in the opposite direction could overset it ... I doubt if man's conscious wisdom is sufficient to accomplish this change.[10]

Nature itself is of course as unintelligent as a hydrogen bomb: the grim fact about human destiny is that intelligence has very little to do with it. In positing the comfort-lovers as one half of the global population, Sir Charles was allowing them an advantage that they do not have: at present they are no more than a quarter. If we take the example of the Jews in America; given their present fertility rate of about 1.5 children per woman, their numbers should halve in about eighty years.

Today there are twice as many Jews as Mormons. By the end of the next century, if one projects current rates, there will be twelve times as many Mormons as Jews – 24 million Mormons, 2 million Jews ...

Today, for every person in the developed nations there are three in the less developed countries. Even though birth rates are coming down in the Third World, a projection by the United Nations shows that, by the year 2100, the ratio will be not three to one, but eighteen to one.

And so the balance of power will probably change. The democracies will lose relative economic potency. They will lose political clout. They will lose political influence ... The world is likely to change in ways we cannot yet fathom.[11]

Alternatively, the gerontocracies will take steps to preserve their supremacy; they will become more authoritarian, more secretive and more militaristic. A military-industrial elite will struggle to control the seething mass of humanity because it has everything to lose. It will lose to the humanity which has nothing to lose. Sir Charles Darwin finds the prospect inexpressibly sad: he foresees a future in which an African professor explains the scientific revolution to his students:

The great series of scientific discoveries which made it possible were due, to a quite preponderating extent to the white race, whose original home had been in Western Europe. However, this race proved unequal to its own greatness. Success sapped its energies and killed its spirit of adventure. They could not believe that the harder world, which we know, would be tolerable. They could not believe, as we know, that happiness has little relation to comfort or luxury. Consequently, they started to limit the numbers of their families in the fruitless expectation that in this way they would restrain the multiplication of the human race. Their numbers started to decrease at first relatively to the other races, and then absolutely; their peoples gradually faded away, and this once great race now survives precariously in a few of the less accessible parts of our earth.[12]

If we die out now, we shall have left monuments far greater than the

Great Pyramid; we will be honoured among the survivors who will learn our names in school. University departments will be set up to document and reconstruct us as human memory would have us. The terror is that we shall undo all the good we have done in freeing human beings from disease and degrading toil by a final demented display of our superhuman inventiveness, the nuclear holocaust. If we leave behind us a poisoned earth and blighted children, the African professor will not be obliged to teach his students who we were, for our names will survive as curses to mankind. The good we have done will be interred with our pampered bones, while our evil lives on after us in a deformed and suffering world.

Sir Charles had a solution for the decline of the comfort-lovers; it was the world wide "enforcement" of contraception. As the comfort-lovers do not rule the world *de jure* but only *de facto*, they themselves cannot enforce anything on a world-wide scale. If the duly constituted authorities are to be got to enforce birth control, we had better conceal the fact that we are anxious to help them in order to ensure the perpetuation of our own supremacy, and so we do. Few of the exponents of population problems would express themselves so egregiously these days. Our desire to coerce expresses itself principally as support for parties who use coercion on their own account in ways that the constitution prevents us from doing in our own "democratic" countries. While legislators retire defeated after struggles to get bills for the "involuntary" sterilisation of welfare mothers, the mentally defective and the unemployed through our parliaments because of the political clout of several minority lobbies, government agencies will be rewarding nations with coercive policies not only by supplying the hardware and expert advice in how to carry out fertility destruction on the mass scale, but with increased military and financial aid. The same lobbies that prevent coercive legislation from passing in our countries will prevent foreign aid money going to support abortion, but will gladly pay 95% of the cost of sterilisations.[13] Another lobby will agitate to prevent the supply of injectables, for different reasons, but with equal ethnocentricity. Such tactics will increase the probability of the eventual adoption of coercive sterilisation policies by limiting the options.

The difficulty about the use of Depo-Provera is that unscrupulous individuals and authorities can administer it without the recipient's consent because it is an injection like any other. This is one of its advantages for the user who does not want to have to persuade others to allow her to exercise freedom of choice in the matter. Women who care about women should realise how important the exercise of such power in the process of emancipation can be, nevertheless it is opposed. Because of the controversy, which began with misgivings about the effects of the drug in the general spectrum of Western medicine, where other methods are just as usable, and the alternative is not dangerous childbirth, the issue became a modish controversy which cannot now be controlled, much to the chagrin of Upjohn who make it. The women of the West do not trust third-world doctors to use Depo any better than their own did, and they are probably right, but will they decide that their governments cannot give moral and physical support to China? It is obvious that the late crop of coercive legislation in China has led to infanticide and forced abortion; the Chinese keep telling us about the infanticides, which are crimes committed by wicked individuals, perhaps because we are being softened up to accept a wave of coercive policies crueller than anything we have yet heard of. The forced abortions are crimes committed by the representatives of the state; anyone who reveals those is liable to find himself discredited very swiftly by the very institutions which accredited him in the first place, bastions though they may be of academic freedom.[14] We do not wish to hear that Chinese policy is brutal because we need to feel secure in the certainty that we do not need to oppose it. We want fewer Chinese more passionately than Hua Guo Feng does. Our support of draconian policies in China probably makes very little difference in regard to their implementation. What is serious about the situation is that it soils us by association, coarsens our understanding of what is meant by democracy. If we leave little on earth but our reputation, it may be sullied beyond redemption. Even the Chinese may despise us for it, when the terrible tale of China in the eighties finally unfolds. The Japanese, I suspect, despise us for it already.

When human groups die out and are replaced by other human groups, their languages and their social systems go with them. Each represents a unique collective human achievement swept into the void. Some students of such matters struggle to construct a record to compensate slightly for such waste, but as graves outnumber beds in this world, so vanished cultures outnumber those which at present exist, which threaten to merge into one monoculture of plastic shoes and brassieres, blue jeans and canned music. That in turn will probably fission into something more various – at least one hopes so; there is as yet little indication that the multifarious peoples of India are bored with Hindi cinema, or that the African in plastic sandals resents the fact the same sandals can be found in Melanesia and South East Asia. Among the rich peoples there are some who quixotically study the ancient kingdoms and crack their jaws to speak languages which never sounded anything like the noises they make, and pore over hieroglyphs hoping to decipher them like a child's puzzle, when the reality to which they gave the clues has ceased to exist and the semantic connections are only to be guessed at. If we care about the Sumerians, the Assyrians, the Phoenicians, the Egyptians, the Greeks and the Romans, it is because they left monuments which are the forerunners of our own culture, or so we hope, for we are anxious to claim the best blood lines, and because their rifled treasures are buried in the massive edifice of our own cultural establishment. The vast kingdoms of Central Africa interest us less than the civilisation of the small island of Crete, because our cultural establishment is not descended from the African. Still less do we care about the pre-literate peoples who died with their way of life. People who left nothing for us to plunder, who left no permanent scars on the ecology, are rewarded by being totally forgotten.

The long-necked Watusi from the watershed of the Nile who swept southwards, displacing the Twa pygmy people and enslaving their masters the Bahutu, were unwise enough to attack the colonial government in 1963 and their serfs, seeing them defeated and the mystique of their supremacy shattered, have been annihilating them ever since. In neighbouring Burundi, the mass of the Hutu population which is ruled by a Tutsi minority is being slaughtered by the Tutsi and is fleeing to Tanzania. In the death-throes of the knightly civilisation of the Watusi some would see the mirror of our own civilisation, which dies off from the top, so that it has to be continually replenished from the lower echelons.[15] We too must be served by an alien helotry in primary and essential industry both at home and abroad. Our very armies are composed of these same helots and their descendants. The aristocratic Tuareg are dying too for raiding and slaving are not roads to dominance these days and the Tuareg culture does not fit them for humbler pursuits. Where they have settled on the fringes of the *bidonvilles* their numbers are rising once more, but those who cling to the knightly way of life are swept hither and thither by desertification and war. For them there is no future.[16] The syphilis that they have borne for centuries has got the upper hand.

In his introduction to Elmer Pendell's *Population on the Loose*, Walter B. Pitkin develops an intriguing theory which would divide the population of the world into cheap nations and dear nations:

> Of course the world does not divide neatly between dear men and cheap men; there are some in between ... Men grow cheaper as we move eastward from the Rhine. Russia is the Great Slave State, and beyond Russia lie the slums where humanity cheapens to zero and perhaps below.
>
> We Americans have on hand 22,796 tons of coal for each of us. The Italians have only one-eighth of a ton each.
>
> Why wonder that the Italians are cheap and we are dear? Or that the Italians all try to move in on us?
>
> We have about 60 times as much iron and 200 times as much coal as the Japanese. Of course the Japs are cheap.[17]

This exalted reasoning contains its germ of truth, especially if for *dear* we substitute the word *costly*. The American will use his tons of coal in electricity, and he will need more to keep him in the manner to which he is accustomed. He will use all his fossil fuels and then require more. The question arises whether the world can afford him and his European counterparts. Other peoples, for example, nomadic herdsmen and hunter-gatherers, have proved too costly, and humbler peasants have spread into their grazing grounds or elected governments who punished them for raiding. It may be a melancholy thought that the Masai are hemmed in, but they are costly in terms of space. A beautiful lifestyle is vanishing but in a crowded world, the need for space constitutes a maladaptation.[18] Peoples who need space respond like caged animals when they lose it; they refuse to breed. After centuries of living according to a rigorous code which kept their numbers in balance with the resources of their habitat, the arrival of powerful strangers destroys all coherence in the system, which therefore disintegrates. Some of the genes of the group may survive, usually through the women who are taken by the interlopers as wives and concubines. For some sociobiologists this measure of survival is understood as sufficient. In these terms the American Indian population is more numerous than it ever was before, but of the four hundred different aboriginal tribes from Asia and their fifty-five language families there is only the dimmest trace. The Plains Indians, the Californian Chumash, the Gabrielino, Fernandeno and Juaneno tribes have left no one to weep for them. The Navaho, the Sioux and the Cherokee may be more numerous now than they were in the sixteenth century but it is doubtful whether their ancestors would recognise them. The Iroquois Confederacy of Five Nations lives on seven reservations. The Osage live on oil cheques and alcohol, led by their womenfolk now that they are all dependants. Aboriginal peoples everywhere have vanished or are vanishing, whether they be the Ainu and the Buryat, last survivors of the paleo-Siberian peoples, the Batwa, the Bushmen, or the Australians, now increasing in numbers, but with most of their languages forgotten, their walkabout territories carved up and brutalised by tourism and cattle-raising, and their blood thinned by the white man's inability to leave aboriginal women alone.

The paradigm for race suicide has always been drawn from the examples of Greece and Rome, rather than from the examples of pre-literate and non-Caucasian societies, for reasons that are obvious. The people of the sub-fertile developed countries are refusing to reproduce for the same reasons as the ruling classes of Greece and Rome, which are the factors which are operating in the Parsee community and among the select company of East Danube merchants described by Geza Roheim.[19] People who make upon the environment demands so heavy that they become increasingly difficult to satisfy, are easily persuaded by a fall or the threat of a fall in their standard of living not to reproduce. Like the dinosaur they simply outgrow the available resource base. The people of the rich nations absolutely require a certain standard of housing. The quantities of space, light and air which are considered essential for the middle-class European child are simply not available in the commercial centres where his parents must live. If they decide to move to commodious suburbs, they have the continually exacerbated problem of crowded transport routes and the extended working day caused by rush-hour conditions. The urban middle class is bitterly conscious of overcrowding: which it is likely to see as a consequence of the reproductive behaviour of its rivals for a place in the sun. Subjectively perceived overcrowding is a contributing cause of lowered fertility. Western civilisation is too vast to die out like Greece and Rome, but it is inevitable that the genetic composition of the dominant groups will change, as it has always done, by absorbing new blood from below. Such a situation only produces alarm and despondency to racists of a certain kidney, because the people who are not reproducing do not, cannot care. The question is strictly academic but ethnocentricity is still such an integral part of the nature even of the most barren academics that they wring their hands at the prospect of a future in which they and their ilk are unrepresented. From the global point of view, it is the astonishing expansion of the Caucasian group which has proved to be ecologically disastrous: its eclipse will be seen by many as an undisguised blessing. Concealed in the low birthrate figures for France, Germany and the UK are the higher rates of the migrant populations who ought to become a higher proportion of the total population because the natives are also providing the high percentage of childless individuals in the whole picture. There is nothing new in the situation, for the elite groups in Europe have always flourished for several generations and died out, to be replaced by more dynamic stocks from below.[20] When the extension of empire made the British the global elite, their entire economy was fattened with the spoils; every Englishman became a maharajah. Now that the plundered peoples have nothing left and the toughness that built empire has withered away, the world's aristocracy is dying out at an even faster rate than appears in the statistics.

We are so squeamish on the point that it is not done to ask who is having the babies in England, but there are rabble-rousers who wish to see an English England, and not a West-Indian-East-Indian-Irish-Portuguese-North African England, who will shout from the rooftops that migrants are outbreeding the native-born English. It hardly matters whether they are or not, for even migrant groups who are passionately attached to their own way of life and convinced that it is superior to what they have found in their country of adoption, cannot turn an anti-child culture into a pro-child culture. They cannot ignore the disincentives to breeding, especially as they are particularly inconvenienced by them. As they work in the lowest-paid sector, wives and husbands must both work; as day-care facilities are totally inadequate they must find the money for child-minding or abandon the children to their own devices. As the children have language and orientation difficulties they need special care and attention which working parents cannot give. As the children become more difficult to control, their parents lament their unwisdom in bearing

them. Before long the most philoprogenitive of migrant groups adopts
the norm of the country of adoption. Women from extended families,
compelled to bring children up without support from other females, soon
register the fact that there is very little fun it it. When family limitation
is presented as an aspect of the progressiveness of the economic system
into which they wish to be integrated as full members, they accept the
small-family norm. The migrant contribution to fertility in Northern
Europe is a concealed bulge in the population pyramid. When it flattens
out, the rate of decrease will be seen to be accelerating. When we subtract
the proportion of illegitimate births in the developed countries, we see
that the parity of married women is even lower than might be thought.
In the United States in 1979, 597,000 of the babies born were illegitimate,
17% of the total.[21] Not all of those were unwanted, but then not all of
the legitimate babies were wanted. Without forced childbirth the
American birthrate would be well below replacement; the same is true
of England, where the growth rate is even lower.

The Caucasian race is nearing the end of a phase of unparalleled
expansion. In the words of the eugenist, Edward Murray East, speaking
of the situation in 1923,

> it has political control of the nine-tenths of the habitable globe ... The Western
> hemisphere is completely within its grasp, on the greater portion of it white
> populations can thrive ... The black zone simply does not count. The negroes,
> even with the help of white contact, cannot compete against white expansion
> ... The various elements of the brown race may indeed throw off the white
> political yoke ... The effort will avail little ... Clamorous propaganda will be
> the beginning and the end of the excitement.[22]

Few would share East's complacency sixty years later, but his remarks
about the Western hemisphere are interesting. Both Canada and the
United States have relatively low population growth rates of 1.5% and
1.0% respectively. The highest growth rates in the area are recorded in
Honduras (3.4%), Venezuela (3.3%), Nicaragua (3.3%), Ecuador (3.1%)
and Paraguay (3.0%). Of these countries only Nicaragua considers that
its fertility level is too high. The countries pursuing pronatalist policies
are, besides Uruguay with the extremely low increase rate of 0.7%,
Argentina, Bolivia and Chile. The lowest increase rate in the hemisphere
is registered in Cuba, at 0.6%.[23] It seems likely that the Caucasian race's
next big push will occur in South America, as the Southern Europeans
perform their own version of the American miracle enacted by the
Northern Europeans – that is, if the multinational conglomerates which
are the ultimate development of North European entrepreneurism allow
them to. The expansion of the white race took place initially as immigration into the new world and the decayed civilisations of Asia; the hybrid
South European-cum-Indian invasion of North America is already well

under way. The difficulty arises when we try to imagine the Mexicans and the Puerto Ricans attempting to subjugate their hosts, for if North European expansionism was without historical parallel their military descendants' power is unprecedented too. At this stage it is clearly absurd to imagine a force of migrant menials taking over, but it is a much more likely event than extinction, and perhaps even more likely than the stabilisation of world population growth with the same proportions of ethnic grouping that characterise it now.

In terms of the reproductive future of the people who are likely to read this book, it looks likely that the decline in the Western birthrate will continue, for the greater the proportion of childless people the more unfamiliar and unmanageable the child appears. Common morality now treats child-bearing as an aberration; there are practically no good reasons left for exercising one's fertility. This discussion of the motivation for child-bearing comes from the preamble to a textbook discussion of sterilisation:

> Fertility as an expression of need for power is becoming increasingly evident in people who feel powerless or unsure of themselves whether on the grounds of poverty, ethnic minority problems, or personal psychological difficulty. Just as a man may feel great satisfaction in proving his virility by impregnating a woman, a woman may feel that her fertility is her power and that she cannot accept interference with it even if she does not want a child. The present, rapidly changing world with its loosening of family ties, changing roles, and fear of loneliness may also create powerful and often unconscious urges for procreation.
>
> The wish for pregnancy itself as proof of personal worth is not uncommon in women. It occurs in young girls in competition with their mothers, in disillusioned or depressed women who want a positive achievement, and in women with poor self-esteem and the need to prove themselves, particularly after some disappointment or loss.[24]

Medical students reading this are already disposed to suspect that desire for issue has very little to do with enlightened self-interest. They already feel little enough compunction when it comes to the reproductive rights of the poor, of ethnic minorities and people who are upset. Most of them will believe in the myth of over-population; what they learn from this kind of pseudo-authoritative writing is that even if people have reasons for wanting children, they are bad reasons and do not need to be respected, especially when the medico can see for himself that the people in question are poor and brown.

Given this mentality, which is expressed so transparently because the writers are conscious of it as orthodoxy, we cannot expect that elective means of day-to-day control of fertility will be developed with any urgency or distributed at all efficiently. Every kind of consideration points to the expansion of current sterilisation practice. The first, in the context of the entry of governments into the delivery of health care, is the undeniable cost-effectiveness of sterilisation when carried out on younger patients of low parity. There is no need of pressure on older individuals who have completed their family size to accept sterilisation; they are already opting for it, in view of the unsatisfactoriness of available contraception. Despite the often-expressed view that voluntarism in family planning is lunacy, a campaign to pressure the younger age groups into accepting sterilisation is not yet acceptable in our societies, but it will become so. Meanwhile there is a considerable number of young people who under various kinds of stress are asking for sterilisation. The signs are that doctors are feeling less and less unwillingness to accede to their demands; in fact, it seems as if the amount of resistance among doctors to the idea of sterilising young and childless people has been exaggerated, judging by the numbers of very young persons who have been sterilised. In countries where there are too many doctors who expect to maintain a very high standard of living, as in the United States, doctors can be found to carry out virtually any elective surgery a patient should dream up. Sterilisation is a great deal easier to justify than sex-change operations. Meanwhile the average citizen of the UK or the USA is wrongly convinced that sterilisation is now reversible.

In 1981, the Centre for Disease Control in Atlanta reported that:

> In the three-year period 1976–1978, 1.9 million women had tubal sterilisations in short-stay hospitals in the United States; just over half these procedures were interval procedures unrelated to a birth or abortion.[25]

The syntax is cunningly chosen: a reporter with a different bias might have said, "Almost half of these sterilisations were performed in conjunction with birth or abortion." We might expect a fairly high repentance rate among that not-quite-half, but surgery that gives rise to a need for further surgery, especially surgery as expensive as tubal reanastomosis, is a good investment. The morality of routinely associating sterilisation with birth or abortion is worrying, to say the least. What can be the hurry, in the rich United States where methods of imposing temporary sterility abound? We have heard the excuse for sterilising, hard on birth or abortion in the Third World, that the patients cannot get back to the hospital easily once they have been let go. The excuse is exaggerated there, because primary health facilities could be organised in such a way that sterilisation went to the people rather than the other way about, but to offer any such explanation in America would be ludicrous. The fact is that women are more likely to accept sterilisation while still suffering the stress of (mismanaged) childbirth or abortion.

> The most significant changes in tubal sterilisation rates between 1975 and 1978 were in the younger and older age-groups; women aged 15–24 had a 31 per cent increase, and those 35–44 had a twenty per cent increase, whereas the rate for women 25–34 was essentially unchanged.[26]

The pushing of sterilisation on artificially receptive individuals has fundamentally changed the nature of infertility practice; nowadays the bulk of an infertility specialist's time and ingenuity is exercised in the attempt to restore fertility deliberately destroyed, and this at a time when the incidence of unwanted sterility is rising. The solutions to the problem are broadly two. Either the surgeons insist that the operation is irreversible and refuse to undertake to reverse it under any circumstances, in which case counselling must be improved and a waiting period insisted upon, both unlikely eventualities, for surgeons can always be found by determined clients. (People who drop out during the waiting period may have found a more willing surgeon rather than changed their minds.) Or sterilisation is routinely accompanied by the collection and storage of germinal material. The problems attaching to this possibility are enormous; the facility should be offered to men and women, but the recovery of ova is much more complicated than the collection of semen. Storage of the material is an expensive and complicated business, relatively easy to manage in the West where child death is rare and children of no economic importance to their parents, and quite beyond the capacity of a peasant culture where a second chance at parenthood could be a life-and-death matter. The likelihood is that both sterilisations and pointless attempts at reanastomosis will be carried out more and more often. The techniques of sterilisation will become simpler. Just how much simpler emerged at the three-day International Workshop on Non-Surgical Methods for Female Tubal Occlusion held in Chicago in June 1982.

> The most intriguing and least known methods, developed in the People's Republic of China, were described by two physicians, Shueh-Ping Tien and Hui-Guo Zheng. Both techniques utilise a thick paste containing phenol. Phenol, or carbolic acid, is a highly caustic chemical that, when injected into the Fallopian tubes, rapidly causes extensive damage to the epithelial tissue that lines the interior of the tubes, or the lumen. After extended exposure to the phenol, the tubes eventually become completely filled with scar tissue.[27]

In order for the paste to get into the tubes, the womb is explored with a sound to determine the lie of the horns and to position the cannula opposite the openings of the tubes. A salt solution is pumped through to see if it runs back through the cervix. If it does not, a tiny amount of saccharin is sent after it. If the patient reports a pain in her lower pelvis, the saccharin has got through the tube and the paste can be pumped in. The paste contains beside the carbolic acid compound, a radio-opaque medium that allows the penetration of the paste to be checked by X-ray and atabrine which "creates long-term damage, inhibiting the tubal repair process and preventing recanalisation." There is no question of reversing a sterilisation done in this manner; the possibility of ovarian or other damage caused by the compound escaping into the peritoneal cavity was not mentioned. Some of the women reported perspiring heavily and feeling dizzy immediately after the procedure; one may be permitted to wonder whether precautions against the possibility of severe shock or air embolism were taken.

> The tubal ostium is tiny, only about 1–2 mm in diameter, and several physicians at the workshop expressed surprise at the level of technical skill achieved by the operators in placing the cannula into such a small opening without actually seeing it ... Tien maintained, however, that the technique is not difficult to learn, and he noted that doctors, nurses and midwives were being trained to perform it ... the training period takes no longer than two weeks.[28]

Doubtless the delight of owning a One-child Glorious Certificate will compensate for much, but it must be more than slightly harrowing to be among the first candidates for tubal occlusion at the hands of your barefoot doctor. Two hundred medical units in twenty-eight Chinese provinces have at least one member trained in the technique and 30,000 women have been sterilised by the method, which is gradually being perfected; the Chinese actually reported on very small samples. Post-operative pregnancy rate is between 1 and 1½ per cent; in one study the ectopic rate was two out of fifteen, which is only to be expected from a method which works by internal scarring in imitation of the action of the gonococcus and its fellow travellers. There are advantages to this method; it is clearly cheap and it may obviate the problem of disrupting the blood supply to the ovaries which bedevils the other methods, but the patients reported two weeks' abdominal "discomfort" for which read *pain*. Pain is a signal that damage is being done, and two weeks is a long time for the signal to last. It seems quite possible, and even likely, that women sterilised by this method will have grossly altered pelvic physiology, with multiple adhesions. Menstrual derangement was reported, but was said to subside after four months.

The Western version of non-surgical female sterilisation uses the quinacrine pellet.

> Quinacrine may cause pain if it leaks through the tubes into the peritoneal cavity; it can also excite the central nervous system if it enters the bloodstream in large amounts, resulting in transient psychosis.[29]

The research on this pleasant substance is being carried out in that well-known bastion of civil rights, Chile, by the promisingly named Dr Jaime Zipper, and, of course, in India. Female mortals in other countries are not threatened by it because the mode of administration is far from perfect and the post-operative pregnancy rates are too high. In Europe testing was abandoned. The only way these methods of non-surgical sterilisation can be perfected is to continue carrying them out experimentally, refining and altering them the while, on a human female population. There cannot be too much consultation with the subjects because their attitude to the procedure should be, as far as possible, neutral. If they are suspicious, they will feel and report bad reactions; if they have been proselytised, they will be over-enthusiastic and interpret genuine symptoms as caused by some other agency. The way in which non-surgical techniques have been developed is of a piece with the way in which all iatric procedures are developed; in the case of non-surgical sterilisation however, the demand has come from the health professionals for a cheaper and easier permanent sterilisation technique.[30] From one point of view it seems as if the trivialisation of fertility destruction is reaching its nadir; from the other, it seems obvious that current methods are too unwieldy and expensive to apply on a mass scale. It is not simply a question of using third-world women as experimental animals; Western women have been involved in trials of all kinds of sterilisation techniques. At present a technique of blocking the tubes by inserting silicone rubber plugs is being tested in England, Belgium and the United States. Women in Canada and Norway are being sterilised by having methylcyanoacrylate pumped into their tubes, along with women in Brazil, India, the Philippines and Venezuela. Both these methods as at present developed require the use of the hysteroscope, which is too costly a piece of equipment for mass use in poor countries; the unimpressive results reported by practitioners with these methods cast some doubt on the veracity of the Chinese claims for the success of their blind method.

The other development on which a good deal of money, time, energy and expertise has been staked so far is the contraceptive vaccine.

Its potential advantages are simplicity of administration, use of paramedical personnel, and the public's generally positive response to vaccination ... A considerable amount of animal experimental work in this area has been carried out in recent years and we now have several leads.[31]

Women can be sensitised to their husband's sperm and their immune response can cause the sperm to be immobilised and die; some infertility is caused in this way.[32] An ethical problem arises if this response is only triggered by the sperm of one man. The research in anti-fertility vaccines has so far concentrated on making the woman's antibodies attack one of the proteins essential to the maintenance of a pregnancy, of which there are several likely candidates. The research, principally funded by the Population Council, has reached the stage of producing mono-clonal antibodies suitable for administration but there are serious problems which will delay the delivery of a usable vaccine indefinitely. Humans are by far the cheapest and most plentiful experimental animals, especially if the process which is to be altered is species-specific, in which case the only alternatives to humans are other anthropoids, such as chimps. The auto-immune response is triggered relatively easily in chimps and other monkeys, which is why the evidence of post-vasectomy serum sickness in members of the genus is not taken very seriously. In any case, the immune response is extremely variable in members of the same species. Not only are researchers faced with formidable dosage problems, they are facing difficulties in establishing the duration of immunogenic in-fertility which also appears extremely variable. The anti-fertility vaccine is now in phase II testing, in which larger numbers of animals are being vaccinated and followed up for one year. Although an anti-fertility vaccine has been used in clinical trials in Brazil, Finland and Sweden, it will be years before it is ready for human administration on any scale.

> ... it should be clear that the development of a pregnancy vaccine is not a quick, inexpensive or straightforward task. Nevertheless the potential impact of this method on world-wide family planning programmes is of such significance that no scientist concerned with global human populations would neglect considera-tion of this approach to a new method development.[33]

Djerassi noted that vaccination could be done by paramedics and that the public had a positive response to vaccination. The public in the developed world has become decidedly leery about vaccination; the public in the third world is not as enthusiastic about vaccination, which has rather intangible results, as it is about injection; so powerful is the mystique of injection that placebo injections must sometimes accompany effective medication by other routes. One of the reasons for the acceptability of Depo-Provera is simply that it is an injection. Other slow-release inject-ables are being developed in the hope of sidestepping the controversy that continues to rage around the use of medroxyprogesterone acetate, which is really another version of the rejection of ovulation-suppressants for steroids of more limited function and lower dosage. The Third World has its infertility injection and will probably continue to have it despite the politicking of concerned groups in the developed world. The beauty of the contraceptive vaccine is not that it can be injected, but that it can be administered even more simply. As John Platt, Professor of Biophysics at the Mental Health Research Institute of the University of Michigan wrote to Carl Djerassi:

> I am not interested in imposing a dictatorial method on the world; I am very concerned about side effects and the long-range effects of the large-scale applica-tion of compounds to populations. But I am also concerned at our inability to do much about the population explosion using our present methods. We have blinded ourselves to the possible degree of public acceptance and to the enormous increase in effectiveness that would result if we could find oral contraceptives that could be put in salt or other foodstuffs and that could be used voluntarily.[34]

Djerassi himself had given great thought to the possibility of putting a sterilant in the water supply, on the analogy of fluoridisation. The most likely candidate for such dispersion would be the vaccine, for uncontrolled dosing of children, old people, animals, Uncle Tom Cobbleigh and all with steroids would produce horrible results in a relatively short time. The vaccine might give people itchy bumps or something of the sort but it would not give them breasts, oedema and tumours. In a spirit of total mischief, one feels like exhorting them to carry on, because the method is only applicable in societies where there is a public, piped water-supply, i.e. in the developed world. The poisoning of wells is the most-hated crime in history; it is rather diverting to reflect what would happen if USAID minions began tipping vaccine into the wells of India and Africa; the substance would dissipate in the underground aquifers or be filtered out by the earth, but before that a considerable number of Peace Corps or VSO workers would have been massacred. The rest of us would roof our houses with corrugated iron or plastic and drink rainwater. The most amusing thing about Platt's communication is that it reflects mental confusion of a fairly dire order, only to be expected in the official of a mental-health institution. People who wish to be infertile may take certain measures to achieve that end; they do not need to have those measures disguised as salt. For Platt the word "voluntary" describes any action taken without a gun in one's ribs. Putting contraceptives in salt might save the world for the aborigines who don't use salt, a very select group. It would be a good way of reducing the use of sodium chloride which would be an excellent outcome, therefore let us encourage him in his delusions. Platt's target is, of course, India:

> If there were an effective and safe contraceptive that could be put into salt, it could be put in at a small number of factories, possibly one or two hundred, all over India, for example. It could be monitored by a small number of biochemical technicians, perhaps with master's degrees, just as chlorine and fluoride in our water, Vitamin D in our milk, iodine in our salt, or other "public health" compounds are monitored in the United States.
>
> This means that such a method would be exceedingly cheap compared with any of our present contraceptive methods, which involve individual application, prescription, or medical examination. If individual examinations or medical examinations were needed for birth control in a country the size of India, with over a hundred million women of child-bearing age, about 100,000 paramedical personnel would have to be trained and kept in the field. To do that, several hundred training centres would have to be set up, staffed by hundreds or thousands of doctors – who must themselves be trained in advance.[35]

There are 180,000 doctors in India, all trained, as Platt so engagingly puts it, "in advance". More than 15,000 Indian doctors "trained in advance" work in hospitals in Britain and the USA. If Professor Platt had ever engaged any of them in conversation he would have learned that there are "too many" doctors in India, rather than too few.[36] If the cost of developing new contraceptive methods were simply paid as doctors' salaries in India, Professor Platt's problem would go some way to resolving itself. What India cannot afford is a vast number of workers trained in nothing but fertility control, because there is so little demand for it, and such an overwhelming demand for basic health services like malaria and parasitic infestation control, burns treatment, stitching for cuts, setting for broken limbs, and re-hydration powder (which should make a dent in the available supplies of salt). Professor Platt and Professor Djerassi, "one of the most active and multi-faceted chemists in America", cannot be expected to get excited about what would happen if the training of doctors in India were completely recast in order to equip them for the rigours of popular medical practice in a peasant economy instead of teaching them to expect the equipment and the standard of care and of reward which is offered in rich countries or what would happen if some of the money thrown away on useless research and luxury procedures was pumped into the Indian exchequer to pay them. Their *what if*s are of a different order. It may be that a certain measure of infantility is to be expected of an innovative genius; perhaps one of the reasons why Djerassi is such a brilliant biochemist is that he has never grasped just how much more there is to people than molecules.

In the developed world, the thoughtful individual will continue to find modern fertility regulation a difficult business, more difficult, I would submit, than the routine practice of a method like *coitus interruptus*. He or she cannot simply learn how fertility regulation is done, because there is no consensus. The array of methods, each with its in-built problems, presents nothing new from the user's point of view because he or, more probably, she has been unable to keep up with the mass of data being issued monthly by the biochemical establishment. Do you know, dear reader, which of the following you and your loved ones are using to regulate your fertility: chlormadinone acetate, cyproterone acetate, diethylstilboestrol, dimethisterone, ethynodiol diacetate, ethynylestradiol, levonorgestrel (sometimes called D-norgestrel), norethisterone, norethisterone acetate, lynestrenol, medoxyprogesterone acetate, megestrol acetate, mestranol, norethynodrel, norgestrel, norgestrienone, quingestanol acetate? Why are they unlikely to be using norethynodrel or lynestrenol? Should they be using megestrol? (Not if they are beagles.) Should the Chinese be using 17-hydroxyprogesterone acetate and 2α, 17α-diethynyl-A-norandrostane -2β, 17β-diol dipropionate?

Perhaps users of the steroid pill should keep samples of the packets of all the kinds they have ever used, in case they may need to know at some later date. To suggest that the bids are not yet in on the oral contraceptive is to raise anxiety, which is useless; the idea behind taking steps is to allay anxiety. Once you have reconstructed your reproductive history, you have at least taken a precaution, not for yourself necessarily, but for your children. There is a difference, however, between adopting a sceptical, investigative attitude, and espousing conspiracy theories. Our enemy is not so much sexism, although sexism there is, as stupidity masked by the professional mystique. The steroid contraceptive has gone through massive changes during the career of a single user. It is as well to study why those changes were deemed necessary. The material is all, or almost all, published and available in special libraries. The difficulties attaching to interpretation are not connected with the hardness of the subject matter but with the mode of argumentation. The legalistic approach to causation, as for example in the case of the IUD, demands positive concrete demonstration of the disease-producing mechanism; in the case of pelvic inflammatory disease, for example, commonsense would find the case proved. The researcher will point to other factors, smoking, exposure to infection, promiscuity, previous history and so forth. The case will be publicly considered moot, while every intern finding a woman admitted as an emergency with severe abdominal pain will ask among his first questions whether she has an IUD. Recent investigations of the degree of public awareness about birth-control methods in a literate and over-informed society showed that users of the various methods were not sure of just what methods they were using, did not know what kind of oral steroid they were taking or called their IUD by the wrong name. The only way they can cope with the controversies that continue to rage is to ignore them and trust in their GPs, a risky business at the best of times. The composition of contraceptive pills has changed radically in the twenty years or so that they have been used; if a long-term sequela of one of the abandoned dosage systems should now emerge, there would be no chance of tracking down the users of those pills and their children. We could take comfort in the idea that we in the developed world have been the guinea-pigs in using oral steroids first, if only the manufacturers had not off-loaded the superseded pills in cut-price mass family-planning projects in the third world.

Research into improved barrier methods goes on, but results seem to be disappointing. A recent study of the Prentif cap, for example, showed a very poor continuation rate of only a half over a one-year period.[37] Two-thirds of the women fitted with this cavity-rim cap complained of the odour, and a fifth of the women who discontinued its use did so on this ground alone. The cap was fitted in one of four sizes and the women were told to fill it with spermicide and leave it in no longer than seven days. A tenth of the sample of 350 users complained that it became dislodged; there were twenty-eight pregnancies. A fifth to a third of the women reported difficulty in inserting and/or removing the cap. The only chance of reinstating the use of barrier methods is if committed women put a good deal of energy and imagination into promoting it; insertion and removal may be difficult but they can be learned. There should be no hard-and-fast rule about the use of spermicide because it ought not to be necessary. Filling the cap with slop simply compromises the fit, especially as the spermicide is unlikely to remain *in situ* and chemically unaltered for seven days. The clinical trial had to aim for comparability and all the patients had to be told the same thing. Only at the level of the neighbourhood clinic would it be possible to reinforce cap use and deal with cases on their merits and with problems as they arose. The variations on the cervical cap are many and there is one to suit the drop-outs from the trial, if only the full range had been utilised. The reactivity of the substance from which the cap is made ought also to be carefully assessed; the odour problem probably has a good deal to do with that. The medical establishment has nothing to gain by reviving barrier methods; there are no fat research fellowships offered by the manufacturers and none of the glamour associated with a breakthrough, still less of the delusions of omnipotence that accompany the development of a vaccine that can be put in salt.

The difficulty raised by the poor clinic trials is that distribution of the cervical cap in countries where testing is required will become or remain illegal. Illegality constitutes no functional disadvantage to a contraceptive, and may in fact strengthen its cultural acceptance in some groups, especially among dissident groups who are deeply suspicious of institutionalised methods. As punks have eagerly adopted the fashion of piercing their ears numerous times, and even their nasal septa, they could also decide for cervical jewellery, individually cast gold and silver or plastic caps to be worn as ornaments when not *in situ*, perhaps. Women less eager to *épater* the squeamish might like to pretend that it is some piece of zoomorphic artwork (which it would be) and keep the secret of its function to themselves. (In case you have never seen a cervix, it could pass as a rather large sea-anemone, with its fronds drawn in.) Those who want a usable barrier method instead of the flabby diaphragm will have to take the matter into their own hands. The cervical cap is guerilla contraception; it is a neat, elegant and economic solution to the contraception problem and it can be made to work again.

The reproductive future holds, as an ever-growing problem, the management of adolescent fertility and adolescent venereal disease, both of which require a single answer, the popularisation of the condom. In essence the problem is simple, and the answer is clear, unlike the problem of managing the fertility of, say, India. Yet we cannot solve it. We do not know how to sell condoms to the young, above all our own young. At a house party in Italy last summer, my hostess was losing sleep because she was certain that her teenage guests were up to something and she was terrified to think that she might return one of the girls to her family pregnant. I suggested that she put a condom under the boys' pillows or in the bathroom cabinet; she was revolted by the idea and it was not so difficult to see why. There is a list of cultural reasons why a mother would not put condoms in her sons' bathroom cabinet. (There are no reasons why a house guest cannot put condoms in a bathroom cabinet.) Mechai, the Thai family planning whizz-kid, in the true gung-ho family-planning tradition presents passers by and visiting diplomats with gaily coloured condoms. It is an old population-lobby party trick, but it will not grab the kids, however effective it has been in Thailand. As a motivation problem getting our kids to use condoms is simpler than turning a woman who has grown up in the living ideology of motherhood into a contraception acceptor, but we cannot do it. Because we cannot handle this, one in ten of our teenagers will be rendered sterile for life, and one in five of the babies born will be the child of a child. As is the case with most of our problems, we have transported it to all the ex-slave nations. It is a real, serious, immediate problem causing palpable suffering and hardship all over the world, and as such it is beneath our immature genius to solve. We prefer global projections and sterilants in salt.

The longed for "male method" of contraception is no nearer now than it ever was. Gossypol, an extract of cotton-seed oil, which was pioneered in China, seems too toxic for every day administration.

Currently, only two techniques are available for widespread control of male fertility, namely condoms and vasectomy. Of the numerous hormonal methods evaluated, the only effective compounds offering any prospects for availability in the near future are testosterone alone or in combination with medroxyprogesterone acetate. However the need for parenteral administration, the failure to suppress spermatogenesis completely in all men, and the long time for suppression and recovery of spermatogenesis, represent the negative aspects of these prospective methods.[38]

The gist of all these observations is that although the universal two-child family has become a marker for after-dinner chit-chat about population, it will not come to pass. It will not come to pass because there are too many sterile people, because there are too many unmarried teenage mothers, because there is too much divorce; these are already large categories and the trends in all three are steadily mounting. More one-parent families mean more children to be raised at public expense, and that means more official interference in what remains of family life. This is not a prediction of chaos. If you try a Galtonian exercise, and undertake to calculate the median family size and typical family structure in which your friends live, you will find that we live in chaos already. We have the power to organise chaos. To some extent we already do, but as the public expense of health and child care grows, there will be a more concerted attempt to avoid handicap before it is manifest in the born. Most of the citizens will not realise what has happened when the hospitals institute routine screening of all pregnancies and all new-borns. Some have done it already. Their justification is the study of epidemiology; we need to know what disease and disability is going to cost us so that we can budget for it, in theory. In practice we spend more on rare diseases than we do on common ones. There will be more sterilisations, too, voluntary and "involuntary," and probably fewer abortions, and certainly more requests for reversal of sterilisation. And governments will set up sperm banks in lead-lined chambers, when it becomes clear that the mutagens are winning. Cancer and the auto-immune diseases will proliferate, but *Homo occidentalis* will not.

Chapter Fourteen

The Myth of Overpopulation

In the exact sense to which modern theory would confine [the term overpopulation] it is of so little service to the discussion of actuality that even the most reputable writers on practical problems use it to denote something less tenuous and equally entitled to the name. Still nearer to the heart of life we find the frank misuse by the journalist, which defeats all clear thinking. In its exact sense it is a term of static economics denoting a state of affairs such that a reduction in the number of the occupants of the area under consideration, while all other circumstances, including the age distribution, remained the same, would be followed by an increase in returns per head.

Sir William Beveridge

On 19 May 1926, Durga Dass Kapur wrote to Marie Stopes from Amritsar, earnestly assuring her of unquestioning adherence to the new faith:

I very acutely realise that all the misery, pain, indebtedness, gloominess, sickness, dirt, prostitution, war, underfeeding, poverty, child mortality, heart-burning, misunderstanding, etc. are deliberately traceable to over-breeding.[1]

Someone with a better sense of humour than the angelic doctor might have suspected that her leg was being pulled. In a sense, this view is quite correct – people who are not born will not be gloomy or in debt because they will not *be*. The Malthusian hypothesis is a sword to slice through the Gordian knot of mounting human misery, and many people, conscious of no desire to wring the withers of the poor, baffled and hurt by the spectacle of their misery, need such a simple explanation. The poor are poor through their own fault. They have outgrown their food supply, the wicked things. The Marquis de Sade was one of the first people to give literary expression to what everybody knows, that the pressure of numbers upon resources is constant and life is easier for the marquises of the world if reproduction is eliminated; his solution was unchastity and the spoliation of humanity by destructive sexual practices, which would leave the world to trees and furry animals, if possible sooner rather than later. Malthus came to the opposite conclusion, that restraint and chastity would have to be urged upon the masses and enforced if possible. He assumed that they would not see the point of self-regulation, partly

because he shared the common view of human sexuality as virtually uncontrollable as well as the middle-class innocence about the ways of
cheating nature. He might have been appalled to realise that his views
inspired the policy of witholding famine relief in India in 1870. In 1870,
the population of India was 290,000,000; India now supports 712,000,000.
In other words, the famine of 1870 was not caused by population out-
growing its resource base. Pressure on resources is constant; no matter
how many people were sterilised by starvation during that famine,
pressure on resources would have continued. Pressure on resources may
even have been intensified by the loss of people to produce food, although,
if the famine followed the usual pattern, the people who died would have
been the least productive, the children, the old, the artisans who
depended upon surplus value, barbers, cobblers, and the like.

Is the world overpopulated? If I must adopt some position on this point,
it will be a highly compromised one. I have been to old Delhi, as Paul
Ehrlich has, but somehow, as usual, I saw the wrong thing. Here follows
the apocalyptic vision of Paul Ehrlich, set out on page one of his bestseller,
under the heading "The Problem."

> I have understood the population problem intellectually for a long time. I came
> to understand it emotionally one stinking hot night in Delhi a few years ago.
> My wife and daughter and I were returning to our hotel in an ancient taxi.
> The seats were hopping with fleas. The only functional gear was third. As we
> crawled through the city, we entered a crowded slum area. The temperature
> was well over 100° F; the air was a haze of dust and smoke. The streets seemed
> alive with people. People eating, people washing, people sleeping. People
> visiting, arguing and screaming. People thrusting their hands through the taxi
> window begging. People defecating and urinating. People clinging to buses.
> People herding animals. People, people, people, people. As we moved slowly
> through the mob, hand horn squawking, the dust, noise, heat and cooking fires
> gave the scene a hellish aspect. Would we ever get to our hotel? All three of
> us were, frankly, frightened. It seemed that anything could happen – but, of
> course, nothing did. Old India hands will laugh at our reaction. We were just
> some over-privileged tourists, unaccustomed to the sights and sounds of India.
> Perhaps, but since that night I've known the feel of over-population.[2]

This then is the problem that Ehrlich and his paymasters and the
gullible public are setting out to solve. It is composed first of heat,
apparently. Some parts of the world are hot and not less likely to be so
when they are more sparsely populated. The only remedy that can be
suggested for this aspect of the problem is that people like Dr Ehrlich who
waste emotional energy in resenting other people's weather had better
stay out of it. Even more alarming than the weather however, was the
taxi. The fact that virtually every car ever put on the roads in India is
still in service is probably intolerable to a citizen of an automobile-
producing nation; some of us are delighted with the ingenuity of Indians

in this regard. The taxi may have been driven in third because there was no other gear, but is more likely to be driven without recourse to the lower gears in order to save petrol. India has only very small reserves of oil and must buy at the market price. The taxi-driver will only realise his minute profit if he husbands every millilitre of petrol. It is a little hard on the passengers, especially if the taxi – which is usually as clean as human hands and little else can make it, because the driver spends so much time waiting for a fare – is full of fleas, something which I have never encountered in India. It is amusing to speculate just how someone as savvy as Ehrlich got himself into this jam; if for example he made the driver empty out a load of goats so he could commandeer the taxi, he was probably driven into the slum as a punishment. As you can hire an immaculate car with a uniformed driver for twenty dollars a day in Delhi, it seems that somebody who should have been looking after Ehrlich threw him to the pi-dogs. If Dr Ehrlich and his fellow-Americans, by the way, were more tolerant of small changes in ambient temperature, and did not instantly squander fuel in raising it or lowering it, their driver might have been able to afford enough petrol and oil to drive his taxi in a more seemly manner, and to maintain it a little better.

If we exclude the carping about the taxi and the temperature, we are left with people, people, people, people. This slum is rather odd in that there are buses and people herding animals in it, so we might guess that Ehrlich did not get himself inside a real slum, where there is no room for buses, taxis or herds, just huts. What he seems to have seen were settlements. The area was certainly not more crowded than Manhattan at three o'clock on a weekday afternoon: the difference is that in Delhi the people were all at pavement level. If they had been nicely shut up in high-rises Ehrlich would not have troubled his head about them, even if he had heard that most of them were drugging themselves with heroin or alcohol or doctors' substitutes. He saw no drunks, no crazy people, no obese people, either, I'll be bound. If he did, he does not say. He does not say that he saw anyone laughing, or men and women playing with their babies. Some of the smells around those tiny fires, made by burning the tips of scrap wood, were spicy and good. Those people had not come there as a couple, years ago, and multiplied until they filled up the area. If he had been less of a ninny and got out of the taxi to talk to the people (who are better at speaking his language than he is at speaking theirs) he might have found out how they got there.

But no. Intellectual understanding precludes investigation. If he had gone into the shanties, he would have been surprised to find that the earthen floors were swept smooth, that the family possessions, most of them the wife's dowry, were neatly hung on poles or standing on a narrow shelf, the brass bowls polished till they shine in the darkness, reflecting every sliver of available light, polished with earth. He did not notice that the people doing their washing-up were not using detergents. Cow-dung smoke and dust are hard on the sinuses but they are less deadly than industrial effluent and exhaust fumes, which Dr Ehrlich seems to prefer. He did not notice the complete absence of the United States' principal product, trash. The greatest insult about all these people living shoulder to shoulder, the visible counterpart of the population planner's nightmare, is that they make do with so little. Such low purchasing power is anathema to men of Ehrlich's kidney. He does not tell us how he treated the beggars, whose presence seems to indicate that he did not get very far off the beaten track. If he had gone to some parts of Delhi in 1970 he would have found American teenagers begging to support their drug habit, much as they do in America. Still, one can sympathise, for the good doctor has had himself sterilised after the birth of one daughter; this matter has been made public presumably in order to show the utter sincerity of his preaching of Zero Population Growth, only to have to contemplate the ghastly vision of the world being taken over by thin brown people who eat, wash, defecate and cling to buses in defiance of him.

In order to feel in his bowels the reality of overpopulation Ehrlich had to go to India; others feel it more strongly when they come across discarded aluminium beer cans in the wilderness. If we agree that the world is over-populated we have still to decide what we mean by the term and what the phenomenon consists in. An Indian Paul Ehrlich might see the sudden exponential increase in the global human population as the result of an ecological disaster which happened about five hundred years ago, namely the explosion of Europe. This was not caused by population pressure, although population pressure there was and always will be, but by the demands of the European trade economy.

What happened when the Europeans risked life and limb in perilous forays into the unknown was a chain reaction caused by the cultural impact of a clever (but not wise) people with great skills and small scruple. They found stable populations living in circumscribed communities with repro-ductive strategies selected for over millennia. Disgusted by these strategies, they outlawed them, or more effectively destroyed them through the demographic catastrophes that followed contact, epidemics, warfare, enslavement and its modern descendant, outwork. The disasters that befell the stable, or stagnant, populations of the southern world could probably not have been averted by the most well-intentioned paternalism on the part of the intruders: nowadays we give hunter-gatherers and swidden agri-culturalists oil cheques or maintenance payments from universities who want to study them. Such a death may be easier but it is certainly more ignominious. After the initial shocks, and systematic annihilation by guns, disease and poison, especially alcohol, the populations of the new world, with a new hybrid base, began to build up the potential for expansion on the model of their *criollo* ruling class: this is the real revenge of

Montezuma. In other words, overpopulation is not something which looms, like the nuclear holocaust; it is something which began to happen in western Eurasia five hundred years ago, and spread like a virus. It is not indigenous anywhere else, with the possible exception of China. Reading an account, like John Hemming's *Red Gold*, of the creation of a state like Brazil, one is struck time and again by the inefficiency of the system which tore out the red dye trees, thousands upon thousands of them, dragged by the Indians to the shore, thousands of Indians, at first eager to deserve steel axes, and then unwilling, driven by fear, because they had all the axes they wanted, but the white man could never have enough of the red dye trees to enrich a handful of merchants and supply a completely inessential commodity.

We wasted people before there was a surplus, buying and selling them cheap, squandering their lives for a pittance, telling ourselves what the eugenists told themselves about the working poor, that they were not really human. We applied *ad hoc* intelligence tests: people who had no written language, no money, no artefacts, people who could not learn to hate us, were non-people and could be buried in the foundations of our empire.

Rubber boots, invented by Amazon Indians who molded the latex right on their feet, had been introduced in the United States early in the nineteenth century. But it was not until the advent of the horseless carriage that the demand for tires, inner tubes and other rubber products was responsible directly for the orgy of lawless greed and inhumanity that makes other terrible episodes in history seem pale by comparison. Upon reviewing the report of Roger Casement, the British consul at Rio de Janeiro, on the atrocities, James Bryce, British ambassador to the United States and a social commentator of some note, declared that, "the method employed in the collection of rubber surpasses in horror anything reported in the civilised world during the last century." According to Casement's report, the Putamayo rubber output of 4,000 tons between 1900 and 1911 was directly responsible for the deaths of 40,000 Indians. The total population of the area shrank during this same period from 50,000 to 7,000. It was estimated that every tonne of rubber from the Amazon valley – gathered primarily by and for British and American firms – had been produced at the cost of two human lives.[3]

What has this to do with the population explosion? The people who suffered that we might have tyres to our cars are exterminated; we will not have done anything to right the wrong done to them if we allow the present inhabitants of their homelands to breed *ad libitum*, obviously. The point is simply that when we see the hopelessness of the slums and barrios, we see the latest stages of an epidemic disease that has become endemic in its later stages. It was the scourge of colonialism that cheapened human life, that made human dignity a nonsense, that showed the people in the hot lands that their destiny was not theirs to command. As long as the situation continues, as long as they have no resource base of their own, as long as they are mocked by the demands of foreign economies, they will have no reason to wish to be fewer. They may wish to escape the pangs of childbirth, they may wish to escape the anguish of seeing children die, but they will not wish to be fewer. There is all the difference in the world between family limitation undertaken for positive reasons and family limitation accepted out of despair. If the second becomes the rule, the world will not be worth living in however few people are in it.

It may seem that these reflections have nothing to do with the question of, say, compulsory sterilisation after the birth of the third child for every-one in the world. As soon as we begin to reflect on the differences in the impact of such a scheme on the North and on the South, we begin to see how the history of the relationship relates to the implementation of such a policy. In the North relatively few people would need to become aware of its existence, for relatively few people have three children and far fewer have four (even fewer of them actually wanted four). Neverthe-less it would mean that a minority, whose religion forbade such mutilation, would be obliged to hold their families at two. Such a scheme might appeal to some as a way of exterminating Catholics. It would, however, raise the question of religious persecution. In the North virtually all of the children born grow to adulthood, and even if they do not, parents do not expect support from their children in their declining years except in the form of state pensions and subsidised health care. The existence of children of our loins is not crucial to our well-being in any way. Sterilisation after three children would probably make very little differ-ence to our birthrate in any event, and might simply land our govern-ments with the bill for sterilisations which the citizens would have had in any case. There is no point in making compulsory operations which are already desirable. The skill and clout of the religious lobbies would probably defeat any compulsory sterilisation legislation if push came to shove.

On the other hand, if global consciousness is a something to be cultivated, perhaps we should lead the way. We keep telling Southern man that the world is too full of people and he should recognise the fact, so perhaps we should be the first to go under the knife, in emulation of our prophet, Dr Ehrlich. Perhaps those of us who are childless (and we are numerous indeed) should wear insignia proclaiming our services to the ecosphere, but we do not merit so much as a No-Child Glorious Certificate or a coat-of-arms saying "One less strain to clutter up the ecosphere." Nobody really believes that anybody is childless out of altruism. In any case, the idea is not population reduction but maintenance of population at current levels. In fact the idea of Zero Population Growth can be interpreted in various fairly sickening ways. The Thai embargo on births in Cambodian refugee camps is called Zero Population Growth too. Zero Population Growth, seen by the simple-minded as the universal two-child family, would be Zero Population Change too, because differential fertility is a principal mechanism of natural selection; differential mortality only works as differential fertility if people die before reproducing. In fact the high incidence of childlessness will protect that mechanism to some extent, although the Northerners may well feel that it is being shielded on the wrong side, by reducing the frequency of their genes in the population. It is an interesting fact that as soon as universal compulsory fertility regulation is accepted in principle, some notion of positive eugenics follows it. The people who will win increased reproductive opportunity will be those who are successful, i.e. the ruling cadres. All of which is probably as good as female infanticide and head-hunting as a way of maintaining population stability; the point is that it is not much better. Success in taking heads might be a better indicator of evolutionary fitness, and more democratic, than the selection of candidates according to success in commerce or politics.

If we turn to the Southern world, we see at once that the implementation of a compulsory sterilisation policy would have a staggering impact, and not principally on the birthrate. It will affect many people, and at a much younger age than in Europe or America – so many, in fact, that the entire health services would be taken up with it. Many children die before they reach adulthood already; if health services are all co-opted into the sterilisation business, more will die. In these countries, older people depend absolutely on their younger kinsfolk for their survival; the quantum of hardship suffered by the average citizen will increase. The hardship suffered by the poorest would increase the most. To think that this would not matter greatly is to perpetuate the mentality which valued rubber above human lives. Besides, the Chinese example goes to prove one thing: once the principle of compulsory fertility limitation is accepted, there is no limit to its application. Three children from the majority, even given higher child-mortality rates, is not few enough; within months of establishment of the precedent the figure could drop to two, and then to one, *because prosperity would not follow.* It is clearly true that economic growth in the South does not keep pace with population increase, but what has not been proved is that it is the population increase itself which eats up the growth. The poor countries are getting poorer; the poor in those countries are getting poorer still. Their share of world trade diminishes, and not because their populations eat up their iron ore and their bauxite and their bananas and their sugar. The more of their agriculture they give over to cash crops for export, the more their manpower is swallowed up in the mines and the factories, the poorer they get, for we are still plundering them. From our point of view we cannot afford to do anything else. We cannot afford to pay the price that, say, clothes cost, unless they are made in sweat-shops on the other side of the world and we are certainly not going to make do with one pair of Taiwan jeans until they hang on our limbs in tatters. We are not going to work for six months to buy a pair of trousers the way plantation workers do. We are going to use power and detergents and immense quantities of water to wash our untattered jeans every time we put them on: this is, after all, our standard of living. We can neither abandon it, mitigate it nor change it, for our economies depend upon our extravagent consumption. When our garments no longer meet our standards, we give them to Oxfam and think ourselves both prudent and charitable.

Because the population debate is conducted in the simplest terms, I am trying to reduce the economic refutation of the ZPG position in equally simple terms. The too-many-people position as maintained by most after-dinner pundits is that if there were fewer people in, say, Italy, there would be more of everything to go round. Looking at the depopulated hillsides of Tuscany and Umbria, one must ask, more of what? Not more olive oil, because olive-oil production is manpower-intensive and very hard work. Only the old people do it as it is, running the perennial risk of falling out of trees they are really too old to climb, especially on cold November days when old muscles seize up. Most of the landowners in the Val d'Esse, for example, give the production of their olive trees away to anyone who will prune and plough and manure and harvest, because even though the market price of virgin olive oil is 6,000 lire a kilo it does not amount to enough money to pay skilled labour even at the lowest rates. The people who still bother with the olives do so because the perfume of the dark-green oil is part of what makes life in these hills worth living. It is sprinkled on bread (which used to be substantial enough to suffice as the staple diet); it is used to dress the salads which are an essential nutriment and the vegetables which are still more central a part of the daily diet than the costly meat. But more and more the younger people are turning to the yellow scentless oil of sunflower seeds, corn and peanuts. The green oil will follow the bitter *pecorino* cheese and the wagonloads of fat black cherries and the perfumed orris root into the void. To Euroveal and Eurochicken (both of which taste of fish) and Eurosalad (iceberg lettuce) will be added Eurosalad-dressing. A way of life has vanished from these hills, where the only peasants' sons who remain have been unable to find wives. The old semantics mean that these fifty- and sixty-year-olds are called *ragazzi*; boys.

Fewer people will not necessarily mean more to go round; more people will not necessarily mean less to go round, because we are not yet committed to making it go round in the first place, unless we are living in China, where everybody has a ration book. It is pointless to talk as if there were a world totalitarian government which will issue ration books to all of us at birth. The farmers of the earth do not deliver all their produce to be stored against scarcity and shared out equally and most of us would be horrified if any such plan was ever mooted. Most attempts to guarantee food distribution by such means to peoples familiar with famine have resulted in falls in production. The farmer will rise at dawn and labour until dark for his family, it seems, but not for the State.

The caste system, which filled the democratic English with horror, was one way of ensuring that food was distributed to those who had no part in producing it, regardless of whether they could lay their hands on cash or not. If the farmer wanted the services of a washerman or a barber he had to feed washermen and barbers. Religious requirements and the association of every human activity with specific groups meant that the farmer could not make his own shoes or cut his children's hair or attend his wife in childbirth. Nowadays the economic function of the caste system has been abolished; only the worst part of it, the mental attitude of hierarchical discrimination, remains. The hungry of India will be fed if they can pay for food. If the price of food rises, and the price of a haircut falls, the barber goes hungry. After centuries of fixed relations between labour and payment in kind, the Indian worker is at the mercy of violent fluctuations. Food production in India has increased much faster than the population increase, but the surplus from the large farms is not immediately redistributed, to be stored unprocessed in family storerooms, cleaned as it is required by the womenfolk, ground on the premises and turned into wholesome fibre and protein-rich food. Now the grain is kept in go-downs, where a proportion of it goes to maintain a population explosion of rats. (The barber and the cobbler protected their grain from rats by storing it in jars.) To put the grain surplus into the bellies of the people, India needs to be able to transport it cheaply from the place of production to the place of eventual distribution, but the roads and the railways lead to the coast, to England. The cement needed for the construction of rat-proof silos is rationed throughout India; most of it is bought and sold on the black market by speculators. The fuel to drive the trains and trucks which would ship the grain is ruinously expensive. Famine in India was not caused by an absolute shortage of food, by failure of crops, or by excess of mouths to feed. It was caused by poverty.

As long as famine is vivid in people's memories, they will not jeopardise their chances of survival by limiting the number of children who can help to scavenge for food, children who may die. A child is never an encumbrance to a beggar: if our economic system causes the pauperisation of the many, and there is no doubt that it does, it also caused the proliferation of paupers. When the farmers had paid the cobbler his wheat for providing their families with chattels, he knew exactly what he and his family had to live on. Towards the end of the season, their bellies would be rumbling as a reminder of what would happen if there should be too many in the cobbler's family. The cobbler's chief problem was to keep his wife and children alive, but even if the problem of too many living children seldom arose, they all realised what it would mean. Such an economy is quite incompatible with capitalism; we would call it stagnant. There is no opening for development; the pots, the shoes, the saris, the charpoys all remained the same. Capitalism means growth. There was wealth in the system, but it went to maintain the rajahs and the temples. Tyranny and superstition, this was called. Outrageous it seemed, that some were born to glitter in gold and jewels, and some to sit meditating and gorging themselves on the offerings of people who had no furniture, no floors to their houses and no money in their pockets. This was called a violent contrast between the rich and the poor and scathing the British officers were about it. Their view of the proper conduct of the Indian economy produced a new group, the industrial proletariat, and a class of *rentiers* which led to growing numbers of landless people, and an export industry which instead of enriching the maharajas and the nawabs, enriched a small island in the North Atlantic. There had been famines in India before the British came, and the rulers had dealt with them – well, not so well, and downright badly. The British were accompanied by famines on an unprecedented scale, during which they continued to export wheat.

Without denying the obvious truth, that if human numbers grow to the point that they outstrip the earth's capacity for food production, some people will starve, I am simply pointing out that we have not yet got to that point and some people are starving already. There is a delusion abroad that the rich countries try to redress the balance by sharing their surplus with the hungry. Many good-hearted people really believe that every gramme of wheat that their farmers produce which is not needed to maintain their own life and health is nobly carried to the feckless people in the hot countries. There are mothers still who urge their children to eat their crusts saying, "Think of all the starving children in India." The irrelevance of that injunction is not more wrong-headed than the idea that the well-run industrial agriculture of the developed world is roped into feeding the poor elsewhere. Governments maintain the price of primary produce in their own countries by subsidies and by buying the surplus. This is considered only fair to the farmers. The surplus is only calculated after the citizens have done their best to consume the available supply, most of which they spoil rather than consume. Four-fifths of American grain production is used to feed beef cattle: only the choicest portions of their huge carcases are considered fit to eat. If the Indians were to slaughter their cows, which seem to live mostly on paper and dust, and eat them in the American fashion there would not be more than four or five meals on each one. Americans who worry about how the Indian economy can support these suppliers of food and heat ought rather to worry about how many acres of corn have gone into the American family meat supply for a week. (Twenty million tonnes of cereal protein produces two million tonnes of meat protein.) Most people in the developed world, even while they waste most of their food products, eat far too much, certainly a great deal more than is necessary to maintain life and health. Thus, most of the surplus is eaten or spoiled by processing of one sort or another; what is available for distribution abroad is what nobody can find any other way of disposing of. Even then, we do not give it away.

Food aid is usually sold, for hard currency or for gold. Susan George summarises the situation admirably in *How the Other Half Dies*:

Title IV was added to PL 480 in 1959. It concerned long-term food supply contracts between the US and the recipient; under its terms the food had to be paid for in dollars or in convertible currency (which amounts to the same thing) over a period of up to twenty years and with interest. In 1966 PL 480 was amended to provide for switching all Title I (local-currency) sales to hard-cash sales: this switch was completed by 1971, although exceptions continued to be made for South Vietnam. "Title I" is the term still used, but now it means *hard currency sales*, the only kind available, Title IV has ceased to exist. The changeover to dollar payments was necessary and logical, first because the US balance of payments showed a deficit owing to the Vietnam war; second because PL 480 had indeed resulted in developing commercial export markets and disposal of surplus was no longer a concern because the food was being *bought*. During the first Food for Peace decade, "it was almost as if the needy nations were doing us a favour by letting us give away or sell under concessional arrangements our unwanted farm surpluses," as Senator McGovern put it. Indeed, during this period, fully a quarter of all US agricultural exports exited through the PL 480 channel. Still, the programme was quietly and gradually fulfilling one of its major aims – that of building up future commercial markets. By fiscal year 1975 ... the proportion of food aid to total agricultural exports had dwindled to only three per cent.[4]

The importance of this is only realised when the full picture of American exports shows only the agricultural sector providing a surplus. Japan, which began by taking $400 million dollars worth of food aid, bought more than $20 billion worth of food in 1975. When the foods were sold against local currencies held in the recipient countries, the funds could subsequently be used for promotion of American products. The principal ingredient of these agricultural exports is not food for people but food for livestock. What the export of American feeding habits to poor countries will eventually bring about is less economical feeding of fewer people at a higher price. Under the provisions of PL 480 private loans can be made to US companies setting up abroad, from the counterpart fund.

In 1966, when the "surplus" concept was dropped in favour of gradual conversion to dollar sales, the law added a certain number of provisions known as "self-help measures" to which recipient country governments were obliged to commit themselves when they contracted for PL 480 aid. These measures vary slightly from country to country, but they include in all cases "creating a favourable environment for private enterprise and investment" and "develop-

ment of the agricultural chemical farm machinery and equipment, transporta-
tion and other necessary industries," the use of "available technical know-how"
as well as programmes to control population growth.[5]

Of course there are hungry people in the world. There are hungry people
who work all the hours of daylight and go to bed empty or half-empty,
only to rise the next morning and go back to work with barely the strength
to carry on. Their faces are drawn not just with hunger but with worry,
for the situation is out of their control. The vicissitudes of meagre
monsoons and floods and droughts and all the other natural disasters were
terrible enough, but the instability of post-colonial economies is even
harder to bear, because it works in one way only. What the primary
producers have to sell grows ever cheaper, and what they must buy grows
ever more costly. This is such an iron law of international commerce that
it affects even a rich country like Australia, whose minute population sits
on a crock of mineral wealth which it is too lazy to extract by its own
endeavours and too mean to invest in on its own behalf. The extraction
is highly mechanised and highly profitable yet the Australians do not have
the power to influence the international market. While the population
lives well the development of the country is stalled. Internal communications and transport facilities are totally inadequate. Industry
and employment are both shrinking. If Australians speed up the
exploitation of their minerals the price falls; if they slow it down the margin
of profit is not sufficient to provide them with the surplus on which the
mass of the population must live. If they demand a bigger pay-off, on
the scale necessary to undertake major development projects and develop
a manufacturing industry of their own, the joint venturers will look for
a cheaper supply of both materials and manpower. When the mineral
wealth is exhausted, not even ghost towns will remain, for the mining
towns are portable and air-travel for the few costs less than roads for the
many. The grazing industry might also vanish, for the squandering of
artesian water by the mining operations is lowering the water-table beyond
the potential for replenishment.

If Australia suffered from population pressure, the hinterland would
be penetrated; population would follow the joint venturers and set up
its shoe-shine stands and brothels and gaming houses and market gardens
and restaurants, which might provide an infrastructure and gradually
result in economic development. Such pressure pushed Europeans like
my grandparents out into Australia in the 1860s and resulted in the
development of cities like Melbourne, which now has more than three
million people. Europeans are still coming; Europeans and other migrants
are the people who actually work in the mining towns, but the great push
has levelled off. The migrants are not desperate now, but demanding –
"bolshie", as Australians say. They will form no attachment to the red

earth, and the administration of the industry does not intend that they should. The object of the exercise seems to be to keep most of Australia as a vast recreation ground; the conservationists have the upper hand. Wilderness must retreat to wilderness again. Unfortunately for the conservationists, who apparently cannot grasp the significance of the fact that aborigines regularly burnt off the scrub, and continue to do so on land that has been taken up for grazing for the last hundred years, in February 1983 devastating fires blazed all along the south-eastern coast, uncheckable because of the policy to keep all bush within a mile of the shore uncleared. The hunter-gatherers were part of the Australian ecology. They kept down competing growth which allowed the tall timber to stand at the same time as they hunted, and did so for so long that fire is built in to the lifecycle of many of the native hardwoods. The Europeans killed them, felled the trees and farmed, then, realising the effect of their depredations, tried to reinstate the earlier situation, which they interpreted as wilderness. All over the world, landscapes, sculpted over thousands of years by the manual labour of peasants, are collapsing. We hear hourly of the destruction of forests for cooking-fuel and the clearing of forests for farming. We do not hear of the sweeping away of the neglected rice terraces as the ditches fill up and the rains carry the topsoil away. We have been waging war on the small farmer for generations; we shall not be able to replace him when he is gone.

For both the hunter-gatherer and the farmer, the earth was not the globe of global consciousness, a ball to be played with, but the matrix from which all else had to spring. While they cleared the scrub by fire, or carried the stones away from the fields and built walls with them to keep the topsoil from the ravages of wind and water, they were holding their world together, not only for themselves, but for those who came after. It was not an easy relationship; peasants do not spend much time admiring the view, any more than a child often remains rapt in contemplation of the beauty of his parent. They cursed the earth as often as they blessed it. They tilled it, and they lay beneath it, or they were burnt or scattered to the vultures in order not to pollute it. It remained the principle which governed every other aspect of life. Even for those who did not work the land, the strength of the farmer's back was as important as the keenness of the hunter's eye. The first bureaucracies supported themselves by taxing the farmer: the harder he worked, the more the bureaucrats proliferated. When the farmers' sweat can no longer sustain the army of bureaucrats, then they look for *Lebensraum*. It is not the farmer's loins which get him into trouble, for he can control them, one way or another. It is his loss of entitlement to the fruits of his labour. Likewise, the worker is not impoverished by his reproductive behaviour, but by his loss of entitlement to the goods and earnings he helps to create. When he becomes helpless in this regard, he abandons conscious control of his fertility, for he has nothing to gain by it except the discomforts of self-restraint. This may seem a very simple and silly description of what has happened to cause the population explosion, for it cannot be denied that world population has exploded, but the thesis of Zero Population Growth is very much sillier.

People who are being pillaged have their inability to control their destiny acted out before their eyes every day. They starve alongside agricultural projects which produce foodstuffs for export; they break laws that they did not know existed; they are expropriated by fraud or because they put their lands in pawn to pay their debts. As soon as they muster their slender resources to cope with one crisis, another appears to take its place. As long as they feel that life is a blessing they can carry on; once they accept a materialist view of their situation, once they see their wretched selves with the eyes of their oppressors, they are finished. Even if they manage to fill their bellies, their hearts will be empty. Perhaps an example will help to make this rather quixotic view comprehensible.

In March 1981 I visited a "well baby" parade in a village near Bangalore. The village was a cluster of gleaming white-washed mud houses, each with its forecourt dressed with fresh cow-dung and decorated with geometric designs in white paste. In the hall, fifty or so people, mostly children with big sisters, waited to be judged according to their wellness. The healthiest children there were the ones whose mothers were labouring in the fields, because they ate raw fruits and berries and peanuts, there being no one at home to cook rice and dal for them, but they got no prizes because they had not had their inoculations. Most of the other babies were actually not very well, with scanty hair, scurfy skin, and running noses, but the organisers of the event had no way of registering the true state of affairs. There was no way the middle and upper castes would learn from the untouchables to feed their children raw food. As usual in India, it seemed totally inappropriate to ask mothers why they had so many children. First of all, they did not actually have so very many. Second, the ones they had did not seem assured of survival. At last a woman appeared who seemed a candidate for a little motivation, for she carried her son on her good arm, while the other hung withered at her side, and she limped. Her life had been blighted by polio. She was pregnant. At my prompting the doctor, who was practically catatonic with depression, roused himself to suggest that she might accept some form of birth control after the arrival of the new baby.

The woman looked at us with a kind of gentle surprise. "It is not necessary," she said. "My sisters-in-law help me and we have land." She hoisted her healthy child up a little higher on her arm and smiled upon us like a queen. He was her victory over disability. Only he could annihilate all the suffering and the weariness of her struggle to live with only one good arm and one good leg. She had won, because she had become that most auspicious of women, the fruitful wife. Nearly everyone in the village had been battered in some way, much of their early potential withered by hunger or scarred by disease or accident. Their children were whole, intact promises of a future, yet so fragile that you held your breath for them. I had always understood that mother and child care assistance had to be given before fertility limitation made sense, but that day I knew it as I know that I am awake. If the family planners could guarantee a future for the children that are born, they could persuade the poor to destroy their fertility, but they cannot. They may pretend that they can, but the poor are not fooled. We do not know how many sterilised men and women have lost their children out of the millions sterilised in India; each one of them is a catastrophe for Indian family planning. The people may say that the death of the children was a punishment for the impiety of mutilating the body; the metaphor comes quite close to the underlying truth. If all those Indian babies are wanted, naked, dirty and hungry as they are, we may all be doomed. Many a *faringhi* traveller waiting in the immigration queue behind three hundred Indians with bed-rolls thinks that the end is pretty nigh. We may believe that there is no time to wait for the plundered peasants of the earth to snap out of their delusions that they and theirs have a future, but in reality we have no choice.

Whether we believe that the world is over-populated or not depends to some extent on how we think people should live. If we in the West think that only our kind of life is worth living, then clearly the numbers that the earth supports will have to be substantially reduced. The world could become a vast luxury hotel, complete with recreational space for us to hunt and ski and mountaineer in, but it must not be forgotten that our luxurious lifestyle demands the services of a huge number of helots, who cannot be paid so much that they can afford rooms in the hotel for themselves. Like Ricardo, we would like to see the supply of helots kept constant, neither falling so low that we have to take out the trash ourselves or becoming so high that we shake in our shoes fearing insurrection in the compound. The official ideology is that the guests in the hotel create all the wealth; only by the extraordinary efficiency of their wealth-creation are all the rest able to survive by merely drudging in the kitchens and the lavatories and the market gardens. At very little cost to himself the guest creates the wealth which is apportioned to them for these worthless but indispensable and time-consuming activities. If this is so, if the capitalist system is actually the best system for creating wealth ever devised, perhaps it could be made less spectacularly unjust; for example, perhaps the cultivation of inessentials which are regarded as essentials, but for which we will not pay a price commensurate with the human labour that they absorb, should be made illegal. Perhaps we should impose the same penalties on the consumption of sugar, tobacco and tea as we do on heroin, so that people brutalised by this kind of cultivation could go back to farming food crops. Perhaps we should outlaw speculation on commodities, which, if it is a way to maintain a "fair" market price, seems to have got a very odd idea of fairness. When primary producers try to do a little speculation on their own behalf, we quickly decide that speculative buying of commodities is not at all fair, as when the London Metal Exchange closed trading in tin, when it was suspected that the government of Malaysia was bidding to force up the price of a ship-load of tin already on the water.

I don't know how many people the earth can support, and I don't believe that anybody else does either; it can certainly support more people on a low calory intake than it can on a high calory intake, but as the world is not a huge soup-kitchen the fact is irrelevant. It is quite probable that the world is overpopulated and has been so for some time but getting into a tizzy about it will not prove helpful. Nothing good can come of fear eating the soul. We cannot take right decisions if we are in a funk. We do not have access to our imagination, if we are convinced that catastrophe lurks just around the corner. We may be living in catastrophe now; perhaps we shall have to adapt to it, or go under. Perhaps catastrophe is the natural human environment, and even though we spend a good deal of energy trying to get away from it, we are programmed for survival amid catastrophe. It is an odd thing that people living precariously have more commitment to the continuity of their line than people safely ensconced in plenty. If this is the case, there is not much we can do about it, for we cannot design a political system which will supply the right proportions of potential catastrophe. If we are to deal with the problem of people at all gracefully, we will have to stop rushing into situations we do not understand encumbered with all kinds of non-solutions. In the past we have tried to avoid this by undertaking all kinds of research, which cost many times what practical help would have cost, and came up with conclusions that were no use to anyone. What does it help to know that when all the statistical correctives are applied to the reproductive histories of a small number of Egyptian women that the death of a child made no difference to overall reproductive performance, did not lead to shorter birth intervals, etc. etc? As we have no plan to kill Egyptian babies, or to keep them alive, there is no way we can use the information.

What this book has tried to show is how false reasoning and obtuseness have distorted an important development in human affairs. I do believe that the crashing blunders of family-planning programmes, especially in India, have actually delayed the coming of the new Saviour, Small Family Norm, as he is affectionately known in family-planning circles; I also believe that unwanted children have been born because of inept family planning, and that some people have died. In the spectrum of global cruelty and mismanagement, the crimes of family planning are very small beer indeed. The money spent, although it is more than the entire international budget for health aid, is a piffling sum compared to the billions spent on "defence". Nevertheless, family planning mismanagement matters, if only because so many thoughtful people have put so much hard work into it in the field. It is cruel to them to train them badly, to pit them against the very people who should be their colleagues and humiliate them by supplying them with train-loads of (unsterilised) Lippes Loops and truckloads of high-dose oestrogen pills. It is not fair to them that they become the tools of half-baked right-wing theory, for their motives are usually very different. The statistics so ingeniously amassed by the rich research institutions are no help in the field, where the full impact of misplaced concretisation of people, who are dynamic, into figures, which are passive, must be felt. Every field-worker eventually realises that overpopulation is not our problem to define and solve; that there may be an alternative definition and an alternative solution, coming from the community with whom he is working. The blind conviction that we have to do something about other people's reproductive behaviour, and that we may have to do it whether they like it or not, derives from the assumption that the world belongs to us, who have so expertly depleted its resources, rather than to them, who have not. Put in this way, the ZPG intellectual position is seen as totally illiberal, yet some – I would say most – liberals hold some such belief.

The only possible coherent motivation in offering family-planning services around the world is a desire to help people, families, individuals, to do what they want, not what we think they ought to want. If we allow the recipients to define their needs, we would save all the thousands of dollars we squander on defining needs. In practice, this is what the field worker has to do, for the information he has from the secretariat or the regional office is useless. There is very little satisfaction to be had in averting births, partly because one is never sure of having actually averted one. There is much more satisfaction to be had from keeping alive the babies who are already there, in improving the health of their mothers, in building gobar gas plants and latrine blocks. There is even more satisfaction in learning from the people just how amazing human beings are, how graceful, how resilient, how funny and how sad. Strange to relate, the poor get more opportunity to develop all these sides of themselves than do the rich, who are much the same the world over.

Let us therefore abandon the rhetoric of crisis, for we *are* the crisis. Let us stop wasting energy in worrying about a world crammed with people standing shoulder to shoulder and counting the babies born every minute (one in every five of them a Chinese and just about all of them foreign) and begin to use our imagination to understand how it is that poverty is created and maintained. Let us get to know Lady Poverty up close, so that we lose our phobia about the poor. If we must be afraid, let us rather be afraid that man, the ecological disaster, now has no enemy but his own kind. Rather than being afraid of the powerless, let us be afraid of the powerful, the rich sterile nations, who, whether they be of the Eastern or the Western variety, have no stake in the future. The birth of every unwanted child is a tragedy, for itself and for the unwilling parents, but in spite of all the attention we have given to the matter, more unwanted children are born to us, the rich, than to them, the poor. This may seem a paradox, but the time gives it proof.

Notes

CHAPTER ONE

A Child is Born

1 John F. BESEMERES, *Socialist Population Politics* (New York 1980) pp. 271, 272.

2 Christopher DRIVER (ed.), *The Good Food Guide* (London 1979) p. 82.

3 ABC Transcript, interview conducted by Bob Clark, 13 July 1978.

4 For a summary of the evidence about the use of drugs during pregnancy see L. D. SABATH, Agneta PHILIPSON and David CHARLES, "Ethics and the use of drugs during pregnancy", *Science*, Vol. 202, 3 November, 1978, pp. 540–541; also, Marcus A. KLINGBERG and Cheri M. PAPIER, "Teratoepidemiology", *Journal of Biosocial Science*, Vol. 11 (1979) pp. 234–251.

5 Robert COUGHLAN, *The Wine of Genius* (London 1952) p. 58.

6 "Battered Women: study shows their plight a 'family problem'", *UTA Magazine*, Vol. 5, No. 1, September 1982, p. 15.

7 Some idea of the complexity of the problem may be gained from Watson A. BOWES, "Obstetrical Medication and Infant Outcome: A Review of the Literature", in *The Effects of Obstetrical Medication on Fetus and Infant* (Monographs of the Society for Research in Child Development, No. 35, pt. iv, pp. 3–23).

8 Sheryl Burt RUZEK, *The Women's Health Movement-Feminist Alternatives to Medical Control* (New York 1978) pp. 59–60.

9 Judith RANDALL, "Too Many Caesarians?", *Parents' Magazine*, November 1978, quoting Dr Albert Havercamp of Denver General Hospital. Frederick M. ETTNER, "Hospital Technology Breeds Pathology", *Women and Health*, Vol. II, No. 2.

10 R. BEARD, M. BRUNDENELL, P. DUNN and D. FAIRWEATHER (eds.) *The Management of Labour:* Proceedings of the Royal College of Obstetricians and Gynaecologists (London 1975) pp. 218–234; Brigitte JORDAN, *Birth in Four Cultures: a Cross-cultural Investigation of Childbirth in Yucatan, Holland, Sweden and the United States* (Montreal 1980) pp. 94–5.

11 *Maternity in Britain: A Survey of Social and Economic Aspects of Pregnancy and Childbirth undertaken by a Joint Committee of the Royal College of Obstetricians and Gynaecologists and the Population Investigation Committee* (Oxford 1948) p. 72.

12 Sheila KITZINGER, *Women as Mothers* (Glasgow 1978) p. 195. This chapter should be read in conjunction with this excellent book, which, while taking a less saturnine view than my own, makes many of the same points in a fuller, more convincing way.

13 JOSS SHAWYER, "Death by Adoption", seen in typescript 1977.

14 Susan BORG and Judith LASKER, *When Pregnancy Fails* (Boston 1981) *passim*.

15 Among the Sande women of Sierra Leone, "The opposite of fat is not thin, but dry, connoting among other things, a dry and barren uterus." C. P. McCORMICK, "Health, Fertility and Birth in Moyamba District, Sierra Leone", *Ethnography of Fertility and Birth* ed. C. P. McCormick (London 1982), p. 122.

16 Although there is very much less literature on pregnancy and child-birth management in other cultures than there would have been if more anthropologists had been women, and women interested in female society, some context for these remarks can be got from H. H. PLOSS and M. and P. BARTELS, *Woman* trans. E. Dingwall (London 1935) Vol. 2, *passim*; K. E. MERSHON, *Seven plus Seven: Mysterious Life-Rituals in Bali* (New York 1971); Richard HESSNEY, "Birth Rites – a Comparative Study", *Eastern Archaeologist*, XXIV, 2, May–August, 1971; Jean Lois DAVITZ, "Childbirth Nigerian Style", *R. N. Magazine*, IV, March 1972; F. LANDA JOCANO, "Maternal and Child Care Among the Tagalogs in Bay, Laguna, Philippines", *Asian Studies*, VIII, 3 December 1970; Joel Simmons KAHN, "Some Aspects of Vietnamese Domestic and Communal Ritual", unpublished M.Phil. thesis, London School of Economics, 1969; Joyce S. MITCHELL, "Life and Birth in New Guinea" *Ms*, I, May, 1973, pp. 21–3; "Rites de la Naissance", *France-Asie* XII, March–May 1956; Helen GIDEON, "A Baby is born in the Punjab", *American Anthropology*, LXIV, pp. 1220–1234.

17 See for example, Kusum NAIR, *Blossoms in the Dust: the Human Factor in Indian Development* (New York 1962): "It was the practice in some Himalayan hill villages to exclude all outsiders from the village during the perinatal period" (p. 137).

18 Hamed AMMAR, *Growing up in an Egyptian Village: Silwa, Province of Aswan* (London 1954) p. 90.

19 JORDAN, *op. cit.*, pp. 26–7.

20 In Stephen A. RICHARDSON and Alan F. GUTTMACHER (eds), *Childbearing: its Social and Psychological Aspects* (Baltimore 1967) pp. 170–171.

21 Mounting criticism of tyrannical and irrational procedures in obstetrics and pressure for the adoption of more rational approaches, such as can be found in Sally INCH, *Birthrights* (London 1982) and Janet and Arthur BALASKAS, *Active Birth* (London 1983) have resulted in changes for the better in some British hospitals. Sheila KITZINGER, *Good Birth*

Guide (London 1983) lists British hospitals which encourage the adoption of alternative postures to the lithotomy position.

22 This case history was made into a film which was shown at the Kennedy International Symposium at the Kennedy Center in Washington on 6 October 1971.

23 Sheila KITZINGER and John A. DAVIS (eds) *The Place of Birth* (London 1978) p.v.

24 See for example, J. C. CALDWELL, "The Economic Rationality of High Fertility: An Investigation Illustrated with Nigerian Survey Data", *Population Studies*, Vol. 31, No. 1 (1976) pp. 5–6.

25 Brij Raj CHAUHAN, *A Rajasthan Village* (Delhi 1967) p. 213.

26 Amrit WILSON, *Finding a Voice: Asian Women in Britain* (London 1978) p. 22.

27 *Ibid.*, p. 25.

28 *Ibid.*, p. 22.

29 AMMAR, *op. cit.* p. 99.

30 Jessie BERNARD, *The Future of Motherhood* (New York 1975) "The Economics of Motherhood", pp. 286–302 *passim*.

31 Elizabeth Warnock FERNEA, *Behind the Veil*.

32 *Ibid.*

33 Ian YOUNG, *The Private Life of Islam* (London 1974) *passim*.

34 E. R. LEACH, *Pul Eliya, A Village in Ceylon* (Cambridge 1971) p. 27.

35 JORDAN, *op. cit.*, pp. 21, 22.

36 Oscar LEWIS, *Life in a Mexican Village: Tepoztlan Restudied* (Urbana 1963) p. 356.

37 Robert REDFIELD, *Tepoztlan – A Mexican Village* (Chicago 1930).

38 Personal observation, Karnataka, March 1981.

39 S. C. DUBE, *India's Changing Villages: Human Factors in Community Development* (Cornell UP, 1958) pp. 75ff.; *cf.* Ayinipalli AIYAPPAN, *Social Revolution in a Kerala Village: A Study in a Kerala Village: A Study in Culture Change* (New York 1965) p. 101.

40 See for example M. VERDERESE and L. M. TURNBULL, *The Traditional Birth Attendant in Maternal and Child Health and Family Planning. A Guide to her Training and Utilisation* (WHO 1975) and J. Y. PENG *et al.*, "Role of the Traditional Birth Attendants in Family Planning", *Proceedings of the International Seminar in Bangkok and Kuala Lumpur 19–26 July, 1974* (Ottawa, International Research and Development Centre, 1974) and S. N. OTOO, "The Traditional management of Puberty and Childbirth among the Ga people, Ghana", *Tropical and Geographical Medicine*, XXV, pp. 88–94 (1973); *cf.* Diana SCULLY, *Men Who Control Women's Health* (Boston 1980) pp. 136ff.

41 KITZINGER, *Women as Mothers*, *op. cit.* p. 109.

CHAPTER TWO

The Importance of Fertility

1 *Sunday Express*, 3 February 1980, p. 7.

2 Julian PITT-RIVERS, "Honour and Social Status", in *Honour and Shame: The Values of Mediterranean Society*, ed. J. G. PERESTIANY (London 1974) p. 45, *cf.* p. 55.

3 J. K. CAMPBELL, "Honour – the Devil", *ibid.* p. 146; *cf.* Pierre Bourdieu, "The Sentiment of Honour in Kabyle Society", *ibid.* p. 198.

4 BOURDIEU, *op. cit*, p. 220.

5 Nancy FRIDAY, *My Secret Garden: Women's Sexual Fantasies* (London 1975) and *Men in Love: Men's Sexual Fantasies: the Triumph of Love over Rage* (London 1980).

6 John B. VICKERY, *The Literary Impact of 'The Golden Bough'* (Princeton 1973) p. 71.

7 Lucy MAIR, *An Introduction to Social Anthropology* (Oxford 1965) p. 22.

8 Sir J. G. FRAZER, "The Myth of Adonis", *The Illustrated Golden Bough*, ed. Mary Douglas (London 1978) p. 123.

9 Karl JUNG, *On Psychic Energy* Par. 75 quoted by Frieda FORDHAM, *An Introduction to Jung's Psychology* (London 1979) pp. 20–21, *cf.* p. 85.

10 W. B. YEATS, "Byzantium", *The Collected Poems* (London 1961) p. 281.

11 J. M. C. CRUM, "Love is come again", *The Oxford Book of Carols* ed. Percy Dearmer, R. Vaughan Williams and Martin Shaw (London 1964) pp. 306–7.

12 Clive JAMES, "A Question of quality," *The Observer*, 3 February 1980.

13 Paul H. GEBHARD, "Situational Factors affecting Human Sexual Behaviour", *Sex and Behaviour*, ed. Frank A. Beach (New York 1965) p. 486; *cf.* Garrett HARDIN, *Nature and Man's Fate* (New York, 1959) p. 311: "There is no such thing as 'reproductive instinct', only an urge for certain sorts of sensual stimulation."

14 F. A. BEACH, *Hormones and Behaviour* (New York 1948) p. 238.

15 Desmond MORRIS, *The Human Zoo* (London 1969) p. 83.

16 *Ibid.*, p. 86.

17 Niko TINBERGEN, *The Study of Instinct* (Oxford 1974) p. 208.

18 Mary D. Salter AINSWORTH (ed.) *Animal Models in Human Psychobiology* (New York 1976) p. 42. R. A. HINDE, *Biological Bases of Human Social Behavior* (New York 1976) pp. 24–5.

19 Seymour S. KETY, "The Inner World of Man: Biochemical Substrates of Affect and Memory", *The Interface between Psychology and Anthropology*, ed. Iago GALDSTON (New York 1971) p. 130.

20 Alex COMFORT, *Nature and Human Nature* (London 1966) p. 28.

21 *Ibid.*, p. 3.

22 Niko TINBERGEN, "Ethology in a Changing World", *Growing Points in Ethology*, ed. P. P. G. Bateson and R. A. Hinde (Cambridge 1976) p. 510.

23 *Ibid.*, p. 520.

24 G. SERBAN, "The Significance of Ethology for Psychiatry" in AINSWORTH *op. cit.*, p. 280.

25 Ilse BLIGNAULT and L. B. BROWN, "Locus of Control and Contraceptive Knowledge, Attitudes and Practice", *British Journal of Medical Psychology*, Vol. 52 (1979) p. 343.

26 Alan SWEEZY, "United Kingdom Policy", *Population Perspective 1972*, ed. Harrison Brown and Alan Sweezy (San Francisco 1972) p. 23.

27 Melvin ZELNIK and John F. KANTNER, "Contraceptive Patterns and Pre-marital Pregnancy among women aged 15–19 in 1976", *Family Planning Perspectives*, Vol. X, No. 3, May–June 1978, p. 135.

28 BLIGNAULT and BROWN *op. cit.*, pp. 339–340.

29 Hans LEHFELDT, "Wilful Exposure to Unwanted Pregnancy", *American Journal of Obstetrics and Gynecology*, Vol. 78, September 1959, p. 662.

30 AINSWORTH, *op. cit.*, p. 86.

31 Edward O. WILSON, *Sociobiology: the New Synthesis* (Cambridge 1975) p. 3.

32 Pierre TEILHARD DE CHARDIN, *L'Avenir de l'homme* (Paris 1959) pp. 300–301, author's translation.

33 COMFORT, *op. cit.*, p. 32.

34 Gertrude E. DOLE, "The Marriages of Pacha: A Woman's Life among the Amahuaca", *Many Sisters: Women in Cross-Cultural Perspective*, ed. Carolyn J. Matthiasson (New York 1976) p. 17: "[Pacho] and her sister-in-law spent some of their free time dancing together and chanting fertility songs. They walked forward and backward hand-in-hand, chanting ditties that are thought to induce pregnancy. These two girls also made sun-dried clay dolls complete with incised lines to represent painted facial designs. Seeds were pressed into the clay to represent eyes and necklaces and the dolls' heads were topped with some of the girls' own hair. These dolls are also said to help pregnancy."

35 Margaret MEAD, *Male and Female* (London 1978) p. 216.

36 *Ibid.*, p. 220.

37 George GILDER, *Sexual Suicide* (New York 1973) pp. 6, 105–6; *cf.* Hugh CARTER and Paul C. GLICK, *Marriage and Divorce, a Social and Economic Study* (Cambridge, Mass., 1970) p. 410; C. LEVI-STRAUSS, *Elementary Structures of Kinship* (London 1970) p. 39; Robin FOX, "Sexual Selection and Human Kinship Systems", in *Sexual Selection and the Descent of Man 1871–1971* (Chicago 1972) p. 299.

38 Raymond C. KELLY, "Witchcraft and Social Relations", *Man and Woman in the New Guinea Highlands*, ed. Paula Brown and Georgeda Buchbinder (Washington 1976) p. 45, *cf.* Alan P. MERRIAM, "Aspects of Sexual Behaviour among the Bala (Basongye)" *Human Sexual Behaviour: Variations in the Ethnographic Spectrum*, ed. Donald Marshall and Robert C. Suggs (New York 1970) p. 85: "When asked to give reasons for intercourse, Bala men, without exception stress having children. This is echoed in their persistent statements that having children is the best thing in life, and that the worst thing in life is to have children die."

39 MEAD, *op. cit.*, p. 225.

CHAPTER THREE

The Curse of Sterility

1 From Morocco: Elizabeth Warnock FERNEA and Basima Qattan BEZIRGAN, *Middle Eastern Muslim Women Speak* (Austin and London 1977).

2 Genesis, 30.1.

3 Among the Aowin people of South-West Ghana, childlessness is a serious social and spiritual disability: "The sterile man or woman is never fully accepted as a member of society. Barren women are suspected of being witches. Men who have no children are called derisive names and at the funeral of a childless person, the corpse is abused as the mourners instruct the spirit of the dead person never to return again." V. EBIN, "Interpretations of Infertility: the Aowin of Western Ghana," *Ethnography of Fertility and Birth*, ed. C. P. McCormick (London 1982) p. 144. *Cf.*, on the misery of childless Yoruba women: T. A. LAMBO, "Neuropsychiatric observations in the western region of Nigeria", *British Medical Journal*, ii, 1388–1394 and J. B. LAWSON and D. B. STEWART, *Obstetrics and Gynaecology in the Tropics and Developing Countries* (London 1967).

4 Vincent CRAPANZANO, *The Hamadsha: a Study in Ethnopsychiatry* (Berkeley 1977) p. 198.

5 Margaret MEAD, *Male and Female*, *op. cit.*, p. 217.

6 AMMAR, *op. cit.*, p. 94. *Cf.* the case of childless women in Ashanti: "Ashanti women become anxious at the merest suspicion that their fertility is impaired ... One of the main reasons that men and women flock in

such numbers to so-called 'fetish-cults' which abound in Ashanti is because these cults offer magical protection against sterility and sexual disorders." Meyer FORTES, "A Demographic Field Study in Ashanti", *Culture and Human Fertility*, ed. Frank Lorimer (UNESCO 1954) p. 226.

7 Elizabeth Warnock FERNEA, *Behind the Veil.*

8 *Ibid.*

9 Personal observation, February–March 1981.

10 Indumati PARIKH, *An Experiment in Community Involvement in Family Planning in a Metropolitan Slum* (Bombay 1978) pp. 5–6.

11 S. P. REYNA, "Age differential, marital instability and venereal disease: factors affecting fertility among the north-west Barma (Chad)", *Population and Social Organisation*, ed. Moni Nag (Yale 1962).

12 The bibliography of depopulation is vast: the following titles merely give an indication of the starting point: A. ROMANIUK, *La Fécondité des femmes congolaises* (Paris/La Haye 1967) p. 63; A. T. RING and R. A. SCRAGG, "A Demographic and Social Study of fertility in rural New Guinea", *Journal of Biosocial Science*, Vol. 5, No. 89 (1972); H. MOUTSINGA, "La stérilité féminine au Gabon en consultation gynécologique journalière", *Médicine dans l'Afrique Noire*, Vol. 20, No. 63 (1973); Anne RETEL-LAURENTIN, *Infécondité et maladies chez les Nzakara, République Centrafricaine* (Paris 1974); F. MERLE and P. PUECH LESTRADE, "Gonococcie et stérilité au Cameroun", *Médicine Tropicale*, Vol. 20, p. 735 (1960); E. S. GRECG *et al.* "Epidemiological Aspects of acute pelvic inflammatory disease in Uganda", *Tropical Doctor*, Vol. 3, 123 (1970); B. K. ADADEVOH (ed.) *Subfertility and infertility in Africa* (Ibadan 1974); Mark A. BELSEY, "The epidemiology of infertility: a review with particular reference to sub-Saharan Africa", *Bulletin of the World Health Organisation*, Vol. 54, 1975, pp. 319–340; Hilde THURNWALD, "Women's Status in Buin Society", *Oceania* 5 (2) 1934, p. 161; Ray PINNEY, *Vanishing Tribes* (London 1968) *passim*; William A. LESSA, "The depopulation of Ulithi", *Human Biology* 27, pp. 161–183; Edward E. HUNT, N. R. KIDDER, D. M. SCHNEIDER and W. D. STEVENS, *The Micronesians of Yap and their Depopulation* (New York 1949).

13 S. KAUL and Anita KALA, "Fertility and family planning in a remote hill area in Himachal Pradesh", *Journal of Family Welfare*, Vol. 23 (1977) No. 3.

14 Andrew COLLVER, "The family cycle in India and the United States", *American Sociological Review*, Vol. 28 (1963), pp. 89–96.

15 Ranajit DUTTA, "Relation of blood groups with Fertility and Infertility: a study in rural India", *International Journal of Fertility*, Vol. 22 (1977), pp. 243–246.

16 S. J. BEHRMAN and Robert W. KISTNER, "A rational approach to the evaluation of infertility", *Progress in Infertility* ed. S. J. Behrman and

R. W. Kistner (Boston 1975) p. 1. At Florida State University, Dr Frank Dougherty found in 1980 that students' median sperm counts were 33% down on the levels shown in a similar study in 1929; 23% of otherwise healthy males were sterile; 27% of the decline was attributable to chlorinated compounds found in the sperm cells, deriving presumably from chlorinated foods and water. (*Not Man Apart*, Friends of the Earth 1980).

17 G. BETTENDORF, *Infertility: Diagnosis and Treatment of Functional Infertility* (Berlin 1978), p. ix.

18 Melvin L. TAYMOR, *Infertility* (New York 1978) p. 29.

19 Ray PINNEY, *Vanishing Tribes* (London 1968) p. 124.

20 Rose E. FRISCH, "Population, Food Intake and Fertility", *Science* No. 199, 6.1.1978, pp. 22ff; *cf.* A. KEYS, J. BROZEK, A. HENSCHEL, O. MICKELSEN and H. L. TAYLOR, *The Biology of Human Starvation* (Minneapolis 1950) Ch. 35, *passim*.

21 Melvin M. TAYMOR and Ellen BRESNICK, "Emotional Stress and Infertility", *Infertility*, Vol. 2, No. 1 (1979), pp. 34–7.

22 TAYMOR, *op. cit* (1978) p. 13.

23 Carl J. PAVERSTEIN and Carlton A. EDDY, "The role of the oviduct in reproduction: our knowledge and our ignorance", *Journal of Reproduction and Fertility*, 55, pp. 223–229.

24 "The sexually transmitted diseases: a challenge to health education", *International Journal of Health Education*, Supplement to Vol. 18, Issue 3, July–September 1975 *passim*.

25 Personal communication from Dr R. D. Catterall, James Pringle House, Middlesex Hospital London; *cf.* Mike MULLER, *The Health of Nations: A North–South Investigation* (London 1983) pp. 98–9.

26 F. Gary CUNNINGHAM and Abe MICKAL, "Pelvic Infections", *Current Obstetric Diagnosis and Treatment* ed. R. C. BENSON (Los Altos 1982) pp. 315–60; Edmund R. NOVAK and J. Donald WOODRUFF, *Gynecologic and Obstetric Pathology with Clinical and Endocrine Relations* (London and Philadelphia 1967) pp. 245–251.

27 J. ORIEL, A. L. JOHNSON, D. BARLOW *et al.* "Infection of the uterine cervix with *Chlamydia trachomatis*", *Journal of Infectious Diseases* Vol. 137, No. 4, (1978) pp. 443–451; J. SCHACHTER, "Chlamydial Infections", *New England Journal of Medicine*, Vol. 29, No. 8 (1978) pp. 428–435; S. PAAVONEN, P. SAIKKU, E. VESTERINEN and K. AHO, "*Chlamydia trachomatis* in acute salpingitis", *British Journal of Venereal Diseases*, Vol. 55, No. 3 (June 1979) pp. 203–6; J. SCHACHTER, G. CAUSSE and M. L. TARIZZO, "Chlamydiae as agents of sexually transmitted diseases", *Bulletin of the World Health Organisation*, Vol. 54 (1976) pp. 245–251.

28 D. A. ESCHENBACH, "Polymicrobial etiology of acute pelvic inflam-

matory disease", *New England Journal of Medicine*, Vol. 293, No. 4 (July 1975) pp. 166–71.

29 W. B. HAGER and B. MAJUMDAR, "Pelvic actinomycosis in women using intrauterine contraceptive devices", *American Journal of Obstetrics and Gynecology*, Vol. 133 (1979) No. 8, p. 60.

30 H. Ian HOGBIN, *Social Change: Josiah Mason Lectures delivered at the University of Birmingham* (London 1958) p. 18.

31 Lidio CIPRIANI, *The Andaman Islanders* (London 1966) pp. 62–5.

32 A. P. ELKIN, *Social Anthropology in Melanesia: A Review of Research* (London 1953) pp. 159–160.

33 *Ibid.*, p. 77.

34 Lewis COTLOW, *The Twilight of the Primitive* (London 1973) pp. 16–17.

35 *Ibid.*, pp. 65–66, *cf.* Edwin BROOKS, René FUERST, John HEMMINGS and Francis HUXLEY, *Tribes of the Amazon Basin in Brazil, 1972* (London 1972) p. 37.

36 *Ibid.*, p. 17, *cf.* BROOKS *et al.*, *op. cit.* pp. 24–5.

37 *Ibid.*, p. 14.

38 *Ibid.*, p. 50.

39 *Ibid.*, p. 57.

40 Claude LEVI-STRAUSS, *World on the Wane* trans. John Russell (London 1961) p. 284 quoting K. OBERG, *Indian Tribes of the Northern Mato Grosso, Brazil* (Washington 1953) pp. 84–5; *cf.* p. 286.

41 *Cf.* COTLOW, *op. cit.*, pp. 160–161.

42 Based upon Mark A. BELSEY, "The epidemiology of infertility: a review with particular reference to sub-Saharan Africa", *Bulletin of the World Health Organisation*, Vol. 54 (1975) pp. 319–340, Table i, p. 321.

43 O. A. LADIPO and A. O. OSOBA, "T. mycoplasma and reproductive failure", *Infertility*, Vol. 2, No. 2 (1979) p. 135.

44 *Cf.* W. O. CHUKUDUBELU, "The male factor in infertility – the Nigerian experience", *International Journal of Fertility*, Vol. 23 (1978) Pt. 3, pp. 238–9.

45 Wilson I. B. ONUIGBO, "Tubal pregnancy in Nigerian Igbos", *International Journal of Fertility*, Vol. 21 (1976) pp. 186ff.

46 Samar KHALAF, *Prostitution in a Changing Society: A Sociological Survey of Prostitution in Beirut* (Beirut 1965) quoting from George C. HOMANS, *The Human Group* (New York 1950) p. 5.

47 *Ibid.*, p. 21.

48 I. SCHAPERA, *Married Life in an African Tribe* (London 1940) p. 197.

49 *Ibid.*, p. 229.

50 *Ibid.*, p. 230.

51 *Cf.* A. T. BRYANT, "Zulu medicine and medicine men", *Annals of the Natal Museum*, ed. E. Warren (London 1916) p. 15: "Leprosy and the

venereal diseases were absolutely unknown," and pp. 50–51; and Colin
TURNBULL, *The Lonely African* (London 1963) pp. 21, 132.

52 R. FARLEY, "Recent changes in Negro fertility", *Demography*,
Vol. 3, pp. 188–203; J. A. MCFALLS Jr., "Impact of venereal disease
on the fertility of the U S black populations 1880–1950", *Social Biology*,
Vol. 2 (1973) p. 19; Verrier ELWIN, *The Tribal World of Verrier Elwin*
(Oxford 1964) pp. 108–9.

53 Amir ANSARI, "Diagnostic procedures for assessment of tubal
patency," *Fertility and Sterility*, Vol. 31, No. 5, May 1979.

54 Jean COHEN, "Results of repeat surgery in tubal sterility", *Infertility*,
Vol. 2, No. 1 (1979) p. 13.

55 Gina Bari KOLATA, "In Vitro Fertilization: Is it Safe and Repeatable?"
Science, Vol. 201 (25 May, 1978) pp. 698–9.

56 Karin G. B. EDSTRÖM, "The relative risks of sterilisation alone and in
combination with abortion", *Bulletin of the World Health Organisation*,
Vol. 52 (1975) pp. 141–148.

57 Victor GOMEL, "Profile of women requesting reversal of sterilisation",
Fertility and Sterility, Vol. 30, No. 1, July 1978, pp. 39–41.

58 Rochelle D. SHAIN, "Acceptability of reversible versus permanent
tubal sterilisation: an analysis of preliminary data", *Fertility and Sterility*,
Vol. 31, No. 1, January 1979, pp. 13–17.

59 Bernard CANTOR and Frank C. RIGGALL, "The choice of sterilising
procedure according to its potential reversibility with microsurgery",
Fertility and Sterility, Vol. 31, No. 1, January 1979, pp. 9–12.

60 Richard STOCK, "Evaluation of sequelae of tubal ligation", *Fertility
and Sterility*, Vol. 29, No. 2, February 1978, pp. 169–174.

61 J. R. NEIL *et al.* "Late Complications of sterilisation by laparoscopy
and tubal ligation", *The Lancet*, 11 October 1975, p. 699; A. D. NOBLE,
"Sterilisation, laparoscopy or laparotomy", *British Medical Journal*, 25
October 1975, p. 227; Geoffrey CHAMBERLAIN and John FFOULKES,
"Long-term effects of laparoscopic sterilisation on menstruation",
Southern Medical Journal, November 1976, p. 1474.

62 Sir Maurice KENDALL, "The World Fertility Survey: Current Status
and Findings", *Population Reports* Series M, No. 3, July 1979, Table 17.

63 Stanwood S. SCHMIDT, "Spermatic granuloma: an often painful
lesion", *Fertility and Sterility*, Vol. 31, No. 2, February 1979, pp. 178–181.

64 Nancy J. ALEXANDER and Deborah J. ANDERSON, "Vasectomy:
consequences of auto-immunity to sperm antigens", *Fertility and
Sterility*, Vol. 32, No. 2, September 1979, pp. 253, 257.

65 A fuller discussion of vasectomy, its advantages and drawbacks can
be found in David and Helen WOLFERS, *Vasectomy and Vasectomania*
(London 1974) *passim*.

66 Not only that, but as Dorothy L. NORTMAN points out, irreversible
sterilisation has little effect on the birthrate, see *Sterilisation and the Birthrate* (New York 1980).

CHAPTER FOUR

Chastity Is a Form of Birth Control

1 C. G. HARTMANN, "On the relative sterility of the adolescent organism", *Science*, Vol. 74 (1931) pp. 226–7; Bronislaw MALINOWSKI, *The Sexual Life of Savages* (London 1932) pp. 166ff; C. G. SELIGMAN, *The Melanesians of British New Guinea* (Cambridge 1910) p. 500; H. I. HOGBIN, "The Native Culture of Wogeo", *Oceania*, Vol. 5 (1935) pp. 320ff; R. F. BARTON, *Philippine Pagans* (London 1938) p. 11.

2 For a résumé of the Catholic teaching on virginity, see J. M. PERRIN, *Virginity* (London 1956) *passim*.

3 J. C. RUSSELL, "The clerical population of mediaeval England", *Traditio*, Vol. 2 (1944) pp. 177–212; *cf.* Eileen POWER, *Mediaeval English Nunneries, c. 1275–1535* (Cambridge 1922).

4 Dr BA HAN, "The Burmese Complex: its roots", *Journal of the Burma Research Society*, Vol. 46, No. 1, June 1963, p. 7.

5 U SEIN TU, "The psychodynamics of Burmese personality", *Journal of the Burma Research Society*, Vol. 47 Part II, December 1964, pp. 263ff.

6 J. STUART, "Why is Burma sparsely peopled?" *Journal of the Burma Research Society*, Vol. 4, Part I, 1914, pp. 1–6.

7 MAUNG BA AUNG, "Why Burma is sparsely populated: a suggestion", *Journal of the Burma Research Society*, Vol. 4, 1914, pp. 224–5.

8 J. HAJNAL, "European marriage patterns in perspective", in *Population in History* (London 1965) ed. D. V. Glass and D. E. C. Eversley.

9 Peter LASLETT, *The World We have Lost* (London 1965) pp. 128–130, 140–141.

10 *Ibid.*, pp. 2–3.

11 Karl G. HEIDER, "Dani sexuality: a low-energy system", *Man*, New Series, Vol. 2, No. 2, p. 188.

12 COTLOW, *op. cit.*, p. 61.

13 Georgeda BUCHBINDER and Roy A. RAPAPORT, "Fertility and death among the Maring", *Man and Woman in the New Guinea Highlands* ed. Paula Brown and Georgeda Buchbinder (Washington 1976) p. 20.

14 Richard SCAGLION, "Seasonal births in an eastern Abelam village", *Human Biology*, Vol. 50 (1978), No. 3, p. 316.

15. Shirley LINDENBAUM, "A wife is the hand of man", Brown and Buchbinder, *op. cit.*, p. 58; *cf.* Margaret MEAD, "The Arapesh," *Cooperation and Competition among Primitive Peoples*, ed. Margaret Mead (London 1937) p. 40 and Hortense POWDERMAKER, *Life in Lesu: the Study of a Melanesian Society in New Ireland* (London 1933) p. 78.

16 J. C. CALDWELL and Pat CALDWELL, "The role of marital sexual abstinence in determining fertility: a study of the Yoruba in Nigeria", *Population Studies*, Vol. 31, No. 2, pp. 195–196 *et passim*.

17 Walter H. SANGREE, "The Bantu Tiriki of western Kenya (Kan-mondo)", *Peoples of Africa*, ed. J. G. Gibbs, Jr. (New York 1965) p. 60.

18 NAG, *op. cit.*, p. 37.

19 CALDWELL and CALDWELL, *op. cit.*, p. 203; *cf.* P. C. LLOYD, "Sexual abstinence among the Yoruba", in GIBBS, *op. cit.*, pp. 566ff.

20 No systematic analysis of the effect of female circumcision on fertility has so far been undertaken: on the one hand it may lower the frequency of marital relations, on the other it may increase the desirability of pregnancy as a way of avoiding them. Sudanese women have told me that even pharaonic circumcision did not affect sexual pleasure (as far as anyone could tell) but it did cause problems in childbirth, leading to higher rates of maternal and infant mortality. Serious damage caused by childbirth may affect a wife's sexual acceptability to her husband, but more impor-tant, in the Sudanese case, is the restitching of the perineum until it is tighter than before.

21 Ian WHITAKER, "The patrilineal kin-group in northern Albania", *Honour and Shame: the Values of Mediterranean Society*, ed. J. G. Peristiany (London and Chicago 1966) p. 199. *Cf.* Henry ORENSTEIN on the formality of the marriage relationship, "symbolised by a taboo on uttering the name of one's spouse. Husband and wife never addressed each other by name ..." (*Gaon: Conflict and Cohesion in an Indian Village*, Princeton 1965, p. 53.)

22 J. D. CAMPBELL, "Honour – the devil", in PERISTIANY, *op. cit.*, p. 156.

23 W. S. MANN, *The Operas of Mozart* (London 1977) p. 451.

24 D. B. McGILVRAY, "Sexual Power and Fertility in Sri Lanka: Batti-coloa Tamils and Moors", *Ethnography of Fertility and Birth*, ed. Carol P. McCormack (London 1982) p. 31.

25 Susan B. WADLEY (ed.), *The Powers of Tamil Women* (Syracuse 1980) p. xii.

26 Amnon ORENT, "Cultural factors inhibiting population growth among the Kafa of south-western Ethiopia", NAG, *op. cit.*, p. 78.

27 *The Collected Works of Mahatma Gandhi* (Ahmedabad 1975) Vol. L, p. 289.

28 *Ibid.*, Vol. LXII, p. 233.

29 *Ibid.*, Vol. LXI, p. 310 (4.8.1935).

30 *Ibid.*, Vol. LXII, p. 262.

31 *Ibid.*, Vol. LXII, p. 310.

32 *Ibid.*, Vol. LXI, p. 417 (*Harijan*, 14 September 1935).

33 Mary DOUGLAS, *Natural Symbols: Explorations in Cosmology* (London 1978) p. 93.

34 Lois PAUL, "Work and sex in a Guatemalan village", *Women, Culture and Society*, ed. Michelle Zimbalist ROSALDO and Louise LAMPHERE (Stanford 1975) p. 297.

35 DOUGLAS, *op. cit.*, p. 113.

36 R. V. SHORT, "The evolution of human reproduction", *Proceedings of the Royal Society of London*, B, Vol. 195 (1976) p. 17.

37 Carol P. McCORMICK, "Adaptation in human fertility and birth", *Ethnography of Fertility and Birth*, ed. C. P. McCormick (London, 1982) p. 9.

38 Melvin KONNER and Carol WORTHMAN, "Nursing frequency, gonadal function and birth spacing among !Kung hunter–gatherers", *Science*, Vol. 207, 15 February 1980, pp. 788–791.

39 John MARSHALL, *Planning For a Family* (London 1965) *passim; cf.* Evelyn BILLINGS and Ann WESTMORE, *The Billings Method: Controlling Fertility Without Drugs or Devices* (Melbourne 1980).

CHAPTER FIVE

Polymorphous Perversity

1 Richard CARLISLE, *Every Woman's Book or What is Love?* (London 1838); Robert Dale OWEN, *Moral Physiology or A Brief and Plain Treatise on the Population Question* (New York 1831); Charles KNOWLTON, *Fruits of Philosophy; or, the Private Companion of Young Married People* (London 1841). Knowlton goes so far as to say, "It is said by those who speak from experience that the act of withdrawal has an effect upon the health similar to temperance in eating" (p. 33).

2 George DRYSDALE, *Physical, Sexual and Natural Religion* (London 1855) p. 349.

3 Eliza Bisbee DUFFY, *What Women Should Know* (Philadelphia 1873) pp. 134–135.

4 Alice STOCKHAM, *Karezza* (Chicago 1896) pp. vi, 24 *et passim*, and *Tokology: A Book of Maternity* (Toronto 1916) p. 325.

5 Edward M. BRECHER, *The Sex Researchers* (London 1970) p. 66.

6 Clive WOOD and Beryl SUITTERS, *The Fight for Acceptance: A History of Contraception* (Aylesbury 1970) p. 27.

7 C. H. R. ROUTH, *The Moral and Physical Evils likely to follow if Practices intended to act as Checks to Population be not strongly discouraged* (London 1879) pp. 11–12.

8 *Proceedings of the Fifth International Neo-Malthusian Conference* (London 1922) p. 247 *cf.* pp. 271, 284–85.

9 C. V. FORD, "Psychological factors influencing the choice of contra-

ceptive method", *Aspects of Human Sexuality*, Vol. 12, No. 1 (1978) p. 91.

10 Helen Singer KAPLAN, *The New Sex Therapy: Active Treatment of Sexual Dysfunctions* (London 1978) Ch. 5, *passim.*

11 Ruth and Edward BRECHER, "The Work of Masters and Johnson", *An Analysis of Human Sexual Response*, ed. R. and E. BRECHER (London 1968) p. 100.

12 John PEEL and Malcolm POTTS, *Textbook of Contraceptive Practice* (Cambridge 1970) pp. 50–51.

13 *Report of the Royal Commission on Population* (London 1949); *cf.* R. HILL, J. M. STYCOS and K. W. BACK, *The Family and Population Control: A Puerto Rican Experiment in Social Change* (New Haven 1959) pp. 163–187; M. POTTS, "Legal Abortion in Eastern Europe", *Eugenics Review*, Vol. 59 (1967) p. 232.

14 M. Shirley EMERSON, "The Personal Factor in Fertility Control", *Journal of Biosocial Science*, Vol. 1, p. 309.

15 Lella Secor FLORENCE, *Progress Report of Birth Control* (London 1956) pp. 83–4, 110 *et passim.*

16 I am indebted for notice of these letters to the late Ruth Hall, who worked through the Stopes correspondence in the British Museum in the course of preparing her *Dear Dr Stopes: Sex in the 1920's* (London 1978).

17 Enid CHARLES, *The Practice of Birth Control* (London 1934) pp. 26, 39, 52.

18 *Family Planning Handbook for Doctors*, ed. Ronald F. KLEINMAN for the IPPF Central Medical Committee (London 1974) pp. 18–19.

19 *Ibid.*, p. 19.

20 B. D. MISRA, "Correlates of Males' Attitudes to Family Planning," *Sociological Contributions to Family Planning Research* ed. D. J. Bogue (Chicago 1967); John KANTNER, "The Place of Conventional methods in Family Planning Programs"; *Family Planning and Population Programs* ed. B. Berelson (Chicago 1966) pp. 403–409. Sheldon W. SEGAL and Christopher TIETZE, "Contraceptive Technology: Current and Prospective Methods", *Reports on Population and Family Planning*, The Population Council (New York 1971).

21 KAPLAN, *op. cit.*, p. 239.

22 Charles TILLY (ed.), *Historical Studies of Changing Fertility* (Princeton 1978) Introduction, pp. 17, 19, 22, 38.

23 Gosta CARLSSON, "The decline of fertility: innovation or adjustment process?" *Population Studies*, Vol. 20 (1967) pp. 149–174 quotes *Befolkningscommissionen, Betänkande i sexualfragen* (Stockholm 1936).

24 Raymond FIRTH, *We the Tikopia* (London 1936) pp. 490–91.

25 Hilda KUPER, "The Swazi of Swaziland", in *Peoples of Africa* ed. J. L. GIBBS, Jr. (New York 1965) p. 491; *cf.* E. TORDAY, "The Principles of Bantu Marriage," *Africa*, Vol. 2, p. 256 and L. S. B. LEAKEY, "Notes

on Kenya Colony," *Journal of the Royal Anthropological Institute*, Vol. 60 (1944).

26 J. CLYDE MITCHELL, "An estimate of fertility in some Yao hamlets in Luwanda district of Southern Nyasaland", *Africa*, Vol. 19, No. 4 (1949) pp. 293–308.

27 John B. WYON and John E. GORDON, *The Khanna Study* (Harvard 1971) p. 141.

28 Shirley GREEN, *The Curious History of Contraception* (London 1971) pp. 126–7, quoting an unidentified 6th-century source.

29 *Chinese Approaches to Family Planning* trans. Robert Dunn, ed. and int. Leo A. ORLEANS (New York and London 1979) pp. 171–2.

30 Peter FRYER, *The Birth-Controllers* (London 1967) pp. 21, 303.

31 Raymond C. KELLY, "Witchcraft and social relations", *Man and Woman in the New Guinea Highlands* (Washington 1976) pp. 40–41.

32 *Ibid.*, p. 43.

33 *Ibid.*, p. 45.

34 Marie Carmichael STOPES, *Married Love: A New Contribution to the Solution of Sex Difficulties* (London 1918) p. 54.

35 Ruth HALL (ed.) *Dear Dr Stopes: Sex in the 1920's* (London 1978) p. 69.

36 Kate MILLETT, *Flying* (New York 1975) pp. 597–8.

37 Havelock ELLIS, "Sexual Inversion", *Studies in the Psychology of Sex*, Vol. II (New York 1936) p. 23.

38 British Society for the Study of Sexual Psychology, *The Social Problem of Sexual Inversion* (London 1915) p. 11.

39 Clifford ALLEN, "Perversions Sexual", *Encyclopedia of Sex*, ed. A. Ellis and A. Abarbanel (London 1961).

40 *Dubbii Amorosi, altri Dubbii. e Sonetti Lussuriosi di Pietro Aretino* (Venice n.d.) pp. 57, 68.

41 *La Philosophie dans le Boudoir* (1975) Vol. 1, p. 98.

CHAPTER SIX

The Short History of Contraception

1 Shirley GREEN, *op. cit.*, p. 97.

2 Carl DJERASSI, *The Politics of Contraception: Birth Control in the Year 2001* (Stanford 1979) p. 17. P. D. HARVEY, "Condoms – a new look", *Family Planning Perspectives*, Vol. 4, No. 4 (1972) pp. 28–39.

3 See the Foreword by Peter HUNTINGFORD to the Brook Advisory Centres Pamphlet, *The Case for the Condom* (London 1979).

4 Almost as venerable as condoms are the vaginal pessaries, creams, gels and so forth; not one is of proven efficacy and not one enhances sexual intercourse, but literally thousands of different kinds of chemical compounds have been used as spermicides. The British FPA recommends a few for use with barrier methods; none for use by itself. A new foaming suppository, Neosampoon, has been used in acceptability trials in Sri Lanka and the Dominican Republic.

5 DJERASSI, *op. cit.*, p. 19.

6 Barbara SEAMAN, *Women and The Crisis in Sex Hormones* (New York 1977) pp. 190–191.

7 Shirley GREEN, *op. cit.*, illustration facing page 73.

8 The letters can be seen in the Stopes collection at the British Library in London.

9 Ruth HALL, *Marie Stopes: A Biography* (London 1977) p. 149.

10 *Ibid.*, pp. 176–7.

11 *Ibid.*, p. 199. Judging from the drawings in publicity material collected by Stopes and now in the British Library, there was no significant difference between the Pro-Race Cap and half a dozen other models; the variety of occlusive devices available in 1920 when Stopes began to interest herself in the subject was enormous.

12 *Ibid.*, p. 229.

13 Muriel Box (ed.) *The Trial of Marie Stopes* (London 1967) pp. 64–5, 147–8, 165–9, etc.

14 HALL, *op. cit.* p. 268.

15 C. TIETZE, H. LEHFELDT and H. LIEBMANN, "The effectiveness of the cervical cap as a contraceptive method", *American Journal of Obstetrics and Gynecology*, Vol. 66 (1955) pp. 904–908; Judith WHARTMAN, "The cervical cap", *Population Reports* Series H, No. 4, January, 1976.

16 DJERASSI, *op. cit.*, "Author's Postscript: The Chemical History of the Pill", pp. 227–256 *passim*.

17 *Ibid.*, p. 249.

18 *Ibid.*, p. 248.

19 Paul VAUGHAN, *The Pill on Trial* (London 1970) p. 31.

20 *Ibid.*, p. 39.

21 *Ibid.*, pp. 33–34.

22 J. HAMMERSTEIN *et al.*, "Clinical pharmacology of contraceptive steroids", *Contraception*, Vol. 20, No. 3, September 1979, p. 193.

23 *Ibid.*, p. 114.

24 DJERASSI, *op. cit.*, Ch. 4, "The fear of cancer," pp. 51–66, *passim*.

25 D. G. JONGMANS and H. J. M. CLAESSEN, *The Neglected Factor: Family Planning and Perception at the Base* (Assen 1974) p. 46.

26 M. BIBBO, M. AL-NAQEEB, I. BACCARINI, W. GILL, M. NEWTON,

K. M. Sleeper, M. Sonek and G. L. Wied, "Follow-up study of male and female offspring of DES treated mothers. A preliminary report", *Journal of Reproductive Medicine*, Vol. 15, No. 29, 1975, and Alvin Siegler, Chun fu Wang and Jan Friberg, "Fertility of the Diethyl-stilboestrol-exposed offspring", *Fertility and Sterility*, Vol. 31, No. 6, June 1979, p. 604.

27 Carol A. Lorber, Suzanne B. Cassidy and Eric Engel, "Is there an embryo-fetal exogenous sex steroid exposure syndrome (EFESSES)?" *Fertility and Sterility*, Vol. 31, No. 1, January 1979, pp. 23–4.

28 *The Sunday Times*, 23 April 1978, p. 6, Oliver Gillie, "Drug company ignored deformity risk for 10 years".

29 Susan Harlap and A. Michael Davies, *The Pill and Births: the Jerusalem Study* (mimeo, Jerusalem 1978) pp. 2, 118–119.

30 P. Petersen, "Seelische Veränderungen bei hormonaler Kontraception der Frau", *Deutsche Arzteblätter*, Vol. 75, No. 18 (1978) pp. 1075–1085, sees the disruption of mood control caused by steroids as disqualifying the oral contraceptive from long-term use. *Cf.* J. Santamaria Martinez, "Aspectos psicologicos de la anti-concepcion", *Ginecología y Obstetrica Mexicana*, Vol. 42, No. 250 (1977) pp. 97–108; E. Ebranti, "Psicopatologia e contracettivi orali", *Sessuologia*, Vol. 14, No. 2 (1973) p. 16; D. Grounds *et al.*, "The contraceptive pill side-effects and personality", *British Journal of Psychiatry*, Vol. 116 (1970) p. 169; A. A. Haspels, "Oral contraceptives and sexuality", *International Congress of Medical Sexology*, Paris (1974); P. W. Adams, W. Wynn and B. P. Rose, *The Lancet*, Vol. 1 (1973) pp. 897–904.

31 Seaman, *op. cit.*, pp. 107–133.

32 Djerassi, *op. cit.*, p. 68.

33 Jean Cohen, "The effects of oral contraceptives on sexual behaviour", *Progress in Sexology. Selected Papers from the Proceedings of the 1976 International Congress of Sexology*, ed. Robert Gemme and Connie Christine Wheeler (New York and London 1977) p. 377.

34 K. S. Moghissi, "The effect of steroidal contraceptives on the reproductive system", *Human Reproduction: Conception and Contraception*, ed. E. S. E. Hafez and T. N. Evans (New York 1979) pp. 530–2; M. Toppozada *et al.* "The protective incidence of progestogen only contraception against vaginal moniliasis", *Contraception*, Vol. 20, No. 2, August 1979, "The use of oral contraceptives of the combined type has been repeatedly shown to increase the incidence of vaginal moniliasis", and J. L. Jackson and W. T. Spain, "Comparative study of combined and sequential anti-ovulatory therapy on vaginal moniliasis", *American Journal of Obstetrics and Gynecology*, Vol. 101 (1968) p. 1134; D. A. Evans *et al.*, "Clearance of Bacteriuria on discontinuing Oral Contraceptives", *British Medical Journal*, Vol. 1, 19 January 1980, p. 152.

35 Cohen, *op. cit.*, p. 377.

36 *Ibid.*, p. 382.

37 Anne DIDDLE *et al.*, "Oral contraception and vulvo-vaginal candidiasis", *Obstetrics and Gynaecology*, Vol. 34 (1969) p. 373.

38 A. L. HILTON *et al.*, "Chlamydia A in the female genital tract", *British Journal of Venereal Disease*, Vol. 50 (1974) pp. 1–10.

39 Stephen MINKIN, "Bangladesh: the Pop Con Game", *Health Right*, Vol. 5 (1979) No. 1, pp. 3–4, 14–15.

40 The advertisement is reproduced in Dianna MELROSE, *Bitter Pills: Medicines and the Third World Poor* (London 1982) pp. 78–9.

41 Saroja REMASWAMY and Tony SMITH, *Practical Contraception* (London 1976), pp. 52–3.

42 The best concise account of the controversy over DMPA is the Special Report by Rachel Beason GOLD and Peters D. WILLSON, "Depo-Provera: New Developments in a Decade-old Controversy", *Family Planning Perspectives*, Vol. 13, No. 1., January/February 1981, pp. 35–39.

43 An article in *Science for the People: a Socialist View of Science, Technology and Medicine*, "Depo-Provera: A clear-cut case?" by Sarah BAREFOOT, states that "it is thought that the majority of 10,000 women involved in monitored trials on DP were Polynesian or Maori women who had not been provided with an interpreter", (p. 5). I am bound to say that my respondents were all middle-class white women who were quite unaware of being involved in a test. Islanders and Maoris would not have been excluded from the testing although it is *a priori* unlikely, given relative numbers, that they would have been the majority. Most of them would have spoken English; I have yet to meet a non-English-speaking Maori.

44 Letter from Dr Colin McCord to Bernard Kervin, 30 April 1980. The Thai case history is compiled from a series of documents copied by William Shawcross from the files at the UN High Commission for Refugees office at Kamput, which he was kind enough to make available to me.

45 Letter from Dr Colin McCord to Mr M. A. Sattar, Secretary Population Control and Family Planning, Ministry of Health and Population Control, Dacca, 31 August 1979, Ref. BGD/79/PO4.

46 Gonoshastaya Kendra, *Progress Report, No. 7*, August 1980, p. 5.

47 Memorandum to UNHCR Field Officers and Medical Co-ordinators at Kamput and Meirut Holding Centres from Dr A. G. Rangaraj, Senior Health Co-ordinator, UNHCR Regional Office, Bangkok, 17 June 1980, "Future Directions in Family Planning for Kampuchean Refugees", p. 2.

48 Comité International de la Croix Rouge, Weekly Report No. 5, Kamput Medical Co-ordinator, S. Rye, 10.4.80, p. 1.

49 Report of Meeting on Family Planning in Kampuchean Holding Centres, 29 August 1980, submitted by Daniel Campbell Susott, Medical Co-ordinator, CCSDPT.

50 Said to have been circulated by OPD 4 in Sa-kaew 1 Camp; copy attached to memorandum, see Note 47.

51 See Note 47.

52 UNFPA *Population Programmes and Projects Vol. 2, Inventory of Population Projects in Developing Countries around the World*, 1980/81, p. 128.

53 See Mike MULLER, *The Health of Nations: a North–South Investigation* (London 1982) pp. 17–61.

54 R. V. SHORT, "The evolution of human reproduction", *Proceedings of the Royal Society of London*, B, Vol. 195 (1976) p. 20.

CHAPTER SEVEN

Abortion and Infanticide

1 Malcolm POTTS and Peter SELMAN, *Society and Fertility* (London 1979) pp. 19–20. *Cf.* R. V. SHORT *loc. cit.* "Normal human semen is notorious for showing an extremely high proportion of morphologically abnormal spermatozoa, often in excess of 40%, whereas the other primates (except the gorilla) have remarkably uniform spermatozoa", and Z. STEIN, M. SUSSER, D. WARBURTON, D. WITTES and J. KLINE, "Spontaneous abortion as a screening device: the effect of fetal survival on the incidence of birth defects", *Americal Journal of Epidemiology*, Vol. 102, p. 275.

2 *Ibid.*, p. 20.

3 E. ALBERMANN and M. R. CREASY, "Factors affecting chromosome abnormalities in human conceptions", *Chromosome Variations in Human Evolution:* Symposia of the Society for the Study of Human Biology No. 14, ed. A. J. Boyce, pp. 83–95; *cf.* F. E. FRENCH and J. M. BIERMAN, "Probabilities of Foetal mortality", *Public Health Reports*, Vol. 77 (1962) pp. 835–847 and A. T. HERTIG, "Implantation of the human ovum: the histogenesis of some aspects of spontaneous abortion", *Progress in Infertility*, ed. S. J. Behrman and R. W. Kistner (1975) pp. 411–438.

4 H. LEHFELDT, C. TIETZE and I. F. GORSTEIN, "Ovarian Pregnancy and the Intrauterine Device", *American Journal of Obstetrics and Gynecology*, Vol. 108 (1970) pp. 1005–1009.

5 J. T. WU and M. C. CHANG, "The physiology of implantation and its inhibition by some agents", *Recent Advances in Fertility Regulation*, ed. CHANG Chai Fen and David GRIFFIN (Geneva 1981) p. 184.

6 V. BERAL, "An epidemiological study of recent trends in ectopic pregnancy", *British Journal of Obstetrics and Gynaecology*, Vol. 82 (1975)

pp. 775–782; M. VESSEY, R. DOLL, R. PETO, B. JOHNSON and P. WIGGINS, "A long-term follow-up of women using different methods of contraception: an interim report", *Journal of Biosocial Science*, Vol. 8 (1976) No. 4, pp. 342–427; C. A. D. RINGROSE, "The occurrence of non-tubal ectopic pregnancies in women with an IUD", *Journal of Reproductive Fertility*, Vol. 55, No. 2, March 1979, pp. 252–7; J. D. STEVEN and I. S. FRASER, "The outcome of pregnancy after failure of intra-uterine contraceptive device", *Journal of Obstetrics and Gynaecology of the British Commonwealth*, Vol. 81 (1974) pp. 282–4; H. S. KAHN and C. W. TYLER, "Mortality associated with the use of IUDs", *Journal of the American Medical Association*, Vol. 234 (1975) pp. 57–59.

7 See for example, R. SNOWDEN, "Pelvic Inflammation, perforation and pregnancy outcome associated with the use of intrauterine devices", The Family Planning Research Unit, University of Exeter, Report No. 15 (1974).

8 X. TACLA, M. MITRA and R. BAEZA, "Post-abortion insertions of the pleated membrane", *International Journal of Gynaecology and Obstetrics*, Vol. 15 (1977) No. 3, pp. 275–8.

9 Indumati PARIKH, *An Experiment in Community Involvement in Family Planning in a Metropolitan Slum* (Centre for the Study of Social Change, Bombay 1978) p. 23, *cf.* pp. 83–84.

10 *Ibid.*, pp. 111–112. *Cf.* Carol VLASSOFF, "Fertility control without modernisation: evidence from a rural Indian community", *Journal of Biosocial Science*, Vol. 11 (1979) p. 328.

11 W. Parker MAULDIN, Dorothy NORTMAN and Frederick F. STEPHAN, Retention of IUDs: an international comparison", *Studies in Family Planning*, No. 18, pp. 1–12.

12 E. D. B. JOHANSEN, "Advantages and disadvantages of the intrauterine device and the hormone implant", *Proceedings of the Royal Society, Series B*, Vol. 194 (1976) p. 83.

13 Terence and Valerie HULL, "Fiji: a study of ethnic plurality and family planning", *Politics of Family Planning*, ed. T. E. Smith (London 1973) p. 190.

14 *Ibid.*, pp. 190–191; also *vide infra*.

15 David NOWLAN, "Dangers of evangelism" *People*, Vol. 8 (1981) No. 2, p. 18.

16 R. T. BURKMAN and the Women's Health Study, "Association between intrauterine devices and pelvic inflammatory disease", *Obstetrics and Gynaecology*, Vol. 57 (1981) p. 269; L. WESTRÖM *et al.*, "The risk of PID in women using IUD compared with non-users", *Lancet* 2 (1976) pp. 221–4; FAULKNER and ORY, "IUDs and acute pelvic inflammatory disease", *Journal of the American Medical Association*, Vol. 235 (1976) pp. 1851–3; B. A. ESCHENBACH, "Acute pelvic inflammatory disease: etiology, risk factors and pathogenesis", *Clinics in Obstetrics and Gyne-*

cology, Vol. 19 (1976) pp. 147–169; I. THALER, E. PALDI and D. STEINER, "IUD and PID", *International Journal of Fertility*, Vol. 23 (1978) No. 1, pp. 69–72.

17 W. D. HAGER and B. MAJUMDAR, "Pelvic actinomycosis in women using intrauterine contraceptive devices", *American Journal of Obstetrics and Gynecology*, Vol. 133 (1979) No. 8, p. 60; D. B. PETITTI and L. MORGENSTERN, "Factors associated with actinomyces-like organisms on Pap smear in IUD users", paper delivered to the Association of Planned Parenthood Physicians, Washington, DC, 30–31 October 1981.

18 M. P. VESSEY and Sir Richard DOLL, FRS, "Evaluation of Existing Methods: is 'the pill' safe enough to continue using?", *Proceedings of the Royal Society*, Series B., Vol. 195 (1976) p. 73. *Cf.* S. D. TARGUM and N. H. WRIGHT, "Association of the intrauterine device and pelvic inflammatory disease: a retrospective pilot study", *American Journal of Epidemiology*, Vol. 100 (1974) pp. 262–271.

19 *FDA Consumer*, November, 1978, p. 21. "PID risk increased sharply among IUD users, British cohort, US case control studies affirm", *Family Planning Perspectives*, Vol. 3, No. 4, July–August 1981; M. P. VESSEY, D. YEATES, R. FLAVELL and K. McPHERSON, "Pelvic inflammatory disease and the intrauterine device: findings in a large cohort study", *British Medical Journal*, Vol. 282 (1981) p. 855.

20 Stanley JOHNSON, *Life Without Birth: A Journey through the Third World in Search of the Population Explosion* (London 1970) pp. 89–90.

21 *Ibid.*, p. 104.

22 *Ibid.*, p. 120.

23 Mark DOWIE and Tracy JOHNSON, "A case of corporate malpractice", *Mother Jones*, November 1976, pp. 36–50.

24 The Medical Device and Drug Advisory Committees on Obstetrics and Gynecology of the US Department of Health, Education and Welfare Food and Drug Administration, *Second Report on Intrauterine Contraceptive Devices* (Washington 1978) p. 7.

25 POTTS and SELMAN, *op. cit.*, pp. 130–131.

26 "Questions and Answers of Family Planning", ed. HAN Hsiang-yang, People's Health Press, in *Chinese Approaches to Family Planning*, trans. Robert DUNN, ed. Leo A. ORLEANS (New York and London 1979) p. 150.

27 *Observer*, 24 April 1980, p. 48, "A Morning After Double".

28 "Postcoital pill legal 'in emergency'," *The Times*, 21 March 1983, commenting on *Post-Coital Contraception: Methods, Services and Prospects*, ed. Helene Graham (London 1983).

29 POTTS and SELMAN, *op. cit.*, p. 129.

30 For a review of the evidence see M. A. KLINGBERG and C. PAPIER, "Teratoepidemiology", *Journal of Biosocial Science*, Vol. 11 (1979) pp. 237–239.

31 E. WEINER, A. A. BERG and I. JOHANSSON, "Copper intrauterine contraceptive devices in adolescent nulliparae", *British Journal of Obstetrics and Gynaecology*, Vol. 83 (1976) p. 204.

32 *Fertility and Contraception in America: Adolescent and Pre-adolescent Pregnancy: hearing before the Select Committee on Population 95th Congress*, Second Session, February 28, March 1 and 2, 1978 (No. 3), Vol. II, p. 1.

33 *Ibid.*, pp. 62–3.

34 See for example G. M. FILSHIE, "Medical and surgical methods of early termination of pregnancy", *Proceedings of the Royal Society, Series B*, Vol. 195, pp. 115–127, and D. A. GRIMES and W. CATES, Jr., "Abortion: Methods and Complications", *Human Reproduction: Conception and Contraception*, ed. E. S. E. HAFEZ (New York 1979) pp. 796–799.

35 DJERASSI, *op. cit.*, p. 77.

36 *Ibid.*, pp. 27–28.

37 In British law the officers of the crown have decided that menstrual regulation is legal as long as two medical practitioners believe pregnancy to exist; the decision was arrived at when the Director of Public Prosecutions was asked to institute proceedings against the providers of the service under the Offences against the Person Act. See *People*, Vol. 6 (1979) No. 3, p. 31.

38 Shushum BHATIA and Lado T. RUZICKA, "Menstrual regulation clients in a village-based family planning programme", *Journal of Biosocial Science*, Vol. 12 (1980) p. 31.

39 N. R. FARNSWORTH *et al.*, "Potential value of plants as sources of new anti-fertility agents", *Journal of Pharmaceutical Sciences*, Vol. 64 (1975), p. 535.

40 James C. MOHR, *Abortion in America: the Origins and Evolution of National Policy, 1800–1900* (Oxford 1978) p. 147.

41 J. F. DASTUR, *Medical Plants of India and Pakistan* (Bombay 1977) p. 181 *et passim*.

42 M. N. LOWENTHAL, I. G. JONES and V. MOHELSKY, "Acute renal failure in Zambian women using traditional herbal remedies", *Journal of Tropical Medicine and Hygiene*, Vol. 77 (1974), No. 8, pp. 190–192.

43 Karin B. EDSTROM, "Early complications and late sequelae of induced abortion: a review of the literature", *WHO Bulletin*, Vol. 52 (1975) pp. 123ff. *Cf.* GRIMES and CATES *op cit.*, pp. 799–813.

44 G. M. FILSHIE, "Medical and surgical methods of early termination of pregnancy", *Proceedings of the Royal Society, Series B*, Vol. 195, pp. 116–118.

45 *Ibid.*, p. 118. See also S. GRECHES, T. K. CHATTERJEE and L. NILES, "Vaginal administration of 15(S) methylprostaglandin F2α methyl ester for induction of mid trimester abortion", *Contraception*, Vol. 16 (1977)

p. 4; S. L. CORSON and R. J. BOLOGNESE, "Abortion of early pregnancy on an outpatient basis using silastic 15(S)15-methyl prostaglandin F2α vaginal devices", *Fertility and Sterility*, Vol. 28 (1977), No. 10, pp. 1056–1062; D. VENGASALADAM, T. H. LEAN and D. A. EDELMAN, "Induction of abortion with 15(S)15-methyl PGE(2α)(Tham)vaginal suppositories", *International Journal of Gynaecology and Obstetrics*, Vol. 15 (1977), No. 1, pp. 93–5.

46 *Ibid*. The first death caused by administration of prostaglandin to induce abortion was reported in the British press in March 1983.

47 Personal communication.

48 C. BREWER, "Induced abortion after feeling foetal movements: its causes and emotional consequences", *Journal of Biosocial Science*, Vol. 10 (1978), No. 2, pp. 203–208.

49 Thomas SZASZ, "The Ethics of Abortion", *Humanist*, October 1966, p. 148.

50 Tongplaew NARKARVONKIT, "Massage Abortion in Thailand", *People*, Vol. 6 (1979), No. 3, p. 30, *cf.* Mona GALLEN, "Abortion Choices in the Philippines", *Journal of Biosocial Science*, Vol. 2 (1970) pp. 281–8.

51 SZASZ, *ibid*.

52 Psychological difficulties concerning therapeutic abortions are more frequent and more severe in physicians, members of the nursing staff and hospital personnel working on or near an abortion service than in patients", L. P. TOURKOW, R. LIDZ and B. L. ROSENFELD, "Psychiatric considerations in fertility inhibition", in HAFEZ, *op. cit.*, p. 862.

53 Napoleon CHAGNON, *Yanomamö: The Fierce People* (New York 1977) pp. 15, 74–5.

54 Doranne JACOBSON, "The Women of North and Central India: Goddesses and Wives", *Women of India*, ed. Tara ALI BEG (Delhi 1958); Mildred LUSCHINSKY, "The Life of Women in a Village in North India," Ph.D. Dissertation, Cornell University, 1962, p. 82; Leigh MINTURN and John T. HITCHCOCK, *The Rajputs of Khalapur, India* (New York 1966) p. 97.

55 J. BIRDSELL, "Some predictions for the Pleistocene based on equilibrium systems among recent hunter–gatherers", in R. LEE and I. DE VORE (eds), *Man the Hunter* (Chicago 1968) pp. 229–249.

56 Marvin HARRIS, *Cannibals and Kings: the Origins of Culture* (London 1978) p. 5. "The insistence upon giving birth in insanitary conditions, and cutting the umbilical cord with dirty implements among relatively sophisticated people seems to be part of an unconscious strategy to ensure that only the fittest children survive. In Keneba, a village in Gambia, more than half the babies die." Barbara THOMPSON, "Infant feeding and child care in a west African village", *Journal of Tropical Paediatrics*, Vol. 13 (1967) No. 3.

57 In coastal southern Sierra Leone, the sisterhood of the Sande decide

which infants shall live and which die: "If the baby is abnormal at birth, it is socially defined as the incarnation of a malevolent spirit. The mother is prevented from feeding it and it is left to die." C. P. McCORMICK, "Health, fertility and birth in Sierra Leone", *Ethnography of Fertility and Birth*, ed. C. P. McCormick (London 1982) p. 129. *Cf.* C. M. FIELD, *Religion and the Ga People* (London 1937) pp. 169–170, 177–178; W. Lloyd WARNER, *A Black Civilisation* (New York 1937) pp. xx–xx; I. SCHAPERA, *The Khoisan Peoples of South Africa* (London 1930) pp. 262–263, 266; George M. FOSTER and Gabriel OSPINA, *Empire's Children: The People of Tzintzuntzan* (Mexico City 1948) pp. 227, 230.

58 Mary ELLISON, *The Black Experience: American Blacks since 1865* (London 1974), on infanticide in the southern United States, pp. 18–19.

59 B. Abbott SEAGRAVES, "The Malthusian proposition and differing nutritional stress: differing implications for man and society", *Malnutrition, Behaviour and Social Organisation*, ed. Lawrence S. Greene (New York 1977) p. 184.

60 Margaret HEWITT, *Wives and Mothers in Victorian Industry* (London 1958) *passim*, and Wanda Franken NEFF, *Victorian Working Women* (London 1929) p. 37.

61 *Report of the Interdepartmental Committee on Physical Deterioration* (London 1903), pp. 44–45.

62 *The Malthusian* for 15 July 1921 (Vol. 45, No. 7) reproduces a letter from Major General John F. O'Ryan to the Women's Professional League Council, dated 25 May 1921: "In the Near East Relief Movement of the American Workers, with supplies available for a given percentage of the population, reported that they had to call upon mothers having several children to designate the children to die and those to be saved by feeding," so that all would not starve when the relief supplies were exhausted.

63 S. CHANDRASEKHAR, *Infant Mortality, Population Growth and Family Planning in India* (London 1972) p. 146; *cf.* H. H. RISLEY and E. A. GAIT, *Census of India*, Vol. 1, Part 1, *Report* (Calcutta 1903) p. 115.

64 Garrett HARDIN, *Population, Evolution and Birth Control* (San Francisco 1969) p. 279.

65 Raymond ILLSLEY and Marion H. HALL, "Psychosocial Aspects of Abortion: a review of issues and needed research", *WHO Bulletin*, Vol. 53 (1976), pp. 83–106.

66 Ann CARTWRIGHT, *The Dignity of Labour? A Study of Childbirth and Induction* (London 1979) Chapter 3, *passim*.

67 Victoria GREENWOOD and Jock YOUNG, *Abortion in Demand* (London 1976) pp. 127–8.

68 Vasile GHETAU, "L'Evolution et la Fécondité en Roumanie", *Population*, Vol. 33(2), March–April 1978, pp. 525–539.

CHAPTER EIGHT

Changing Concepts of Sexuality

1 Michel FOUCAULT, *The History of Sexuality: Volume One: an Introduction*, trans. Robert Hurley (London 1981) *passim*.

2 Wilhelm REICH, *The Function of the Orgasm: Sex-economic Problems of Biological Energy* (New York 1942) pp. xxii–xxiii, 73–93.

3 Paul ROBINSON, *The Sexual Radicals* (London 1973) p. 62.

4 FOUCAULT, *op. cit.*, p. 197.

5 Robin McKIE, "Men of science have tiff over sex", *Observer*, 4 March 1982.

6 Richard P. MICHAEL and Doris ZUMPE, "Potency in male rhesus monkeys: effects of continuously receptive females", *Science*, Vol. 200 (28 April 1978) p. 451.

7 *Ibid.*, p. 453.

8 John BALE, *The Actes of Englysh Votaryes comprehendynge their vnchast practyses and examples by all ages* (London 1546) *passim*.

9 John GAGNON and William SIMON: *Sexual Conduct: the Sources of Human Sexuality* (Chicago 1973).

10 Donald S. MARSHALL and Robert C. SUGGS, *Human Sexual Behaviour: Variations in the Ethnographic Spectrum* (New York, 1970).

11 *Vide supra*, pp. 123–133.

12 George FRANKL, *The Failure of the Sexual Revolution* (London 1974) p. 54.

13 *Ibid.*, p. 36.

14 FOUCAULT, *op. cit.*, pp. 57–68.

15 Wilhelm REICH, *The Sexual Revolution: Towards a Self-governing Character Structure*, trans. Theodore P. Wolfe (New York 1969) p. 74.

16 Melvin KONNER and Carol WORTHMAN, "Nursing frequency, gonadal function and birth spacing among !Kung hunter–gatherers", *Science*, Vol. 207 (15 February 1980) pp. 788–791.

17 Personal communication.

18 E. ELKAN, "Evolution of female orgastic ability – a biological survey", *International Journal of Sexology*, Vol. 2, 1948, pp. 1–13; 84–93. *Cf.* L. M. TERMAN, *Psychological Factors in Marital Happiness* (New York 1938).

19 Daniel G. BROWN, "Female orgasm and sexual inadequacy", *An Analysis of Human Sexual Response*, ed. R. and E. BRECHER (London 1968) p. 153.

20 Eustace CHESSER, *The Sexual, Marital and Family Relationships of the English Woman* (London 1956) p. 421.

21 Mary S. CALDERONE, "Human sexuality – battleground or peace-

ground?'', *Progress in Sexology: Selected papers from the Proceedings of the 1976 International Congress of Sexology*, ed. Robert GEMME and Connie Christine WHEELER (New York and London 1977) p. 588.

22 Joseph Josy LEVY, "The sexology program at the Université du Quebec à Montreal", *Progress in Sexology, op. cit.*, pp. 566–570.

23 Quoted from their brochure, *Human Loving: Sexuality and Intimacy A Multidisciplinary Holistic Approach* (Stanford 1978).

24 CALDERONE, *op. cit.*, p. 589.

25 See for example the discussions of the Government's Education Bill in British newspapers for February, 1980.

26 Anne SCOTT, "New approach to teenage problems in Panama", *People*, Vol. 8 (1981), No. 2, p. 27.

27 ROBINSON, *op. cit.*, p. 25.

28 Emmanuel LeRoy LADURIE, *Montaillou: Cathars and Catholics in a French Village 1294–1324*, trans. Barbara Bray (London 1980) pp. 30, 209.

CHAPTER NINE

The Fate of the Family

1 Nafis SADIK, "Simplify, simplify", *People*, Vol. 8 (1981), No. 2, p. 8.

2 Ferdinand MOUNT, *The Subversive Family* (London 1981) p. 54.

3 Friedrich ENGELS, *Der Ursprung der Familie, des Privateigenthums und des Staates* (Stuttgart 1884) p. xx.

4 MOUNT, *op. cit.*, p. 26.

5 *Ibid.*, p. 16.

6 *Ibid.*, *cf.* Ch. XII, "The Recovery of Divorce", *passim*.

7 Peter LASLETT, "Introduction: the History of the Family", *Household and Family in Past Time*, ed. P. Laslett (Cambridge 1972) *passim*.

8 Robert SUGGS, "Sex and Personality in the Marquesas", MARSHALL and SUGGS, *op. cit.*, pp. 165ff.

9 LASLETT, *op. cit.*, p. 1.

10 E.g. E. A. HAMMEL, "The Zadruga as Process", LASLETT, *op cit.*, pp. 335–375.

11 LASLETT, *op. cit.*, Preface, p. ix.

12 *Ibid.*

13 Jack GOODY, "The Evolution of the Family", LASLETT, *op. cit.*, p. 104.

14 *Ibid.*, p. 110.

15 Frances Moore LAPPE, Joseph COLLINS and David KINLEY, *Aid as Obstacle: Twenty Questions about our Foreign Aid to the Hungry* (San Francisco 1980) pp. 113–114.

16 Jane MORTON, "How far do family ties go? The Indian answer", *The Times*, 12 May 1982.

17 *Ibid.*

18 *Ibid.*

19 John DEMOS, "Demography and psychology in the historical study of family life: a personal report", LASLETT, *op. cit.*, p. 562.

20 GOODY, *op. cit.*, pp. 103–4.

21 Peter LASLETT, *Family Life and Illicit Love in Earlier Generations: Essays in Historical Sociology* (Cambridge 1977) p. 60.

22 W. J. GOODE, *World Revolution and Family Patterns* (New York 1963) p. 7.

23 Robin FOX, *Kinship and Marriage: an Anthropological Perspective* (London 1981), pp. 13–14.

24 David COOPER, *The Death of the Family* (London 1980) p. 74.

25 E. R. LEACH, *A Runaway World* (London 1968) pp. 44–45.

CHAPTER TEN

Eugenics

1 Jane Hume CLAPPERTON, *Scientific Meliorism* (London 1885) p. 342; letter dated 20 November 1878.

2 Matthew ARNOLD, *Culture and Anarchy* (London 1869) pp. 245–246.

3 CLAPPERTON, *op. cit.*, p. 88, quoting A. R. WALLACE, *The Action of Natural Selection on Man*.

5 *Ibid.*, p. 373.

6 W. R. GREG, *Enigmas of Life* (London 1872) p. 105.

7 Arthur KEITH, "Galton's Place among anthropologists", *Eugenics Review*, Vol. 12 (1920–21), No. 1, p. 20.

8 Francis GALTON, "Eugenics, its definition, scope and aims", *Sociological Papers* (London 1905) p. 47.

9 Francis GALTON, *Memories of my Life* (London 1908) p. xx.

10 Cited by C. P. Blacker in *Eugenics: Galton and After* (London 1956) p. 104; *cf.* GALTON, *Memories of my life, op. cit.*, p. 322.

11 GALTON, *Memories of My Life, op. cit.*, p. 323.

12 Karl PEARSON, "On the relation of fertility in man to social status and on the changes in this relation that have taken place in the last fifty years", Drapers Company Research Memoirs.

13 Karl PEARSON, "On the correlation of fertility with social value", *Eugenics Laboratory Memoirs*, Vol. 18 (1913).

14 Karl PEARSON and Margaret MOUL, "The problem of alien immigration into Great Britain, illustrated by an examination of Russian and Polish Jewish children", Eugenics Laboratory Memoirs, *Annals of Eugenics*, Vol. 1 (1925).

15 Leon F. WHITNEY, *The Case for Sterilisation* (New York 1934) p. 126.

16 *Eugenics Review*, Vol. 14 (1912) pp. 204–5.

17 See E. S. GOSNEY and Paul POPENOE, *Collected Papers on Human Sterilisation in California* (Pasadena 1930); *Journal of Criminal Law and Criminology*, August 1918; and J. H. LANDMAN, *The History of Human Sterilisation in the United States* (New York 1929); Paul POPENOE and Roswell Hill JOHNSON, *Applied Eugenics* (New York 1918) pp. 192 ff; and Donald K. PICKENS, *Eugenics and the Progressives* (Nashville 1968) p. 82.

18 For an insight into Davenport's views, see "The life of the commonwealth takes precedence over the right of reproduction of the individual", *Proceedings of the World Population Conference*, ed. Margaret SANGER (New York 1927) p. 242.

19 H. H. LAUGHLIN, *Eugenical Sterilisation in the United States: Eugenics Record Office Report No. 1* (New York 1913) p. 20.

20 H. H. LAUGHLIN, "Immigration Control", in Chamber of Commerce of the State of New York: *A Report of the Special Committee on Immigration and the Alien Insane submitting a Study on Immigration Control by H.H.L.* (New York 1934) p. 7.

21 Nils von HOFSTEN, "Sterilisation in Sweden", *Journal of Heredity*, Vol. 40, No. 9 (September 1949), pp. 243–7.

22 George Bernard SHAW, *Sociological Papers* (London 1904) pp. 74–5.

23 Arabella KENEALY, "A study of degeneracy", *Eugenics Review*, Vol. 3, No. 1, pp. 39, 43.

24 Anna MARTIN, *The Married Working Woman* (London 1911) p. 47.

25 Anna MARTIN, *The Mother and Social Reform* (London 1913) p. 3.

26 Sidney WEBB, "Eugenics and the Poor Law: the Minority Report" (1909), reprinted in *Eugenics Review*, Vol. 60 (1968), p. 75.

27 Bertrand RUSSELL, "Marriage and the Population Question", *International Journal of Ethics*, Vol. 26, No. 4 (July 1916), p. 461.

28 L. BURLINGAME, *Heredity and Social Problems* (New York 1940) p. 278.

29 C. P. BLACKER, *Birth Control and the State. A Plea and a Forecast* (London 1926) p. 37–38.

30 E. W. McBRIDE, in answer to F. A. E. Crew, *Eugenics Review*, Vol. 12 (1920–21), No. 1, p. 43.

31 E. W. McBRIDE, in a review of the second report of the National Birth-rate Commission, *Problems of Population and Parenthood*, ed. Sir James Marchant, in *Eugenics Review*, Vol. 12 (1920–21), No. 3, p. 221.

32 In an article for *Nature* quoted by J. B. S. HALDANE, *Heredity and Politics* (London 1938) pp. 170–71.

33 *Better Unborn*, Eugenics Society pamphlet (n.d., 1932?). In view of the fact that Huxley was associated with the eugenics movement all his life, it is interesting to note that an aunt went into irreversible melancholia after the birth of a child and pined to death, one of his brothers hanged himself, and the other, Aldous, suffered from interstitial keratitis. The cause of this suffering was not genetic, but congenital syphilis, although it seems that the family does carry the gene for high myopia.

34 L. S. PENROSE, *Mental Defect* (London 1933) pp. 170–71.

35 R. B. CATTELL, *The Fight for our National Intelligence* (London 1937) p. 127.

36 *Ibid.*, Introduction, p. v.

37 *Ibid.*, p. 141.

38 J. B. S. HALDANE, *Heredity and Politics* (London 1938) p. 7.

39 *Ibid.*, pp. 86–87.

40 *Ibid.*, p. 120.

41 C. L. BURT, *Intelligence and Fertility* (London 1946) p. 5.

42 See L. S. HEARNSHAW, *Cyril Burt, Psychologist* (London 1979) *passim* for a full account of Burt's methods.

43 Buck *vs.* Bell (1926), 247 US 200.

44 *Ibid.*, p. 202. For an excellent discussion of the issues raised in such cases, see Robert BAKER, "Social control and medical models in genetics", *Genetics Now: Ethical Issues in Genetic Research*, ed. John J. Buckley, Jr. (Washington 1978) pp. 75–139.

45 Gunnar DAHLBERG, *Race, Reason and Rubbish* (New York 1943) p. 235.

46 E. S. GOSNEY and Paul POPENOE, *Sterilisation for Human Betterment: a Summary of Results of 6,000 Operations in California 1909–1929* (New York 1929) p. 6.

47 Moya WOODSIDE, *Sterilisation in North Carolina: a Sociological and Psychological Study* (Chapel Hill 1950) p. xiv.

48 *Ibid.*, p. 6.

49 WHITNEY, *op. cit.*, p. 137.

50 *Ibid.*, p. 147.

51 WOODSIDE, *op. cit.*, pp. 10–11.

52 *Ibid.*, pp. 16–17.

53 *Ibid.*, p. 17.

54 *Ibid.*, pp. 17–18.

55 C. B. DAVENPORT and Lt-Col. A. G. LANE, "Defects of drafted men", *Scientific Monthly*, February, 1920.

56 WOODSIDE, *op. cit.*

57 Faith SCHENK and A. S. PARKES, "The activities of the Eugenics Society", *Eugenics Review*, Vol. 60 (1968), p. 154.

58 *Ibid.*, p. 155.

59 *Vide infra re* the activities at the Marie Stopes Memorial Clinic.

60 Claudia DREIFUS (ed.) *Seizing Our Bodies: The Politics of Women's Health* (New York 1977), "Sterilising the Poor"; Barbara CARESS, "Sterilisation: Women Fit to be Tied", *Health/PAC Bulletin 62*, Jan–Feb 1975, pp. 1–6, 10–12; Judith COBURN, "Sterilisation Regulation: Debate not Quelled by HEW Document", *Science*, Vol. 183, March 1974, pp. 935–9; Judith HERMAN, "Forced Sterilisation", *Sister Courage*, January 1976; Jeanie ROSOFF, *Memorandum: DHEW Proposed Regulations on Sterilisation*, PP/WP Washington 1974; *Sterilisation Abuse of Women: The Facts*, Mimeograph, NY Committee to end Sterilisation Abuse, 1975; "Sterilisation Guidelines Criticised by ACLU", *The Spokeswoman* 4, November 1974, p. 2.

61 Quoted in Thomas B. LITTLEWOOD, *The Politics of Population Control* (Notre Dame 1977), pp. 126–8.

62 *Ibid.*, p. 125.

63 BAKER, *op. cit.*, pp. 79–84.

64 *Family Planning Digest*, Vol. 1, No. 1 (January 1972), p. xx.

65 Eugenics Society, *Schedule for Pre-Marital Investigation* (London, n.d.).

66 Marcus A. KLINGBERG and Cheri M. PAPIER, "Teratoepidemiology", *Journal of Biosocial Science*, Vol. 11 (1979), p. 233, "Known cytogenic abnormalities and hereditary transmission account for about 25% of congenital defects, but the aetiology of the vast majority remains undetermined."

67 G. A. MACHING and J. A. CRIOLLA, "Chromosome constitution of 500 infants dying during the perinatal period with an appendix concerning other genetic disorders among these infants", *Humangenetik*, Vol. 23 (1974), No. 3, pp. 183–198; Charles R. SCRIVER, "Genetics and medicine: an evolving relationship", *Science*, Vol. 200 (1978), pp. 946–952; L. F. HINMAN III, "Legal considerations and pre-natal genetic diagnosis", *Clinics in Obstetrics and Gynecology*, Vol. 19 (1976), No. 4, pp. 965–972; S. L. B. DUNCANS, "Problems of pre-natal screening programme for Down's Syndrome", *Journal of Biosocial Science*, Vol. 10 (1978), No. 2, pp. 141–6.

68 *Vide supra*, pp. 9–12.

69 Hermann J. MULLER, *Out of the Night: A Biologist's View of the Future* (London 1936); *cf.* Herbert BREWER, "Eutelegenesis", *Eugenics Review*, Vol. 27 (1935–6), p. 121.

70 C. von EHRENFELS, "Die konstitutive Verderblichkeit der Monogamie und die Unentbehrlichkeit einer Sexualreform", *Archive für Rassen- und*

Gesellschaftsbiologie, Vol. 5, Nos 5 and 6 (September–October and November–December 1907), pp. 615–651 and 803–830.

71 SCHENK and PARKES, *op. cit.*, pp. 152–3.

72 Gordon WOLSTENHOLME (ed.) *Man and His Future: A Ciba Foundation Volume* (London 1963) p. 17.

73 *Ibid.*, p. 18.

74 *Ibid.*

75 Hermann J. MULLER, "The Dominance of Economics over Eugenics: A Paper delivered at the Third International Eugenics Conference", *Birth Control Review*, Vol. 16, No. 6 (October 1932), p. 236.

76 WOLSTENHOLME, *op. cit.*, p. 259.

77 *Ibid.*, pp. 274–5.

78 *Ibid.*, p. 281.

79 *Ibid.*, p. 282.

80 Robert K. GRAHAM, *The Future of Man* (North Quincey 1970) p. 134.

81 *Ibid.*, p. 158.

CHAPTER ELEVEN

The Population Lobby

1 Dr WATERS (*pseud.*), *Every Woman's Book; or, What is Love* (London 1838) Sig. B2, publisher's preface, dated 1828.

2 *Ibid.*, p. 23.

3 *Ibid.*, p. 25.

4 *Ibid.*, p. 41.

5 *Ibid.*, p. 38.

6 *Ibid.*, p. 25.

7 Charles KNOWLTON, *The Fruits of Philosophy or, The Private Companion of Young Married People* (London 1841) pp. 30–33.

8 Annie BESANT, *An Autobiography* (London 1893) pp. 205–214.

9 G. M. WILLIAMS, *The Passionate Pilgrim* (London n.d.) p. 91.

10 Annie BESANT, *The Law of Population: Its Consequences and its Bearing Upon Human Conduct and Morals* (London n.d.) pp. 33–35.

11 Edith HOW-MARTYN and Mary BREED, *The Birth Control Movement in England* (London 1930) pp. 10–11.

12 Victor ROBINSON, *Pioneers of Birth Control in England and America* (New York 1919) p. 55.

13 How-Martyn and Breed, *op. cit.*, p. 13.

14 H. A. Allbutt, *The Wife's Handbook* (2nd edition, revised, London 1886) p. 47.

15 *Ibid.*

16 *Ibid.*, p. 48.

17 *Ibid.*

18 C. P. Gerritsen, letter to *The Malthusian*, Vol. 2, No. 1, March 1879.

19 H. De Vries in *Proceedings of the Fifth International Neo-malthusian and Birth Control Conference*, ed. Raymond Pierpoint (London 1922).

20 Margaret Sanger, *An Autobiography* (London 1939) p. 145.

21 Medical Committee of the National Birth-rate Commission, *Medical Aspects of Contraception* (London 1927) p. 51.

22 *The Malthusian*, Vol. 44, No. 10, p. 74, quoting *The Birth Control Review* for September 1920.

23 *The Malthusian*, Vol. 44, No. 11, p. 85, letter dated 15 November 1920.

24 Sanger, *An Autobiography*, *op. cit.*, p. 109. (All the copies of *Family Limitation* that I have seen feature a single unhelpful illustration of the small Mensinga pessary, from a block that remained unchanged through all editions.)

25 Sanger, *An Autobiography*, *op. cit.*, p. 28.

26 Margaret Sanger, *The Pivot of Civilization* (New York 1921) p. 123.

27 *Birth Control Review*, October 1926.

28 Sanger, *An Autobiography*, *op. cit.*, p. 366; see also David M. Kennedy, *Birth Control in America: the Career of Margaret Sanger* (New Haven and London 1970), Ch. 4 "Revolution and Repression: The Changing Ideology of Birth Control", *passim*.

29 Robinson, *op. cit.*, p. 79.

30 Guy Aldred, *No Traitor's Gait* (London 1955–1963), Vol. II, No. 5 (1959), pp. 401, 404 and 406, and Vol. III, No. 1, *passim*.

31 See Madeleine Gray, *Margaret Sanger: a Biography of the Champion of Birth Control* (New York 1979) and David M. Kennedy, *Birth Control in America: the Career of Margaret Sanger* (New Haven and London 1970) *passim*. (My own judgement is rather harsher than either Kennedy's or Gray's).

32 Margaret Sanger, *My Fight for Birth Control* (London 1932) p. 101.

33 Letter from British Library Collection, quoted by Ruth Hall, *Marie Stopes: A Biography* (London 1977) p. 120.

34 Edward Carpenter, *Love's Coming of Age* (London 1902) pp. 22–23.

35 Marie Stopes, *Married Love: A New Contribution to the Solution of Sex Difficulties* (Fifth edition, London 1918) p. 90.

36 *Ibid.*, p. 20.

37 *Ibid.*, pp. 51–52.

38 *Vide supra*, pp. 119–122.

39 *Daily Mail*, 13 June 1919.

40 Parliamentary Questionnaire, 8 November 1922. British Library Add. MS. 58560.

41 Marie STOPES to Rev. Alfred Smith, Superintendent, Royal Association in Aid of the Deaf and Dumb, 10 October 1924, British Library Collection.

42 Muriel SEGAL, *Australian Women's Weekly*, 19 April 1934.

43 Letter of 30 December 1949, to "May", British Library Collection.

44 SCHENK and PARKES, *op. cit.*, pp. 153–4.

45 Anne HARDY, "Stopes to conquer", *Guardian*, 31 March 1976, p. 11; *Observer*, 3 August 1980, report of resignations by Lady Brook, Peter Huntingford and Mrs Helen Grahame; 31 August 1980, *News of the World*, report of criticism of policies by British National Marriage Guidance Council; *Pulse*, 29 November 1980, report on new direction, offering post-coital IUD insertion.

46 Norman HAIRE, *Birth Control Methods* (London 1937); Courtenay BEALE, *Wise Wedlock* (London 1930).

47 Muriel BOX, *The Trial of Marie Stopes* (London 1967) pp. 105–7.

48 Marie STOPES, *A New Gospel to All Peoples. A Revelation of God Uniting Physiology and the Religions of Man* (privately printed, June 1920).

49 *The Malthusian*, Vol. 44, No. 6, 15 June 1920.

50 *The Malthusian*, Vol. 45, 4 April 1921.

51 See letter from Dr Robinson to Mary Ware Dennett, from MWD to Dr Robinson, dated 29 May 1931 and Robinson's reply of 1 June 1931, British Library Collection.

52 HALL, *op. cit.*, p. 246.

53 Marie STOPES, *A Letter to Working Mothers* (London 1927) p. 11.

54 BOX, *op. cit.*, pp. 64–65. An interesting insight into Stopes' relationship with this eminent gentleman is provided by a letter from him dated 26 May 1921, "The nation which most effectually adopts eugenic ideals will be bound to rule the world ... We may not at once be able to get rid of homosexuals but an enlightened nation will have no use for them." (Homosexuality is, of course, not a hereditary defect.)

55 BOX, *op. cit.*, pp. 101–2, 135, 147–8, 167–8 etc.

56 There are numerous examples in the Stopes correspondence in the British Library Collection, but all are protected from publication at present for obvious reasons: they include attempts to remonstrate with her, "I must beg you once more not to treat them [the facts alleged] as personal reflection. If a satisfactory method of birth control is to be discovered then surely all the facts relating to the subject must be carefully recorded and considered," and outright lies from Stopes: "Yours is the first case of failure we have had in more than 3,000 people who have used the clinic" (5 July 1922).

57 Marie STOPES, *The First Five Thousand. Being the First Report of the First Birth Control Clinic in the British Empire, "The Mothers' Clinic for*

Constructive Birth Control" at *61*, *Marlborough Road, Holloway, London, N.19* (London 1925).

58 Box, *op. cit.*, pp. 292–4.

59 Letter from MCS to Shaw Desmond, 8 November 1946, British Library Collection.

60 *Birth Control News*, Vol. 3, July 1922.

61 Bertrand Russell to Marie Stopes, 30 January 1923, British Library Collection.

62 Marie Stopes to F. A. E. Crew, 22 February 1927, "You might like to know that I myself, the doctors at the clinic and everyone connected with the Society for Constructive Birth Control has [*sic*] refused to give evidence before Marchant's Committee as it is not properly constituted and is biased. We do not trust it. Of course, what I would prefer is that you also refuse." British Library Collection.

63 National Birth-Rate Commission, *Medical Aspects of Contraception: Report and Evidence* (London 1927) pp. 54–56.

64 Helena WRIGHT, "Fifty years of family planning", *Family Planning*, Vol. 20, No. 4 (January 1972), p. 76.

65 See letter to Ernest Thurtle, 18 October 1927, British Library Collection.

66 *E.g.* letter to R. A. Morton, 1 June 1942, another to Captain Jaggard, 25 June 1942, British Library Collection.

67 Stopes' first husband, Reginald Ruggles Gates, went on to function perfectly adequately as the husband of another woman whose efforts to retrieve his reputation have been completely unavailing. Much of the evidence adduced is irrelevant, but we are left with what amounts to a categorical denial that Stopes was *virgo intacta* at the time of the annulment hearing. No alternative explanation of the findings of the learned gentlemen has ever been suggested. Before she had been married four years, Stopes was seeking advice on Verdon Roe's "flagging virility" (Hall, *op. cit.*, p. 203); in 1938 he wrote a statement giving her permission to take a lover, referring to her suffering "sex deprivation for all these years", a document dictated apparently by Stopes herself (*Ibid.*, pp. 277–8).

68 WRIGHT, *op. cit.*, p. 77.

69 Linda GORDON, *Woman's Body, Woman's Right: A Social History of Birth Control in America* (New York 1976) p. 284.

70 UNFPA, *Population Programmes and Projects. Vol. 1. Guide to Sources of International Population Assistance 1982* (New York 1982) p. 247.

71 *Ibid.*, p. 244.

72 Lawrence LADER, *Breeding Ourselves to Death* (New York 1971), pp. 109–111. This is the source for all material relating to Moore's role in creating the international birth-control establishment.

73 *Ibid.*, p. 3.

74 Paul EHRLICH, *The Population Bomb* (London 1971) Sig. A2v.

75 LADER, *op. cit.*, p. 55.

76 *Ibid.*, p. 3.

77 GRAY, *op. cit.*, p. 428; photograph in LADER, *op. cit.*, p. 8.

78 Thomas B. LITTLEWOOD, *The Politics of Population Control* (Notre Dame 1977) p. 51.

79 Philip HAUSER, "America's Population Crisis", *Look*, 21 November 1961, pp. 30–31; see also LITTLEWOOD, *op. cit.*, p. 41.

80 LITTLEWOOD, *op. cit.*, p. 42.

81 *Ibid.*, pp. 79–80.

82 Donald P. WARWICK, *Bitter Pills: Population Policies and their Implementation in Eight Developing Countries* (Cambridge 1982) p. 46.

83 Based on an interview in the *St Louis Post-Dispatch*, 22 April 1977, and Warwick, *op. cit.*, pp. 46–51.

84 UNFPA, *op. cit.*, pp. 124–6.

85 LADER, *op. cit.*, p. 64.

CHAPTER TWELVE

Governments as Family Planners

1 LITTLEWOOD, Thomas B. *The Politics of Population Control* (Notre Dame 1977) p. 45; *cf.* Lincoln PASHUTE, "Economics versus racial discrimination in provision of birth control services in the United States", *Research in Population Economics*, Vol. 1 (1978), pp. 189–196.

2 Data from the *People* "Fertility and Family Planning" wallchart (July 1982).

3 The Kenyan *Sunday Nation* (12 October 1980) quoted Dr Yusuf Eraj of Nairobi as saying, "With the money spent on one demographer who comes from Europe, lives in the capital of an African country, runs a car, enjoys his holidays, almost four doctors can be employed in any city."

4 UNFPA, *Population Programmes and Projects. Vol. 2. Inventory of Population Projects in Developing Countries around the World 1980/81*, p. 52.

5 WHO, *Annual Report 1982: WHO Special Programme of Research Development and Research Training in Human Reproduction* (New York 1983), p. 61–62.

6 Egon DICZFALUSY and Britt Marie LANDGREN, "New Delivery Systems: Vaginal Devices", *Recent Advances in Fertility Regulation*, ed. Chang Chai Fen and David Griffin (New York 1981) pp. 60–66.

7 Japan Organisation for Co-operation in Family Planning (JOICFP), *Bird's Eye View of Family Planning in Japan* (Tokyo 1982) p. 10.

8 *Ibid.*, p. 21.

9 JOICFP, *Where there's a Will: the Story of a Countryside Health Nurse* (Tokyo 1981), p. 5.

10 *Ibid.*, pp. 6, 14–15, 21.

11 *Ibid.*, p. 19.

12 JOICFP, *Bird's Eye View, op. cit.*, pp. 43, 38.

13 *International Herald Tribune*, 7 February 1978.

14 For a more detailed discussion see Y. Scott MATSUMOTO, *Demographic Research in Japan 1955–70: a Survey and a Selected Bibliography, Papers of the East–West population Institute*, No. 30, April 1974.

15 UNFPA, *op. cit.*, Vol. I. *Guide to Sources of International Population Assistance*, 1982, p. 221.

16 LITTLEWOOD, *op. cit.*, p. 55.

17 Donald P. WARWICK, *Bitter Pills: Population Policies and their Implementation in Eight Developing Countries* (Cambridge 1982) p. 52.

18 Government of India, Ministry of Family Planning, *Centre Calling*, Vol. 10, No. 9, September 1975, p. 14.

19 Margaret SANGER, *An Autobiography* (London 1939) pp. 458–461; *cf.* Mahadev DESAI, report of interview with Sanger, *Harijan*, 25 January 1936, and Beryl SUITTERS, *Be Brave and Angry: Chronicles of the IPPF* (London 1973), pp. 14–16.

20 GRAY, *op. cit.*, pp. 422–3; *cf.* SUITTERS, *op. cit.*, p. 48.

21 See also the remarks of Vasant P. PETHE, *Population Policy and Compulsion in Family Planning* (Poona 1981) pp. 22–23 and D. M. POTTS, "The Implementation of Family Planning Programmes", *Proceedings of the Royal Society, Series B*, Vol. 195 (1976) p. 214.

22 Amram SCHEINFELD, *The New You and Heredity* (New York 1956) p. 543.

23 SUITTERS, *op. cit.*, pp. 161–2, 197–9.

24 UNFPA, *op. cit.*, Vol. 1, p. 207.

25 UNFPA, *op. cit.*, Vol. 2, pp. 180–81.

26 Roberto CUCA and Catherine S. PIERCE, *Experiments in Family Planning: Lessons from the Developing World* (Washington 1977) p. 132.

27 *Vide supra*, p. 119–120.

28 Population Council, "India: the Singur Study", *Studies in Family Planning*, Vol. 1 (1963), No. 1, pp. 1–4.

29 The first Union Minister for Health, Rajkumari Amrit Kaur tried repeatedly to explain this point to the foreigners, but her opposition was put down to her religious allegiance and obscurantism and simply ignored. (SUITTERS, *op. cit.* pp. 63–64).

30 Robert REPETTO, "A Case Study of the Madras Vasectomy Program", *Studies in Family Planning*, No. 31 (May 1968), pp. 8–16.

31 V. Dutt MULLICK, L. V. PHATAK, A. K. JAIN and R. CHABRA, *Preliminary Report on the Field Trials of Copper T (T Cu 200) Devices* (Delhi 1974); *cf. Centre Calling*, Vol. 3 (1968), No. 4, p. 2 and Vol. 4 (1969), No. 5, p. 6.

32 Carol VLASSOFF, "Fertility control without modernisation: evidence from a rural Indian community", *Journal of Biosocial Science*, Vol. 11 (1979), p. 326. *Cf.* Ketayun GOULD, "Sex and contraception in Sherapur: family planning in a North Indian village", *Economic and Political Weekly*, Vol. 4 (1969), pp. 1887–1892, and "Family Planning: a politically suicidal issue", *Economic and Social Weekly*, Vol. 4 (1969), pp. 1513–18, and L. E. BLICKENSTAFF, "Sociology of family planning", *Journal of the Christian Medical Association of India* Vol. 42 (1967), pp. 32–4.

33 *Ibid.*, p. 330.

34 WARWICK, *op. cit.*, p. 61. Gamble's credibility was apparently unaffected by his attempt to promote salt as a spermicide, claiming non-existent successful trials at the Margaret Sanger Research Bureau in 1955. (SUITTERS, *op. cit.*, pp. 102–5).

35 *Centre Calling*, Vol. 2 (1967), No. 9, p. 5.

36 Karan SINGH, *Population, Poverty and the Future of India* (Delhi 1975) p. 117.

37 WARWICK, *op. cit.*, p. 28.

38 CUCA and PIERCE, *op. cit.*, pp. 143–145.

39 Kingsley DAVIS, "Population policy: will current programs succeed?" *Science*, Vol. 158, pp. 730–39, 10 November 1967.

40 Bernard BERELSON, "Beyond family planning", *Studies in Family Planning*, No. 38 (New York 1969).

41 Lyle SAUNDERS, *Beyond Family Planning: A Ford Foundation Reprint* SR/44 n.d., p. 3.

42 *Ibid.*, p. 10.

43 Meredith MINKLER, "Consultants or colleagues: the role of the US population advisers in India", *Population and Development Review*, December 1971.

44 D. M. POTTS, "The implementation of family planning programmes", *Proceedings of the Royal Society*, Series B, Vol. 195 (1976) p. 218.

45 John ROWLEY, "Chojiro Kunii: man and message", *People*, Vol. 9 (1982), No. 3, p. 23.

46 Rural Health Research Centre, *The Narangwal Population Study: Integrated Health and Family Planning Services* (Narangwal 1975).

47 David G. MANDELBAUM, *Human Fertility in India: Social Components and Policy Perspectives* (Berkeley 1974) p. 9, quoting "Population control in India", *Population Bulletin*, Vol. 26 (1970), No. 12, p. 31.

48 John MARSHALL, "Culture and contraception: response determinants to a family planning program in a North Indian village", unpublished Doctoral Dissertation, University of Hawaii 1972.

49 Government of Kerala, *The Story of the Ernakulam Experiment in Family Planning* (Cochin 1971).

50 V. H. THAKOR and Vinod M. PATEL, "The Gujurat States' massive vasectomy campaign", *Studies in Family Planning*, Vol. 3 (1972) No. 8, pp. 186–192.

51 Interview for Independence Day issue of *The Illustrated Weekly*, 1972, reprinted in Kushwant SINGH, *Mrs Gandhi Returns* (New Delhi 1979) pp. 45–6.

52 SINGH, *op. cit.*, p. 81.

53 Nancy S. HENLEY and Sagar C. JAIN, *Family Planning in Haryana: Evaluation of a State Program in India* (Chapel Hill 1977) p. 13.

54 Quoted by MANDELBAUM, *op. cit.*, p. 79.

55 M. E. KHAN and C. V. S. PRASAD, *Fertility Control in India* (New Delhi 1980).

56 SINGH, *op. cit.*, p. 84: transcript of the inaugural address to the joint meeting of the Central Councils for Health and Family Planning, New Delhi, 17 April 1975.

57 *Ibid.*, speech to the Lokh Sabha, 1 August 1975, in the debate on the New Economic Programme.

58 *Ibid.*, p. 116.

59 *Centre Calling*, Vol. 10 (1975), No. 3, p. 8.

60 *Ibid.*, p. 16.

61 *Centre Calling*, Vol. 10 (1975), No. 4, p. 1.

62 V. A. PAI PANDANIKER, R. N. BISHNOI and O. P. SHARMA, *Family Planning Under the Emergency: Policy Implications of Incentives and Disincentives* (New Delhi 1979) Ch. iii, The New Policy Measures, *passim*.

63 Figures in this section are taken from the *Shah Commission of Enquiry Third and Final Report*, 6 August 1978, especially p. 207, Table "Sterilisation Targets and Achievement".

64 Shah Commission, *op. cit.*, p. 165, *cf.* Satya PRAKASH and Kuldeepak SHARMA, *Administering Family Planning* (Rohtak 1979) p. 95.

65 Shah Commission, *op. cit.*, p. 178.

66 Satya PRAKASH and Kuldeepak SHARMA, *Administering Family Planning* (Rohtak 1979) *passim*.

67 Shah Commission, *op. cit.*, p. 31.

68 *Centre Calling*, Vol. 10 (1975), No. 11, leader on p. 3. Such views had not been so frankly expressed since Sir Julian Huxley and C. P. Blacker visited the 6th International Conference at Delhi, which was also attended by the American eugenist, Frederick Osborn (SUITTERS, *op. cit.*, pp. 171–172).

69 S. R. GROVER, "After-effects of vasectomy", *Journal of Family Welfare*, Vol. 33 (1977), No. 4, pp. 51, 54.

70 *Centre Calling*, Vol. 10 (1975), No. 10, p. 7.

71 *Guardian*, 15 July 1980; *Indian Express*, 30 August 1980; *Pioneer* (Lucknow), 13 September 1980.

72 *Centre Calling*, Vol. 11 (1976), No. 3, p. 2.

73 Inter-regional seminar on Primary Health Care, Yexian County, Shandon Province, 26 June 1982. Revised draft report by UNICEF 14 July 1982.

74 International Planned Parenthood Federation, "Family Planning in the People's Republic of China: report on the first IPPF visit" (June 1972).

75 The Victor-Bostrom Fund and the Population Crisis Committee, *Population and Family Planning in the People's Republic of China* (Washington 1971).

76 *China's Experience in Population Control: the Elusive Model*, prepared for the Committee of Foreign Affairs of the US House of Representatives by the Congress Research Service of the Library of Congress, September 1974, p. 3.

77 PI-CHAO Chen, "The Chinese Experience", *People*, Vol. 6 (1979), No. 2, p. 17.

78 *Ibid.*

79 *New York Times*, 24 April 1979.

80 *People's Daily*, 19 May 1979.

81 Xinhua News Agency, June 1979.

82 *New York Times*, 27 July 1979.

83 *International Herald Tribune*, 26 February 1981.

84 *International Herald Tribune*, 22 July 1980.

85 Xinhua News Agency, 18 February 1981.

86 *Daily Telegraph*, 6 January 1981.

87 *International Herald Tribune*, 7 March 1980.

88 *Guardian*, 8 September 1980.

89 Xinhua News Agency, 27 January 1981.

90 *International Herald Tribune*, 31 August 1981.

91 *Daily Telegraph*, 27 August 1980.

92 *Population Bulletin* (Population Information Centre, Sri Lanka).

93 *The Times*, 4 September 1980.

94 Mark G. FIELD, "The re-legalisation of abortion in Soviet Russia", *New England Journal of Medicine*, Vol. 255, No. 9, pp. 421ff.

95 Maggie JONES, "State attempts to stem decline", *People*, Vol. 7 (1980), No. 1, pp. 19–20.

96 P. CHAUNU, G.-F. DUMONT, J. LE GRAND and A. SAUVY, *La France ridée* (Paris 1979) p. 42, *cf.* p. 59; Population Division, Department of International Economic and Social Affairs, UN Secretariat, *Population Policy Briefs: The Current Situation in Developed Countries*, ESA/P/WP 72, 6 January 1981; Maurice KIRK, *Demographic and Social Change in Europe 1975–2000*, (Council of Europe 1981).

97 Nusret H. FISEK, "Social Problems of Migrant Labour", in Milos MACURA, *The Effect of Current Demographic Change in Europe on Social Structure* (Belgrade 1979) p. 69.

CHAPTER THIRTEEN

The Reproductive Future

1 Chief of Division of Family Health, Government of Haiti, in *People*, Vol. 8 (1981), No. 2, p. 5.

2 D. M. POTTS, "The implementation of family planning programmes", *Proceedings of the Royal Society, Series B*, No. 195 (1976) p. 220.

3 Alva MYRDAL, *Nation and Family* (New York and London 1941), pp. 87–88.

4 Eckehard KULKE, *The Parsees in India: A Minority as Agent of Social Change* (New Delhi 1978) p. 41.

5 Bernard BERELSON, "An evaluation of the effects of population control programs", *Studies in Family Planning*, Vol. 5, No. 1, 1974, pp. 2–12.

6 Alva MYRDAL, *op. cit.*, pp. 88–89. Also of interest in this context is J. M. KEYNES's Galton lecture, delivered in 1937, "Some economic consequences of a declining population", *Eugenics Review*, Vol. 9 (1938–1939), pp. 13ff.

7 Clellan Stearns FORD, *A Comparative Study of Human Reproduction* (Yale 1945) p. 86.

8 *Ibid.*, p. 87.

9 Ashley MONTAGU *Man and Aggression* (New York 1968) p. 11.

10 Sir Charles DARWIN, *Problems of World Population* (London 1958) p. 19.

11 Ben WATTENBERG, "The Tale of Two Birthrates", *International Herald Tribune*, 3 March 1983.

12 DARWIN, *op. cit.*, pp. 40–41.

13 Thomas B. LITTLEWOOD, *The Politics of Population Control* (Notre Dame 1977), p. 12; Rachel Benson GOLD, "Publicly Funded Abortions in FY 1980 and FY 1981", *Family Planning Perspectives*, Vol. 14, No. 4 (July–August 1982), p. 204; Women's League for Peace and Freedom, *Pax et Libertas*, Vol. 46, December 1981, p. 10.

14 See for example the case of Stephen Mosher of Stanford University as reported in *New Scientist*, Vol. 97 (3 March 1983), p. 567.

15 *The Times*, 9 September 161, p. 7 and 30 October 1963, p. 11.

16 Jeremy KEENAN, *The Tuareg: People of Ahaggar* (London 1977) pp. 4–5, *et passim.*

17 Walter PITKIN in Elmer PENDELL, *Population on the Loose* (New York 1951) p. xii.

18 Soloman Ole SAIBULL and Rachel CARR, *Herd and Spear: the Masai of East Africa* (London 1981) *passim.*

19 Rudolf ANDORKA, *Determinants of Fertility in Advanced Societies* (London 1978) pp. 93–98 and Geza ROHEIM, *Psychoanalysis and Anthropology* (New York 1950) p. 496.

20 Etienne VAN DER WALLE, "The View from the Past: Population Change and Group Survival", in *Zero Population Growth for Whom? Differential Fertility and Minority Group Survival,* ed. Milton HIMMEL-FARB and Victor BARAS (Westport 1979) pp. 6–25.

21 United States Bureau of the Census, *Monthly Vital Statistics Reports,* Vol. 30 (1981), No. 6, Supplement 2.

22 Edward Murray EAST, *Mankind at the Crossroads* (New York 1923) pp. 116–117.

23 Figures from *World Population Prospects as Assessed in 1980,* UN Department of International Economic and Social Affairs (Population Studies No. 78) ST/ESA/SER.A/78, 1981 and *Selected Demographic Indicators by Country 1950–2000,* UN Department of International Economic and Social Affairs, ST/ESA/SER.R/38, 1980.

24 L. P. TOURKOW, R. LIDZ and B. L. ROSENFELD, "Psychiatric Considerations in Fertility Inhibition", *Human Reproduction: Conception and Contraception,* ed. E. S. E. HAFEZ (New York 1979) pp. 857–8.

25 Center for Disease Control, *Surgical Sterilisation Surveillance: Tubal Sterilisation 1976–1978* quoted in *International Family Planning Perspectives,* Vol. 13 (1981) No. 5, p. 236.

26 *Ibid.*

27 Michael KLITSCH, "Sterilisation without surgery", *International Family Planning Perspectives,* Vol. 8, No. 3, September 1982, p. 101.

28 *Ibid.,* p. 102.

29 *Ibid.*

30 Elton KESSEL and Stephen MUMFORD, "Potential demand for voluntary female sterilisation in the 1980s: the compelling need for a non-surgical method", *Fertility and Sterility,* June 1982.

31 Karl DJERASSI, *The Politics of Contraception: Birth Control in the Year 2001* (Stanford 1979) p. 161.

32 Barry BOETTCHER, "Immunity to spermatozoa", *Clinics in Obstetrics and Gynecology,* Vol. 6, No. 3, December, 1979.

33 Vernon C. STEVENS, "Vaccines against pregnancy", *Recent Advances in Fertility Regulation* ed. Chang Chai Fen and David Griffin (WHO, 1981), p. 213. *Cf.* Ralph M. RICHARDS, "Female sterilisation using

chemical agents", *Research Frontiers in Fertility Regulation*, Vol. 1, No. 5, December 1981, Population Council, *Annual Report* (8.2.USA.7.3.Pop), J. P. HEAR. (ed.) *Immunological Aspects of Reproduction and Fertility Control* (MTP Press Ltd 1980).

34 DJERASSI, *op. cit.*, pp. 177–8. Putting a sterilant in salt was proposed by N. C. WRIGHT at the CIBA Symposium on *Man and his Future* (ed. WOLSTENHOLME, London 1963). (Wright was the Deputy Director-General of the Food and Agriculture Organisation at the time.) PIRIE pointed out that the Swiss thought of putting fluoride in salt but found that salt consumption was too uneven to provide the basis for any kind of dosing system (pp. 103–104).

35 DJERASSI, *op. cit.*, pp. 178–179.

36 WHO report summarised in the *International Herald Tribune* 23 June 1980.

37 J. P. KOCH, "The Prentif contraceptive cervical cap: a contemporary study of its clinic safety and effectiveness", *Contraception*. Vol. 25, 1982 p. 135, and "The Prentif contraceptive cervical cap: acceptability aspects and their implications for future cap design", *Contraception*, Vol. 25, 1982, p. 161.

38 D. M. DE KRETSER, "Fertility regulation in the male: recent developments", FEN and GRIFFIN, *op. cit.*, p. 119.

<hr />

CHAPTER FOURTEEN

The Myth of Overpopulation

1 British Library Collection.

2 Paul EHRLICH, *The Population Bomb* (London 1971).

3 Lewis COTLOW, *The Twilight of the Primitive* (London 1973) pp. 16–17.

4 Susan GEORGE, *How the Other Half Dies* (London 1977) p. 196.

5 *Ibid.*, p. 203.

Index